Public Finance and Public Policy

Responsibilities and Limitations of Government

This textbook systematically sets out the issues involved in public finance and public policy. A recurring theme is the decision when to assign responsibility to government to levy taxes to finance public spending and choose the public policies that accompany public finance. Ten chapters cover markets and property, collective benefits, voting, market corrections, social justice, political processes and redistribution, taxation, user pricing, the size of government, and public policy toward health, education, and provision for retirement. Also included are topics such as the rule of law, national defense, government bureaucracy, public policies that prohibit markets when there are willing buyers and sellers, and global environmental issues.

The book is designed as a text for courses in public finance or public economics, with additions from political economy or aspects of public choice. The presentation begins by presupposing no more than an elementary background in economics and proceeds to introduce and explain analytical concepts as required. Supplements include presentations suitable for upper-level undergraduates. Graduate students will find that the text defines fundamental questions and provides guidance to the literature. All chapters contain question sets.

Arye L. Hillman is the William Gittes Professor of Economics at Bar-Ilan University in Israel. He has a PhD in economics from the University of Pennsylvania, has taught as a visiting professor at UCLA and Princeton, and has been an invited lecturer at universities around the world. He is an editor of the *European Journal of Political Economy* and serves as a member of the editorial or advisory board of other professional journals. A Research Fellow of the Centre for Economic Policy Research in London and of CESifo in Munich, he has also been a Fellow of the Japanese Society for the Promotion of Science and a visiting collaborating researcher at the International Monetary Fund and the World Bank in Washington, D.C. Professor Hillman was jointly awarded the Max-Planck Prize in Economics in 1995 for his contributions to the study of political economy.

Public Finance and Public Policy

Responsibilities and Limitations of Government

Arye L. Hillman

Bar-Ilan University, Israel

CAMBRIDGE
UNIVERSITY PRESS

PUBLISHED BY THE PRESS SYNDICATE OF THE UNIVERSITY OF CAMBRIDGE
The Pitt Building, Trumpington Street, Cambridge, United Kingdom

CAMBRIDGE UNIVERSITY PRESS
The Edinburgh Building, Cambridge CB2 2RU, UK
40 West 20th Street, New York, NY 10011-4211, USA
477 Williamstown Road, Port Melbourne, VIC 3207, Australia
Ruiz de Alarcón 13, 28014 Madrid, Spain
Dock House, The Waterfront, Cape Town 8001, South Africa

http://www.cambridge.org

First published 2003

Printed in the United States of America

Typefaces Times Ten 10/13 pt. *and* Helvetica   *System* LaTeX 2_ε [TB]

A catalog record for this book is available from the British Library.

Library of Congress Cataloging in Publication Data

Hillman, Arye L.
    Public finance and public policy : responsibilities and limitations of government /
Arye L. Hillman.
    p.   cm.
    Includes bibliographical references and index.
    ISBN 0-521-80641-0 – ISBN 0-521-00114-5 (pb.)
    1. Finance, Public.   2. Economic policy.   3. Taxation.   I. Title.
HJ141 .H54   2003
336–dc21   2002031203

ISBN 0 521 80641 0 hardback
ISBN 0 521 00114 5 paperback

For Jeannette

and Tamara, Ilana, Eli, and Benjamin

and Yitzi, Hovav, Galit, and Yael

and Dafna, Yishai, Mayan, Ya'ara, Dov, Shani, Ze'ev, Lior, Hallel, Harel, and Raphael, and the others

and for my mother and in memory of my father, to whom some governments were kinder than others.

Be cautious with the government, for they do not make advances to a man except for their own need. They seem like friends in the hour of their advantage, but they do not stand by a man in his hour of adversity.

Rabban Gamliel, around the year 230

Pray for the peace of the government; for, except for the fear of that, we should have swallowed each other alive.

R. Hanina, born around the year 20

The Jerusalem Talmud (Sayings of the Fathers)

Contents

Preface

This book sets out and addresses the basic questions of public finance and accompanying public policy. The questions have in common the choice between personal market decisions to earn and spend income and collective decisions of taxation and spending by government.

The book covers topics for a course in public finance or public economics, with additional topics such as voting and political principal-agent problems that are part of political economy and were introduced to the economics literature through public choice.

The book is designed to be used at different levels.

(1) The book is a text for students who begin with no more than an understanding of the basics of supply and demand.
(2) With the supplements included, the book is a text for advanced undergraduate students.
(3) For graduate students and researchers, the book defines and organizes the basic themes of public finance and accompanying public policy and provides guidance to the literature.

There are ten chapters. Chapter 1 on *markets and property* provides an overview of competitive markets, looks at criteria for evaluating efficiency and social justice, and points out why government has responsibilities, but why there are also limitations of government. The chapter also studies the role of property rights in allowing markets to function and in avoiding the inefficiency and contestability of the anarchy that can arise without the rule of law. Outcomes of maximal government are described and compared with minimal government, to set the bounds for choosing the responsibilities of government.

Chapter 2 on *collective benefits* describes voluntary financing outcomes for different types of public goods and sets out the case for a role for government in financing public goods. The information problems that governments face when designing public spending on public goods are described, and resolution of these problems is considered using cost-benefit analysis, schemes that provide incentives for truthful revelation of preferences, and locational choice. The chapter also studies public finance for public goods through taxation and government borrowing.

Chapter 3 studies *voting on public spending for public goods* and evaluates the outcomes of public spending decisions determined by majority voting and through political competition. The chapter also looks at the implementation of collective decisions through government bureaucracy.

Chapter 4 on *market corrections* studies resolution of externalities by private means and by public policy, and also considers public policies that suppress or disallow markets.

Chapter 5 on *social justice* studies the role of government as a provider of social insurance, investigates the incentive effects of entitlements provided by government, and considers prospects for achieving social justice without government through private charity and social mobility.

Chapter 6 on *politics and redistribution* studies redistribution through majority voting and the limits to such redistribution, the role of interest groups in public policy and why there are political incentives to accommodate special interest policies, and the relation between public policy and rent-seeking behavior.

Chapter 7 on *taxation* studies properties of different taxes, investigates whether an ideal tax system can be designed, and looks at problems of tax evasion and a shadow economy.

Chapter 8 investigates *user prices* as an alternative to taxation for financing public goods. Public policy toward natural monopoly is also considered.

Chapter 9 addresses the question *how much government?* Federal structures of government and the consequences of tax competition among governments are investigated, and the benefits and costs of multiple government are evaluated. Also addressed is the extent to which trust among people and voluntary cooperation can reduce the need for government. Reasons for the growth of government are considered, and the case for constitutional restraint on government is evaluated.

Chapter 10 investigates public policy choices for *health care and health insurance, education, and provision for old age*. In each case, markets allow private supply and private spending decisions, but government is in general involved through public finance and public policy.

A postscript brings together conclusions about why views on public finance and public policy can differ. Supplements provide additions and more advanced treatment of topics.

Chapters are divided into three subsections. References and related literature at the end of each subsection provide a guide to further reading, and questions provide a framework for review and further discussion. Some of the questions ask for statistics and contemporary descriptions of public finance and public policy. Economic statistics and descriptions of public policy become dated, and contemporary statistics and descriptions of public policies are available from websites of national and local governments and international institutions.

Government from the vantage point of a student

As a student, you may have combined study with work and paid some taxes; however, you may not personally have had to pay a substantial part of your income in taxes. When people pay a substantial part of personal income in taxes, they may begin to ask questions about whether the taxation is fair and justified. Questions about whether government is spending tax revenue in the most beneficial ways may also be raised. People may ask themselves whether they agree with the assignment of responsibilities to different levels of government and whether it is reasonable that they are paying taxes to finance past government borrowing. They may ask about the social justice of having to pay social security taxes that may not provide for their own future, and whether welfare programs have achieved the appropriate balance between satisfying social objectives and providing incentives for self-reliance. They might want to see a different role for government in education, or they might be concerned about the quality of health care and coverage of health insurance and ask what role government could have in possible improvements. They may also ask themselves whether, as citizens and voters, they have sufficient control over political decisions that affect taxation and public spending. Most basically, people may ask how much of their incomes they want to choose to spend themselves and how much they want government to take from them in taxes to finance public spending. These questions arise throughout this book. Economics students have the advantage of asking these questions as part of their studies. Others will, perhaps, confront these questions for the first time as they pay the taxes that finance spending by government, and as they contemplate how public policies – including decisions about the level of taxes and about how tax revenue is spent – affect their personal lives and the society in which they live.

1

MARKETS AND PROPERTY

1.1

A First Account

The most important question that can perhaps be asked in economics is when should we forgo the personal decisions of markets, where we choose how we earn and spend income, and instead rely on decisions of government. This book addresses this fundamental question.

The background for our study is the existence of markets. Markets allow people voluntarily to buy and sell. Assigning responsibilities to government in general requires taxes, which are not voluntary.

We shall be happy with markets, if markets achieve two basic objectives: (1) efficiency and (2) social justice. We shall presently more precisely define these objectives. If markets cannot achieve these objectives, we need to consider replacing the private decisions made in markets with the collective decisions of public finance and public policy made through government.

We shall begin our investigation with markets where neither public finance nor public policy is present. From this starting point without government, we shall investigate whether or how public finance and public policy can improve outcomes of private, individually made, market decisions.

1.1.1 The market and efficiency

A case for the virtue of private market decisions without government can be traced back at least to the writings of Adam Smith (1723–90). On a number of occasions, Smith, who was a professor of moral philosophy,[1] referred in his writings to an invisible hand that guides personal self-interest to outcomes that benefit an entire society.

Voluntary market decisions are necessarily personally beneficial, since a person who believes that a market decision is not in his or her best interest can simply choose not to buy or not to sell. The invisible hand, according to Adam Smith, ensures that personally beneficial market decisions are also socially beneficial.[2] The social benefit provided by the invisible hand can be identified as efficiency. The invisible hand does not promise social justice.

The invisible hand, according to Adam Smith, allowed virtuous men and women to pursue self-interest through markets without feelings of guilt. We see elements

---

[1] Adam Smith first studied at Glasgow University in Scotland and then at Oxford University in England. After his studies, he returned to Glasgow to take a position as professor of logic; in the following year, he became professor of moral philosophy.

[2] The idea of the invisible hand appears in Smith's book *The Theory of Moral Sentiments* first published in 1759 and also makes an appearance in his book *An Enquiry into the Causes of the Wealth of Nations* first published in 1776. The invisible hand has become part of the folklore of economics. For accounts of Smith's intentions when using the idea of the invisible hand, see Macafie (1959), Rothschild (1994), and Grammy (2000). Overviews of Smith's writings and ideas include Reisman (1975) and Tribe (1999).

of moral philosophy in this suggestion: People who pursue self-interest through markets should not feel guilty for not having broader social objectives because the invisible hand will direct their personal self-interest to the good of all society. That is, through markets people do social good by doing personal good for themselves.

Adam Smith also pointed out that social good achieved through the invisible hand is unintentional. People do not purposefully set out to do social good when making self-interested market decisions. The absence of *intent* to do social good was seen by Adam Smith as a virtue because hypocrisy could be absent from market decisions. Smith wrote (1776/1937, p. 423):

> *I have never known much good done by those who affected to trade for the public good.*

Adam Smith would thus advise us to be wary of persons who, when offering to buy or sell, claim to have objectives other than their own personal self-interest. We should be cautious when offers to buy or sell are accompanied by claims of altruistic motives. The saying, "do not look a gift horse in the mouth," advises us not to examine too closely the quality of a gift that we are offered.[3] In a market, however, gifts are not given. Rather, money and goods change hands. Adam Smith advised us to beware of gifts or bargains in markets. To achieve both private and social good, people need only profess to seek their own personal benefit when they offer to buy or sell.

Efficiency in a competitive market

There is no formal proof in Adam Smith's writings that personal self-interest expressed through market decisions benefits a society. In the centuries since Smith's writings, various ways of more formally confirming the social benefit of markets have become available. The simplest means of proof is to look at a single competitive market, as in Figure 1.1, where market demand expresses marginal benefit of buyers through willingness to pay, and market supply expresses the marginal cost of sellers.[4] In a competitive market, individual buyers and sellers do not influence market prices. Buyers choose quantities to buy by setting the market price equal to their personal marginal benefit MB. Sellers choose quantities to sell by setting the market price equal to their marginal cost of supply MC. Since the market price is the same for all buyers, all buyers have the same realized personal MB from their purchase decisions. Market demand in Figure 1.1 thus reflects the equalized personal MB of all buyers. The market supply function likewise reflects the common MC of sellers. At point E in Figure 1.1, the total quantity demanded by all buyers is equal to the total quantity supplied by all sellers, and the price that buyers are willing to pay is equal to the price that sellers require in order

---

[3] Examination of the condition of the teeth of a horse will reveal the age and health of the horse.
[4] More elaborate proofs of the efficiency of markets are provided in Supplements 1A and 1B.

Price

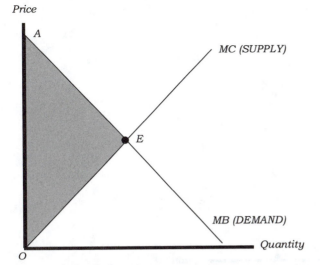

Figure 1.1. The efficiency of a competitive market.
Demand expresses marginal benefit *MB* of buyers. Supply expresses marginal cost *MC* of suppliers. At point *E* where demand equals supply, *MB* and *MC* are equal, and $W = B - C$ is therefore maximized. Maximal *W* is the area *AEO*.

to supply.[5] We confirm Adam Smith's claim that personal market decisions are socially beneficial, if we show that the market outcome at point *E* is efficient. Of course, we would then have defined social benefit as efficiency.

We define an outcome as efficient, if net social benefit

$$W = B - C \qquad (1.1)$$

is maximized, where *B* is total benefit and *C* is total cost. In seeking maximal net social benefit *W*, we are not asking how total benefits *B* and total costs *C* are distributed in a population. We are not asking whether the people who benefit or incur costs are rich or poor. Such questions are distributional; we ask distributional questions when we seek an objective of social justice.

In the market shown in Figure 1.1, *B* is the total benefit of all buyers in the market, and *C* is the total cost of all suppliers. *W* is the net benefit to society from existence of the market.

Efficiency to maximize $W = B - C$ requires that a quantity of output be supplied and sold for which

$$MB = MC. \qquad (1.2)$$

Because *MB* of buyers is indicated by the demand function and *MC* of sellers is indicated by the supply function, the output at which $MB = MC$ is at point *E*

---

[5] The demand and supply functions in Figure 1.1 are shown as linear. Linearity is only for exposition. The negative slope of demand indicates diminishing *MB* of buyers, and the positive slope of supply indicates increasing *MC* of suppliers.

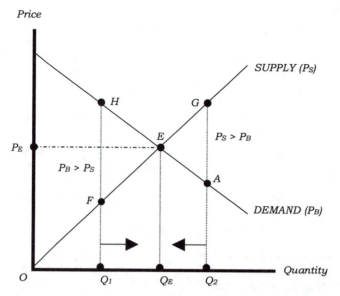

Figure 1.2. The competitive market adjustment mechanism.
The competitive adjustment mechanism moves the market to the equilibrium output Q_E.

where demand and supply are equal. The outcome at point E in Figure 1.1 is therefore efficient and is, moreover, the only efficient outcome.[6] The shaded area AEO is the maximal value of $W = B - C$ that the market can offer.[7]

If the market is not at the efficient point E but somewhere else, a competitive adjustment mechanism will bring the market to point E. Once at point E, the market will stay there. The competitive adjustment mechanism is illustrated in Figure 1.2. The price that buyers are willing to pay for additional output is shown as P_B. This price is determined from the demand function. The price that suppliers require to provide additional output is P_S. This price is given from the supply function. At quantity Q_1 in Figure 1.2, the price P_B that buyers are willing to pay for additional output exceeds the price P_S that suppliers require to supply additional output. Since buyers are willing to pay a higher price than sellers ask to supply more output, output supplied increases from Q_1. Output supplied continues to increase until the efficient output Q_E at point E is reached. At output Q_E, the price P_B that buyers are willing to pay and the price P_S that suppliers require in

---

[6] A second-order condition is satisfied at point E. See Supplement 1A.

[7] The area under the demand function measures the total benefit B for any quantity of output provided to buyers by summing MBs from quantities of output. The area under the supply function measures the total cost C of supplying a quantity of output by summing MCs of supply. Therefore, $W = B - C$ is the difference between the areas under the demand and supply functions. This difference reaches a maximal value at point E. We shall often use the area under the demand function to measure total benefit and the area under the supply function to measure total cost. The area under the demand function is an approximation for total benefit. The approximation is in general reasonable. See Robert Willig (1976).

order to supply are equal to the price P_E. Output now stays constant. E is therefore the point of market *equilibrium*.[8]

With market supply originally the quantity Q_2 shown in Figure 1.2, buyers' willingness to pay for additional output P_B (given from the demand function) is less than the price P_S (given from the supply function) that sellers require to provide more output. Buyers are therefore unwilling to pay the price that suppliers require to maintain supply at the quantity Q_2, and output supplied falls. The output decline stops at the equilibrium output Q_E at point E.

Whether the market begins from an output such as Q_1 less than Q_E or from an output such as Q_2 greater than Q_E, the competitive adjustment mechanism thus brings the market to the efficient output Q_E at the equilibrium point E.[9]

We have now shown that the equilibrium of a competitive market is efficient. The market could be for a product or service supplied for consumption, or it could be for a factor of production. Buyers and sellers make self-interested decisions (buyers choose quantities to purchase according to $P = MB$ and sellers choose quantities to supply according to $P = MC$), and the market adjusts to the efficient equilibrium if not already at the equilibrium. We have therefore confirmed Adam Smith's proposal that the market is guided to efficiency by individual self-interest *as if* by an invisible hand, and that buyers and sellers have no reason to feel guilty about making personally self-interested decisions, provided the decisions are made in competitive markets and provided that the social objective is efficiency.[10]

A first responsibility of government: competition
The efficiency achieved through markets requires that markets be competitive. A first responsibility of government is thus the preservation and protection of competitive markets.[11] This responsibility of government requires an antimonopoly or

---

[8] During adjustment to the market equilibrium, price is changing. Since no individual buyer or seller can influence a market price in a competitive market, we might ask how prices ever change. Calling on the "invisible hand" to change market prices is not an adequate answer. The condition that no buyer or seller can influence price is a characteristic only of the market equilibrium. When the market is not in equilibrium, individual offers to buy or sell influence market prices. See Supplement 1A on how prices change in a competitive market.

[9] From Figure 1.2, we also confirm that nonequilibrium outputs such as Q_1 and Q_2 are not efficient outputs. At quantity Q_1, there is a loss equal to HEF from the market not being at the efficient point E. At the quantity Q_2, there is a loss equal to GEA.

[10] Adam Smith did not use the ideas of supply and demand to make his case for the virtue of the market. Alfred Marshall (1842–1924) much later introduced the ideas of market supply and demand. Marshall resolved a problem that had been debated for centuries, which is whether the price (or value) of a good is due to the cost of production or reflects personal benefit expressed in willingness of people to pay. Marshall showed that neither cost nor benefit alone *caused* value. Rather market price (or market value) was determined by supply and demand interacting simultaneously in markets.

[11] The responsibility of government to ensure competition includes international free trade. A foreign supplier may offer buyers the lowest price or the best quality, or a foreign buyer may offer a better price than is available in a seller's home market. International free trade permits buyers and sellers to take advantage of *all* market opportunities when making decisions to buy or sell. See Supplement 1B. Adam Smith included the benefits from free trade in the benefits from markets. More formal statements of the gains from free trade followed, for example Murray Kemp (1962).

antitrust agency that pursues a public policy of ensuring competition.[12] The persons employed in the government's antitrust agency receive incomes that are publicly financed. The implementation of public policy through the antitrust agency thus requires taxes and public spending.

1.1.2 Individual freedom

Competitive markets are a basis for individual freedom. A single seller in a market can restrict individual freedom by arbitrarily refusing to sell, and a single buyer can arbitrarily refuse to buy. In a competitive market, the personal attributes or beliefs or social and ethnic background of a buyer or seller do not influence buying or selling opportunities. The presence of many buyers and sellers makes a competitive market anonymous and impersonal, so there can be no adverse discrimination.

There is also individual freedom in that market decisions involve neither compulsion nor obligation. No one is telling anyone else what to do.

1.1.3 Spontaneous order

Individual freedom is related to the idea of spontaneous order. Spontaneous order differs from order that some people impose on others. In competitive markets, order arises spontaneously, as markets achieve efficiency through voluntary decisions. The idea of spontaneous order through voluntary market decisions has sometimes been viewed as a puzzle and with suspicion, since the way in which markets function may not be immediately evident to the human eye (hence the invisible hand). Some people have been led to wonder why the outcome of market decisions is not chaos rather than the adjustment to market equilibrium.

Suspicions about independent market decisions have at times led to proposals to impose order through a visible hand of government, to preempt the perceived anarchy of the market. The market is however not anarchic. Order emerges spontaneously through independent personal decisions. No imposed order is required by men and women who might want to control decisions for others.

---

[12] The responsibility of government to ensure competitive markets can be subtle. A single seller does not necessarily indicate monopoly. The test of monopoly is whether artificial barriers exist that deter sellers who wish to sell. A single seller might achieve market dominance by providing a better product or service or by selling at a low price, in which case a single seller is not an indication of monopoly but the consequence of competition. For example, in a famous case in the 1960s, the U.S. government accused IBM of being a monopolist in the market for computers. IBM's successful defense was that the company's market successes were due to continual quality improvement and low prices in the face of potential competitors waiting to enter the market. At the time, IBM produced mainframe (large) computers. By the 1990s, personal desktops and laptops had the computing power of the previous mainframe computers, and IBM confronted new competition that ended its previous dominance of the market for computers, without the intervention of government. When we call upon government to ensure that markets are competitive, we therefore add the qualification that success should not be penalized, and that allowance should be made for the technological competition that can give temporary market dominance to innovating firms. To provide incentives for innovation and the creation of new knowledge, governments also provide innovating firms with *legal* monopolies, through patent protection.

For example, there is spontaneous order at a fruit and vegetable market. Farmers arrive at the market with produce for sale. Farmers independently make individual supply decisions for the produce that they bring to the market, without coordinating their personal decisions. The government has issued no directives about the types of products and the quantities that should be brought to the market. Buyers also arrive at the market to make their purchases. In the course of a day, numerous transactions take place between farmers and buyers. At the end of the day, the farmers will have left their stalls, their produce sold, to return the next day with new supplies. Buyers also return the next day to purchase the produce that they seek. Spontaneous order is present. Every buyer and seller knows "what to do" without instructions from anyone else.

Spontaneous order extends to market relations among different goods. Producers supply goods not only for consumption but also to other producers, who use the purchased inputs in the stages of their own production activities. In the web of market interdependence, foreign producers supply imported goods, and domestically produced goods are sold in foreign countries. Foreign producers might use these goods as inputs to produce goods that are exported back for consumption or for use by other domestic producers.

Spontaneous order in the market is made possible by the information about value revealed by market prices. When all individual buyers set their personal MB equal to the price revealed in the market and likewise all individual sellers set their personal MC equal to the market price, we have

$$MB = P_E = MC \tag{1.3}$$

at the market price where demand equals supply. This ensures that net social benefit $W = B - C$ is maximized. Spontaneous order is thereby achieved through voluntary independent personal decisions that establish the equality between MB and MC required for market efficiency. Moreover, to participate in markets for their own advantage, individuals need only to know their own personal MB or own personal MC.

1.1.4 Responsibilities of government: why the market may not be enough

Governments have the responsibility of certifying private ownership and protecting lives and property through the rule of law. In Section 1.2, we shall elaborate on this responsibility of government. The two responsibilities of overseeing competitive markets and ensuring the rule of law define a minimal government.

A minimal government is usually not enough. Markets may fail to achieve efficiency. In that case, government has a responsibility to correct the inefficiencies. In the chapters that follow, we shall identify market efficiencies from a number of sources. We shall see that markets are inefficient or ineffective when spending benefits a number of people at the same time. Such collective benefits arise in many cases that range from spending on roads to national defense to disease prevention.

Markets also do not ensure efficiency when individual market decisions affect others, whether adversely or beneficially. For example, there may be damage to the environment. Societies may also decide to prohibit particular markets. Questions also arise concerning social justice. If markets do not ensure social justice, a society may decide that government has a responsibility to amend market outcomes by taxation and income redistribution.

1.1.5 Normative and positive questions

As we investigate the responsibilities of government, we need to ask both normative and positive questions. A *normative question* enquires whether a public policy can improve on markets, or whether public finance is socially beneficial. *Positive questions* seek explanations and predictions, without judgments about whether policies or outcomes are desirable.

The distinction between normative and positive questions is in particular important for studying political processes that redistribute income. We need to consider whether political decisions about public finance and public policy are consistent with normatively justifiable objectives.

The normative and positive distinction is also important for questions about taxes. Normative questions ask about the taxes that ought to be imposed. Positive questions ask why different taxes are imposed, about the effects of the different taxes, and about why taxes are sometimes not paid.

To ask and answer normative questions, we require norms that allow us to judge whether an outcome or a change is justified as efficient or as socially just.

1.1.6 Pareto efficiency

Normative questions about efficiency can be posed by using the criterion that an outcome is efficient if net social welfare $W = B - C$ is maximized. This is the procedure we followed when we enquired about the efficiency of a competitive market. We can also use an alternative definition of efficiency, called *Pareto efficiency*, after Vilfredo Pareto (1848–1923).

Pareto efficiency for production is achieved when no more of any one good can be produced without giving up some quantity of another good. Pareto efficiency for consumption is achieved when an allocation of goods or income among people cannot be changed to make someone better off, without making someone else worse off.

Pareto efficiency therefore defines absence of waste. No more can be produced without giving something up. No person in society can be made better off unless at the expense of someone else.

Decisions to buy and sell in a competitive market are Pareto efficient. We have seen that competitive markets result in outcomes where $W = B - C$ is maximized. At the same time, since individual decisions to buy and sell are voluntary, no one can be worse off as a consequence of a personal market decision. Since there are only gainers, the efficiency achieved by a market in maximizing $W = B - C$ also results in outcomes that are Pareto efficient.[13]

While personal decisions made in markets are Pareto-efficient, the same is not necessarily so for public policy decisions. A public policy decision can increase net social benefit $W = B - C$, without benefiting everybody. For example, a road that benefits many people could be built through someone's house. The Pareto criterion for efficiency is not satisfied if the owners of the house are worse off as a consequence of the public-policy decision to build the road, although total benefits from the road exceed total costs including the costs imposed on the people who lose their house.

If total benefits exceed total costs so that $W = B - C > 0$, the people who gain from construction of the road gain more than the losers lose. The gainers can thus compensate the losers for their loss and still be better off. After the losers have been compensated, the Pareto criterion will be satisfied because some people are better off and no one is worse off.

Any public policy that is justified by the efficiency criterion that the policy increases $W = B - C$ also allows the Pareto criterion to be satisfied through compensation of any losers from the public policy. The compensation may however only be possible in principle, and not in practice. We know the identity of the people who have lost when construction of a road requires that their houses be destroyed. In other cases, identification of the losers may not be possible. As an example, we can consider the introduction in the nineteenth century of steam technology to replace sails as the means of propulsion of ships. Because of the change in technology, people who had skills and knowledge associated with furling and unfurling sails lost income. It would have been very difficult to compensate all people with such skills for the losses they incurred because of the new steam technology. The market introduced steam technology without compensation to the losers. Yet, because the change in technology increased the total income of society, the losers could in principle have been compensated and the gainers would still have been better off. Requiring actual compensation would have been an impediment to the introduction of the new technology because of the administrative complexities of identifying and certifying who should be compensated and by how much. The problem is complex. It involves not just identifying the losers and determining how much each loser lost but also identifying the gainers and determining how much each gainer should contribute to the fund to compensate the losers. A further complexity is that future gainers from a new technology may not yet have been born.

There were gainers and losers when the personal computer was introduced. Before the advent of the personal computer, typing was a specialized skill, and few people did their own typing. The introduction of personal computers disadvantaged typists because many people learned to do their own typing. Insistence

---

[13] Supplement 1B develops the concept of Pareto efficiency achieved through markets.

on actual compensation of losers would have made the introduction of personal computers contingent on identifying all gainers (i.e., all people who gained from using a personal computer) and determining how much each gained. It would have also been necessary to identify all people who lost income as a consequence of the introduction of the personal computer and to establish how much they lost. An administrative office would have been required to implement the compensating income transfers from the gainers to the losers. If compensation had been required, the personal computer would never have been introduced.

These examples show that administrative and information costs of making compensating payments can be too high to make compensation to losers feasible. When the identities of the gainers and losers and the values of the gains and losses are clear, we might however insist that the gainers compensate the losers. The compensation to the losers might be paid by the government on behalf of the gainers. For example, in the case of the road, we would not expect each gainer individually to compensate the owners of the house. The administrative costs of such individual compensation could be prohibitive. We would not expect the owners of the house to place a toll booth or electronic monitor where the house had been. The government would provide the compensation to the owners of the house through an income transfer financed by taxes.

The compensation is not designed to ensure efficiency. A public policy is efficient if, in principle, the gainers can compensate the losers and still be better off. That is, a public policy is efficient if, for society as a whole, $W = B - C$ is maximized. A desire to provide actual compensation reflects a concern for social justice. Compensation may be socially just. When some people lose from an efficient policy and compensation is not possible or is prohibitively costly, a society faces a conflict between the objective of efficiency and the objective of social justice.

Insistence on actual compensation to losers would have resulted in public policies banning both steam technology and the personal computer, and many other new technologies that have, on the whole, benefited society. As another example, new awareness of damage to the environment may lead to a decision to close a factory that is polluting a lake because ongoing production in the factory is not warranted once the damage to the environment has been included in costs. That is, with the damage to the environment included in costs, total benefit B from the factory's output is less than total cost C. If the factory was constructed before social concern about pollution, should the owners be compensated because new awareness of the harm inflicted by pollution has resulted in the closing of the factory? Most people would agree that if the owners of the factory have lost because of a change in society's environmental standards, the owners of the factory should be compensated.

Should the employees who lose their jobs also be compensated? Should people who have incurred a loss through a decline in the value of their houses because of reduced demand for housing after the closing of the factory be compensated? Should suppliers who supplied inputs used by the factory be compensated? Should the advertising agency that had the account for the factory be compensated? Should consumers with a special liking for the products of the factory be compensated?

At some stage in the list of people who have lost, a society that seeks efficiency may decide to forego the actual compensation required to satisfy the Pareto criterion that no one lose because of a change. A judgment might be made, for example, that the advertising agency should not be compensated for the closing of the factory. Such judgments involve considerations of social justice. The closing of the factory is justified because for society the costs C of the existence of the factory exceed the benefits B. The benefits lost by the closing of the factory include the former gains of the advertising agency that had the account for the factory's products.

A society that emphasizes efficiency might choose to adopt a general rule that a public-policy decision is justified when $W = B - C > 0$ increases. Such a society does not investigate the distribution of the benefits B and costs C among the population. The intention is that, by proceeding with all changes and public policies that increase $W = B - C$, all people over time will come to benefit, even if on some occasions some people lose.

1.1.7 Social justice

We have two quite precise ways of expressing the social objective of efficiency, through the net social benefit criterion $W = B - C$ and through Pareto efficiency. Social justice, the other objective that societies seek, is a more elusive concept to express than efficiency.

Social justice through actual compensation

One way to express the objective of social justice is insistence on actual compensation whenever somebody loses from a public policy. Many of the fundamental disagreements that arise in economics, and in politics, can be traced to different positions on whether social justice through actual compensation for losers is required before a government can proceed with efficient public policies.

Social justice through competitive markets

Do competitive markets provide incomes that are socially just? A competitive market provides individuals with incomes according to the value of personal contributions to production.[14] As a result, personal incomes earned in competitive markets are consistent with social justice, if we make the judgment that people should be rewarded according to the value of their personal contributions to a

---

[14] We can express profits of a competitive firm as $P \cdot Q(L) - wL$, where P is the competitively determined price, Q is output, w is the competitively determined wage paid to labor, and L is the amount of labor employed. The output Q depends positively on L. The firm maximizes profits by hiring labor so that $P\partial Q/\partial L = w$, so that the wage received by labor is equal to the value of labor's marginal product, which is the value of the marginal contribution of labor to production.

society's output. If we make this judgment, a competitive market is both efficient and socially just. Personal reward determined by the value of personal contributions to production however provides no or low income for people who are incapacitated. Moreover, some people may object to personal ability determining personal income because of the element of luck in innate ability. Luck also determines ability to earn income through support and encouragement to study received from parents. Some people may consequently regard the inequality resulting from market-determined outcomes as unjust and rather may view social justice as requiring equality.

Social justice as equality

Suppose that three people each have incomes of $1,000 and all benefit equally when they spend the money. A proposed public policy would result in a new outcome where person 1 has $1,200, person 2 has $1,300, and person 3 has $1,400. The change introduced by the public policy satisfies the efficiency condition that $W = B - C > 0$. The public policy also provides a Pareto improvement because all three persons are better off (and no one is worse off). Yet, because incomes are no longer equal, the change has resulted in a departure from social justice defined as equality. We see therefore that defining social justice as equality and insisting that no policy violate equality can be inconsistent with efficiency. In this example, if the three persons cannot equally share their gains, or if the gains are not transferable among the three people, insistence on social justice defined by equality requires person 2 to throw away $100 of benefit and person 3 to throw away $200 of benefit.

Water in the desert

Conflict that can arise between efficiency and social justice defined as equality is described in circumstances where two people are in a desert with enough water for one of them to survive. A discussion of these circumstances is found in the Talmud.[15] The Talmud relates:

> *Two people were traveling along the way and one of them had in his possession a flask of water. If both drink, they both die. However, if one drinks, he will reach a populated area.*

The water belongs to one of the travelers. The question that is asked is whether the person with the water should share the water with the other person. As is usual in the Talmud, more than a single answer is given. One answer is consistent with justice defined as equality and the other answer is consistent with Pareto efficiency.

---

[15] Compilation of the Jerusalem Talmud was completed around 1,600 years ago and the Talmud Bavli was completed some 100 years later. The example that follows is from the Talmud Bavli. In the Talmud, the opinions of people who did not live at the same time are often compared.

The view guided by social justice defined as equality is that the water should be divided. Dividing the water results in equality of outcomes, even though neither person has enough water to survive.[16]

The alternative view is that the person who has possession of the water should drink the water. In that case, a Pareto-efficient outcome is achieved, since one person alive is preferable to no one left alive.[17]

We should note that the issue was not whether one should give up one's own life for the life of another.[18] Sharing the water saves no one's life. Rather, the question is whether the person with the water should give up his or her own life, when the only purpose is to satisfy a principle of equality.[19]

Social justice and equal opportunity

Social justice can also be defined as equal opportunity. Using a lottery to determine who receives the water is socially just in terms of providing equal opportunity if the lottery assigns the water with equal probabilities. After the outcome of the lottery is known, one person has all the water, which is efficient.

The use of a lottery to assign the water presupposes that neither person owns the water in the first place. If the water were owned by one of the travelers, the lottery would require the owner of the water to donate the water as a prize in the lottery. In the circumstances of the two persons in the desert, one person owns the water, and so an obligation to offer the water as the prize for a lottery contradicts rights of ownership. A lottery is a socially just way of assigning the water only if there is no identified owner of the water.

Social justice and "survival of the fittest"

Consider two people in a desert without water. They see a flask of water lying ahead of them, and both set off in a run to be the first to reach the flask. The faster runner will reach the flask first and claim the water. Because the amount of water in the flask is only enough to allow one person to survive, it is efficient for one person to have all the water. Is it however fair, or socially just, that the faster runner has been able to claim the water? Alternatively, if one of the two travelers has better eyesight than the other, or is more perceptive by nature, this person

---

[16] The reason given for this view was that *it is better that both should drink and die than that one should witness the death of his fellow.* This was the view of Ben-Petura.

[17] This was the view of R. Akiva (c.50–135). The term "Pareto efficiency" was of course not used. This was before Pareto's time.

[18] The different views are alternative interpretations of the principle that we should care about others and not only care about ourselves.

[19] Adherents to Ben-Petura's position might counter that personal benefit should include the feeling of sharing a common fate by sharing the water. R. Akiva's position was that this type of suicide was not desirable behavior, and that *your life takes precedence over your fellow's life.* So, if you have the water and the water can save only one life, you should use the water to save yourself. R. Akiva was sensitive to the plight of the poor. He had been a shepherd and had married the daughter of a wealthy man, who disowned his daughter for marrying below the status of her family. After beginning his studies at the age of forty by learning the alphabet together with his young son, R. Akiva went on to become one of the most prominent of scholars.

will see and claim the water before the other traveler is aware of the presence of the water. Is it fair or socially just that the more alert person, or the person with better eyesight, obtains the water?

When different abilities determine who claims the water, the rule is survival of the fittest. Because differences in initial abilities influence who succeeds in obtaining the water, equality of opportunity is not present as it was in the case of a lottery.

One person might have the water through prior claim based on original owner-ship or through success in a lottery, and the second person might steal the water or appropriate the water by physical force. The outcome is again determined by the principle of survival of the fittest and is again efficient. The means whereby the water was obtained are now evidently not socially just. The principle of survival of the fittest does not, however, seek to accommodate social justice.

Social justice as the right of possession

Another definition of social justice is the right to possess what one rightfully owns. In the case of the water in the desert, use of the water by a person who owns the water is by this definition socially just, as well as efficient.

On the other hand, there can be disputes about rightful ownership. An example of such a dispute is provided by a problem that confronted Solomon, king of Israel some 3,000 years ago. In his court in Jerusalem, Solomon was confronted by two women who both claimed to be the mother of the same baby. Both women had given birth around the same time, but only one baby had survived. We see that in this case there is an indivisibility, as in the case of water in the desert. Babies cannot be divided. There was no evidence to support either woman's claim that she was the mother of the living child. Solomon faced a problem of asymmetric information. That is, he did not know the identity of the true mother, although each of the two women did know who the true mother was. Solomon decreed that, unless one of the two women renounced her claim to the baby, the baby would be cut in half and divided between the two claimants. The true mother thereupon renounced her claim, but the false claimant did not. Solomon decreed that the baby should be given to the woman who had renounced her claim to save the life of the child, and the true mother thereby received her child. The outcome was efficient since the baby was not divided, and the outcome was also just when justice is defined, not as equal division, but as right of possession by a true owner.

The two women who claimed the same baby are identified as harlots. We might ask why this identification was necessary, or important. An answer is that, since a harlot had low status in society, we are shown that all persons should be provided with equal access to justice without regard for their social status. In receiving the harlots and judging their case, Solomon demonstrated the principle of equality for all persons before the law.

Envy

An anecdote describes two farmers in different societies looking at the well-kept cow of a neighbor. In one society the farmer thinks to himself: "What a beautiful cow; I wish that I had a cow like that; I will work hard, and soon I will also be able to afford to buy such a cow." In another society, the farmer looks at the well-fed cow of his neighbor and thinks to himself: "I wish that cow would die." This second farmer might attempt to achieve equality by killing his neighbor's cow, or he might also promote the idea that cows should not be privately owned. We see here two different responses to inequality. In the first case, there is tolerance for inequality, and the farmer believes that, even if disadvantaged today, he can do better tomorrow. Perhaps the farmer who is envious of his neighbor's cow lives in a society that does not offer opportunities to aspire to obtain a similar cow by personal effort.

The response to inequality of the first farmer is efficient; the response of the second farmer is inefficient. The first farmer's response is to attempt to make himself better off without making anyone else worse off. The second farmer's response does not add to his own possessions but would make the neighbor worse off (by having the cow die).

In the case of the disputed baby, the false claimant was acting with the same envy as the farmer who wishes for the inefficient outcome where his neighbor's cow dies. Had the false claimant to the baby responded in the same way as the true mother and declared that she would rather give up the child to see the child live, there would have been no way of distinguishing between the two claims. The false claimant was, however, prepared to accept an inefficient outcome and to destroy, out of envy. As in the case of the envious farmer, she was content to have nothing, provided the other had nothing.

Incentives and social justice

Conflicts between social justice and efficiency can arise through the effect of incentives on behavior. Social justice can, for example, be regarded to require welfare payments to teenage mothers who have no means of support. A society with a social conscience does not allow a mother and her baby to be destitute on the streets. Nevertheless, welfare payments might encourage teenage pregnancy by reducing the personal cost of the mother. Teenage pregnancy is inefficient because the disruption to the mother's education diminishes prospects for a future self-reliant life and more taxes are needed to finance present and possibly future welfare payments. A case might consequently be made for government not providing welfare payments to destitute teenage mothers. Such a case, if it were made, would be based on efficiency, through effects of welfare payments on incentives and behavior before a child is born. The case in favor of providing welfare payments is based on social justice after the child has been born.

A policy could be announced that, as of a future date, income support will no longer be provided to anyone. This announcement may, however, have little credibility because people may not believe that they will be left to starve if they do not support themselves.[20] Providing no income support would make clear society's

---

[20] The type of problem we have identified here is known as moral hazard. We shall return to moral hazard in subsequent chapters.

preference that people be self-reliant. Yet such a policy might be viewed as socially unjust. We see that there can be a conflict between incentives for self-reliant behavior and perceptions of social justice.

1.1.8 Limitations of government

We have now described normative criteria for efficiency and for social justice, and we have seen that objectives of efficiency and social justice, or social conscience, can conflict. Responsibilities for government are introduced when markets fail to achieve efficiency or fail to satisfy a definition that has been chosen for social justice. Decisions by government may also be required about the choice between efficiency and social justice. We shall elaborate on the responsibilities of government in coming chapters.

There are also limitations on calling on government. The limitations take the following forms.

(1) Inadequate information is a limitation on government. We shall see that government may simply not have the information required to fulfill designated responsibilities.

(2) Government may not be able to please everybody. When decisions are made by majority voting, the majority will be pleased, but not the minority.

(3) When calling on government, voters and taxpayers can confront a principal-agent problem. A *principal-agent problem* arises when an agent, who should act faithfully on behalf of a principal, is able to make self-interested decisions that are to the disadvantage of the agent. The agent in our case is government. The principal is the voter or taxpayer on whose behalf government should be faithfully and benevolently acting. Elected political representatives and people who have chosen careers in government bureaucracy may be able to make self-interested decisions about public finance and public policy that are not in the broad public interest. A principal-agent problem can be solved if the principals (voters and taxpayers) can design an incentive scheme that will lead the agent (government) to act in the interest of the principal. Principal-agent problems are not always readily resolvable.

The principal-agent problem

We shall briefly expand on the principal-agent problem, since the idea of a principal-agent problem will recur a number of times as we study responsibilities and limitations of government. Principal-agent problems are associated with asymmetric information. That is, some people know what others do not. Taxpayers and voters in particular have imperfect information about decisions made by their representatives in government. The personal benefits from public spending decisions and public policies often reach taxpayers in circuitous and uncertain ways. When people spend their own money directly, they generally do so with adequate knowledge of the relation between personal costs and benefits. They usually do not have the same knowledge about personal benefits and costs for taxes paid to finance public spending.[21]

Taxpayers may not attempt to find out about personal benefits and costs from taxation and public spending. They may rather choose to remain *rationally ignorant*. People choose to be rationally ignorant because acquiring information about how taxes are spent is a personally costly activity, and the personal benefit from being informed about how tax revenue is spent may be less than the personal cost of obtaining the information. It is rational to be ignorant, or to choose not to know, if our personal costs of acquiring information exceed our personal benefits.

Still, some taxpayers might diligently set out to learn how taxes are spent by looking at published statements of government budgets. The taxpayers seeking information about public finance would then find that statements of government budgets provide only broad pictures of public spending and not the detailed accounts of spending required for a systematic evaluation of taxpayers' costs and benefits. For example, the statement of a government budget does not reveal whether a government official requires the assistance of three secretaries or four.

Corporate governance

Principal-agent problems also arise in the private sector and are expressed in problems of corporate governance. Shareholders as owners of a firm want profits or long-term market value to be maximized, whereas management of the firm may have personal objectives that contradict shareholder interests. Managers of private corporations can have more personal secretaries than are required for the most profitable operation of the company and may assign themselves unnecessary entertainment budgets.

To resolve principal-agent problems, the private sector has monitoring and incentive mechanisms. Incentives for efficiency of management can be provided in private firms through stock option schemes that tie managers' incomes and wealth to the value of a company's shares. The stock-option schemes attempt to resolve the principal-agent problem by giving managers incentives to act in shareholders' interests to maximize the value of the company's shares (although stock-option schemes can also be used to the disadvantage of shareholders in offering excessive rewards to management). Management in private firms is also monitored and disciplined by private owners who can replace inadequately performing managers. In large corporations where no one owns a significant share of the company, auditing firms and financial analysts in investment banks and brokerages monitor managerial performance. If the performance of management is revealed to be inadequate, financial analysts downgrade the firm in their stock-market evaluations, and the share price of the company falls. This is a market signal for the dismissal of

[21] This lack of knowledge is different from the limitation on calling on government because the government lacks adequate information to achieve designated objectives. Here the problem is not inadequate information by government, but inadequate information by taxpayers and voters about the behavior of government.

management. New owners might buy the company's stock at the depressed prices and install replacement management. A firm may also be compelled to declare bankruptcy because of a fall in demand or new competition. The bankruptcy is the consequence of the firm's inability to maintain profits. Through bankruptcy, or subsequent reorganization of the firm, the losses cease.

The monitoring and performance incentives present in the private sector cannot be used in government departments and agencies. Neither private owners nor asset market valuations exist to act as a discipline on government agencies and departments. The discipline of ultimately facing a cash constraint or reporting profits and losses does not confront government agencies. Tax-financed government departments or agencies cannot go bankrupt.

Corruption

Corruption sometimes occurs in government. For example, a public-health inspector can accept a bribe not to report a public-health infringement in a restaurant. The health inspector and the owner of the restaurant privately gain at the expense of the health of the public. A corrupt public-health inspector might also ask for a bribe not to report an untrue infringement; the inspector in that case seeks to impose a personal tax on the restaurant owner. The tax imposed by the public-health inspector is extortion and is an addition to the official taxes that the restaurant owner pays to the government. The possibility of corruption is a further limitation of calling on government.

In the private sector, there can be dishonesty in the actions of management and culpability in the actions of the auditing firms and analysts on whom shareholders rely to protect their interests and to provide information. Managers may withhold information from shareholders about lower earnings or earnings growth, and privately profit from the insider information while others who are less well-informed continue to buy stock that will ultimately severely decline in value. In these cases, there is asymmetric information, and a principal-agent problem again arises because the principals (shareholders) are unable to monitor and control the actions of agents (management).

The consequences of dishonest management and the culpability of auditors are, however, limited. Eventually losses can no longer be hidden by misreporting and by accounting misrepresentation, and the inappropriate actions of managers, auditors, investment banks, and analysts are revealed. There is a personal cost for the people who have acted dishonestly (some people may go to jail, while others may pay fines).[22] Through the information that is revealed and subsequent bankruptcy, acts of abuse by managers and auditors cease. There is not the same market discipline to contain corruption in government.

---

[22] The limited accountability of managers to shareholders and the potential for fraud is the basis of a case for public policy toward corporate governance. The policies include insider-trading laws that prohibit the use of privileged information for personal benefit; regulations about reporting assets, liabilities, and cash flows in corporate accounts; and criminal penalties for managers, corporate officers, and auditors who perpetrate or facilitate fraud.

The discipline of financial markets

We shall not be concerned with the responsibilities (and limitations) of government that relate to macroeconomic policy. Macroeconomic policy focuses on broad economic aggregates and asks questions about fiscal and monetary policy, exchange rates, and the role of central banks. Macroeconomic policy has however one implication of interest to us. We have observed that markets do not discipline government agencies, which cannot become bankrupt; however, from a macroeconomic perspective, markets do discipline public policy. Financial markets discipline governments when a government's macroeconomic policies are inappropriate. If government spending or inflation is excessive, financial markets can increase the interest rate that a government pays when borrowing, or foreign exchange markets can devalue the national currency.

1.1.9 The private cost of public finance

Markets and public finance are distinguished by respective private and public spending. Public spending is financed by taxes and government borrowing or the sale of bonds. Some governments have also financed public spending through inflationary financing (i.e., governments have sometimes simply printed money to finance their spending). Lotteries also sometimes provide governments with revenue. The different sources of public finance all ultimately place the burden of payment on private individuals. Taxes are current obligations to pay money to the government. Government bonds require future taxes to enable the government to repay past borrowing and to pay interest on the loans that people have made to government. Inflationary financing is a form of taxation through reductions in the value of money and other nominal assets that private individuals hold. Lotteries provide governments with revenue by exploiting people's unbounded optimism or their lack of understanding of objective probabilities. For both private and public spending, private individuals pay. In the words of the Milton Friedman (Nobel Laureate 1976), "there is no free lunch." Individuals always pay, even if (or especially if) government provides something for "nothing."

1.1.10 Summary

We can now summarize. We have seen that Adam Smith's claim of social benefit from private market decisions can be given formal expression in the efficiency of competitive markets where efficiency is expressed as maximal net social benefit. Market outcomes are also Pareto efficient since, through voluntary market decisions, people are made better off and no one is made worse off. Because efficiency requires that markets be competitive, a responsibility of government is identified through an antitrust or antimonopoly agency.

Competitive markets also ensure individual freedom. Order is spontaneous through freely made personal decisions and is not imposed through the will of some people over others.

There are nonetheless circumstances where markets do not result in efficiency. In chapters that follow, we shall study how public policy and public finance can improve efficiency. Markets also cannot necessarily ensure social justice or outcomes consistent with social conscience. We shall accordingly also study responsibilities of government directed at achieving social justice.

We have seen that efficiency and social justice can be irreconcilable when social justice is defined as requiring compensation for all losers from public policies, and, as the water-in-the-desert example showed, when social justice is defined as requiring equal outcomes for everybody. Incentives for efficient behavior and social justice or social conscience can also conflict. Some rules for distribution (survival of the fittest) place no weight at all on social justice. On the hand, a quest for equality may place no weight on efficiency (as when the water is divided). We have noted that social justice can also be defined as respect for rightful possession, as in the case of the disputed baby. We have seen that envy and efficiency are related.

We have noted that there are limitations on taxpayers and voters calling on government to take corrective action when markets have failed to provide efficiency or social justice. Government may have inadequate information to fulfill its responsibilities. Because collective decisions are required, government may be unable to please everybody. As well, a political principal-agent problem limits the accountability of government to taxpayers; government departments are not subject to the financial discipline of private firms, and incentives that can be used in private firms are not available for addressing the political principal-agent problem. Financial markets can, however, discipline a government's macroeconomic policies.

Corruption can sometimes be a problem in government. While dishonest behavior can likewise arise in the private sector, limitations on functioning without profits in the private sector in the end reveal the dishonest behavior.

We finally noted that although private and public spending differ in terms of who makes the decisions regarding how money is spent (the private individual or the government), it is private individuals who finance both private and public spending.

References and related literature

On the writings of Adam Smith, see Macafie (1959), Reisman (1975), Evensky (1993), and Tribe (1999); for interpretations of the invisible hand, see Rothschild (1994) and Grammy (2000). On normative and positive analysis, see Friedman (1953). On rational ignorance, see Downs (1957). On macroeconomics, see Drazen (2000).

Downs, A., 1957. *An Economic Theory of Democracy*. Harper and Row, New York.
Drazen, A., 2000. *Political Economy in Macroeconomics*. Princeton University Press, Princeton, New Jersey.
Evensky, J., 1993. Ethics and the invisible hand. *Journal of Economic Perspectives* 7, 197–205.

Friedman, M., 1953. The methodology of positive economics. In *Essays in Positive Economics*, University of Chicago Press, Chicago. Reprinted 1994 in *The Philosophy of Economics*, D. M. Hausman (ed.). Cambridge University Press, New York, 180–213.

Grammy, W. D., 2000. What did Smith mean by the invisible hand? *Journal of Political Economy* 108, 441–65.

Kemp, M. C., 1962. The gains from international trade. *Economic Journal* 72, 803–19.

Macafie, A. L. 1959. Adam Smith's Moral Sentiments as foundation for his Wealth of Nations. *Oxford Economic Papers* 2, 209–28.

Pareto, V., 1909. *Manuel d'economique politique*. Girard and Briere, Paris.

Reisman, D. A., 1975. *Adam Smith's Sociological Economics*. Croon Helm, London and Barnes & Noble, New York.

Rothschild, E., 1994. Adam Smith and the invisible hand. *American Economic Review, Papers and Proceedings* 84, 319–22.

Smith, A., (1759) 1976. *The Theory of Moral Sentiments*. Oxford University Press, Oxford.

Smith, A., (1776) 1937. *An Enquiry into the Nature and Causes of the Wealth of Nations*, E. Cannan (ed.). Modern Library Edition. Random House, New York.

Tribe, K., 1999. Adam Smith: Critical theorist. *Journal of Economic Literature* 37, 609–32.

Willig, R. D., 1976. Consumer's surplus without apology. *American Economic Review* 66, 589–97.

Questions for discussion

1. Adam Smith was a professor of moral philosophy. How does his case for the market reflect ethical considerations?

2. What is the meaning of "spontaneous order achieved through the market"? How is spontaneous order related to efficiency and to individual freedom?

3. Efficiency and personal freedom are two distinct benefits of competitive markets. How do competitive markets assure personal freedom?

4. Maximal net social benefit $W = B - C$ and Pareto efficiency are two definitions of efficiency. What is the relation between the two definitions? What is the role of compensation in the definitions?

5. Explain how self-interested decisions of individual buyers and sellers in competitive markets assure efficiency through maximal $W = B - C$. How can we be assured that competitive market outcomes are Pareto efficient? (See also Supplement 1A.)

6. When not in equilibrium, how do competitive markets adjust to the market equilibrium price and quantity? What happens when there is more than a single market equilibrium? (See also Supplement 1A.)

7. How do competitive markets assure efficiency in an economy when we account for the relation between product and factor markets? (See Supplement 1B.)

8. Preserving competition is the first responsibility that we identified for government. Is the presence of a single seller sufficient to prove that a market is not competitive?

9. When a public policy is proposed for which total benefits exceed total costs (i.e., $W = B - C > 0$) but some people lose, would you insist on actual compensation for losers before agreeing to implement the policy? Explain.

10. What is the difference between a normative statement and a positive statement? Do you believe that people are more likely to disagree over normative or positive statements?

11. What are the different ways in which social justice can be defined? In particular, compare the social justice of rewards in a competitive market (where people are paid the value of their marginal contribution) to social justice defined as equality.

12. Which of the two positions do you support regarding sharing of the water in the situation described in the water-in-the-desert example? What is the reason for your decision?

13. What are your views, as normative and positive statements, on survival of the fittest as a rule for determining who benefits from the water?

14. Would you expect a society where people are more envious of each other to be less efficient than a society where there is less envy and greater tolerance for inequality? What is the relation between envy and efficiency? Consider a society of 100 people where 100 tons of wheat and a horse are available to be shared among the population. Only one person can have ownership of the horse. What would you say to a person who suggests that the horse be given away to someone in another country or society rather than be assigned to someone in the society by a lottery, because the envy due to one person ultimately owning the horse is not worth the expected benefit from the opportunity to own the horse through the lottery? Would your position change if there were twenty horses or seventy horses or ninety horses?

15. The case of water in the desert is an allegory for broader cases of indivisibilies that arise in a society. What are such cases?

16. What is a principal-agent problem? How is the idea of rational ignorance of taxpayers related to the principal-agent problem between taxpayers and decision makers in government?

17. How does the principal-agent problem between taxpayers and government differ from the principal-agent problem between shareholders and management in a private company?

18. Why does public finance imply private finance in one way or another?

19. In the place where you live or study, what is the division between private spending and public expenditure of government? What share of national income is paid to governments in taxes?

20. How many levels of government are involved in taxation and public spending in the place where you live or study? What are the primary responsibilities of the different levels of government?

1.2
Property Rights and the Rule of Law

In showing how competitive markets achieve efficiency, we have taken for granted the presence of the rule of law. The rule of law allows property rights or rights of ownership to be certified and protected. It is a responsibility of government to ensure the rule of law.

1.2.1 Principles of the rule of law
The principles of the rule of law specify rights of ownership of possessions and property, as well as basic human rights, including the right to be free of coerced subservience to others, the right not to be kidnapped and enslaved or raped, and

the right to life itself. Under anarchy without the rule of law, the strong can prevail over the weak, and possessions and life are not safe.

The rule of law is not the same as the rule of government. When there is no rule of law, there may be the rule by government. Without the protection provided by the rule of law, arbitrary and whimsical rule of men or women who control government can subvert the law, so that the "law" becomes a means of appropriation and repression rather than a means of ensuring basic individual rights.

The rule of law is inconsistent with laws and regulations that are retroactive. It is a contradiction of the rule of law for people to be accused today of crimes committed yesterday that were not designated as crimes yesterday. If laws can be retroactive, *anything* that a person did in the past can be arbitrarily transformed from legal to illegal. By not allowing retroactive laws, the rule of law ensures that property that belonged to someone yesterday belongs to the same person today, unless the property was voluntarily sold or given away.[1]

Markets and the rule of law

The benefits from markets that we outlined in Section 1.1 are based on the rule of law. We can identify different types of markets: (1) markets for goods and for consumer services; (2) factor markets, for factors of production such as labor; and (3) asset markets and associated financial and credit markets. By certifying ownership, the rule of law allows the various markets to function.

In product and asset markets, buyers know that sellers have the right to sell. Buyers also know that, after payment has been made, new ownership is defined through the sale of property to the buyer.

In labor markets, the rule of law provides property rights to the value of a person's output. People who are not assured that the output they produce (or the value of the output) belongs to them lack incentives to be productive.

Asset markets mobilize resources for investment and allow individuals to spread risk by diversifying sources of income. Without property rights certified by the rule of law, assets cannot be traded. For example, a family cannot exchange its house for another house. Suppose that this family lived in the house it built but that the right of possession was not recognized by law and, hence, was not protected by the rule of law. In addition to being unable to sell the house, the family could also not have borrowed through a mortgage to finance the construction of the house. Nor could the house be used as collateral for a loan. Also, insurance cannot be bought against damage to the house because the house does not have a legally defined owner who can enter into an insurance contract. Without certified property rights, the house provides shelter, but cannot perform the additional function of providing real backing for financial assets. In general, without certified

---

[1] Besides ensuring respect for property rights, the rule of law includes legal means of solving disputes and provision for bankruptcy to protect rights of debtors and creditors.

property rights, credit markets are restricted because without defined ownership of assets collateral or security for loans cannot be provided. A house cannot, for example, be the backing for part of a portfolio of mortgages without the tradability of the mortgage that is facilitated by property rights through the rule of law, since the holder of the mortgage must be able to certify ownership to a part of the value of the house. Similarly, without the rule of law to certify property rights, a factory cannot be owned by a firm that in turn has diverse shareholders who diversify assets and spread risk through ownership of different types of stocks. Without the rule of law, physical property can therefore exist, but a society is denied the benefits of asset markets and financial services that rely on defined property rights.

Productive use of resources and the rule of law

A nomadic hunter-gatherer population roaming where land is plentiful would not require private property rights to land.[2] When competition for natural resources becomes sufficiently intense – by animals in the wild and by people for fodder for domesticated animals – private property rights to grazing land become valuable. Property rights likewise become valuable when crops are planted, when a house is built, or when any type of output that requires input and effort can be physically appropriated by others. Without the rule of law to define property rights, these valuable possessions become contestable by force. Appropriation, extortion, and theft, but not the market, are the means of acquiring the wealth and goods of others, and a person can only have as much property as he or she is capable of successfully defending.

The activities of appropriation, extortion, theft, and defense use resources and personal time and initiative in socially wasteful ways. The resources and time could be used productively in ways that *add* to a society's output and wealth, rather than being used in attempts to appropriate and defend wealth or possessions that *already exist*. When the rule of law protects private property rights, people's time and initiative can be used for productive purposes.

The benefits from the rule of law

We can therefore identify two types of benefits from the rule of law:

(1) Without the rule of law, markets cannot exist, and a society loses the benefits of market exchange whether for products, labor, or assets and financial services.

(2) Without markets, people still could be self-sufficient and live by using their own abilities and resources to provide for themselves. Nonetheless, a second social loss arises in the absence of the rule of law because of incentives to use resources to appropriate property.

---

[2] The rule of law would still be required to protect personal freedom, life, and personal possessions.

An example where the rule of law saved lives

Prisoners were once private property protected by the rule of law. Bruno Frey and Heinz Buhofer (1988) describe a case (from the battle of Poitiers in 1356) where a prisoner was claimed as a personal property, but the captor, after seeing someone else whom he could capture, went off to stake a claim to another prisoner. A new captor then appeared and claimed the first prisoner as his own. Legal ownership of the prisoner could be contested, and prisoners were privately valuable for ransom or for servitude. The original captor appealed in court to retrieve possession of the prisoner; however, the judge ruled that the claim to legal possession had been forfeited when the prisoner had been abandoned. When property rights to prisoners ceased, prisoners became collective possessions of the state; the state had no personal incentive to keep prisoners alive, so mass slaughter in warfare began. The end of certifiable private rights to prisoners therefore resulted in loss of life that could have been preserved through private property rights.

Justice and efficiency

The appropriation of property when property rights are absent can be unjust. The rule of law ensures that property that belongs to someone else is not obtainable through force but requires the voluntary exchange of a market (or a truly voluntary gift).

What, however, would we say of the activities of the legendary English thief Robin Hood, who robbed the "rich" and gave the proceeds to the "poor"? Robin Hood did not respect the property rights of the rich. In Robin Hood's view, the rich had unfairly appropriated the property of the poor in the first place; therefore, he viewed his activities of appropriation as socially just. Irrespective of views of social justice, Robin Hood's activities were socially inefficient. The society of Robin Hood's time would have been better off if Robin Hood had chosen productive employment rather than spending time in robbery and appropriation.

Yet, for Robin Hood to have had an incentive to choose productive activity in preference to theft, he would have required assurances that his own property rights were to be protected so that he could benefit from his own production. Had government (in the form the sheriff of Nottingham) protected the property of everybody, Robin Hood would have had reason to be productive and not be a thief. Because the sheriff failed to respect the property rights of the common people, Robin Hood felt under no obligation to honor the rights of possession of the sheriff and the nobility whom the sheriff represented. He accordingly spent his time unproductively ensconced in the forest, coming out every now and then to take property by force and then returning the property that he had taken to its rightful owners.

Independent of the ethical merit of returning property to rightful owners, the focus on appropriation rather than production made the life of Robin Hood unproductive – as were the lives of the sheriff and his henchmen who robbed the poor in the first place.

TABLE 1.1. THE PRISONERS' DILEMMA WITHOUT THE RULE OF LAW

	Person 2 only produces	Person 2 uses resources to steal
Person 1 only produces	3, 3	1, 4
Person 1 uses resources to steal	4, 1	2, 2

1.2.2 The inefficiency of anarchy

Circumstances known as the prisoners' dilemma provide a way of describing the social loss from appropriation when the rule of law does not protect property rights. We shall first explain the dilemma without reference to prisoners. Later we shall see how prisoners were involved, and how the dilemma received its name.

We can consider two identical people in a situation of anarchy without the rule of law. We view the two people as representing the whole of a society, and our conclusions will apply to larger populations. Each person faces the same *strategic* decision whether to use time and resources productively or to steal from the other.[3]

We shall refer to decisions to *steal*, although, in an anarchic society, a legal and judicial system does not exist to certify private ownership and theft is therefore not strictly definable as illegal. There is nonetheless a conception of natural rights of possession. For example, natural rights of possession were present when people cleared a field and planted and tended a crop. The crop belonged naturally to the persons who cleared the field and planted and cared for the crop because the crop would not exist without their effort. More generally, natural rights of possession are present when a person produces something with his or her own effort. That is, output or wealth belongs naturally to those who make the effort to create it – we would add, however, without violating anyone else's natural property rights. We define theft in anarchy as people taking property that, by natural right of possession, belongs to others.

Table 1.1 shows the four possible outcomes of the two persons' decisions regarding productive effort and appropriation or theft. Each person can choose to be exclusively productive or to use some time and effort to appropriate from the other. No resources are used in defense because defense is ineffective. A decision to appropriate always yields a return.

The first number in a cell shows the personal benefit from the outcome to person 1 and the second number indicates the personal benefit to person 2. Since the two persons represent the society, the sum of their benefits is the total benefit

---

[3] A decision is strategic when the benefit to one person from a decision depends on the decision made by another person. In competitive markets, decisions are not strategic because people buy and sell at the market price without being influenced by, and without influencing, the decisions of other buyers and sellers.

to society. An outcome is socially efficient when the sum of personal benefits of the two persons is maximized.

The numbers in Table 1.1 also indicate rankings of outcomes for each person. When both persons use all their resources productively, they each have personal benefits of 3. When they each use some resources to steal from one another, they both have personal benefits of 2. The outcomes (3, 3) and (2, 2) are symmetric. The two people were identical before they make their decisions, and they receive identical benefits after they both make the same decision.

The outcomes (4, 1) and (1, 4) provide asymmetric benefits. In these two cases, the person who steals has a benefit of 4, and the person who only uses resources productively has a benefit of 1. The best personal outcome 4 is obtained by stealing when the other person does not steal. The lowest benefit 1 is obtained by a person who does not steal when the other does.

The efficient outcome for society is (3, 3), where both persons use all their resources productively and no resources are wastefully used in taking output from the other. At (3, 3), total benefit is $(3 + 3) = 6$, which is the largest possible total benefit.

The next best outcome for society as a whole is an asymmetric outcome (4, 1) or (1, 4), where total benefit for society is 5. The worst outcome for the society is (2, 2), where both persons use resources (including time and initiative) to steal from one another. In this case, the total benefit for the society is a minimal 4.

The equilibrium outcome

Table 1.1 describes a game because people are strategically interacting with one another and the benefit to one person depends on what the other does. The game in Table 1.1 is noncooperative because the two individuals do not cooperate with one another when making decisions. That is, the game is noncooperative because each person independently makes a decision without consulting or coordinating with the other.

With each person making a decision based on personal self-interest, which outcome can we expect? We are looking for an equilibrium outcome of the two persons' simultaneous decisions (they decide at the same time).

In an equilibrium outcome, there is no tendency for change to another outcome. The definition that we shall use for the concept of equilibrium is called a *Nash equilibrium*.[4] In a Nash equilibrium, a person cannot gain by changing his or her decision, given the decisions that others have made. That is, people could change their minds, but they do not.

There is a unique Nash equilibrium in Table 1.1 at the outcome (2, 2) where both persons choose to steal. When at (2, 2), the two persons cannot independently change their decisions to improve their benefits, given the decision that the other

---

[4] Nash equilibrium is named after John Nash, who received the Nobel Prize in economics in 1995 (see Nash 1951). The equilibrium is also called Cournot-Nash, with reference to the nineteenth-century French economist and engineer Augustin Cournot (1801–77) who formulated a similar idea (Cournot 1838).

has made. A change of mind by either person not to steal, given the decision of the other to steal, reduces personal benefit from 2 to 1.

The efficient outcome at (3, 3) is not a Nash equilibrium. At (3, 3) neither person is using resources to steal from the other. Given that the other person is not stealing, a personally better outcome is achieved by changing to stealing. Stealing when the other person is not stealing increases personal benefit from 3 to 4. A gain from a change of mind by one person is sufficient for an outcome not to be a Nash equilibrium. Here both persons are identical and have the same incentive to change their decisions, which leads to the inefficient outcome (2, 2), where they both steal.

Dominant strategies

In the game in Table 1.1, each person has a *dominant* strategy. "Strategy" here is another word for decision. A dominant strategy or decision exists when a person's best course of action does not depend on the other person's decision. The dominant strategy in Table 1.1 is to steal. That is, stealing is the best decision whether or not the other person decides to steal.

We can confirm that stealing is a dominant strategy by looking at the structure of personal benefits in Table 1.1. Consider the decision of person 1. Person 1 asks: what should I do, if person 2 decides not to steal. Person 1's choice in column 1, where person 2 does not steal, is between a personal benefit of 3 from choosing to be productive and a personal benefit of 4 from choosing to steal. If person 2 does not steal, person 1's best response is therefore to steal.

Then person 1 asks: what however should I do if person 2 decides to steal? The choice for person 1 in column 2, where person 2 steals, is between a personal benefit of 1, should person 1 not steal, and a personal benefit of 2 should person 1 steal. If person 2 steals, the best response of person 1 is therefore again to steal.

That is, no matter what the decision of person 2, person 1's best decision is to steal. Stealing is therefore person 1's dominant strategy.[5]

Since the two persons in Table 1.1 are identical, the best personal decision for person 1 is also the best personal decision for person 2. Person 2 therefore has the same dominant strategy of deciding to steal.

The inefficiency of independent personal self-interested decisions

Since the dominant strategy of both persons is to steal, this is what they do. They steal rather than using their efforts and resources in exclusively productive ways. The society accordingly finds itself at the inefficient Nash equilibrium (2, 2).[6]

The Nash equilibrium (2, 2) is the worst outcome for society as a whole, since the total benefits (2 + 2 = 4) are the lowest among the possible outcomes. The

---

[5] Or we can say that stealing strictly dominates not stealing.
[6] Whenever people have dominant strategies, the outcome of applying the dominant strategies is a Nash equilibrium.

Nash equilibrium at (2, 2) is also quite clearly Pareto inefficient. A move from (2, 2) to (3, 3) makes both persons individually better off. It is clearly worthwhile for the society composed of the two persons to find a way to move from (2, 2) to (3, 3).

Promises and credibility

Suppose that the two persons simply agreed to move to (3, 3) from (2, 2) by promising not to steal from one other. A promise is only credible if people gain from following through with their promises. We have seen that, at (3, 3), each person has a personal incentive to deviate from the behavior that would sustain (3, 3). That is, (3, 3) is not a Nash equilibrium. Since keeping a promise not to steal is in neither person's self-interest, and since there is no means of enforcing promises (or contracts) because there is no rule of law, neither person may have reason to believe the other's promise. With promises to cooperate not credible, the equilibrium can only be at (2, 2), where individual decisions are made independently and noncooperatively.[7]

Simultaneous and sequential decisions

We have viewed the two persons as making decisions simultaneously (or, if not exactly simultaneously, each person decides without knowing the decision that the other has made). The two persons have full information about the possible outcomes of their combined decisions. Each knows that the dominant strategy is to steal. The simultaneous personal decisions are thus to steal, which results in the inefficient outcome (2, 2).

Decisions could also be made sequentially. Person 1 might, for example, decide first. Person 1's dominant strategy is to steal, independently of the decision that person 2 will make. When it is the turn of person 2 to decide, person 2 will also

---

[7] The name "prisoners' dilemma" comes from a situation where the police have evidence to convict two prisoners of a minor crime but suspect that they have committed a serious crime for which the police have no evidence. The prisoners know that there is no evidence regarding the major crime and that they can be convicted of the major crime only if one of them confesses and implicates the other. The police take the prisoners to separate rooms and present each prisoner independently with the following alternatives. (1) If neither prisoner confesses to the serious crime, they will both be convicted of the minor crime, for which the sentence is light (e.g., two years in jail). (2) If one of them confesses to the major crime and the other does not, the prisoner who confesses will receive a relatively lenient sentence (e.g., one year in jail), whereas the prisoner who did not confess will receive a very harsh sentence (e.g., ten years in jail). (3) If both prisoners confess, they each receive quite a severe sentence (e.g., seven years in jail), but less severe than the sentence of a prisoner who does not confess when the other does (which is ten years). The prisoners confront a dilemma: if neither confesses, there is no evidence regarding the serious crime, but the dominant strategy is to confess to the serious crime for which there is no evidence. Each prisoner reasons along the following lines: "Either my partner will confess or he will not. If he confesses, my best decision is also to confess (seven years in jail is better than ten). If he does not confess, again my best decision is to confess (one year in jail is better than two)". Hence, whatever decision the other makes, each prisoner's personal best response is to confess to the major crime. We can observe a potentially unjust aspect of this situation, which is that in the Nash equilibrium the two prisoners confess to the major crime whether they have committed the major crime or not.

decide to steal because stealing is person 2's dominant strategy. Person 1 when deciding first knows that person 2 will decide to steal, and when deciding first chooses to steal. Person 2, when deciding second, responds to person 1's decision to steal by also stealing. Through sequential decisions, the two persons again arrive at the inefficient equilibrium (2, 2).

Repeated interactions in small and large populations

We have considered a single encounter between the two persons. If the two people met each other in repeated interactions, might they cooperate? They both clearly benefit from cooperation to achieve (3, 3) in place of (2, 2). If they could each develop a personal reputation for cooperation, so that each person believes that the other will cooperate, each person could safely decide not to steal, and the outcome would be (3, 3). That is, the problem, or dilemma, could be resolved if the two persons had reason to trust one another to honor a promise not to steal from the other.

We shall return to such repeated interactions (or repeated games) in a later chapter. At this point, we can note that there is no personal incentive for cooperation in repeated situations of the prisoners' dilemma if the number of interactions is known in advance and is finite. To see why this is so, consider two people who know that they going to interact ten times. They both know that, in the tenth interaction, there is no value to having a reputation for being the sort of person who cooperates, since the value of reputation is in influencing future behavior of the other person, but there is no future if the tenth interaction is known to be the last.

There is therefore no personal incentive not to steal in the tenth interaction because reputation has no value in the tenth and final interaction. Both persons however also know that reputation for cooperating has no value in the ninth interaction because, when they find themselves in the ninth interaction, both persons know there will be no cooperation in the tenth interaction. Nor then does reputation have a value in the eighth interaction, nor in any of the preceding interactions. By a process of backward induction, reputation never has value when the number of interactions is known and finite, and there is no incentive for cooperation beginning from the first interaction.

If interactions are known to go on forever, or for long but uncertain periods of time, and if the future is sufficiently important for both persons,[8] reputation for cooperating can have ongoing value. People then might cooperate and the efficient outcome (3, 3) can be repeatedly achieved.

However, a problem stands in the way of cooperation in repeated interactions in large populations. When two people know one other, personal reputation for cooperating is valuable. In large populations where people are anonymous, personal reputation has no value because nobody knows the reputation

---

[8] The future must be important because the benefit from reputation is in the future. Another way of saying that the future needs to be sufficiently important is that the rate at which people discount future benefits must be sufficiently low.

TABLE 1.2. A PENALTY FOR STEALING

	Person 2 only produces	Person 2 uses resources to steal
Person 1 only produces	3, 3	1, 2
Person 1 uses resources to steal	2, 1	0, 0

of the other people whom they might encounter. There is therefore no point in cooperating.

The personal benefit from external enforcement
Rather than hoping to rely on cooperation through decisions in repeated interactions, the efficient outcome (3, 3) can be achieved by *imposing* the rule of law. The rule of law requires external enforcement to ensure that people do not steal. The rule of law imposed through external enforcement is a responsibility of government, since government has a monopoly on legal coercion.

By using the legal right of coercion to apply the rule of law, government can ensure the efficient outcome where all resources are used productively. We have now a seeming paradox. The paradox is that usually we do not expect people to benefit from coercion. Yet, in the prisoners' dilemma, people do benefit from coercion and indeed wish to be coerced. For, in being coerced by government not to steal, people are made personally better off.

Markets and the prisoners' dilemma
In a competitive market, Adam Smith's idea of an invisible hand describes how independent, personally beneficial decisions achieve efficiency for the population at large. In the interaction in anarchy described by the prisoners' dilemma, the invisible hand fails because personal decisions that people independently make in their own best interest result in the inefficient Nash equilibrium.

Legal deterrence
Table 1.2 shows how legal deterrence implemented through the rule of law can achieve efficiency. A penalty of 2 is set as punishment for theft. This penalty is subtracted from personal benefit whenever a decision has been made to steal.[9] The penalty changes the dominant strategy (or dominant decision), which is now not to steal. Consider again person 1's decision. In Table 1.2, if person 2 does not steal, person 1's best response is also not to steal, since 3 > 2. If person 2 does decide to steal, person 1's best response is still not to steal, since 1 > 0. The dominant strategy of person 1 is therefore not to steal. Likewise, the dominant strategy of person 2 is not to steal.

---

[9] A person who steals when the other does not receives $(4 - 2) = 2$. When both steal, each receives $(2 - 2) = 0$.

We can note that, in Table 1.2, no actual punishment is ever necessary, since personal rational behavior in Table 1.2 is never to steal. Therefore, the rule of law does not punish but instead rationally deters.

Rather than government protecting property rights through the rule of law, individuals could take private actions to defend their property. Protection provided by government through the rule of law has however the advantage that, by changing incentives, government provides collective benefit to the entire population at once. Everybody benefits from the changed incentives that move the society to the efficient outcome (3, 3).

Credible threats of punishment

Incentives are changed and deterrence is provided, only if the threat of punishment is credible. Credibility requires that the threat of punishment could be implemented if required. For threat of punishment to be an effective deterrent, the means must exist to implement the punishment. Resources therefore must be expended to make the threat of punishment credible. Credible deterrence is accordingly not costless. Public spending is required on the institutions of the rule of law, including the court system and police. Therefore, with changed incentives through penalties, punishment is never required because it is not rational to steal, but the reason why punishment is never required is that the threat of punishment is credible.

Private costs and public spending

We expect credible deterrence provided through the rule of law by government to use fewer resources than individuals would use in total for private defense. Another reason for preferring the rule of law through government to private spending on defense is that private spending protects according to an individual's ability to pay for personal protection. Protection of property rights through private spending is therefore more akin to anarchy than to the rule of law because in anarchy personal power relative to others determines the possessions that people have. It is a principle of the rule of law that people are equal before the law.[10] The rule of law therefore cannot be based on private capabilities or private spending, which cannot be relied upon to provide the equality before the law that defines the presence of the rule of law.

1.2.3 Ethical behavior

We have considered people who make decisions based on personal material benefit from stealing and not stealing. The government resolves the prisoners' dilemma that people confront in making this decision by imposing the rule of law

---

[10] Hence, as noted in Section 1.1, when King Solomon judged the two women who claimed the same child, the women were identified as harlots, to demonstrate that all people are equal before the law, even those at the lowest status of society.

TABLE 1.3. ETHICAL RESTRAINT

	Person 2 only produces	Person 2 uses resources to steal
Person 1 only produces	5, 3	3, 4
Person 1 uses resources to steal	1, 1	2, 2

and announcing a credible threat of punishment. Collective benefit makes the rule of law through government more efficient (or less costly) than expending personal resources for personal defense. Moreover, we have observed that personal defense is inconsistent with the principle of equality before the law. This has provided the basis for a case for government to provide and oversee the rule of law. Yet people guided by ethical principles do not need the deterrence imposed by government not to take the property of others. In the situation described in Table 1.3, person 1 has personal ethical inhibitions about stealing or appropriating other people's property. Person 2's benefits remain as described in the prisoners' dilemma.

Person 1 feels best off when no one steals (where person 1's benefit is 5). The worst outcome for person 1 (with benefit 1) is where he or she steals when the other person does not. This outcome in contrast yielded the personally highest benefit in the prisoners' dilemma.[11]

The dominant strategy of person 1 is *not to* steal: no matter what person 2 decides to do, person 1 feels better off when not stealing. Person 1 will therefore not steal. Person 2's best response when person 1 does not steal is to decide to steal. The outcome is then (3, 4) where person 2 steals from person 1, but person 1 does not steal from person 2. This outcome is a Nash equilibrium.[12]

The outcome (3, 4) in Table 1.3 where person 2 steals from person 1 while person 1 is honest and only uses resources productively is better for society at large than the outcome at (2, 2) where both persons waste resources in stealing from one another. Ethical behavior, however, is costly in material terms for person 1, who is victimized by person 2's predatory behavior.

The efficient outcome for society in Table 1.3 is (5, 3), where no resources are wastefully used in stealing.[13] The outcome (5, 3) is not a Nash equilibrium because person 2 can do better by switching to stealing, which moves the outcome to (3, 4).

Achieving and maintaining the efficient outcome (5, 3) therefore again requires changing incentives (for person 2) through the rule of law. A penalty of 2 for stealing changes the dominant strategy of person 2 to not stealing and establishes the efficient outcome (5, 3).

[11] Person 1 also prefers not stealing even if the other person does steal (where the benefit is 3) to an outcome where he or she steals and person 2 also steals (where the benefit is 2).

[12] A change to stealing decreases person 1's benefit from 3 to 2. A change to not stealing reduces person 2's benefit from 4 to 3.

[13] The total (5 + 3) exceeds (3 + 4).

TABLE 1.4. THE WEAK AND THE STRONG

	Person 2 (strong) uses resources to appropriate	Person 2 (strong) is only productive
Person 1 (weak) produces	2, 27	12, 20
Person 1 (weak) does not work beyond subsistence	4, 17	4, 20

Efficiency is therefore achieved through the rule of law. At the same time, there is *social justice* because the rule of law protects honest people from victimization.

In the prisoners' dilemma, since both persons are made better off by the rule of law, both would vote to introduce the rule of law. The same consensus to introduce the rule of law is not present when one person behaves ethically. The rule of law improves the personal outcome for the ethical person 1 but is disadvantageous for predatory person 2.

Since the implementation of rule of law is efficient, the gainer (the honest person 1) could compensate the loser (the predatory person 2) and still be better off after the rule of law has been introduced.[14] However, should honest person 1 be required to compensate predatory person 2 in order for the rule of law to be implemented? Note that this question is normative. A requirement by person 2 to receive compensation for the rule of law is extortion, and is itself inconsistent with the rule of law.

Of course, there is no need for external enforcement through the rule of law imposed by government, if person 2 is also honest. If person 2 also respects the property rights of others, the efficient (and socially just) outcome is obtained through voluntary behavior without government.[15]

1.2.4 The strong and the weak

When some people are honest and others not, we have an *asymmetry* in the population. Asymmetry is also present when some people are strong and some people are weak, and the weak have no means of defense against the strong.

With the rule of law absent, Table 1.4 shows outcomes of the different decisions that the strong and weak can make. The first number is the benefit from an outcome to person 1 who is weak, and the second number is the benefit to person 2 who is strong. The weak decide whether to work. The strong decide between using all their resources productively and using some resources in attempting to take output

---

[14] There is benefit of 8 in total in the efficient outcome (5, 3) compared to 7 in the Nash equilibrium (3, 4).

[15] In Table 1.3, we replace the benefits for person 2 with the benefits for person 1. The efficient outcome (5, 5) is then the unique Nash equilibrium.

from the weak. The decision facing the strong is as in the prisoners' dilemma. The weak however cannot (or do not) reciprocally take from the strong.[16]

The society described in Table 1.4 faces two sources of inefficiency:

(1) The use of resources by the strong to appropriate output of the weak is wasteful. The resources could be productively used to add to available output.
(2) It is inefficient for the weak to have to choose to be idle because they fear appropriation of their output by the strong.

We see in Table 1.4 that the strong produce 20 and the weak produce 12 when all resources are used productively. The efficient outcome for society is (12, 20). The sum $(12 + 20) = 32$ is greater than the total available in any other outcome.

Let us now look for a Nash equilibrium.[17] The efficient outcome (12, 20) is not a Nash equilibrium because the strong can do better by appropriating the output of the weak and moving to (2, 27). The strong then have 27 instead of 20.

We arrive at the values of (2, 27) in the following way:

(1) Appropriation is costly for the strong, who use 3 in terms of output lost by diverting resources to taking output from the weak.
(2) The weak require 2 for subsistence (so that they do not starve), and the strong leave the weak with this subsistence consumption. The weak therefore have 2.
(3) The strong take $10 = (12 - 2)$ from the weak (the weak have produced 12), and, since the strong have incurred a cost of 3 in using resources for appropriation, the strong have $20 + 10 - 3 = 27$.

The outcome (2, 27), where the weak work but lose above-subsistence output to the strong, is also not a Nash equilibrium. The weak can now do better by not producing beyond their subsistence needs. This moves the outcome to (4, 17). These values are obtained as follows:

(1) The benefit of 4 for the weak consists of their subsistence consumption 2, plus a benefit of 2 from leisure, or the additional benefit of 2 may derive not from leisure but from the satisfaction that the strong have come to the fields of the weak and there is nothing for the strong to appropriate. The benefit of 4 obtained by the weak when they do not work cannot be appropriated.
(2) The strong have 17 because they have come to the fields of the weak to find that the weak have not worked and have incurred a cost of 3 in the unsuccessful attempt at appropriation. The cost of appropriation 3 is deducted from the output of 20 the strong could have produced if they had used all their resources productively, which leaves the strong with 17.

---

[16] We shall view the strong and the weak as collective groups. Person 1 in Table 1.4 represents the weak and person 2 represents the strong.

[17] That is, we are looking for an outcome where neither the strong nor the weak have an incentive to change their decision, given the decision of the other.

The outcome (4, 17) is not a Nash equilibrium because the strong can again do better, by not using resources to attempt appropriation. That is, if there is nothing to appropriate because the weak have not worked, the strong have had no reason to expend resources on appropriation. The outcome then moves to (4, 20), where the strong use all their resources productively, and the weak do not work beyond subsistence.

The outcome (4, 20) is also not a Nash equilibrium. If the strong do not set out to appropriate, the weak can do better by working. A decision by the weak to work moves the outcome back to (12, 20).

We began at (12, 20) and have returned to this outcome without finding a Nash equilibrium. The cycle among the different alternative outcomes begins again. Unlike the case of the prisoners' dilemma, there is no Nash equilibrium because, in every outcome, either the strong or the weak have an incentive to change their minds about the decision they have made.

There is no dominant strategy

We can usually begin looking for a Nash equilibrium by looking for dominant strategies. We can see, however, that there is no dominant strategy for either the weak or the strong. If the weak work, the best response of the strong is to appropriate. If the weak do not work, the best response of the strong is not to use resources in appropriation. If the strong use resources in appropriation, the best response of the weak is not to work. If the strong do not attempt to appropriate, the best response of the weak is to work. The best response of both the weak and the strong depends on what the other has decided to do, giving no dominant strategy for either.

The uncertainty confronting the weak and the strong

The weak and the strong both confront uncertainty. The uncertainty confronting the weak is whether their output will be appropriated if they work. The uncertainty confronting the strong is whether the weak have worked and so have output that can be appropriated.

Mixed strategies

We have not found a Nash equilibrium because we have restricted ourselves to looking for decisions made with certainty. We can find an equilibrium where the strong and weak make decisions based on probabilities of taking different actions. An equilibrium where people make decisions with certainty is called a pure-strategy equilibrium. An equilibrium where people make decisions based on probabilities is called a mixed-strategy equilibrium.[18]

---

[18] As an example of a mixed strategy, suppose that we are presented with two identical closed boxes. We are told that one box contains a diamond and the other a pencil, and that we can choose between the contents of the two boxes. If we have no way of knowing where the diamond is, we can do no better than randomize our decision. That is, we can flip a coin to decide. Our decision rule of flipping

If the strong could be certain that the weak will be productive, they would choose to appropriate with certainty. If the strong could be certain that the weak will not work, they would with certainty choose not to use resources in appropriation. Since the strong do not know what the weak will do, they can randomize or *mix* their decisions whether or not to use resources in appropriation.

Similarly, if the weak could be certain that the strong intend to appropriate, they would not produce above subsistence. If the weak could be certain that the strong did not intend to appropriate, they would with certainty use their resources productively. Since the weak do not know what the strong will do, they can also randomize or mix their decision whether to work.

A mixed-strategy equilibrium is a Nash equilibrium because no one has an incentive to change the choice of randomizing behavior, given the choice of randomizing behavior of others. The equilibrium randomizing behavior of the strong and the weak is in general not probabilities of 50 percent of taking different actions. That is, flipping a coin is in general not the best decision rule. For a game as in Table 1.4, we need to find the precise probabilities that define the randomization of the mixed-strategy equilibrium.

The solution in Table 1.4 is that the weak decide, "we will work with 30 percent probability and not work with 70 percent probability." The strong decide that "we will travel to the fields of the weak to appropriate their output with probability 80 percent and we will stay home and be productive in our own fields with probability 20 percent." That is, if P_W is the probability that the weak work and P_S is the probability that the strong steal, the mixed-strategy Nash equilibrium in Table 1.4 is $P_W = 0.3$ and $P_S = 0.8$. If we changed the numbers in Table 1.4, we would of course obtain different probabilities of the weak and the strong taking their respective actions.

We derive a mixed-strategy equilibrium by finding the probabilities that make the strong and the weak *indifferent* between their alternatives choices. We look first at the decision of the strong.

The strong

The strong in Table 1.4 can always achieve 20 with certainty by being exclusively productive and using no resources in attempts at appropriation. The strong will therefore never rationally choose the uncertain alternative of appropriation, if choosing that alternative leaves them on average (because of the uncertainty) with less than the 20 they can obtain with certainty by using all their resources productively.

If the strong arrive at the fields of the weak and find that the weak have chosen to work, the strong obtain 27. If the weak have not chosen to work, the strong obtain 17. The expected benefit (the benefit on average to the strong) from

a coin gives each box a 50 percent chance of being chosen. This is our mixed strategy. We have mixed the strategies (decisions) to assign a 50 percent probability to choosing either box.

choosing to appropriate is therefore

$$27P_W + 17(1 - P_W),$$

where P_W is the probability that the weak decide to work. In an equilibrium, this expected benefit from appropriation for the strong has to be equal to the benefit of 20 that the strong can obtain with certainty from working. The strong are indifferent between using all their resources productively and trying to appropriate the output of the weak, when

$$27P_W + 17(1 - P_W) = 20.$$

This implies that $P_W = 0.3$. That is, the strong are indifferent between their two alternative decisions of being exclusively productive and setting out to take from the weak, if the weak work in the fields with a probability of 30 percent.

The weak

We can similarly consider the alternatives facing the weak. The weak can always obtain a benefit of 4 by choosing not to work. The benefit of the weak when they work beyond subsistence depends on the probability P_S that the strong will come to their fields to take their output.

If the weak work and the strong come to take their output, the weak are left with their subsistence of 2. If the strong do not come to take their output, the weak have 12. The expected benefit of the weak when they work is therefore

$$2P_S + 12(1 - P_S).$$

Since the weak can always obtain 4 by not working beyond subsistence needs, they are indifferent between working and not working when

$$2P_S + 12(1 - P_S) = 4.$$

The weak are therefore indifferent between working and not working when $P_S = 0.8$, that is, when the probability that the strong steal is 80 percent.

The different outcomes

The equilibrium for the behavior of strong and weak is based on mixed strategies, because the weak and the strong mix their respective strategies or decisions in the ways that we have established. The mixing is done through the strong coming to the fields of the weak to appropriate with probability 80 percent and the weak working with probability 30 percent.

There are four different outcomes in Table 1.4. To obtain the likelihood of each of the different outcomes, we derive the *joint probabilities* of the different outcomes.[19] The joint probabilities are set out in Table 1.5. The sum of the joint probabilities of the four outcomes of course equals one.

---

[19] The joint probability of an outcome is found by multiplying the probabilities that the strong and the weak jointly make the decisions that result in that outcome.

TABLE 1.5. PROBABILITIES OF OUTCOMES FOR THE WEAK
AND THE STRONG

	Person 2 (strong) uses resources to appropriate	Person 2 (strong) is only productive
Person 1 (weak) produces	$(0.3) \cdot (0.8) = 24\%$	$(0.3) \cdot (0.2) = 6\%$
Person 1 (weak) does not work beyond subsistence	$(0.7) \cdot (0.8) = 56\%$	$(0.7) \cdot (0.2) = 14\%$

We see that the most likely outcome is the least efficient, since, with 56 percent probability, the strong use resources on intended appropriation and the weak do not work. The efficient outcome where all resources are used productively arises with probability of only 6 percent. We also see that with a probability of 24 percent the weak work and the strong successfully appropriate, and with a probability of 14 percent the weak do not work and the strong have not attempted to appropriate. All outcomes where resources are used by the strong in appropriation and/or the weak do not work above subsistence are inefficient.

The burden of inefficiency
In the mixed-strategy equilibrium, the strong obtain 20, since this is the benefit they can have with certainty by using all their resources productively and not attempting to appropriate. The strong always do as well as they would by using all their resources productively.

The weak can obtain 4 with certainty if they do not work beyond subsistence and also receive 4 on average in the mixed-strategy equilibrium. The weak therefore do as well as they would if they did not work beyond subsistence.

Total benefit on average in the mixed-strategy equilibrium is $24 = (20 + 4)$. This is less than the total benefit of $32 = (12 + 20)$ when all resources are used productively. The efficiency loss from the absence of the rule of law is therefore $8 = (32 - 24)$.

The behavior of the strong is the reason for inefficiency. There would be no inefficiency if the strong respected the rights of possession of the weak. The strong are in control, and they would never behave in a way that harms themselves. Because the mixed strategy equilibrium provides the society with total benefit on average of $24 = (20 + 4)$, with 20 for the strong and 4 for the weak,[20] we see that the entire burden of inefficiency falls on the weak.

Laziness of the weak
Some people observing the behavior of the weak might be tempted to refer to the weak as "lazy" because the weak do not always work beyond subsistence. The

---

[20] We can also obtain 24 as the expected total benefit of the society by multiplying benefits by probabilities of each outcome in Table 1.5.

weak are, however, not lazy. The weak are responding rationally to the possibility that the strong may come to appropriate their output.

Increased efficiency when the weak are less productive

Let us now change one of the values in Table 1.4 to consider a society where the weak produce only 10 when they work, and not 12. When we recompute the probabilities of the mixed-strategy equilibrium for this society, we find that $P_S = 0.75$ and $P_W = 0.375$.[21] That is, the strong, instead of setting out to appropriate with probability 80 percent, set out to appropriate with probability 75 percent. The weak, instead of working with probability 30 percent, now work with probability 37.5 percent.

In the mixed-strategy equilibrium, the total output on average is as before $(20 + 4) = 24$.[22] The total potential output of the society with the less productive weak is $(20 + 10) = 30$. The efficiency loss from the predatory behavior of the strong is $(30 - 24) = 6$, and not 8 as before.

For the resources that it has, the society with the less productive weak is therefore more efficient.

The society with the less productive weak is relatively more efficient (is closer to its potential maximal output) because in this society the strong are less likely to expend resources on attempted appropriation and the weak are more likely to work. The weak are less attractive prey for the predatory strong because, if the strong come to the fields of the weak and find that the weak have worked, there will be less for the strong to take. Therefore, the strong come to the fields of the weak to appropriate with lower probability, and the weak work with higher probability.

The benefits of the rule of law

In the type of society we have described, the rule of law does not protect the weak from the predatory strong. However, if property rights were protected by the rule of law, the efficient outcome for the society would be attained where resources are always used productively.

In our first example, without the rule of law, the efficient outcome is obtained with probability of only 6 percent (as shown in Table 1.5). That is, an inefficient outcome arises with probability 94 percent. The least efficient outcome (where the strong expend resources on attempted appropriation and at the same time the weak do not work beyond subsistence) is the most likely outcome (with 56 percent

---

[21] For the strong, we have $20 = P_W 25 + (1 - P_W)17$, and so $P_W = 0.375$. For the weak, we have $4 = P_S 2 + (1 - P_S)10$, and so $P_S = 0.75$.

[22] Reducing the output that the weak can produce when working full time from 12 to 10 does not change the output of 20, which the strong can produce when working full time, nor the benefit of 4 to the weak when they do not work above subsistence. The values of 20 for the strong and 4 for the weak determine the benefits that the strong and the weak, respectively, obtain in the mixed-strategy equilibrium because these are the values the strong and the weak can assure themselves with certainty.

probability). The rule of law eliminates the likelihood of inefficiency. There is also social justice, since the predatory behavior of the strong ceases.

The unethical world of Nietzsche

Our description of the behavior of the strong without the rule of law corresponds to a society without ethics that was described by the German philosopher Friedrich Nietzsche (1846–1900). Nietzsche believed that ethics and conscience were the invention of the weak to protect themselves against the strong and that, in a natural state of the world, the strong do as they wish to the weak. Just as a strong animal in nature eats a weak animal, so among humans the strong impose their will on the weak. In interpreting Nietzsche, we should recall our distinction between a normative view of the world as we would like it to be and a positive statement that explains and predicts behavior. Nietzsche did not recommend inhumane behavior by the strong as normatively desirable. He simply observed that morality and conscience defend the weak against the strong, and predicted that in a world without morality and conscience the strong would impose their will on the weak.[23]

Slavery and feudalism

We have not considered the possibility that the strong might deprive the weak of their liberty and force the weak to work. Slavery was historically prominent in many parts of the world, and persisted into the twenty-first century in some places. Feudalism was a form of near-slavery. Under feudalism, the nobility owned the land, which was worked by serfs who served the feudal lords and who in general did not have freedom to leave.

1.2.5 Roving and stationary bandits

If we refer to the strong as "bandits," we can distinguish between stationary and roving bandits.[24] A roving bandit has no reason to care about the weak tomorrow, since, when tomorrow comes, the roving bandit will be elsewhere preying on other weak. Stationary bandits know, however, that the weak who are their prey today will also be their prey tomorrow. Since stationary bandits care about the future and roving bandits do not, we can expect stationary bandits to behave more benevolently toward the weak than roving bandits behave.

Single interactions and repeated encounters

We derived the mixed-strategy equilibrium by looking at a single interaction between the strong and the weak. In a single interaction, the strong behave like roving bandits because there are no repeated encounters with the weak.

---

[23] Nietzsche may have become insane when he dwelt on the logical consequences of his writings. He spent the last part of his life in an insane asylum believing that he was the devil.

[24] The distinction between the predatory behavior of stationary and roving bandits was emphasized by Mancur Olson (1932–98), who was a professor at the University of Maryland. See Olson (2000).

When the encounters between the strong and the same weak are repeated over time, and if the strong care sufficiently about the future, the strong behave like stationary bandits. Repeated encounters therefore take us from the behavior of a roving bandit to the behavior of a stationary bandit.

The more efficient behavior of the stationary bandit

Stationary bandits can do better for themselves than adopting the randomizing behavior described by the mixed-strategy equilibrium. The behavioral possibilities available to stationary bandits also improve outcomes for the weak. Stationary bandit behavior thus provides a Pareto improvement over roving bandit behavior because both the strong and the weak can be made better off.

In our example in Table 1.4, the strong acting as roving bandits in one-time encounters appropriate with a probability of 80 percent, and the weak work with a probability of 30 percent. Suppose that there are repeated encounters. We can then view roving bandit behavior in repeated encounters as the strong appropriating 80 percent of the time when the weak work 30 percent of the time.

If the weak could be provided with incentives to work all the time, the strong and the weak could share the additional output that the weak would produce. This is useful for the strong only if the strong are present in the future to benefit from the sharing of the additional output produced by the weak. That is, to benefit from the additional future output, the strong must be stationary bandits.

The strong as stationary bandits understand that it is efficient for the weak to work all the time and not just 30 percent of the time. The strong therefore have an interest in devising incentives that result in the weak consistently working. The strong know that the weak will be prepared to work consistently, if appropriation of output of the weak is not as rapacious as in the roving-bandit (i.e., mixed-strategy) equilibrium. That is, since the weak obtain 4 in the roving-bandit equilibrium, the weak will be prepared to work consistently if the strong assure them a benefit of more than 4 in each period of time. With a benefit of more than 4, the weak will no longer be indifferent between working and not working but will choose to work.

The strong can make many different decisions that over the course of time leave the weak with a benefit of more than 4 on average. One of the many possibilities is that the strong announce that they will continue to appropriate 80 percent of the time, but that they will take only 7 from the weak every time they appropriate and not 10 as in Table 1.4. The weak (who produce 12) are therefore left with 5 whenever the strong appropriate. The expected benefit of the weak from working now exceeds the benefit of 4 at which the weak were indifferent between working and not working; therefore, the weak consistently work (instead of working with probability 30 percent).[25]

---

[25] If the strong appropriate 80 percent of the time and take 7 when they appropriate (and so leave the weak with 5), the expected benefit of the weak if they work consistently is $(0.8)5 + (0.2)12 = 6.4$, which is greater than 4.

TABLE 1.6. 100 REPEATED ENCOUNTERS WITH STATIONARY BANDITS	Strong	Weak
Output produced when the strong are stationary bandits	+2,000	+1,200
Loss through the cost of appropriation	−240	
Amount the strong take from the weak	+560	−560
Benefits when the strong are stationary bandits	2,320	640
Benefits when the strong are roving bandits	2,000	400
Gain from stationary bandits compared to roving bandits	320	240

Table 1.6 shows the benefits from stationary-bandit behavior. There are 100 repeated encounters between the strong and the weak. The strong can choose to behave in each encounter as roving bandits, in which case they follow the behavior of the mixed-strategy equilibrium and appropriate 80 percent of the time, taking 10 every time they appropriate. Alternatively, the strong can behave as stationary bandits; they can appropriate 80 percent of the time but take only 7 every time they appropriate. The weak respond differently to roving- and stationary-bandit behavior. When confronting roving bandits, the weak work 30 percent of the time; when confronting stationary bandits, the weak choose to work all the time.[26]

From Table 1.6, we see that, when the strong are stationary bandits, benefits are 2,320 for the strong[27] and 640 for the weak.[28] When the strong are roving bandits, benefits are 2,000 for the strong and 400 for the weak.[29]

Stationary-bandit behavior is therefore efficient compared to roving-bandit behavior. The strong (the bandits) and the weak are both better off when the strong behave as stationary bandits. A change from roving- to stationary-bandit behavior gives the strong an additional benefit of 320 and the weak an additional benefit of 240.

The example in Table 1.6 is one of infinitely many possibilities for mutual gain to the strong and the weak from stationary-bandit behavior by the strong. Gains are present to be shared whenever the strong leave the weak with more than 4,

[26] In Table 1.4, after 100 repeated interactions as stationary bandits, the strong have 2,000 from production (100 times their each-period production of 20) minus 240 lost as the cost of appropriation (a cost of 3 is incurred in each act of appropriation and there are 80 acts of appropriation). With stationary-bandit behavior by the strong, the weak work consistently and produce 1,200 (100 times their per-period output of 12) and lose 560 through appropriation (the weak lose 7 every time appropriation takes place, and the strong appropriate 80 percent of the time). The values in Table 1.6 presuppose a zero discount rate. Otherwise, for a positive discount rate, we would need to discount future benefits at the rate of discount to reflect the lower valuation placed on the future when compared to present benefits at any point in time. We shall consider discount rates in Chapter 2.

[27] The stationary bandit has 2,000 minus the amount of 240 lost in using resources to appropriate, plus the 560 that has been taken from the weak.

[28] The weak produce 1,200 but lose 560 in appropriation by the strong.

[29] That is, we have the outcomes of the one-period mixed strategy equilibrium, multiplied 100 times for each interaction.

since the weak then consistently work. The gains can in turn be shared in many different ways.

In the example in Table 1.6, stationary-bandit behavior takes the form of the strong announcing that they will appropriate 80 percent of the time and that they will take 7 when they appropriate. The strong could be less generous and announce that they will appropriate 80 percent of the time but take 8 each time. As long as the strong take less than 10 when they appropriate, the weak still have an incentive to work consistently, and the additional output of the weak exists to be shared (through appropriation) with the strong.

Stationary-bandit behavior could also, for example, take the form of the strong announcing that they will take 10 whenever they appropriate, but that they will appropriate only 70 percent of the time (and not 80 percent of the time). Since the benefit to the weak from working consistently is again greater than 4, the weak work consistently, and the additional output that the weak produce makes both the weak and strong better off.[30]

A self-enforcing contract without enforcement by government

Contracts are usually enforced through the rule of law imposed by government.[31] The gains from stationary-bandit behavior are, however, sustainable as a *self-enforcing contract* without the need for enforcement by government through the rule of law.

The self-enforcing contract regarding behavior of the strong and the weak is implicit rather than explicit and follows from incentives. The weak know that, when they work, part of their output will be appropriated by the strong. When the strong act as stationary bandits, the weak work consistently and put up with appropriation of some of their output because the randomizing behavior of the mixed-strategy equilibrium gives the weak an outcome where they have less. The strong will also have less if they change unilaterally from acting as stationary bandits to mixed-strategy roving-bandit behavior. When the strong act as stationary bandits, there is therefore an implicit contract between weak and strong that is self-enforcing because both the strong and the weak have *personal incentives* to continue to honor the contract.

---

[30] We have encountered here an application of a general conclusion known as the folk theorem for repeated games. This theorem says that, when people who meet each other in repeated encounters care sufficiently about the future, there are infinitely many solutions for repeated games. The conclusion is known as a folk theorem because the result was generally known before the formal analysis was published.

[31] A need for contracts arises when transactions are subject to contingencies. Contracts often accompany market transactions when a sequence of moves takes place by buyers and sellers before a transaction between a buyer and a seller is completed (e.g., dates of payment and delivery of output may be contractually specified, with predetermined penalties imposed for delayed payment by the buyer or delayed delivery by the seller).

The self-enforcing contract is based on reputation. The strong could, at any point in time, leave the weak with less than 4. The weak would then have to decide what to do in the next period. They might understandably no longer trust the strong and revert to the mixed strategy in the next period and work with the 30 percent probability. The strong would then lose (see Table 1.6). The strong therefore have an interest in preserving their reputation of behaving as they announced they would (i.e., as stationary and not roving bandits). The weak similarly benefit from preserving their reputation for consistently working. If the implicit contract were to be abrogated, the strong and the weak would revert to the roving-bandit mixed-strategy equilibrium, and both would be worse off.

Why are all bandits not stationary bandits?

Since stationary-bandit behavior benefits both strong and weak compared to roving-bandit behavior, why are not all bandits stationary bandits? Bandits who do not expect to be around for repeated interactions to take place have no incentive to moderate their predatory behavior because the benefits from moderating predatory behavior come from the effect of the reputation of the strong on the *future* behavior of the weak.

The rule of law

When the strong act as stationary bandits, there is no efficiency loss from the weak not working because the weak work all the time. An efficiency loss, however, remains through the resources used by the strong to appropriate.

Social injustice also remains when the strong, whether as roving or stationary bandits, appropriate the output of the weak. The inefficiency and the social injustice end when the rule of law to protect property rights is introduced.

1.2.6 Private response to failure of the rule of law

We have now described anarchy in three situations: (1) under symmetric conditions of the prisoners' dilemma where personal decisions are based only on material benefit, (2) where some people are honest or ethically restrained from taking the property of others, and (3) when the strong feel no ethical restraint in taking from the weak. In each case, the rule of law ensures an efficient outcome. In the latter two cases, the rule of law also results in social justice.

In practice, governments do not guarantee protection of property and life through the rule of law. Victims of crime cannot, for example, successfully sue governments for being negligent in failing to protect them against criminals.

Failure of the rule of law differs from anarchy because government exists to implement the rule of law, but deterrence has been ineffective. In terms of strong and weak, some of the strong do not obey the law and continue to prey on the weak.

When the rule of law fails to protect, potential victims can be expected to seek private solutions. One private solution is insurance. People may put up with loss of property to predators and spread their risk through insurance. The insurance eliminates uncertainty about personal losses. Each insured person makes a pre-determined payment to the insurance company and no longer bears risk. For example, if thieves steal 2 percent of cars, the owners of the cars can accept the likelihood of theft as part of the cost of owning cars and can pool their risk through insurance payments that cover the loss of the stolen cars. Insurance can also be supplemented or replaced by private spending on personal protection.[32] The private spending on insurance and personal protection is in addition to the taxes that are paid to finance spending by government on providing the rule of law.

Predators who seek to do harm

Peaceful people can confront predators whose personal objectives are not material gain, but who for reasons of malice seek simply to inflict maximal harm. The harm that the predators can do (through loss of life) may be too great for risk to be spread through insurance, and effective personal defensive measures may also be unavailable. With any individual in society a potential victim and with private options for defense unavailable, protection can only be provided through the rule of law enforced by government.[33]

1.2.7 Unfavorable views on property rights

We have described benefits from property rights; however, property rights have sometimes been viewed unfavorably. One unfavorable view has been that private property rights make people greedy rather than magnanimous and pleasant because property rights are an incentive for people to strive to accumulate ever more private wealth.

Property rights have also been viewed unfavorably because of limitations on the redistribution of wealth. For example, with property rights preserved, a feudal society remains forever feudal, or wealth remains unequally distributed in an agricultural society where a royal family or nobility owns all or much of the land. Land is bequeathed to the hereditary kings and queens and nobility, and inequality is maintained because property rights are protected by the rule of law. Revolutions have taken place to end the bequeathed inequality of hereditary monarchy and nobility. We shall not, however, be concerned with revolution in this book. Nor shall we be concerned with societies where the greater part of wealth consists of land. Our discussion of property rights has been in the context of benefits that

---

[32] For example, cars can be protected from theft through alarm and ignition systems, and homes can be protected through surveillance systems and alarms or private security services.

[33] When we consider the rule of law, we focus on avoiding anarchy within a society. In Chapter 2, we shall consider the related issue of national defense against aggression from outside a society.

are provided against the alternative of anarchy – or against the alternative of the rule of men and women over others without adherence to the principles of the rule of law.

In the final section of this chapter, we shall look at societies that attempted to eliminate greed and inequality by banning or restricting private property. We shall see that these societies were unsuccessful compared to societies where the rule of law protects private property rights. Moreover, greed became exaggerated when the stakes were control over all the property of the society. Before looking at the outcomes in societies that disallowed private property, we can summarize our conclusions from this section.

1.2.8 Summary

In this section we have considered the responsibility of government to provide the rule of law. We have noted that the rule of law is not the same as the rule of government. The rule of law is not rule by government, but rule based on principles among which protection of property and life are prominent. Government *oversees* the rule of law but does not determine the fundamental principles of the rule of law.

Property rights allow ownership to be specified and certified so that the benefits of markets for goods can be realized. People can be paid according to the value of their production. Property rights also allow the functioning of asset markets and the provision of financial services.

Moreover, without the rule of law, there are incentives to appropriate rather than to be productive. The incentive for appropriative rather than productive behavior has been explained in terms of the prisoners' dilemma. Independent self-interested behavior, which through the invisible hand is a virtue in a competitive market, becomes a source of social inefficiency and personal loss under the conditions of the prisoners' dilemma.

The inefficiency can be eliminated by credible penalties that change rational behavior so that the property rights of others are respected. We have noted that deterrence is based on the existence of a credible threat of punishment, and so requires public spending to provide the presence of the institutions of the rule of law that allow punishment if necessary. Although individuals can take private measures to protect themselves and their property, it is in general more efficient for government to use deterrence to provide protection collectively through the rule of law. Moreover, private spending on protection is inconsistent with the principle of equality before the law.

We first considered anarchy under the conditions of the prisoners' dilemma where people care only about personal material gain and are not bound by ethical restraint. When a population is divided into people who are guided by ethical principles and people who place no ethical restraints on their behavior, the rule of law provides efficiency and also protects ethical people against victimization.

We also examined the sources of inefficiency in a society where the strong behave unethically toward the weak. In single encounters without the rule of law, the strong use resources to attempt to take from the weak, and the weak do not consistently work. The weak are not lazy but are responding to the predatory behavior of the strong. We have also seen that the more productive the weak are, the more inefficient the society is. In repeated interactions where the strong care about the future and act as stationary rather than roving bandits, the strong can provide incentives for the weak to work consistently, but the society remains inefficient (and unjust) because of the predatory behavior of the strong. The inefficiency and the injustice are brought to an end by the rule of law, which protects the output and property of the weak against the strong.

We have observed that the rule of law does not always provide effective deterrence. When the damage that can be done by predators is small, insurance allows pooling of risk. When the harm done by predators is too great for reliance on insurance as a sole solution, private spending on personal protection often supplements public spending on providing the rule of law. We have noted the limitations on private protective measures when a society confronts uncompromising predators.

We also observed that, despite the benefits in facilitating markets and preempting anarchy, private property rights protected by the rule of law have not always been viewed favorably by everybody.

References and related literature

On the rule of law and competition, see Mann (1997). On the development and protection of property rights, see Demsetz (1976), Umbeck (1981), Sudgen (1986), Skaperdas (1992), Wärneryd (1993), Grossman and Kim (1995). On the relation between asset markets and property rights, see de Soto (2000). On the weak and the strong, see Hillman (2000, 2004). On roving and stationary bandits, see Olson (2000). On advantages of the "weak," see Hirshleifer (1991). On the hope that moral revival will change the behavior of predators, see Grossman and Kim (2000). For the writings of Nietzsche, see, for example, Nietzsche (1997). On repeated games, see Aumann (1986).

Aumann, R., 1986. Repeated games. In *Issues in Contemporary Microeconomics*, G. Feiwel (ed.), Macmillan, London, 209–42.

Cournot, A., 1838. *Recherches sur les Principes Mathematiques de la Theorie des Richesses*. English edition: 1897. *Researches into the Mathematical Principles of the Theory of Wealth*, N. Bacon (ed.). Macmillan, London.

Demsetz, H., 1976. Toward a theory of property rights. *American Economic Review* 57, 347–59.

de Soto, H., 2000. *The Mystery of Capital*. Basic Books, New York.

Frey, B. S. and H. Buhofer, 1988. Prisoners and property rights. *Journal of Law and Economics* 31, 19–46.

Grossman, H. I. and M. Kim, 1995. Swords or plowshares: A theory of security to the claims to property. *Journal of Political Economy* 102, 1275–88.

Grossman, H. I. and M. Kim, 2000. Predators, moral decay, and moral revivals. *European Journal of Political Economy* 16, 173–87.

Hillman, A. L., 2000. Poverty, inequality, and unethical behavior of the strong. International Monetary Fund, Fiscal Affairs Department, working paper WP/00/187, Washington, D.C.

Hillman, A. L., 2004. Nietzschean development failures. *Public Choice*.

Hirshleifer, J. 1991. The paradox of power. *Economics and Politics* 3, 177–200.

Mann, H. G., 1997. The judiciary and free markets. *Harvard Journal of Law and Public Policy* 21, 11–37.

Nash, J. F., 1951. Non-cooperative games. *Annals of Mathematics* 54, 286–95.

Nietzsche, F., 1997. *Beyond Good and Evil: Prelude to a Philosophy of the Future.* Dover Publications, New York.

Olson, M., 2000. *Power and Prosperity.* Basic Books, New York.

Skaperdas, S., 1992. Cooperation, conflict, and power in the absence of property rights. *American Economic Review* 82, 720–39.

Sudgen, R., 1986. *The Economics of Rights, Cooperation, and Welfare.* Basil Blackwell, Oxford.

Umbeck, J., 1981. Might makes right: A theory of the foundation and initial distribution of property rights. *Economic Enquiry* 19, 38–59.

Wärneryd, K., 1993. Anarchy, uncertainty, and the emergence of property rights. *Economics and Politics* 5, 1–14.

Questions for discussion

1. Why is the rule of law not the same as rule by government?
2. Why does the existence of markets require the rule of law?
3. What is the relation between asset markets and the rule of law?
4. Why is absence of the rule of law a source of inefficiency, even when people do not buy or sell in markets?
5. If Robin Hood has justice on his side, why might we find his behavior socially undesirable? Were Robin Hood and the legal authority, the Sheriff of Nottingham, caught in a prisoners' dilemma?
6. Explain the meaning of dominant strategy and Nash equilibrium? Is the outcome of following dominant strategies always a Nash equilibrium?
7. How has the invisible hand failed in the prisoners' dilemma? How is the failure related to the paradox of personal benefit from coercion?
8. What is the difference between preemption and punishment? What is the role of a credible threat of punishment in resolving the prisoners' dilemma?
9. What is the advantage of government in protecting property rights through the rule of law compared to private personal protection?
10. In Table 1.3, where person 1 does not steal for ethical reasons, confirm that (3, 4) is the only Nash equilibrium.
11. Reformulate Table 1.3 when both persons behave ethically in respecting each other's property rights. How do the dominant strategies establish the new Nash equilibrium? Why is the Nash equilibrium now efficient?

12. In an anarchic situation where the weak cannot defend themselves against appropriation by the strong, what are the sources of inefficiency? If the weak choose sometimes not to work, does this indicate that the weak are lazy?

13. With roving-bandit behavior (single interactions), how does absence of the rule of law affect the distribution of income or wealth between strong and weak?

14. In Table 1.4, recompute the roving-bandit mixed-strategy probabilities of the strong stealing and the weak working, when the weak can produce 18 rather than 12 by using their resources productively. What are the new probabilities of the different possible outcomes? With the weak *more* productive, what has happened to efficiency of the society, where efficiency is defined as the equilibrium output relative to the potential maximal output of the society?

15. In Table 1.4, recompute the roving-bandit mixed-strategy probabilities of the strong stealing and the weak working, and the probabilities of the different possible outcomes, when the cost incurred by the strong when they attempt to appropriate is 6 and not 3. Has the society become more efficient in terms of total output on average produced?

16. Why does the roving bandit impose more inefficiency on a society than the stationary bandit? Provide another example of the improvement in efficiency from the change from roving- to stationary-bandit behavior shown in Table 1.6. Why are there many possible outcomes of stationary-bandit behavior?

17. When the rule of law is absent, why do the weak have an incentive to invest in themselves through "human capital" (i.e., by increasing personal skills and knowledge) rather than by improving the productivity of agricultural land? Is it reasonable that, by cultural transmission between generations, the weak would end up valuing education more than the strong?

18. What is the role of insurance when enforcement of the rule of law is imperfect? What are the limits of insurance as a solution to disrespect for the rule of law? Is insurance appeasement?

19. Do you believe that government should guarantee the rule of law and pay compensation when individuals have not been protected by the rule of law?

20. Do you believe that it is reasonable that members of a society could behave according to the principles of the rule of law without government? Does the number of people in the society affect your answer? Is your answer related to the strategic interactions among people considered in this section?

1.3

Life under Maximal Government

The two responsibilities identified in the previous sections – (1) ensuring competitive markets and (2) providing the institutions of the rule of law – define the functions of minimal government. In fulfilling these responsibilities, government has only an oversight role and leaves individuals to make personal decisions through markets and private property. We shall now look at maximal government where neither markets nor private property exist. In practice, societies generally find themselves somewhere between the limiting cases of minimal and maximal government.

1.3.1 Collective property

Maximal government has often taken the form of rule by a king or queen, or dictator, who has governed for personal benefit and for the benefit of a few privileged sycophants. Another path to maximal government is through collective property. Under collective property, resources and goods produced, with the exception of some personal possessions, are owned by society at large and not individually.[1] The primary justification for choosing collective property is social equality, or social justice. When collective property replaces private property, private wealth can no longer be a source of social inequality.[2] Collective property leads to maximal government because government, which oversees and controls the collective property, thereby controls the society's resources.

Markets cannot coexist with collective property because, as we saw in Section 1.2, markets require private property that individuals can exchange or buy and sell. With collective property, the decisions of a planning bureaucracy replace markets. The planning bureaucracy is accountable to the political masters who control the collective property.

We do not have to theorize or guess about the characteristics of life under maximal government with collective property. We can look at the experiences of societies that had collective property throughout a large part of the twentieth century. We can judge the experiences of these societies by three criteria: (1) personal freedom, (2) social justice, and (3) efficiency.

1.3.2 Personal freedom

Writing in 1944, in his book *The Road to Serfdom*, Friedrich von Hayek (1899–1992, Nobel Prize in economics 1974) pointed out how collective property is a catalyst for personal power over other people. A person who controls the collective property of a society, controls the society. Hayek wrote:

> *collectivists must create power – power over men wielded by other men – and their success will depend on the extent to which they achieve such power* (p. 144).

Societies with markets and private property also offer personal benefits from political success and political power. Private property however limits political power. When property is private, political decisions can be made about

---

[1] Collective property is also called communal or social property. As we noted at the end of Section 1.2, the feeling of unfairness when private property is unequally distributed in the hands of privileged hereditary kings or queens or noble families has often resulted in rebellion or revolution. If successful, the revolutions usually redistributed property, which remained private. A revolution in Russia in 1917 was influenced by the ideas of Karl Marx (1818–83) and Frederick Engels (1820–95). Marx and Engels wrote the *Communist Manifesto* in 1847 and proposed collective property as the solution to problems of social and economic inequality. The 1917 revolution introduced collective property in Russia and was the forerunner to collective property in a large part of the world, until the collapse of collective property with limited exceptions around 1990.

[2] Supplement 1C describes other reasons why people believed collective property might be desirable.

taxation and public spending, but not about how to allocate or assign society's entire wealth. Hayek remarked that personal power in a society where the rule of law protects private property is "never power over the whole life of a person," whereas, in a society with collective property, personal control over collective property "creates a degree of dependence scarcely distinguishable from slavery."

Adam Smith had observed that markets dissipate personal power. He had noted that, in societies with only limited opportunities for exchange in markets, people use their wealth to expand their personal power by hiring private armies to take the property, and lives, of others. Markets, on the other hand, allow personal wealth to be used to purchase goods and to acquire personal possessions, rather than to control people. Although Adam Smith was writing before the advent (and demise) of the societies based on collective property, his observations apply to societies where there are no markets and the measure of personal success is personal control over collective property – and thereby control over people.[3]

1.3.3 Information and efficiency

Lenin (1870–1924), who had led the Russian Revolution of 1917, described how collective property would transform a society into an egalitarian single extended firm and family. Lenin envisaged the day when:

> *The whole of society will have become a single office and a single factory with equality of work and equality of pay.*[4]

To make efficient decisions, the "single office and single factory" required information about the *entire economy*. In contrast, individuals making decisions in markets need and use only the limited information that is required for their own personal decisions. In a market economy, there is therefore no need for anyone to collect information about the entire economy.

A bureaucracy that has replaced markets faces an impossible task in seeking information about values of output and inputs, because the markets that can reveal the information do not exist. Because of information problems, the people working in the planning bureaucracies of the economies with collective property resorted to simple rules to make economic decisions. The bureaucracies treated people

---

[3] Leon Trotsky (1937) observed that "where the sole employer is the State, opposition means death by slow starvation. The old principle: who does not work shall not eat, has been replaced by a new one: who does not obey does not eat" (cited by Hayek 1944, p. 119). Trotsky (1879–1940) participated in the 1917 Russian revolution, but fled Russia in 1929, making his way to Mexico where he sought safety. In 1940, he was assassinated. Hayek also fled his native land but was more fortunate. He left Austria in 1938 when Austria united with Germany, took positions at the London School of Economics and the University of Chicago, and went on to receive the Nobel Prize in economics.

[4] Quoted by Hayek, 1944, p. 119.

as having identical needs. They also used the simple rule of giving instructions throughout the economy to repeat previous production. These simple rules required the least information. All people were treated as if they wanted the same output, and the output was produced by replicating the past.[5]

Instructions to factories to repeat previous output sustain outdated production technologies. Innovation and product improvement do not take place when producers are told to replicate yesterday's goods produced using yesterday's technologies.[6] The planning bureaucracies designed and produced the nuclear reactor at Chernobyl, the melt down of which in 1986 was an ecological disaster. The planning bureaucracies were grossly negligent of the environment in other ways, caring little for the damage to health from pollution or for sustainability of the gifts of nature.[7] For the population, the planners provided small cramped housing where a number of families often shared communal kitchens and bathrooms. Goods were shabby. There was no market competition that could offer choice of improved products. The planning bureaucracies had an official monopoly on supply, on everything.[8]

Adam Smith predicted that economic misfortune would follow if the decisions of government officials were allowed to replace personal market decisions. In his words:

> *The statesman who would attempt to direct private people in what manner they ought employ their capitals, would ... assume an authority which could be safely trusted, not only to no single person, but to no council or senate whatever, and which would nowhere be so dangerous as in the hands of a man who had folly and presumption enough to fancy himself fit to exercise it.* (Smith, 1776/1937, p. 423)

Adam Smith was here remarking on the vanity, and the dangers to society, of men and women who seek to make decisions on behalf of others, and who believe in the superiority of their abilities over the personal market decisions that allow people to choose what they want for themselves.

---

[5] The people working in the planning bureaucracies also wished to avoid personal failure. By using the rule of replication of the past, they hoped that they would do no worse in the present than in the past.

[6] The best personal strategy for an on-line manager or worker was to abide precisely by the planning bureaucracy's instructions. If a manager exercised independent discretion that reduced costs of production or improved quality, the gains were not personal but were collective. A manager who unsuccessfully attempted improvisation, or innovation, or quality improvement was, on the other hand, subject to penalties. Personal innovation was not only illegal but also irrational. International trade also offered little prospect for obtaining improved products. The economy, which had no domestic markets, was also closed to foreign markets.

[7] It is instructive to study the Aral Sea.

[8] When success depended on mobilizing resources for a single-minded purpose, there were exceptions to the technological backwardness. The planning bureaucracies sent the first man into space, and their military technology often matched and sometimes surpassed that of private-property market economies.

1.3.4 The fatal conceit

When property is collective, there is a problem of how to have private incentives that will encourage people to be productive, because whatever a person produces belongs in principle to everybody. In an attempt to solve the problem of the lack of personal incentives to be productive, a new model of personal behavior was introduced to accompany the collective property. The new model of behavior called on people to contribute according to their ability while consuming according to their needs. The planning bureaucracies would determine people's "needs." With personal needs determined, there was no necessary relation between a person's contribution to production and personal income or consumption.[9]

The new model of production according to ability accompanied by consumption according to need (determined by others) was in direct contradiction to Adam Smith's model of market behavior. As we observed in Section 1.1, Smith sought to reconcile personal benefits in markets with benefit to society. The new model, however, asked people to pursue the good of society without incentives for personal gain.

Hayek described the attempt to re-engineer human nature through the new model of people contributing without regard for personal gain as "the fatal conceit."[10] He pointed out that markets and private property had over the course of time been the only means of consistently providing wealth and personal happiness. Hayek's case for private property and the market was evolutionary. Markets, private property, and personal incentives had evolved over time to be the most successful means of organizing economic behavior. Whereas markets and private property allowed people to follow their natural inclinations to better themselves, the new model of behavior was unnatural in asking people to contribute to the benefit of others without caring about their own rewards. Hayek predicted that the attempt to base economic organization on the new model of personal behavior would fail.

Hayek's prediction did not endear him to many people who had become convinced of the injustices of markets and private property, and who wished to see the new model of personal behavior succeed. Hayek was criticized for challenging a virtuous model of personal behavior where men and women voluntarily give of themselves to others, and where a sense of community and common good replace the self-interest and individualism (and greed) of markets and private property. The idea of collective property had won the hearts and minds of many people, and Hayek's warnings about the conceit of those who wished to re-engineer human nature were, at his time, for many people not politically correct.

---

[9] Exceptional deeds were recognized and rewarded with medals, certificates, praise, and, sometimes, special privileges. Questioning of the virtue of the new model of personal behavior could, on the other hand, result in exile to far-away desolate wastelands or to being confined to an insane asylum. Children were taught at school about the virtue of the new model of behavior and were encouraged to inform the police whenever they detected dissent, including in their own family.

[10] Hayek (1988).

1.3.5 Privilege and social justice

When property is collective, with no link between personal contributions and personal rewards, privilege often determines how well a person fares. In a market, people buy what they want (if they have the means). When markets do not exist, personal connections and the ability to request and receive favors are more important than an individual's knowledge and abilities. Personal effort is therefore directed toward networking, so as to build the personal relationships that are the source of the privileged favors. A society with collective property and planners is not a meritocracy where people who are diligent and work hard are rewarded. The society is rather made up of bastions of privilege that are in turn based on private benefit derived from control over collective property.

The idea underlying collective property was that envy would be eliminated through an end to private wealth. Yet, with collective property, people knew that, if someone had more than they had, privilege was in all likelihood involved. Envy persisted under collective property and was perhaps present to a greater degree than where there are markets and private property. Because privilege influenced what people received, the social justice through equality that was the objective of social property was not achieved.[11]

People can become cynical when consumption opportunities depend on privilege and favors rather than on personal effort and productive contributions. Social justice and equality are not served when a person's most valuable asset is the personal ability to please others who, by controlling collective property, are in a position to hand out privileged favors.[12]

1.3.6 Soft budgets

Although markets require private property, there have been attempts to combine markets with collective property. When collective property coexists with markets, people buy and sell what is not theirs.

János Kornai (1983) described the combination of markets and collective property as subject to "contradictions and dilemmas." Kornai in particular identified a problem of "soft" budget constraints. A "hard" budget constraint is binding and credible. With a hard budget constraint, there is a budget, and, when the money is exhausted, there is no more. Under a soft budget constraint, when money is exhausted, more becomes available. A soft budget therefore does not bind on

---

[11] The principle was that all people should be equal. Engels (1884/1972) claimed that women had been better off when there was tribal communal property than they were in societies based on private property and the family. According to Engels, private property and the family were means whereby men subjugated women.

[12] The person dispensing privileged favors might, for example, be the manager of a supermarket who preferentially allocates goods that are in short supply. There were many shortages and the system of collective property was also known as a shortage economy. Higher market prices could have eliminated the shortages, but there were no markets that could allow suppliers to respond to higher prices by increasing supply. With supply limited and often sporadic, and of various qualities, the supermarket manager knew when new supplies would be arriving, and the best quality could be kept for personal privileged assignment.

spending.[13] Under a soft budget, a threat that there will be no more money is therefore not credible. Factories, which are collective property, are then like a government department or agency that receives money from the government and cannot go bankrupt no matter what it does. Because of the soft budget, there is no incentive to use resources efficiently.[14]

The cow and the milk

To describe the different ownership possibilities in a society, we can use the example of a cow and milk. In a market economy with private property, the cow and the milk are privately owned. In an economy with collective property where a planning bureaucracy replaces markets, the cow and the milk are collectively owned, but there can be private benefit from being in a position to distribute the milk through privileged favors. A third way is to combine collective property with markets: cows are collective property that cannot be bought or sold, but there is a market in which milk can be sold. People can benefit personally from the privilege of being in a position to sell the milk. The cow as collective property benefits from a soft budget, since the government is responsible for collective property. Spending on the cow is therefore inefficient. At the same time, some people are permitted to sell the cow's milk in the market. The people selling the milk are accountable to neither planners nor private owners. Because of the personal benefits from being allowed to sell the milk produced by the state's cow, there is no assurance that division of the milk will be socially just.[15]

1.3.7 Conclusions

When in Sections 1.1 and 1.2 we made the case for the efficiency of markets and private property, we did not propose that *only* private property and markets could provide efficiency. We have now seen, however, that abandoning private property and markets results in inefficiency, loss of personal freedom, and no assurance of social justice.

The maximal government that emerges from the abandonment of private property and markets contrasts with the minimal government that has the limited responsibilities of ensuring competitive markets and providing the rule of law. The minimal government allows individuals to own their own property and to make their own decisions in markets, and the market links personal rewards to personal effort.

---

[13] An example of a soft budget is when a child, who has been given lunch money at the beginning of a week for the entire week, announces in midweek that he or she has no money left to buy lunch the next day. Since parents will not normally allow a child to go hungry, the budget constraint confronting the child is soft. The child, knowing the budget constraint is soft, can safely spend the lunch money by midweek.

[14] The soft budget is not the only reason why the combination of collective property and markets is inefficient. See Supplement 1C, which looks at the decisions made by a labor-managed firm.

[15] In principle, the milk should not be sold for private benefit, since the milk, like the cow, is collective property.

We shall not return to maximal government, nor shall we return to collective property. We shall study public finance and public policy when private property and markets are the foundations for social and economic organization.

As we proceed, however, hints will at times appear of the presence of the types of problems that arise with maximal government. The taxes required for public finance create gaps between the value of the productive contributions that people make and the personal rewards they receive, and attempting to preserve personal incentives to be productive under conditions of high taxation is similar to asking people to contribute according to their ability without regard for personal reward. Government bureaucracies confront information problems when making decisions about public finance, and political decision makers can have considerable flexibility when deciding on who benefits from public policy. Government bureaucracies and agencies at the same time can confront soft budgets, since the bureaucracies and agencies are financed by public finance and not by market revenue. Government property and government revenue are, moreover, collective property.

References and related literature

On principles and underlying ideas of socialism, see Marx (1857–8/1994, 1887), Engels (1884/1972), Lange (1938). For critiques, see von Mises (1951), Pejovich (1987), Hayek (1944, 1988). On the treatment of Hayek by contemporaries, see Caldwell (1998). On the soft budget, see Kornai (1983), Schaffer (1989). On the labor-managed firm (Supplement 1D), see Bonin and Putterman (1987), Hillman and Milanovic (1992).

Bonin, J. P. and L. Putterman, 1987. *Economics of Cooperation and the Labor-Managed Economy.* Harwood Academic Publishers, Chur.

Caldwell, B., 1998. Hayek and socialism. *Journal of Economic Literature* 35, 1856–90.

Engels, F., (1884) 1972. *The Origin of the Family, Private Property and the State.* Pathfinder Press, New York.

Hayek von, F. A., 1944. *The Road to Serfdom.* University of Chicago Press, Chicago. Reprinted 1972.

Hayek von, F. A., 1988. *The Fatal Conceit: The Errors of Socialism*, W. W. Bartley III (ed.). Routledge, London.

Hillman, A. L. and B. Milanovic (eds.), 1992. *The Transition from Socialism in Eastern Europe: Domestic Restructuring and Foreign Trade.* The World Bank, Washington, D.C.

Kornai, J., 1983. *Contradictions and Dilemmas: Studies on the Socialist Economy and Society.* Corvina, Budapest and MIT Press, Cambridge, Massachusetts.

Lange, O., 1938. *On the Economic Meaning of Socialism*, B. E. Lippincott (ed.). University of Minnesota Press, Minneapolis.

Marx, K., 1887 (date of original publication). *Capital: A Critical Analysis of Capitalist Production*, F. Engels (ed.). Progress Publishers, Moscow.

Pejovich, S., 1987. Freedom, property rights, and innovation in socialism. *Kyklos* 40, 461–75.

Schaffer, M., 1989. The credible commitment problem in the center-enterprise relationship. *Journal of Comparative Economics* 13, 359–82.

Smith, A., (1776) 1937. *An Enquiry into the Nature and Causes of the Wealth of Nations*,
    E. Cannan (ed.). Modern Library Edition, Random House, New York.
von Mises, L., 1951. *Socialism*. Yale University Press, New Haven, Connecticut.

Questions for discussion

1. Suppose somebody proposes that replacement of private property by collective property will result in a virtuous socially just society. How would you respond?
2. What is the basis of Hayek's observation that collective property results in loss of individual freedom?
3. Information has different roles in societies with collective and private property. How do the roles differ? How is efficiency affected?
4. How do incentives for innovation differ under private property rights and collective property?
5. Anarchy can in principle be brought to an end by the rule of law protecting either private or collective property. Yet why might the idea of theft have different meanings in the two cases?
6. What was the "fatal conceit" proposed by Hayek?
7. How does privilege naturally arise to compromise social justice when property is collective?
8. What is a soft budget? What is the relation between a soft budget and efficiency?
9. Ownership of a cow and milk can be used to characterize means of social and economic organization. How is personal self-interest pursued under the combinations of ownership of the cow and the milk?
10. In markets, owners of capital usually hire labor; labor does not make employment decisions. With collective property, there are no private owners of capital. How is efficiency affected when employees then make employment decisions? (See Supplement 1D).
11. A starting point for study of the responsibilities and limitations of government can be either maximal government or minimal government. That is, we could look for exceptions to maximal government; or we could look for responsibilities of government when there are markets and private property. If there had been no historical experience with maximal government, the choice between maximal and minimal government as starting points would have to be made using only theoretical or hypothetical arguments. (See also Supplement 1C.) Do you believe that the theoretical and hypothetical arguments would convince many people of the merits of maximal government organized around collective property? Why do think that, historically, more people were convinced of the case for collective property (and maximal government) in Europe (the old world) than in the United States (the new world)?
12. Some attributes of a society with maximal government organized around collective property can appear in democratic societies with private property and markets, although by no means to the same degree. What are these attributes?

2

COLLECTIVE BENEFITS

In this chapter we shall consider goods that simultaneously benefit a number of people independently of who pays. We shall investigate the consequences of voluntary payments for public goods and information problems that arise in seeking to determine efficient spending on public goods, as well as the provision of public goods through taxation and public spending.

2.1

Public Goods

2.1.1 From private to collective benefits

In the well–known story by Daniel Defoe (first edition 1719), Robinson Crusoe is shipwrecked on an island and finds himself in a state of isolation. Alone on the island, Crusoe has no social contact with others. Since he is alone, his consumption is privately his own. There are no goods from which he benefits collectively with others, and no questions arise of sharing costs with others.

Shared benefits and costs arise if Crusoe does not live on the island alone. Suppose he lives in a household with others. A house then provides collective benefit through shelter to all members of the household. The household confronts collective decisions about the size of the house and the assignment of rooms within the house. Other collective decisions might include the dinner menu. If the island had electricity, the refrigerator would provide collective benefit to household members, as would a dishwasher and washing machine. Decisions about spending and supply for these goods that provide collective benefits are made within the household.

When the population of the island grows to two households and three, and beyond, other goods provide collective benefits. A decision may, for example, have to be made about how many hours each household should contribute to building an infrastructure of trails and paths, or decisions may have to be made about keeping watch for passing ships or how to share the cost of building and maintaining a lighthouse. These are public goods that benefit the entire public or population on the island.

A public good is not public because supply is decided by public policy or because the goods are publicly financed through a government on the island. The identifying aspect of a public good is not whether it is paid for privately or publicly financed, but whether one person or a number of people benefit. Only one person at a time benefits from a private good. The benefit from a public good is collective, to a number of people.

We expect many types of public goods to be introduced as the island's population increases. A defense force is set up to provide security for the inhabitants of the island. The rule of law is put in place through police and a judicial system. An antitrust (or antimonopoly) agency is set up to oversee the maintenance of competitive markets. Trails and paths become roads and highways. Bridges are built. National and local parks are established. Television and radio transmission are introduced. Telecommunications facilities are made available that allow use of telephones, fax machines, and the internet. Preventive immunization programs protect against infectious and contagious diseases. Public transportation is introduced (public transportation provides a public good, not because the transportation is available to the public, but because a number of people simultaneously benefit from a bus or tram or train). A meteorological service provides a public good by providing weather forecasts. Education provides a public good through the benefits to all the population from more educated fellow citizens. A museum, library, and perhaps a zoo also provide collective benefit to the island's residents. Embassies and consulates are established in faraway places.

The knowledge provided by inventions and innovations is a public good. People can use new knowledge for their personal benefit once the knowledge has been made available. For example, research may reveal that certain types of consumption or behavior are detrimental to personal health, allowing people to make changes that improve their well-being.[1]

Public goods also take the form of an option to use a good or service. Many people simultaneously benefit from the option to use an ambulance or hospital or to call the fire department. Everybody prefers that such options remain only options. Yet although no one may wish to use these services (there are exceptions, for example, maternity wards of the hospital), the option to use the service provides a public-good benefit to all potential users. The same is true of a lifeguard at a beach and of firemen. We prefer that a lifeguard have nothing to do and that firemen likewise be idle. Nonetheless, we wish lifeguards and firemen to be on call should we need them.

Pure and impure public goods

Public goods can be pure or impure. A pure public good provides the same level of benefit for everybody independently of the number of users. The benefit to any one person is therefore not at the expense of any other person.

Figure 2.1a shows benefits from a pure public good. Individual benefit is constant as the number of users increases. A pure public good can also be a local public good. That is, the benefits can be locally available to people in an area. Noncongested local roads, local police protection, or local public health services are pure public goods that benefit people in a particular area.

Individual benefit from an impure public good declines with the number of users because of congestion effects. The same public good may at different times be pure or impure (i.e., congestible). A highway at 3A.M. may be a pure public good, whereas at 8A.M., when choked with peak hour traffic, the same highway becomes an impure public good. Figure 2.1b shows benefits from a public good that is pure up to a number n_1 of users, after which congestion begins and the benefit from use declines as the number of users increases. After the number of users has reached n_2, the public good yields negative benefit. We can imagine cars not moving on a congested highway; reflecting the common negative benefit, after n_2 cars are on the highway, people are in principle prepared to pay to leave the highway.

---

[1] Knowledge can also be proprietary, in which case knowledge constitutes intellectual property rights. Firms have an interest in protecting these proprietary rights, and the granting of patents allows property rights to knowledge to be certified and protected.

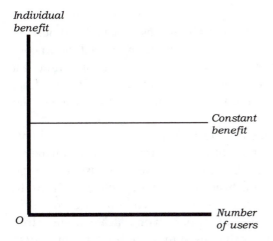

Figure 2.1a. In the case of a pure public good, individual benefits are independent of the number of users.

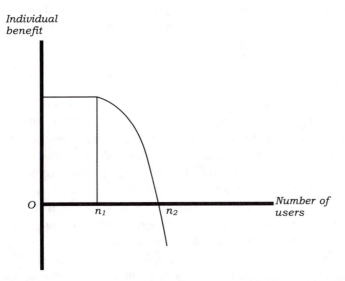

Figure 2.1b. A public good that becomes subject to congestion.

When we refer to public goods, we shall mean pure public goods or public goods that are not congested, unless we indicate otherwise.

Exclusion and free riders

It is often impossible to exclude people from the benefits of public goods. The rule of law, for example, protects everybody from anarchy. Public health programs like-wise benefit everybody by eradicating communicative diseases. When exclusion from benefit does not or cannot take place, a person can benefit from spending on public goods by others. We shall call attempts to benefit without personally paying free-riding behavior. To illustrate free riding, suppose that a number of people on Crusoe's island have fishing boats and that Crusoe proposes that a lighthouse be built. Some boat owners might claim that they feel under no obligation to contribute to the financing of a lighthouse because they are quite happy without a lighthouse. After the lighthouse has been constructed without their participation, they nonetheless benefit from the additional safety due to the presence of the lighthouse.

Means could be available to exclude free riders from the benefits of the lighthouse. Someone could be stationed in the lighthouse to turn off the light whenever a free rider is seen in the vicinity. Once the lighthouse exists, exclusion from the benefits of the lighthouse is inefficient. Exclusion from a pure public good is Pareto inefficient because allowing additional users to benefit makes no one worse off. Exclusion also requires resources: the time of the person on watch to exclude free riders could be used productively rather than used to make some people worse off through exclusion.

If everybody on the island attempted to free ride, there would of course be no lighthouse. The population would consist exclusively of prospective free riders – prospective because, when all people attempt to free ride, no one pays and no public good is supplied on which to ride free.

Public goods and natural monopoly

The lighthouse is a classic example of a pure public good. All owners of ships and boats benefit from a lighthouse. A lighthouse reveals the location of the entrance to a port or the location of dangerous rocks; in former times, lighthouses provided sailors with information about their location as they navigated their way along a coastline. A lighthouse in a given location is a natural monopoly. That is, duplication of the service provided by the lighthouse by building another lighthouse in the same location is wasteful because there is no benefit from the second lighthouse. Monopoly or a single supplier is therefore natural. Competitive supply would unnecessarily increase costs because of the unnecessary duplication. When two or more lighthouses are in the same location, it is also impossible to identify which lighthouse is the source of benefit to sailors using the lights for navigation, and therefore impossible to know which lighthouse owner to pay if payments are levied for entering a port at night through guidance from the lighthouse beacons.

Ronald Coase[2] (1974) studied lighthouses in the United Kingdom in the nineteenth century and found that lighthouses were privately constructed, while government took responsibility for ensuring that ship owners paid for the services provided by the lighthouses. The government eventually bought the lighthouses from the private owners. Private supply of a public good was thereby transformed to public supply of a public good.

---

[2] Ronald Coase of the University of Chicago received the Nobel Prize in economics in 1991.

The lighthouse example illustrates the principle that all pure public goods are natural monopolies. The converse is not true. All natural monopolies do not provide public goods. For example, the delivery of electricity supply to a house is a natural monopoly (because it is wasteful to duplicate the infrastructure of high-tension wires), but electricity provides private benefits to a household.

Public inputs

A lighthouse is strictly speaking a public input and not a public good. The benefit from the lighthouse is an input into fishing or sea transportation and is not a good for final consumption. A road or bridge is likewise a public input that is collectively used to provide transportation. Many public goods are public inputs. We shall at times distinguish public goods from public inputs; however, in general, what we have to say about public goods also applies to public inputs.

Collective harm

Public goods sometimes do collective harm rather than collective good. For example, damage to the environment harms everybody. We shall use the term public "good" to describe collective harm as well as collective good.

Private goods and public goods

When a quantity X of a private good is available for consumption by n people, the sum of the quantities consumed by the population is the total quantity X available for consumption. That is, if individual i consumes a quantity x_i of a private good,

$$\sum_{j=1}^{n} x_j = X. \tag{2.1}$$

When n people collectively benefit from a quantity G of a public good, the same quantity G is available for everyone; therefore,

$$G_1 = G_2 = \cdots = G_n = G. \tag{2.2}$$

Expression (2.2) applies to both pure and impure (or congestible) public goods. When a public good is congestible, the level or quality of service declines with the number of users (as in Figure 2.1b after n_1 users), but the availability of the public good remains the same for everybody. Everybody caught in a traffic jam on a highway receives the same benefit from the congested highway, even if the common benefit has been reduced by the inability of the cars to move.

The equal supply of a public good to all persons does not imply that all people value public goods equally. On the contrary, we expect individuals' valuations of public goods to differ. When a Mozart symphony is played in a room (the music is a public good), some people will enjoy the music, whereas others may find the music unappealing and may prefer jazz or hard rock. Those people who enjoy the Mozart symphony are in principle prepared to pay to hear the music. People who find the music unappealing should be prepared to pay to have the music stopped.

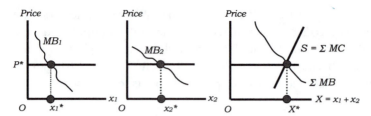

Figure 2.2. Market demand for a private good.

2.1.2 Voluntary payment for public goods

The example of music illustrates that people have different demands (or willingness to pay) for public goods, just as they have different demands for private goods.

Figure 2.2 shows a market demand function $\sum MB$ for private goods derived by summing the individual demands MB_1 and MB_2 of two persons. Market demand $\sum MB$ for the private good is obtained by asking the question: at any price, what is the total demand? In Figure 2.2 at the market equilibrium price P^*, individual 1 chooses to purchase the quantity x_1^* and individual 2 chooses to purchase the quantity x_2^*. Total market demand at price P^* is therefore $X^* = (x_1^* + x_2^*)$. Repeating the summation of individual demands for all prices results in the complete private-good market demand function $\sum MB$.

In the market equilibrium for a private good, consumers choose *different* consumption quantities when confronting the *same* market price. For public goods, people are supplied with the same quantity: by the definition of a public good, the quantity available for one person is also the quantity available to all other people. In Figure 2.3, we see the same quantity G^* of a public good available to two persons with different demands MB_1 and MB_2. Person 1 values the quantity G^* at P_1^* and person 2 values the same quantity G^* at P_2^*.

The combined valuations, or combined willingness to pay of the two persons for the quantity G^*, is $P^* = (P_1^* + P_2^*)$, as shown at point E. When we sum valuations of the two persons for all possible quantities of the public good, we obtain the combined market valuation of the public good, or combined market demand $\sum MB$. Individual valuations to establish total demand for a public good are therefore summed vertically over different quantities. In contrast, for private goods, individual demands to establish total market demand are summed horizontally over different prices.

For both private and public goods, total demand is thus found by summing individual demands to obtain $\sum MB$, but the way in which the summation takes place differs. The difference reflects the different questions that are being asked when establishing total market demand for private and public goods. For private goods, the price is the same for everybody and the question is which quantities are people willing to buy at different prices. For public goods, the quantity is the same for everybody and the question underlying market demand is how much are people willing to pay in total for different determining quantities.

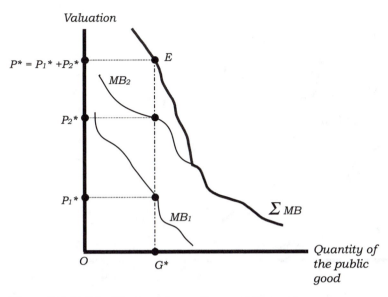

Figure 2.3. Total willingness to pay for a public good.
The total demand or willingness to pay $\sum MB$ of a population for a public good is found by summing individual *MB*s vertically for different quantities.

In a market for private goods as in Figure 2.2, individuals voluntarily pay the price P^* for consumption, and any person who does not pay is excluded from benefit. For the public good in Figure 2.3, benefit does not require personal payment if no one is (or can be) excluded from benefit. Whereas people pay for private goods because they are excluded (or exclude themselves) if they do not pay, the same incentive is not present to personally pay for public goods because of the possibility of benefiting from the spending of others.

We can consider what a market for a public good would look like, if people paid for public goods in the same voluntary way that they pay for private goods. A market requires a demand and a supply function. We have a demand function for public goods from Figure 2.3 where individuals' valuations of a public good are summed for different quantities.

The supply function for a public good is in principle the same as the supply function for a private good. The inputs required for public goods are generally available in markets and can be competitively supplied. For example, if the public good is the protection provided by police officers in a patrol car, the police officers are hired in labor markets, and the police vehicle is purchased in a market. The marginal cost MC of supply of a police patrol is the combined marginal cost of an additional police car and the officers who staff the car. The same principle of market supply applies to inputs for other public goods. For national defense, payments for personnel and equipment are similarly determined in markets. For foreign representation, salaries of the diplomats and their support staff, the cost of the embassy building, the furnishings, and the expenses incurred in hosting

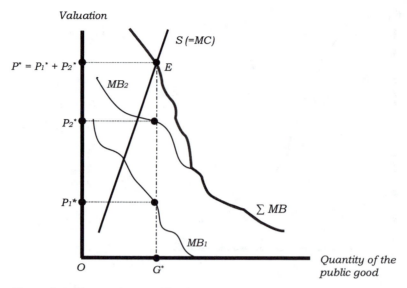

Figure 2.4. The market equilibrium for a public good.
People pay different prices for the same quantity.

diplomatic receptions together determine marginal cost MC of the public good. With inputs purchased in competitive markets, the competitive supply function for a public good is the (horizontal) sum of MC functions of all prospective suppliers, just as for a private good.[3] The difference between markets for private and public goods is only in demand, through the different means that individual MBs are added to obtain total demand.

Figure 2.4 shows a competitive supply function S for a public good and the combined valuation or demand $\sum MB$ of two people for the public good (any number of people could in principle benefit from the public good). Supply and demand in Figure 2.4 are equal at the point E, where quantity is G^* and price is P^*.

We see that at point E in Figure 2.4 that supply is equal to demand in the market for the public good

$$\sum_{j=1}^{n} MB_j = MC, \tag{2.3}$$

where, in our case with two people, $n = 2$. The supply function indicates MC of supply. The market demand function was constructed by vertically adding marginal benefits for different quantities, and so market demand indicates $\sum MB$. At the point E where supply and demand are equal, $\sum MB$ therefore equals MC.

---

[3] When supply of the inputs to provide the public good is competitive, supply of the benefits of a pure public good is nonetheless a natural monopoly because additional people can benefit without additional spending on the inputs required to provide a pure public good.

At the point E, the cost of the public good is shared among the population. Person 1 pays a price P_1^* and person 2 pays a price P_2^*. The individual prices are determined by each person's personal benefit from the public good according to

$$P_1^* = MB_1, \qquad P_2^* = MB_2. \tag{2.4}$$

The sum of the personal prices equals the price of the public good:

$$P^* = P_1^* + P_2^*. \tag{2.5}$$

That is, each person pays a share of the price of the public good, which is consistent with the simultaneous benefits to both persons.

We have now established the characteristics of a market for public goods if people were voluntarily to share costs of supply. We can now also ask the question: is the outcome of voluntary payment for public goods supplied through a market efficient?

To answer this question, we can apply the same indicator of efficiency that we used when investigating the efficiency of a competitive market for private goods, except that we take into account that everybody benefits (in personally different ways) from public goods. With n people benefiting from a public good, efficiency is achieved by choosing supply of a quantity of a public good to maximize:

$$W = \sum_{j=1}^{n} B_j - C. \tag{2.6}$$

In expression (2.6), we sum the benefits of all n beneficiaries of the public good, and we subtract the total cost of supplying the public good. It follows from (2.6) that supply of a public good is efficient when

$$\sum_{j=1}^{n} MB_j = MC. \tag{2.7}$$

Expression (2.7), which describes efficient supply of public goods, is precisely the same as expression (2.3), which describes the market equilibrium in Figure 2.4 attained through voluntary payments for public goods. The market outcome achieved through the voluntary payments shown in (2.4) is therefore efficient.[4]

There has been no reason to anticipate that the market outcome that would be achieved though voluntary sharing of costs of a public good would not be efficient. The market is efficient for private goods. For public goods, the only change is in the way we have summed individual demands or valuations to establish total market demand.

Implementing the public-good market is, however, all but impossible. For private goods, individuals face prices that are the same for everybody and choose

[4] The condition (2.7), or equivalently (2.3), is known as the Samuelson rule for efficient supply of a public good, after the MIT economist Paul Samuelson (who received the Nobel Prize in economics 1970). In Supplement 2A, the equivalent condition is derived for efficient allocation of resources to production of public and private goods.

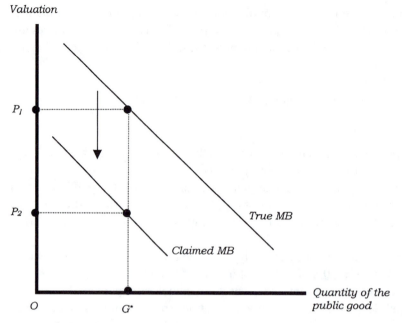

Valuation

Figure 2.5. The gain from deception.
By deceptively misrepresenting personal benefit, individuals can reduce personal contributions to voluntary financing of a public good.

different quantities. For public goods, individuals who face quantities that are the same for everybody are being asked to pay the different personal prices determined by expression (2.4). The different personal prices depend on personal individual subjective benefits MB, which people only know about themselves. Asking people to contribute to the cost of public goods according to their MB is, in effect, asking people to choose their own contributions to the costs of supplying public goods. In these circumstances, there may be a temptation for people to declare low personal benefit and thereby determine low personal prices for themselves even if their benefits are high.

Figure 2.5 shows the personal gain from acting deceptively rather than paying according to true personal MB. By understating true marginal benefit, the individual in Figure 2.5 reduces personal payment for the quantity G^* from P_1 to P_2.

We might feel that it is unfair or dishonest for people to behave deceptively. Beyond the ethical perspective, deceptive behavior results in an inefficient outcome for society. Figure 2.6 shows the downward shift in $\sum MB$ of the population when everybody, or many people, deceptively claim low personal benefit from a public good and underpay. Total spending on the public good is reduced to provide only the quantity G^o, and the public good is underprovided relative to the efficient quantity G^*.

If all people voluntarily paid according to their true personal benefit, markets would efficiently provide public goods. Adam Smith's invisible hand, and

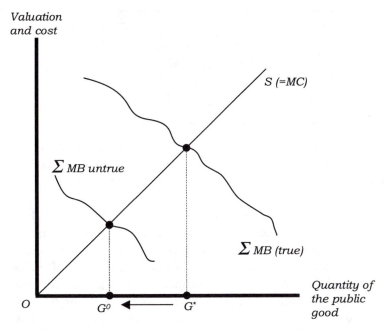

Figure 2.6. Undersupply of a public good due to misrepresented personal benefits.

spontaneous order of the market to achieve efficiency, would then apply to public goods as well as to private goods. We can *describe* a market for public goods that could in principle result in efficient spending on public goods through voluntary personal payments. Self-interested personal behavior (the same self-interested personal behavior that provides efficiency in markets for private goods) however stands in the way of efficient voluntary spending on public goods. Because personal benefit is subjective information, we would, moreover, never know whether voluntary personal payments reflect true personal benefit.

2.1.3 The prisoners' dilemma and public goods

Voluntary payment for public goods is another case of the prisoners' dilemma. We previously encountered the prisoners' dilemma when individuals under anarchy faced the choice between respecting the property of others or stealing. The prisoners' dilemma for voluntary payment of public goods has the same structure as the prisoners' dilemma of anarchy. In Table 2.1, two identical persons face the decision whether voluntarily to contribute to financing of a public good according to their true personal benefit or to misrepresent personal benefit and not contribute. The first number in Table 2.1 is again the benefit to person 1 and the second number is the benefit of person 2. The numbers indicate, besides personal benefits, the *rankings* of the outcomes by the two persons, with 4 indicating the most preferred outcome and 1 the least preferred.

The best personal outcome 4 is when the public good is supplied through the spending of the other person. The next best personal outcome 3 is that both persons

TABLE 2.1. THE PUBLIC-GOOD PRISONERS' DILEMMA

	Person 2 contributes	Person 2 deceives
Person 1 contributes	3, 3	1, 4
Person 1 deceives	4, 1	2, 2

share the cost of financing the public good. The next best personal outcome 2 is that neither contributes to finance the public good. The worst personal outcome 1 occurs when a person spends to provide the public good while the other person contributes nothing or free rides.[5]

The dominant strategy for each person is not to pay for the public good. That is, independently of the decision made by the other, each person's best personal decision is to behave deceptively. Consider the decision of person 1. If person 2 decides to contribute to financing the public good, person 1 is best off being deceptive and free riding on person 2's payments (since 4 > 3). If person 2 decides *not* to contribute to paying for the public good, person 1's best response is again not to contribute (since 2 > 1). Whatever person 2 decides to do, person 1's best response is thus not to contribute to financing the public good.

The two persons in Table 2.1 confront the same incentives. With decisions made simultaneously, the Nash equilibrium is the outcome (2, 2) where neither person contributes to providing the public good.[6]

Rather than decisions being made simultaneously, decisions could be made sequentially. The equilibrium is then again (2, 2). Suppose person 1 decides first. Person 1 knows that, if he or she contributes to financing the public good, person 2 will not contribute, in which the case the outcome will be (1, 4), that is, 1 for person 1 and 4 for person 2. If person 1 decides first and does not contribute, the outcome will be (2, 2). Person 1, or whoever decides first, therefore does not contribute. The best response of the person who decides second is also not to contribute.

The Nash equilibrium outcome at (2, 2) is inefficient. Both persons are better off at (3, 3) where they contribute to spending on the public good. That is, (3, 3) is a Pareto improvement compared to (2, 2) because both persons are better off (and no one is worse off) at (3, 3).

---

[5] For example, suppose that efficient spending on a lighthouse is $1,000, which in the efficient outcome (3, 3) is equally financed by private individual payments of $500 each. If the benefits from efficient spending on the lighthouse are $700 each, a net benefit of $200 each is provided in the efficient outcome. If only person 1 pays, the lighthouse provided by person 1's spending of $500 yields a benefit to each person of $400. Person 1 has a net loss of ($500 − $400) = $100 and person 2 has gain of $400. If neither person pays, each receives zero. In this example, the best personal outcome at 4 is $400 through successful free riding. The next best personal outcome at 3 is $200 through voluntary mutual payment to achieve efficient supply. The next best outcome at 2 is zero, where no payment is made and the public good is not supplied. The worst personal outcome at 1 is a loss of $100 from paying for the public good when the other person free rides.

[6] (2, 2) is a Nash equilibrium because a change of mind at (2, 2) by either person to contribute to financing the public good reduces personal benefit from 2 to 1.

The efficient outcome (3, 3) is not a Nash equilibrium because at (3, 3) each person can personally do better by not contributing to spending on the public good, given that the other is contributing. When each person acts in a personally self-interested way and attempts to rely on spending on the public good by the other, the outcome moves from (3, 3) to the inefficient Nash equilibrium (2, 2).

One person might wish to be honest and pay for the public good in accord with true personal benefit. The honest person would then be exploited by the free riding of the other person. If person 1 were honest, the outcome would be (1, 4).

When both persons act deceptively (but rationally) they find themselves at the Nash equilibrium (2, 2). Both gain when a government achieves the efficient outcome (3, 3) by levying compulsory taxes that finance the public good through public spending. As in the case of anarchy, the paradox of benefit from coercion is present. Everyone is better off because of the coercive intervention of government.

Large populations
With more than two people, the same inefficiency arises when voluntary payments are intended to finance public goods. Independent personal decisions result in an inefficient multiperson Nash equilibrium. With large populations, we can also ask how voluntary contributions to paying for public goods are affected by increases in the size of the population. Supplement 2B describes voluntary contributions to public goods in large populations and investigates free-riding behavior as the population increases.

Income distribution
The distribution of income in a population can affect voluntary contributions to finance public goods. Supplement 2C shows the relation between total voluntary contributions to a public good and income distribution.

2.1.4 Volunteer-type public goods
In the circumstances of the prisoners' dilemma, if n people were each voluntarily to contribute a quantity z_i of a public good, the total amount of the public good that would be available to the population of n persons is the sum of the individual contributions:

$$G = \sum_{j=1}^{n} z_j. \qquad (2.8)$$

The summation in expression (2.8) might not be over actual quantities z_i of the public good that people individually contribute. More usually, people contribute money to finance supply of a public good. In that case, with P the price of a unit of the public good, the sum of individuals' contributions is $\sum P z_i$, which is the total amount of money available for spending on the public good.

In some cases, supply or spending on a public good is not determined by the sum of individuals' contributions as described in expression (2.8). Rather, once one person has provided the public good, there is no need for anyone else to do so. In such cases, the question is who, if anybody, will provide the public good for the benefit of everybody else. The person who provides the public good can be described as a volunteer – even though he or she may prefer someone else to have volunteered.

Personal security can be provided as a volunteer-type public good. Government has the responsibility of providing personal security by ensuring the rule of law and protecting life and property. Yet, as we observed in Chapter 1, governments do not guarantee the protection of life or property. People can therefore find themselves needing help, when the help can only come from other people. For example, help might be required to move a disabled car to the side of the road. Or help may be required to thwart assault or robbery. All bystanders may feel better when help is provided to a person in need, but it may take only one bystander to act to provide the assistance. The person being helped receives private benefit from the assistance that is given. The public good is the benefit to all people who are pleased that the person in need was helped. Although everyone feels better because of the assistance that has been provided, the person who provides the assistance incurs a personal cost.

A similar situation arises if passengers lining up to board a plane notice that a person is acting suspiciously. People may not wish to voice their suspicions to security personnel because of personal cost through the embarrassment in being mistaken about the intentions of the suspicious person. A passenger who brings the suspicious person to the attention of the security personnel incurs the personal cost. However, everyone benefits when the suspicious person is brought to the attention of security personnel, who investigate and find that the suspicious person is harmless – or not.

Another example of a volunteer-type public good is removing a rock from a road. A person who stops to remove the rock from the road incurs a personal cost, but his or her action benefits other drivers. The question is who, if anybody, will stop to move the rock to the side of the road? Or if a bottle has been broken on a path, who if anybody will pick up the broken glass? When someone is creating a disturbance in a movie theater, who will ask the person causing the disturbance to be quiet? Or, if two exams are scheduled at unreasonably close times, who if anybody will arrange rescheduling of the exams for everybody? If at least one person must be present at a meeting to represent a group of people, who will come to the meeting? A story from the Netherlands tells of a boy who placed his finger in a hole in a dyke to stem the inflow of water that would have flooded the land. The boy is a hero in the story because he personally provided a public good to the rest of the population, although, in the nature of public goods, by his actions he also personally benefited, by saving himself.

When, as in these cases, the actions of one person are sufficient to provide a public good from which other people freely benefit, the quantity of the public good supplied through the contributions of n people is defined as

$$G = \max\{z_1, z_2, \ldots, z_n\}. \tag{2.9}$$

It is still true that the quantity of the public good *received* by any person is the same as the quantity received by anyone else. That is,

$$G = \max\{z_1, z_2, \ldots, z_n\} = G_1 = G_2 = \cdots = G_n. \qquad (2.9a)$$

Expression (2.9) shows that the quantity G that is supplied to everybody is the largest of the n individual contributions (and not the sum of the individual contributions as in the case of a prisoners' dilemma-type public good). After the largest individual contribution has determined how much is supplied to everybody, the other personal contributions do not affect availability of the public good. Costs of providing less than the maximal contribution have been needlessly incurred.

For example, suppose that four people each incur personal costs in respectively providing quantities (4, 7, 10, 15) of a public good. The amount available for all is then 15, and the costs incurred by the three people who provide the smaller amounts (4, 7, 10) have no effect on the amount of the public good that is available.

An outcome where three persons individually contribute (4, 7, 10) when another person contributes 15 cannot be a Nash equilibrium because the three persons making the contributions (4, 7, 10) are better off contributing zero given that the fourth person is contributing 15. It is efficient for one person to provide a volunteer-type public good. Free riding is thus efficient. For public goods described by the prisoners' dilemma, free riding was inefficient.

Efficient supply of a volunteer public good may require contributions from not one person as we have described but two or three persons, or some other subsegment of a population. For example, three people might be required to push a disabled car to the side of the road or to overpower a mugger. We shall now proceed with the case where only one person is required to provide the public good. The conclusions are similar when the contribution of more than one person is required. The identifying characteristic of the volunteer-type public good is that not everybody in a population is required to contribute for the public good to be efficiently provided, so that free riding is efficient. There is no altruism or personal satisfaction from providing the public good. Everybody prefers that someone else incur the personal cost of providing the public good.

Who volunteers to provide the public good?

If the contribution of only one person is required to provide public-good benefits for everybody, who will bear the personal cost of providing the public good? When individuals differ in benefits from the public good and everyone knows each other's benefits, a high-benefit person may well provide the public good. Or if personal costs of providing the public good differ and are known to all, the person with the lowest costs might be more inclined to provide the public good than others. A group of hikers may have lost their way and need help. The fittest person might volunteer to go for help (the lowest-cost person). Or a hiker who needs special medication may volunteer to go for help, to ensure that he or she receives the medication on time (the highest-benefit person then goes). The maximum-benefit or minimum-cost person is maximizing personal benefit by

TABLE 2.2. VOLUNTEER-TYPE PUBLIC GOODS

	Person 2 provides the public good	Person 2 does not provide the public good
Person 1 provides the public good	10, 10	10, 12
Person 1 does not provide the public good	12, 10	2, 2

volunteering. A volunteer may make the calculation that the best personal chance of being rescued is to go for help personally rather than to rely on others. There is no need for altruism in the personal decision. Self-interest suffices, and others gain because of the public-good nature of the benefit.

Because everyone prefers that, if possible, the cost of volunteering be imposed on someone else, we might expect a game of "chicken" to emerge, where people wait for others to act to provide the public good. It is possible that no one might provide the public good.

Let us consider two identical individuals for whom a public good provides a common benefit 12. The personal cost of providing the public good is 2. It is sufficient for one person to incur the cost 2 for the public good to be provided.

Let us now look at Table 2.2, which describes a symmetric game. When neither person provides the public good, both persons have a benefit of 2. A person who provides the public good has a benefit of $(12 - 2) = 10$. The best personal outcome 12 is when the other person incurs the cost of providing the public good. Each person knows the benefits and costs of the other; therefore, the two persons know they have identical benefits and costs.[7]

In Table 2.2, the total benefit when both persons provide the public good is $(10 + 10) = 20$. This is not a Nash equilibrium, because, given that one person is providing the public good, the other person can do better by not providing the public good (and so obtaining a benefit of 12 rather than 10).

The minimum total benefit is $(2 + 2) = 4$ when neither person provides the public good. This is also not a Nash equilibrium, because either person can do personally better by providing the public good.

Nash equilibria in Table 2.2 are (12, 10) and (10, 12) where one person personally provides the public good and the other does not. At these outcomes, given that one person is providing the public good, no person can do better by changing

---

[7] That is, there is common knowledge, which means that people know each other's costs and benefits, and also that people know that people know, and they know that people know that they know, and so on. The formal definition of "common knowledge" differs from the definition of "public knowledge," where people know each other's costs and benefits, but do not know that other people know. Behavior under common knowledge and public knowledge differs. People react differently when they know that other people know. The interactions among people that we have been considering are based on common knowledge.

the decision that each has made. The Nash equilibria are efficient. Total benefit is a maximal $(12 + 10) = 22$. Unlike the case of the prisoners' dilemma, efficiency does not require contributions of both people to the public good.[8]

In the case of the prisoners' dilemma, there is a dominant strategy: not to contribute to the public good. For volunteer public goods, there is no dominant strategy. If the other person provides the public good, the best response is not to provide the public good. If the other person does not provide the public good, the best response is to provide the public good.

Neither person knows whether the other will provide the public good. Each person can only make a decision based on the probabilities of the possible actions taken by the other. That is, we have mixed-strategy solutions where individuals act probabilistically.[9]

To establish the mixed strategy equilibrium, we can consider the decision facing person 1 in Table 2.2. By personally providing the public good, person 1 obtains a benefit of 10 with certainty, independently of the decision of person 2. The benefit for person 1 from not providing the public good depends on the decision made by person 2.

Let P_2 be the probability that person 2 will provide the public good. With person 1 not providing the public good, if person 2 provides the public good, person 1 has a benefit of 12, and if person 2 does not provide the public good, person 1 has a benefit of 2. Person 1's expected benefit (or benefit on average) by not acting to supply the public good is therefore

$$12P_2 + 2(1 - P_2). \tag{2.10}$$

A mixed strategy for person 1 is defined by person 1 being indifferent between providing and not providing the public good. To determine the mixed-strategy equilibrium, we set expression (2.10) equal to the assured benefit of 10 that person 1 receives by personally supplying the public good:

$$12P_2 + 2(1 - P_2) = 10. \tag{2.11}$$

We can solve equation (2.11) to obtain the probability $P_2 = 0.8$.

Because behavior of the two persons is symmetric, the solution for the probability P_1 that person 1 will act to provide the public good is the same as for P_2. When benefits are as described in Table 2.2, each person thus personally provides the public good with 80 percent probability.[10]

If each person provides the public good with 80 percent probability, what is the probability that the public good will be supplied? To answer this question, we look

---

[8] For volunteer public goods, there is one efficient Nash equilibrium for as many persons as there are, since an efficient equilibrium requires that one person alone contribute to provide the public good.

[9] We previously encountered mixed strategies in Chapter 1 in the interaction between the strong and the weak without the rule of law.

[10] This means, for example, that each person puts eight red balls and two blue balls in a box, and randomly draws a ball from the box. If the ball that is drawn is red, the person provides the public good; if the ball is blue, the person does not provide the public good.

TABLE 2.3. PROBABILITIES OF THE OUTCOMES IN TABLE 2.2

	Person 2 provides the public good	Person 2 does not provide the public good
Person 1 provides the public good	$(0.8)(0.8) = 0.64$	$(0.8)(0.2) = 0.16$
Person 1 does not provide the public good	$(0.2)(0.8) = 0.16$	$(0.2)(0.2) = 0.04$

TABLE 2.4. HIGH BENEFIT FROM SUPPLY BY OTHERS

	Person 2 provides the public good	Person 2 does not provide the public good
Person 1 provides the public good	10, 10	10, 22
Person 1 does not provide the public good	22, 10	2, 2

at the probabilities of obtaining each of the four possible outcomes in Table 2.2. That is, we compute the joint probability of the two persons making the decisions that lead to a particular outcome. The resulting probabilities are shown in Table 2.3.

We see that the outcome where the public good is not provided (when neither person provides the public good) arises with a probability of 4 percent. In the other three cases, the public good is provided (since it is sufficient that one person provides the public good); therefore, the probability that the public good will be provided is $(64 + 32) = 96$ percent. Although the probability that the public good will be provided is quite high, the probability of an *efficient* outcome is only $(0.16 + 0.16) = 32$ percent. A wasteful duplicative outcome occurs with probability of 64 percent.

Another example

The probability of the public good being provided is high in Table 2.3, because of the small difference between the individual benefit 10 from personally providing the public good and the individual benefit 12 when someone else provides the public good. Table 2.4 shows an example where the personal cost of providing the public good, and therefore the benefit when someone else provides the public good, is more substantial (22 instead of 12 in Table 2.2). The mixed-strategy equilibrium is now determined from

$$22 P_2 + 2(1 - P_2) = 10, \tag{2.11a}$$

and the probability that a person provides the public good is 0.4.

TABLE 2.5. PROBABILITIES OF THE OUTCOMES IN TABLE 2.4

	Person 2 provides the public good	Person 2 does not provide the public good
Person 1 provides the public good	$(0.4)(0.4) = 0.16$	$(0.4)(0.6) = 0.24$
Person 1 does not provide the public good	$(0.6)(0.4) = 0.24$	$(0.6)(0.6) = 0.36$

TABLE 2.6. THE GENERAL FORM OF VOLUNTEER-TYPE PUBLIC GOODS

	Person 2 provides the public good	Person 2 does not provide the public good
Person 1 provides the public good	$b - c, b - c$	$b - c, b$
Person 1 does not provide the public good	$b, b - c$	a, a

We see in Table 2.5 that the public good is now not provided with 36 percent probability (and so, with probability 64 percent, the public good *is* provided). Each efficient outcome where one person provides the public good occurs with probability 24 percent, and the probability of efficient supply is therefore 48 percent. Comparing Tables 2.3 and 2.5, we see that the probability of the public good not being provided at all has increased (from 4 percent to 36 percent). The probability of an efficient outcome has also increased (from 32 to 48 percent), but not as drastically as the probability that the public good will not be provided at all.

We can also consider an example where there are substantial personal losses if the public good is not provided. For example, in Table 2.2, suppose that there is a loss each of 88 when the public good is not provided. The probability that an individual will personally supply the public good is then $P = 0.98$. If the personal loss from not supplying the public good is high enough, each individual will personally supply the public good with near certainty.

The general form of the volunteer-type public good

Table 2.6 shows the general form of the structure of personal benefits for volunteer-type public goods. The benefit from the public good is b and the personal cost of providing the public good is c. If the public good is not provided, each person has a benefit a.

In Table 2.6, a personal benefit of $b - c$ is obtainable with certainty independently of the decision of the other person by personally providing the public good rather than relying on the other person. With P as the probability that the other person will provide the public good, a mixed strategy is determined from

$$b - c = Pb + (1 - P)a, \qquad (2.12)$$

and therefore

$$P = 1 - \frac{c}{b - a} < 1. \qquad (2.13)$$

When we substitute the values for a, b, and c that were used in Tables 2.2 and 2.4, we obtain the outcomes in Tables 2.3 and 2.5. We see from expression (2.13) that the probability P that an individual will personally supply a public good increases with the benefit b from the public good. The probability P declines with the personal cost c of providing the public good, and with the personal benefit a available without the public good.

Sequential decisions
We have been looking at simultaneous decisions, or decisions made by one person without knowing the decision made by the other person. If decisions are made sequentially, and if the personal loss from deferment of benefits to the future is not too great, the first person with the opportunity to make a decision chooses not to supply the public good, and the second person's best personal response is to act to provide the public good. The decision of the second person to supply the public good is, of course, hardly volunteering. The second person knows that, if the public good is to be supplied at all, he or she must incur the cost, and personal benefit is maximized by supplying the public good if no one else does. The outcome obtained through sequential decisions is efficient. One person (the second to decide) supplies the public good. Sequential decisions thus determine which of the two efficient Nash equilibria will be obtained. The first person to decide imposes the cost of supply on the second person.

Large populations and information
With larger populations and with sequential decisions, each person can choose to leave provision of the public good to the next person, if there is a next person. If the number of people is some finite number, for example 20, then the 20th person provides the public good. The last person will provide the public good, since, as in the case of two people, the last person has no one else to rely on, or onto whom to move the cost of supplying the public good, since there is no one else left. A more complicated situation arises when there is uncertainty about how many people might provide the public good, so that the 19th person, for example, is not sure whether there is a 20th person. Individuals then have to match the personal benefit obtained with certainty through personal supply against the expected benefit of relying on someone else to supply, when there may be no one else.

We can also consider simultaneous decisions with many people. We might also want to take into account that people in general do not know each other's benefits or costs associated with supply of the public good. We could therefore introduce the additional uncertainty that arises when people have incomplete information about each other's incentives to provide the public good. In such circumstances, does a larger population increase the overall likelihood that the public good will be provided? We know that the larger the population, the greater is the likelihood that at least one person will provide the public good. At the same time, however, the greater the population, the greater the number of other people on whom each individual can hope to rely to provide the public good; that is, as the population increases, there is increased free riding, in the form of a reduced personal probability of providing the public good. The two effects counter one another. Therefore, an increase in population can increase or decrease the probability of supply when decisions are made simultaneously and people are uncertain about each other's benefits from the public good or each other's personal costs of supply.[11]

Volunteering and social norms

A volunteer bears a personal cost in providing the public good for personal benefit and (in the nature of public goods) inadvertently or unintentionally benefits everyone else. That is, the intent in providing the public good is not altruistically to benefit others. If a person helps someone in distress, the reason is that the personal MB of providing assistance exceeds the personal MC, conditional on expectations or beliefs about the likelihood of someone else providing help. If someone stops to move a rock to the side of the road, it is because of the personal inconvenience of having to drive around or over the rock, or because the rock may still be there tomorrow when the same person travels the same route. The intention underlying moving the rock was not to provide benefit to others (although others benefit). The volunteer would prefer that someone else volunteer.

Collective benefits within a household often take the form of personally provided volunteer-type public goods. For example, it may be sufficient for one person to cook a meal or do the grocery shopping or clean or tidy the house, or replace a light bulb or fuse. In such cases, the problem of supply of volunteer-type public goods is often solved by convention. The conventions within a household are established by repeated personal contact and may involve specialization or taking turns. Within broader society, we cannot rely on similar sharing conventions for different people performing tasks. However, social norms can influence people's decisions to volunteer to provide a public good. Social norms reflect people's self-expectations about how they feel they should act in different situations and are inculcated from the society in which they live. Social norms thus introduce outside influences on personal decisions. For example, people who stop to help a stranded driver, even if they are on their way to a movie and will be late because they have stopped to help, are responding to the social norm of helping others in distress and are not relying on the likelihood that others will provide help.

---

[11] When a population becomes very large, the probability that the public good is supplied approaches a finite limit (see Xiaopeng Xu, 2001).

Social norms can reduce free-riding behavior though stigma (disapproval by others) or conscience (self-disapproval of a person's own behavior). Social norms thereby affect the likelihood that volunteer-type public goods will be provided. A society where the social norm is to take personal responsibility to provide volunteer-type public goods will be a better society in which to live than a society where the norm is to wait for others to act, although, when decisions are simultaneous, unnecessary duplication may occur.

Public finance

It may require only one police officer patrolling a neighborhood to provide personal security for all the inhabitants. The benefits from the police officer on patrol are however not provided through a voluntary act of personal responsibility. Because the salary of the police officer is publicly financed, there is no uncertainty about whether the public good will be provided. When government can take responsibility for supply, the uncertainty inherent in people relying on one another to provide the public good is avoided. When there is public finance, we have a prisoners' dilemma-type public good rather than a volunteer-type public good.

2.1.5 Weakest-link public goods

Another form of public good is known as weakest-link. Such public goods have the characteristic that the amount available is the *least amount* that is voluntarily financed by any member of a population. That is, the quantity of the public good available is

$$G = \min\{z_1, z_2, \ldots, z_n\}, \tag{2.14}$$

where person i pays for an amount z_i. As with prisoners' dilemma-type and volunteer-type public goods, the quantity of the public good G that is supplied to a population is the same for everybody. If, for example, three persons personally provide 5, 7, and 12, the amount available to everybody is the smallest amount 5. The resources that individuals use in providing more than 5 have been wasted. The amount 5 is available because each person has individually provided at least 5.

To describe weakest-link public goods, Jack Hirshleifer (1983) used the example of a wall that protects homes on an island against encroaching waves. Homeowners could construct individual segments of a protective wall along the shore facing their houses. The level of protection against the sea was determined by the minimal height of any one individual's wall, since encroaching water can enter anywhere along the shore of the island and then flow on and spread out to flood all houses on the island. Weakest-link public goods arise in such cases where the lowest standard of behavior or benefit determines the overall standard.

Table 2.7 shows an example of benefits from a weakest-link public good for two persons. Each person has a benefit of 24 if both pay for the public good (both build a wall along their part of the seashore and the island is not flooded). They each have a benefit of 10 if neither pays for the public good (the island is flooded,

TABLE 2.7. A WEAKEST-LINK PUBLIC GOOD

	Person 2 provides the public good	Person 2 does not provide the public good
Person 1 provides the public good	24, 24	4, 10
Person 1 does not provide the public good	10, 4	10, 10

TABLE 2.8. THE GENERAL CASE OF WEAKEST-LINK PUBLIC GOODS

	Person 2 provides the public good	Person 2 does not provide the public good
Person 1 provides the public good	b, b	c, a
Person 1 does not provide the public good	a, c	a, a

but neither has spent money on the sea wall). The lowest personal benefit is 4, for a person who builds a wall when the other does not.

There is a Nash equilibrium at (24, 24) where both persons build a wall. There is also a Nash equilibrium at (10, 10) where neither person builds a wall. That is, at both (24, 24) and (10, 10), no person can do personally better by independently changing his or her decision. The efficient equilibrium is the Nash equilibrium at $(24 + 24) = 48$, where both persons build a protective wall. This is also the personally most advantageous outcome for each person.

There is no dominant strategy for making individual decisions. Whether one person's best decision is to build a wall depends on whether the other person builds a wall. The best personal decision, given the decision of the other person, is to duplicate the decision of the other person. When decisions are simultaneous, neither person knows what to do with certainty. Randomization through a mixed strategy is again a solution, with each person building the wall with some probability.

Table 2.8 describes the general structure of benefits for weakest-link public goods. The best personal return b (24 in the example of Table 2.7) is available when each person pays for the public good, and the individually worst return c (4 in Table 2.7) is that of a person who pays for the public good when the other does not. An intermediate return a (equal to 10 in Table 2.7) is available with certainty by not paying for the public good. Hence $c < a < b$.

To find the equilibrium in mixed strategies, we again set equal the benefits from the alternative decisions to pay for or not pay for the public good. A decision not to

TABLE 2.9. PROBABILITIES OF THE OUTCOMES IN TABLE 2.7

	Person 2 provides the public good	Person 2 does not provide the public good
Person 1 provides the public good	$(0.3)(0.3) = 0.09$	$(0.3)(0.7) = 0.21$
Person 1 does not provide the public good	$(0.7)(0.3) = 0.21$	$(0.7)(0.7) = 0.49$

pay provides the return a with certainty. A decision to pay provides the expected benefit $Pc + (1 - P)b$, where P is the probability that the other person will *not* provide the public good. The mixed-strategy equilibrium is again found from the condition describing indifference between paying and not paying,

$$a = Pc + (1 - P)b. \tag{2.15}$$

From the expression (2.15), the probability that a person will not supply the public good is therefore

$$P = \frac{b - a}{b - c} < 1. \tag{2.16}$$

Since behavior is symmetric, this is the equilibrium probability for both persons. For the values in Table 2.7, we find that $P = 0.7$. That is, each person *does not* build the wall with probability 70 percent (or each *does* pay for the public good with probability 30 percent).

Table 2.9 shows the probabilities of the different outcomes when each person pays for the public good with a probability of 30 percent. We see in Table 2.9 that an efficient outcome where both persons pay for the public good is achieved with only probability of 9 percent. With probability 49 percent, neither person pays for the public good. With probability $(21 + 21) = 42$ percent, there is an inefficient outcome where one person has used resources in an attempt to provide the public good, and there is no public good because the other person has not also paid.

With weakest-link public goods, a society faces a coordination problem. There is no free-rider problem. Free riding is not possible. Everybody wants to provide the public good, but one person's actions alone cannot provide the public good. Coordinated provision by everybody is required. When the size of the population increases, the coordination problem becomes more extensive.

Sequential decisions

Table 2.9 describes probabilities associated with simultaneous decisions. Sequential decisions solve the coordination problem. When two people make sequential decisions, the first person to decide pays for the public good (builds the sea wall at a requisite height) and the personally best response of the second person is to do likewise. The outcome of sequential decisions is therefore the efficient Nash equilibrium where the public good is provided and benefits in Table 2.7 are (24, 24). The same efficient outcome is in principle achieved through sequential decisions in a large population. The person deciding first pays, and so gives a signal to the people who decide thereafter that the efficient outcome with everybody cooperating to provide the public good can be achieved. With rational behavior, we expect the efficient outcome from sequential decisions to be that everyone pays so that the public good is provided.

A coordinating role of government

If sequential decisions are not possible, a superior solution to the uncertainty of randomizing behavior is for government to coordinate individual decisions. In the example of the sea wall, a government can ensure that private decisions are coordinated by a public policy of mandating minimum heights for compulsory privately financed sea walls. Alternatively, the government can provide the wall through compulsory taxation and public finance. The coordinating role of government for weakest-link public goods is similar to the role of government in resolving the prisoners' dilemma. In the prisoners' dilemma, the role of government is, however, to avoid free riding, whereas free riding is impossible for weakest-link public goods. A weakest-link public good is almost a private good. Every person has a self-interest in paying for a weakest-link public good, provided everyone else pays.

Different standards

We have described weakest-link public goods with people wanting the same standards. In the example of the protective wall, everyone wants the same height for the wall. People might, however, have different standards, or different demands for weakest-link public goods. For example, some people may want protection against tidal waves that occur with very low probability, whereas others may want a seawall that covers reasonable contingencies. The people who want a very high wall could pay the people who want lower walls to increase the height of the wall, but this could lead to free-riding behavior by people who in fact want a high wall but change their declared preference in an attempt to be paid to increase the height of their part of the wall. More generally, people may reduce standards to be paid to increase their standards. The role of government is then to set and enforce standards to avoid such opportunistic behavior.

2.1.6 National defense as a public good

National defense is a public good for which benefit depends not only on a country's own spending, but also on the aggressive capability of the potential adversary. The smaller the aggressive capability of a potential adversary, the smaller the defense spending required to provide a given level of national security.

In Table 2.10, the decisions of two countries' governments regarding military spending define a prisoners' dilemma. The decisions are to spend or not to spend. The best outcome 4 for a country in Table 2.10 is when the adversary does not

TABLE 2.10. MILITARY SPENDING BY TWO COUNTRIES AS A
PRISONERS' DILEMMA

	Country 2 does not spend	Country 2 spends
Country 1 does not spend	3, 3	1, 4
Country 1 spends	4, 1	2, 2

spend and a country does. The next best outcome is 3, where neither country
spends. The outcome giving a benefit of 2 occurs when both countries spend and
neutralize one another. The worst outcome 1 is where a country does not spend and
the adversary does. The dominant strategy is to spend on defense. Both countries
undertake military spending but neutralize one another, giving a return of 2 for
each. The efficient outcome where both countries have a return of 3 requires
neither country to undertake military spending.

The countries may not trust one another, and a promise not to develop weapons
secretly can be difficult to monitor. The outcome is then the inefficient Nash
equilibrium at (2, 2). The Nash equilibrium at (2, 2) is sometimes described as the
outcome of an "arms race." The countries would have been better off escaping the
inefficient Nash equilibrium by finding a way to cooperate in reducing national
defense spending. Such cooperation has often taken place through treaties that
place limits on particular types of weapons and defensive systems that countries
can have. Efforts are then, however, sometimes redirected into finding new ways
to expand military capabilities that are outside of the treaties. The treaties are
also sometimes not honored: some countries have developed nuclear capability
and biological weapons, although their governments signed treaties that obligated
them not to do so.

Military alliances

Since the national security from defense spending is a pure public good, the benefits from military spending by one country can be freely provided to people in
other countries. Consequently, there are incentives for the formation of defense
coalitions or military alliances among countries. Within such coalitions, the individual member countries are making contributions to finance defense spending
that benefits all members of the coalition. Free-riding problems can arise in defense coalitions, with governments of some participating countries attempting to
underpay and still receiving the benefits of being members of the coalition. Free
riding can also take the form of declaring that a common adversary is a friend.

Free riding within a country

Defense-related free-riding problems can also arise within a country. A person
may claim that he or she objects to participating in defense (or in the military) as a

TABLE 2.11. PERSONAL DECISIONS TO CONTRIBUTE TO DEFENSE AS A
PRISONERS' DILEMMA

	Person 2 contributes	Person 2 avoids contributing
Person 1 contributes	3, 3	1, 4
Person 1 avoids contributing	4, 1	2, 2

matter of principle. If the need for defense is not imagined but real, this person is free riding on the efforts of others. The prisoners' dilemma that then arises within the population of a country is shown in Table 2.11, where two persons face the decision whether to contribute to national defense. The Nash equilibrium is at (2, 2) where neither person contributes.

We can combine the prisoners' dilemma within a country in Table 2.11 with the prisoners' dilemma between countries in Table 2.10. The people inside a country may be in the Nash equilibrium (2, 2) in Table 2.11 and not contribute to defense. At the same time, the adversary in Table 2.10 may spend on military capability (since this is the dominant strategy). The outcome in the prisoners' dilemma *between* countries is then unfortunate for the country where the population has chosen to attempt to free ride in defense preparations, since there is no defense.

Besides financing defense through public spending, governments have at times used conscription, or compulsory participation of the population in defense, to avoid free riding that might take place. At the same time, rather than seeking to free ride, people have often volunteered to participate in contributing to defense of their country when national security has been threatened.

When the participation of everybody in national defense is not required, defense can be publicly financed through payments to people who choose a military career. The role of government is then to coordinate payments through taxation to those people who choose military careers. There is a "volunteer" army because people voluntarily choose military careers. The volunteer army is not however an example of a volunteer-type public good because the "volunteers" are not volunteering to incur costs personally for the benefits of others but are being paid.

Technology and capabilities

The Nash equilibrium in military spending at (2, 2) in Table 2.10 is a symmetric outcome where countries have equal capabilities that maintain a balance of power. Capabilities need not, however, be symmetric. A larger richer country can mobilize more resources for military capability than a smaller poorer country. A smaller country may therefore be at the mercy of a larger aggressive country. In numerous cases throughout history, the outcome has not been the symmetric equilibrium in the prisoners' dilemma where both countries spend on military capability and neutralize one another through a balance of power, but rather wars have taken place. The wars have often been won by the side with the larger population and with more resources available for mobilization. At other times, however, motivation and determination, and a sense of justice, have proved to be more decisive than population and resources available, in particular when people are defending their country against a foreign invader.

Technology has changed the role of country size and resources in determining military effectiveness. Capabilities of inflicting damage through nuclear, chemical, and biological warfare have made the size of a country's population and the resources available less important, and have increased the vulnerability of civilian populations. Private markets in nuclear, chemical, and biological weapons also increase the potential for harm to a country's population.[12]

Democracy

Democracies do not wage war on one another, nor do democracies initiate conflict.[13] Democracies have, however, often been attacked by countries with autocratic regimes. Historical precedent suggests that democracy in all countries is a means of ending international conflict and ultimately eliminating the need for defense spending.

2.1.7 Defense against terror

Terror is the intentional wanton killing and maiming of people going about their everyday life. Usual military preparedness can be ineffective in preempting terror attacks.[14]

When the reason for conflict is a dispute over territory or wealth, compromises are possible. Compromises are, however, impossible when enemies set out to inflict harm because they disagree with other peoples' beliefs and values.[15]

---

[12] Private supply of weapons of mass-destruction in particular became available when in 1991 the former Soviet Union separated into fifteen different government jurisdictions with access to military technology and equipment. The transition from collective property to private ownership in some of these countries included sale for private profit of the technology, equipment, and knowledge for weapons of mass destruction.

[13] Democracies have sometimes supported dictatorial regimes or kingdoms against other democratic regimes. Also, in countries with autocratic governments, the purpose of military spending is often not to provide external defense but to protect the autocratic government from internal dissent.

[14] On September 11, 2001, the United States was attacked not by a foreign army nor with missiles, but by nineteen terrorists who did not use usual military weapons and who were from different countries (fifteen of the attackers were citizens of one country, the kingdom of Saudi Arabia). The attack demonstrated how foreign aggressors could use implements and technologies of everyday life to carry out intentions of doing harm. People in other countries have also been victims of terror attacks.

[15] Absence of democratic values and absence of the rule of law can result in deep and widespread poverty in foreign countries. The foreign response can sometimes be jealousy and malice toward the richer societies that have democratic values and the rule of law. Terror does not, however, usually originate among poor people. For example, the terrorists who attacked the United States on September 11, 2001, were not from the poorer segments of their society.

The personal costs of terror

Defense against terror imposes personal costs on a population beyond the taxes that finance defense spending. The costs arise through expenses and inconveniences imposed on people in day-to-day life. The cost of air travel increases when increased security is required. There are personal costs when harmful bacteria can be delivered by mail, because of the need to examine carefully each letter we receive. There are personal costs in the anxiety of knowing that foreigners who wish us harm might have access to nerve gas, to the virus that causes smallpox and to other chemical or biological weapons, or to bombs containing radioactive material or nuclear weapons that can be transported in suitcases. The greatest private cost is of course incurred when people lose their lives or are maimed.

The cost of terror through social dilemmas

Terror imposes a cost through the social dilemmas that arise in preempting intent to do harm. A principle of a civilized society is absence of discrimination based on color or creed. However, discrimination is efficient if there is prior evidence that people with identifiable visible attributes are statistically more likely to do harm than others. Use of such profiles to discriminate in questioning people contradicts civil liberties. Efficient preemption may nonetheless require discrimination in stopping, questioning, and (if regarded as necessary) searching people. For example, 350 people might be waiting to board a plane, and prior evidence may indicate that *only* people fitting particular profiles have ever taken over and crashed planes. If there are four people with these attributes among the passengers waiting to board the plane, should all 350 passengers be thoroughly searched and questioned, or should special attention be directed at the four that fit the profile? Equal treatment of all 350 passengers is costly in terms of passengers' time and security personnel. Discrimination against the four, on the other hand, violates the principle that people should be treated equally, and as innocent of wrong-doing unless proven otherwise. A cost of terror is the social dilemma that terror imposes on a civil society because of the efficiency of profiling.

In general, defense spending is based on the premise that adversaries wish to stay alive. Defense is difficult when adversaries place a low value on their own lives, and becomes more difficult when adversaries look forward to death because of a belief in rewards in an after-life when death is incurred in a battle against nonbelievers. A further social dilemma arises when terrorists are prepared to die, or look forward to dying, since the only form of effective defense is then preemption of intentions by stopping terrorists before they have been able to inflict harm. Another fundamental principle of a civil society is then violated because of terror. Perpetrators should in principle be punished because of what they have done and not because of what they intend to do. Again, terror imposes costs by undermining the principles of civilized society.

Defense against terror can also impose a cost through social divisions. The social divisions arise when some people declare that we should attempt to understand terrorists rather than preempt terror, while other people take the position that it is more important to preempt terror than to understand and empathize with terrorists.

2.1.8 Public finance and public supply

For defense spending, and for prisoners' dilemma-type public goods in general (and for some possible instances of weakest-link public goods), we have identified a responsibility for taxation and public finance by government. Responsibility of government to finance public goods is not the same as a case for government supply. The advantage of government over voluntary payment for public goods is that government can overcome the free-rider problem by imposing the compulsory legal obligation to pay taxes.

When we refer to supply of public goods, we need to be clear about whether we mean supply of the inputs required to provide a public good or supply of the benefits from a public good. The distinction is important because supply of the benefits from a public good is a natural monopoly, but supply of the inputs into a public good is in general not. For example, supply of the benefits from national defense is a natural monopoly because cost-minimizing supply requires a single supplier. Supply of the equipment that is an input into defense is not a natural monopoly: there are and can be many competing suppliers. When we identify the condition for efficient supply of public goods as $\sum MB = MC$, the MC is the marginal cost of the inputs that provide public-good benefits (i.e., MC is for example the marginal cost of purchasing additional defense equipment).

Efficiency in supply of public goods has different aspects that are common to all three types of public goods that we have considered.

(1) One aspect of efficiency is given by the condition $\sum MB = MC$, which determines efficient supply of the inputs that provide public-good benefits (e.g., efficient defense spending).

(2) A second aspect of efficiency concerns access to public-good benefits. Efficient access requires that everyone who so wishes should be able to benefit from a public good because the addition of one more person who benefits harms nobody, by the definition of a pure public good.[16]

(3) Because allowing free access to benefits from a public good is efficient, it is wasteful to expend resources on replicating a public good. As we have noted, supply of the benefits of a public good is a natural monopoly.

The case for supply of public goods by government, as distinct from public finance through government, is related to access to benefits and natural monopoly. Government might take responsibility for supply, to ensure efficient free access and to avoid private monopoly in supply. We shall return in Chapter 8 to issues

---

[16] When a public good is not pure but is congestible, efficient access to the public good may require limiting access, to prevent a decline in personal benefit through congestion. We shall consider efficient access to congestible public goods in Chapter 8.

of public and private supply of benefits from public goods and natural monopoly. At this point, we keep in mind the distinction between public finance and public supply. We note that free-riding incentives and the benefits of compulsory taxation make a case for public *finance* of public goods, and not necessarily for public supply of public goods. We also note that when government finances public goods, the inputs or equipment can be supplied by competing private suppliers (or private contractors).

2.1.9 Summary

In Chapter 1, we set out a case for efficiency of personal voluntary decisions in competitive markets when private spending provides private benefit. Public goods provide collective benefits from private spending. That is, people spend for their own benefit, but their spending also benefits others. We have seen that markets could supply efficient quantities of public goods if, as with private goods, people were willing to pay for public goods voluntarily in accord with personal benefit. However, because benefits from spending on public goods are available when others have paid, there is a personal incentive to seek to free ride on the spending of others. Because of the incentive to free ride or understate benefit, voluntary financing of public goods through markets is not efficient.

We have expressed the free-rider problem for public goods in terms of a prisoners' dilemma. Under the conditions of the prisoners' dilemma, the individually rational decision is to attempt to free ride on the payments of others, but the efficient outcome for a society requires voluntary payments according to true personal marginal benefit. In the Nash-equilibrium outcome, everyone acts deceptively. Honest people who do not wish to act deceptively are disadvantaged because their payments finance benefits for the people who have chosen to free ride. The public-good prisoners' dilemma is the basis for a case for giving government responsibility for financing public goods through compulsory taxation.

We have also looked at two categories of public goods where incentives and benefits differ from the prisoners' dilemma. For volunteer-type public goods, it is sufficient that one person (or a subgroup of the population) personally provide the public good. In these cases, when individual decisions are made simultaneously, a society confronts uncertainty about whether a public good be efficiently provided, and about whether a public good will be provided at all. When personal decisions about supply of volunteer-type public goods are sequential, the burden of supply is shifted to the last person who it is known will have the opportunity to supply, but there may be uncertainty about who will be last. Because personal actions are the source of collective benefit, volunteer-type public goods are not the responsibility of government. Social norms affect the likelihood that volunteer-type public goods are supplied.

We also identified weakest-link public goods where efficient supply requires coordination of individual decisions. Contrary to the situation described by the prisoners' dilemma, incentives for free-riding behavior are not present. People want to pay for weakest-link public goods when there is an assurance that everyone else will also spend on the public good. Government can solve the coordination problem by using compulsory taxes and public finance to eliminate the risk that someone might not contribute. For weakest-link public goods, sequential decisions achieve efficiency without government.

We have considered spending on national defense and defense against terror as cases of public goods. National defense and defense against terror have special characteristics. National defense involves a prisoners' dilemma both between countries and inside a country. Defense against terror involves public spending; however, terror imposes personal costs on people and compels societies to confront dilemmas when defending themselves.

We have noted that public-good efficiency has different aspects. The condition $\sum MB = MC$ identifies efficient supply of inputs or efficient spending. Efficient access requires use by everybody who wishes to benefit. Efficient supply of benefits is a natural monopoly. The case we have made in this section for government responsibility relates to financing public goods. Efficient access and natural monopoly introduce the separate question of whether government should be involved in directly supplying (as opposed to financing) public-good benefits.

We shall proceed now to look more closely at public finance for public goods. Since volunteer-type public goods are not the responsibilities of government, we shall not consider such goods in investigating public finance for public goods. For weakest-link public goods, not only do sequential private decisions offer an efficient solution without government, but there are also no incentives for individuals to free ride. Our focus as we continue will be public goods characterized by the disincentive for personal voluntary finance described by the conditions of the prisoners' dilemma.

References and related literature

For the condition establishing efficient supply of public goods, see Samuelson (1954). On diversity in tastes for music, see Prieto-Rodriguez and Férnandez-Blanco (2000). On volunteer and weakest-link public goods, see Hirshleifer (1983), Diekman (1985), Harrison and Hirshleifer (1989), Sandler (1992), Cornes (1993), and Xu (2001). On the economics of defense, see Sandler and Hartley (1995). For a perspective on democracy and defense, see Garfinkel (1994). On statistical discrimination, see Arrow (1972) and Borooah (2001).

Arrow, K. J., 1972. Some mathematical models of race in the labor market. In *Racial Discrimination in Economic Life*, A. H. Pascal (ed.). D. C. Heath, Lexington, Massachusetts, 197–204.
Borooah, V. K., 2001. Racial bias in police stops and searches: An economic analysis. *European Journal of Political Economy* 17, 17–37.
Coase, R. H., 1974. The lighthouse in economics. *Journal of Law and Economics* 17, 357–76.
Cornes, R., 1993. Dyke maintenance and other stories: Some neglected types of public goods. *Quarterly Journal of Economics* 108, 259–71.

Diekman, A., 1985. The volunteer's dilemma. *Journal of Conflict Resolution* 29, 605–10.

Garfinkel, M. R., 1994. Domestic politics and international conflict. *American Economic Review* 84, 1294–1309.

Harrison, G. and J. Hirshleifer, 1989. An experimental evaluation of weakest-link/best-shot public goods. *Journal of Political Economy* 97, 201–23.

Hirshleifer, J., 1983. From weakest link to best-shot: The voluntary provision of public goods. *Public Choice* 41, 371–86 (and 1985, 46, 221–3).

Prieto-Rodriguez, J. and V. Férnandez-Blanco, 2000. Are popular and classical music listeners the same people? *Journal of Cultural Economics* 24, 147–64.

Samuelson, P. A., 1954. The pure theory of public expenditure. *Review of Economics and Statistics* 36, 387–9.

Sandler, T., 1992. *Collective Action: Theory and Applications.* The Univeristy of Michigan Press, Ann Arbor.

Sandler, T. and K. Hartley, 1995. *The Economics of Defense.* Cambridge University Press, New York.

Xu, X., 2001. Group size and the private supply of a best-shot public good. *European Journal of Political Economy* 17, 897–904.

Questions for discussion

1. List the public goods from which you benefit in the course of a day. Include in your list "option demands." Classify the public goods according to whether the prisoners' dilemma, volunteer-type public goods, or weakest-link public goods apply.

2. What is the logic underlying the condition for efficient voluntary spending on public goods? What is the difference between summation of benefits to establish total demand for private and public goods?

3. For the prisoners' dilemma-type public goods in your list, if people were asked voluntarily to finance these public goods through anonymous contributions, which, if any, of the public goods do you believe would receive voluntary financing that approaches efficient total spending for the public good?

4. In the prisoners' dilemma that arises under conditions of anarchy (where people decide whether to steal), the Nash equilibrium results in mutual harm (due to resources and time wastefully used in stealing). In the case of the public-good prisoners' dilemma, the Nash equilibrium results in failure to benefit (through unavailability of the efficient quantity of the public good). Are the consequences of noncooperation the same in the prisoners' dilemma of anarchy and in the public-good prisoners' dilemma? That is, does it matter for the analysis of the prisoners' dilemma whether the Nash equilibrium results in mutual harm or failure to benefit?

5. In anonymous prisoners' dilemma situations, people sometimes voluntarily contribute to financing of public goods and do not attempt to free ride in the way predicted by the prisoners' dilemma. In particular, in experiments conducted with students, there is less free-riding than might be predicted. Economics students, however, often tend to free ride more than other students. Do you have suggestions regarding how to explain the different behavior of the economics students?

6. In one society, a driver who sees a rock on the road stops and moves the rock to the side of the road. In another society, the driver swerves around the rock and continues

on his or her way, even though the same driver will be passing along the same stretch of road the next day. How would you explain the different behavior in the two societies? What are the influences affecting the probability that a volunteer-type public good will be provided, efficiently or inefficiently?

7. In the case of weakest-link-type public goods, how does changing the structure of benefits (or the payoffs) change the likelihood of achieving efficient outcomes?

8. How does increasing the size of the population affect the likelihoods of supply of volunteer-type and weakest-link public goods?

9. How do outcomes of simultaneous and sequential decisions differ for volunteer and weakest-link public goods? Do you think that in practice the simultaneous or sequential scenarios are more relevant?

10. How do social norms affect the likelihood of supply of volunteer-type public goods?

11. What are the special characteristics of national defense as a public good?

12. For national defense as a public good, how does the prisoners' dilemma arise both between countries and within countries? What is the relationship between the internal and external prisoners' dilemmas?

13. What do you believe is the reason that, in general, democracies do not go to war against one another? Why do you think wars have usually begun by an attack on a democracy by a nondemocratic country?

14. What makes defense against terror different from national defense to deter foreign aggression?

15. What are the costs imposed on a society by terror?

16. Why is a case for public finance for public goods not necessarily a case for public supply of public goods?

17. What is the condition for efficient supply of a combination of public and private goods? Show that this condition is the same as the requirement that the sum of MBs from a public good equals MC. Why are there many efficient outcomes? (See Supplement 2A.)

18. How does an increase in the size of a group that benefits from a public good affect total voluntary contributions to finance the public good? What are the different considerations that affect total private voluntary contributions as population size increases? (See Supplement 2B.)

19. How does income distribution within a group of beneficiaries affect total voluntary contributions to finance a public good? Would you expect total voluntary contributions to increase when income distribution in the group becomes less equal? (See Supplement 2C.)

20. How does the need to achieve a minimal total contribution before a public good can even begin to be provided affect voluntary contributions? (See Supplement 2D.)

2.2

Information and Public Goods

2.2.1 Information and public spending

We have seen that public goods can involve different types of strategic interactions, but that public finance for public goods involves most prominently the conditions of the prisoners' dilemma. Under the conditions of the prisoners' dilemma, the quantity of a public good supplied is the sum of individual contributions. When n people are contributing and individual i contributes z_i, the quantity available to the entire population of n persons is

$$G = \sum_{j=1}^{n} z_j. \tag{2.17}$$

When public goods are publicly financed, the individual contributions in (2.17) are provided through compulsory payment of taxes. The taxes resolve the free-rider problem of the prisoners' dilemma by making payment compulsory, thereby allowing the public good to be financed. Society thereby benefits when government uses its authority to compel financing through taxation to solve the prisoners' dilemma.

The circumstances described by the prisoners' dilemma, however, make the solution of calling on government to finance public goods look easier than might be the case in practice. In the symmetric prisoners' dilemma that we have described, individuals have identical valuations of a public good, and total spending required for efficient supply of the public good is known. The government thus has the easy task of levying equal taxes to finance known public-spending requirements.[1] The task of levying taxes to finance public goods efficiently becomes more difficult when people's benefits differ. For a population of n people with different benefits, efficient pricing of public goods requires personal taxes T_i for person i per unit of the public good that satisfy

$$T_i = MB_i \qquad 1 = 1, \dots, n. \tag{2.18}$$

The tax T_i replaces the price that people do not voluntarily and truthfully pay when they choose to free ride.

To set the taxes in (2.18), a government requires information about the different personal marginal benefits MB_i of the people in the population. The different valuations of the public good are, however, private information that individuals do not have an incentive to truthfully reveal when they know that the information they provide will determine their tax payments.

Also, without true information on personal MBs, the government cannot use the efficiency condition

$$\sum_{j=1}^{n} MB_j = MC \tag{2.19}$$

to determine efficient quantities of public goods.

For example, in Figure 2.7, a public good is competitively available under conditions of constant cost $(AC = MC)$ at a per-unit cost or price P. To establish the efficient quantity G^*, the government needs to know the different marginal

---

[1] For example, if the spending required to provide the public good is F, two identical persons can be asked to pay an equal share $\frac{1}{2}F$. The prisoners' dilemma is therefore resolved by a tax of $\frac{1}{2}F$ on each person, which finances the public good and achieves an efficient outcome.

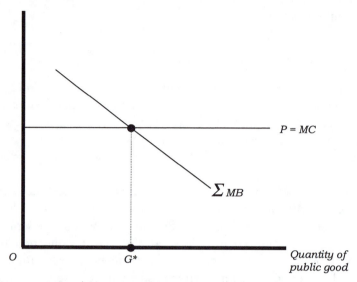

*Price and valuation of
the public good*

P = MC

$\Sigma\, MB$

O   *G**   *Quantity of
public good*

Figure 2.7. The information problem facing government.

To determine efficient supply G^* of a public good, a government requires information about benefits to the population $\sum MB$ from the public good and information about the marginal cost of supply MC.

benefits of all the people in the population so that the individual marginal benefits can be summed to determine $\sum MB$.

In the special conditions of the prisoners' dilemma where people are identical and the cost of financing the efficient quantity of the public good is known, the known cost can be divided through identical taxes on the identical people. When we move outside of these special conditions, a government confronts the same information problem that was the justification in the first place for asking government to take responsibility for ensuring efficient supply of public goods.

2.2.2 The ideal Lindahl solution and information problems

We shall now consider a mechanism that identifies efficient spending on public goods and provides the benchmark that a government should seek to duplicate in decisions about public-good supply. The mechanism, proposed by the Swedish economist Knut Wicksell in 1896 and set out in 1919 by Erik Lindahl, returns us to the idea of a market for public goods that we considered in Section 2.1.

In Figure 2.8, the horizontal axis measures the quantity of a public good G to be supplied without exclusion to all people in a population. The inputs that provide the public good are available at a unit-cost or price P.

A population of two people – person 1 and person 2 – shares the cost of the public good by paying proportions of the price P for each unit supplied. The share

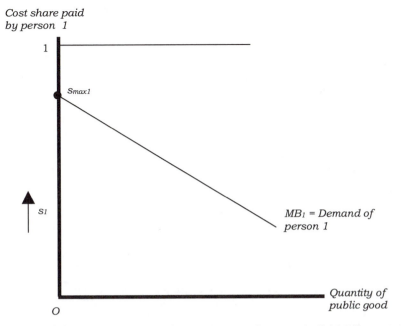

Figure 2.8. Demand for a public good depends on an individual's cost share.

of the price P paid by person 1 is measured on the vertical axis in Figure 2.8 and is denoted s_1. The share s_1 determines the personal price P_1 paid for units of the public good by person 1 as

$$P_1 = s_1 P. \tag{2.20}$$

In Figure 2.8, MB_1 shows the change in demand of person 1 for the public good as the cost share s_1 changes. We have a usual negatively sloped demand function, with the difference, however, that individual demand depends not on the price P of the public good, which is given, but on the share s_1 of the price that person 1 pays. We see in Figure 2.8 that person 1 is not prepared to contribute to financing the public good at all, if he or she has to pay a cost share greater than s_{max1}.

Figure 2.9 adds the demand function MB_2 of person 2. This demand function has its origin at 0_2 (the origin for person 1 is at 0_1). Person 2's demand is zero if he or she has to pay a cost share greater than s_{max2}. Person 2's demand for the public good increases along MB_2 as the cost share s_2 falls in the direction of 0_2.

The cost shares of the two persons sum to one:

$$s_1 + s_2 = 1. \tag{2.21}$$

For person 1, the willingness of person 2 to pay for the public good as expressed by MB_2 provides free supply of the public good. This is so since, by the nonexcludable nature of the benefit from the public good, any quantity financed by person 2 is available to person 1. Similarly, demand of person 1 is supply for person 2.

Cost shares

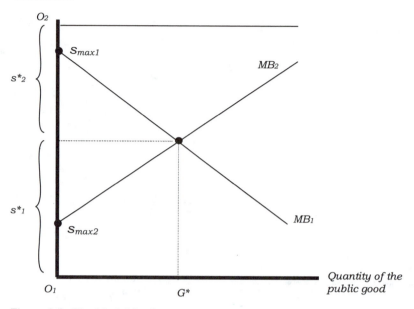

Figure 2.9. The Lindahl voluntary–payment consensus.

There is consensus that the quantity G^* should be supplied when cost shares are s_1^* and s_2^*. The quantity G^* is efficient supply.

We can therefore interpret Figure 2.9 as showing demand and supply in a market. The quantity supplied in this market is G^* where $MB_1 = MB_2$. At the quantity G^*, the two individuals' cost shares are s_1^* and s_2^*.

When the cost shares are s_1^* and s_2^*, there is consensus regarding the quantity of the public good the two individuals wish to see supplied. Both want the quantity G^*. The consensus ensures Pareto efficiency. The consensus could be broken by one of the two persons vetoing the choice of G^*. Because there is consensus rather than veto, both persons must necessarily gain when they share the cost of supplying the quantity G^* in the proportions s_1^* and s_2^*.

For each person, the personal payment P_i for the consensus quantity G^* is equal to personal marginal benefit, that is,

$$P_i \equiv s_i^* P = MB_i(G^*) \qquad i = 1, 2. \tag{2.22}$$

Summing over the two individuals, we have

$$P_1 + P_2 = (s_1^* + s_2^*)P = MB_1 + MB_2 = \sum MB. \tag{2.23}$$

If the price P of the public good is given in a competitive market and equal to the marginal cost of supply MC, it follows from (2.23) that the Lindahl consensus outcome satisfies the condition for efficient public-good supply

$$\sum MB = MC. \tag{2.24}$$

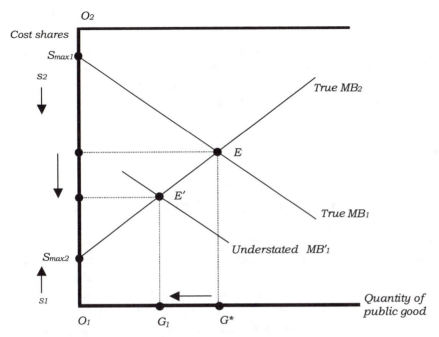

Figure 2.10. Reducing the cost share by understatement of benefit.

The information problem again

The Lindahl mechanism for determining efficient financing and supply of a public good is subject to the individual incentive to misrepresent true personal marginal benefit. Figure 2.10 shows how person 1 gains by declaring demand to be MB'_1 rather than the true MB_1. By understating demand, person 1 moves the consensus quantity from G^* to G_1. At G_1, person 1 has a lower cost share, at the expense of a higher cost share for person 2.

Person 1 will not wish to understate benefit too much. The amount of the public good that is supplied is a consensus quantity, and person 2's supply falls when his or her cost share is increased by person 1's understatement of benefit. Person 1 certainly would not wish to deceptively raise person 2's cost share so much that person 2 is willing to provide nothing. This would happen in Figure 2.10 if person 2's cost share were raised to s_{max2} or beyond.[2]

Person 2 confronts the same incentives to misrepresent personal benefit as does person 1. The mutual incentives to understate true benefit that we identified in the prisoners' dilemma as underlying free riding are therefore once more present, and the public good is undersupplied.

The Lindahl mechanism provides the solution for a government seeking efficient spending on a public good. The mechanism also makes clear the scope of the

[2] If person 1 knew the location of person 2's MB function, he or she could use this information to determine a strategically personal optimal understatement of benefit. Person 1 does not, however, know the precise location of MB_2, which is person 2's private information.

information problem facing a government in determining efficient public-good supply.

In practice, application of the Lindahl mechanism would involve the numerous people who benefit from different public goods. The large number of people complicates use of the Lindahl mechanism. In principle, however, if everybody reported true personal benefits, the efficient cost shares and efficient consensus quantity could be computed. The problem standing in the way of efficient public good supply is the incentive for personal gain by understating benefit.

2.2.3 Cost–benefit analysis and information problems

If people lack the incentive to reveal true personal benefit from public goods, governments have to look for other means of obtaining information that might help them identify the efficient Lindahl supply of a public good. Cost-benefit analysis is a direct measurement procedure for identifying efficient public-good supply. For the public good shown in Figure 2.11, the purpose of cost-benefit analysis is to compute the benefits $\sum MB$ in order to determine the efficient quantity G^*. If some components of marginal cost MC of the public good were not revealed in markets, cost-benefit analysis would include direct computation of the unknown part of costs.

With n people identified as benefiting from the project in Figure 2.11, the project is socially worthwhile if, for some choice of supply of the public good, total benefit

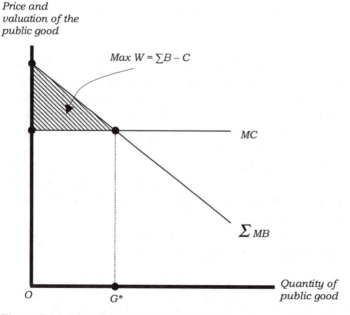

Figure 2.11. Identifying an efficient project using cost-benefit analysis.

to the population of n people exceeds total cost, that is, if

$$W = \sum_{j=1}^{n} B_j - C > 0. \tag{2.25}$$

The task of cost-benefit analysis is to reveal the particular value of supply that maximizes (2.25). Maximizing (2.25) requires

$$\sum_{j=1}^{n} MB_j = MC, \tag{2.26}$$

subject to total net benefit given by (2.25) being positive. In Figure 2.11, we see that total net benefit W in (2.25) is positive at the efficient quantity G^*. The shaded area indicates the maximal net benefit W obtainable from the project.

Figure 2.11 looks like a market. Cost-benefit analysis looks for substitutes for absent market information about benefits, or costs.

The public project in Figure 2.11 could be a new foreign embassy. The costs of building construction, salaries, furniture, and diplomatic entertainment might be known and provide the value of MC, but information may not be available about the benefits $\sum B$ provided by the new embassy. The benefits are not observed as values in markets. To measure the benefits, we need to know how taxpayers or citizens personally value the proposed new foreign embassy. Alternatively, the project in Figure 2.11 could be a public zoo. The scale G of the project is then defined by the number of animals and the types of facilities provided for the animals. The cost of animals and providing the animals with shelter and food may be known (as MC in Figure 2.11), but benefit $\sum B$ to the population from the zoo may be unknown. To measure benefit, estimates are required of how many people would visit the zoo and how much they value seeing the animals. When rare species of animals are protected in the zoo, values are also required for the benefits of sustaining biodiversity. If the public project is a bridge or a highway, estimating $\sum MB$ requires establishing the number of users, the value of the users' time, and the time saved by the bridge or highway. The project might also contribute to public safety by reducing road injuries or fatalities. Estimates are then required of the value of a life saved, and the value of a reduction in the probability of someone being injured in a road accident. If the project is a new building to expand a government department, estimates of the benefits to taxpayers from the activities of the government officials who are to occupy the new building are required. For a crime prevention program, estimates of benefits from the envisaged reduction in crime are required. If the project provides public health protection, estimates of the value of benefits from the reduced probability of contracting different diseases are required.

Cost-benefit analysis can involve complex relationships. Increasing the water supply can require a dam that will reduce the habitat of a rare toad, in which case valuations are required of the costs of reduced biodiversity because of the adverse effect on the habitat of the toad. In some countries, some people believe that the ground-up horn of a rhino is an aphrodisiac, and this belief has threatened the viability of rhino populations. The benefits of public finance to support a research program that develops medicinal substitutes for the supposed aphrodisiacal properties of the rhino horn include reducing the threat to rhino populations. We then, however, need to measure the benefit (to ourselves and to the rhinos) of making rhinos safer.

Cost-benefit analysis can also be applied to government regulations. There are costs and benefits associated with compulsory seatbelts. Safety regulations for work conditions similarly increase costs but save workers from injury or death.

The value of life

Cost-benefit analysis often includes computations of the value of life and of the benefits from increased probabilities of saving lives. One approach to placing a value on loss of life is to compute the income that a person would have earned, had the person lived to retirement age. When someone unfortunately dies young, do we then, however, for consistency have to include as benefits the savings from not having to pay pension or social security payments after retirement? For example, when governments have sued tobacco companies for costs incurred by the state in treating people who have become ill from use of tobacco products, there have been suggestions that penalties paid by the tobacco companies should be reduced by the savings in social security payments for the people who died before reaching retirement age.

Cost-benefit analysis may require comparisons of the value of life of different people. For example, decisions may have to be made between allocating public funds to support research to find cures for diseases that mainly affect children or diseases that mainly affect adults and older people. An adult may have made investments in education and may have knowledge and experience that has high market value and provides high personal income. A child has not yet made investments in education and has no knowledge and experience that provides market income. A strict economic approach based on the value of investments and income lost can value the life of the child less than the value of the life of an older person who has already made investments in education.

The value of a life is, however, more than the economic losses from the absence of life (or the economic gains through saving of social security payments). According to one view, the value of a life has no bound, and saving one life is equivalent to saving the world, since saving a life saves the world of the person whose life has been saved. Difficult choices arise because unbounded resources are not available to save lives.

Valuation over time

The benefits and costs of public-good projects generally extend over time. For most types of public-good projects, costs are incurred today, and benefits accrue over time in the future. When a bridge or a highway is built, a museum is established, or a foreign embassy is built, the costs are mostly in the present and the benefits become available over time in the future. Sometimes, however, the benefits are obtained today, and the costs are imposed on future generations, as, for example, when there is environment damage.

Let us consider a project that provides net benefits of $(\sum B_0 - C_0)$ during the first year, and then $(\sum B_1 - C_1)$ during the following year, and then $(\sum B_2 - C_2)$ in the next year, and so on for some ongoing period of time. Because the project provides public-good benefits, the benefits $\sum B_0, \sum B_1$, and $\sum B_2$ are summed over the population. A decision how to compare benefits and costs at different periods of time must be made. This decision is made through choice of a discount rate. That is, a rate is chosen at which to "discount" the future. A higher discount rate, or higher discounting of the future, places a higher value on present costs and benefits than on costs and benefits in the future. In contrast, a lower discount rate places higher weight on the future. A zero discount rate gives the same weight to benefits and costs at any time in the future as to benefits and costs in the present.

Choice of the discount rate can affect conclusions about whether a project merits public finance. The environment, for example, provides benefits that reach far into the future. When a project harms the environment, the lower the rate of discount chosen for the project, the more likely the project will be rejected, because of the greater weight given to future environmental benefits.

We can consider as an example a project that requires a one-time public expenditure this year and provides a one-time benefit next year. The cost today is C_0, and benefits next year summed over the population of beneficiaries are $\sum B_1$. With the rate of discount given as i, the cost-benefit criterion for justification of public finance for the project is

$$W = \frac{\sum B_1}{(1+i)} - C_0 > 0. \tag{2.27}$$

If $\sum B_1 = 105$ and $C_0 = 100$, it follows from (2.27) that the project is justified if the rate of discount i is less than 5 percent. Choosing a discount rate of more than 5 percent ensures a decision to reject public finance for the project. Choosing a discount rate of less than 5 percent on the contrary ensures a decision to provide public finance for the project.

Because of the sensitivity of the choice of the discount rate for desirability of a public investment, cost-benefit studies usually include "sensitivity analysis" to see how conclusions change with the rate of discount. Another procedure is to estimate the rate of return of the project and to decide whether this rate of return is reasonable. In the preceding example, the return on the project is 5 percent.

A project may have a time horizon of N years. That is, the project may be expected to provide benefits or to incur costs over N years. If the discount rate has been chosen as zero, so that all future benefits and costs are valued as if they were incurred today, the net benefit over time from the project is the undiscounted sum:

$$W = \left(\sum B_0 - C_0\right) + \left(\sum B_1 - C_1\right) + \cdots + \left(\sum B_N - C_N\right). \tag{2.28}$$

To discount the future, we choose a positive discount rate, which discounts (or lowers) future costs and benefits. With a positive discount rate given by i, the cost-benefit criterion for a public investment is

$$W = (B_0 - C_0) + \frac{\sum B_1 - C_1}{(1+i)} + \frac{\sum B_2 - C_2}{(1+i)^2} + \cdots + \frac{\sum B_N - C_N}{(1+i)^N} > 0. \quad (2.29)$$

Expression (2.29) shows the present value of the costs and benefits associated with the project. As we move out in time in (2.29) to include future benefits and costs, we reapply the discount rate again every year that passes. The further we go into the future, the smaller our valuation today of the future year's benefits and costs is. We see that, when the discount rate i is zero, (2.29) becomes the straight summation of net benefits over time as shown in (2.28). When the discount placed on the future is infinity, all terms in (2.29) except today's values disappear, and we have the limiting case that all that matters is today and now.

When $i > 0$, we can define

$$\delta \equiv \frac{1}{1+i} < 1. \tag{2.30}$$

This provides another way of expressing the discount rate. When we substitute (2.30) into the expression for present value (2.29), we have

$$W = \left(\sum B_0 - C_0\right) + \delta \left(\sum B_1 - C_1\right) + \delta^2 \left(\sum B_2 - C_2\right) + \cdots \tag{2.31}$$

where δ is a number less than one that discounts the future.

In the special case where benefits and costs are the same in each year and extend indefinitely into the future, the property of the sum of an infinite series can be used to express the present value of a project as

$$W = \frac{\sum B_i - C_i}{i}. \tag{2.32}$$

How should the discount rate be chosen? If private capital markets reflect the time preference of people in society, we might want to consider using the market rate of interest as the social rate of discount for valuing future costs and benefits of public investments. The market rate of interest indicates the compensation that has to be paid to people for deferring consumption to the future and thereby reflects the market's valuation of time preference. If we wish to define a separate social rate of discount that differs from the market interest rate, we need to make a case that private capital markets are not efficient, or that there is something defective about the concept of discounting that results in the market rate of interest not accurately measuring society's time preference. For example, we might believe that the environment is a gift of nature that is not the possession of any generation to do with as it wishes, and that the discount rate applied to the preservation of the environment should therefore be zero. That is, we might believe that future generations should be treated equally with us in placing a value on environmental benefits and costs.

The distinction between social and private risk is another reason that might lead us to conclude that the social rate of discount for evaluating costs and benefits of public projects is lower than the market rate of interest. Private capital markets

TABLE 2.12. THE CHOICE BETWEEN A SUBWAY AND A HIGHWAY

	Subway	Highway
Cost C	1,400 once	400 every 10 years
Benefit each year B_i	60 per year	50 per year
A time horizon of 50 years		
$\quad$ Undiscounted total benefit $\sum B_i$	3,000	2,500
$\quad$ Undiscounted net benefit $\sum(B_i - C)$	1,600	500
$\quad$ Gain from choosing the subway	1,100	
A time horizon of 100 years		
$\quad$ Undiscounted total benefit $\sum B_i$	6,000	5,000
$\quad$ Undiscounted net benefit $\sum(B_i - C)$	4,600	1,000
$\quad$ Gain from choosing the subway	3,600	
Discounted at $i = 5\%$		
$\quad$ Total benefit $\sum B_i$	1,200	405 every 10 years
$\quad$ Total net benefit $\sum(B_i - C)$	−200	+5 every ten years

make allowance for risk, whereas public investment proposals spread risk over all the population, and so should perhaps be evaluated at a low risk-free discount rate.

Also, we have used a constant discount rate over time to compare present and future benefits and costs, but the discount rate might change over time. Future beneficiaries of the public good provided by the public investment may not find acceptable the discount rate we have chosen. Problems of time inconsistency can also arise in choice of the discount rate: that is, we ourselves may find that the discount rate we have chosen is inappropriate in the future, and we may regret that we did not choose another discount rate that places more weight on the future, when we ourselves arrive into the future.

Often cost-benefit analysis involves not evaluating whether a project is worthwhile but choosing between alternative public investments. As an example, we can consider the choice between public investment in a subway system and highway expansion. Table 2.12 shows a subway system that requires initial nonrepeated public spending of 1,400 and provides indefinite benefits of 60 per year. Expanding a highway system costs 400 (including environmental costs through deteriorated air quality) and provides benefits of 50 per year for 10 years. After 10 years, the volume of traffic on the highway grows to cause congestion, and the highway system again must be expanded.

We see in Table 2.12 that a society that does not discount the future and that has a time horizon of 50 years will choose the investment in the subway. The gain from choosing the subway is 1,100.[3] The subway is yet more worthwhile if,

---

[3] The benefits $\sum B_i$ from the subway over 50 years are 3,000, and the cost is 1,400, giving net benefit $\sum(B_i - C)$ of 1,600. The benefits $\sum B_i$ from the highway over 50 years are 2,500, and the cost is 2,000 (the cost is 400 every 10 years), giving net benefit $\sum(B_i - C)$ of 500.

without discounting, the time horizon is 100 years. The gain from choosing public investment in the subway rather than the road system is then 3,600.[4]

We can also compare public investment in the subway and highway when a discount rate of 5 percent is used. In that case, public investment in expanding the highway system every 10 years is preferable to building the subway.[5]

Our example comparing public investment in the subway with public investment in highway expansion has used constant benefits over time, whereas in practice we can expect benefits to increase over time, in particular from the subway, which can be used to run trains with increasing frequency and with more carriages if demand increases over time. We could elaborate by changing benefits over time, as well as by allowing for different maintenance costs of the subway and the highway system and by including the different costs of mass-transit equipment and subway personnel compared with costs incurred in bus travel and travel in private automobiles and the costs of parking. We could also include the environmental cost of expanding the highway system and computations for projected loss of life and injury through highway accidents against the probability of a subway accident. All these elements of cost and benefit are subsumed in our simple example. The purpose of our example is not to provide detailed evaluations of a case where actual costs and benefits are compared for a subway system and highway expansion. Such detailed evaluation would be required in an actual cost-benefit comparison of the public-investment alternatives. The purpose of the example is to show how the discount rate affects the choice between alternative public investment projects when costs and benefits of different projects are distributed differently over time. We have noted that time-consistency problems can arise in choice of discount rates. People, for their personal decisions, might choose very high discounts for present decisions and then lament in the future that their past behavior was based on such high discount rates.[6] The same type of lament expressing time inconsistency can arise for collective decisions about public investments that provide public goods. We can imagine a lament that "it is a shame that we always expand the highway system instead of building a subway" and that "had we built the subway in the past, we would not have to pay taxes now to expand the road system, and also air quality would have been better." In the example, with the

---

[4] The benefits $\sum B_i$ from the subway are then 6,000, which after subtracting the initial cost of 1,400 gives total net benefit from the subway of $\sum(B_i - C)$ of 4,600. Over 100 years, the highway requires 10 repeated investments of 400, so the cost is 4,000. The benefit $\sum B_i$ from the highway over 100 years is 5,000, giving net benefit of $\sum(B_i - C)$ of 1,000 from the highway.

[5] Since the subway provides benefits of 60 per year forever, we can use formula (2.32) to compute the present value of an indefinite flow of benefits of 60 discounted at 5 percent, which gives 1,200. Since the cost of building the subway is 1,400, the subway has a negative present value, equal to -200. Highway expansion costs 400 every 10 years and provides benefits of 50 per year. The present value of benefits of 50 per year for 10 years discounted at 5 percent is approximately 405, which exceeds the cost of 400.

[6] A high discount rate indicates a preference for immediate benefit while future costs are discounted. For example, people who have used harmful drugs for immediate gratification can come to regret their choice of a high personal discount rate when they suffer the adverse consequences of their past drug use in the future.

discount rate at 5 percent, it never pays at any point in time to incur the cost of building the subway; however, expanding the highway system every 10 years is worthwhile.

Note that the source of the lament is not that other people in the future benefit from a current generation's public spending. The cost-benefit criterion does ask who benefits. The same people who lament that the subway was not built in the past can themselves have collectively decided in the past not to build the subway because of the discount rate applied to the choice between public investment in the subway and expansion of the highway system. The case for a zero or low discount rate is to avoid such lament (or time inconsistency) in public investment decisions.

If the correct discount rate is 5 percent, the correct decision is being made to expand the highway system rather than the subway. That is, if 5 percent reflects an accurate real rate of return required for public investment, public investment for the subway is not justified, while highway expansion every 10 years is justified. In our example, the outcome of cost-benefit analysis can change, and the subway can be chosen in preference to highway expansion, if the discount rate is reduced sufficiently, or if new increased population estimates show increased benefit from use of the subway, perhaps from the avoidance of environmental costs of highway expansion.

Information limitations

Cost-benefit analysis is used because market valuations do not exist for benefits from public goods. In Chapter 1, we considered an economy with collective property and without markets, and we observed how political decision makers confronted information problems when attempting to make indirect estimates of cost and benefit to replace missing market valuations. Cost-benefit analysis introduces the same types of problems at the level of justification of public projects. With market valuations for public-good benefits unavailable, we seek alternative indirect means of computing $\sum MB$, or we seek an alternative means of computing costs that we do not know. The information we are seeking is only accurately revealed in markets, by people revealing their valuations through willingness to pay or willingness to sell.

Also, the further we go into the future, the greater the uncertainty about values of costs and benefits. We do not know whether changes will take place that will alter our own valuations of future benefits or costs, and we cannot be certain of the valuations of yet unborn populations.

Distributional effects

Cost–benefit analysis is a means of attempting to provide information to solve an efficiency problem. We are attempting to find the *efficient* consensus spending on public goods that would be revealed through the Lindahl voluntary payment mechanism if the Lindahl mechanism were feasible. Social justice is not a consideration when the objective is efficient supply of a public good. However, questions of social justice enter cost-benefit analysis when we care about who benefits, or who pays. For example, when the proposed public investment is a bridge, distributional issues related to social justice enter when someone asks whether the bridge benefits low- or high-income persons.

Who benefits from a bridge can have efficiency consequences that enter into cost-benefit analysis. We expect a bridge to provide greater benefits for high-income persons than for low-income persons because high-income persons have high value of time, and part of measuring the benefits from the bridge is the value of time saved in travel.

Low-income people might, however, have low incomes because they are cut off from high-income employment opportunities by the absence of a bridge. Cost-benefit analysis should then take into account a future increase in the incomes of present low-income people when determining whether public investment to build the bridge is warranted. In this case, there are efficiency consequences of benefit provided to low-income persons.

A case based on fairness or social justice in cost-benefit calculations would propose that benefits or costs should not be measured without taking into account whether poor or rich people benefit or incur a cost. The cost-benefit criterion would then become a mixture of considerations of efficiency and social justice. We would need to know how much weight to put on efficiency and how much weight to put on social justice. A social criterion that incorporates both efficiency and social justice and allows different weights to be placed on efficiency and social justice is known as a social welfare function. We leave issues that arise when decisions are required based on both efficiency and social justice to Chapter 5. Suppose, however, that the people whom a publicly financed project is intended to benefit are targeted beneficiaries whom a society wants to help on social justice grounds. If public investment in the project is not justified on efficiency grounds by cost-benefit analysis, the intended beneficiaries of the project are better off if they are given the public money directly than if the public money is used to finance the proposed public spending.[7]

2.2.4 Incentive mechanisms for truthful reporting

A government could attempt to obtain the personal Lindahl prices required for the efficient consensus financing and supply solution by asking people to declare their benefits from a public good. However, when people know that their declared benefit determines how much they pay, we expect people to understate personal benefit.[8] A government could also ask people to declare their personal valuations

---

[7] If $100 of proposed present public spending provides benefits with a present value of $90, the cost-benefit criterion for efficient public spending is not satisfied. The intended beneficiaries of public spending are then better off receiving the $100 directly. The direct transfer of $100 will provide benefits of $100 and more because the benefit from personal spending in a market exceeds the value of the money spent (see Chapter 1).

[8] As we have previously noted, we would not know whether or by how much people are understating personal benefit because only they know their own true benefit.

TABLE 2.13. AN EXAMPLE OF THE
CLARKE TAX

Person 1	Person 2	Person 3
100	70	−80
Tax = 10	Tax = 0	Tax = 0

of benefit from public goods after they have been assured that the public goods will be publicly financed through general taxation and that their reported personal valuations of benefit will not be used to determine their personal payments for financing the public good. Since financing is then through general taxes, people with low tax obligations (because of low income) have reason to declare high personal benefit and to ask for high public spending on public goods because of their small contribution to financing public spending. People who pay higher taxes might also take the view that "government" is paying when stating their personal benefit. Benefits reported without an obligation to pay can therefore lead to overstatement of true benefits, and thereby to overprovision of public goods. Such overprovision of publicly financed public goods then contrasts with the underprovision suggested when people are asked to make voluntary payments for public goods as through the Lindahl mechanism.

Is there a way, however, that incentives can be provided for people to voluntarily and truthfully report their benefits from public goods? Let us look at Table 2.13, which describes the benefits of two people from a publicly financed public good and the loss imposed by the public good on a third person. The public-good project might be a lighthouse. Persons 1 and 2 have boats and benefit from the lighthouse, although differently. Person 3 has no boat but has a house that is in the path of the lighthouse beacon and is disturbed by the rotation of the beacon at night.

The loss of 80 to person 3 is less than the combined benefits of 100 of person 1 and 70 of person 2. Since the total benefit is $\sum B = 170$ and the total loss is $C = 80$, public spending on the project is justified by the cost-benefit criterion.

The government, however, does not know the benefits of persons 1 and 2 and the cost imposed on person 3. We now impose the following rules for a procedure whereby the government asks people to indicate their benefit or loss from the public good:

(1) A person pays a tax if the information about personal loss or benefit that the person declares changes the cost-benefit calculation regarding whether the public good is to be supplied. That is, people pay for being decisive in making a difference in determining whether public spending takes place.

(2) The amount of the tax that a person pays is equal to the net loss imposed on all others as a result of that person's changing the public spending decision.

(3) The money collected from the taxes that people pay is not used to finance the project, nor is the tax revenue distributed in any other way that benefits the persons involved. The tax revenue is transferred to the government budget and is spent in a way such that benefits to the people involved in declaring their benefits or costs for the public good are negligible.

The tax with these properties is known as the Clarke tax, after Edward Clarke who proposed this tax in the early 1970s. The Clarke tax solves the public-good information problem. When faced with the Clarke tax, people have an incentive to declare their true benefits or true losses.

Let us now return to Table 2.13. To determine the Clarke tax of each of the three persons in Table 2.13, we consider whether a person's truthful statement of benefit or loss changes the cost-benefit calculation for whether the public good should be provided.

We start with person 1. We see in Table 2.13 that, when person 1 does not participate in the cost-benefit valuation and person 2 and person 3 truthfully report their valuations, spending on the public good does not pass the cost-benefit test. The loss of 80 imposed on person 3 exceeds the benefit of 70 for person 2. By participating and declaring true benefit of 100, person 1 changes the outcome of cost-benefit valuation. The addition of person 1's true declaration of benefit makes total net benefits from the project positive; that is, $(100 + 70 - 80) = 90$. By providing information about personal benefit and changing the cost-benefit outcome, person 1 has provided a benefit of 70 to person 2 and imposed a loss of 80 on person 3. Person 1 therefore pays a Clarke tax of $(80 - 70) = 10$.

Person 2 pays a tax of zero, since, with or without person 2's participation in supplying personal information, the project passes the cost-benefit test (since the benefit of 100 of person 1 is in any event greater the loss of 80 incurred by person 3). Person 2's participation therefore does not affect whether the public good is provided. Person 3 also pays no tax because, with or without person 3's participation, benefits exceed costs.

The dominant strategy of each person is to reveal truthfully personal benefit or loss from the public good. Person 1 gains from paying a tax of 10 and switching the decision in favor of the project. The gain for person 1 from changing the public spending decision is 100, which exceeds the tax of 10. Person 1 cannot manipulate the amount of the tax paid by declaring other than true benefit. Person 1's tax is determined by the net cost imposed on person 2 and person 3 by changing the cost-benefit decision. Since the tax is determined by the valuations of the other two people and not by person 1's declaration of his or her own benefit, person 1 has no reason to misrepresent personal benefit by declaring a value other than the true 100.

Person 2 also has no reason to misrepresent true valuation of benefit. Person 2 benefits from the public good and pays zero tax when revealing true benefit.

Person 3 loses 80 from the public good. Since the combined benefit of person 1 and person 2 is 170, person 3 could block the project by lying and declaring a loss of 171. Such misrepresentation to block the project is however not in person 3's interest. By declaring a loss of 171 to block the project, person 3 faces a Clarke tax of 170, since this is the cost imposed on person 1 and person 2 if the project is blocked. The tax of 170 that person 3 would pay to block the project exceeds person 3's loss of 80 if the project proceeds. Person 3 therefore has no incentive to report an untruthful loss to block the project.[9]

No one therefore has an incentive to misrepresent true benefits or losses. The dominant strategy is to report true benefit, and the Nash equilibrium is that everyone reports true benefit. The Nash equilibrium is achieved (e.g., as in the prisoners' dilemma) through simultaneous decisions. Given that everyone truthfully reports personal benefits or losses, the best personal response that anyone can make is also to report personal benefit or loss truthfully.

The role of the revenue from the Clarke tax

As we have noted, a condition for the effectiveness of the Clarke tax is that the revenue from the tax not be used to finance the public good. In particular, if the Clarke tax is to reveal true personal benefits or costs, the Clarke tax cannot finance the public good.

To see why this condition is required, we can consider the tax paid in Table 2.13 by person 1. Because the value of person 1's tax is determined by the net loss that person 1 imposes on person 2 and person 3, these persons would have an incentive to increase person 1's tax if they were to benefit from the tax paid by person 1. For example, person 2 could deceptively claim a benefit of zero rather than the true benefit of 70. The Clarke tax of person 1 would then increase to 80. Or person 3 could increase person 1's tax by claiming a greater loss than the true loss of 80. The requirement that people affected by the cost-benefit decision not benefit from the revenue from the Clarke tax eliminates the incentive for such misrepresentation of personal benefit or cost to increase other people's tax payments.[10]

An example with two projects

Table 2.14 shows an example where a decision is required between public finance for one of two projects, A or B. In this example, three people each have a positive benefit from the two alternative projects. The total benefit from project A is 170, which exceeds the total benefit from project B of 160. Project A would therefore be

---

[9] A claimed loss by person 3 of 171 is the minimum that blocks the project. By declaring a loss of 1,000, person 3 still pays the same Clarke tax of 170, since the Clarke tax is determined by the losses imposed on person 1 and person 2 and not by person 3's declared loss.

[10] Person 2 could decrease person 1's Clarke tax by claiming higher than true benefit of 70. Person 1 would be prepared to pay person 2 for this deception. Suppose, for example, that person 2 deceptively claimed a benefit of 81. Then the project is accepted whether or not the declaration of benefit of person 1 is involved in the cost-benefit decision, and, since person 1 is no longer decisive in determining whether the public good is provided, person 1 no longer pays a tax. Nor is person 2 decisive, and so person 2 also pays no tax. Such deception eliminates payment of the Clarke tax but does not change the outcome that the project in Table 2.13 satisfies the test of cost-benefit analysis.

TABLE 2.14. AN EXAMPLE OF THE CLARKE TAX
WITH TWO PROJECTS

	Person 1	Person 2	Person 3
Project A	70	80	20
Project B	30	50	80
Clarke tax	Tax = 30	Tax = 20	Tax = 0

chosen in preference to project B, if the government knew the personal valuations in Table 2.14. To obtain information to determine whether project A or project B should be publicly financed, the government applies the Clarke tax.

If person 1 does not participate in the cost-benefit calculation, project B is chosen in preference to project A (since without person 1 the total benefit from project A is 100 and the total benefit from project B is 130). When person 1 participates truthfully in the cost-benefit calculation, the decision changes to project A (since the total benefit from project A is then 170, against total benefit from project B of 160). Since participation by person 1 changes the cost-benefit outcome, person 1 pays a Clarke tax, which is given as 30 by the value of the net loss imposed on person 2 and person 3 from the change (person 2 gains 30 and person 3 loses 60 from the change from financing project B to financing project A).

The participation of person 2 likewise changes the decision about which public project is chosen.[11] The Clarke tax for person 2 is 20.[12] The participation of person 3 does not change the decision regarding the choice between projects A and B, and the Clarke tax for person 3 is therefore zero.[13]

The dominant strategy is again to declare true benefit, and in the Nash equilibrium true personal benefits from the two projects are revealed.

Use of the Clarke tax

No government ever appears to have used the Clarke tax as a means of providing incentives to reveal true personal benefits and losses from public spending. Implementation of the Clarke tax would require simultaneous interaction among the large numbers of people who usually benefit from publicly financed public goods.

If the difficulties of implementing the Clarke tax could be overcome, we might expect resistance to the tax by taxpayers. There might be complaints of unfairness, in particular if high personal taxes are determined for low-income persons.

---

[11] Without the participation of person 2, the benefit from project B is 110 and the benefit from project A is 90; with the participation of person 2, the benefit from A is again 170 and the benefit from B is 160.

[12] Person 1 gains 40 from person 2's participation, and person 3 loses 60.

[13] Without the participation of person 3, the benefit from project A is 150 and the benefit from project B is 80. With person 3's participation, the benefit from project A is 170 and from project B 160.

The taxes moreover do not finance the public good. In fact, we have seen that the Clarke tax should *not* be used to finance the public goods for which information about costs and benefits is being sought. The Clarke tax is an incentive mechanism to lead people to reveal information truthfully, and people may not accept that there is justice in the idea of paying taxes only for the purpose of revealing information. For political reasons, a government might also not like the uncertainty of not knowing how the Clarke mechanism will determine tax obligations for different people.

2.2.5 Information and locational choice

Another approach to solving the public-good information problem is through people choosing location from among alternative government jurisdictions. When governments offer alternative quantities of tax-financed public goods, people reveal their willingness to pay for the public goods through their willingness to locate in a government's jurisdiction. The mechanism for choosing taxes to pay for public goods through locational choice is often called the Tiebout mechanism, after Charles Tiebout (1924–68) who in 1956 proposed the locational mechanism as a solution for the public-good information problem. Tiebout made his proposal in response to the claim that the free-rider problem made efficient personal voluntary spending on public goods impossible. Although taxes paid to governments are compulsory, locational choice makes taxes voluntary because taxes can be avoided by moving to another government jurisdiction. Free riding is at the same time impossible, since location in a jurisdiction is an obligation to pay the taxes that finance public spending in the jurisdiction.

Figure 2.12 shows how locational choice solves the free-rider problem. In Figure 2.12, one person has low personal benefits MB_L from a public good, and the other person has high marginal benefits MB_H. The reason for the different personal valuations of the public good can be different preferences: one person can value the public good more than the other. MB_L and MB_H can also reflect different demands resulting from different incomes: one person may have higher income and so have higher demand for the public good.

Let us consider both people initially in the same tax jurisdiction where they pay taxes to the same government. Both pay a tax T *per unit* to finance public spending on the public good. The tax T is like a price paid per unit of the public good.

When the tax *per unit* is T, the low-benefit person's preferred choice of the quantity of the public good in Figure 2.12 is G_L, determined at the point J where the tax per unit (acting as a price) equals this person's marginal benefit:

$$T = MB_L. \tag{2.33}$$

The area VJT in Figure 2.12 shows the low-benefit person's maximized benefit when supply of the public good is determined by expression (2.33).[14]

---

[14] Area VJT is determined by deducting total personal taxes $OTJG_L$ from total personal benefit VJG_LO.

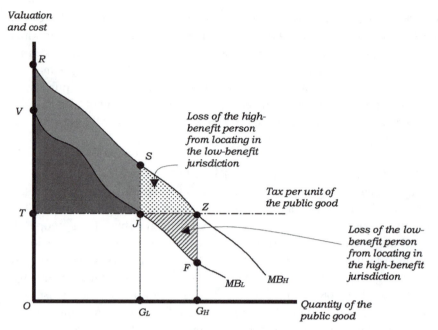

Figure 2.12. Sorting of low- and high-benefit people by locational choice.

When faced with the same tax T per unit of the public good, the high-benefit person ideally wants the government to supply the greater quantity of the public good G_H, which is determined at the point Z in Figure 2.12 where

$$T = MB_H. \tag{2.34}$$

The benefit to the high-benefit person from his or her ideal supply G_H is RZT.[15]

The jurisdiction in which the low- and high-benefit people are located may offer neither the quantity G_L nor the quantity G_H. However, two alternative jurisdictions may offer public spending on these quantities at the same tax per unit T. By relocating to the jurisdiction that offers his or her preferred public spending, each person achieves an outcome as if the public good were supplied in a competitive market at a price equal to the per unit tax T. That is, in moving to separate tax jurisdictions, the two people choose supply of the public good to suit themselves and each achieves maximal benefit as through choice in a competitive market.

After the two people have relocated to the jurisdictions offering their preferred quantities, neither has an incentive to misrepresent personal valuation of the public good. The person with high marginal benefit MB_H cannot gain by claiming to be a low-benefit person with marginal benefit MB_L. Such a claim would require the high-benefit person to locate in the jurisdiction that offers the low quantity G_L of the public good. In Figure 2.12, the high-benefit person

---

[15] Area RZT is determined by deducting total personal taxes $OTZG_H$ from total personal benefit $ORZG_H$.

would lose SJZ by changing locations.[16] Therefore, the high-benefit person's best decision is to remain in the high-benefit jurisdiction.

The low-benefit person likewise loses from pretending to be a high-benefit person. By locating in the jurisdiction that provides G_H, the low-benefit person would be contributing through taxes toward financing a greater supply of the public good than he or she wants. In Figure 2.12, the loss to the low-benefit person from locating in the high-benefit jurisdiction is area JZF.[17]

Locational sorting therefore results in each person receiving access to and financing a personally efficient quantity of the public good, with no incentive to misrepresent preferences. This was Charles Tiebout's case for choice among government jurisdictions solving the public-good information problem and achieving efficient financing and supply of public goods.

The sharing of costs

We have described the low- and high-benefit individuals as paying the same tax T per unit of the public good in their separate locations. Let us now consider how the per-unit tax T is determined. The public good is available at a price P, which is a jurisdiction's marginal cost MC for supply of the public good. The per-unit tax T is determined by sharing the price or unit cost among taxpayers. If there are n taxpayers in a jurisdiction,

$$T = \frac{P}{n}. \tag{2.35}$$

Therefore if per-unit taxes are to be the same in two different jurisdictions, the number of taxpayers sharing costs of the public good must also be the same. If the number of taxpayers in the two jurisdictions differs, the jurisdiction with the higher population has a lower per-unit tax because more taxpayers are sharing the cost or price P of each unit of the public good supplied.

We noted in Section 2.1 that pure public goods are natural monopolies because benefits to additional people can be provided without increasing spending. That is, a pure public good is there for all people to use, and benefit for any person is independent of the number of users.

Because of the natural-monopoly aspect of supply, efficient cost sharing requires that all beneficiaries or users be located in one jurisdiction. The ideal outcome is as described by the Lindahl solution. That is, ideally all people are together in the same jurisdiction where they pay shares of the cost of the public good according to their different marginal benefits and a quantity of the public good that everyone agrees on (the Lindahl consensus quantity) is supplied. However, the Lindahl solution requires being able to distinguish between low- and high-benefit

---

[16] By locating in the low-benefit jurisdiction, the high-benefit person reduces taxes from $OTZG_H$ to $OTJG_L$, that is, taxes decline by G_LJZG_H. However, total benefit declines by G_LSZG_H. The difference between the decline in benefit and the decline in taxes is the loss SJZ.

[17] By locating in the high-benefit jurisdiction, the low-benefit person pays additional taxes G_LJZG_H and receives additional benefit G_LJFG_H. The net loss is JZF.

people so that cost shares can be set according to benefit. In general, however, there is asymmetric information: that is, individuals know their own type as low or high-benefit, while a government knows that low- and high-benefit people may be present in its jurisdiction but cannot tell the two types of people apart. In the absence of information on individual benefits, the government can only reasonably set the same per-unit tax for everybody. Then, rather than the Lindahl consensus, there is disagreement on the quantity of the public good that low- and high-benefit people wish to have supplied, when, as in Figure 2.12, low- and high-benefit people are in the same jurisdiction.

Of n people located in a jurisdiction, suppose n_L are low-benefit people with marginal benefit MB_L and n_H are high-benefit people with marginal benefit MB_H. The government does not know this division (nor does anyone else). If the n_L low-benefit people were to form their own jurisdiction, the per-unit tax for financing public spending on the public good would be

$$T_L = \frac{P}{n_L}. \tag{2.36}$$

The per-unit tax if the n_H high-benefit people form their own jurisdiction is

$$T_H = \frac{P}{n_H}. \tag{2.37}$$

The per-unit taxes given by expressions (2.36) and (2.37) each exceed the per-unit tax given by expression (2.35) when all n people share the cost of the public good.

The decision whether to form a separate jurisdiction

Let us suppose that the quantity (or quality) of the public good supplied in a government jurisdiction is determined by majority voting.[18] When all n people are in the same jurisdiction, if high-benefit people are the majority (i.e., if $n_H > n_L$), the quantity of the public good chosen is G_H in Figure 2.12. Low-benefit people then face the decision whether to remain in the all-inclusive jurisdiction or to leave to form their own jurisdiction. In their own jurisdiction, they can choose public spending on the public good according to their own preferences.

High-benefit people prefer that low-benefit people not leave to form their own jurisdiction. By leaving, the low-benefit people increase costs for the high-benefit people: in place of the per-unit tax given by expression (2.35), high-benefit people are left paying the higher tax per unit given by expression (2.37). The high-benefit population cannot make compensating payments to induce low-benefit people to stay and share costs. Within the jurisdiction, low-benefit people are indistinguishable from high-benefit people. People might claim to be low-benefit when they are actually high-benefit so as to obtain the payment not to leave. The only credible act that a low-benefit person can undertake to demonstrate his or her type is to leave and join the separate low-benefit jurisdiction.

---

[18] We shall examine majority voting as a means of making collective decisions about public goods in more detail in Chapter 3.

If, alternatively, low-benefit people are the majority in the all-inclusive jurisdiction, majority voting results in public spending to supply the quantity of the public good G_L in Figure 2.12. The high-benefit minority then faces the question whether the gains from choosing public spending on the public good according to their own preferences in a separate jurisdiction justify the higher cost per person (or higher per-unit tax) in expression (2.37). Because of the gains from sharing costs among a larger number of taxpayers, the low-benefit majority does not want the high-benefit minority to leave.

Let us consider the case where there are equal numbers of low- and high-benefit people. The per-unit tax is then the same in two separate jurisdictions (since equal numbers in each jurisdiction are sharing the price P of the public good). In Figure 2.13, T shows the tax per unit for financing the public good determined by expression (2.35) when the entire population is located in a single all-inclusive jurisdiction. When the population is divided into separate groups, the per-unit tax given by expression (2.36) or (2.37) is precisely $2T$ as shown in Figure 2.13 (since, compared to the all-inclusive jurisdiction, half as many people are sharing the price of the public good in the separate jurisdictions). In the separate jurisdictions, each group by consensus (since everyone in the group has the same preferences) chooses public spending by setting the per-unit tax $2T$ equal to the common marginal benefit in the jurisdiction. Therefore, the separate low-benefit jurisdiction chooses the quantity G_{LI} at point E and the separate high-benefit jurisdiction chooses the quantity G_{HI} at point D.

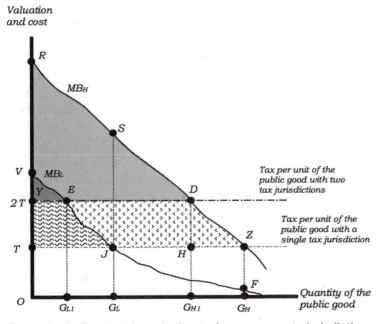

Figure 2.13. The decision whether to form a separate jurisdiction.

The quantities G_{LI} and G_{HI} are efficient supplies of the public goods to the populations in the two separate jurisdictions. When the quantity G_{LI} is supplied to the n_L people in the separate low-benefit jurisdiction, the condition is satisfied that

$$\sum_{j=1}^{n_L} MB_L = MC. \tag{2.38}$$

Correspondingly, when the quantity G_{HI} is supplied to the n_H high-benefit people in a separate jurisdiction,

$$\sum_{j=1}^{n_H} MB_H = MC. \tag{2.39}$$

The information problem that can deter efficient spending on public goods in thus solved by people locationally sorting themselves according to benefit.[19]

A better outcome for a group than described by expression (2.38) or (2.39) in a separate jurisdiction is obtainable in the all-inclusive jurisdiction, if the group can choose public spending according to its preferences and the other group is present to participate in sharing costs. In Figure 2.13, low-benefit people are best off if they can choose G_L when the high-benefit population participates in sharing costs so that the per-unit tax is T. The after-tax benefit of a low-benefit person VJT in the all-inclusive jurisdiction is greater than the after-tax benefit VEY when the low-benefit population forms a separate jurisdiction. Similarly, high-benefit people are best off when low-benefit people contribute to financing their preferred quantity G_H in the all-inclusive jurisdiction. A high-benefit person then has benefit RZT after paying taxes, compared to an after-tax benefit of RDY in a separate jurisdiction of high-benefit people. In each case, the group determining public spending in the combined jurisdiction benefits by imposing its preferences on the other group that wants different public spending.

Still, if preferences of the two groups are sufficiently similar, no group has an incentive to form a separate jurisdiction even if the other group is determining public spending. The limiting case is where preferences are nearly identical so that the choice of one group is very close to the choice of the other in the all-inclusive jurisdiction.

However, when preferences are sufficiently diverse, incentives to form separate groups arise. Then, when high-benefit voters are in the majority and determine supply in the all-inclusive jurisdiction, it may be in the interest of the low-benefit population to form their own jurisdiction.[20] Similarly, with sufficiently diverse

---

[19] We have defined $2T$ as the per-unit tax when the price P of the public good is equally shared in separate populations (which we have defined as of equal sizes). Therefore $P/n_H = P/n_L = 2T$. If the public good is supplied in a competitive market, we have $P = MC$. Conditions (2.38) and (2.39) follow because $2T = P/n_L = MB_L$ at point E and $2T = P/n_H = MB_H$ at point D (where $n_L MB_L = \sum MB_L$ and $n_H MB_H = \sum MB_H$).

[20] In Figure 2.13, low-benefit people would supply G_{LI} to themselves in a separate jurisdiction. Their per-unit tax will have doubled to $2T$, but they avoid paying for a quantity of the public good that

preferences, the high-benefit population may be better off in a separate jurisdiction when low-benefit voters determine supply in the all-inclusive jurisdiction.[21] It is of course sufficient for one group to form its own jurisdiction for separation to occur.

If low- and high-benefit people remain together in the same jurisdiction, the low-benefit people can help the high-benefit people pay for public goods, and can benefit from public goods that high-benefit people would provide in any event if the low-benefit people were not present. We can return to the example of the lighthouse. A large lighthouse can serve low-benefit users, even though low-benefit users ideally want a smaller lighthouse. That is, the low-benefit users have small boats and do not travel far enough from shore to need a large lighthouse, but a large lighthouse serves their purposes. The equivalent of two separate jurisdictions is to build two lighthouses side-by-side, one large for high-benefit users and one small for low-benefit users.

As another example, we can consider two groups of people who own either cars or trucks. A road that both car and truck owners would use is to be built between two locations. The road will not become congested and is therefore a pure public good. Truck owners benefit from greater spending to provide a road suitable for heavy trucks. Owners of cars and trucks could finance separate roads, which is, however, wasteful because cars can use a road suitable for trucks. Owners of cars have no incentive to increase their costs by participating in the additional spending required to make the road suitable for trucks. Owners of trucks might propose that car owners pay for the road that accommodates cars, while the truck owners pay for upgrading the road to accommodate trucks. Car owners might say: you truck owners are going to build the road anyway to accommodate trucks, so why not allow cars to use the road without payment. In these proposals for sharing costs, the per-unit tax is not equal for low- and high-benefit users. The two groups are attempting to shift costs onto one other. If the truck owners attempt to place too great a share of the costs on the car owners, the car owners have an incentive to build their own road. If the car owners attempt to free ride and do not offer to contribute to the road on the grounds that any road suitable for trucks will in any event be more than enough for cars, the truck owners may finance their own separate road and exclude cars.

When car and truck owners share the financing of one road, their combined efficient spending provides a better quality road than either group would independently provide for themselves. Figure 2.14 shows efficient supply G_{LI} and G_{HI}, respectively determined according to expressions (2.38) and (2.39) in separate

is more than they want. Low-benefit people compare after-tax benefit in the combined jurisdiction when G_H is supplied (total benefit VFG_HO minus total tax payments $OTZG_H$) with after-tax benefit VEY in the separate homogeneous jurisdiction. If the latter is greater than the former, they are better off forming their own jurisdiction.

[21] In a separate jurisdiction, high-benefit people pay the higher per-unit tax $2T$ and supply themselves the quantity G_{HI}. In Figure 2.13, to decide whether it is in their interest to form a separate jurisdiction, high-benefit people compare their after-tax benefit $RSJT$ in the combined jurisdiction when G_L is supplied with their after-tax benefit RDY in the separate jurisdiction.

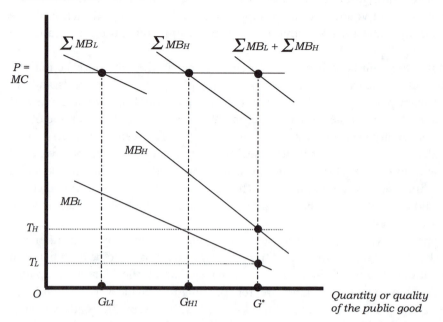

Taxes and cost

Figure 2.14. The efficient Lindahl solution compared to separate efficient supply by low- and high-benefit populations.

groups of low- and high-benefit users. In contrast, the efficient Lindahl solution keeps everyone in one group and determines the efficient consensus quantity as G^* where the combined marginal benefits of the entire population of low- and high-benefit users are equal to price $P(=MC)$; costs are shared with low-benefit users paying T_L per unit and high-benefit users paying T_H.[22] That is, in terms of our example, there is consensus on the quality G^* of the one road that everybody uses and car owners pay a lower cost share than truck owners. The quantity or quality G^* is moreover greater than that which either group provides to itself in the efficient supply outcomes with segmented populations.

In the example of the road, people are identifiable as low- or high-benefit by the vehicle they own, so perhaps the Lindahl solution is attainable. Rather than a road, the public good might be police patrols, a museum, diplomatic representation, defense, and so on, for which low- and high-benefit people are not distinguishable. A high-benefit person will want large spending, and a low-benefit person will want low spending. The public-good information problem stands in the way of sharing costs according to benefit in a combined jurisdiction, and segmentation into separate tax jurisdictions will take place, if this is to the advantage of one of the groups.

Consequently, although division of the population into different sharing groups increases costs per taxpayer, nonetheless best personal choices may involve people

---

[22] In Figure 2.14, all *MB*s are summed vertically. In the efficient Lindahl solution, $P = MC = n_L T_L + n_H T_H$. That is, the combined per-unit tax payments of all users finance the price of the public good.

joining together to ensure the public spending that they want. In Figure 2.14, with the efficient Lindahl outcome at G^* unattainable because of inability to distinguish between low- and high-benefit users in a combined jurisdiction, low-benefit users may be better off financing and receiving G_{LI} in a separate jurisdiction. Or high-benefit users may be similarly better off financing and receiving G_{HI} in their own separate jurisdiction then remaining in a combined jurisdiction that does not cater to their preferences.

Different types of public goods

Locational choice is provides efficient cost-sharing arrangements when different people want completely different public goods. Retired persons can for example locate in jurisdictions where taxes do not finance schools, as can other people who pursue lifestyles without children. Older people can choose locations where community facilities cater to their leisure preferences and health needs. People with young children can seek locations where taxes finance parks, play facilities, and day care.

Congestible and local public goods

Partitioning populations into separate jurisdictions also results in efficient cost-sharing arrangements when public goods are congestible, or if public goods provide local benefits that decline with distance from the location of the public good. For such congestible and local public goods, supply is no longer a natural monopoly. The benefits of reduced costs through a larger sharing group are matched against decline in benefits because of congestion, or decline in benefits when, as the population increases, people are located further from the local public good.

Other requirements for a locational choice mechanism

If choice of public goods is to take place through location, jobs and employment opportunities must be available in the government jurisdiction that provides the public goods that a person seeks, or be available close by.

Also, if locational choice is to be an approximation to a competitive market for congestible and local public goods, choices through location must be broad enough to replicate the supply offers that would be provided through markets. Because public goods come in bundles in each jurisdiction, large numbers of alternative jurisdictions may be required to offer the sought-after combinations of quality and quantity. The number of jurisdictions may not be large enough to offer competitive alternatives for every bundle of public goods.

The use of information to adjust supply

Cost–benefit analysis and the Clarke tax are intended to provide the information that allows *governments* to make decisions about public finance for public goods. The locational choice mechanism is different in describing *individuals* or groups of people choosing public goods through locational decisions.

We can expect governments to respond to individuals' location and relocation decisions when making decisions about taxation and public spending. That is, we expect governments to use the *information* provided by taxpayers' location and relocation decisions when choosing supplies of public goods. People who seek the same public goods cannot usually spontaneously form new tax jurisdictions that accommodate their preferences. Boundaries of existing jurisdictions are usually historically fixed and difficult to change. However, the responsiveness of government to information provided through locational choice allows changes in taxation and public spending to match individuals' preferences. In this way, the information provided by locational choice is used in a way similar to the information that would be provided through cost-benefit analysis or the Clarke tax to assist government in making efficient decisions about public spending on public goods.

2.2.6 Conclusions

If not for the information problem, a government could efficiently finance and supply public goods using the personal taxes of the Lindahl mechanism. However, just as the Lindahl mechanism is impractical when payments are voluntary, so government cannot use the Lindahl mechanism to determine efficient public spending. Without information about people's preferences for spending on public goods, and lacking other information that markets do not offer, a government can attempt to use cost-benefit analysis to compute efficient spending on public goods directly. We have seen that cost-benefit analysis requires decisions about the discount rate that compares present and future costs and benefits, and that values have to be set for benefits and costs that are not revealed in markets.

We have considered the Clarke tax as a means of solving the government's information problem. The Clarke tax can in principle lead people truthfully to reveal personal benefits and costs associated with public good projects. In contrast to the efficient Lindahl consensus solution that sets personal payments to finance a public good, Clarke taxes do not finance public goods. On the contrary, the mechanism requires that tax revenue explicitly not to be used for financing public projects. We can speculate that taxpayers might regard the Clarke tax with suspicion or consider the mechanism "unfair," in particular because Clarke taxes do not finance public goods.

When government jurisdictions offer different quantities or qualities of public goods, people reveal information about their willingness to pay for public goods through locational choice. If locational choice is to be an efficient mechanism for revealing information about benefits from public goods, partitioning of a population according to willingness to pay must be efficient. For pure public goods, partitioning of people with different preferences for public spending is inefficient because pure public goods are natural monopolies. Locational choice can, therefore, solve the information problem of public-good supply but at the expense of inefficiently small populations sharing costs.

The inefficiently small populations arise through incentives to form separate tax jurisdictions based on common valuations of public goods when in a combined jurisdiction low- and high-benefit people pay the same taxes. The Lindahl solution would eliminate incentives for inefficient partitioning of populations, by providing incentives for low- and high-benefit people to remain in the same tax jurisdiction. The incentives to maintain a combined tax jurisdiction are provided through the low Lindahl taxes paid by low-benefit people and high Lindahl taxes paid by high-benefit people, and through the consensus quantity that low- and high-benefit people both want to have supplied when together in the same tax jurisdiction. The information problem makes the Lindahl outcome unattainable because of the inability to set the different taxes for low- and high-benefit people. With the same tax paid by everybody without regard for valuation of the benefits from public goods, inefficient segmentation becomes a possible outcome. The choice between combined and segmented tax jurisdictions hinges on the balance between lower taxes in combined tax jurisdictions and greater compatibility of personal preferences with public spending in segmented populations.

Locational choice is an effective mechanism for solving the public-good information problem when groups of people seek different types of public goods, and when benefits from sharing costs in larger populations are matched against congestion or distance effects as populations become larger. Nonetheless, then, for efficient outcomes, sufficient locational choice must be available to approximate choice in competitive markets.

References and related literature

On the ideal consensus solution for public goods, see Wicksell (1896) and Lindahl (1919). On the Clarke tax, see Tideman and Tullock (1976) and Clarke (1980). For further investigation of preference revelation mechanisms, see Groves and Ledyard (1977). Tiebout (1956) proposed locational choice as an alternative to a market for public goods. On cost-benefit analysis, see Hammond (1989), Gramlich (1990), Darvish-Lecker and Eckstein (1991), and Graham (1992). For the case against a positive discount rate, see Price (1993). On the valuation of safety and life, see Vicusi and Moore (1991). On offsetting savings of costs of early death, see Viscusi (1999). On distributional weights in cost-benefit calculations, see Harberger (1978).

Clarke, E. H., 1980. *Demand Revelation and the Provision of Public Goods*. Ballinger, Cambridge, Massachusetts.

Darvish-Lecker, T. and S. Eckstein, 1991. Optimizing foreign loan conditions for a public sector project. *Journal of Policy Modeling* 13, 529–50.

Graham, D. A., 1992. Public expenditure under uncertainty: The net benefit criteria. *American Economic Review* 82, 822–46.

Gramlich, E. M., 1990. *Cost-Benefit Analysis of Government Programs*, 2nd edition. Prentice Hall, Englewood Cliffs, New Jersey.

Groves, T. and J. Ledyard, 1977. Optimal allocation of public goods: A solution to the free-rider problem. *Econometrica* 45, 783–809.

Hammond, P., 1989. Principles for evaluating public sector projects. In *Surveys in Public Sector Economics*, P. Hare (ed.). Basil Blackwell, Oxford, 15–44.

Harberger, A. B., 1978. On the use of distributional weights in social cost-benefit analysis. *Journal of Political Economy* 86, S87–S120.

Lindahl, E., 1919. Positive losung, die gerichtigkeit der besteuerung, Lund. Reprinted as Just taxation – a positive solution. In *Classics in the Theory of Public Finance*, R. A. Musgrave and A. T. Peacock (eds.), 1967, St Martin's Press, New York, 168–76.

Price, C., 1993. *Time, Discounting, and Value*. Blackwell, Oxford.

Tideman, N. and G. Tullock, 1976. A new and superior process for making social choices. *Journal of Political Economy* 84, 1145–59.

Tiebout, C. M., 1956. A pure theory of local expenditures. *Journal of Political Economy* 64, 416–24.

Viscusi, W. K., 1999. The government composition of the insurance costs of smoking. *Journal of Law and Economics* 42, 575–609.

Viscusi, V. K. and M. J. Moore, 1991. Rates of time preference and valuations of the duration of life. *Journal of Public Economics* 38, 297–317.

Wicksell, K., 1896. A new principle of just taxation. *Finanztheoretische Untersuchnung*, Jena. Reprinted in *Classics in the Theory of Public Finance*, R. A. Musgrave and A. T. Peacock (eds.), 1967, St Martin's Press, New York, 72–118.

Questions for discussion

1. The prisoners' dilemma suggests that government can achieve efficiency by using legal coercion to compel tax payments to finance public goods. Why is the problem confronting government in determining efficient spending on public goods more complicated than indicated in the symmetric prisoners' dilemma?

2. What is the ideal Lindahl solution for spending on public goods? Why is the Lindahl solution like a market? Why is consensus an important attribute of the Lindahl voluntary financing solution? What prevents government from implementing the Lindahl solution?

3. Cost-benefit analysis of public spending is a means of attempting to overcome the information problem associated with determining efficient spending on public goods. How do the characteristics of public goods call for but also impede use of cost-benefit analysis?

4. How does choice of the discount rate affect decisions based on cost-benefit analysis?

5. When nonrenewable resources or biodiversity is involved, do you believe that positive rates of discount should be applied for evaluating public projects?

6. Do you believe that there is a general case for a zero discount rate for evaluating costs and benefits over time of public spending? That is, do you believe that future generations should have the same weight in the computation of costs and benefits from public spending as present generations?

7. Are there reasons for believing that the market rate of interest does not reflect the discount rate that should be used in cost-benefit analysis for public spending?

8. Publicly financed projects sometimes increase the probability that people will live longer or avoid injury (as when government finances highway improvement, provides subsidies for medical research, provides security personnel at airports, or finances

police or national defense). If you were asked to do a cost-benefit analysis of public spending in such cases, how would you value an increase in the likelihood that a person's life will be saved?

9. "The Clarke tax is a means of obtaining information and not a means of financing public spending on public goods." Explain this statement.

10. Provide another example of the use of the Clarke tax, when the problem facing the government is to choose between the financing of two different projects.

11. We do not see the Clarke tax used in practice to obtain information about private costs and benefits from publicly funded projects. Why do you think governments are reluctant to use the Clarke tax?

12. If the locational mechanism for revealing information about willingness to pay for public goods is to be efficient, partitioning of the population according to benefits from public goods must also be efficient. Explain why, against the background of this observation, locational choice can solve the public-good information problem but the outcome is an inefficient partitioning of a population.

13. In Figure 2.13, show the costs and benefits for low- and high-benefit people from being in a combined tax jurisdiction and separate tax jurisdictions. In Figure 2.13, will low- or high-benefit people wish to be in a combined tax jurisdiction for financing of the public good when the other group determines public spending?

14. Why is the locational mechanism an effective way of resolving the public-good information problem when local public goods are congestible, or when people want public spending on distinctly different types of public goods?

15. Elaborate on the statement: "Public goods introduce a responsibility for government, but information requirements introduce a limitation on what we can expect government to achieve."

2.3

Public Finance for Public Goods

We saw in Section 2.2 that financing and supply of public goods is ideally determined by the Lindahl consensus solution, but that governments lack the information about personal benefits required for implementing the Lindahl solution. Cost-benefit calculations, the Clarke tax, and locational choice are means of hoping to solve the information problem. We shall now set aside the information problem and consider how to finance public spending on public goods.

We would have liked to have unambiguously solved the information problem about *how much to spend* before beginning to consider *how to finance public spending* on a public good. We do not, however, have an unambiguous solution to the information problem. Therefore, we shall now take the view that the government somehow knows the benefits to the population from a public good and also knows the costs of supplying the public good. Perhaps information was obtained through accurate cost-benefit analysis, or perhaps the government jurisdiction consists of people who have revealed their similar preferences through locational choice. We shall therefore now regard $\sum MB$ for the population and the MC of the public good as known to the government, where MC is determined by the market prices of the inputs used to provide a public good.

We shall be concerned with taxes when public goods are not congestible or congested. When public goods become congested, the purpose of taxation can be not to finance a public good but to discourage excessive use and so reduce congestion. For pure public goods or public goods that are not congested, the reason for taxation is to finance public spending.[1]

Public goods can be financed by user prices rather than taxation. User prices require the ability to exclude from benefit people who do not pay, as for example excluding users from a toll road or bridge if they do not pay. People could also, for example, pay a user price every time they call upon the police for assistance. The user charges could finance the police budget, so avoiding the need for taxation and public finance.[2] If user prices were imposed for calling for police assistance, victims would be paying for police services and people with insufficient money would be denied the protection of the rule of law, which would result in a situation that is socially undesirable and unethical. Since user charges for police assistance would discourage people from reporting crimes, criminals would also have greater opportunities to repeat their crimes. The police also provide a public good through deterrence of crime, and it is not possible to charge directly for the benefits of deterrence. User charges are therefore not levied to finance the costs of police protection. Where exclusion from benefit of people who do not pay is possible, voluntary private payment is, however, in principle an alternative to compulsory taxation of public finance. We shall return to considering user pricing as an alternative to taxation and public finance for public goods.

Here, we shall now consider taxation and public finance as the means of paying for public goods. After the public goods have been financed through taxation, the benefits from publicly financed public goods are then available without further payment to everybody. As we have previously noted, such free access to publicly financed public goods is efficient, since an additional person benefiting does not reduce the benefit to any other person.

2.3.1 Taxes and public finance

The personal Lindahl prices provide efficient financing for public goods, but the Lindahl solution cannot be implemented. If the efficient Lindahl prices could somehow be charged to finance public goods, the payments would be in the market for a public good. That is, if Lindhal prices were possible, people would voluntarily and directly finance public goods.

---

[1] In Chapter 8, where we investigate user prices as an alternative to taxation, we shall consider situations where the objective is to deter use of congestible public goods.

[2] Such user prices would not be the unattainable personal Lindahl prices that differ among individuals according to personal benefit. User prices are in general uniform prices for everybody.

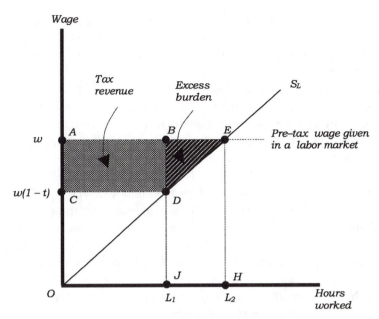

Figure 2.15. The excess burden of an income tax.

The voluntary Lindahl payments that would take place within a market for public goods contrast with financing of public goods through compulsory taxes that are levied on buyers and sellers *in other markets* and not in the market for the public good itself. The taxes in other markets can be taxes on incomes earned in the labor market or sales taxes on private spending on private goods. The taxes in other markets are an intrusion into these other markets. The intrusion has a cost, through a personal efficiency loss for taxpayers.

To see how the personal efficiency loss arises, we can consider a tax on income. Figure 2.15 shows an individual's supply of labor function S_L (for labor supplied during a week, or month, or year). The supply of labor function shows the substitution between hours worked and free time when the net-of-tax wage that the individual receives changes. As the net-of-tax wage increases, the individual substitutes income-earning activity for free time and labor supply (or effort) increases.[3]

---

[3] Hence the slope of the labor supply function S_L in Figure 2.15 is positive. The labor supply function is, however, more complex than just a substitution response to a change in the net-of-tax wage. When the net-of-tax wage changes, an individual responds through an income effect as well as a substitution response. Whereas the substitution effect leads labor supply to increase when the net-of-tax wage increases, the income effect has the opposite consequence of leading labor supply to decrease when the net-of-tax wage increases. The reason is that demand for free time increases with income, and when personal income increases because of a higher net-of-tax wage, the individual wants more free time and so chooses to work less. There are therefore two countervailing effects on labor supply when the net-of-tax wage increases. In Figure 2.15 and in subsequent representations of labor supply, we do not include the income effect and focus only on the substitution effect. Supplement 2E provides a representation of labor supply that includes the income effect.

In Figure 2.15, at the individual's market-determined wage w with no taxation, the individual chooses to work L_2 hours. An income tax at a constant t percent reduces the net-of-tax wage per hour to $w(1 - t)$, and the individual responds by decreasing hours worked to L_1.

The tax of t percent is levied on the *tax base* of L_1 hours worked. After the tax has been introduced, the employer continues to pay the competitively determined market wage w. The individual's pre-tax income in Figure 2.15 is $ABJO$ and net-of-tax income is $CDJO$. The difference between gross income and net income is the money $ABCD$ paid as taxes to the government.

We see in Figure 2.15 that the tax has created a gap between the cost of labor to the employer w and the wage received by the employee $w(1 - t)$. The tax has also resulted in a change in market behavior, indicated by the decline in labor supply from L_2 to L_1. The change in market behavior has occurred through a *substitution response*, with the individual substituting free time for productive time. The substitution response is the source of a personal efficiency loss.

The presence of the personal efficiency loss due to the tax is revealed when we ask the individual in Figure 2.15 one of two questions:

(1) How much are you prepared to pay the government, in return for the government *not* levying the income tax on you?
(2) How much does the government have to give you to *compensate* you for the tax that has been levied on you?

The first question presumes that the tax is not levied and asks how much the individual is willing to pay to keep the tax at bay. The second question presumes that the tax is in place and asks how much the individual has to be paid as compensation for the tax having been levied.

Let us suppose that, in answering the questions, the individual in Figure 2.15 feels no benefit from the taxes paid to the government. The individual then wants the money paid in taxes returned. Still, the answer to the question how much the individual is prepared to pay to avoid paying the tax is more than the money paid in taxes. The answer to the second question about how much the individual has to be compensated for having had to pay the tax is also more than the value of the money paid in taxes. In both cases, there is an *excess burden* of taxation beyond the value of the money paid in taxes.

The excess burden of taxation is the area DBE in Figure 2.15. The individual in Figure 2.15 is prepared to pay an amount of money DBE that is more than the value of the tax to avoid paying the tax, and has to be compensated by the amount of money DBE more than the value of the tax for having paid the tax.[4]

---

[4] In Figure 2.15, DBE is the excess burden of taxation obtained through the answers to both questions about payment to avoid the tax and compensation for the tax. Supplement 2E shows that, when income effects are included, the answers to the two questions differ, and different measures are obtained for the excess burden of taxation.

Why is DBE a personal loss from taxation?

When labor is supplied, a personal cost is incurred through free time that would otherwise have been available. The personal cost is expressed through the labor supply function S_L, which is a personal MC function for labor supplied. The area under the function S_L is correspondingly the personal total cost of supplying labor.[5] We can now proceed through the following steps:

(1) Before the tax is imposed, the individual's benefit from market participation in Figure 2.15 is OAE, which is the benefit or income $AEHO$ from supplying L_2 hours of labor minus the cost OEH of supplying these hours of labor.

(2) After the tax is imposed, the individual's benefit from market participation is OCD, which is the difference between post-tax income $CDJO$ and the personal cost ODJ in terms of free time forgone of supplying L_1 hours of labor.

(3) The effect of the tax has therefore been to reduce the gain from market participation by $(AEO - CDO) = AEDC$.

(4) $AEDC$ has two components. One component is the tax revenue $ABCD$ paid to the government. The second component is DBE, which is the additional personal loss from the tax in excess of the tax revenue paid to the government.

The efficiency loss of taxation

We have been viewing the individual who is being taxed as not feeling benefit from the tax paid to the government. Taxes, however, finance public spending on public goods, and the public goods can be a source of benefit for the taxpayer.[6] There is, however, no prospect for gain associated with the excess burden DBE in Figure 2.15. The excess burden is purely and simply an efficiency loss, or a waste.

The efficiency loss DBE is borne personally by the taxpayer in Figure 2.15. The personal efficiency loss is not directly observed as any sum of money. It is something that a person had before the tax but that disappeared after the tax. No sum of money equal to the excess burden of taxation changes hands. The excess burden of taxation is invisible.

When the supply-of-labor function S_L is linear as in Figure 2.15, we have the special circumstances where the area DBE is a triangle.[7] We can then use the formula for the area of a triangle to establish the area of DBE, and thereby to determine the loss through the excess burden of taxation. We then find that the

---

[5] Adding the marginal costs for increases in labor supplied gives the total cost.

[6] When public goods are financed by taxation and not by voluntary payments, individuals' taxes may finance public goods from which they do not benefit. We shall more explicitly see why this is so in Chapter 3, where we consider determination of spending on tax-financed public goods through voting.

[7] There is no reason why the supply-of-labor function S_L should necessarily be linear. All that we require is that the slope be positive, to reflect the increased attractiveness of substituting hours worked for free time or leisure as the net-of-tax wage increases.

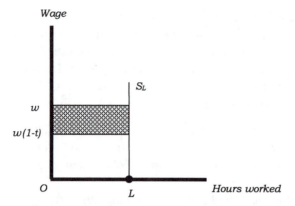

Figure 2.16. An income tax without an excess burden.

measure of the excess burden of taxation is given by

$$\frac{1}{2} w L \, \varepsilon_S t^2. \tag{2.40}$$

In this expression, ε_S is the elasticity[8] of the labor supply function S_L.[9]

Figure 2.16 shows a case where there is no excess burden of taxation. There is no substitution between hours worked and the individual's free time (the elasticity ε_S is zero); consequently, before and after the tax, the individual chooses to work the same number of hours L.

Because labor supplied is independent of the net-of-tax wage, the tax in Figure 2.16 has not affected the individual's market behavior. Without a change in market behavior (without a substitution response), there is no excess burden

---

[8] The elasticity ε_S measures the percentage change in substitution of labor supply in place of free time as the net-of-tax wage increases. The elasticity ε_S is a positive number (labor supply increases when the net-of-tax wage increases). The excess burden of taxation given by area of the triangle DBE in Figure 2.15 depends on the slope of the labor supply function S_L. The slope depends on whether we are measuring labor supply in terms of hours or weeks or months; it also depends on whether we are measuring the wage in dollars or euros or some other currency. Converting the slope to a percentage change, or elasticity, eliminates any effects from the units of measurement of time or money.

[9] To derive the expression in (2.40), we observe that the area of the triangle DBE in Figure 2.15 is

$$\frac{1}{2} \Delta w \Delta L = \frac{1}{2} t w \Delta L$$
$$= \frac{1}{2} t^2 w L \frac{\Delta L}{\Delta w} \frac{w}{L}$$
$$= \frac{1}{2} t^2 w L \varepsilon_S.$$

The elasticity ε_S is in general not a constant number. ε_S would be constant if the measurements on the axes in Figure 2.15 were in terms of logarithms. In that case, a constant slope for the function S_L would precisely measure the elasticity of labor supply. In (2.40), the measure of the excess burden of taxation is properly appropriate only for small changes in a tax. For small changes in taxes, we are not moving very far along the supply function, and we can make the approximation that ε_S can be treated as constant. For large changes in taxes, determining the excess burden of taxation requires decomposing the tax into small parts and adding (integrating over) the values of the excess burden for the sequence of small tax changes.

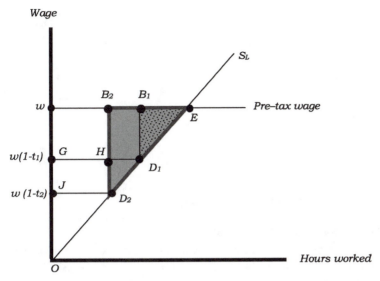

Figure 2.17. The relation between the excess burden and the rate of taxation.

An increase in the tax rate increases the excess burden. The tax revenue received by the government can increase or decrease.

of taxation. Substituting $\varepsilon_S = 0$ into the expression (2.40) correspondingly gives a value of zero for the excess burden of taxation.[10]

The expression (2.40) indicates that the excess burden of taxation increases with the square of the rate of taxation. In Figure 2.17, when the tax rate increases from t_1 to t_2, the excess burden of taxation increases from $B_1 D_1 E$ to $B_2 D_2 E$.

The change in tax revenue

The tax revenue received by the government by levying a tax of t percent is

$$R = twL. \tag{2.41}$$

The wage w in (2.41) is fixed in the market (this is the individual's pre-tax market determined wage w in Figure 2.15, or Figure 2.17). When the tax rate t increases, because of the substitution response in use of personal time, the number of hours worked L declines. An increased tax rate t increases tax revenue given by (2.41), if the number of hours worked does not decline too much in response to the increased rate of taxation, that is, if the substitution response in hours worked to increased taxation is not too large. In the case shown in Figure 2.17, an increase in the rate of taxation increases tax revenue if GHD_2J is greater than $B_1 B_2 HD_1$.

Tax revenue can therefore in principle increase or decrease when the tax rate is increased.[11] We shall suppose in continuing our investigation of public finance for

---

[10] In Figure 2.16, we see no equivalent of the triangle BDE that appears in Figure 2.15.

[11] From (2.41), we can establish that the change in tax revenue when the rate of taxation increases is given by $wL(1 - \varepsilon_S)$. We recall that the labor-supply elasticity ε_S is a positive number. Whether

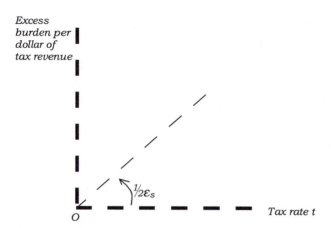

Figure 2.18. The excess burden per dollar of tax revenue.

The excess burden per dollar of tax revenue increases with the rate of taxation and with the responsiveness of work or effort decisions to changes in tax rates.

public goods that tax revenue increases when the tax rate is increased. We make this supposition because the government is, after all, interested in increased tax revenue to finance public goods and would not (at least knowingly) increase the tax rate if tax revenue did not increase.

The efficiency loss of collecting tax revenue

We have now identified an efficiency loss of using taxation to finance public goods. The efficiency loss is the excess burden of taxation imposed on the taxpayer paying a tax. This efficiency loss is a cost of calling on government to levy taxes to finance public goods.

To find the efficiency loss (or excess burden) per dollar or euro or any other currency of tax revenue collected, we divide the total excess burden of taxation given by (2.40) by the tax revenue given by (2.41), which gives

$$\frac{1}{2}\varepsilon_S t. \tag{2.42}$$

From the expression (2.42), we see that:

(1) The excess burden per dollar of tax revenue is greater, the greater is the individual's substitution response away from income-earning activity (or work) as measured by the labor-supply elasticity ε_S.
(2) The excess burden per dollar of tax revenue increases with the rate of taxation.

Figure 2.18 shows these relationships.

tax revenue increases or decreases when the rate of taxation is increased depends on whether the substitution elasticity ε_S is greater or less than 1.

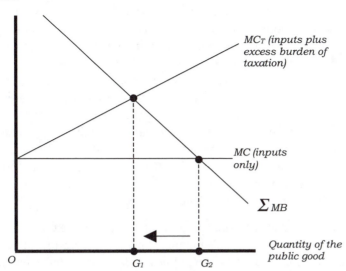

Figure 2.19. Efficient spending on tax-financed public goods.

Because of the excess burden of taxation, the efficient quantity G_1 of a tax-financed public good is less than the efficient quantity G_2 when payment is voluntary.

In Figure 2.18, we see that the excess burden per dollar of tax revenue increases as the tax rate increases for any value of the substitution elasticity ε_s. At the same time, the greater the substitution elasticity ε_S is, the greater the personal loss imposed through the excess burden of taxation at any tax rate.

The excess burden of taxation and efficient public spending

Figure 2.19 shows how the excess burden of taxation affects efficient public spending on public goods. $\sum MB$ is the sum of marginal benefits to a population from a public good. MC shows the marginal cost of the inputs used for supply of the public good. We see that $\sum MB = MC$ at the quantity G_2 in Figure 2.19. The efficiency condition $\sum MB = MC$ does not, however, make allowance for the loss through the excess burden of taxation when spending on public goods is publicly financed. Rather, the efficiency condition $\sum MB = MC$ presumes that a public good is voluntarily financed within the market for the public good, and not through compulsory taxes that intrude into other markets.

MC_T in Figure 2.19 includes, in addition to the market cost of the inputs for the public good given by MC, the personal loss incurred by taxpayers through the excess burden of taxation when the public good is publicly financed. If the government can accurately determine $\sum MB$, efficient public spending can be determined at the quantity G_1 where $\sum MB = MC_T$. Because of the excess burden of taxation, efficient supply of a tax-financed public good is therefore less than efficient supply if payment could be voluntary.

The following relations underlie Figure 2.19:

(1) Increased quantities of the public good require increased tax revenue. Increased tax revenue is obtained by increasing the rate of taxation (we have supposed that the government would not increase the rate of taxation if tax revenue did not increase).

(2) Each additional dollar of tax revenue results in an increased excess burden of taxation, as shown by expression (2.42). MC_T therefore increases as the quantity of the public good financed by taxation increases.[12]

(3) Since increasing tax revenue to finance greater quantities of public goods requires increases in the rate of taxation, the difference between MC and MC_T increases as the quantity of the public good financed through public spending increases.

(4) Efficient public spending is determined where $\sum MB = MC_T$.

In Section 2.1, we introduced a role for government to levy taxes to finance public goods because of the prisoners' dilemma and free-riding incentives for misrepresentation of personal benefit when public goods are voluntarily financed. We see, however, that, because of the excess burden of taxation, we do not call upon government to duplicate efficient supply of voluntarily financed public goods.

In a special case, as in Figure 2.16, where there is no excess burden of taxation, MC and MC_T in Figure 2.19 coincide, and G_1 and G_2 therefore also coincide. However, when taxes affect effort decisions and willingness to work, the excess burden of taxation creates a gap between MC and MC_T, and efficient public-good supply through public finance is less than efficient supply through private spending.[13]

How large is the excess burden?

Estimating the size of the excess burden of taxation is an empirical task that requires us to look at how people respond in their labor supply or effort decisions to increased taxes. Information on substitution between work and free time allows us to measure the elasticity ε_S and to determine the excess burden of taxation for observed tax rates. Empirical measurement of the excess burden of taxation has provided different answers. Estimates have ranged from low to high values.[14]

---

[12] Figure 2.19 shows MC_T as a straight line. There is no reason for MC_T to be a straight line. The straight line is only for convenience.

[13] Recall from Section 1.3 Hayek's critique of the proposal that people should be prepared to work without regard for reward, based on his observation that it is part of human nature that personal incentives matter for determining personal work effort. If Hayek was correct, we can rule out the case in Figure 2.16 where labor supply is independent of the wage. All cases are then as in Figure 2.19 where efficient publicly financed supply G_1 is necessarily less than efficient voluntarily financed supply G_2.

[14] For example, a study in 1984 by Browning and Johnson reported a value of $3.49 as the efficiency loss from a dollar of income taxes in the United States. A study in 1988 by Ballard reported a value of only $0.781 for the excess burden per dollar of the income tax in the United States. These and other studies use different procedures. The Browning-Johnson estimate was a cost-benefit ratio

One of the problems encountered in measuring the excess burden of taxation is to isolate the substitution response measured by the elasticity ε_S. The substitution response is not directly observable in market labor supply decisions.[15] Other information problems must also be overcome in order to directly measure the excess burden of taxation.[16]

An alternative to direct measurement of the excess burden of taxation is to use suggestive values for the labor-supply market substitution response ε_S in simulated models of an entire economy. Researchers who believe that individuals do not have much choice other than to work inflexible hours designated by the conditions and requirements of a job might choose to base their measures of the excess burden of taxation on low values of the labor supply elasticity ε_S. Researchers who believe that individuals have considerable flexibility in choosing effort and hours worked might conversely base measurement of the excess burden of taxation on high values for the labor supply elasticity ε_S. Both types of researchers might adjust their prior beliefs in the light of evidence. The choice made for ε_S for use in simulations of how an economy responds to a tax change will be reflected in the indicated size of the excess burden that emerges from the simulation results.[17]

Individual behavior and aggregation
Figure 2.15 has described an individual's labor supply decision and an individual's personal excess burden of taxation. Measures of the excess burden of taxation usually involve the combined taxes paid by the many taxpayers in an economy. That is, measures of the excess burden of taxation are based on aggregates or totals for a population of taxpayers and for public spending in general. The focus on the aggregate (or the average) hides high excess burdens of taxation for some individuals and low excess burdens for others.

Figure 2.19 describes spending on one particular public good. The excess burden of taxes that finance any one public good is usually part of the excess burden of taxes that finance all public spending. That is, in general, particular taxes are not associated with the financing of particular public goods.[18]

Measures of the excess burden of taxation are therefore usually aggregate measures for all taxpayers and for all tax-financed public spending. However, the

for tax-financed equal grants to the population, whereas the estimate by Ballard was a marginal welfare cost of collecting a dollar in tax revenue. Allgood and Snow (1998) estimated that the marginal welfare cost (or efficiency loss) per dollar of income paid in taxes in the United States was between 13 and 28 cents.

[15] See Supplement 2E.

[16] See Supplement 2F.

[17] The simulations include prespecified utility or supply-of-labor functions that contain a prespecified substitution effect through the value of ε_S, which in turn determines the excess burden for any level of taxation.

[18] When revenue from a tax is designated for financing a particular public good, the financing of the public good is through benefit taxation that is similar to a user price. The excess burden of taxation that finances a public good is, for example, identifiable when a tax is designated or "ear marked" to finance that particular public good, as for example when gasoline (or petroleum) taxes finance highways.

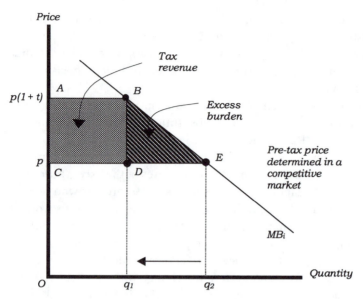

Figure 2.20. The excess burden of a sales tax.

excess burden of taxation is nonetheless a cost personally borne by the individual taxpayers who pay taxes to finance public spending. Returning to Figure 2.15, we see that the excess burden is personally determined by an individual's responses to a tax. Although the excess burden is personally borne, we can refer to the excess burden as a social cost of taxation, since the loss through the excess burden is imposed on all taxpayers in a society.

2.3.2 Taxation when income is spent

We have been considering the excess burden of taxation when income is taxed at the time it is earned. Income can also be taxed when it spent, through a sales tax. The principles underlying the excess burden of taxation then do not change. In Figure 2.20, tax revenue is provided through a sales tax. MB_i is an individual's demand for a good that provides private benefits, and p is a competitively determined market price. When confronting the market price p, the individual in Figure 2.20 chooses to purchase the quantity q_2. A sales tax at rate t increases the price the individual pays to $P(1 + t)$, and the quantity purchased declines from q_2 to q_1. The revenue from the tax in Figure 2.20 is $ABDC$.

If we ask the person being taxed the question how much are you prepared to pay to avoid having the tax imposed, or how much do you need to be compensated for having the tax imposed, in either case we obtain the answer $ABEC$. This exceeds the value of the tax revenue paid by DBE, which is the excess burden of the sales tax. The area of DBE in Figure 2.20 is

$$\frac{1}{2}pq\varepsilon_D t^2, \tag{2.43}$$

where ε_D is the elasticity of the demand function.

The individual demand elasticity ε_D appears in the expression (2.43) for the personal excess burden of a sales tax. The individual supply elasticity ε_S appears in the similar expression (2.40), which measures the personal excess burden of an income tax. In the labor market where the income tax is imposed, the individual is a supplier (or seller), and so the substitution response to a tax is expressed through the supply elasticity. For a sales tax, the substitution response to the tax takes place in a market where the individual is buying and is therefore expressed through the demand elasticity.

From (2.43), we can establish the efficiency cost per dollar of tax revenue from a sales tax as

$$\frac{1}{2}\varepsilon_D t. \tag{2.44}$$

2.3.3 Taxes without an excess burden

Are there situations as in Figure 2.16 where taxes have no excess burden? Another way of asking this question is whether taxes can be found that do not result in substitution responses in individuals' market behavior. We can consider a number of possibilities for taxes that have no excess burden.

Property taxes

A tax on unimproved land has no excess burden. The value of unimproved land is determined by the location of the land. A tax cannot change the location of the land. Land is therefore trapped with no substitution response that might allow "escape" from the tax.

A property tax on improved land does, however, have an excess burden. The value of improved land includes the value of properties built on the land (housing or commercial buildings or factories). A tax on the value of improved land is a tax on adding to the value of a property through further investment. The substitution effect in response to a tax is that some investment is not undertaken because of the increased tax liability when value-improving investments are made.

Taxes on investments in property also have substitution effects through allowances in the tax code for depreciation. When investments in property can be depreciated over time, investors receive their money back through the tax depreciation allowances, and they face the question where to reinvest. If taxes have become excessive, they can choose to reinvest elsewhere. The substitution effect then occurs through the changed location of investment.[19]

Taxes on essential and addictive goods

A tax on goods or services that people demand at any price, such as essential medicines, will not lead to market substitution, and such taxes have no excess

---

[19] Sometimes owners simply abandon properties. The owners have calculated that it is preferable to abandon the properties rather than to retain ownership and make necessary investments in renovations on the property because of the property taxes that would be incurred.

burden. Questions of ethics and social justice, however, arise when taxes are levied on essential goods such as medicines. Governments also tax addictive goods such as tobacco and alcohol, for which, because of addiction, there are low or no substitution effects.

A lump-sum tax

A tax with no substitution responses is sometimes called a lump-sum tax. A lump-sum tax can take the form of a "head" tax. A head tax is paid because the taxpayer "exists" (or has a head). The only possible substitution response that permits an escape from the head tax is "ceasing to exist," by leaving the jurisdiction of the government that imposes the tax.

A head tax opens possibilities for discrimination among people. Since each head tax is associated with a head, taxes can be set based on whose head is being taxed. Such taxes are undesirable because of the scope for arbitrariness and for violation of principles of fairness.

A poll tax

A tax with no market substitution responses is also sometimes known as a poll tax. The term "poll" in this popular usage has lost its historical meaning of a tax paid for the right to participate in a poll (or vote).[20] A literal poll tax has an effect on behavior in discouraging people from voting. If public spending is determined by voting, a poll tax, by influencing who votes, can affect decisions about public finance for public goods.

Different taxes

Governments can choose from among different taxes to finance public spending. Income can be taxed, and spending can be taxed in various ways, or property can be taxed. Governments also choose a structure for income taxes. We shall return to the issues of the choice of taxes and the structure of income taxation in Chapter 7, where we shall also consider problems of tax evasion. Our objective at this point has been to point out that taxes impose personal efficiency losses through the excess burden of taxation. Inviting a government to use taxes to finance supply of public goods because of failure of voluntary financing (due to free riding in the prisoners' dilemma or equivalently the impossibility of implementing personal Lindahl prices that reflect true personal MB) therefore comes at a cost, through the efficiency loss imposed on taxpayers by the excess burden of taxation.

2.3.4 Administrative and emotional costs of taxation

Taxation to finance public spending imposes personal losses on individuals in addition to the excess burden of taxation. Legal requirements to comply with tax obligations require taxpayers to collect and report information. A burden is

---

[20] Poll taxes were, for example, used in some states of the United States as payment for the right to vote (the last remaining poll taxes were abolished the United States in 1963).

imposed on taxpayers through the time spent in complying with the tax-reporting obligations. Accountants, tax advisors, and lawyers also spend time working on tax-related matters for clients or employers. Taxpayers are, of course, entitled to seek professional advice to reduce legal tax obligations. The time and initiative of taxpayers, and the abilities of accountants, tax advisors, and lawyers could, however, be used in more socially productive ways than meeting tax-reporting obligations or finding ways to reduce tax payments. Government employees who spend their time processing taxpayers' files and auditing tax returns could also use their time and initiative more productively.

In addition, some people experience personal emotional distress when, in the course of tax audits, strangers with the backing of the law investigate the details of their private lives.

The administrative and emotional costs of taxation supplement the personal efficiency losses imposed through the excess burden of taxation.

2.3.5 Deferred taxation: Government borrowing

Rather than being financed by current taxation, public spending can be financed through government borrowing, or the sale of bonds to the public. When a government borrows money from the public by selling bonds, the government is making a commitment to pay interest over time to bondholders and to repay the value of the bond at the end of the life of the bond. To be able to pay the interest and to repay the value of the bond, the government will require a future source of finance. The government will require future taxes, or will be required to borrow again. That is, eventually, when the loan is repaid, taxes will need to be levied. Bond financing of government spending is therefore deferred taxation, including a deferred excess burden of taxation.

By deferring tax obligations to the future, bond financing allows the tax burden of financing public goods, as well as the excess burden of taxation, to be transferred to future taxpayers. A government's budget in general includes expenditures to finance interest payments, and also expenditures to redeem bonds that have become due for repayment. The expenditures on interest and on repayment of bonds are obligations on present taxpayers from past decisions to finance government spending through bond financing.

Bond financing and the user-pays principle

When the benefits from public spending extend over the lives of different generations of taxpayers, bond financing or government borrowing is an application of the user-pays principle. Future generations who benefit from a public-good project may be unborn or may be children or students when the project is initiated and completed. Through government borrowing by the sale of bonds to the public, the future generations participate in the cost of the public goods from which they benefit, by paying future taxes.

We can consider a bridge. The costs of building the bridge are incurred at the time the public investment is made. The costs consist of the resources used in the project. These resources are withdrawn from other use by generations alive when the bridge is built. Bond financing permits the generation supplying the resources for building the bridge to be compensated, by spreading the financing of the bridge over future generations of taxpayers.

A two-period example

Spreading the financing of a public project over time requires that generations overlap in time. A public-good project might for example benefit two generations X and Y that overlap during two periods of time. In the first period, generation X works, pays taxes T_X, and lends the government B_X (generation X buys government bonds of value B_X). Together the taxes T_X and the sale of bonds B_X finance the resource cost C of the project:

$$C = T_X + B_X. \tag{2.45}$$

Generation X has provided the resources and the initial financing C for the project, partly in payment of taxes T_X and partly by lending the government the value of the bonds B_X.

In the next period, a new generation Y begins to work and to pay taxes. Generation Y pays T_Y in taxes, which is its share of the cost of the project. The tax revenue T_Y is used to repay the bonds B_X to generation X.

If the interest rate is i, generation Y also pays taxes to finance the interest on the bond, so

$$T_Y = B_X(1 + i). \tag{2.46}$$

Generation X thus receives back the face value of the bond plus interest. The interest paid is generation X's return for having deferred consumption to provide resources for the public-good project. Through bond financing, the burden of financing has consequently been spread over the two generations X and Y that benefit from the public project.

A three-period example

Table 2.15 shows a public project that provides benefits for three periods of time. There are three generations of beneficiaries. At each point in time, only two of the

---

TABLE 2.15. BOND FINANCING FOR A PUBLIC GOOD

Period 1	Period 2	Period 3
$T_X = 400$	$T_Y = 400$	$T_Z = 400$
$B_X = 800$	$B_Y = 400$	
	$B_X = 800 = T_Y + B_Y$	$B_Y = 400 = T_Z$
$D_1 = -800$	$D_2 = -400$	$D_3 = 0$
	Total cost: $C = 1{,}200 = T_X + T_Y + T_Z$	

generations are simultaneously alive. Generation X is working and paying taxes when the project is undertaken, and again bears the total initial cost of the project, through loss of alternative use of the resources that the project used.

The total cost of the project in Table 2.15 is 1,200 (dollars or euro or other currency). For simplicity, let us use an interest rate of zero. In the initial period when the project is undertaken, generation X pays $T_X = 400$ in taxes and lends the government $B_X = 800$. This provides the public finance of 1,200 for the project.

In the second period, generation Y pays taxes of $T_Y = 400$ and lends the government $B_Y = 400$. The sum of money $800 = T_Y + B_Y$ is paid by the government to generation X to redeem the bonds B_X. Generation X consumes this 800 and passes from the scene, to be replaced by generation Z.

In the third period, generation Z pays taxes of $T_Z = 400$. The taxes of 400 paid by generation Z are used to repay the bonds held by generation Y.

After the completion of the three-period life of the project, each of the three generations has contributed equal tax shares of 400 to finance the project. The total taxes paid equal the total cost. That is, $C = 1,200 = T_X + T_Y + T_Z$.

After the transactions of period 1, the government has a debt of $D_1 = -800$. The debt is the excess of government spending over tax revenue. The debt is equal to the value of the bonds B_X sold to generation X.

In period 2, the government repaid 800 and borrowed 400, giving an end-of-period 2 debt of $D_2 = -400$.

In period 3, the government repaid the debt of 400 and did not borrow. The debt at the end of period 3 is therefore zero. Over the life of the project, the government budget for financing the project is balanced.

The example in Table 2.15 has a zero interest rate. With a positive interest rate, taxes paid are greater than 400 for generations Y and Z, to provide financing for the interest due on the government's bonds.

Default on government bonds

Generation Z could gain by reneging and refusing to transfer its share of the cost of the project to generation Y. Generation Z can do this by electing a government that declares that it will not honor the bonds held by generation Y. That is, although bonds are a government obligation to repay a loan, a government might declare that it does not recognize repayment obligations for debts of a previous government. In general, governments honor the sovereign debt obligations of previous governments. Yet, if a government did not pay the interest due and defaulted on bonds that had been issued in the past, the public project would continue to provide the same benefits to all generations. The project was completed in period 1 and the only change if a government reneges on honoring bond redemption obligations is in intergenerational income distribution.

Unequal tax sharing

Unintended intergenerational income redistribution can occur if the benefits from a project persist longer than originally envisaged. Suppose that it was thought that the project in Table 2.15 would provide benefits for three periods, but the project continues to provide benefits into a fourth period. The generation earning income in the fourth period contributes nothing but nonetheless benefits.

Unequal intergenerational sharing can also arise by design. Generation X might altruistically pay the entire cost of the project, leaving future generations with a legacy of free benefits.

Generation X could also fund the entire project by issuing bonds, thereby shifting the entire burden of taxation for financing of the project onto future generations.

In times of economic growth, later generations are better off than earlier generations. If a judgment is made that future generations should pay more than preceding generations, bond financing will be used disproportionately relative to taxation when the project is initially undertaken.

Bond financing for the benefit of a present generation

Our example has supposed that the revenue received from the sale of government bonds is used to finance a project that provides benefits over time to future generations. The initial generation X might, however, use the money received from the sale of bonds for its own exclusive benefit. That is, the revenue from the sale of bonds might be used to provide income transfers to finance present consumption of members of generation X. No benefit is then provided to future generations. The future generations have, however, been bequeathed a tax liability to finance the interest and the repayment of the government bonds.

We see that bond financing can be politically sensitive. Bond financing can in particular place burdens of taxation and associated excess burdens on people who cannot object (they are unborn or are children when the government bonds are sold).

There is no assurance in general that bond financing will be used for projects that benefit future generations who incur tax liabilities. Future generations can be protected by constitutional limitations on allowable government budgetary deficits or by limitations on the stock of national debt (the national debt consists of the outstanding bonds that governments issued in the past and that have not been redeemed). We shall return to questions of constitutional limitations on government in Chapter 9.

Does it matter whether public finance is by taxes or bonds?

Whether a government uses taxes or borrows to finance public spending does not matter for an individual, if the same individual in any event pays the taxes that finance repayment of the government loan. Suppose that an individual is given the gift of a government bond of $1,000 that will be redeemed in 10 years time. The bond pays interest (say 5 percent annually). At the same time, suppose that the individual knows that after 10 years he or she will be personally obliged to finance the repayment of the bond, and during the 10 years he or she also must personally finance the interest payments on the bond. That is, the gift of the bond is accompanied by future tax liabilities of the same value. Every year through the 10 years of the bond, the individual pays to finance the interest that is received, and in the 10th year the individual pay taxes of $1,000 to finance redemption of the bond. The gift of the bond is worth precisely nothing.

Whether taxation or government borrowing is used to finance public spending matters when payment of the interest and future repayment of the bond can be shifted to future generations, as in our examples with overlapping generations.

Nonetheless, equivalence between tax and bond financing is restored, if older generations make compensating income or wealth transfers to younger generations, or in particular to their children. The circumstances where the compensating payments are made are known as Ricardian equivalence, after David Ricardo (1772–1823).[21]

Ricardian equivalence occurs when members of an older generation voluntarily neutralize the intergenerational effects of government decisions to use bond financing. Voluntary income or wealth transfers are made to compensate younger generations for the future taxes they will need to pay to finance interest and redemptions of government bonds.

Generation Y might consist of the children of generation X. When a government finances public spending that benefits generation X through bond financing and transfers the burden of taxes into the future onto generation Y, the parents in generation X can compensate their children in generation Y through gifts or bequests. The parents thereby return to their children the gift that they received from the government through bond financing.

Intergenerational altruism by parents with regard to children therefore makes taxation and bond financing equivalent. The equivalence requires parents to compute the value of their children's future tax liabilities that are due to government borrowing from which the parents have benefited. The parents can then provide compensation for the children's future tax obligations.

Ricardian equivalence requires that adequate physical wealth be available that can be transferred between generations. Investments in education and experience (known as human capital) are embodied in a person and cannot be transferred to other persons. A desire by parents to return to children gifts that were received through bond financing can therefore affect forms of investment, since Ricardian equivalence requires parents to have sufficient transferable physical assets or wealth to compensate the children.

Governments sometimes tax gifts or bequests. Such taxes are a tax on the parental behavior that underlies Ricardian equivalence. The taxes on gifts and bequests are taxes on intergenerational altruism. Through taxes on gifts and

---

[21] David Ricardo followed Adam Smith as a prominent thinker and expositor of economic themes. Ricardo was descended from Jews who came to England from Spain and Portugal; he became a member of parliament and is known for setting out the principle of comparative advantage and advocating free trade (the principle of comparative advantage shows that everyone gains from market transactions, even a person who is relatively inefficient in every productive activity relative to other people).

bequests, a government encourages people to consume their wealth rather than to transfer their wealth to others, in particular their children.

Fiscal illusion in the choice between tax and bond financing

Do people recognize that government bonds are future tax obligations? The failure to recognize the relation between bond financing and future taxes is a form of fiscal illusion. If there is fiscal illusion, Ricardian equivalence will not hold. People will not be aware of the intergenerational income transfer taking place through bond financing, and the income transfers that compensate for future taxes on the next generation will not be made.

When, because of fiscal illusion, government borrowing is not recognized as requiring future taxes, public spending can be greater than voters may want. That is, a government might use fiscal illusion to increase government revenue beyond taxpayers' preferred present and future taxation levels.

Why might a government use fiscal illusion to increase public spending against taxpayers' wishes (i.e., beyond the public spending that taxpayers would want if they understood that bond financing requires future taxes)? An answer requires considering the possibility that people in government might seek revenue to be spent for their own personal benefit. The spending of the revenue might be directly beneficial to people in government by allowing increased salaries and paying for better offices and increased travel. The increased public spending might be indirectly beneficial by allowing political decision makers to increase political support and to obtain more campaign contributions for financing future elections. Self-serving behavior by people in government would not be possible, if taxpayers controlled government decisions about public finance. We noted, however, in Chapter 1 that, because of a principal-agent problem between taxpayers and government, government may be able to make decisions about public finance without being accountable to taxpayers.[22]

Taxpayers can vote to replace political decision makers who use government revenue for personal benefit (people who have chosen careers in government bureaucracies cannot be so readily replaced). Fiscal illusion about the future tax obligations of bond financing may, however, allow government to extract more revenue from taxpayers than taxpayers notice, and so disciplining of political decision makers through elections may not take place. Future governments, along with taxpayers in the future, may then come to face the problems of a legacy of accumulated government debt, with accompanying redemption and interest payment obligations.

There are therefore two reasons why government budgetary deficits financed by government borrowing through the sale of bonds can be undesirable. Taxpayers might knowingly use bond financing to impose socially unjustified tax obligations

---

[22] The agent-agent problem is that taxpayers should be the principals who determine public-finance decisions, but people in government, who should be taxpayers' agents, have discretion that inverts the principal-agent relationship.

on other future taxpayers. Or, taking advantage of fiscal illusion, political decision makers might use bond financing to increase government revenue for personal benefit, by deferring taxes for the same taxpayers to the future. In both cases, future governments may face political problems when they discover that they must impose taxes to pay for past government spending.

A case for constitutional restraint

We see the basis for a case for constitutional restraint on governments raising revenue through the sale of bonds. In principle, bond financing of government spending is justified only to ensure that future generations participate in paying for past public spending from which they benefited, that is, as a means of spreading payments over time to match the benefits that different generations receive from past public investments. In the absence of constitutional restraint, there is no assurance that government borrowing will only be used for this purpose.

2.3.6 Who pays a tax?

Let us now consider a government that has identified particular groups on whom it wishes to levy taxes to finance public spending. The principle according to which the government wishes to distribute the burden (and excess burden) of taxation might be ability to pay. Alternatively, the principle might be that people who benefit from particular public spending ought to pay taxes that match the spending (as in the case of intergenerational financing through bonds). Either principle for assigning tax payments requires that a government be able to identify who pays a tax, so that the tax can be levied on the intended taxpayer.

Ricardian equivalence indicates that a government may not be able to control the burden (and excess burden) of taxation through bond financing, since older generations can voluntarily compensate younger generations for a government's intergenerational income transfers.

Quite generally, and not only in the case of intergenerational income transfers, the person who pays a tax is not necessarily the person whom a government legally obligates to pay the tax. The identity of who pays a tax depends not on who has the legal obligation to deliver tax revenue to the government, but on substitution responses in markets (the same types of substitution responses also underlie the excess burden of taxation). In other terminology, the legal incidence of a tax (i.e., the legal obligation to pay a tax) does not necessarily correspond to the economic incidence of a tax (i.e., the determination of who pays the tax). To see why this is so, we can look at the competitive market shown in Figure 2.21.[23]

When there is no tax, the competitive market outcome in Figure 2.21 is a price P, and a quantity supplied Q_2 at the point E. When a unit tax t (the tax is a fixed sum of money per unit of output) is levied on sellers, the sellers are obliged to deliver

---

[23] That is, we are now looking at a market, and not at an individual's response in a market. We looked at an individual's response in a market when we identified the excess burden of taxation.

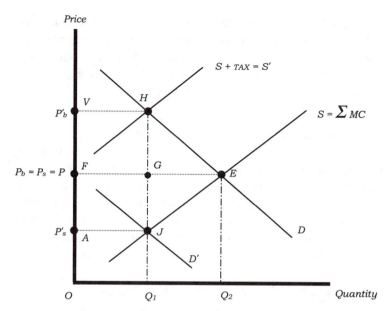

Figure 2.21. The payment of a tax is independent of whether the tax is levied on buyers or sellers.

The sharing of the payment of a tax between buyers and sellers is determined by the substitution possibilities of buyers and sellers.

the tax to the government. Sellers respond to the tax as if they face an additional cost of production. Individual sellers make supply decisions according to the price they receive for supplying goods. In Figure 2.21, the price received by sellers is shown as P_s. With no tax, P_s is equal to the market price P. After the tax has been levied, the price that sellers receive covers the MC of production and also the per-unit tax t that sellers pay to the government. The tax t therefore defines a new market supply function S', which includes the additional cost imposed on sellers by their obligation to pay the tax. The post-tax market outcome in Figure 2.21 is at the point H, at the intersection of the tax-inclusive supply function S' and demand D.

Together points H and J describe the post-tax market outcome. Point H shows the post-tax price P'_b that buyers pay. Point J shows the post-tax price P'_s that sellers receive. The difference $VA = HJ$ is the tax.

Although the tax has been levied on sellers, we see in Figure 2.21 that the payment of the tax is divided between sellers and buyers. The division of tax payments is determined by the location of the point G. The part of the tax paid by sellers is $FA (= GJ)$, which is equal to the fall in price for sellers from P to P'_s. The share of the tax paid by buyers is $VF (= GH)$, which is equal to the increase in the price paid by buyers from P to P'_b.

Government revenue from the tax in Figure 2.21 is $VHJA$. The payment of this tax revenue can be viewed as divided between sellers and buyers, with sellers paying $FGJA$ and buyers paying $VFGH$.

A tax levied on buyers

The legal obligation to pay the same tax might be placed on buyers. The outcome is then precisely the same as when the legal obligation to pay the tax is placed on sellers.

Buyers choose quantities along the demand function D. The demand by buyers depends on the price they pay, and not on how much of the money they pay goes to sellers and how much is delivered to the government through the tax.

Sellers, however, do care about how much of the price that buyers pay they receive and how much is delivered to the government in taxes. In making supply decisions, sellers deduct the tax paid to the government from the price paid by buyers to determine the price that they receive.

When the tax has been levied on buyers, as far as sellers are concerned, the demand function is no longer D but D'. That is, after the tax, sellers confront the new demand function D', which expresses buyers' willingness to pay along the demand function D after deduction of the tax that goes to the government.

The supply decision of sellers is determined where the demand function D' intersects the supply function S, which in Figure 2.21 occurs at point J. In the post-tax outcome at point J, buyers pay the same price P_b' and sellers receive the price P_s' as when the legal obligation to pay the tax is placed on sellers. With post-tax prices received by sellers and paid by buyers precisely the same, the distribution of the payment of the tax is also the same. Therefore, it does not matter for the burden of payment of the tax whether buyers or sellers have the legal obligation to deliver the tax revenue to the government.

The excess burden of taxation again

Now let us return to the excess burden of taxation. When we considered the excess burden of taxation in a labor market, we took the wage confronting suppliers of labor to be determined in the market. When looking at the excess burden of a tax on goods, we similarly took the market price confronting buyers of goods to be market-determined. The excess burden of taxation fell entirely on the individual supplying labor at the fixed market wage, or purchasing goods at the fixed market price.

In Figure 2.21, we are not looking at the behavior of an individual who faces market-determined prices, but at a market where price is determined by supply and demand, and by taxes. The excess burden of taxation in Figure 2.21 depends on substitution responses from both demand and supply sides of the market. Suppliers adjust to taxes (or substitute) along the supply function. Buyers adjust to taxes (or substitute) along the demand function. The excess burden of taxation in Figure 2.21 is made up of two triangles – GEJ from substitution along the supply function and HGE from substitution along the demand function. The total excess burden of taxation EJH is the sum of these triangles and is measured by a formula that adds the separate excess burdens of adjustments (or substitutions) in demand and supply. With substitution in demand in response to the tax given by the demand elasticity ε_D, and substitution in supply given by supply elasticity

ε_S, the excess burden EJH is measured by

$$\frac{1}{2}\frac{pqt^2}{\frac{1}{\varepsilon_D}+\frac{1}{\varepsilon_S}}. \tag{2.47}$$

The formula (2.47) reduces to (2.40) when ε_D is infinity (e.g., the market wage is given) and to (2.43) when ε_S is infinity (e.g., the market supply price for a good is given).

Sellers and buyers share the excess burden of taxation in Figure 2.21 just as they share payment of the tax. Point G, which determines the shares of taxes paid by buyers and sellers, also determines the sharing of the excess burden of taxation. Of the total excess burden EJH, GHE is incurred by buyers, and GJE is incurred by sellers. The formula (2.47) is the sum of the areas of these two triangles.

We have been interpreting Figure 2.21 as showing a market for goods, where income is spent. We can also view Figure 2.21 as a labor market where income is earned rather than as a market for goods. The conclusions about sharing the burden of the tax payment and sharing the excess burden of taxation then remain the same.

For example, it does not matter whether an employment (or payroll) tax is levied on employers or whether an income tax is levied on employees. The legal obligation to transfer tax revenue to the government does not affect who actually pays the tax and does not affect who bears the accompanying excess burden of taxation.

A tax is paid by persons who do not have substitution opportunities that allow escape from the tax. The means of escape is to respond by substitution or "leaving" the market where the tax has been imposed. In Figure 2.22a, suppliers (of labor or of goods) do not change their responses when the price that they

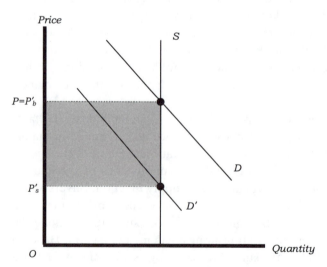

Figure 2.22a. A tax paid by sellers.

The tax is paid entirely by suppliers, since suppliers have no substitution possibilities to escape the tax. There is also no excess burden of the tax.

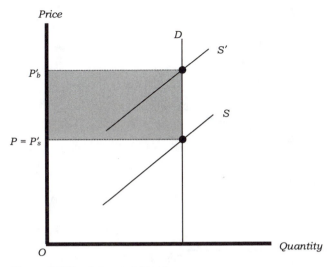

Figure 2.22b. A tax paid by buyers.
The tax is paid entirely by buyers, who have no substitution opportunities to escape the tax. There is no excess burden.

receive falls. They cannot (and do not) escape the tax, and the tax is entirely paid by sellers. We see correspondingly in Figure 2.22a that the tax does not change the price paid by buyers. After the tax, $P = P'_b$, while the price P'_s received by suppliers (of goods or of labor) falls by the full amount of the tax. Since there is no substitution response by the persons who pay the tax (i.e., by suppliers), there is also no excess burden of taxation.

In Figure 2.22b the quantity demanded remains unchanged when the price that buyers pay changes. Buyers therefore now do not (or cannot) escape the tax. The tax increases the price paid by buyers to P'_b, but does not affect the price received by suppliers (we see that $P = P'_s$). The tax is paid entirely by persons on the demand side of the market (buyers seeking goods or employers hiring labor). There is again no excess burden due to taxation, since again there has been no substitution response by the persons who pay the tax.

In the limiting cases shown in Figures 2.22a and 2.22b, the tax is paid entirely by people on one side of the market, and there is no escape from the tax because there is no substitution response (substitution out of the market is the escape from the tax). When persons on one side of the market cannot escape the tax, there is no excess burden of taxation.

Figure 2.21 is the more general case where both buyers and sellers adjust their market behavior in response to the tax (through willingness to buy or willingness to supply), and the tax payment is shared; an excess burden of taxation is also shared.

Ability to pay?

Let us now consider as an example of a market for loans where lenders are "rich" and borrowers are "poor." Suppose that, for ability-to-pay reasons, a government

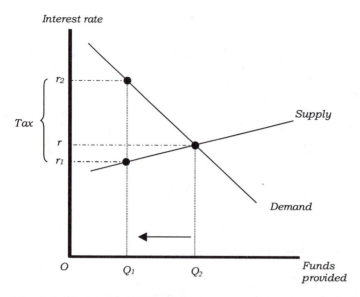

Figure 2.23. A tax is levied on lenders, but borrowers pay the larger part of the tax.

decides to levy a tax on the rich lenders. The lenders may, however, readily be able to move their money out of the government's tax jurisdiction to escape the tax. A "tax" on the rich lenders is then primarily paid by the poor borrowers. Figure 2.23 shows why this is so.

In Figure 2.23, the interest rate on credit is shown on the vertical axis, and funds provided for loans are shown on the horizontal axis. Before the tax, the interest rate is r, and loans are equal to Q_2. A tax on the interest rate received by lenders increases the cost of borrowing to r_2, and loans fall to Q_1. The interest rate received by lenders falls to r_1. The tax is the difference between r_2 and r_1.

We see that, contrary to the government's intention of imposing a tax on lenders, the tax is for the most part paid by borrowers. Since borrowers pay the major part of the tax, the objective formulated as ability-to-pay taxation has not been achieved. We also see that the excess burden of the tax falls primarily on borrowers.

As another example, suppose that the government decides on ability-to-pay grounds that employers should pay for the health insurance of employees. If the labor market is as described in Figure 2.22a, employees pay the tax even though the legal obligation to pay is on employers. In a labor market with supply and demand as in Figure 2.21, the tax payment is divided between employers and employees, as is the excess burden of taxation. Only if the labor market has the characteristics of Figure 2.22b do employers actually pay employees' total health insurance costs.[24]

---

[24] The excess burden of taxation would be avoided if health insurance were voluntarily purchased on a user-pays basis in the market for health insurance rather than being financed through taxation in the labor market. As we have noted, the excess burden arises when taxes intrude into another market, while there can be no excess burden of taxation when there is voluntary payment within a market.

Market substitution responses can therefore frustrate intentions of government to determine who pays a tax. Tax payments and the excess burden can fall on those who have the least ability to pay a tax, and who can least afford the personal loss due to the excess burden of taxation.

2.3.7 Economy-wide effects of taxes

We have been looking at who pays a tax and at the excess burden of taxation in one market. Taxes also affect incomes and result in excess burdens through links among the different markets in an economy. Consider for example a tax on income from capital. Such a tax discourages investment and encourages people to move their capital elsewhere if they can. The income received by labor depends, however, on the accompanying capital that is used in production together with labor. When the availability of accompanying capital falls, the income received by labor generally falls. A tax on income from capital therefore decreases the future income of labor.

A tax might alternatively be imposed on goods or services supplied by people with particular specialized skills. The effect of such a tax is to reduce the incomes of these specialized people. The tax reduces demand for these people's services. Specialized people cannot substitute to apply their specialized skills in other lines of work, and their incomes fall in response to the decline in demand for the services for which they have specialized skills.

Interdependencies among markets can be subtle and can result in unintended effects of taxes. A sales tax on toothbrushes, for example, benefits dentists. If, because of the increased demand for their services, dentists play less golf, demand for golf clubs and for the services of golf caddies at the local golf course falls. Golf club manufacturers and caddies then lose because of a sales tax on toothbrushes.[25] Rather than taxing toothbrushes, governments might subsidize toothbrushes to promote dental care. The same effects then arise in the opposite direction. Or a government might limit imports of foreign sugar, to allow domestic sugar producers to receive higher prices. The restrictions on sugar imports then reduce the incomes of dentists and again affect incomes of golf club manufacturers and golf caddies.

To understand how a particular tax affects incomes throughout an economy, we therefore need to be able to trace through the complete effect of the tax through all markets. To trace through such linkages, economists construct computable general equilibrium models of an entire economy. We have noted how such models are used to measure the economy-wide excess burden of a tax. The models are *general equilibrium* because they attempt to provide a general or all-encompassing picture of all the markets in an entire economy.[26] The models are computable because

---

[25] Dentists play less golf because of a substitution effect. An income effect would lead dentists to play more golf, and the tax on toothbrushes would increase the incomes of golf club manufacturers and golf caddies. On substitution and income effects, see Supplement 2E.

[26] Supplement 1B presents a simplified version of a general equilibrium picture of an economy.

the purpose of the models is not only to describe the linkages among markets in an economy, but also to compute the effects throughout the economy of changes in a particular tax.

The models are attempts to describe how a tax in one market affects incomes and creates excess burdens in the many markets of an economy. We noted in Chapter 1 the problems encountered when planners replaced markets. The problems of planning an economy are similar to the problems of constructing an accurate computable general equilibrium model that simulates an economy. In either case, there is inadequate information, and guesses must be made.[27] Yet, without the guidance of an accurate general equilibrium model, a government is subject to information limitations and cannot know how a tax affects incomes and excess burdens throughout an economy.

2.3.8 Responses to a government budget surplus

We have been concerned in this section with taxation to provide revenue for public spending. A government can have surplus revenue. Revenue can exceed spending requirements because of a period of unanticipated prosperity or because of miscalculations in projections of government revenue.

When there is surplus revenue, a question arises as to what to do with the surplus. The surplus can be used to reduce present taxes, or to repay past government borrowing (the government can buy back previously issued government bonds in the market for bonds). When the surplus is used to reduce taxation, the distribution of benefits corresponds to the distribution of the reduced burden of taxation (including the reduced excess burden of taxation). When the surplus is used to repay government borrowing, the beneficiaries are future taxpayers, who will be required to pay less in future taxes. When a government budget surplus becomes available, pressures can also arise for government to spend the surplus revenue in particular ways rather than to take advantage of the surplus to reduce present or future taxes. The decision about how to use a government budget surplus can therefore often be distributional and political.

2.3.9 Summary

We have been led to consider public finance for public goods because of problems with voluntary payment for public goods. The taxes that provide revenue for public spending in general have an excess burden because of substitution responses that are characteristic of market behavior. The excess burden of taxation is a personal efficiency loss imposed on individual taxpayers. The personal efficiency loss incurred through the excess burden of taxation reduces efficient public spending on public goods below efficient voluntary financed private spending.

Public spending can also be financed by sale of bonds or government borrowing. Taxes are then deferred to the future. Bond financing can be used to match future

---

[27] We have noted how guesses about labor supply elasticities in particular must be made to determine values for the excess burden of taxation. Similar guesses are required for other parameters of the models. The guesses can be quite informed when empirical evidence allows broad agreement about characteristics of the markets in an economy.

benefits from public investment with future tax payments. Bond financing can also be used to distribute taxation over generations independently of the intergenerational distribution of benefits from public spending. A present generation can spend on itself and transfer taxes to future generations. Fiscal illusion, whereby people do not view government bonds as future tax obligations, can also be used by governments to increase public spending above levels that a society would want if fiscal illusion were not present. We noted that, because of the possibilities for bequeathing tax obligations to future generations and because of fiscal illusion, there is a case for constitutional restraint on public spending financed through government borrowing.

We have also observed that older generations can neutralize intergenerational income redistribution that a government intended through bond financing by voluntary transfers of income or wealth to younger generations. A government then cannot implement intergenerational income redistribution through bond financing. Such neutralization of intergenerational distributional consequences of bond financing requires that there be no fiscal illusion regarding future tax obligations of bond financing.

We have also seen that a government cannot determine who pays a tax by simply requiring that specified people (buyers or sellers in a market) deliver the tax revenue to the government. The burden of payment of a tax (and the additional personal loss due to the excess burden of taxation) is determined by the characteristics of supply and demand in the market where the tax is levied. To determine who pays a tax, or the excess burden associated with a tax, a government also needs to be able to trace through the effects of a tax on substitution decisions in all the markets of the economy.

Taxes and government borrowing provide governments with revenue for spending, but sometimes governments can have a surplus of revenue over intended public expenditures. Questions then arise about what to do with the surplus, which can be used to reduce taxes, to reduce government borrowing or repay past government debt, or to increase public spending.

References and related literature

On the excess burden of taxation, see Mayshar (1990), Triest (1990), Fullerton (1991), and Usher (1991). On the consequences of the excess burden for public finance of public goods, see Pigou (1947), Atkinson and Stern (1974), Widasin (1984), and Kaplow (1996). For estimates of the excess burden of taxation, see Browning and Johnson (1984), Ballard (1988), and Allgood and Snow (1998). On tax administration and compliance costs of taxation, see Slemrod and Sorum (1984) and Stanford, Godwin, and Hardwick (1989). On Ricardian equivalence, see Barro (1974), Drazen (1978), and Bernheim (1987). On fiscal illusion and bond financing, see Buchanan and Wagner (1977). On computable general equilibrium models of taxation, see Ballard et al. (1985).

Allgood, S. and A. Snow, 1998. The marginal cost of raising tax revenue and redistributing income. *Journal of Political Economy* 106, 1246–73.

Atkinson, A. B. and N. H. Stern, 1974. Pigou, taxation, and public goods. *Review of Economic Studies* 41, 119–28.

Ballard, C. L., 1988. The marginal efficiency cost of redistribution. *American Economic Review* 78, 1019–33.

Ballard, C. L., D. Fullerton, J. B. Shoven and J. Whalley, 1985. *A General Equilibrium Model for Tax Policy Evaluation*. University of Chicago Press, Chicago.

Barro, R. J. 1974. Are government bonds net wealth? *Journal of Political Economy* 82, 1095–1117.

Bernheim, B. D., 1987. Ricardian equivalence: An evaluation of theory and evidence. In *NBER Macroeconomics Annual*, S. Fisher (ed.). MIT Press, Cambridge, Massachusetts, 263–304.

Browning, E. K. and W. R. Johnson, 1984. The trade off between equality and efficiency. *Journal of Political Economy* 92, 175–203.

Buchanan, J. M. and R. Wagner, 1977. *Democracy in Deficit*. Academic Press, New York.

Drazen, A., 1978. Government debt, human capital, and bequests in a life-cycle model. *Journal of Political Economy* 86, 505–16.

Fullerton, D. 1991. Reconciling recent estimates of the marginal welfare cost of taxation. *American Economic Review* 81, 302–8.

Mayshar, J., 1990. On measures of excess burden and their application. *Journal of Public Economics* 43, 263–89.

Kaplow, L., 1996. The optimal supply of public goods and the distortionary cost of taxation. *National Tax Journal* 49, 273–91.

Pigou, A. C., 1947. *A Study of Public Finance*. Macmillan, London.

Slemrod, J. and N. Sorum, 1984. The compliance cost of the U.S. individual tax system. *National Tax Journal* 37, 461–74.

Stanford, C. T., M. Godwin and P. Hardwick, 1989. *Administrative and Compliance Costs of Taxation*. Fiscal Publications, Bath.

Triest, R. K., 1990. The relationship between the marginal cost of public funds and marginal additional personal loss due to taxation. *American Economic Review* 80, 557–66.

Usher, D., 1991. The hidden costs of public expenditures. In *More Taxing than Taxes*, R. M. Bird (ed.). ICS Press, San Francisco, 11–65.

Widasin, D., 1984. On public good provision with distortionary taxation. *Economic Enquiry* 22, 227–43.

Questions for discussion

1. The excess burden of a tax arises because of intrusion into other markets of compulsory payments to finance public spending. What is the nature of this "intrusion"? How does the intrusion create an efficiency loss?

2. What are the determinants of the excess burden per dollar of tax revenue raised by a government?

3. Why is the excess burden of taxation invisible?

4. The excess burden of taxation is a personal loss borne by individual taxpayers; nevertheless, it is sometimes referred to as a "social cost." Why is the term "social loss" used?

5. Why do income effects give rise to different measures of the excess burden of taxation? (See Supplement 2E.)

6. How does the excess burden of taxation affect the relation between efficient private voluntary spending on public goods and public spending on public goods?

7. What are the problems encountered in statistically measuring the excess burden of taxation? (See Supplement 2F.)

8. "A head tax has no excess burden and should be used to finance public spending." Do you agree with this statement? Explain.

9. What are costs of taxation besides the excess burden?

10. Why is government borrowing to finance public spending "deferred taxation"?

11. Suppose a public project will provide benefits for three periods of time. The total cost of the project is 3,000, and benefits are divided over time such that the generation working in period 1 has 50 percent of the benefits, the generation working in period 2 has 30 percent of the benefits, and the generation working in period 3 has the remaining 20 percent of the benefits. With an interest rate of 5 percent, show how bond financing can distribute financing of the project commensurate with the distribution of benefits (each generation lives for 2 periods, the period when it is working and a further period when it is retired).

12. What is the justification for financing public spending through government borrowing rather than taxation?

13. What is the relation between fiscal illusion by taxpayers and bond financing? What type of behavior by political decision makers is facilitated by fiscal illusion of taxpayers regarding bond financing? Do you believe that people are subject to fiscal illusion? Explain.

14. What is the case for constitutional restraint on government borrowing?

15. What is Ricardian equivalence? What information is required for people to act in the way suggested by Ricardian equivalence? Do you believe that people have this information? Explain. If people had the information, do you believe that they would behave in the way described by Ricardian equivalence?

16. Explain why a legal obligation to pay a tax to the government does not affect who actually pays the tax. Why is this important?

17. What is the relation between the distribution of payment of a tax and the distribution of the excess burden of the tax between buyers and sellers? Why is there no excess burden of a tax when one side of the market (buyers or sellers) pays the entire tax?

18. Suppose a debate takes place on whether employers should pay health insurance for employees or whether employees should pay for their own health insurance. Formulate a position in this debate that includes reference to who pays a tax and the excess burden of taxation.

19. How does the presence of many markets in an economy affect a government's ability to determine who pays a tax and who bears the excess burden of taxation?

20. When a government has a budgetary surplus, are the principles of deciding how to use the surplus revenue the same as the principles of deciding how to increase tax revenue to finance additional public spending?

3

VOTING AND PUBLIC GOODS

Since public goods provide collective benefits, public spending on public goods is often decided by voting. We now begin an investigation of voting as a means of making collective decisions about public spending on public goods. We shall also consider the implementation of collective decisions by a government bureaucracy.

3.1
Majority Voting and Public Goods

3.1.1 Voting and consensus

Public goods provide collective benefits. Voting is a corresponding means of making collective decisions. That is, the quantity of a public good is the same for all people in a population, and voting is a means of determining the common quantity that will be supplied. Decisions made by voting require a rule indicating how a collective decision is to be made.

One voting rule is that a collective decision requires consensus among voters. With a consensus rule, an individual voter can block or veto any proposal. The personal ability to block or veto ensures that a collective decision made by consensus is Pareto-efficient because a voter who is made worse off by any proposal can veto the proposal.

Because of the ability of only one voter to block or veto under the consensus rule, other voting rules have been proposed. For example, a rule might be that support of 90 percent of voters is required for a collective decision. Under a consensus rule, one voter can block, but under a 90 percent rule it takes 10 percent of voters to block. People might behave opportunistically to block proposals in order to extort personal benefits. That is, even if people benefit from a public spending proposal, they might claim personal loss and try to extort personal benefits in return for agreeing to support the proposal. A consensus rule has maximal opportunities for such extortion because each and every voter can block. Voting rules requiring less than consensus make such opportunistic behavior more difficult, or impossible, because of the cooperation required among voters with extortionary intentions. Also, if voting is anonymous, opportunistic blocking to extort benefits cannot take place because voters cannot identify one another.

If voting results in an outcome of consensus, we know, however, that a proposal for financing and supplying public goods is Pareto-efficient. Each person has compared his or her payment obligations with the personal benefit from the public spending proposal and has decided to support the proposal.

We recall that consensus is a characteristic of the efficient Lindahl public-good solution. In Chapter 2, we considered the Lindahl solution for financing public goods through voluntary personal payments. We can also apply the Lindahl solution to decisions made by voting, with compulsory taxes and public finance replacing private voluntary payments.

In Figure 3.1, MB_1, MB_2, and MB_3 are the marginal benefits from spending on a public good for three taxpayers, and $\sum MB$ is the sum of the taxpayers' marginal benefits for different quantities. The public good is available in a competitive market at the price P, which is shown in Figure 3.1. The price P is the marginal cost (and also average cost) of the public good. Efficient spending on the public

Valuation and cost

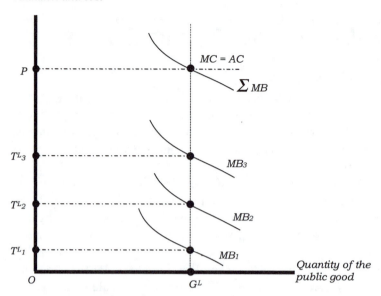

Figure 3.1. Consensus when taxes equal Lindahl prices.

If individual tax payments are equal to Lindahl prices, voting results in a consensus in favor of the efficient quantity.

good requires supplying the quantity G^L, since this is the quantity where the condition for efficient supply $\sum MB = MC$ is satisfied.

Suppose that the government knew and so could set the personal Lindahl per-unit tax payments T^{L_i} ($i = 1, 2, 3$) shown in Figure 3.1. Individuals' per-unit taxes sum to the price of the public good,

$$\sum T_i = P. \tag{3.1}$$

With the price in particular shared among taxpayers according to Lindahl cost shares as in Figure 3.1, each taxpayer would vote for public spending to supply the efficient quantity G^L of the public good. We see in Figure 3.1 that, with the Lindahl tax shares T^{L_1}, T^{L_2}, and T^{L_3}, each individual taxpayer's personally preferred choice of supply of the public good is precisely the efficient quantity G^L. The personal marginal cost to each taxpayer is the tax share T_i that he or she pays. A taxpayer's preferred choice of public-good supply is determined where this personal marginal cost is equal to marginal benefit so that

$$T_i = MB_i \qquad i = 1, 2, 3. \tag{3.2}$$

When asked to vote, all three taxpayers in Figure 3.1 therefore vote for public spending on the quantity G^L.

Taxpayers only vote by consensus for the efficient quantity G^L if, before voting takes place, they know that their tax shares for financing the public good are the personal Lindahl prices T^{L_1}, T^{L_2}, and T^{L_3}. However, contrary to our supposition, a government cannot be expected to know individuals' Lindahl prices. Consequently, Lindahl prices cannot be set as personal tax shares when taxpayers are asked to vote on public spending on public goods. That is, a government does not know the locations of MB_1, MB_2, and MB_3 in Figure 3.1. If the individual MBs were known, the government could follow the procedure of summing the individual MBs to determine $\sum MB$, which could be set equal to the price P, which is the MC of supply of the public good. Through the condition $\sum MB = MC$, the government could determine the efficient quantity G^L, and the efficient tax shares T^{L_1}, T^{L_2}, and T^{L_3} could then be found, as in Figure 3.1, through the values of the different individual MBs at the quantity G_L.

Only individual taxpayers, however, know the location of their personal MB function in Figure 3.1, and the taxpayers have no incentive to truthfully reveal personal marginal benefits when they know that the information they provide will be used to set their personal tax payments. We saw in Chapter 2 that there is a disincentive to reveal benefits from public goods truthfully when payments are voluntary. The same disincentive remains present when collective decisions about individuals' taxes and spending on public goods are made by voting.

3.1.2 Majority voting and the median voter

Although information to allow setting the Lindahl tax-shares is unavailable, taxes are still required to allow public spending on public goods to take place. Suppose that the government decides that taxpayers should make equal tax contributions to financing a public good. This tax rule is arbitrary, and we shall later consider other tax rules. With each person in a population of n taxpayers paying an equal share of the price (or cost) of the public good

$$T_i = \frac{P}{n} \qquad i = 1, \ldots, n \text{ taxpayers.} \tag{3.3}$$

With three taxpayers, for example, as in Figure 3.2, each taxpayer therefore pays a third of the price of the public good.

With equal tax shares, we see in Figure 3.2 that taxpayer 1 wants G_1 of the public good to be supplied, taxpayer 2 wants G_2, and taxpayer 3 wants G_3. Every taxpayer therefore wants a different quantity. There is no consensus. To resolve the disagreement, we can ask the taxpayers in Figure 3.2 to vote, on the understanding that the majority determines the collective choice.

Since the taxpayers disagree about the desirable quantity of the public good, we cannot ask them to vote on the question: how much of the public good do you want to see supplied? We would then obtain the different replies G_1, G_2, and G_3, with no majority for any quantity.

We can however put the following alternative question to the voters: do you favor an increase in supply in the public good? When a majority votes to increase the quantity, the quantity is increased. When a majority votes against increasing the quantity, the quantity stays as it is, in which case there is an equilibrium. More

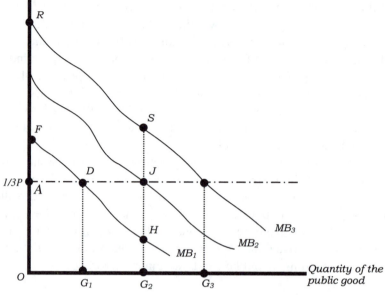

Figure 3.2. Determination of public spending by majority voting.
The outcome of majority voting is public spending on the quantity of the public good that is personally desired by the median voter.

specifically, in that case there would be a *majority-voting equilibrium* for supply of a public good.

In Figure 3.2, suppose that the three taxpayers are asked to vote on whether they favor an increase in supply beyond G_1. The quantity G_1 is the preferred supply of taxpayer 1. Taxpayer 1 wants no more than G_1 and so votes against an increase in supply. For voters 2 and 3, the benefits of increased supply beyond G_1 however exceed the personal cost in tax payments. That is, for these taxpayers,

$$MB_i(G_1) > T_i \qquad i = 2, 3. \tag{3.4}$$

Taxpayers 2 and 3 therefore vote in favor of increasing supply beyond G_1, and there is a majority in favor of increasing supply. Since there is majority support to increase supply beyond G_1, this quantity is not the equilibrium supply.

Voting then continues for quantities larger than G_1. At G_2, taxpayer 2 joins with taxpayer 1 in opposing any further increased supply. With the majority (taxpayers 1 and 2) voting against increasing supply beyond G_2, the quantity G_2 is the equilibrium supply determined by majority voting.

The costs and benefits for other voters from the median voter's choice

Majority voting has not resulted in consensus. Taxpayer 2 in Figure 3.2 is the median voter, or the voter whose vote has been instrumental in determining the majority-voting equilibrium. The collective choice G_2 determined by majority voting is the preferred choice of the median voter. Reflecting the absence of consensus, the median voter's choice of public-good supply is excessive from the viewpoint of taxpayer 1 and not enough from the viewpoint of taxpayer 3.

A low-benefit (or low-demand) taxpayer such as taxpayer 1 can lose from the supply of the public good determined by majority voting. In Figure 3.2, taxpayer 1 obtains total benefit of FHG_2O from supply G_2 and pays (as does everyone else) AJG_2O as a personal share of financing the public good. The cost to taxpayer 1 exceeds the benefit from the public good, if DJH exceeds ADF.

A high-benefit taxpayer such as taxpayer 3 benefits from the supply G_2 determined by majority voting. Taxpayer 3's total benefit from supply G_2 is RSG_2O, which is greater than taxpayer 3's total tax payment AJG_2O. Taxpayer 3 would however benefit more if supply of the public good were expanded beyond G_2 and would have maximal personal benefit if the quantity supplied were G_3.

The identity of the median voter

In Figure 3.2, taxpayer 2 is always the median voter. This is so because the MB functions of the different taxpayers never intersect.

In Figure 3.3, two taxpayers' MB functions do intersect. Since different taxpayers' valuations of the public good are independent of one another, there is no reason why MB functions of different taxpayers should not intersect.

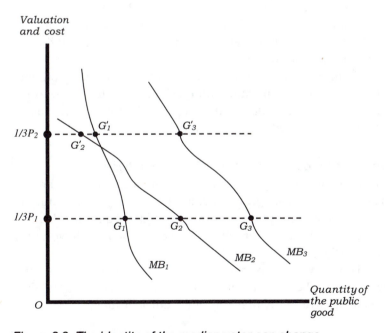

Figure 3.3. The identity of the median voter can change.

When the price of the public good is P_1, voter 2 is the median voter, and public spending on the quantity G_2 is the median-voter equilibrium. When the price of the public good is P_2, voter 1 is the median voter, and public spending on the quantity G'_1 is the median-voter equilibrium.

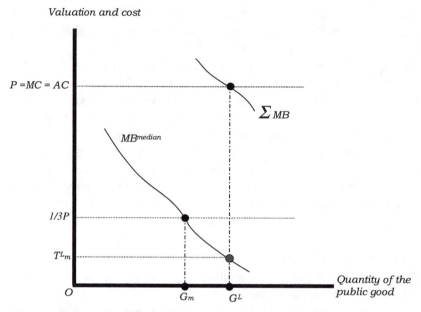

Figure 3.4. Majority voting does not ensure efficient spending on public goods.

We see that the identity of the median voter in Figure 3.3 depends on the price of the public good. If the price (or unit cost) is P_1, taxpayer 2 is the median voter, and the equilibrium quantity determined by majority voting is G_2. If the price of the public good is P_2, taxpayer 1 is however the median voter and the equilibrium quantity is this taxpayer's preferred choice G'_1.

The median voter is like a dictator whose personal preferred choice determines the collective choice. In a large population, no one can be quite sure who the median voter is. The virtue of the median voter as dictator is also that the median voter in general does not know that he or she is the median voter.

Does the median voter choose efficient supply of the public good?

Does choice of spending on public goods decided by the median voter through majority voting result in efficient supply of a public good? In Figure 3.4, efficient supply is determined in the usual manner by setting $\sum MB$ equal to MC. The efficient quantity is G^L. We see however that the choice by the median voter G_m is less than efficient supply.

There is in general no necessary reason to expect the choice of the median voter to result in efficient supply. The median voter's choice can exceed or be less than efficient supply, or might fortuitously precisely equal efficient supply.

The distribution of valuations

In Figure 3.4, T^{L_m} is the median voter's Lindahl tax-share. The median voter would make the efficient choice G^L, if the median voter confronted this tax share when voting took place to determine public spending on the public good. The median voter's choice in Figure 3.4 is, however, not determined by the personal Lindahl tax-share but by the equal tax shares that taxpayers face when voting.

Under special circumstances, the median voter would still choose efficient public spending even though taxes are determined by equal cost sharing rather than efficient Lindahl willingness to pay. With taxpayers paying equal cost shares, the median voter chooses efficient public spending if the valuation of the public good by the median voter is also the average valuation of the population.

To see why this is so, we can consider a population with n voters. Average MB for the population is

$$MB^{average} \equiv \frac{\sum_{j=1}^{n} MB_j}{n}. \tag{3.5}$$

With equal sharing of costs, the preferred supply of the voter with the average valuation of the public good is determined by

$$MB^{average} = \frac{P}{n} = \frac{MC}{n}. \tag{3.6}$$

In (3.6), $P = MC$, since the public good is supplied in a competitive market; therefore, (3.6) can be equivalently expressed as

$$n \cdot MB^{average} = MC. \tag{3.7}$$

Expression (3.7) is another way of expressing the condition $\sum MB = MC$ for efficient public-good supply. If the median voter happens to have the average MB of the population, then, in addition to expression (3.7), we also have

$$n \cdot MB^{median} = MC. \tag{3.8}$$

This confirms that the median voter chooses efficient public spending for a public good, if the median voter has the average MB in the population. That is, the condition for efficient supply in the form of the expression (3.7) is satisfied with median voter's valuation.

Whether the median voter's choice is efficient therefore depends on the distribution of MBs in a population. The distribution can reflect different preferences or different incomes.

Preferences might be normally distributed as in Figure 3.5a. In that case, since median and average coincide, collective choice through majority voting by the median voter would be efficient. However, the distribution of income or wealth in a population is in general skewed as in Figure 3.5b, with the median less than the average. In that case, the median voter chooses less-than-efficient public spending on a public good.

We observed a tendency for undersupply of public goods when financing is by voluntary payment. With the median voter choosing supply, undersupply can arise. However, the reason for undersupply is not now free riding, since each taxpayer is contributing to financing the public good. Undersupply is a consequence of valuation by the median voter that is lower than average valuation of the population.

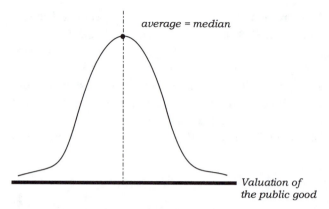

Figure 3.5a. Valuations are normally distributed.

With equal cost sharing, majority voting results in efficient supply, if the median voter has the average valuation of a public good.

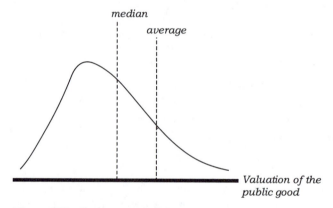

Figure 3.5b. Average exceeds the mean.

The valuation of the median voter is less than the valuation of the voter with average valuation.

With a skewed distribution of marginal benefits as in Figure 3.5b, choice by the median voter can also result in oversupply. This occurs when low-income people value public goods more highly than high-income people. Low-income people might wish to have access to publicly financed shared facilities, such as recreational amenities or state schools, whereas high-income persons might prefer private recreational amenities and private schools. In that case, the valuation or marginal benefit of the median voter exceeds the average valuation or marginal benefit, and the outcome of majority voting is oversupply of a public good relative to the efficient quantity.

Progressive taxes

We have been considering equal sharing through taxation of the costs of public goods. In Figure 3.6, we see personal taxes (T_1, T_2, T_3) that are not equal but

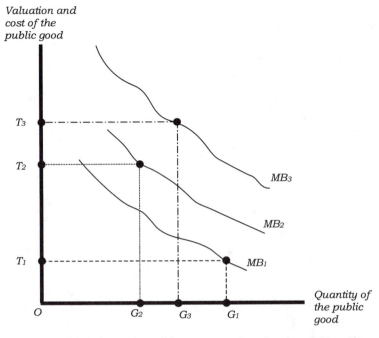

Figure 3.6. Majority voting with a progressive structure of taxation.

increase with individual demand or marginal benefit. The taxes are progressive if higher demand for public goods reflects higher personal incomes.

With the taxes in Figure 3.6, the median voter is taxpayer 3, who is decisive in determining the collective choice through majority voting as G_3. The choice by the median voter could only fortuitously be efficient.

A government could try to make a guess at the values of the efficient Lindahl taxes. The government would know that its guess had been successful, if, when asked to vote on quantities of a public good, all taxpayers voted for the same quantity (which would be the Lindahl consensus quantity G^L in Figure 3.1).

Because it is the median voter who determines the quantity of the public good under majority voting, efficient supply could be achieved if the government could guess just the personal Lindahl price of the median voter. If the guess were correct (e.g., T^{L_2} in Figure 3.1 or T^{L_m} in Figure 3.4), majority voting would result in choice of the efficient quantity of the public good. Guessing the personal tax that would lead the median voter to make the efficient choice is a difficult task for a government. Even if the median voter could be identified before a vote takes place, the median voter has no incentive to reveal true personal benefit because the government is determining the median voter's personal tax payments based on this information.

3.1.3 Instability of majority voting

We are now going to look at *cycling*, which is a problem of majority voting. Majority voting can fail to achieve a stable collective decision because of indefinite cycles

TABLE 3.1. RANKINGS OF ALTERNATIVE PUBLIC PROJECTS		
Taxpayer 1	Taxpayer 2	Taxpayer 3
X	Y	Z
Y	X	Y
Z	Z	X

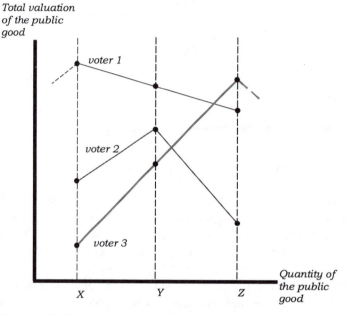

Figure 3.7. Rankings of the alternatives by taxpayers in Table 3.1: preferences of all three taxpayers are single-peaked.

among alternatives. To demonstrate the problem, we reduce choice of quantities of a public good to three alternatives X, Y, and Z. X is a small quantity, Y is an intermediate quantity, and Z is a large quantity. Figure 3.7 shows the ranking of three voters over the three alternatives. Table 3.1 shows the same information.

Using the rankings among alternatives in Figure 3.7 and Table 3.1, we can ask taxpayers to vote in pairwise votes. The outcome of voting is that Y has a majority over X (by two votes to one) and Y has a majority over Z (by two votes to one). Matched against any alternative, Y wins by majority voting. That is, alternative Y is the *Condorcet winner*, named after the Marquis de Condorcet who wrote about such pairwise voting in 1792.

In Table 3.1 and Figure 3.7, preferences of all voters are *single-peaked*. Voter 1 has a single peak for utility at X, voter 2 has a single peak at Y, and voter 3 has a single peak at Z.

TABLE 3.2. RANKINGS IN FIGURE 3.8		
Taxpayer 1	Taxpayer 2	Taxpayer 3
X	Y	Z
Y	Z	X
Z	X	Y

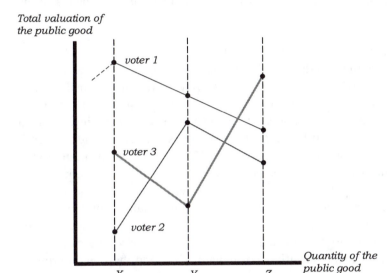

Figure 3.8. The rankings of the alternatives by taxpayers in Table 3.2: preferences of voter 3 are not single-peaked.

Let us now look at the rankings of voters in Table 3.2 and as illustrated in Figure 3.8. We see that in this case taxpayer or voter 3 does not have single-peaked preferences. Voter 3 prefers the extremes Z and X to the middle alternative Y. With the rankings of alternatives in Table 3.2 and Figure 3.8, majority voting provides the following results: X has a majority over Y, Y has a majority over Z, and Z has a majority over X. Majority voting therefore does not provide a stable collective choice. Any alternative can always be defeated by another alternative, and so there is no Condorcet winner. The instability of majority voting has occurred because voter 3 has two peaks for preferred outcomes, not a single peak.

The alternatives X, Y, and Z could indicate quality rather than quantity of a public good. In that case, voter 3 in Figure 3.8 wants a high standard rather than a mediocre standard; if a high standard cannot be provided, voter 3 prefers a minimum standard. The non-single-peaked preferences of voter 3 in Figure 3.8 can also arise naturally when the choice is among altogether different public-good projects and not differing quantities or qualities of the same public good. For example, the choice may be among the alternatives of (X) increased education expenditures, (Y) increased entertainment budgets for diplomatic personnel in embassies abroad, and (Z) a new national park. There is then no reason to expect a personal ranking of preferences among the alternative projects to have a single peak.

The previous median voter outcomes

In Figure 3.2, the outcome of majority voting was stable at the preferred choice of the median voter at G_2 because preferences of voters in Figure 3.2 are single-peaked. Voters' benefits are respectively maximized, or have single peaks, at the quantities G_1, G_2, and G_3.

Choice of the agenda

When cycling occurs, the agenda, or order in which voting on the alternatives takes place, determines the winning outcome. With taxpayers' rankings as in Table 3.2, suppose that a vote is first taken on a choice between X and Y. Then X has a majority over Y, and Y is eliminated; in the next round of voting, Z has a majority over X, so Z wins. If however the first vote is between Y and Z, then Y eliminates Z, and X wins with a majority over Y. Alternatively, if the first vote is between alternatives Z and X, Z has a majority over X so X is eliminated, leaving Y to win over Z. The order of voting on alternatives – or the agenda for voting – determines the winning choice. The winning alternative can therefore be determined by control over the order of voting. We see the importance of being the person with the ability to set the agenda for the order of voting. Setting the agenda determines which alternative is eliminated first, and thereby determines the alternative that will emerge as the winner from majority voting.

When there is cycling, collective choice through majority voting is therefore subject to manipulation by setting the agenda for voting, or the order in which voting takes place. Indeed, when cycling among alternatives occurs, a stable decision can be reached only by imposing the additional constraints on the order of voting that entail manipulation. Without additional constraints that eliminate one of the alternatives, majority voting can result in continual cycling among alternatives, with any one alternative continually being defeated by another alternative.

Stable outcomes with preferences that are not single-peaked

When preferences are not single-peaked, cycling can occur as we have shown, but cycling is not necessary. For example, all voters might have the same non-single-peaked preferences and prefer small and large spending on a particular public good to an intermediate expenditure. Although preferences are not single-peaked, there is then a stable outcome of majority voting, by consensus.

3.1.4 Majority voting and cost-benefit valuation

We now leave the issue of stability of outcomes under majority voting and return to our primary question, which is whether majority voting results in efficient collective decisions for public goods. We would want a public good project chosen

TABLE 3.3. VALUATIONS OF THE PROJECT THAT WINS BY
MAJORITY VOTING

Project Y: the winner by majority voting in Table 3.1	Cost to the taxpayer of the project	Taxpayer benefit from the project	Taxpayer net benefit from the project
Taxpayer 1	100	30	−70
Taxpayer 2	100	130	30
Taxpayer 3	100	110	10
Total	Total cost = 300	Total benefit = 270	Total net benefit = −30

by majority voting to satisfy the cost-benefit criterion that total benefits for society exceed total costs, that is, that $W = B − C > 0$. With this criterion satisfied, taxes levied to finance public spending on a public good project are justified on efficiency grounds.

Let us return to the stable outcome of majority voting in Table 3.1. Table 3.1 does not provide information that allows a cost-benefit evaluation of the outcome of voting. The information provided in Table 3.1 is about taxpayers' rankings of the different projects. No information is provided about values of costs and benefits for each project. To justify public spending on the winning project in Table 3.1 (which is project Y), we would want to be able to confirm that the project satisfies the cost-benefit condition that $W = B − C > 0$.

Suppose that values of benefits and costs for project Y for the three voters in Table 3.1 are as shown in Table 3.3. Project Y has a total cost of 300, and the project is financed by equal cost sharing among taxpayers, with each taxpayer paying 100. Taxpayers' benefits from the project (each taxpayer's benefit is private information known only to the taxpayer personally) are, respectively, 30, 130, and 110. The total benefit from the project is therefore 270. Total benefit 270 is less than the total cost 300. The total net benefit $W = B − C$ is −30 (a negative number), and so public spending on the project is not justified. Yet project Y was chosen as the Condorcet winner under majority voting. We conclude that a project that is a Condorcet winner need not satisfy the cost-benefit criterion that $W = B − C > 0$.

Table 3.4 shows taxpayer valuations for project X, which in Table 3.1 lost to project Y by majority voting. Total cost of the project in Table 3.4 is again 300, with equal cost shares of 100. Project X provides positive benefit to taxpayer 1 (we saw in Table 3.1 that taxpayer 1 prefers X to the other alternatives) and results in losses for taxpayers 2 and 3. Total benefit 650 exceeds total cost 300. There is a positive net benefit of 350 from the project, and so project X satisfies the cost-benefit condition $W = B − C > 0$. Public spending on the project is thus socially justified.

With majority voting, project X, for which taxation and public spending are socially justified, lost to project Y, for which taxation and public spending are not socially justified. In the vote between Y and X, taxpayers 2 and 3 voted in favor of

TABLE 3.4. VALUATIONS OF THE PROJECT THAT LOSES BY
MAJORITY VOTING

Project X: a loser by majority voting in Table 3.1	Cost to the taxpayer of the project	Taxpayer benefit from the project	Taxpayer net benefit from the project
Taxpayer 1	100	500	400
Taxpayer 2	100	80	−20
Taxpayer 3	100	70	−30
Total	Total cost = 300	Total benefit = 650	Total net benefit = 350

Y and only taxpayer 1 voted in favor of X. A project with positive net benefit to society (of 350) was defeated by a project with negative net benefit (of -30).

Such outcomes are possible because voting decisions are based only on personal rankings of alternatives and do not take into account other voters' benefits and losses. Nor do differences in personal benefit from different projects affect an individual's voting decision. Only the rankings of values of net benefits of alternatives matter for voting.

By not accounting for information about valuations, majority voting cannot distinguish between circumstances where gainers who are in the majority have small benefits with losers who are in the minority having large losses, and other circumstances where the majority has large benefits while the minority has small losses. In either case, the majority votes in favor of the project. Similarly, majority voting cannot distinguish between circumstances where losers who are in the majority have small losses while gainers who are in the minority have large benefits, and other circumstances where losers who are in the majority have large losses while the gainers who are the minority have small benefits. In both cases again, the majority votes against the project.

Since rankings and not valuations of alternatives matter for determining voting outcomes, it is not surprising that collective decisions made by majority voting can contradict the decisions based on a comparision of total costs and benefits that underlie cost-benefit evaluation. Voting is insensitive to how much losers lose and how much gainers gain. Yet how much losers lose and how much gainers gain is essential information for determining whether public spending on a project is justified by the cost-benefit criterion $W = B - C > 0$.

A continuum of choices

We have been looking at choices from among three alternative projects X or Y or Z. The same conclusions about efficiency and majority-voting decisions apply when decisions are made from a continuum of choices.

Let us look at the project shown in Figure 3.9a. Under majority voting, a median voter paying a tax T_m chooses the quantity G_m. The project is, however, not socially

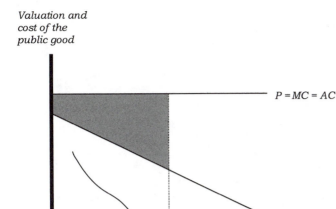

Valuation and cost of the public good

$P = MC = AC$

$\sum MB$

T_m

MB^{median}

Quantity of the public good

O G_m

Figure 3.9a. Inefficient choice by the median voter.
The median voter chooses a project that is not justified by cost-benefit valuation. The loss to society from public spending on the project is the shaded area.

justified. The efficient quantity where $\sum MB = MC$ is zero. By providing the public good at the quantity determined by the median voter, society incurs a total loss equal to the shaded area.

Figure 3.9b shows an alternative situation where the median voter opposes any supply of the public good, since the personal marginal benefit of the median voter from the project never exceeds the tax-share T_m faced by the median voter in contributing to financing the public good. The project is socially justified because total benefit exceeds total cost, and the efficient quantity is G^*. With the median voter determining the collective decision under majority voting, the project is rejected, and society incurs a loss given by the shaded area. The social loss is the benefit to society that would have been available, had efficient public spending been approved for the public good.

We see again that: (1) majority voting can result in rejection of public spending for projects that are socially justified through cost-benefit valuation, and (2) majority voting can result in approval of public spending on projects that are socially unjustified.

3.1.5 A market for votes

In Chapter 1, we noted the compensation criteria associated with Pareto efficiency. Change is justified as Pareto efficient, if gainers can compensate losers and still gain; change is not justified when losers can compensate the gainers and be better

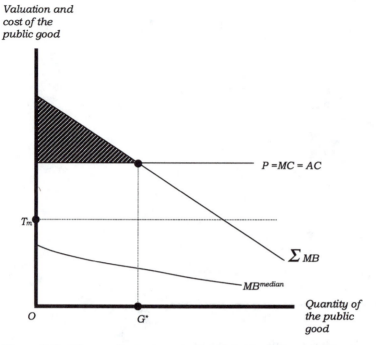

Figure 3.9b. The median voter rejects efficient public spending.
The median voter votes against public spending on a public project that is justified by cost-benefit valuation. The loss to society is the shaded area.

off without the change. Can compensation offer a means of ensuring that the outcome of majority voting is always efficient public spending as determined by cost-benefit valuation?

To consider the role of compensation, we return to the choice between projects Y and X in Tables 3.3 and 3.4. We see that taxpayer 1 gains 400 from project X, and taxpayers 2 and 3 gain in total 40 from project Y. The net gain from replacing spending on project Y with spending on project X is 360. Taxpayer 1 can more than compensate taxpayers 2 and 3 for changing their votes in favor of project X and still be better off. After taxpayer 1 has made compensating payments to taxpayers 2 and 3, there is a consensus among all three taxpayers in favor of the socially worthwhile project.

A Pareto improvement where all taxpayers are better off can therefore be achieved through payments that lead people to change how they vote. That is, escape from inefficiency is possible, if there is a market in which votes can be bought and sold.[1]

---

[1] Taxpayer 1 need not, of course, compensate both taxpayers 2 and 3 to obtain majority support for project X. To have majority support, it is sufficient that taxpayer 1 persuade either taxpayer 2 or 3 to vote in favor of project X rather than Y. If a Pareto improvement is to take place, both taxpayers 2 and 3 need to be compensated.

Markets in votes are, however, in general not allowed because of the objection that personal income or wealth should not determine how many votes a person controls. Rather, democracy should allow citizens to have equal influence through voting without regard for personal income or wealth. That is, the principle of "one person one vote" contradicts a market for votes.

A second case against permitting a market in votes is based on the value of aggregated votes. In a large population of voters, a rational voter will correctly perceive that it is very unlikely that his or her single vote will affect the outcome of majority voting. The value of a single vote that a person sells in a market for votes would correspondingly be quite low. A single vote is however not similarly valueless to the buyer of the vote, if the buyer can buy enough votes. As the number of votes in the hands of the buyer increases, the probability increases that the accumulated votes can be used decisively. There is value added by aggregation, since the value of the total number of votes exceeds the sum of the negligible values of single votes. A person or group that buys votes can therefore undermine democracy, by accumulating votes at small cost and benefiting from influence over public policy decisions about taxation and public spending.[2]

Because of these objections, markets in votes are usually illegal. However, because of the illegality, inefficiencies that can arise due to majority voting cannot be corrected by compensating people for changing their vote.

3.1.6 Political coalitions and logrolling

Although markets in which people pay money for votes are usually illegal, vote trading among elected political representatives can legally take place. The vote trading among political representatives takes the form: "If you vote for my preferred project, I will vote for your preferred project." This type of vote trading is known as logrolling because one person can cut down a tree, whereas it takes the cooperation of two to roll the log.

Does trading of votes through logrolling ensure efficient public spending decisions as outcomes of majority voting? To answer this question, we look at Table 3.5 where three politicians face a vote on three projects D, E, and F. Taxes will be collected, and each project will be publicly financed through the government budget, if there is majority support for funding the project. The projects are therefore now not alternatives as we previously considered. Every project can be financed, if a majority can be found in favor of the project.

The final column in Table 3.5 shows the net benefit to society as a whole from a project. Each project provides positive net benefit. Public spending on each project is therefore justified as efficient by cost-benefit valuation.

The three projects have, however, different distributional effects. Each project provides positive benefit to only one politician's constituency. In a vote on whether

---

[2] Citizens need not be the only buyers in a market for votes. Foreign interests could buy votes and use the votes by proxy through people with citizenship who have the right to vote. The foreign interests might want to reduce national defense spending or to secure income transfers for themselves (i.e., foreign aid).

		TABLE 3.5. LOGROLLING WITH EFFICIENT PROJECTS		
Project	Politician 1	Politician 2	Politician 3	Net Benefit
D	110	−20	−30	60
E	−20	100	−30	50
F	−30	−30	100	40

to finance each project separately, only representative 1 therefore supports project D, only representative 2 supports project E, and only representative 3 supports project F.[3]

When put to a separate vote, each project is therefore rejected by majority voting by two-to-one. Public spending on all three projects is, however, socially worthwhile.

Two political representatives who form a coalition will have a majority in favor of the projects that each wants to have funded through public spending. The possible coalitions are made up of representatives $(1, 2), (2, 3)$, and $(1, 3)$. These coalitions respectively provide majority support for pairs of projects (D, E), (E, F), and (F, D).

We can denote the benefits from a combination of projects i and j by

$$V_{ij} = (B_1, B_2, B_3),$$

where B_i is the benefit from the formation of the coalition to the constituency of representative i. When representatives 1 and 2 form a coalition to support projects D and E, the benefits to the three constituencies are

$$V_{12}(D, E) = (90, 80, -60).$$

Representatives 1 and 3 can form a coalition that provides benefits

$$V_{13}(D, F) = (80, -50, 70).$$

Representatives 2 and 3 can form a coalition that provides benefits

$$V_{23}(E, F) = (-50, 70, 70).$$

The coalition that provides maximal benefit to any two constituencies is therefore between representatives 1 and 2.

The constituency of representative 1 gains 90 from the coalition of its representative with representative 2 and gains 80 from a coalition with representative 3. Representative 2 is therefore the preferred coalition partner for representative 1.

[3] Political representatives need not always make voting decisions based on constituent interest. Campaign contributions can affect how a political representative votes. We leave these other influences until Chapter 6.

The gain to the constituency of representative 2 from its representative forming a coalition with representative 3 is 70, which is less than the gain of 80 from the coalition with representative 1. Representative 1 is therefore reciprocally representative 2's preferred coalition partner.

Representatives 1 and 2 therefore combine their votes to vote in favor of projects D and E and to vote against project F. This leaves the constituency of representative 3 with a loss of 60.

Project F provides positive benefit and should also be financed. Logrolling has resulted in public finance for two of three efficient projects. Indeed, the two most valuable projects are accepted by majority voting. Without logrolling, no efficient project would be financed.

The outcome is, however, unfortunate for the constituency of representative 3, which loses from both projects for which public finance is provided. Representative 3's constituency is paying taxes that finance two projects from which the constituency has a net loss.

When logrolling takes place, no money changes hands to influence decisions about voting. The coalitions are based on trades of votes alone. If monetary payments were permitted among the representatives, all three projects would be supported by consensus. Every project has a positive net benefit, and so financing and implementing each project is Pareto-improving after compensating payments by the gainers to the losers. That is, the constituency that gains from each project in Table 3.5 can compensate the two losing constituencies and still be better off.

For example, after representatives 1 and 2 have formed their coalition, monetary payments allow the constituency of representative 3 to compensate the constituencies of representatives 1 and 2 for supporting public spending on project F.[4]

When gainers and losers are the people in the representatives' constituencies, a means of making the compensating transfers among the constituencies must be available. The costs of organizing the payments from constituencies of gainers to constituencies of losers are however high or prohibitive.[5] Also, it is doubtful whether the compensating payments between constituencies could be legally made because the monetary payments influence how political representatives vote.

---

[4] In Table 3.5, the constituents of representative 3 gain 100 from project F, while the constituents of representatives 2 and 3 together lose 60. There is therefore a gain of 40 to be shared when public funding is provided for project F.

[5] People in the constituency of gainers might not voluntarily finance the compensating payments. Taxes would then have to be levied on the individuals in the constituencies of gainers to provide the revenue for transfer to the constituencies of losers. Computing the individual payments required from gainers and the individual transfers to losers is also a difficult task. The gains from the Pareto-improving change to fund efficient projects justified by cost-benefit valuation can be shared in different ways. When projects provide public-good benefits within a constituency, the gains are available to everybody in the constituency and the problem of financing compensating payments is the problem of how to finance public goods.

TABLE 3.6. LOGROLLING WITH INEFFICIENT PROJECTS

Project	Politician 1	Politician 2	Politician 3	Net benefit of the project
D	50	−40	−30	−20
E	−40	50	−30	−20
F	−40	−30	20	−50

Socially unjustified projects

Table 3.6 shows three projects, none of which is socially justified by cost-benefit analysis. Each project has a negative net value. Still, each representative's constituency has an interest in a particular project being funded. Representatives can again gain from majority coalitions formed through logrolling to provide tax funding for the project that benefits their constituencies.

A coalition between politicians 1 and 2 in Table 3.6 results in funding for projects D and E and provides benefits of $V_{12}(D, E) = (10, 10, -60)$. A coalition between politicians 1 and 3 provides funding for projects D and F and provides benefits of $V_{13}(D, F) = (10, -70, -10)$. A coalition between politicians 2 and 3 provides funding for projects E and F, with benefits $V_{23}(E, F) = (-80, 20, -10)$.

Only the coalition between politicians 1 and 2 provides positive benefit for the two coalition members.[6] The coalition that forms is therefore between politicians 1 and 2, and funding for projects D and E receives majority support.

Logrolling or vote trading has therefore resulted in majority support for two inefficient projects not justified by cost-benefit analysis.

The inefficiency could again be avoided if votes could be traded for money. The constituency of politician 3 loses 60 from the combination of projects D and E, while the constituencies of politicians 1 and 2 gain only 20 in total from the two projects. The constituency of politician 3 could therefore compensate the constituencies of politicians 1 and 2 for losses from not proceeding with funding for projects D and E and still gain. Once more, mechanisms that would readily allow the compensating payments to be made do not exist and would be of doubtful legality if they did exist.

3.1.7 The incentive for secession

Taxpayers participate in collective decisions to provide themselves with the collective benefits of public goods. If the collective benefits are not provided, taxpayers have no reason to participate in a collective decision-making body. If the losses for

---

[6] Although in the example in Table 3.6 only one logrolling coalition provides positive benefits for coalition members, other examples are possible where no project is justified by cost-benefit analysis and two coalitions provide positive net benefits to political constituencies.

a group of taxpayers are systematic, the group might be led to consider secession from the collective decision-making body.

As we noted in Chapter 2 when we considered locational choice as a means of solving the public-good information problem, the majority has an interest in opposing the secession of a minority, since the presence of the minority as taxpayers is a source of advantage for the majority.

Secession and consensus

When secession by a minority is possible, the option of secession transforms the collective decision-making rule from majority voting to consensus, since anyone who does not agree with a majority decision can secede and thereby avoid contributing to financing a project. When secession is possible, all persons who remain and contribute to financing a project do so voluntarily, so there can be no losers from a project. There is no minority to be disadvantaged by the vote of a majority. No inefficient projects are then financed through majority voting by a majority imposing costs on a minority.

3.1.8 Voting and locational choice

Secession of groups of taxpayers has sometimes occurred when taxpayers have been geographically concentrated. The disadvantaged taxpayers have asked for jurisdictional independence, or for fiscal independence, to finance their own public goods.

By seceding to form populations with similar requirements for public spending on public goods, people sort themselves into groups where a majority does not disadvantage a minority. The sorting can also take place through locational choice by individuals from among pre-existing government jurisdictions that provide different quantities or different types of public goods. Locational choice therefore also allows the problem of the majority-minority conflict that arises with majority voting to be solved. Without disadvantaging minorities of voters, retired people can form majorities in a location to collectively finance public goods consistent with their preferences. Families with children can form majorities to collectively finance schools without imposing taxes on people who do not envisage that their life-styles will be consistent with having children and so do not require schools. By creating more homogeneous populations of voters in such ways, locational sorting by individual choice among government jurisdictions can eliminate disagreement between majorities and minorities of voters over the quantities and types of public goods that are to be publicly financed.[7]

---

[7] We observed in Chapter 2 that the effectiveness of the locational sorting mechanism for financing public goods depends on the locational flexibility of people (their willingness or ability to move, which can depend on employment opportunities) and on the availability of a sufficient range of alternative jurisdictions that provide different public goods.

TABLE 3.7. VOTING AND THE PUBLIC-GOOD PRISONERS' DILEMMA

	Group 2 pays	Group 2 does not pay
Group 1 pays	3, 3	1, 4
Group 1 does not pay	4, 1	2, 2

3.1.9 Checks and balances

Rules can also protect a minority of taxpayers from the votes of the majority, through constitutional restraint against discrimination through voting. To see how such constitutional restraint protects a minority *and so assures efficiency*, we can look at Table 3.7, which returns us to the public-good prisoners' dilemma.

In Table 3.7 there are two groups of voters rather than two persons. For individuals and groups alike, the dominant strategy in Table 3.7 is to attempt to free ride, and the outcome of voluntary independent private-spending decisions for the public good is at (2, 2), and not the efficient outcome (3, 3).

Rather than voluntary spending, we can consider situations where decisions about public finance for public goods are made by voting. At (2, 2), no public goods are provided. At (3, 3), public goods are provided that symmetrically benefit both groups. At (4, 1) and (1, 4), a minority loses by paying taxes to finance public goods that benefit the majority.

If group 1 is in the majority, the outcome of majority voting is (4, 1) where group 1 benefits and group 2 pays. If group 2 is in the majority, the outcome of majority voting is (1, 4) where group 2 benefits and group 1 pays.

Majority voting thus results in an outcome that differs from voluntary personal financing decisions. We saw in Chapter 2 that voluntary financing results in the symmetric inefficient outcome at (2, 2). Majority voting results in an asymmetric outcome (4, 1) or (1, 4) depending on who is in the majority.

A rule can be introduced that forbids discriminatory (i.e., asymmetric) outcomes. The rule disallows the outcomes at (4, 1) and (1, 4), and so the vote is between (2, 2) and (3, 3).

When confronted with the choice between (2, 2) and (3, 3), members of both groups vote by consensus in favor of (3, 3), which is the alternative that gives higher personal benefit.

A rule forbidding discrimination in outcomes of majority voting on issues of public finance is therefore equivalent to a consensus rule. The rule of nondiscrimination eliminates outcomes where there is a division of voters into a majority and minority. The minority that is in evitable under majority voting can be protected by "checks and balances" provided through a nondiscrimination rule. Checks and balances are also provided by an independent judiciary, duplicated legislative bodies (such as a house of representatives and a senate) and divisions of political authority between executive and legislative branches of government.

3.1.10 Summary

We have considered majority voting as a means of making collective decisions about public spending on public goods. Majority voting is an alternative to making decisions about public spending on public goods by cost-benefit analysis of public projects.

We have seen that a consensus voting rule would ensure efficient public spending on public goods. Achieving the efficient consensus through voting would require voters to face their Lindahl prices as tax payments when voting takes place, and government does not know people's Lindahl prices.

With the Lindahl prices unknown, we considered an equal cost-sharing rule for determining personal tax payments to finance public goods and we looked at the majority voting equilibrium where the median voter is decisive in determining public spending. Majority voting in general pleases only the median voter. With the equal tax shares, even though it is possible for the median voter to make an efficient choice, in general the median voter does not vote for efficient public spending on public goods.

Majority voting can be subject to cycling. Because of cycling, there may be no determinate Condorcet winner. When cycling occurs, the order of voting (or the agenda) determines the outcome of majority voting.

Where stable outcomes of majority voting exist, collective decisions made by majority voting need not be consistent with the cost-benefit requirement for social desirability of a project that $W = B - C > 0$. We have seen that a public-good project that is the Condorcet winner may not be socially justified. A socially justified project can therefore be rejected through majority voting in favor of a project that is not socially justified.

"Popularity" through majority voting therefore does not ensure efficiency. The inconsistencies that can arise between majority voting and cost-benefit valuation are due to the type of information that people use to make voting decisions. Decisions about how to vote are based on personal rankings of alternatives and are not sensitive to values of personal benefits and costs nor to costs or benefits imposed on others. Taxpayers who are a minority may therefore lose more than the majority gains.

The minority may consequently be prepared to pay substantially more to change the outcome than the members of the majority need to be paid to change their vote. A market for buying and selling votes would rescue majority voting from the possibility of inconsistency with benefit-cost valuation. However, markets in which votes can be directly bought and sold are in general not allowed on the grounds that such markets contradict basic principles of democracy.

Legal vote trading takes place among politicians, not through money in exchange for votes, but through the exchange of votes for votes in a process known as logrolling. We have seen that when majority voting takes place under conditions of logrolling, there is no assurance that socially justified projects (i.e., projects that are efficient by cost-benefit valuation) receive majority support, while there can be majority support for projects that are not socially justified. Monetary payments for votes as an accompaniment of logrolling would ensure efficient collective decisions. However, monetary payments among elected representatives in exchange for votes are in general not permitted. Also, mechanisms that would allow compensating payments between gainers and losers in different political representatives' constituencies do not in general exist.

The problems of majority voting underlie incentives for a minority to wish to secede from a collective decision-making body. Secession is a change toward more homogeneous voting populations. That is, after secession, populations of voters are more similar in public-spending requirements. Secession is in general opposed by the majority, which has a financial incentive to keep the minority in its tax jurisdiction.

Problems of majority voting can be resolved or moderated by locational sorting for supply and financing of public goods. Secession then takes place, not through minority groups collectively exiting a collective-decision making body, but through individual location decisions.

A means of protecting a minority under majority voting is to limit outcomes to taxation and public spending decisions that are not discriminatory. When we look at voting decisions in the context of a prisoners' dilemma of public-good supply, a rule that limits choice to symmetric outcomes ensures efficient collective decisions where public finance does not disadvantage a minority with preferences that differ from the majority. Such a nondiscrimination rule is part of a system of checks and balances to accompany collective decisions made through majority voting.

In Chapter 1, the invisible hand allowed a case to be made for efficiency based on aggregation of personal market decisions. We have seen in this section that there is no assurance of efficient outcomes when personal decisions are aggregated through voting. Contrary to the assured personal benefits from voluntary transactions in markets, nor is there assurance that an individual necessarily gains from decisions made by majority voting – unless adequate checks and balances are present.

References and related literature

On voting rules, see Buchanan and Tullock (1962), Wickström (1986), and Guttman (1998). On cycling and single-peaked preferences, see Black (1948). On the median voter and efficient decisions, see Bowen (1943) and Bergstrom (1979). On inconsistency between majority voting and cost-benefit analysis, see Tullock (1959). For a perspective on markets for votes, see Kochin and Kochin (1998). On logrolling and extensions, see Bernholz (1977). On secession, see Buchanan and Faith (1987). On locational choice and voting, see Kollman, Miller, and Page (1997). On checks and balances, see Persson, Roland, and Tabellini (1997).

Bergstrom, T. C., 1979. When does majority rule provide public goods efficiency? *Scandinavian Journal of Economics* 81, 217–26.
Bernholz, P., 1977. Prisoners' dilemma, logrolling, and cyclical group preferences. *Public Choice* 29, 73–84.

Black, D., 1948. On the rationale of group decision making. *Journal of Political Economy* 56, 23–34. Reprinted 1969 in *Readings in Welfare Economics*. K. J. Arrow and T. Scitovsky (eds.). Richard D. Irwin, Homewood, Illinois, 133–46.

Bowen, H. R., 1943. The interpretation of voting in the allocation of economic resources. *Quarterly Journal of Economics* 58, 27–48. Reprinted 1969 in *Readings in Welfare Economics*. K. J. Arrow and T. Scitovsky (eds.). Richard D. Irwin, Homewood, Illinois, 115–32.

Buchanan, J. M. and R. L. Faith, 1987. Secession and the limits of taxation. *American Economic Review* 77, 1023–31.

Buchanan, J. M. and G. Tullock, 1962. *The Calculus of Consent: Logical Foundations of Constitutional Democracy*. University of Michigan Press, Ann Arbor.

Guttman, J. M., 1998. Unanimity and majority rule: The calculus of consent reconsidered. *European Journal of Political Economy* 14, 189–207.

Kochin, M. S. and L. A. Kochin, 1998. When is buying votes wrong? *Public Choice* 97, 645–62.

Kollman, K., J. H. Miller, and S. E. Page, 1997. Political institutions and sorting in a Tiebout model. *American Economic Review* 87, 977–92.

Persson, T., G. Roland and G. Tabellini, 1997. Separation of powers and political accountability. *Quarterly Journal of Economics* 112, 1163–1202.

Tullock, G., 1959. Problems of majority voting. *Journal of Political Economy* 67, 571–9. Reprinted 1969 in *Readings in Welfare Economics*. K. J. Arrow and T. Scitovsky (eds.). Richard D. Irwin, Homewood, Illinois, 169–78.

Wickström, B-A., 1986. Optimal majorities for decision rules of varying importance. *Public Choice* 48, 273–90.

Questions for discussion

1. "A Pareto improvement is assured if there has been agreement by a consensus vote." Do you agree? Is the converse true? That is, does Pareto efficiency imply the presence of consensus? What roles do compensation and extortion have in your answer?

2. If voters know that their Lindahl prices will determine their taxes, will voting result in efficient public spending on public goods? Why is a voting outcome using Lindahl prices to determine taxes not feasible? Could voting result in the efficient Lindahl outcome by chance?

3. "Public spending determined by a median voter only pleases the median voter." Does this statement suggest problems because the median voter is dictating public spending to others? Can the choice by the median voter be efficient public spending? Explain.

4. What is the relation between single-peaked preferences and the stability of collective decisions made by majority voting? Are individual preferences over public spending alternatives that are not single-peaked irrational? Explain

5. Why can setting the agenda for majority voting be decisive in determining the collective decision that is made?

6. In the votes that take place in Tables 3.3 and 3.4, suppose that taxpayer 1 compensates taxpayer 2 for voting for X instead of Y but does not compensate taxpayer 3. Is the coalition between taxpayers 1 and 2 stable? That is, can taxpayer 3 make any offer of compensating payment to again change the outcome of majority voting? Explain.

7. How would a market for votes prevent inefficient public spending determined through majority voting?

8. Why are markets in which citizens can buy and sell votes in general illegal?

9. Do you think logrolling should be allowed or banned? Would it be easy to ban logrolling? Explain.

10. Would the introduction of a market where politicians can buy or sell votes for money with their constituents' interests in mind change your view of logrolling?

11. Why does no mechanism exist that would allow compensating monetary payments for votes among constituencies of different elected representatives? If such a mechanism did exist or could be implemented, would you propose that the mechanism be legally allowed?

12. In Table 3.6, only one logrolling agreement can provide positive benefits to members of a logrolling coalition. Rather than the constituency of representative 3 receiving a benefit of 20 from project F, suppose that the benefit is 40. What are the benefits now from different possible logrolling agreements for each representative's constituency? What differences now arise compared to the case where the benefits to the constituency of representative 3 from project F were 20?

13. Why does majority voting provide incentives for secession from a collective decision-making body that decides on taxes and public spending? Why would we expect a majority to oppose secession?

14. Individual secession takes place when individuals leave one government jurisdiction for another that provides different combinations and quantities of public goods and levies different taxes. How does such locational choice contribute to solving problems when decisions about public finance are made by majority voting?

15. Restraint on the outcomes expressed through the prisoners' dilemma ensures that majority voting does not disadvantage a minority of voters. What is the nature of the restraint?

16. Identify checks and balances in collective decision-making procedures in the place where you live or study. Are the checks and balances equally present at all levels of government? Would you expect checks and balances to be more prominent at federal or central levels of government than at local levels of government? How does your answer relate to personal locational choices available among governments?

17. What is the general conclusion that you draw about the comparison between personal decisions made in markets and collective decisions made through majority voting?

18. In the light of your answer to question 17, do you agree with the statement, "personal market decisions where possible are preferable to collective decisions made through majority voting on both efficiency and social-justice grounds." Explain.

3.2

Political Competition and Public Spending

The conclusions about majority voting in Section 3.1 apply whether taxpayers vote directly on public spending or elected representatives vote on behalf of taxpayers. When voting is by elected representatives, there will have been previous *political competition* among candidates who sought to be chosen as taxpayers' representatives. In the competition for elected office, the political candidates will have announced their policies, and the winning candidate will have been chosen by voters. In this section, we investigate the characteristics of policy determination through such political competition. Our objective is to establish whether political competition provides taxpayers with a satisfactory means for making collective decisions about taxation and public spending on public goods.

3.2.1 Direct and representative democracy

Under direct democracy, taxpayers decide directly on issues of public finance. For example, they can vote on whether public spending should be financed through taxation or government borrowing, on how high taxes should be and the form of taxation, and on the purposes of public spending.

In general, however, voters' decisions are made not through direct democracy but under representative democracy. Under representative democracy, voters elect representatives who vote on their behalf.

The prevalence of representative democracy reflects the high costs of seeking each individual voter's opinion on each issue. There may also have been a feeling that public spending decisions should be made by political representatives, who could dedicate their time to studying the issues to be decided, and who would therefore be in a position to make better informed decisions than voters at large.

Over time, information technology has diminished the costs of direct voting. Coded transmission through the internet and e-mail can allow voters to express views on issues under conditions of confidentiality, while at the same time allowing verification that people have the right to vote and that they have only voted once on each issue. Communications technology has provided means for voters to become better informed. The internet provides information with an immediacy that was not possible when systems of representative democracy were first established.

Switzerland provides comparative evidence on differences between direct and representative democracy. In Switzerland, some cantons rely more on direct democracy than others. The evidence from Switzerland on collective decision making in the two types of voting systems indicates that taxpayers are personally better informed about issues when decisions are made under direct democracy. There is a smaller incentive for "rational ignorance" under direct democracy because voters participate directly in the collective decision through the votes they cast. Because information is more useful, voters rationally acquire more information. Besides voters being better informed, there appears to be greater personal satisfaction among the population under direct democracy because of greater personal involvement in collective decisions. Under direct democracy, substantive issues of public finance become part of everyday discussion among voters. People ask each other, "how are you going to vote?" and "why?"[1]

---

[1] Lars Feld and Gebhard Kirchgässner (2000) reviewed the Swiss evidence on comparisons between direct and representative democracy.

TABLE 3.8. OSTROGORSKI'S PARADOX

	A = Stadium	B = Freeway	C = Museum of modern art
Group 1 (20%)	No (candidate 1)	No (candidate 1)	Yes (candidate 2)
Group 2 (20%)	No (candidate 1)	Yes (candidate 2)	No (candidate 1)
Group 3 (20%)	Yes (candidate 2)	No (candidate 1)	No (candidate 1)
Group 4 (40%)	Yes (candidate 2)	Yes (candidate 2)	Yes (candidate 2)

Ostrogorski's paradox

The outcomes of voting under direct and representative democracy need not co-incide. The failure of direct voting and outcomes under representative democracy to coincide is known as Ostrogorski's paradox (after Moise Ostrogorski, 1903; see also Hannu Nurmi 1997, 1999). Table 3.8 illustrates Ostrogorski's paradox for three public spending proposals A, B, and C. Project A is, for example, a sports stadium, project B is a freeway, and project C is a museum of modern art. Taxes can be levied to finance any and all projects, if there is majority support from voters.

The voters in Table 3.8 are divided into four groups with different preferences for public spending. A "yes" indicates that a group favors a project, whereas a "no" indicates that a group opposes a project. We see that voters in group 1 oppose the stadium and the freeway but favor the museum. Voters in group 2 oppose the stadium and the museum but favor the freeway. Voters in group 3 oppose the freeway and the museum but favor the stadium. Voters in group 4 are in favor of all three projects. Groups 1, 2, and 3 each contain 20 percent of voters, and group 4 contains the remaining 40 percent of voters.

In a vote under direct democracy, voters decide on each issue separately. There are then three distinct questions on which a vote is taken, whether to levy taxes to finance projects A, B, and C.

When a vote is taken directly on whether to use public funds for project A (the stadium), a majority votes in favor (the majority consists of 40 percent in group 4 plus the 20 percent in group 3). When a vote is taken directly on project B (whether to construct the freeway), a majority votes in favor (the 40 percent in group 4 plus the 20 percent in group 2). When a vote is taken directly on project C (whether to use tax proceeds for the museum of modern art), a majority also votes in favor (the 40 percent in group 4 plus the 20 percent in group 1). Under direct voting, therefore, voters support taxation and public spending for all three projects.

Under representative democracy, two competing candidates announce policies regarding all three projects. That is, under representative democracy, issues are bundled rather than decided separately. Voters support a political candidate whose position regarding the bundled issues more closely approximates their spending preferences for the three projects.

Candidate 1 opposes public spending on any of the projects. Candidate 2 favors government spending on all the projects. In Table 3.8, wherever there is a "no" regarding public spending, we therefore see candidate 1, and wherever there is a "yes" regarding public spending we see candidate 2.

When a vote is taken, voters in groups 1, 2, and 3 vote for candidate 1. This candidate supports their position on two issues, while candidate 2 supports their position on only one issue. Voters in group 4 however support candidate 2, whose pro-spending position coincides precisely with their preference for spending on all projects.

The outcome of political competition is therefore that candidate 1 wins with 60 percent of the vote, against 40 percent for candidate 2. No public spending therefore takes place for any of the projects. Correspondingly, no taxes are levied or bonds sold to finance any of the projects.

The public spending outcome under representative democracy is therefore the precise opposite of the outcome under direct democracy. Under direct democracy, a majority supports each project. Under representative democracy, political competition results in the election of the candidate who has declared that he or she will implement none of the projects.

Which outcome is preferred?

We do not know from the information in Table 3.8 whether the outcome of direct or representative democracy is preferred. When a group favors a project, we presume the net benefits to the voters in the group from the project are positive; when a group objects to a project, we can presume that the project imposes a net cost on the voters in that group. To determine whether a project is socially justified, we need to be able to add the benefits and the costs for the different groups of taxpayers. We established in Section 3.1 that the outcome of majority voting cannot reveal whether a project is socially justified (i.e., efficient) by the benefit-cost criterion. The projects in Table 3.8 may or may not be justified, and so we cannot make a judgment about the efficiency consequences of Ostrogorski's paradox.

Representative democracy can save a society from inefficient projects that would be accepted under direct majority voting and can just as well stop efficient projects. The disconcerting aspect of Ostrogorski's paradox is the contradiction between outcomes of majority voting under direct democracy and representative democracy.

3.2.2 Political competition with a single policy issue

Ostrogorski's paradox provides an example of political competition as a means of making collective decisions. We shall now investigate political competition more generally. We begin with the simplest setting for political competition. *Two* candidates for political office take policy positions regarding public spending on a

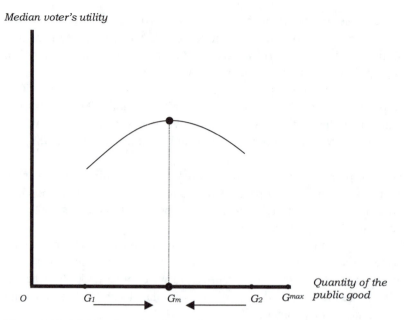

Figure 3.10. The preferred policy of the median voter is a stable equilibrium for policies of two candidates.

single public good. The supply of this public good is the only collective decision that voters face. Figure 3.10 shows the quantity of the public good.

Taxpayers know their tax obligations for financing the public good. Given their tax obligations, they choose their personally preferred supply of the public good along the line in Figure 3.10.

Taxpayers' preferences are single peaked (see Section 3.1); that is, each taxpayer has a unique preferred quantity, and the utility of a taxpayer declines when quantities provided are further away from the preferred quantity. Figure 3.10 shows the median voter's utility from availability of the public good. Utility of the median voter declines with departures from G_m, which is the preferred quantity of the median voter. G^{max} is the maximal quantity sought by any voter. The distribution of taxpayers over the range of quantities (or public spending) is uniform, and taxpayers vote for a candidate who proposes supply of the public good that is closest to their preferred choice. All voters vote; there are no abstentions. Two political candidates choose their policy positions with the objective of winning the election.

Suppose that candidate 1 begins with a proposal that quantity G_1 should be provided and that candidate 2 proposes a quantity G_2. The policy proposals G_1 and G_2 are not an equilibrium. We apply the Nash equilibrium: in an equilibrium, no candidate wishes to change his or her announced policy, given the announced policy of the competing candidate.

The candidates are assured of support from voters whose preferences are more extreme than their policy pronouncements. That is, in Figure 3.10, all taxpayers who ideally want G_1 or less vote for candidate 1 when candidate 1 announces the policy G_1, and all taxpayers who ideally want G_2 or more vote for candidate 2. Taxpayers who want quantities between G_1 and G_2 make their voting decisions based on whether their preferred supply is closer to G_1 or G_2.

Under these conditions, the candidates have incentives to move their policies to the preferred supply of the median voter. The equilibrium is where both candidates propose to supply the quantity sought by the median voter.

A candidate requires more than 50 percent of the votes to win. It is in principle possible to have support from more than 50 percent of voters without having the support of the median voter. For example, the support of 50 percent of voters might be sought from the 25 percent of voters seeking lowest public-good supply and the 26 percent seeking highest public-good supply. A winning majority would then not include the median voter. Such a voter coalition could not however be an equilibrium. There is only one equilibrium outcome of political competition, and this is where candidates have both announced the supply G_m in Figure 3.10 sought by the median voter. In the equilibrium, the candidates and their policies are therefore indistinguishable, and the median voter is decisive.

The idea underlying convergence of policies is associated with Harold Hotelling (1895–1973), and the outcome is known as the Hotelling equilibrium. See Hotelling (1929). The outcome of convergence of candidates' policies is a Nash equilibrium because, given the policy position taken by the opposing candidate, a candidate cannot improve his or her election prospects by taking any another policy position.

Abstention and alienation

When candidates converge to the Hotelling equilibrium, they rely on continued maintained support from "locked-in" voters on the left or right of their policy position in Figure 3.10. Voters may, however, be alienated by the perceived opportunism of a candidate in moving to the middle to attract the support of the median voter and may respond by abstaining from voting. If abstentions are known in advance, a new constituency of voters who do not abstain is defined, and the median voter of the new constituency determines the equilibrium policy. If for example the voters on the extreme left of the spectrum in Figure 3.10 announce that they intend to abstain, the median voter is moved further to the right. The announced abstention has therefore come at a cost to those abstaining because the position of the median voter that determines the equilibrium policy has been moved further from the preferred policies of the abstainers.

However, if abstentions are random and unknown to the candidates before the election, candidates can do no better than to announce the median voter's policy for the entire population of voters.

A third candidate

A third person with political aspirations might observe the two candidates du- plicating the median voters' preferred position. The third person might become a candidate for political office and announce a policy that appeals to one of the

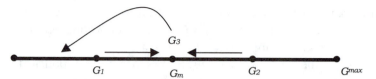

Figure 3.11. Absence of a stable equilibrium policy with three candidates.

extremes of the electorate. The change from two to three candidates has profound consequences. There is now no equilibrium policy. Figure 3.11 describes a political contest with three candidates. Candidate 3 has initially chosen the policy G_3 at the preferred policy of the median voter, and candidates 1 and 2 initially announce the policies of public spending to supply the quantities G_1 and G_2. Candidates 1 and 2 have, however, incentives to change their policies to converge to the median voter's position at G_m.

As the policy positions of candidates 1 and 2 converge toward G_m, political support from voters for candidate 3 declines because more taxpayers find their personally preferred positions closer to the policies of the two candidates who are converging toward the median position. At some point, in response to the decline in political support as candidates 1 and 2 converge toward G_m, candidate 3 will decide to jump, either to the left or the right. In Figure 3.11, the jump is to the left. The jump of candidate 3 places candidate 1 in the middle. Candidate 1 will then in turn have an incentive to jump as candidates 2 and 3 converge toward the middle.

The jumps in policy by the candidate in the middle take place because winning an election requires more than the support of just the median voter. To win, a candidate requires the support of an additional 50 percent of voters *besides* the median voter. Positioning of policy at the median voter's preferred policy G_m therefore cannot ensure a candidate electoral success. Indeed, such positioning ensures defeat when other candidates are drawing away political support by converging toward the median.

Since the candidate positioned in the middle near the median voter eventually jumps, there is no equilibrium for political competition among three candidates.

When the political contest is extended to more than three candidates, stability can be restored, depending on how many candidates there are.[2]

Why complete policy convergence is not observed

The complete duplication of policy positions predicted by the two-candidate model of political competition is not usually observed. Duplication eliminates the basis for a political contest by giving voters no way of choosing between candidates.

In Figure 3.10, the preferred policy of the median voter may, however, not be known to the two candidates. The candidates may conduct opinion polls in an attempt to identify the position of the median voter but still may not know the policy preferences of the median voter with certainty. Candidates with different

---

[2] See Selten (1971) and Supplement 3A.

perceptions of the identity of the median voter might then choose different policies. The candidate who wins the election is the candidate who is more accurate in identifying the position of the median voter.

Even if the location of the median voter is known, the candidates have reason *not* to duplicate their policies. When policies are precisely duplicated, the candidates present themselves to voters as an identical Tweedledum and Tweedledee.[3] The candidates might be seeking campaign contributions, but if the candidates announce precisely the same policy they receive no campaign contributions because political contributors have no reason to prefer one candidate to the other. Candidates provide incentives for political contributors to give them money by distinguishing themselves from one another, by moving away from each other's policy positions. The more they move away from one another's policies, the more campaign contributions they can hope to receive from political contributors.[4]

Another reason for incomplete convergence is ideological commitment by political candidates. The behavioral hypothesis underlying policy convergence is that candidates choose policies to win elections. An alternative behavioral hypothesis is that candidates have policy principles that they are not prepared to compromise, and that they participate in elections with the hope (perhaps forlorn) of winning an election in order to implement their preferred policies. Candidates' own policy preferences, and not the preferred policy of the median voter, then determine their policy pronouncements. For example, in Figure 3.10, the candidate declaring a policy of G_1 may believe as a matter of principle that taxation and public spending should be modest and may not be prepared to compromise his or her principles by converging to the median policy. A candidate adhering to principles always loses against a more flexible candidate who chooses a policy pronouncement with the intent of winning the election.

3.2.3 Political competition with multiple issues

We now turn our attention to a contest between two political candidates when there are two separate policy issues. The two issues are public spending on two different public goods. We shall see that in general increasing the number of issues from one to two eliminates stable outcomes of majority voting for two-candidate political contests.

A voter's preferences over supplies of two public goods

Figure 3.12 shows quantities of two public goods X and Y. Preferred public spending for voter 1 on the public goods is at the point 1. That is, voter 1 ideally wants the quantities X_1 and Y_1 of the two public goods. Voter 1's utility declines as the distance from the preferred point 1 increases in any direction.

---

[3] Tweedledum and Tweedledee are identical characters in Lewis Carroll's nineteenth-century children's story *Alice in Wonderland*.

[4] In Chapter 6, we investigate in more detail the trade-off that politicians confront between voter support and campaign contributions to finance political expenses.

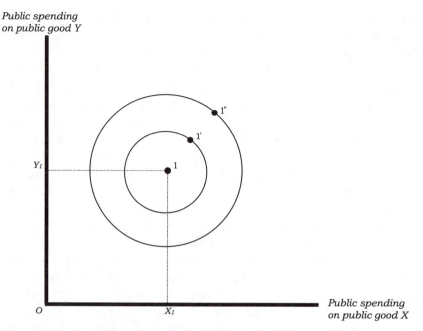

Figure 3.12. A voter's preferred combination of public spending.

Point 1 is the voter's preferred public spending point. The voter's utility decreases with the distance from point 1, and the voter is indifferent between spending alternatives on a circle (points on a circle are equidistant from the preferred point 1).

In Figure 3.12, the indifference curves that define fixed utility levels are concentric circles around point 1.[5] Point 1′ on the inner circle provides more of both public goods than point 1. Point 1″ in turn provides more of both public goods than point 1′. Nonetheless, point 1 with less of both public goods is preferred to either point 1′ or point 1″. Usually more goods are preferred to fewer goods, but this is not the case in Figure 3.12. The reason is that the voter in Figure 3.12 derives utility from goods other than the two public goods X and Y. Let us denote voter 1's private consumption of all other goods by Z. The voter's utility is made up of the benefit from the public goods X and Y, as well as the benefit from private consumption Z. Figure 3.12 shows only the benefit from the two public goods X and Y. That is, Figure 3.12 separates the utility from the public goods from the utility derived from private consumption.

Public spending on the public goods X and Y is financed by taxes, and spending on other goods Z is privately financed through personal market expenditure. Voter 1 in Figure 3.12 has a limited demand for spending on the public goods because personal income left after payment of taxes to finance the supply of the public goods is available to be spent on other consumption Z. That is, voter 1

---

[5] Voter 1 is indifferent in Figure 3.12 among all points on any concentric circle. All points on a circle are equally distant from the preferred point 1, and voter 1 is therefore indifferent among the alternative points on a concentric circle. The voter is better off at a point on the inner circle than the outer circle because the inner circle is closer to the preferred point 1.

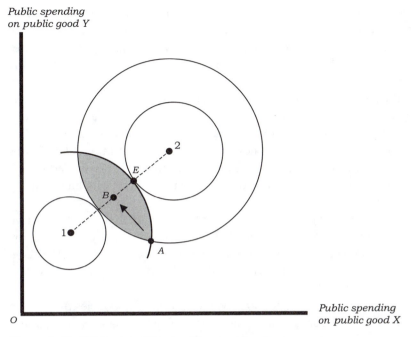

Figure 3.13. Efficient public spending proposals.
Public spending proposals on the contract curve are efficient. Through majority voting, an efficient proposal will always defeat an inefficient proposal.

wants to have income available for personal spending on private consumption Z. Because of the voter's demand for private consumption Z, the voter ideally wants to be taxed no more than the personal taxes required to finance the quantities of the public goods at point 1, when others are also paying taxes determined by their tax obligations.

A political candidate can be assured of voter 1's support by proposing to supply the combination of public goods at voter 1's ideal point 1. If, however, no candidate proposes precisely the combination of public-good supply at point 1, the voter will support a candidate whose supply proposal for public goods is closest to point 1.

Figure 3.13 introduces preferences for public spending of an additional voter, whose preferred spending is at point 2. We see that voter 2 ideally wants more of both public goods to be supplied than voter 1 (i.e., the second voter ideally wants greater public spending on public goods than voter 1).

The contract curve

We define a contract curve as the line that joins points of tangency of voters' indifference curves. The contract curve in Figure 3.13 for voters 1 and 2 is the straight line joining points 1 and 2.

All points on the contract curve are Pareto-efficient. That is, once on the contract curve, it is not possible to move to another combination of supply of the public goods without making at least one of the voters worse off.

For example, beginning from point E in Figure 3.13, moving toward point 1 along the contract curve makes voter 1 better off and makes voter 2 worse off. Moving toward point 2 along the contract curve conversely makes voter 2 better off and voter 1 worse off. Moving off the contract curve makes one or both of the voters worse off.[6]

A political candidate whose policy proposal is on the contract curve always defeats a candidate who proposes a policy off the contract curve. For example, suppose that, with two candidates for political office, candidate 1 proposes public goods supply at the point A, which is not on the contract curve. Candidate 2 wins the support of voters 1 and 2 by proposing a policy anywhere in the shaded area in Figure 3.13, since points in the shaded area provide both voters with higher utility than at the point A.

In particular, by choosing a policy such as at the point B on the contract curve in Figure 3.13, candidate 2 assures that there is no possible policy response by candidate 1 that can win away the support of both voters. For, as we have seen, once on the contract curve, there is no alternative policy that can make both voters better off.

We therefore conclude that candidates will only announce policies that are on a contract curve. When looking for equilibrium policy pronouncements (where candidates have no incentive to change their pronouncements), we can therefore confine our attention to policies on a contract curve.

Three voters

Three voters allow us to consider outcomes of majority voting. Figure 3.14 introduces a third voter, whose preferred public-good supply is at point 3.

There are now three contract curves. One contract curve joins each pair of voters' preferred points. The three contract curves make a triangle joining the points 1, 2, and 3.

Suppose that candidate 1 has chosen a policy position at the point E in Figure 3.14 on the contract curve for voters 1 and 3. Because E is on the contract curve for voters 1 and 3, indifference curves (the circles) of these voters are tangential at the point E.

An indifference curve (the dark curve) of voter 2 also passes through point E.[7] The indifference curve of voter 2 can be used to define points on the other contract curves where two voters prefer the spending policy to candidate 1's policy position E. On the contract curve for voters 1 and 2, all points on the wide gray area are preferred by voters 1 and 2 to the point E. In particular, voters 1 and 2 prefer the policy at point S to that at point E. A second candidate who announces

---

[6] Only one of the voters is worse off when the move off the contract curve is along an indifference curve; for example, a move from point E in Figure 3.13 along the inner concentric circle of voter 2 makes voter 2 no worse off, but voter 1's utility falls. A move off the contract curve from the point B to a point inside the gray area makes both persons worse off.

[7] An indifference curve (circle) for every voter passes through each and every point so that, at each point, we know a voter's utility.

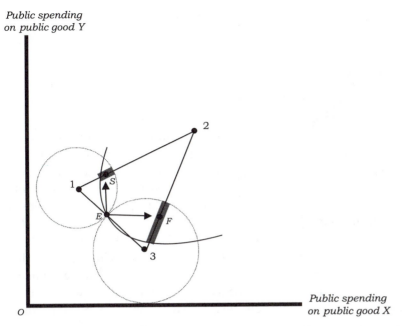

Figure 3.14. *The instability of spending proposals with political competition between two candidates with two issues.*

Public spending proposals such as those at points *S* and *F* defeat the proposal at *E* by majority voting. Since the public spending proposal at *E* was an arbitrary choice, any public spending proposal can always be defeated through majority voting by other proposals. There is no stable outcome.

the spending policy at *S* when candidate 1 has announced the spending policy at *E* therefore wins the election because voters 1 and 2 support the second candidate, and only voter 3 supports candidate 1 (since voter 3 is better off at *E* than at *S*).

Alternatively, when candidate 1 has announced the policy at *E*, candidate 2 can also win the election by announcing a policy such as that at *F*. After candidate 2 has announced the policy at *F*, candidate 1 whose policy is at *E* has the support of only voter 1. Voters 2 and 3 are better off at *F* than at *E* and support candidate 2.[8]

Suppose that candidate 2 responds to candidate 1's policy at *E* by announcing the policy at *S*. Candidate 2 would win the election if candidate 1 maintained the original policy announcement at *E*. Once candidate 2 has chosen *S*, candidate 1 can however readily find a policy that defeats *S*. There are points on the contract curves for voters 1 and 3, and also on the contract curve for voters 2 and 3, that provide majority support for public spending and taxation policies relative to *S*.

---

[8] Point *E* is off the contact curve for voters 2 and 3, while point *F* is on the contract curve for these two voters. As we have seen, a point can always be found on the contract curve that makes two voters better off, compared to a point off the contract curve.

Or, similarly, candidate 1 can find a policy that defeats F.[9] The process is never-ending, with no stable outcome.

The implications for incumbency

There is no Nash equilibrium in policy pronouncements in Figure 3.14 with candidates making simultaneous pronouncements. With sequential declarations, there is an advantage to being the last candidate to take a policy position. The last candidate to choose a policy position is able to take an assured winning policy position, if the other candidate has declared and maintains his or her policy. Political incumbents are therefore at a disadvantage when seeking reelection because voters will have observed an incumbent's policy during the incumbent politician's time in office, which provides a competing candidate with the opportunity to choose a different policy with majority support.

Incumbency is not, however, in general a disadvantage. Rather, incumbents often systematically win reelection. The success of incumbents in winning reelection suggests that reputation is a source of political advantage. The incumbent's reliability is known, but that of the challenger is not. An incumbent's reelection prospects can also be enhanced by political favors that have been possible during the incumbent's term in office.[10]

A case where a stable median-voter policy exists

Figure 3.15 shows a case where a stable outcome of political competition exists. In Figure 3.15, the preferred policies of all three voters lie along the same straight line GH, which combines all contract curves for the three voters. This is of course a very special case that could occur only coincidentally. In this case, the two separate issues of how much to spend on X and how much to spend on Y have been reduced to a single issue, which is where along the line GH public spending should be. Voter 2 is the median voter on this single issue, and the unique stable equilibrium outcome of majority voting is voter 2's preferred point 2.[11]

The relative price of the public goods and total public spending

Suppose that the slope of GH happened to be the relative price of the two public goods X and Y. In that case, besides being the all-inclusive contract curve, the line GH also describes a level of public spending on the two public goods. We can then interpret the voters in Figure 3.15 as agreeing on the level of public spending but disagreeing on the composition of public spending between the public goods X and Y.

---

[9] Such policies exist on the contract curve between voters 1 and 2 or on the contract curve between voters 1 and 3.

[10] The saying, "better the devil that you know than the devil you do not know," may guide voters who are imperfectly informed about political candidates who are challenging incumbents.

[11] The vote determines movement along the contract curve. At any point, voters are asked the question, do you want to move further toward the point 2? Whether the point 2 is approached from below or above along the contract curve, there is a majority in favor of change at every point except at point 2.

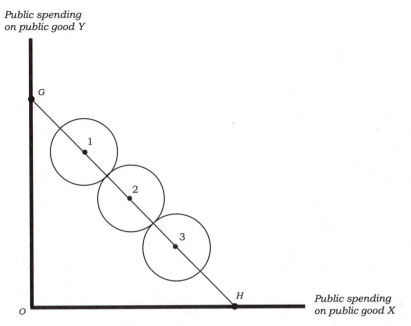

*Public spending
on public good Y*

*Public spending
on public good X*

Figure 3.15. A stable policy proposal.

Choice of public spending on public goods X and Y is a single issue, which is choice along the line GH. There is a stable median-voter equilibrium at the point 2.

In general, the relative price of the public goods is not equal to the slope of the contract curve. There is no necessary relation between the relative price of public goods and the slope of a contract curve.[12] Figure 3.16 repeats Figure 3.15 for the more usual case where the slope of the contract curve and the relative price of the public goods differ. The relative price of the public goods is indicated as the common slope of the dotted lines.[13]

Each voter in Figure 3.16 not only wants a different combination of public goods along the contract curve but also a different level of public spending.[14] A stable majority-voting equilibrium in figure 3.16 again exists at the preferred outcome of the median voter 2 at point 2.

All that is required for the existence of a stable outcome of majority voting as in Figures 3.15 and 3.16 is that the contract curve for the voters form one straight line. The relative price of public goods has no role in determining the existence of the stable majority-voting equilibrium. Nor does the relative price of the public

[12] For example, the contract curve can have a positive slope, while the slope of the line indicating the relative price of public goods is always negative.
[13] The relative price of the public goods, under conditions of competitive supply is the relation between the MC of public good X and the MC of public good Y.
[14] The preferred level of public spending is given by the value of the combination of public goods at a voter's preferred point. The valuation of the public goods is at the relative price given by the slope of the dotted lines.

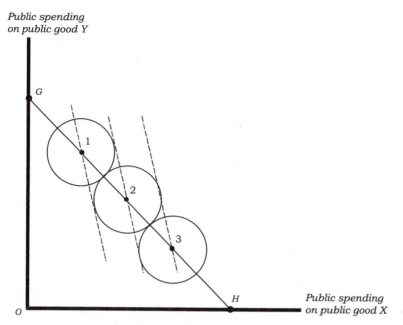

Figure 3.16. The relative price of public goods and the contract curve.

goods have a role in the conclusion that, with two candidates and two policy questions, there is no stable policy equilibrium for majority voting in the general case.

3.2.4 Principled political behavior

We have described political candidates as declaring policy positions with the objective of gaining majority support from voters to win elections. An alternative view is that political candidates have principles about the type of policies they wish to implement, and that the reason they wish to win elections is to be able to implement their preferred policies.

We have observed how, in the case of political competition between two candidates with a single issue, principled candidates confront a problem when their chosen policy positions do not have the support of a majority of voters. By adhering to principles and maintaining policy positions that do not have majority support, political candidates can only resign themselves to electoral defeat.

To see the similar consequences of principled policy positions taken by political candidates when there are two issues, we return to Figure 3.14. Let us again simplify by supposing that the slope of the contract curve joining points 1 and 3 in Figure 3.14 is also the relative price of the two public goods.[15] The contract curve joining points 1 and 3 then also represents a level of public spending on the two public goods. Voter 2 in Figure 3.14 seeks greater total public spending for public

[15] As we have noted, the relative price of the public goods in general differs from the slope of the contract curve.

goods than voters 1 and 3. Voters 1 and 3 agree about the level of public spending but disagree about the composition of spending between the two public goods.

Voters 1 and 3 have a substantive disagreement with voter 2 over the "size of government," or about total taxes that should be collected by government for financing public spending. Voter 2 wants high government tax revenue and high public spending, while voters 1 and 3 want tax revenue and public spending to be more modest. Voter 2 might favor high taxes and public spending because he or she has low income and pays lower taxes than voters 1 and 3. Or voter 2 might pay the same in taxes as voters 1 and 3 but might simply prefer more of the public goods at the expense of lower private consumption.

A political candidate who personally sympathizes with voter 2's preference for high taxation and public spending could, as a matter of principle, take a policy position at the preferred point 2 of voter 2. This candidate might, moreover, as a matter of personal integrity, maintain an announced policy of high taxes and public spending in the face of the opportunity to change to a policy position that wins more votes.

The candidate who prefers high taxation and high spending might maintain this policy position in the hope that voters' preferences will change, or in the hope that voters will prefer a committed candidate to a candidate who opportunistically responds to perceived changes in voters' preferences. Nonetheless, principled behavior by a political candidate will in general not help to win an election when the preferences of the majority of voters are closer to the policy position of the other candidate. The candidate precommitted by principle to a position (*any* position) will always lose because an opposing candidate who chooses policy declarations strategically can always choose a policy that will have majority support over a maintained policy position.

Voters with principles

We have described voters as maximizing personal benefit or utility by supporting a political candidate whose policy provides a voter with highest personal benefit. Voters may however be guided by principles that extend beyond their personal benefit when they vote. To illustrate voter principles, we return once more to Figure 3.14. With the contract curve between voters 1 and 3 again indicating the relative price of the two public goods, suppose that voters 1 and 3 decide, as a matter of principle, that they will not support higher public spending than indicated by the position of their contract curve. These voters therefore support a candidate who proposes a policy along their contract curve in preference to a candidate with a policy position that offers them higher personal utility but that requires greater public spending and taxation. When in Figure 3.14 a candidate has announced the policy at the point E on the contract curve between voters 1 and 3, voter 1 will therefore continue to support this candidate in preference to a candidate who proposes the policy at S, even though voter 1's personal benefit is higher at S.[16] Voter 3

---

[16] That is, at point F, voter 3 is on a higher indifference curve than he or she is at point E.

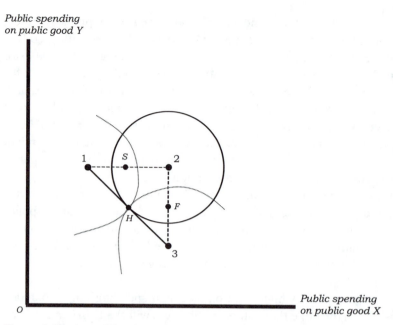

*Public spending
on public good Y*

*Public spending
on public good X*

Figure 3.17. A coalition based on preference for low public spending.

Voters 1 and 3 oppose greater public spending than along the line joining points 1 and 3. Voter 2 is the decisive median voter.

will similarly not support a candidate who proposes the policy at F, although voter 3's personal benefit is higher at point F. Voters 1 and 3 both subordinate personal utility to the principle of limiting public spending and taxation.

Although voters 1 and 3 agree on the principle of containing public spending and taxation, voter 1 wants the composition of spending to be at point 1, while voter 3 wants the combination of public spending to be at point 3. In these circumstances, voter 2 now becomes the decisive voter. We see this in Figure 3.17.

In Figure 3.17, voter 2's utility is maximized on the contract curve of voters 1 and 3 at point H. The policy position at H is a majority-voting equilibrium. Along the contract curve, voters 2 and 3 oppose a movement away from H toward point 1, while voters 1 and 2 oppose a movement away from H toward point 3. There is no majority support for a movement away from H to a point below the contract curve between 1 and 3. As a matter of principle, voters 1 and 3 reject higher public spending than at H and so reject any point above the contract curve. Therefore, there is no majority support for a change of policy from H, and accordingly H is a majority-voting policy equilibrium.

Figure 3.18 shows a converse case where voter 2 ideally wants less public spending on public goods (and less taxation) than voters 1 and 3. With voters 1 and 3 committed on principle to greater public spending than that sought by voter 2, voter 2 is once more the decisive voter, and there is a stable majority-voting equilibrium at the point H'.

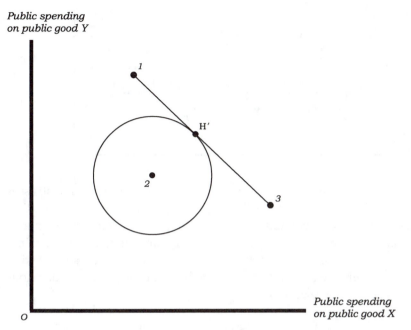

Figure 3.18. A coalition based on preference for high public spending.
Voters 1 and 3 favor high public spending, and voter 2 is the decisive voter.

The personal economic cost of principled behavior

Commitment to principle, whether by candidates or voters, thus results in policy stability. However, commitment to principle has a personal price. Principled candidates deny themselves policy flexibility and lose elections. Voters who maintain principled positions refrain from supporting policies that could increase their well-being defined in terms of personal economic benefits. Principled voters do not, however, have utility functions that depend on quantities of goods consumed alone. Their perception of their welfare depends on their self-discipline in adhering to their principles, in this case regarding the size of government or levels of taxation and public spending.

The incentive to form "political parties"

In Figures 3.17 and 3.18, neither voter 1 nor voter 3 might be sure about whether the other can be trusted to maintain a principled position. Voter 1 could harm voter 3 by deviating from the principle regarding the size of public spending to support policies based on personal economic self-benefit. Similarly, voter 3 could harm taxpayer 1.[17] If the voters distrust one another, we return to the instability of outcomes of political competition under majority voting, since, without the constraint of voting according to principle, no policy has sustainable majority

---

[17] In Figure 3.17, if voter 3 supports a political candidate who announces the policy at F, voter 1 loses. In the same way, by supporting a candidate who announces the policy at S, voter 1 reduces voter 3's welfare.

TABLE 3.9. ELIMINATION TWO-ROUND VOTING

Ranking of group 1 (4 voters)	Ranking of group 2 (2 voters)	Ranking of group 3 (3 voters)
A	B	C
B	C	B
C	A	A

support over any other. A means for voters 1 and 3 to avoid mutual distrust is for a coalition between them to be formalized as a "political party." The political party serves the purpose of committing members to a principle regarding public spending (small in Figure 3.17 or large in Figure 3.18) and eliminates uncertainty about whether voters will support policies (that we have seen necessarily exist) that will improve their personal well-being by departure from principled decisions about taxation and public spending.

3.2.5 Systems of voting
In the preceding cases of political competition, winning candidates are chosen by majority voting. Other systems of voting are also used. We shall now consider other voting systems.

Elimination two-round voting
A commonly used system of voting allows for a second-round of voting if (with more than two candidates) no candidate receives a majority (over 50 percent) in the first round. The two candidates with the greatest number of votes in the first round proceed to the second round, and all other candidates are eliminated.

In Table 3.9, we see the ranking of three groups of taxpayers over three alternative projects A, B, and C. Three candidates compete for political office. Each candidate represents one of the three groups. In a first round of voting, the candidate representing group 1 receives four votes, the candidate of group 2 receives two votes, and the candidate of group 3 receives three votes. No candidate wins by majority voting (a majority over 50 percent) in the first round.

A second round of voting then takes place, with the candidate of group 2, who received the lowest number of votes in the first round, eliminated. In the second round, voters in group 2 vote for the candidate of group 3, since these voters prefer C to A. The candidate of group 3 therefore wins in the second round, and the project C is financed, through public spending.

The Condorcet winner in Table 3.9 is, however, B.[18] The system of elimination two-round voting has therefore not selected the Condorcet winner.

---

[18] We see in Table 3.9 that B defeats A by 5 votes to 4, and B defeats C by 6 votes to 3.

TABLE 3.10. PLURALITY OR SIMPLE MAJORITY VOTING		
Ranking of group 1 (3 voters)	Ranking of group 2 (2 voters)	Ranking of group 3 (2 voters)
A	B	C
B	C	B
C	A	A

Plurality or simple majority voting

The system of elimination using two-round voting is based on majority voting. In an alternative to majority voting, a simple majority (any majority with possibly less than 50 percent support, or in other words a plurality) is sufficient to win a political contest. There is one round of voting in which voters vote for their preferred choice.

When there are two candidates, plurality voting is equivalent to majority voting.

When there are more than two candidates, the winning candidate does not need the support of more than 50 percent of the voters. In Table 3.10, we see seven voters divided into three groups. When voting takes place under a plurality rule, the candidate of group 1 wins (since the candidate of group 1 has the support of three voters, and the other two candidates each have the support of two voters). Project A, which is the preferred project of group 1, is therefore financed through the government budget.

By majority voting, project B is preferred to project A by four votes to three, and project B is preferred to project C by five votes to two. Project B is the Condorcet winner, but the candidate whose constituency wants project A has won the election.

Moreover, the winning project A under plurality voting can be the least-favored alternative under majority voting. That is, the winner under the plurality rule can be the Condorcet loser. We see this is the case in Table 3.10, where project A chosen under plurality voting is defeated by both projects B and C, in each case by four votes to three.

Under plurality voting, a Condorcet winner therefore need not be chosen as the collective choice, and the collective choice can be the Condorcet loser from among the alternatives. Nevertheless, the plurality or simple majority rule is commonly used for making collective decisions. The rule provides a determinate collective decision because it is immune to the instabilities of cycling.

Approval voting

Under the plurality voting rule, voters are permitted to vote only once. Under a system of voting known as approval voting, voters can vote simultaneously for more than one alternative of which they approve. Approval voting is a system of one-round voting, like plurality voting. Plurality voting is a special case of approval voting where voters are limited to one vote.

TABLE 3.11. APPROVAL VOTING WITH FOUR ALTERNATIVES

Ranking of group 1 (4 voters)	Ranking of group 2 (3 voters)	Ranking of group 3 (2 voters)
A	B	C
D	D	B
B	C	D
C	A	A

Let us look again at Table 3.10. Under approval voting, the seven voters in the three groups in Table 3.10 can vote for as many alternatives as they wish. Voters in group 1 have an incentive to avoid the outcome C, and voters in groups 2 and 3 have an incentive to avoid an outcome of A. Approval voting allows voters to vote for their preferred alternative, and also to vote for their intermediate choice as a form of insurance. If voters use their option to vote for more than a single alternative in this way, when we add the votes, we find seven votes for B, four votes for C, and three votes for A. In this example, alternative B, which is the Condorcet winner under majority voting, therefore wins. Alternative A, which wins under a simple majority voting rule, is in last place under approval voting, reflecting the disapproval of A by a majority when matched against B or C.

Table 3.11 shows another example, where there are four candidates or proposals A, B, C, and D. There are four voters in group 1, three voters in group 2, and two voters in group 3. B is the Condorcet winner.[19]

Under approval voting, suppose that all voters decide to vote for their first two preferred alternatives. Alternative D then wins.[20]

With voters using approval voting to seek insurance by voting for their first two preferred alternatives, the collective choice is therefore not the Condorcet winner B. Approval voting has rather resulted in a win for D, which is the first choice of no group.

With three alternatives as in Table 3.10 and voters voting for their first two choices, the spreading of votes among different alternatives resulted in choice by approval voting of the Condorcet winner. The example in Table 3.11 shows that, when the number of alternatives is increased to four, approval voting cannot be relied upon to choose the Condorcet winner.

Voters could also decide not to exercise the option of multiple votes but to vote for only their first-ranked alternative. The outcome of approval voting is then the same as plurality voting. We have seen that there is no assurance that the Condorcet winner is chosen by plurality (or simple majority) voting.

---

[19] B wins over A by five votes to four, B wins over C by seven votes to two, and B wins over D by five votes to four.

[20] D receives seven votes, B receives five votes, A receives four votes, and C receives two votes.

TABLE 3.12. UNCERTAINTY AND APPROVAL VOTING		
Ranking of group 1 (5 voters)	Ranking of group 2 (2 voters)	Ranking of group 3 (2 voters)
A	B	C
B	C	B
C	A	A

Uncertainty and strategic decisions also affect the outcome of approval voting. We can expect voters to be imperfectly informed about each other's preferences. The effect of this uncertainty can be to prevent a collective decision in favor of the preferred choice of the majority.

In Table 3.12, the five voters in group 1 are an absolute majority of voters and prefer A. These voters may not, however, know that they form an absolute majority. To avoid their most undesirable outcome C, the five voters in group 1 might each decide to vote for their second choice B as well as for their preferred choice A. Through the support of group 1's voters (who are a majority), B then wins. Group 1 composing the majority however prefers A.

Under approval voting, outcomes are influenced by decisions regarding how many candidates to vote for. The voters in group 1 in the example in Table 3.12 made a decision because of uncertainty about the number of voters in each group (in particular in this case in their own group), to vote for their preferred choice A, and, as insurance, also to vote for B. Had group 1's voters chosen to vote only for A, their preferred alternative would have won.

Under plurality voting, voters might also not vote for their true preferred alternative because they do not regard their preferred choice as a realistic prospect. Approval voting allows voters the personal satisfaction of voting for their true first choice, even if the likelihood of that choice winning is low. By allowing a voter simultaneously to vote for more than one alternative, approval voting expands the scope for voters' expressing their preferences.

A problem in comparing decisions made by approval voting with the outcome of other systems of voting is that information about voters' preferences is not enough to determine the outcome of approval voting. We also need to know how many alternatives a voter will choose to vote for.

Proportional representation
Under proportional representation, political parties have representatives in a collective decision-making body in proportion to the number of voters that voted for them.[21] Voters vote once for one party.

---

[21] In general, this is qualified by the need for a political party to receive some minimum number of votes before being allowed representation.

TABLE 3.13. PROPORTIONAL REPRESENTATION		
Ranking of group 1 (30,000 voters)	Ranking of group 2 (20,000 voters)	Ranking of group 3 (20,000 voters)
A	B	C
B	C	B
C	A	A

In Table 3.13, suppose that there is one representative for each 10,000 votes received. In an election that takes place based on Table 3.13, party 1 (representing group 1) would receive three seats in the collective decision-making body, and parties 2 and 3 would each have two seats.

The proposals A, B, and C in Table 3.13 could be different levels of public spending and taxation. Project B, which is the preferred choice of group 2, is the Condorcet winner under majority voting.[22]

In a simultaneous vote on the alternatives (rather than the pairwise vote that establishes the Condorcet winner) party 2 (representing group 2) does not have enough votes alone to implement its preferred project B. No party alone has a majority. A coalition between at least two of the parties is required to establish a majority. Coalitions require compromises.

Along a dimension for the amount of public spending for which $A < B < C$, natural coalitions consist of the middle party 2 together with one of the extremes 1 or 3. Which coalition partner will party 2 prefer? We see that party 2 prefers C to A. Party 2 therefore has an incentive to choose party 3 as a coalition partner, since a coalition between parties 2 and 3 results in public spending on B and also C.

Party 2 has another reason for preferring party 3 as a coalition partner. By keeping the coalition as small as is necessary, party 2 minimizes the compromise that it is required to make in public spending. In a coalition with party 1, party 2 would be a minority partner. In a coalition with party 3, party 2 is an equal partner.

The smallest winning coalition is desirable for coalition members because minimizing the size of the winning coalition results in the least sharing required with others in the coalition. The smallest-sized coalition on which a majority can be based also provides the largest-sized minority on whom costs can be imposed through majority voting.

Under proportional representation, there can be problems of coalition instability. To illustrate, let us return to Table 3.13. Suppose now that the alternatives A, B, and C are not how much to spend, but are three different public projects to be financed through public spending. Parties 2 and 3 can form a coalition on the basis of an agreement that half of public spending will finance project B and half will finance project C. Party 1, which has been excluded from this coalition, can

[22] B defeats A by four votes to three, and B defeats C by five votes to two.

"bribe" one of the included parties to leave and join it in a new coalition. Party 1 can offer either party 2 or 3 more than half of public spending for its preferred project. The benefit to party 1 from the new coalition is public spending on its preferred project A, as compared with no public spending on A when party 1 is excluded from the governing coalition. Suppose that party 3 leaves the original coalition to join party 1 in a new coalition. The new coalition of parties 1 and 3 is however also not stable. Party 2, which is now excluded, can likewise offer terms for a new coalition that are preferred by party 1 or party 3.

Efficiency and voting outcomes again

We have considered different voting rules and compared the outcomes of the rules with the Condorcet winner. Our conclusions from Section 3.1 indicate that none of the voting rules can assure that public spending is efficient in satisfying the cost-benefit rule that $W = B - C > 0$. Whether the voting rule is elimination two-round voting, plurality or approval voting, or proportional representation, total costs for the winning project can exceed total benefits.

3.2.6 Summary

We began this section by observing the contradictory outcomes that can emerge from direct majority voting and political competition (i.e., from direct and representative democracy). We have also seen that political competition has problematical features. In a single-issue political contest between two political candidates, the candidates converge to the median voter's preferred policy. However, with three candidates in a single-issue contest, no stable equilibrium policy exists.[23] In a two-issue contest with two candidates, there is in general no stable outcome for policies chosen by majority voting through political competition. In special circumstances, however, a stable majority-voting outcome with two issues and two candidates is obtained. This occurs when voters' preferred policies define a common line on which contract curves between different voters coincide. A stable outcome is also obtainable when, with two issues and two candidates, candidates do not choose policy positions to maximize support from voters but adhere to principles when choosing policy declarations. A principled candidate loses against a pragmatic candidate when voters support candidates whose policies provide them with highest personal benefit. A stable outcome also arises when voters are constrained by principle in choosing between the policies proposed by competing candidates. Shared principles underlie the formation of political parties that provide means of commitment for voters supporting policies based on principle and not personal benefit.

We have also investigated different systems of voting. We saw that, with more than two candidates, when majority voting is combined with a two-round elimination system of voting, the winner of political competition need not be the

---

[23] More than three candidates can restore stability, but need not. See Supplement 3A.

Condorcet winner. Nor need political competition result in the choice of the Condorcet winner under a simple majority or plurality rule. Approval voting, which is a variation on the simple majority rule that allows voters to vote simultaneously for as many alternatives as they wish, also does not in general ensure choice of the Condorcet winner, although under some circumstances tendencies can be introduced that increase the likelihood of success of intermediate proposals rather than extremes. Strategic aspects enter into both plurality and approval voting when voters do not know the preferences of other voters. We have also seen that the coalitions that may be required to achieve majorities under a system of proportional representation are prone to instability.

We have compared the outcomes of voting under different systems to the Condorcet winner (i.e., the collective choice that defeats all alternatives in pairwise direct votes). We observed in Section 3.1 that we have no assurance that a proposal for public spending and taxation that is a Condorcet winner is socially justified by cost-benefit valuation. We saw that a Condorcet winner can fail the cost-benefit test. Also, we saw that an inefficient Condorcet winner can defeat an efficient public spending and taxation proposal. Efficiency of public-spending decisions made through voting mechanisms requires that spending and taxation proposals, whether or not Condorcet winners, pass the test of cost-benefit valuation.

References and related literature

On political competition, see Downs (1957) and Ursprung (1991). On incomplete divergence of policy positions, see Ursprung (1990). For an application of political competition to the determination of public policies, see Hillman and Ursprung (1988). On voting paradoxes, see Nurmi (1997, 1999). The Ostrogorski paradox originally appeared in Ostrogorski (1903). On approval voting, see Brams and Fishburn (1983) and Yilmaz (1999). Osborne and Silvinsky (1996) consider the decision to become a candidate for political office. Merrill and Grofman (1999) propose a unified theory of voting.

Brams, S. and P. C. Fishburn, 1983. *Approval Voting*. Birkhäuser, Boston.
Downs, A., 1957. *An Economic Theory of Democracy*. Harper and Row, New York.
Feld, L. P. and G. Kirshgässner, 2000. Direct democracy, political culture, and the outcome of economic policy: A report on the Swiss experience. *European Journal of Political Economy* 16, 287–306.
Hillman, A. L. and H. W. Ursprung, 1988. Domestic politics, foreign interests and international trade policy. *American Economic Review* 78, 729–45.
Hotelling, H., 1929. Stability in competition. *Economic Journal* 39, 41–57.
Merrill, S., III and B. Grofman, 1999. *A Unified Theory of Voting: Directional and Proximity Spatial Models*. Cambridge University Press, New York.
Nurmi, H., 1997. Compound majority paradoxes and proportional representation. *European Journal of Political Economy* 13, 443–54.
Nurmi, H., 1999. *Voting Paradoxes and How to Deal with Them*. Springer, Berlin.

Osborne, M. J. and A. Silvinsky, 1996. A model of political competition with citizen-candidates. *Quarterly Journal of Economics* 111, 65–96.

Ostrogorski, M., 1903. *La démocratie et l'organisation des partis politiques*. Calmann-Levy, Paris (2 volumes).

Selten, R., 1971. Anwendungen der Spieltheorie auf die Politische Wissenschaft. In *Politik und Wissenschaft*, H. Maier (ed.). Beck, München, 287–320.

Ursprung, H. W., 1990. Public goods, rent dissipation, and candidate competition. *Economics and Politics* 2, 115–32.

Ursprung, H. W., 1991. Economic policies and political competition. In *Markets and Politicians: Politicized Economic Choice*, A. L. Hillman (ed.). Kluwer Academic Publishers, Boston and Dordrecht, 1–25.

Yilmaz, M., 1999. Can we improve upon approval voting? *European Journal of Political Economy* 15, 89–100.

Questions for discussion

1. Historically, representative democracy was introduced because of the costs of communicating with voters. With the availability of information technology that reduces the costs of individual voters expressing their opinions on different questions, do you believe that representative democracy should be replaced by direct democracy? Explain.

2. What are the reasons for Ostrogorski's paradox?

3. With political competition between two candidates and a single policy, the candidates converge in their positions to the policy position sought by the median voter. In elections that have taken place, have you observed such convergence between candidates, perhaps to the extent that the candidates are barely distinguishable from each other on the major issue of the election? If convergence of the candidates to a common policy has not taken place, what do you believe are the main reasons?

4. Have you observed instability in candidates' policy decisions when there are three candidates and there is one policy issue? What conclusion can be drawn from the absence of instability?

5. With two candidates and two policy issues, and with candidates caring only to win elections and voters seeking maximal personal benefit from policies, why is there no stable policy position for the competing candidates?

6. With two candidates and two policy issues, what happens when one candidate takes a principled stance and does not adjust policy in response to the policy announcement of the competing candidate? Have you observed such principled behavior by political candidates?

7. With two candidates and two policy issues, why do stable policies emerge when voters have additional principled concerns beyond their own personal benefit from policies?

8. Given the attributes of voting systems that we have considered, are you happy with the voting systems that are used in the place where you live or study? Explain. If you would like to see a change in the system of voting, which alternative system of choosing elected representatives would you like to see used?

9. What are the characteristics of outcomes of approval voting compared to other voting systems? Would you support use of approval voting for electing political representatives? Explain.

10. We have described candidates as proposing policies and voters as choosing policies by voting for candidates. An alternative view is that political candidates cannot commit themselves to implementing the policies that they have announced after they are elected, and voters therefore chose among candidates based not on announced future policies but on past policies and past performance by political incumbents. That is, the alternative view sees voters as voting *retrospectively* and not as voting on the basis of anticipated future implementation of political candidates' announced policies. Do you believe that, in the place where you live or study, voters vote retroactively or make forward-looking decisions based on political candidates' election promises? Cite examples. What do you believe are the characteristics of people who choose to become candidates for political office? Does you answer affect whether voters look to the future or vote retrospectively to reward or punish incumbent politicians?

11. If you live or study in a country or other government jurisdiction where elections are based on proportional representation, have you noticed coalition instability in the formation of governing majorities? Are there advantages of proportional representation compared to other systems of voting?

12. We concluded our investigation of direct majority voting in Section 3.1 by observing that it is preferable, if possible, to make personal decisions through markets rather than to rely on collective decisions made through majority voting. How does our study of political competition and representative democracy in this section affect this general conclusion?

3.3

The Implementation of Collective Decisions by Government Bureaucracy

After collective decisions have been determined by voting, implementation of the decisions requires a government bureaucracy. The elected political representatives, who are the legislative branch of government under representative democracy, decide on taxation and public spending on behalf of voters, and the government bureaucracy, which is the *executive* branch of government, implements the decisions. The tax administration (e.g., the Internal Revenue Service in the United States and the Treasury in other countries) collects the taxes that have been voted upon, while other government bureaucracies implement and administer public spending. There are also government bureaucracies that have regulatory tasks: in particular, we observed in Chapter 1 that a minimal task of government is to ensure competitive markets, which requires a regulatory authority. We also noted in Chapter 1 that the second task of minimal government is to ensure the rule of law, in particular to provide the certification and protection of private property rights necessary for markets to function. This task is the responsibility of the judicial branch of government, which also requires an attendant bureaucracy to administer the court system, police, and other security agencies. Bureaucracy is therefore an essential component of government. Without bureaucracy, the decisions made regarding public finance and public policy could not be implemented.

A government bureaucracy is also necessary when there is direct democracy. Taxpayers as voters then directly decide issues of taxation and public spending (rather than delegating these decisions to political representatives). The government bureaucracy is still required to implement and administer the voters' decisions.

We proceed now to look more closely at government bureaucracies. In so doing, we shall use the terms "government officials," "bureaucrats," and "civil servants" interchangeably. Each of these terms describes career employment in a government bureaucracy.

3.3.1 The principal-agent problem

We encountered the idea of a principal-agent problem between taxpayers and government in Chapter 1 when we compared the characteristics of private spending through markets and public spending through government. We recall that a principal-agent problem is present whenever a principal, who should be the decision maker, cannot entirely control the behavior of an agent to whom tasks or decisions have been delegated. The principal-agent problem is the result of (1) differences in objectives of the principal and the agent and (2) imperfect monitoring and control of the agent by the principal. The reason for imperfect monitoring can be that the principal does not observe the behavior of the agent or that actions taken by the agent may not be verifiable by the principal. There is then a problem of asymmetric information: the agent knows what he or she is doing, but the principal cannot monitor or observe the agent's actions. A principal-agent problem is solved when the principal can design an incentive scheme for the agent so that the agent is led to behave in the way that the principal wishes. There is no assurance, however, that an incentive scheme to solve a principal-agent problem can always be designed.

Principal-agent problems are common in different circumstances. Principal-agent problems arise between employer and employee when an employer wishes an employee to exert maximum effort and the employee wishes to exert less effort. Principal-agent problems also arise between managers and a firm's stockholders when stockholders want managers to maximize shareholder value in the stock market and managers wish to expand the size of the firm beyond the firm's core competencies.[1] Principal-agent problems can also arise between parent and child: the parent may wish the child to score high grades in exams, but the child may

---

[1] Managers want the firm to be larger because of the greater benefits managers can then often assign themselves. Managers also benefit from diversification in the firm's activities through the insurance provided against declines in profitability in particular activities. Shareholders can however better achieve diversification of risk through a portfolio of shares in companies that focus on their core competencies.

prefer not to study. The child can decide not to study and to attribute a low grade not to low effort but to an inordinately difficult exam or an "unfair" teacher. There is asymmetric information when the child knows the reason for the low grade but the parent cannot acquire this information: in particular, it may be impossible for the parent to measure the seriousness of the effort that the child puts into studying.

In this section, we are interested in the particular principal-agent problem that arises between taxpayers and the government bureaucracy.[2]

Monopolies and rents

Civil servants employed in the department of defense have the responsibility of managing the government budget designated for national defense. The employees of the department of state or foreign affairs oversee public spending associated with foreign policy and the staffing of embassies and consulates. Civil servants in the government bureaucracy are responsible for administering spending decisions on public health, national highways, national parks, and so forth, across the spectrum of public goods financed by government. These and other government bureaucracies are usually monopolies with regard to designated responsibilities. There is only one department of defense, only one government department that deals with foreign policy, or one department that verifies citizenship or issues passports for foreign travel. Similarly, one government department manages the public health programs that are aimed at preempting epidemics of infectious and contagious diseases, and one government agency handles tenders for road construction.

In a market with private supply, such monopoly positions would allow monopoly profits to be earned. Similarly, rents from government monopoly positions can be available to government bureaucrats. A rent is defined as a payment or benefit that someone receives beyond the payment necessary for carrying out an assigned task. A monopoly profit is a form of a rent because a competitive firm would be willing to supply at a lower price than the monopolist. That is, monopoly profit is not a necessary incentive for supply; rather, monopoly profit is an unnecessary excess payment or a rent.

A person might choose to work for government, even though a higher salary is available in the private sector. For some people, however, employment in a government bureaucracy can provide benefits or rents in the form of low effort and stress, low workload, and other benefits associated with on-the-job quality of life. Employment in a government bureaucracy can for some people also offer financial benefits or rents in the form of higher salaries than in the private sector. As we observed in Chapter 1, government bureaucracies cannot go bankrupt and incomes of government bureaucrats are assured from tax revenues.

The owners of a private monopoly have incentives to minimize costs of production because lower costs increase profits. Civil servants in a government

---

[2] In Chapter 6, we shall consider principal-agent problems that can arise between taxpayers and political representatives.

bureaucracy do not confront the same incentives to minimize costs of the activities that they undertake. We shall see presently that incentives in a government bureaucracy can be precisely the opposite, to maximize costs.

3.3.2 Dedicated career bureaucrats

A vision of bureaucrats who are dedicated to serving the public interest was set out by Max Weber (1947). Weber (1864–1920) described career bureaucrats who seek the best for the taxpayers. Dedicated Weberian bureaucrats have a self-image of themselves as honest and faithful to the public interest. Their behavior reflects their perception of themselves as responsible public servants. They maximize personal utility, but, as dedicated bureaucrats, their utility is based on personal satisfaction from behavior in the public interest. They derive personal utility from the social good that they do through their efforts in the government bureaucracy.

Weber thus described a culture of dedication to the public interest and presented a normative view of how the ideal bureaucrat should behave. Weber's normative model of good bureaucracy supposes that the dominant personal motive of a civil servant is solely to serve (as the name "public servant" implies) the public interest. If bureaucrats behave according to the model of Max Weber, there is no principal-agent problem between taxpayers and government bureaucracy.

3.3.3 Self-interest within a government bureaucracy

The invisible hand that we associated with Adam Smith in Chapter 1 directs private self-interest to social good through personal decisions made in competitive markets that supply private goods. We have seen that, under the conditions of the prisoners' dilemma and in other strategic situations associated with public goods, private self-interest does not result in the best social outcome. We have also seen that outcomes are not necessarily socially beneficial when private self-interest is expressed through voting. Private self-interest expressed through decisions made in government bureaucracies likewise need not result in outcomes that are in society's best interest. That is, Weber's vision of dedicated public servants acting in the social good may not be realized.

A departure from the Weber's vision takes place if bureaucrats or civil servants behave in the way that economic analysis views people generally as behaving, that is, as doing their personal best for themselves. The hypothesis about behavior in economic analysis is that people rationally act to maximize personal benefit.

Contrary to the hypothesis of self-interested behavior, people can be altruistic, or have a social conscience. They may also be concerned with their self-images as ethical people. The consequence can then be the socially responsible behavior of the career bureaucrat described by Max Weber. By adhering to the socially responsible model of behavior, people can accept positions in a government bureaucracy, fulfill their obligations to taxpayers and society with integrity, and take pride in their personal contributions in directing the hand of government to a better outcome for society.

Nevertheless, economic behavior in markets outside of a government bureaucracy is based on the pursuit of personal self-interest, and not altruism or social conscience. We recall moreover from Chapter 1 Adam Smith's observation that we should be wary of people who claim they are acting other than in their own personal best interest.

If the underlying premise describing people's motives is self-interest, consistency requires that we consider the consequences of self-interested behavior when people are employed in a government bureaucracy. Otherwise, we require an explanation for why people in a government bureaucracy will choose to act for the benefit of society and not for their own personal benefit. Max Weber offered such an explanation, although Weber's picture of government bureaucracy is normative (what ought to be) rather than necessarily positive (a prediction about what will be).

Personal benefit of bureaucrats

Private self-interest enters bureaucratic behavior if civil servants have personal objectives related to their personal careers and their personal incomes. Careers and incomes of civil servants are often advanced by larger government budgets. The larger the budget that a bureaucrat manages, in general the greater is the bureaucrat's own personal income and prestige.

The objective of maximizing the budget that a bureaucrat controls can be achieved by personal progression up a bureaucratic hierarchy. The larger and more extensive the hierarchy is, the more advantageous promotion opportunities are. Also, the larger and more extensive the hierarchy is, the greater are in general the benefits for the higher-level officials, who preside over a larger bureaucracy of subordinates. The prestige of government officials is also often related to the number of other bureaucrats who are their subordinates in the hierarchy.

Government officials therefore have incentives to maximize the size of bureaucracy over which they preside and the size of the budget that they control. However, maximization of the size of the bureaucratic hierarchy and maximization of the budgets of government agencies is contrary to interests of taxpayers. Taxpayers prefer that a government bureaucracy carry out its designated tasks in ways that minimize the tax burden (and the excess burden of taxation).

The contrasting objectives of taxpayers and public officials set the ground for a principal-agent problem. In seeking least-cost implementation of collective decisions within a modest but effective government bureaucracy, taxpayers, who are principals, have the precisely opposite objective of government bureaucrats who are their agents.

Creating demand to be satisfied by government bureaucracy

If personal welfare of employees in government bureaucracies increases with the budgets they control, there are incentives for government officials to create demand for the public goods that are under the administrative responsibility of the bureaucracy. The consequences of these incentives can be unappealing for taxpayers and citizens. Government officials who are responsible for administering an unemployment compensation program might, for example, not have an interest in reduced unemployment because this would diminish the demand for their bureaucratic services. Government social workers tending to the needs of marginally functioning or destitute people can have an interest in the persistence of personal adversity to preserve the client base that justifies their government jobs. To create demand for their services, officials in the state department or foreign service have an interest in justifying the need for embassies and consulates in foreign locations.

The bureaucratic self-interest in demand creation differs from a suggestion that the self-interest of a police department is in the perpetuation of crime, or that a fire department has an interest in there being fires to put out. It is illegal for police and fire departments to create demand for their services. It is not in general illegal, however, for government officials to create demand for their services, or to act to preempt decisions that would reduce the demand for their services.

Information problems

When officials in the state department or the foreign service, for example, declare the need for more diplomatic staff, or for larger foreign embassy entertainment budgets, taxpayers can have difficulty verifying that the proposed increased expenditures are justified for the assigned tasks of the government bureaucrats (and diplomats) requesting the budget increases. The categorization of internal documents and memos describing behavior and activities as available on "a need-to-know" basis only, or as "confidential," makes external verification of the justification of budgets of government bureaucracies yet more difficult.

Individual taxpayers lack the incentive, in any event, to personally investigate whether the budget of a government bureaucracy is justified. Individuals rather tend to be rationally ignorant, because of the time, and perhaps also money, required to gather information about the justification for budgets of government bureaucracies as compared to the limited personal benefit from having the information.

The benefits from any taxpayer acting on information that he or she has acquired about a government bureaucracy are in general collective. All taxpayers benefit when a bureaucracy is made to be more cost-effective and responsive to taxpayers' needs. Because of the public-good aspect of benefits from taxpayer action, individual taxpayers confront the public-good prisoners' dilemma – or free-rider problem described in Chapter 2. There is an incentive to rely on others to incur the costs of becoming informed about the bureaucracy and acting on the information.

Ambiguities in measuring output

There are ambiguities in measuring output of a government bureaucracy. The inability to measure bureaucrats' achievements compounds the problem of rational ignorance and the free-rider problem of information acquisition.

Ambiguities regarding measurement of output can also arise within firms in the private sector of an economy. In private firms, profit motives and private ownership provide incentives for private monitoring and evaluation of the worth of employees' activities. Private judgments are made about imperfectly measurable outputs of employees, and management is rewarded for the ability to be accurate in making such judgments. The accuracy of the judgment of management is revealed in the profits of the business or production enterprise.

The same rewards for judgment cannot apply to government agencies and departments. Profitability cannot be a criterion for evaluating bureaucratic efficiency because the output of government agencies and departments is generally not sold in markets.

Substitution of visible activities

Absence of means of accurate measurement of output can lead employees in bureaucracies to focus their efforts on activities that are not productive but are visible. Paperwork and forms, multiplicity of network messages that are not informative, expansion of data files, and unnecessary meetings can become components of bureaucratic activity because these activities are observable and can be measured in terms of output or time. The same activities are also a means of increasing demand for the services of the bureaucracy.

Expert advice

Expert advice may be required before civil servants can make public-spending decisions. We observed in Chapter 2 that cost-benefit analysis by professional experts is an aid to deciding on the merits of public-spending proposals. In general, there are many experts who are willing to be hired to undertake cost-benefit analysis. The public officials who request cost-benefit evaluations are, however, exclusive buyers of advice about their own proposed spending projects. Because of the personal gain from greater public spending and from more projects to manage, public officials may wish to avoid having public projects rejected. Public officials might therefore look favorably on positive evaluations of proposed projects. Margins for discretionary judgment exist in cost-benefit valuation because the benefits and costs that are evaluated are not directly observed as values in markets. Consultants who provide cost-benefit valuations can be aware that they will be competing with other consultants on contracts for cost-benefit valuation in the future, when public officials will again assign consulting contracts for evaluations of proposed publicly financed projects. The personal incentives of experts wishing to be awarded consulting contracts in the future can result in a reluctance to find that public projects do not pass the test of cost-benefit analysis.

3.3.4 The Thomas-à-Becket effect

The principal-agent problem between taxpayers and government bureaucracy disappears when only well-meaning benevolent persons with a Weberian culture choose careers in government service. The benevolence or altruism required for Max Weber's socially benevolent bureaucratic culture requires a transformation from the self-interested individual behavior of the private sector. An example that is commonly used to illustrate the required personal transformation is the principled behavior of Thomas-à-Becket, after whom the Thomas-à-Becket effect is named. Thomas-à-Becket (1118–70) was a close friend of the English king Henry II, who in 1162 appointed him to the position of archbishop of Canterbury. The king had expected that his friend would be a compliant cleric who would support him in disagreements with the church in Rome. Upon becoming archbishop, Thomas-à-Becket however took the side of the church that he now headed in England. The king is said to have proclaimed: "Who will rid me of this meddlesome priest?" Whether the king's question was intended as rhetorical or not, four of the king's knights took the question as a command and proceeded to Canterbury where they murdered Thomas-à-Becket on December 29, 1170. The king had been rid of the "meddlesome" principled priest.

Thomas-à-Beckett went to his death rather than betray the trust of the public office to which he had been appointed. Appeals to the Thomas-à-Beckett effect look for the same fortitude from government officials. The Thomas-à-Beckett effect anticipates that government bureaucrats and officials realize that the private self-interest that guides behavior of private individuals in markets is inappropriate for the behavior of government officials. The hope is that, as did Thomas-à-Becket, government officials will act in the public interest and will not follow their personal interest, and that they will detach themselves from the influence of former friendships and personal relationships to devote themselves to the responsibilities of serving the interests of the public.

3.3.5 A contract between taxpayers and bureaucrats

Without the personal transformation envisaged by the Thomas-à-Becket effect, resolution of the taxpayer-bureaucrat principal-agent problem requires a contract that provides incentives for a bureaucracy to make the decisions that are in the interest of taxpayers. The contract could specify that the head of the bureaucracy will personally receive a share of efficiency savings during the course of a period of office. Although output of the bureaucracy may not be precisely (or imprecisely) measurable, the costs of inputs in a government bureaucracy are measurable through the bureaucracy's budget. A sufficiently large personal reward for efficiency enhancement can transform the self-interest of senior career bureaucrats to consistency with the interest of taxpayers.

In private firms, incentive mechanisms used in attempts to resolve principal-agent problems include stock options for senior management. Stock options cannot be used in government bureaucracies because government bureaucracies do not have the private ownership that is required for stock to be issued and traded. We also do not observe the use of incentive-based cost-saving contracts to resolve the principal-agent problem between taxpayers and government bureaucracies. The use of such incentive-based contracts would be an acknowledgment that behavior within the government bureaucracy differs from the behavior described in the exemplary model of Max Weber. Weber's bureaucrats do not require incentive mechanisms to act in the public interest.

3.3.6 Political representatives and government bureaucracy

Taxpayers might look to elected political representatives to monitor the government bureaucracy. The monitoring can be done through high-level political appointments who head government bureaucracies or through committees of elected representatives who have oversight roles. Whether the monitoring is effective in solving the principal-agent problem between taxpayers and the bureaucracy depends on the information available to the political monitors and on the political control exercised over the bureaucracies.

Political monitoring is impeded if civil servants in government bureaucracies have longer job tenure than elected politicians. The longer job tenure allows career bureaucrats to become better informed than politicians or political appointees about the inner workings of government bureaucracies, in particular about the behind-the-scenes mechanisms that determine how public spending is dispensed. Because of career bureaucrats' longer tenure and informational advantages, political appointments to head the bureaucracy can come to rely on the career bureaucracy for information, including information about the resource needs of the bureaucracy. Elected representatives, and representatives' assistants and support staff, often rely on government bureaucracies for information.

Because elected representatives depend on bureaucrats for information, the effectiveness of political monitoring and oversight in restraining bureaucratic propensities for excessive spending is limited. The desire for electoral popularity can provide elected representatives with incentives to keep taxation low and to constrain budget-expanding tendencies of bureaucracy. However, if information limitations (or asymmetric information) prevent political representatives from effectively monitoring bureaucrats, a principal-agent problem arises between bureaucrats and the elected political representatives. The bureaucrats are again principals, and the elected political representatives become the agents. The principal-agent problem between taxpayers and government bureaucracy is then supplemented by the principal-agent problem between elected representatives and bureaucracy.

Criteria for political success and for advance in a bureaucracy

Different criteria usually apply for political success and for personal advancement within a government bureaucracy. A senior career government bureaucrat responsible for economic issues often requires formal qualifications for the position. The same educational attainments may not be necessary for political appointments within government bureaucracies. A political appointment may be a reward for political loyalty rather than a reflection of competence or expertise in the field of responsibility of the government department. The politically appointed bureaucrat may then have all the more reason for deferring to the expertise and experience of the career bureaucrats, and the bureaucratic discretion that is the basis for the principal-agent problem between elected representative and bureaucrat is further enhanced.

The type of political system
The type of political system influences the control exercised by elected politicians over bureaucracy. In a parliamentary political system, career government bureaucrats may tend to outlast politicians who, in their political careers, rotate among ministries or go in and out of elected office. In a presidential system such as that in the United States, political seniority determined through length of political tenure provides advantages in appointments to congressional oversight committees. The oversight committees in turn can influence budgets of the bureaucracies so that career bureaucrats are given incentives to comply with objectives sought by political representatives.

The behavior of career bureaucrats becomes consistent with that of Max Weber's dedicated civil servants, if the objectives of the political representatives who have oversight over the bureaucracies are the same as the objectives of taxpayers. If political objectives are not the same as those of taxpayers, taxpayers are left confronting a principal-agent problem because of the differences between the objectives of the taxpayers and the objectives of the politicians who oversee the bureaucracies.[3]

3.3.7 Spending on public goods
In Chapter 2, we identified a tendency for underprovision of public goods due to the incentives of people to free ride on the payments of others. The incentive to free ride was the basis for a case for delegating responsibility for financing public goods to government. The principal-agent problem between taxpayer and bureaucracy suggests that delegation of responsibility for financing public-good supply to government can have the effect of increasing spending on public goods beyond the spending that taxpayers want.

The bureaucratic incentive to increase public spending does not necessarily imply oversupply of public goods. The incentive is to spend more, and not necessarily to supply more; some of the spending may be to pay for the expanded government bureaucracy. Nonetheless, because bureaucratic benefits increase with the size of the budget administered by the bureaucracy, the result of delegating responsibility for public goods to government can be oversupply – in contrast with the undersupply anticipated to result from voluntary private payment.

---

[3] We shall return in Chapter 6 and Chapter 8 to circumstances where political control over government bureaucracies is used to achieve regulatory objectives that politicians seek.

3.3.8 Government bureaucracies in poorer countries

There is a difference between corruption and opportunism: corruption is illegal and opportunism is not. The line between opportunism and corruption can, however, be finely drawn. The scope for personal gain by bureaucratic corruption can be substantial because government bureaucrats administer the receipt of government revenue from taxpayers and the spending of the government budget.

In the bureaucratic culture described by Max Weber, there is neither opportunism nor corruption because career civil servants take pride in serving the public interest. When the norm is to be a dedicated civil servant, opportunism or corruption within a government bureaucracy is moreover perceived as aberrant behavior by a bureaucrat's co-workers. Corrupt or opportunist bureaucrats are dismissed. Corruption may also result in criminal penalties.

There are societies, however, where self-serving corrupt behavior can be the norm in government bureaucracies rather than being deviate behavior that is ostracized or punished. In some poorer countries of the world, government bureaucrats have been known to pay for their jobs. The willingness to pay for a position in the government bureaucracy reflects the anticipated personal gains from corruption, and not the high incomes of civil servants. In the countries where corruption is endemic, official salaries of government bureaucrats are often minimal, and it is taken for granted that a government official's income will be supplemented through bribes that are paid in return for providing private benefits through corrupt administration of public finance.

Whether a country's bureaucrats seek their own personal benefit or serve the public interest is a reflection of a society's social norms and ethical values. Either trustworthy behavior or corruption may be the social norm. Which is the social norm determines the degree of intolerance exhibited in a society to government bureaucrats acting in their personal self-interest rather than the public interest.

3.3.9 Conclusions

In Sections 3.1 and 3.2, we considered collective decisions about public finance made through voting. The collective decisions require a government bureaucracy for implementation. The government bureaucracy administers procedures for tax collection and public spending. We have contrasted two visions of the way in which the bureaucracy behaves. The vision of Max Weber describes dedicated civil servants who serve the public interest. Another view sees government officials as having personal objectives associated with incomes and career progression, and as pursuing these personal interests within bureaucratic hierarchies. The personal objectives of government officials then differ from the objectives of taxpayers, and, because taxpayers cannot effectively monitor and control the behavior of bureaucrats, the ground is set for a principal-agent problem.

The principal-agent problem can result in more public spending than taxpayers would choose if they were fully informed about the bureaucracy, and if they could control the bureaucracy. The excess public spending is the source of personal benefits in the form of rents within the bureaucracy. The personal benefits or rents reflect the bureaucracy's monopoly in the services provided to taxpayers.

The principal-agent problem between taxpayers and bureaucracy is the result of asymmetric information. Taxpayers have incentives to be rationally ignorant of behavior in bureaucratic decisions; there are free-riding problems because of the collective benefits from acquiring information to improve the outcomes of bureaucratic behavior; and the information sought might be difficult to quantify and measure in the first place because of the intrinsically unobservable nature of the output of government bureaucracies. The response of government officials to the non-observable nature of bureaucratic output can be to provide visible but not socially productive activities.

A basis for optimism for resolution of the principal-agent problem is the personality change known as the Thomas-à-Beckett effect. The hope or prediction is that people who are self-interested personal optimizers when subject to the invisible hand of the private market economy are transformed into socially minded and dedicated servants of the public interest when placed in positions of responsibility for collecting and choosing how to spend public funds.

The principal-agent problem between taxpayers and government bureaucracy can also be resolved by a contract that provides rewards for more cost-effective management of government agencies and administrative offices. However, such contracts face the problems of measuring output, and in general the incentive-based mechanisms available for addressing the principal-agent problem in the private sector are not available in government bureaucracies.

Government bureaucracies can also be monitored by political appointments and by oversight committees made up of elected representatives. We saw, however, that information problems limit prospects for monitoring career bureaucrats by politicians or political appointments.

The principal-agent problem between taxpayers and government is ameliorated by a culture of integrity and public-mindedness in public service. The principal-agent problem would not arise at all under the model of exemplary bureaucratic conduct set out by Max Weber. With a culture of dedication to public service in a government bureaucracy, procedures for selecting government bureaucrats can be sufficiently discerning to ensure that only socially responsible persons embark on career opportunities and successfully advance their careers in government agencies and departments. The culture is self-sustaining through social norms of behavior. Where the norms described by Max Weber have taken hold, self-interested bureaucratic behavior cannot survive, and persons who do not have Weber's norms do not seek positions as civil servants.

Extreme cases of the principle-agent problem between citizens and government bureaucracy arise in societies with overt cultures of corruption. We are interested not so much in endemically corrupt societies, but in societies where overt self-serving bureaucratic behavior at taxpayer expense is not tolerated. Nonetheless, more covert self-serving behavior can take place through activities that increase demand for the services of government bureaucracies, and so expand the budgets of the bureaucracies.

We were concerned in Chapter 2 that public goods would be undersupplied through voluntary payments because of the prisoners' dilemma and the free-rider problem; hence, we proposed public goods as a responsibility of government. We have now seen that because of the incentives for excess spending in government bureaucracies, delegating responsibility for public goods to government can result in more being spent on public goods than taxpayers want (although more public goods might not be supplied because of spending within the bureaucracy).

References and related literature

On the behavior of government bureaucracies, see Weber (1947), Downs (1967), Niskanen (1971), Borcherding (1977), Rowley and Elgin (1988), Tirole (1994), Breton (1995), and Heckman, Heinrich, and Smith (1997). On the U.S. federal bureaucracy, see Johnson and Libecap (1994). On the ability of political representatives to control decisions of government bureaucracies or agencies, see Ferejohn and Shipan (1990). For a study of the attributes of bureaucrats, see Rauch (1995).

Breton, A., 1995. Organizational hierarchies and bureaucracies: An interpretative essay. *European Journal of Political Economy* 11, 411–40.

Borcherding, T. E. (ed.), 1977. *Budgets and Bureaucrats: The Sources of Government Growth*. Duke University Press, Durham, North Carolina.

Downs, A., 1967. *Inside Bureaucracy*. Little, Brown, Boston.

Ferejohn, J. A. and C. Shipan, 1990. Congressional influence on bureaucracy. *Journal of Law, Economics, and Organization* 6, 1–20.

Heckman, J., C. Heinrich and J. Smith, 1997. Assessing the performance standards in public bureaucracies. *American Economic Review*, 87, 387–95.

Johnson, R. and G. Libecap, 1994. *The Federal Civil Service and the Problem of Bureaucracy: The Economics and Politics of Institutional Change*. University of Chicago Press and NBER, Chicago.

Niskanen, W., 1971. *Bureaucracy and Representative Government*. Aldine, Chicago.

Rauch, J., 1995. Bureaucracy, infrastructure and growth: Evidence from U.S. cities during the progressive era. *American Economic Review* 85, 968–79.

Rowley, C. K. and R. Elgin, 1988. Government and its bureaucracy: A bilateral bargaining versus principal-agent approach. In *The Political Economy of Rent Seeking*, C. K. Rowley, R. Tollison, and G. Tullock (eds.). Kluwer Academic Publishes, Boston and Dordrecht, 267–90.

Tirole, J., 1994. The internal organization of government. *Oxford Economic Papers* 46, 1–29.

Weber, M., 1947. *The Theory of Social and Economic Organization*. W. Hodge, Edinburgh.

Questions for discussion

1. What is the basis for the principal-agent problem that can arise between taxpayers and a government bureaucracy?

2. How is the principal-agent problem affected by the characteristic that government bureaucracies are in general monopolies?

3. The dedicated civil servants described by Max Weber appear to exist more so in some societies than in others. Why do you think that is so?

4. In the place where you live or study, is it more accurate to describe career government bureaucrats as more interested in furthering their own careers by increasing the budgets they control or as dedicated to serving the public as described by Weber? Do you have any evidence?

5. If you have no evidence regarding behavior in government bureaucracies, is this because you are rationally ignorant (i.e., you have had no incentive to invest in finding information)? Or is it because information on behavior within government bureaucracies is simply unavailable? What does rational ignorance or unavailability of information imply about the prospects for existence of a principal-agent problem between taxpayers and government bureaucrats?

6. Do you believe that the Thomas-à-Beckett effect is a credible basis for change in behavior when a person takes a position inside a government bureaucracy? Explain.

7. How is the principal-agent problem between taxpayers and government bureaucracy related to the non-observability of much of bureaucratic output? If excess paperwork is a means whereby government bureaucrats provide signals that allow measurable output, how would you expect information technology that substitutes for paperwork to change the behavior of government bureaucrats?

8. In the private sector, incentive schemes allow principals (e.g., shareholders) to align the interests of agents (management) with their own objectives. What are the impediments that stand in the way of using similar schemes for solving the principal-agent problem between taxpayers and government bureaucracy?

9. In Section 1.3, we came across the idea of a soft budget. How is the idea of a soft budget related to the principal-agent problem between taxpayers and government bureaucracy?

10. How does political culture affect norms of behavior in a government bureaucracy? Do you think that government bureaucrats should be paid high incomes?

11. In the place where you live or study, how does the political system affect the incentives and the ability of political representatives to monitor government bureaucracy? What are the sources of information asymmetries between political representatives and bureaucracy? How do these information asymmetries affect the ability of political representatives to monitor government bureaucracy?

12. How does the principal-agent problem between taxpayers and government bureaucracy affect conclusions about efficient public spending on public goods?

4

MARKET CORRECTIONS

When introducing public goods, we began with a person living in isolation and considered relationships that arose through collective benefits and shared costs when the population increased. When a person who lives in isolation is joined by other people, a further source of interrelation arises if personal market decisions fail to account for costs imposed on others or benefits provided to others. We shall now consider such benefits or costs associated with other people's decisions that are not accounted for (or internalized in) market decisions. In this chapter, we shall also consider decisions to prohibit markets.

4.1

Private Solutions for Externalities

4.1.1 Social interaction and market externalities

Alone on his island, Robinson Crusoe might fish in a stream. The stream has no defined private owners, which does not matter when Crusoe is alone on the island. Other people might then arrive on the island. When one of the new arrivals sets up a factory upstream that pollutes the water in which Crusoe fishes, the stream no longer supports the same number of fish, and Crusoe incurs a loss because he catches fewer fish. The owner of the factory has imposed a negative externality on Crusoe. The owner of the factory would, in contrast, impose a positive externality on Crusoe if the factory were to discharge nutrients on which fish feed, and which thereby increased the number of fish that Crusoe catches.

Whether imposing a negative or positive externality, the owner of the factory behaves, as the invisible hand requires, with the intention of maximizing private benefit or profits from a private market decision. The factory owner is however not taking into account the costs imposed on Crusoe by pollutants, or alternatively is not taking into account the benefits provided to Crusoe's fishing by nutrients emitted into the stream. Because the costs or benefits are not taken into account by the owner of the factory, the market outcome is not efficient.

Figure 4.1 illustrates the case of a negative externality. The market demand function $D = \sum MB$ accounts for all private benefits from consumption of a private good. Competitive market supply $S = \sum MC$ is, however, based only on private MC that producers pay for inputs and does not, for example, include a cost due to damage to the environment. Social MC is defined as the combined private costs of production and the environmental costs imposed on society. The supply function S' in Figure 4.1 is the sum of social MC. That is, social MC of production consists of the producers' private costs plus the additional costs of environmental damage caused by the decision to produce.

The market equilibrium determined by the supply function S that includes only private costs is at the point C, where total production is Q_2. The supply function S', which reflects true costs of production for society, determines efficient output as Q_1. A reduction in output from Q_2 to the socially efficient quantity Q_1 provides a gain equal to the area ABC.[1] Equivalently, ABC is the efficiency loss to society when production is at Q_2 rather than Q_1.

Externalities and public goods are different ways in which the decisions of one person affect the well-being of another and are two different reasons why private decisions in markets can fail to result in efficient outcomes. Externalities and public

---

[1] The reduction in consumption from Q_2 to Q_1 reduces total benefit from consumption by the area $BCDE$. The true cost to society inclusive of environmental damage of the output $(Q_2 - Q_1)$ is $ABED$. The difference is ABC.

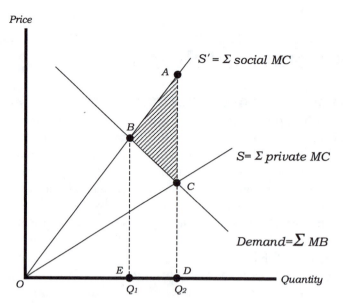

Figure 4.1. The gain from correction of a market externality.

Correction of the externality by a reduction in output from Q_2 to Q_1 provides a gain to society of *ABC*.

goods often appear together. The example of Crusoe's fishing affected by the up-stream factory involves two people, Crusoe and the owner of the factory. This is a one-to-one personal externality. There are no public-good aspects involved. A public good provides benefit to a number of people simultaneously or harms a number of people simultaneously. If pollution of the stream were to affect many people, the pollution would be at the same time a (negative) public good as well as an externality. A public-good free-rider problem would be present if the people adversely affected by the pollution sought to rely on others who are affected to take action to resolve the pollution problem. If, for example, legal action against the factory is required, each adversely affected person could wait for someone else to begin legal proceedings and to pay the costs of litigation. Resolving an externality problem when more than one person is affected by the externality therefore requires resolving a problem of collective action.

When two people fish in the stream, actions taken by one person to reduce or eliminate pollution in the stream provide benefit to the other person, and the public-good free-rider problem accompanies the externality because of the collective benefits from the personal actions to reduce pollution in the stream. The public-good problem and the externality problem, however, involve relationships between different people. The public-good problem is between the two people who fish in the stream. The externality problem is between each person who fishes in the stream and the owner of the factory that pollutes the stream.

When two people fish in the stream, there is an additional externality problem that we might expect to be present. The two people fishing in the stream might impose negative externalities on one another because they are competing for the same fish. They may each catch too many fish and by their overfishing deplete the future stock of fish. This type of externality is known as the tragedy of the commons. We shall presently return to the tragedy of the commons. The "commons" refers to common ownership, or absence of private ownership, in this case absence of property rights to the fish in the stream, and the "tragedy" is the depletion of the common resource, here the fish.

Who affects whom?

The factory-fishing example and the case of two people fishing both describe a negative externality between two producers. An environmental externality, as when factories pollute the air that people breath or pollute a beach is, between producers and individuals in general. These are examples of adverse externalities imposed by producers on the individuals in a society. Instances of beneficial externalities by producers on consumers appear to be uncommon. One example of a beneficial externality due to a producer decision is the benefit provided to an individual who likes the smell of freshly baked bread and lives in the proximity of a bakery. More usually, people are adversely affected by production decisions. Air quality or the quality of water in a river or at a beach deteriorates because of effluents, or people are disturbed by noise from trucks or planes. The adverse externality due to production may be purely aesthetic, as when people are disturbed by the presence of a factory on the street where they live. The behavior of people toward one another can also be a source of negative externalities: a neighbor may host noisy and boisterous parties into the early hours of the morning, or a driver may endanger others on the road.

The absence of intent

When we described in Chapter 1 how competitive markets are socially beneficial in providing efficiency (when there are no public goods, and when there are no externalities), we observed that the social benefit was an *unintended* consequence of self-interested personal market decisions. That is, although people seek to do good for themselves through their market decisions to buy and sell, the outcome is unintentionally socially beneficial. The people who create externalities likewise do not intend to harm or benefit others. There is no goodwill intended from a positive externality and no malice intended from a negative externality. Farmers who clear rain forests are seeking to expand the land they can cultivate and do not consider how their land-clearing activities affect the global climate. The contribution of the land clearing of any one farmer to global warming is an incidental and unintended consequence of activities undertaken in the farmer's own private interest.

The absence of intent associated with externalities likewise applies when the externalities are beneficial. For example, there are positive dynamic externalities from education as, over time, better students become better teachers and professors, who in turn produce better students, who become better teachers and professors, and so on. Such beneficial externalities associated with education are an unintended consequence of individuals' private education decisions.

A neighbor who has a noisy air conditioner does not intend to inconvenience others. People who leave trash in the hallway of an apartment building or who dispose of bottles by throwing them out of cars while driving also do not necessarily intend to harm or inconvenience others. They are just pleasing themselves. Nonetheless, we see that negative externalities involve a lack of consideration for others.

A person might act with a lack of consideration of consequences for others because of the absence of a legal obligation to take into account the effect of a personal decision on others. If, for example, polluting a stream or having a noisy air conditioner or throwing bottles out of cars is illegal, then the rule of law makes imposing negative externalities illegal. If not all people are law-abiding and enforcement of the law is imperfect, the rule of law will of course not prevent negative externalities.

Personal interactions that are not externalities

Not all personal interactions involve externalities. Let us return to the example where two people are in the desert and there is enough water for one to survive. In this case, we might want to conclude that one person drinking the water imposes a very serious negative externality on the other. One person drinking the water is not, however, a case of an externality. Externalities involve inefficiencies. One person drinking the water is a Pareto-efficient outcome because it is not possible to make one person better off without making someone else worse off by changing the behavior of the person drinking the water. Alternatively, two people in the desert might see a water bottle ahead and set off in a run to reach the water bottle. The person who reaches the water first drinks the water. This situation describes a contest that someone has won and another person has lost. We do not in general associate winning and losing contests with externalities. In any assignment of a quantity of a good that provides private benefit, one person has less if another person has more, but no externality that can be corrected to improve efficiency is present.[2]

Let us consider an ice cream vendor who brings a given quantity of ice cream to a beach. When the day turns out to be hotter than had been predicted by the weather forecasters, more people come to the beach than the vendor had expected. The vendor realizes that demand for ice cream will be higher than anticipated and increases the price of ice cream. People have now affected one another by their decisions to come to the beach, through the increased price of ice cream. Although the increase in price is due directly to the decision of more people to come to the beach, the increased price of ice cream is not a case of an externality. There is no externality because the market has *internalized* the increased demand through an increase in the market price. The congestion that people might impose on one another at the beach *is*, however, an externality when people compete for space

---

[2] In Figure 4.1, correction of the externality by contracting output from Q_2 to Q_1 resulted in an efficiency gain of ABC. The gain ABC could be distributed among the population to make everybody better off while making no one worse off.

or kick sand on one another as they walk to the water. Or, at the end of the day, when the people at the beach decide to go home, negative externalities are present through congestion on the road leading from the beach.

We can think of externalities as reflecting missing markets. A positive externality is something that a person is prepared to pay to have, and a negative externality is something a person is prepared to pay to eliminate or avoid, but the payments cannot be made because the required markets do not exist. For example, if someone smokes in our presence and we find this unpleasant, we could offer to pay the person who is smoking to stop. Alternatively, the person smoking could compensate us for the inconvenience of his or her smoking. These payments would be made in the first case in a market for "smoking a cigarette" and in the second case in a market for "not smoking a cigarette." Which case applies depends on who has legal rights, that is, on whether the non-smoker has the legal right to clean air or the smoker has the legal right to smoke. The externality of interaction between smokers and non-smokers arises because neither of these markets exists; otherwise, the market would internalize the externality, and there would be no externality. A reason why a market does not exist may be that neither person has the legal rights required for the market to exist. The smoker may not have the right to sell "not smoking cigarettes" while the non-smoker may not have the right to sell "permission to smoke cigarettes."

We have identified minimal responsibilities of government to be (1) ensuring the rule of law, in particular certification and protection of property rights, and (2) preserving competitive markets. Perhaps externality problems can be solved with such minimal government. In the remainder of this section, we shall consider resolution of externality problems with minimal government through private property rights and the creation of markets. In Section 4.2, we shall consider more active roles for government in resolving externality problems.

4.1.2 The tragedy of the commons and private ownership

In early societies, natural resources were abundant relative to demands of the population. People could graze their domesticated animals on land that had no private owners, that is, on land that was "common" or was the "village common." Negative externalities arose when the common land could no longer efficiently accommodate everyone's animals. The inefficiency took the form of overgrazing. Too many animals grazing on the common resulted in inadequate food for the animals and disturbed the natural balance that had allowed the pasture grass to replenish itself through sustainable growth. The overgrazing gave rise to a situation known "as the tragedy of the commons." Because of overcrowding, no animal could find enough to eat on the common, and animals starved.

Private ownership can rescue a society from the tragedy of the commons. A private owner has an interest in maximizing the value of grazing land. The private owner will therefore internalize the effect of the size of the grazing herd on the feeding capacity of the land by taking into account the reduction in the amount of feed grass available to all other animals when deciding whether to add another animal to the grazing flock. Under the free-access conditions of the common, a person who owned 10 percent of the animals feeding on the common would internalize 10 percent of the externalities among animals but would ignore the negative externalities imposed by his or her animals on the other 90 percent of animals feeding on the common. Another example of a common-access resource is fishing, which we already considered. Overfishing results in depletion of the future fishing stock because too few fish are left to breed. A private owner will restrict the number of fish caught to preserve the stock of fish. Similarly, the private owners of a forest have an incentive to ensure that the forest is replenished rather than stripped bare. The private owners know that a tree not cut down will still belong to them in the future.

Highway congestion is also an example of the tragedy of the commons. Drivers who enter the highway do not take into account the adverse effect of their presence on the ability of other drivers to reach their destination. At peak congested periods, nobody might move on the highway. If the highway were privately owned, the private owner would maximize profits by selling a service that we can call "noncongested travel." The private owner would recognize that drivers' willingness to pay to use the highway depends on the number of other users on the highway at any point in time and would internalize the crowding externalities by charging an appropriate user price for access to the road, or a road toll. Since only those people willing to pay the toll use the road, congestion declines or is eliminated. Users of the road are better off because they are provided with access to noncongested travel and have voluntarily paid the price of access to the road. People who do not pay to use the road have to find alternative free routes, use public transportation that may be available, or choose to travel at different times when the road is not congested and when the private owner of the road should then charge a lower road toll.

The prisoners' dilemma of the tragedy of the commons

The formal problem of the tragedy of the commons is set out in Supplement 4A. The problem has the character of a prisoners' dilemma. By taking advantage of free access to a common resource such as a pasture field or fishing ground or highway, users impose negative externalities on one another. Everybody would be better off if an agreement could be reached whereby each person reduces personal use so that overall use is at the efficient level. The dominant strategy of each individual is, however, to maximize personal benefit by taking advantage of free access. Table 4.1 shows the prisoners' dilemma for two people who graze their sheep on a village common. The efficient outcome is where both herders restrict the number of sheep they graze on the field (they then receive a benefit of 14 each, and the combined 28 is the maximum value of total benefits). If one herder restricts the number of sheep on the common but the other does not, the outcome is disadvantageous for the herder who has voluntarily restricted the size of the flock (the herder restricting the size of the flock has a benefit of 1 and the herder

TABLE 4.1. THE TRAGEDY OF THE COMMONS AS A PRISONERS' DILEMMA

	Herder 2 restricts the number of sheep	Herder 2 places a large number of sheep on the common
Herder 1 restricts the number of sheep	14, 14	1, 20
Herder 1 places a large number of sheep on the common	20, 1	3, 3

not restricting personal use of the commons has a benefit of 20). Each herder's dominant strategy is to place a large number of sheep on the common. If the other herder restricts usage, the best personal response is to exploit the common. If the other herder does not restrict the number of sheep, the best individual decision is again to exploit the common. The Nash equilibrium is therefore where neither herder restricts the size of the flock, which gives benefits of 3 to each herder.

Private ownership eliminates the strategic decisions and resolves the externality problem. Users of the common might come to an agreement that the common will be converted to private ownership, with each herder receiving shares in a private firm that owns the common. The shares in the private firm will be more valuable than the combined value of free access for all sheep herders because the privately owned firm will internalize the negative externalities that were due to free access, by charging a user price for access to the grazing ground. After private ownership is introduced, each sheep herder has two separate roles. One role is as a shareholder in the private firm. The second role is as a herder of sheep who uses the grazing ground. Access to the grazing ground is by payment to the firm, which then distributes the profits from payments for using the grazing ground to the owners. All sheep herders are better off after they have paid the user price for access of sheep to the grazing ground and have received their dividends from the firm in which they have part ownership. In terms of Table 4.1, the firm pays each sheep herder a dividend of 14, whereas with free access to the common each sheep herder would receive a benefit of 3.

Conservation and the commons

The externalities in the tragedy of the commons have a time dimension. A private owner of a field takes into account that sheep will require grass in the future and ensures that the sheep do not eat the roots of the grass, so allowing the grass to be a sustainable resource over time. The incentive to conserve for the future is likewise present if a fishing area is privately owned. The private owner has an incentive not to overfish so as to allow the fish to reproduce so that there will be fish in the future. When there is free access and no private ownership, the owners of fishing trawlers reason that most of the future benefit from conservation of fish will go to others, who will have access to tomorrow's fish through open access to fishing areas. When fishing areas in international waters are open to common access, fishing areas are therefore overfished. In the case of a forest, with free access without private ownership, there is similarly a private incentive to strip the forest of trees today because trees left will in all likelihood be felled by someone else. Private ownership therefore encourages conservation of renewable depletable resources, while common access encourages depletion.

Private ownership resolves the inefficiency of the tragedy of the commons, but there are also distributional consequences. Everybody who wishes to do so can freely graze animals on common grazing land. Private ownership is, however, accompanied by the obligation to pay owners of the land for the right to graze an animal. If the commons have been privatized in a way that gives a share of ownership to all persons who previously used the common (by issuing shares in a firm), all previous users can be made better off in the manner we have described through dividends received from private ownership. If, however, assignment of private property rights to the former common land makes select people the owners, the people who previously used the commons freely and did not receive a share in the private property rights have to pay the private owners for use. We see that considerations of social justice arise when previously common property is transformed to private property. The transformation of common property to private property is, however, efficient, by introducing the private incentives that resolve the externality problem.

Bees and apples

James Meade (1952)[3] described a beekeeper and the owner of an apple orchard located in proximity to one another. The beekeeper and the owner of the apple orchard mutually benefit from externalities that are the consequence of the production activities of the other. The owner of the apple orchard benefits from the bees because the bees pollinate the apple trees. The beekeeper benefits from the presence of the apple orchard because the trees in the orchard provide nectar for the bees' production of honey. Each producer thus confers a reciprocal benefit on the other. The reciprocal benefits are, however, not taken into account in the private decisions of the beekeeper and the owner of the orchard when they make their respective decisions about how many apple trees to plant and how many bees to keep.

Figure 4.2 shows the decision problem of the beekeeper, who sells honey (the output) and can buy bees (the input) in competitive markets. The market price at which a bee can be bought is shown as P_{bees}. In Figure 4.2 the honey producer chooses the privately profit-maximizing number of bees to keep q_1.

---

[3] James Meade (1907–95), who was a professor at the London School of Economics and at the University of Cambridge, and received the Nobel Prize in economics in 1977.

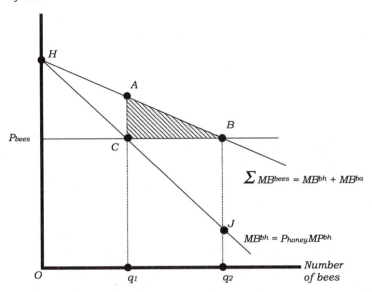

Figure 4.2. The gain from common private ownership.
Private ownership internalizes externalities. *ABC* is the gain from joint private ownership of the bees and the orchard.

In choosing the personally beneficial number of bees q_1, the beekeeper is not taking into account the benefit that the bees provide to the owner of the orchard. At q_1, the beekeeper is providing a free benefit, equal to the area HAC in Figure 4.2, to the owner of the orchard.[4] This free benefit is the positive externality. The total benefit from the bees is the bees' contribution to honey production, plus the bees' contribution through pollination to the fruit grown in the orchard. In Figure 4.2, the combined marginal benefit is shown as

$$\sum MB^{bees} = MB^{bh} + MB^{ba}. \tag{4.1}$$

In expression (4.1), MB^{bh} is the value of the marginal product of bees to the beekeeper and MB^{ba} is the value of the marginal product of bees to the owner of the apple orchard. While the beekeeper values bees for their honey alone, the

---

[4] The marginal cost of a bee is the price P_{bees} of a bee. The marginal benefit from keeping bees is the value of the marginal product of bees in honey production,

$$MB^{bh} = P_{honey}MP^{bh},$$

where P_{honey} is the price received for honey and MP^{bh} is the honey production of the marginal bee. The beekeeper maximizes profits by setting the marginal cost of a bee equal to the marginal benefit from keeping a bee, that is, by setting

$$P_{bees} = MB^{bh} \equiv P_{honey}MP^{bh},$$

which determines q_1 in Figure 4.2.

efficient number of bees is determined by valuing the contribution of bees to both honey and apples.

The efficient number of bees in Figure 4.2 is q_2, where the combined marginal benefit in expression (4.1) of bees in honey and apple production is equal to the price of a bee, that is, where

$$\sum MB^{bees} = P^{bee} = MC^{bee}. \tag{4.2}$$

The efficient decision regarding the number of bees thus requires summing the benefits of bees in honey production and pollination.

By independently expanding the number of bees to the efficient number q_2, the beekeeper would incur a personal loss equal to the area BCJ. If the beekeeper were to buy the orchard and then increase the number of bees to q_2, he or she would gain ABC.[5]

ABC in Figure 4.2 is one part of the efficiency gain from joint private ownership. We can follow the preceding steps for the decision about the size of the apple orchard. We can do this by changing the label *bees* in Figure 4.2 to apple trees and honey to apples, and considering the private decision of the owner of the apple orchard. The owner of the apple orchard chooses the number of apple trees to plant based on the value of apples and neglects the value of the apple trees as inputs into the production of honey. Under separate ownership, the owner of the orchard has too few apple trees. Under common ownership, the externality from the apple trees to honey production is internalized, and the number of apple trees is expanded to the efficient size.

When the bees and the apple orchard are separately owned, potential benefit is therefore lost because of the mutual neglect of the positive externalities that the activity of each provides for the other. There is therefore a private incentive for common private ownership of the bees and the orchard. Under common private ownership, private behavior is efficient, because the common owner internalizes (or takes into account) all consequences of private decisions. To achieve common ownership, the beekeeper can buy the orchard or the owner of the orchard could buy the bees. Or the two producers could merge into a single firm. The value of the gain from common ownership is revealed by market valuation of combined commonly owned honey-apple production. The gains from common private ownership can be shared based on the market value.

The presence of the gains to be shared confirms that common private ownership achieves a Pareto-improving change where both producers gain. At the same time, no one else loses. We see that the path to efficiency is through private profit maximization, where joint profits are maximized under common private ownership.

---

[5] Increasing the number of bees from q_1 to q_2 yields a value of additional product of the bees given by ABq_2q_1, at a cost of the additional bees CBq_2q_1.

Externalities and mergers and acquisitions

The term "synergies" rather than "externalities" is often used to describe benefits from common ownership. All mergers and acquisitions are, however, not necessarily justified by mutually beneficial externalities or synergies between firms. Managers may have personal reasons to seek mergers and to make acquisitions of other firms. Management's incomes may increase with the size of the firm. Mergers and acquisitions may also be motivated by the benefits to producers from reduced market competition. We observed in Section 3.3, when comparing principal-agent problems in the private sector with principal-agent problems between taxpayers and government bureaucracy, that managers in private firms also have an interest in a diversified portfolio of businesses, to provide self-insurance in the event that some of the different businesses do not perform well. The attention of managers is then drawn away from "core" activities in which they have expertise, which is a disadvantage to shareholders of the firm. Shareholders will tend to hold diversified portfolios of shares for purposes of risk spreading and will not require the diversification that managers seek through mergers and acquisitions. Investment banks also have incentives to encourage mergers and acquisitions to earn advisory fees. Because of these incentives of management and investment bankers, when two firms merge or one firm acquires the other, we cannot be certain that we are witnessing an efficiency-enhancing response to mutually beneficial reciprocal externalities.

Unidirectional negative externalities

In the honey–apples example, the externality is (1) reciprocal and (2) mutually beneficial. In the example of the pollution of the stream by the factory, the externality was unidirectional (the factory affected fishing in the stream, but people fishing in the stream did not affect the output of the factory) and negative (the factory adversely affected the number of fish in the stream). The externality in this case can again be internalized through common ownership of the factory and the fishing enterprise, which would allow joint profits from the two production activities to be maximized and would result in internalization of the negative externality by a reduction in the output of the factory to increase the number of fish in the stream. The externality is internalized if the people fishing in the stream buy the factory, or the factory can buy the rights to fish in the stream.

Profits of the factory and fishing enterprise under joint private ownership might be maximized by a level of output of the factory that makes the stream inhospitable for fish. Alternatively a decision would be taken to close down the factory, if this maximizes joint profits of the factory and the fishing enterprise. The owners who close down the factory might also be environmentalists who want an unpolluted stream for aesthetic value.

Public inputs and externalities

We recall that the condition for efficient supply of a public good is $\sum MB = MC$. The expression (4.1) for efficient resolution of an externality has the same general form as this condition for efficiency in public-good supply. In the expression (4.1), the combined marginal benefit that bees provide to the honey producer and to the owner of the orchard is equal to the marginal cost of bees, which is the price of bees in a competitive market. There is therefore a similarity between the conditions for efficient resolution of externalities and efficient supply of a public good.

The contribution of bees to production indeed has public-good properties. The bees are a public input into production of honey and apples. The public-good, or public-input, nature of the bees is reflected in the characteristic that a bee's honey production is not at the expense of the value of the bee's contribution to apple production. Bees simultaneously provide benefit to the beekeeper through honey and to the owner of the apple orchard by pollinating the apple trees.

Bees therefore provide collective benefit to both producers. Because bees provide a public input, we expect the condition for efficient use of bees to satisfy the condition for efficient supply of a public good (or public input).

Bees provide beneficial public inputs, but a public input can also be associated with a negative externality and so detract from rather than add to the value of production. The factory that pollutes the stream uses a public input that affects both the output of the factory (positively) and the return to time spent fishing (negatively).

A contractual alternative to common private ownership

Although common private ownership allows externalities to be efficiently internalized through private decisions, the beekeeper and the owner of the apple orchard could also keep their independent ownership and enter into a contractual agreement that ensures the efficient number of bees and efficient number of apple trees. The contract could provide the owner of the orchard with compensation, paid by the beekeeper, for increasing the number of apple trees. The beekeeper could at the same time receive compensation, paid by the owner of the apple orchard, for increasing the number of bees. The owner of the orchard and the beekeeper could thereby both profit by sharing the gains from the efficient internalization of the mutual externalities. The question is: which organizational form is more efficient (or equivalently more profitable), common ownership or separate ownership with contractual relations?

Common ownership can be more costly than the contractual agreement, if the costs of organizing production in the joint firm increase because of more extensive monitoring and coordination tasks confronting management in the enlarged firm. There can be few or no benefits from common management, if the knowledge required for growing and marketing apples has little to do with the knowledge required for keeping bees and marketing honey, and, if, in the combined firm, management cannot specialize to core expertise and is obliged to oversee both types of production and marketing activities. On the other hand, apples and honey could be two separate divisions of the same firm, where each division applies specialized knowledge to its own task.

A problem with the contractual solution is that contracts may be incomplete. A complete contract specifies responsibilities and courses of action for all contingencies. An incomplete contract does not include all contingencies. A rare unanticipated disease might for example strike the apple trees, and there might be disagreement about whether the owner of the apple orchard had taken all due precautions to avoid the disease. Legal costs can be high when disagreements about contact compliance arise. The legal costs are avoided by common private ownership.

4.1.3 Legal rights, private negotiation, and the Coase theorem

Common private ownership as in the case of privatization of the commons or joint private ownership of separate production facilities as in the case of the apples and the honey cannot resolve externality problems that arise among people, since people are not owned (jointly or otherwise) and one person cannot buy another. People can, however, pay to change each other's behavior.

It has been proposed that externalities among people can be – or indeed will be – voluntarily internalized by private negotiation, provided that the costs of reaching agreement are not too high. The proposal is known as the Coase theorem (named after Ronald Coase of the University of Chicago law school, who received the Nobel Prize in economics in 1991).

To explain the reasoning behind the Coase theorem, we can consider two people in a classroom. Person S (a smoker) likes to smoke cigarettes and person N (a non-smoker) does not like cigarette smoke. In Figure 4.3, MB_S is the declining marginal benefit from smoking cigarettes of person S. This marginal benefit is

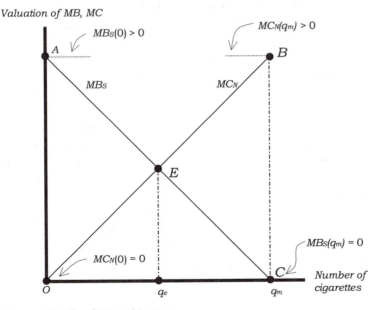

Figure 4.3. The Coase theorem.

The outcome of private negotiation is at the point E whether the smoker or non-smoker has legal rights to the quality of the air.

measured after payment of the price of cigarettes. MC_N is the increasing marginal cost imposed on the non-smoker N by the smoker's cigarettes.

The MB and MC functions in Figure 4.3 thus describe benefits and costs of different persons. Maximizing $W = B - C$, where the benefits B are those of the smoker and the costs C are those of the non-smoker, achieves an efficient outcome. In seeking efficiency, we do not ask about the distribution of benefits and costs between the smoker and non-smoker. We want to maximize the difference between total benefit and total cost independently of how the benefits and costs are distributed in the population.

The smoker, person S, might have the legal right to smoke as he or she pleases. The smoker cares only to maximize personal utility and does not take into account (or internalize) the costs that smoking imposes on the non-smoker. If the smoker can freely decide, the smoker chooses to smoke q_m cigarettes, determined in Figure 4.3 where $MB_S = 0$. Maximized total benefit for the smoker is the area ACO under the smoker's MB function.

We observe, however, that, at q_m,

$$MC_N(q_m) > MB_S(q_m) = 0. \tag{4.3}$$

That is, the MC imposed on the non-smoker when the smoker chooses to smoke q_m cigarettes exceeds the smoker's MB from the last cigarette smoked. The non-smoker therefore has ample scope to pay the smoker not to smoke the last cigarette. That is, the smoker receives zero marginal net satisfaction (after paying for the cigarette) from the last cigarette and can be overcompensated by the non-smoker for the loss of satisfaction from the last cigarette by being paid any positive payment of money. There is therefore potential for Pareto improvement. A Pareto improvement is achieved by person N(the non-smoker) paying person S(the smoker) not to smoke the last cigarette.

The process of compensation (or overcompensation) for not smoking a cigarette can continue, until the number of cigarettes smoked declines in Figure 4.3 to q_e. At this number of cigarettes, the MB to the smoker is equal to the MC imposed on the non-smoker. For values smaller than q_e, the non-smoker cannot compensate the smoker for not smoking and still be better off after paying the compensation. The equilibrium outcome of the process of compensation is therefore q_e.

The equilibrium at q_e is efficient, since $W = B - C$ is maximized. We see that the point E in Figure 4.3 has the characteristics of a market equilibrium. The market is for "not smoking cigarettes."

The reduction in the number of cigarettes from q_m to q_e results in a total gain equal to the area of the triangle EBC.[6] This gain can be divided between the smoker and the non-smoker. How the gain will be distributed is unclear. The market for "not smoking a cigarette" has only one buyer and one seller and is

---

[6] The total cost imposed on the non-smoker from $(q_m - q_s)$ cigarettes is $q_e EBq_m$. The total benefit to the smoker from these cigarettes is $q_e Eq_m$. The difference is the net gain EBC available to be shared.

therefore not a competitive market where price is determined by impersonal supply and demand. We know however that the gain EBC exists to be realized. It would be irrational for the smoker and the non-smoker not to come to an agreement on sharing the gain. There are many possible ways of sharing the gain EBC. The problem is similar to cutting a cake, for which one solution is "you cut and I choose which share I want." This rule results, of course, in equal sharing of the cake, or of the gain.

More generally, we can look at the division of gains as the outcome of a bargaining process over time, with the smoker and the non-smoker making sequential offers and counteroffers until an agreement on sharing the gain is reached. We might think that it could take a long time for an agreement to be reached through bargaining. The individuals involved in the bargaining process can, however, be expected to have positive time preference: that is, they can be expected to prefer to have their shares of the gains today rather than tomorrow. The longer they tie each other up in inconclusive bargaining, the less they therefore have to share. We can think of the value of the total gain available for distribution as shrinking over time, to reflect the preference for present over future gains. The two persons therefore each have an incentive to reach an agreement as soon as possible.

The agreement that is reached will reflect the bargaining power of the two individuals. A way of measuring bargaining power is patience or the discount rate that a person applies to the future. A more patient person has a lower discount rate (discounts the future less) and has more bargaining power because he or she is prepared to wait longer for an agreement to be reached.

The more patient person has a smaller loss from deferring agreement to the future, but, if both persons are fully informed about each other's bargaining power or patience, they have a mutual incentive to come to an agreement on sharing the gains immediately. Immediate agreement avoids the loss that is incurred from deferring agreement to the future. Immediate agreement is an efficient bargaining outcome because there is no loss needlessly incurred in waiting for an agreement to be reached.

Bargaining is more complex when people have incomplete information about each other's patience or time preference. Beliefs about the patience of the other person then matter. Bargaining under incomplete information about time preference of the other person can result in many possible outcomes and is inefficient when people defer reaching agreement.

A change in the law that gives the non-smoker legal rights to air quality

The compensating payments that we have described are based on the legal right of the smoker to smoke. The market created has been in "not inhaling other people's cigarette smoke." Person N(the non-smoker) might alternatively have the legal right to determine air quality. Let us return to Figure 4.3. When the non-smoker has legal rights and chooses not to permit smoking at all, the outcome is that

$$MB_S(0) > MC_N(0) = 0. \qquad (4.4)$$

That is, now the MB of the smoker from the first cigarette exceeds the MC imposed on the non-smoker. The smoker can therefore overcompensate the non-smoker for being allowed to smoke a first cigarette. Permitting smoking of one cigarette is therefore a Pareto improvement compared to prohibition of smoking. The smoker can continue to overcompensate the non-smoker for being allowed further cigarettes so long as $MB_S > MC_N$, that is, until the number of cigarettes smoked is again q_e.

A market has now been created for "the right to smoke a cigarette." The total gain to be shared from the creation of this market is AEO in Figure 4.3. Again, the smoker and the non-smoker can bargain over how they will share the gain from the creation of the market, and it is irrational for them not to bargain to find a way to share the benefit.

The Coase theorem

We can now state a general conclusion known as the Coase theorem:

(1) When an externality is present, efficiency is achieved by assignment of legal rights that allows creation of a market and bargaining over the division of the efficiency gains.

(2) The efficient voluntary resolution of an externality problem is independent of who has legal rights.

Both parts of the Coase theorem have qualifications that we need to add. Before considering the qualifications, let us consider the message of the Coase theorem. As we observed in Chapter 1, legal rights (or property rights) establish the right to sell and underlie willingness to buy. The Coase theorem tells that, when legal rights have been specified, two affected parties can create a market and use the market to achieve an efficient outcome by mutually beneficial trades that internalize the externality. Part (2) of the theorem states that the efficient outcome does not depend on who has legal rights: we see in Figure 4.3 that the efficient outcome is q_e, whether the smoker or the non-smoker has legal rights.

4.1.4 The consequences of assignment of legal rights

Although the Coase theorem states that legal rights do not make a difference for the efficient outcome, assignment of legal rights can, however, affect the outcome of Coase-type negotiations in various ways.

Income effects

The assignment of legal rights determines who makes and who receives payments, and therefore affects people's incomes. A significant income effect associated with these payments influences the positions of the MB and MC functions. For example, in Figure 4.4a, the smoker has legal rights, and the smoker's demand for cigarettes increases because of payments received from the non-smoker. The increased demand moves the marginal benefit of the smoker to MB'_S, and the efficient outcome is at q'_e and not q_e.

*Valuation of marginal cost and
marginal benefit*

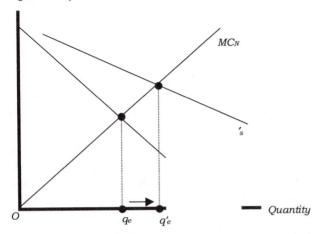

Figure 4.4a. An income effect when the polluter has legal rights.

*Valuation of marginal cost
and marginal benefit*

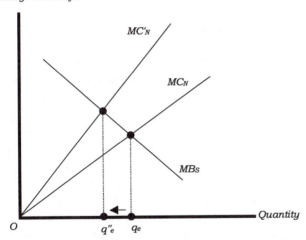

Figure 4.4b. An income effect when the victim has legal rights.

If the non-smoker has legal rights, the non-smoker receives payments from the smoker, which might increase the non-smoker's demand for clean air. The non-smoker's willingness to suffer smoke then declines. In Figure 4.4b, this is expressed in a new marginal cost function of the non-smoker MC'_N. The number of cigarettes allowed to the smoker in the market for permission to smoke is then q''_e and not q_e.

When income effects are significant, the outcome of Coase-bargaining to resolve externality problems therefore depends on who has legal rights. The Coase theorem as previously stated requires that income effects associated with legal rights be insignificant. For goods or activities that are small parts of people's budgets, this is reasonable. In our example, the question is whether this applies to the smoker's demand for cigarettes and the non-smoker's willingness to pay to avoid cigarette smoke.

Incentives and negligence

The Coase theorem takes the assignment of legal rights as predetermined. In our example, either the smoker or the non-smoker has legal rights, and the path to the efficient Coase bargaining solution proceeds from there. An assignment of legal rights can, however, be defined as efficient or inefficient by the incentive to minimize damage. For example, the level of pollution may depend on the care taken by a producer to avoid incidents of pollution. The *cost of negligence* is higher when the public has legal rights than when the owners of a factory have legal rights. If the owners of the factory have legal rights, the cost of negligence for the factory owners is zero because the factory owners do not have to pay for the damage due to negligence in causing pollution. As another example, the incentive to take care to avoid oil spills is greater when cost of negligence is imposed on the owners of the tankers. The assignment of legal rights can therefore matter in affecting the likelihood that a negative externality will arise.

4.1.5 Failures of the Coase theorem

The Coase theorem implies that we should never observe an uncorrected externality because any externality that has existed will have been internalized to the mutual advantage of the affected parties. We do, however, observe noninternalized externalities. That is, contrary to the prediction of the Coase theorem, externalities persist.

Externalities may persist because of unresolved disputes about who has legal rights. If legal rights are not defined, there may simply be a situation of anarchy where the strong exert their will on the weak – although then, with the strong assigning legal rights to themselves, the Coase theorem still predicts voluntary negotiation to achieve an efficient outcome such as at q_e in Figure 4.3.

There may be a dispute about the value of damage, or about whether damage was at all incurred. The value of the damage can be subjective, and as a consequence not observable. We can consider externalities on a crowded beach where people attempt to apply the Coase theorem. Subjective valuations can make the crowding either a negative or positive externality, depending on people's subjective tastes. Some people might like the fun atmosphere of a crowded beach and might find attractive the opportunities for making new friends by having other people in close proximity. Congestion or crowding is, for these people, a positive externality. The positive externality is expressed in a form of behavior known as herd effects, which reflects the idea that people like to go to places where other people go. A beach or bar or restaurant is consequently popular because it is popular. For those seeking solitude or introspection, or a little private space, crowding is, on the contrary, a negative externality; such people are prepared to pay others to move away and leave them some personal space. To resolve externality problems when benefits and costs are private subjective information, we require means of obtaining truthful private information as for example whether a person on a beach likes or dislikes proximity to others. Therefore, we confront a problem similar to the information problem that arose when we sought to determine efficient spending on public goods. Because of the subjective information required, the negotiation and bargaining required to obtain mutual benefit through the Coase theorem can be long and intensive, and perhaps unpleasant. People will not begin to negotiate if the costs of negotiation and bargaining are anticipated to exceed the benefits that can be obtained from resolution of an externality.

Of course, the information problem affects only subjective valuations. If people fishing in a stream kept certified records of the number of fish they caught before a factory began polluting the stream, they could provide objective information verifying the value of the losses due to the polluting activities of the factory. If, however, the complaint is that the pollution is destroying the aesthetic quality of the stream or is preventing recreational enjoyment from the stream, there is a problem of asymmetric information because only the complainants know the value of the loss from aesthetic deterioration or enjoyment from recreation.

The idea of transactions costs refers to a broad category of costs that arise in the course of attempting to establish market conditions of exchange between buyers and sellers, including in particular the costs of negotiation and bargaining when there is no established market price. Where a market already exists, the market establishes a price. When there is no market and attempts are made to create a market, the market does not exist to provide information about price. The price will determine the sharing of the benefits from resolution of the externality by determining, for example, how much the smoker pays the non-smoker for the right to smoke or how much the non-smoker pays the smoker not to smoke; or how much factory owners pay for releasing pollutants into a steam or into the air, or, if factory owners happen to have legal rights, how much they will receive for not releasing the pollutants.

Asymmetric subjective information creates transactions costs in reaching a Coase-type agreement because of possibilities for opportunistic behavior. When a smoker has legal rights, the smoker might decide to exaggerate the number of cigarettes he or she intends to smoke in order to create a large supply of "not-smoking cigarettes" that the non-smoker can pay for. If legal rights are with the non-smoker, the non-smoker can exaggerate the personal losses from cigarette smoke to increase payments received from the smoker in the market for permission to smoke. Opportunistic behavior or deception can therefore be present on either side.

Perhaps assigning legal rights to one side might be efficient in keeping transactions costs to a minimum and allowing the Coase market to be created. If the victim has less scope for misrepresentation or opportunistic behavior than the polluter, it is efficient to assign legal rights to the victim. Assignment of legal rights to a person harmed by pollution would then not reflect a judgment regarding an individual's natural right to clean air. The right to clean air is rather assigned on efficiency grounds because Coase negotiations when a person adversely affected by pollution has legal rights to clean air will more closely approximate an efficient outcome than Coase negotiations when the polluter has legal rights to pollute. When assignment of legal rights affects efficiency through transactions costs, we see again that the Coase theorem's prediction of an efficient outcome independent of the initial assignment of property rights is not accurate.

There can be transactions costs when people do not opportunistically use personal information in an attempt to extract a larger share of the gains from the creation of a market that internalizes externalities. At a crowded road intersection, some people are in a hurry and others have no pressing commitments. The drivers in a hurry have a high value of time, and are willing to pay the low-value-of-time people for priority access through the intersection. A market for priority access could in principle be created. In such a market, high-value-of-time drivers would pay low-value-of-time drivers for priority. Pedestrians wishing to cross the road might also become involved in this market. The market would provide mutual gain through the voluntary transactions of market participants. The existence of the market would require that someone have the legal right to sell priority access. There would be a natural monopoly in the market for priority access through the intersection: the market could not be competitive because, with different sellers of priority, the externalities would not be internalized.[7] Markets allowing transactions between high- and low-value-of-time drivers at an intersection do not exist because the transactions costs of organizing such markets are excessive relative to the benefits. Even if people do not use personal information about benefits and costs to behave opportunistically, there are high costs of communicating willingness to pay for priority access and communicating willingness to receive payment for deferring to others. Drivers will have passed through the intersection without the creation of a Coase market in less time than required for sorting on the basis of willingness to pay for priority access to have taken place, that is, in less time than required for prices for priority access to be negotiated and paid and for paths to be cleared for those who purchased priority access.

In the example of priority access at an intersection, we have downplayed the role of subjective or asymmetric information. Because of subjective asymmetric information, drivers at the intersection do not know each other's valuations of priority access when a person is on the demand side of the market or how much a person is prepared to accept to provide priority access when a person is on the supply side of the market. Whether a person is on the demand side or the supply side of a market depends of course on the price, which is undetermined and is the object of the Coase negotiations and bargaining.

---

[7] When there are alternative routes that people could take to avoid the intersection, the number of alternative routes affects the monopoly power of natural monopolists who control access through any one intersection. When there are two consecutive intersections, the pricing behavior of the natural monopolist for the first intersection affects the demand for priority access facing the natural monopolist for the second intersection.

Because of externalities, access through an intersection might be regulated by traffic lights or by a rule that indicates who has priority. Some of the externalities are then resolved through people waiting their turn in an orderly manner before passing through the intersection, but externalities persist. The externalities are present because low-value-of-time people keep high-value-of-time people waiting, when the high-value-of-time people would have been prepared to pay for priority access and low-value-of-time people would have been prepared to give up their places in exchange for the payments that high-value-of-time people were prepared to make.

Markets as predicted by our example of externalities between smokers and non-smokers also do not in general exist. Smokers once had legal rights to smoke where and as they wished. By the end of the twentieth century, legal rights had changed to be with non-smokers. When legal rights were with smokers, non-smokers rarely attempted to pay smokers not to smoke, and, when non-smokers have legal rights, smokers in general do not attempt to pay to be allowed to smoke. The transactions costs of creating the markets predicted by the Coase theorem appear to be too high.

Personal unwillingness to create markets

The Coase theorem can fail even without high transactions costs because of personal unwillingness to create markets. Let us consider an example where the costs of creating a market are low. There is a line at the post office, and you do not have time to wait. There is an externality problem because other people who arrived first have priority in the line. A market can be created by offering a person at the front of the line money in return for the place in the line. No other people would lose their place.

Yet people may not be prepared to accept payment for giving up their place in the line. They may feel insulted by an offer to buy their place in the line and may think that a place in the line should not be for sale (in particular because they believe that they have earned their place in the line through costs of frustration in waiting). If the offer of payment is regarded as illegitimate, then the offer can come to be regarded as an attempted bribe rather than as an offer of payment.

We might expect the view that a place in the line is not for sale can change by offering enough money. If a place in the line were sold, there might also be complaints from other people whose positions in the line are unaffected by the transaction. Although their places in the line do not change, they may complain that the transaction is "unfair." The unfairness is expressed in the view: "I have been waiting in the line for my turn. It is unfair that you come along and use money to buy a place before me at the front of the line."

In the case of smoking, when a smoker has the legal right to smoke, the smoker might be similarly offended by an offer of payment of money to stop smoking. The smoker might be prepared to stop smoking without payment, if asked nicely to do so as a favor.

Personal aversion to creating, and buying and selling, in markets can therefore stand in the way of realizing the predictions of the Coase theorem. People may feel that there are things that should not be done for money, but that they may be willing to do for free if the circumstances are appropriate. For example, if people think that a case is justifiable, they may be prepared to give up their place in a line without payment.

Collective action

When we describe externalities as involving only two people (e.g., the owner of an orchard and the owner of honeybees, a person fishing in a steam and a factory owner, a smoker and a non-smoker), we separate the concept of externalities from the concept of public goods. Often whenever one individual is affected by an externality, we can expect that other individuals will also be affected. A factory that pollutes the environment harms a number of people simultaneously. Similarly, there are effects on many people when aircraft noise disturbs residents, when people dump garbage in corridors or parks, or when a road becomes congested. When an externality has public-good characteristics, free-rider problems arise in resolving the externality problem. The free-rider problems are distinct from transactions costs of negotiation and bargaining. Transactions costs are present when an externality involves only two people and there are no public-good aspects.

When many people are affected by externalities and externalities have therefore public-good characteristics, prospects for achieving the efficient private resolution predicted by the Coase theorem depend on the effectiveness of collective action by the members of the affected population. Suppose that it becomes known that a factory has changed its production process and is emitting effluents that are harmful to the health of children whose school is in the vicinity of the factory. We can expect the parents of the children to be very concerned, yet we can imagine that any parent acting alone may feel inadequate in confronting a polluting factory. The costs of organizing parents for collective action are reduced by the parents' common characteristic that their children attend the same school. They can immediately identify and contact one other, so enabling them to call a meeting at which to devise a program of collective action against the factory. Some parents might however think strategically that: "this issue is so important that nearly everybody will surely participate in organizing and financing collective action to solve the problem and so my presence at the meeting is unimportant, and I do not have to attend." If enough parents think in this way, free riding prevails over effective collective action.[8]

4.1.6 Location and market capitalization

A decision often has to be made about where to locate a facility that has accompanying negative externalities. The facility could be an airport. A location could also be sought for a waste storage facility, a prison, a communications antenna, a

---

[8] Supplement 2B considers more formally and extensively how the size of a population affects free riding and organization for collective action.

rehabilitation center for drug addicts, a police station, a school, or the route of a highway. Residents might object to having any of these facilities near their neighborhoods or near their houses. The inconvenience or disturbance, or perceived health hazard, would reduce the value of residents' homes.

The owners of the proposed facilities could offer to compensate residents for the decline in property values. The compensation is an application of the Coase theorem where the residents have legal rights. After compensation has been paid for the decline in market value of the houses, the houses continue to have lower market values than similar houses in other locations not adversely affected by the presence of neighboring facilities with negative externalities. People who subsequently buy the houses from the original owners (who received compensation) pay the lower prices for the houses. The lower housing prices are the compensation to the new residents for the negative externalities.

Refusal to accept compensation

We observed that it is sometimes difficult to create markets to internalize externalities because people refuse to accept payment. We considered the refusal of people to accept compensating payments for giving up their place in a line. The same type of refusal can confront offers to pay compensation for locating facilities with negative externalities near people's houses. People can express moral outrage or indignation at the suggestion that they should be compensated, for example, for having a nuclear waste disposal site near their houses. The indignation expresses the feeling that there is no compensation that could be paid to justify accepting the proposal to place the site near a person's house, and that it is an insult even to be asked.

The indignation can have a moral basis. People can feel that it is immoral or unethical to accept money for agreeing to the location of such sites near their houses. The indignation is sometimes known by the acronym NIMBY, which stands for "not in my backyard." That is, the disposal site, the prison, the drug habilitation center, and the like must be put somewhere because of the social benefit or social need, but everyone prefers that the location be far from them, even though the consensus is that the site is necessary somewhere.

Compensation for the location of the undesirable facility may be refused because of uncertainty about future effects on people's health. Cigarette smoking was regarded for a many years as elegant and as not harmful. Asbestos was regarded as a safe construction material until a link was established to cancer. People may fear that even low-dose radiation from a waste disposal site or from a communications antenna can be harmful to health through a sufficient cumulative effect over a period of years. Because of the uncertainty, there can be a feeling of discomfort from having the suspect facility nearby. There can also be a feeling of guilt when a house located near the suspect facility is sold to someone else.

Why poor people are more affected by negative externalities

It is uncommon for communities to accept compensation for accepting the location of a facility with adverse externalities. More commonly, such facilities are placed far from people's houses. Over time, however, as demand for housing grows, houses can begin to encroach upon the facility. The more adverse the externality associated with the facility, the lower the price of the land around the facility is, and the lower the prices of houses are. Therefore, the people who move into the houses around the facility are generally poor, low-income people, who cannot afford higher-priced housing. Correspondingly, if health problems occur, the people adversely affected tend to be the same poorer, lower-income people.

4.1.7 Consideration for others

The virtue of markets proposed by Adam Smith was that personal self-interest without consideration for others would result in efficiency. A person could therefore be self-centered and completely self-interested without feeling guilt, as long as the egotistical and self-interested behavior took place through competitive markets. The presence of externalities compromises ethical equivalence between self-interested behavior and the social good. Ethical behavior in the presence of externalities calls not for self-interested behavior but for regard for other people.

Externality problems would not arise if people were considerate of others. There is a question, however, of who should be considerate of whom. A non-smoker who has legal rights can be considerate by allowing a smoker to smoke without requiring the payments suggested by the Coase theorem. If the cigarette smoke makes the non-smoker feel unwell, being considerate means that the non-smoker is willing to accept personal harm. For the smoker, being considerate means deferring the cigarette or finding another place to smoke where no one is inconvenienced, even if the smoker has legal rights.

4.1.8 Social norms

Social norms are a way of internalizing externalities. A social norm is a form of behavior that people adopt because everybody else is behaving in the same way. Social norms are the basis for social conventions that can override personal preferences. People may follow social norms to avoid being ostracized by the people around them or because of personal disutility from behaving differently from the norm or convention. For example, the social norm may be to wait patiently in line and not to push or shove. A person who does push or shove is ostracized and may not be permitted to have his or her way. Externalities are not internalized when the social norm is that positioning in a queue is a free-for-all affair.

An individual may not personally feel inhibitions about littering a hiking trail in a nature reserve, whereas the social norm may be not to litter. The person may then not litter in the presence of others to avoid being socially ostracized, and the negative externality of littering is internalized by adapting personal behavior to social norms. The internalization of an externality has taken place not through the creation of a Coase-type market but through the private incentive to conform to avoid the personal cost of being seen by others as deviating from the social norm of not littering.

On the other hand, personal values may be to be considerate, when the social norm is to be inconsiderate. For example, littering a hiking trail may contradict an individual's personal values but the social norm may be to litter. Personal dilemmas can then arise because of threshold effects in externalities. We can consider a person who begins a hike valuing a litter-free hiking trail and fully intending to carry personal litter out of the nature reserve rather than throwing litter on the trail. The intention not to litter is consistent with the individual's sense of self-identity as a responsible, socially aware, considerate person. What does this person do when there is litter all along the trail that other people have left? Faced with the litter that already exists, considerate hikers might feel that they might just as well add their own litter to the piles of litter that exist. By adding to the litter, an individual is conforming to the social norm of littering the trail. Given all the litter that already exists, the effect of the additional litter is small and inconsequential. Although the personal value of the hiker is not to litter, personal values can become subordinated to an inferior social norm, and people might add to the extensive litter that others have left.

Personal values could continue to guide personal behavior, and people may decide not to add their own litter to the pile. They may even pick up the litter that others have left and take it out of the nature reserve, a response that is an example of the volunteer-type of public good described in Chapter 2. The public good is the benefit provided to others who also value a litter-free trail.

4.1.9 Conclusions

When we described the efficiency of competitive markets in Chapter 1, we did not consider the possibility that some benefits might not be included in personal valuations of benefit that underlie market demand, or that some costs might not be included in private valuations of cost that underlie market supply. Benefits or costs can however be left out of market valuations. The benefits or costs external to markets are unintentional consequences of personal self-interested decisions.

There is always a personal self-interest in internalizing externalities. Externalities cause inefficiency, and correction of the inefficiency allows gains that people can share. Personal self-interest should therefore always lead to voluntary elimination (or internalization) of externalities.

The voluntary elimination of externalities can occur through common private ownership, as in the tragedy of the commons (where externalities are negative) and in the example of the apples and the bees (where externalities are positive). Whenever externalities affect producers, we can expect the quest for private profit to result in internalization of externalities.

When externalities affect people's subjective utility or well-being, we cannot look to joint ownership to resolve externality problems. Nonetheless, there are still private mutual gains from resolution of externalities. The Coase theorem tells us that rational individuals will act to realize these mutual gains, which are the counterpart to mutual profit of producers, through the creation of markets that internalize externalities. The prediction of the Coase theorem is that, once legal rights are specified, markets will be created in which personal voluntary payments can be made (and accepted) that resolve the inefficiencies of externalities, and that the efficient outcomes that arise are independent of who has legal rights. Because resolving externality problems provides opportunities for Pareto improvement through mutual gain, affected individuals have an incentive to come to an agreement about sharing gains through negotiation and bargaining.

The designation of legal rights however affects the outcome of Coase negotiation and bargaining when there are significant income effects, and also when legal rights affect incentives to take precautions and avoid negligence (e.g., avoidance of oil spills).

The incentive to internalize externalities for mutual benefit suggests that we should never observe the presence of externalities.[9] Externalities exist (or persist) and the predictions of the Coase theorem fail to be realized, when transactions costs of creating the markets that would internalize an externality exceed the benefits that would be available to be shared if the market were created.

The predictions of the Coase theorem also fail to be realized when people are unwilling to accept payment for changing their behavior, or refuse to accept payment for giving up or providing something. People do not like to think that they are being bribed, and they think they are being bribed if they regard the offer of payment that is being made as somehow illegitimate.

The predictions of the Coase theorem also fail to be realized because in many cases public-good characteristics accompany externalities, so that resolution of externality problems requires collective action. The actions required to internalize externalities are then subject to public-good free-rider problems.

We have observed that markets internalize externalities through changes in the market value of land and houses. The Coase theorem is then compromised when people are not willing to accept payment as compensation for the location of facilities with adverse externalities near their homes. When a facility does have adverse externalities, it is usually poorer people who live in such locations, because of the cheap price of housing.

The Coase theorem makes clear how absence of legal (or property) rights underlies externality problems. After the designation of legal rights, we know who has a legal right to do what to whom. The Coase theorem can therefore be understood as another perspective on the role of private property in ensuring market efficiency. Without property rights, there is anarchy, and people can impose various externalities on others at will. The strong simply have their way, or a majority has its way (the majority could vote to place dangerous facilities near the houses of the minority). Neither the will of the strong nor the greater numbers of the majority ensures efficient resolution of externality problems. Legal rights

---

[9] The presence of an externality problem requires, of course, the recognition of the external effect. When people did not know that asbestos was dangerous or that cigarette smoke was dangerous, there was no externality problem (although some people simply "did not like" cigarette smoke before the dangers to health were documented).

are required so as to provide the prospect for an efficient outcome through the prediction of the Coase theorem.

We have noted that externalities would not exist if people showed consideration toward one another, although a question of who should show consideration to whom would then arise.

We have also observed that social norms are a means of internalization of externalities.

Minimal government that does no more than certify and enforce legal rights so that the Coase theorem can be applied may not be sufficient for efficient resolution of externality problems because of the problems that we have noted (transactions costs of negotiation and bargaining, unwillingness to accept payments, and free-rider incentives that arise because of the collective or public-good character of externalities). Nor may consideration for others or social norms resolve externality problems. In Section 4.2, we shall consider the resolution of externality problems through active public policies of government.

References and related literature

On the nature of externalities, see Scitovsky (1954) and Heller and Starrett (1976). On the apples and bees, see Meade (1952). On the tradegy of the commons, see Levhari and Mirman (1980), Cornes and Sandler (1983), de Meza and Gould (1987), and Ostrom, Gardener, and Walker (1994). On the Coase theorem, see Coase (1960), Schweitzer (1988), and Demsetz (1996). On information and externalities, see Farrell (1987) and Greenwood and McAfee (1991). On efficient bargaining outcomes, see Rubinstein (1982). On bargaining outcomes with incomplete information about time preferences, see Fudenberg and Tirole (1993, Chapter 10). On collective action, see Olson (1965). On location and externalities, see Kunruether and Easterling (1990), Gerrard (1994), and Frey, Oberholzer-Gee, and Eichenberger (1996). On measurement of external effects through market capitalization, see Smith and Huang (1995) and Jeanrenaud and Soguel (1999). On social norms and externalities, see Arrow (1971) and Fershtman and Weiss (1998).

Arrow, K. J., 1971. Political and economic evaluation of social effects and externalities. In *Frontiers of Quantitative Economics*, M. D. Intriligator (ed.). North-Holland, Amsterdam, 3–25.

Coase, R. C., 1960. The problem of social cost. *Journal of Law and Economics* 3, 1–44.

Cornes, R. and T. Sandler, 1983. On commons and tragedies. *American Economic Review* 73, 787–92.

de Meza, D. and J. R. Gould, 1987. Free access versus private property in a resource: Income distribution compared. *Journal of Political Economy* 100, 1317–25.

Demsetz, H., 1996. The core disagreement between Pigou, the profession, and Coase in the analyses of the externality question. *European Journal of Political Economy* 12, 565–79.

Farrell, J., 1987. Information and the Coase theorem. *Journal of Economic Perspectives* 1, 113–29.

Fershtman, H. and Y. Weiss, 1998. Social rewards, externalities, and stable preferences. *Journal of Public Economics* 70, 53–73.

Frey, B. S., F. Oberholzer-Gee and R. Eichenberger, 1996. The old lady visits your backyard: A tale of morals and markets. *Journal of Political Economy* 104, 1297–1313.

Fudenberg, D. and J. Tirole, 1993. *Game Theory*. MIT Press, Cambridge, Massachusetts.

Gerrard, M. B., 1994. *Whose Backyard, Whose Risk: Fear and Fairness in Toxic and Nuclear Waste Siting*. MIT Press, Cambridge, Massachusetts.

Greenwood, J. and R. P. McAfee, 1991. Externalities and asymmetric information. *Quarterly Journal of Economics* 105, 103–21.

Heller, W. P. and D. A. Starrett, 1976. On the nature of externalities. In *Theory and Measurement of Economic Externalities*, S. A. Y. Lin (ed.). Academic Press, New York, 9–21.

Jeanrenaud, C. and N. Soguel (eds.), 1999. *Valuing the Cost of Smoking*. Kluwer Academic Publishers, Boston and Dordrecht.

Kunreuther, H. and D. Easterling, 1990. Are risk-benefit tradeoffs possible in siting hazardous facilities? *American Economic Review, Papers and Proceedings* 80, 252–6.

Levhari, D. and L. Mirman, 1980. The great fish war: an example using a dynamic Cournot-Nash solution. *Bell Journal of Economics* 11, 322–34.

Meade, J. E., 1952. External economies and diseconomies in a competitive situation. *Economic Journal* 62, 54–67. Reprinted 1969 in *Readings in Welfare Economics*, K. J. Arrow and T. Scitovsky (eds.). Richard D. Irwin, Homewood, Illinois, 185–98.

Olson, M., 1965. *The Logic of Collective Action*. Harvard University Press, Cambridge, Massachusetts.

Ostrom, E., R. Gardener and J. Walker, 1994. *Rules, Games, and Common-Pool Resources*. University of Michigan Press, Ann Arbor.

Rubinstein, A., 1982. Perfect equilibrium in a bargaining model. *Econometrica* 50, 97–109.

Schweitzer, U., 1988. Externalities and the Coase theorem: Hypothesis or result? *Journal of Institutional and Theoretical Economics* 144, 245–66.

Scitovsky, T., 1954. Two concepts of external economies. *Journal of Political Economy* 17, 143–51. Reprinted 1969 in *Readings in Welfare Economics*, K. J. Arrow and T. Scitovsky (eds.). Richard D. Irwin, Homewood, Illinois, 242–54.

Smith, V. K. and J-C. Huang, 1995. Can markets value air quality?: A meta-analysis of hedonic property value models. *Journal of Political Economy* 103, 296–313.

Questions for discussion

1. Why can an externality be defined as the consequence of a missing market?
2. Give examples of interactions among people (where the behavior or decision of one person affects other people) that are not externalities. If unpredicted heavy rain results in an increase in the price of umbrellas, has the rain created an externality through the higher price of umbrellas?
3. What is the relation between externalities and intent to harm or benefit others? How would you reply to someone who declares that he or she did not intend to do harm (i.e., create a negative externality) by throwing a bottle from a car window?
4. List the major negative externalities that you encounter in the course of a day, including the sources of the externalities. How many further negative externalities would you encounter in the absence of legal rights that preempt negative externalities?
5. List positive externalities that you encounter.

6. Which of the externalities that you encounter are examples of the tragedy of the commons? Why have these externalities not been resolved by private ownership? (See also Supplement 4A.)

7. In the case of the benefits from the bees in providing honey and apples, how do private property rights restore the relation between efficiency achieved through markets and the quest for personal gain?

8. Honey and pollinating apple trees can be described as joint products of bees' activities. How are these joint products related to the idea of public inputs?

9. How do private property rights facilitate sustainable conservation of renewable natural resources such as forests and fishing stocks? Would private property rights help endangered species of animals? In some cases, people sensitive to sustaining biodiversity and the environment are against private property rights for natural resources and natural endowments and prefer collective or government ownership. What could be the basis for this preference?

10. What are the predictions of the Coase theorem?

11. Bargaining theory suggests that people should instantaneously agree on the sharing of benefits from resolving an externality problem. What aspects of bargaining stand in the way of instantaneous agreement and give rise to bargaining costs? What are the bargaining costs in these cases?

12. In negotiations to resolve an externality when legal rights are not defined, arguments arise about who should pay whom. In these cases, a preamble to negotiations is often a court case to determine legal rights. What considerations should enter into determination of legal rights?

13. The Coase theorem predicts we should never see an externality. How do transactions costs explain the persistence of externalities? How are the transactions costs related to asymmetric or subjective information? Can you give examples from the externalities that you face in day-to-day life of transactions costs that stand in the way of resolving externality problems?

14. Are there times when you would like to create a market for "someone to stop bothering you" in some way? Or perhaps you would like more attention from a particular person. Is one of the reasons why you do not attempt to create a Coase-type market that you think offering money will be counterproductive? What are the general circumstances in which an offer of money in an attempt to create a market might be counterproductive?

15. Resolution of externalities requires collective action when many people are affected by an externality at the same time. Does your personal list of externalities include cases for which the large size of the affected group prevents voluntary resolution of the externalities?

16. After people living in an area have received a large sum of money as compensation for the construction of a waste disposal facility near their houses, why would we expect the population in the area to change? Will the change in the population living near the disposal facility be efficient? Will the outcome be unfair (define what you mean by "fair")?

17. How do people's attitudes toward others through showing consideration influence resolution of externality problems? Can showing consideration toward others be a complete substitute for specification of legal rights?

18. What is a social norm, and how do social norms or conventions affect private resolution of externality problems? Can you identify externality problems that you would confront if behavior were not determined by social norms and conventions? Do some of the social norms or conventions contradict your own personal values?

19. The neighbors are having a loud party, and the noise bothers you because you do not like the music. You go to the neighbor's house and conduct a poll asking everyone present including the neighbors how much they would have to be paid for the party

to stop and for the guests to go home. Everyone tells the truth. You find that the sum of money that you would have to pay exceeds your benefit from stopping the party. What do you conclude about efficiency and fairness of the consequent outcome? In this situation, would you expect people to tell the truth? If there were no party, but the neighbor was alone at home listening to the music, would you expect the outcome to change?

20. The Coase theorem predicts that externalities should not exist because of the mutual gains from voluntary private actions to internalize externalities. Summarize the principal reasons why externalities nonetheless persist.

4.2

Public Policy and Externalities

4.2.1 The case for government

In Section 4.1, we considered private solutions to externality problems. We saw that externalities can be privately resolved through minimal government that allows legal rights to be established. We also observed that there are impediments to relying on private solutions to externality problems. If transactions costs are so high as to exceed the benefits to be shared from creating a market, there are no efficiency gains from private creation of the market, and the market will not be privately created even if legal rights are specified. Free-rider problems and unwillingness to participate in markets can also stand in the way of private resolution of externality problems.

The case for government to take responsibility for correcting externalities rests on government having lower transactions costs than private individuals. Or on government being able to overcome free-rider problems that deter the collective action required for private resolution, or being able to circumvent the inhibitions of people who are unwilling to participate in particular markets.

When setting out to resolve externality problems through public policy, government still faces subjective, and therefore unknown, costs and benefits associated with an externality. A role therefore reappears for the Clarke tax as a means of providing information about public policy. Or a government can use cost-benefit analysis to determine public policy when externalities are present. In Chapter 2, we viewed the reason for cost-benefit analysis as being to reveal information about the value of benefits provided from public goods. The indirect measurement of benefits was a means of approximating values of personal benefits that could not be directly observed because of preference misrepresentation or free-riding behavior. Market values are likewise absent, and cost-benefit analysis is required, when costs or benefits take the form of externalities.

Positive externalities associated with education are, for example, part of the cost-benefit valuation of a new school, and positive externalities from reduced probabilities of infection or contagion are part of the benefits of a public-health project. In cost-benefit valuation of whether to widen a road, the benefits consist of a reduction in negative externalities through reduced crowding on the road. The widening of the road may also affect biodiversity by restricting the habitat of animals, and there are other externalities through effects on the environment through vehicle emissions.

The results of cost-benefit analysis can change when relevant externalities are forgotten and so left out of the computations or are not appropriately valued. A sufficiently high value placed on animal habitats or on archeological sites can, for example, change a decision that a dam or road is socially worthwhile.

In another example, there are externalities associated with the construction of nuclear power stations. The source of the externalities is the need to dispose of and store nuclear waste, and the possible need eventually to decommission (or close down) power plants. When cost-benefit studies of nuclear power stations are undertaken, the externalities are far in the future. When the future costs are excessively discounted, a project can be given a positive present value, but future generations will confront externalities through future costs of decommissioning nuclear power stations and disposing of and storing of waste.[1]

Valuation of costs or benefits that arise as externalities is therefore often part of cost-benefit analysis. As with public goods, the reason for cost-benefit analysis when there are externalities is absence of values revealed in markets. We noted in Section 4.1 that externalities reflect missing markets.

In many cases, there is broad consensus about costs and benefits to be included in cost-benefit valuation, even though measurement may be imprecise or am-biguous. For example, there is broad consensus about environmental and health externalities, as well as externalities associated with education.

The source of externalities can also be a subjective feeling of personal like or dislike. As a hypothetical example, we can consider someone who has an aversion to the color purple. Such a person is willing to pay not to see the color purple and is prepared to pay people not to wear purple clothes. It is impractical for a person with an aversion to the color purple to go around offering money to people to change their clothing from purple to another color. The person with the aversion to the color purple might, however, form a collective action group by seeking out other people with a dislike of the color purple. The collective action group could make wearing of purple clothes an election issue or could lobby government to implement legislation that makes purple clothing illegal.

Public policy that makes the color purple illegal would not be very sensible, and governments have rarely enacted laws regarding the color of clothing. There have been times nonetheless when legal discrimination has been based on the color of

---

[1] Warren Young (1998) investigated the economics of nuclear power stations. Young concluded that neglect or discounting of costs due to future externalities from disposal of nuclear waste resulted in the construction of nuclear power plants that do not pass a properly specified test of cost-benefit analysis.

a person's skin or ethnic background. A prohibition on wearing purple clothing is an annoyance but compliance is possible. Changing one's skin color is not like changing one's clothing. Changing one's parents or ethnicity is impossible.

The question is not, however, whether compliance is readily possible. The question is rather about rights to declare externalities and to propose resolution of the externalities as a responsibility of government. Civilized societies place bounds on externalities that can either be declared by governments or determined through collective choice of voters. A constitution (i.e., a set of rules about allowable laws) provides protection against unethical and idiosyncratic declarations of negative externalities.[2]

We now consider resolution of externality problems through the public policy of government. We shall see that there are different ways in which governments can use public policy to resolve externality problems, and that political considerations can affect public policy decisions.

4.2.2 Taxes and subsidies

Charles Pigou (1877–1959), writing in *The Economics of Welfare* (1920/1962), proposed that governments should use taxes or subsidies to correct for failure of self-interested buyers and sellers to account for effects of their decisions on others. To see how Pigovian taxes and subsidies (named after Pigou) can resolve externality problems, we can look at Figure 4.5, which shows a negative externality due to the output of an industry. The negative externality might, for example, be harm to the environment. Market demand is D and competitive market supply determined by *private* costs is $\sum(PRIVATE\ MC)$. The marginal cost of production inclusive of the cost of environmental damage is $\sum(SOCIAL\ MC)$. The difference between *private MC* and *social MC* measures the damage incurred because of the negative externality for each addition to output. In Figure 4.5, this difference increases with output. That is, marginal environmental damage increases as output expands.

The competitive market outcome when production decisions are based on private valuation of cost in Figure 4.5 is at point F. Socially efficient output, however, is at point E. Efficiency therefore requires that output be decreased from Q_2 to Q_1. The efficiency gain to society from the output reduction from Q_2 to Q_1 is the shaded area GEF. Private voluntary action, if feasible, would realize this gain.

---

[2] Because of ambiguities that can arise, enforcement of antidiscrimination laws can sometimes be difficult in employer-employee and landlord-tenant relations. Gary Becker (1971) of the University of Chicago (who received the Nobel Prize in economics in 1992) proposed, however, that markets internalize externalities associated with discrimination, since an employer who discriminates on racial grounds may miss out on the best person for the job, or a landlord may miss out on the most responsible tenant. An employer or landlord therefore personally pays for any discrimination because the externality is internalized through a cost imposed on a person who discriminates. However, when markets are not competitive in offering alternative identical employment or housing possibilities, a cost of discrimination falls on the victim because people lose from discrimination when they do not have alternatives as good as the opportunities they were denied through discrimination.

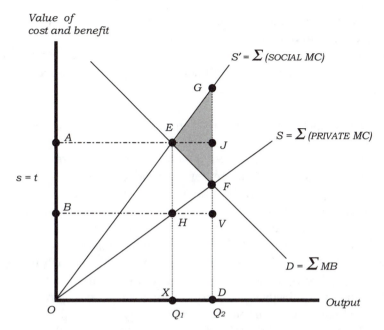

Figure 4.5. Use of Pigovian taxes or subsidies to correct an adverse externality.

When private voluntary resolution is not feasible, a tax or a subsidy can move the outcome from F to E.

The corrected efficient market equilibrium at point E can be achieved by the government setting a per-unit tax on output,

$$t = \sum \text{SOCIAL } MC\,(Q_1) - \sum \text{PRIVATE } MC\,(Q_1). \tag{4.5}$$

The level of the tax in Figure 4.5 is $AB = EH$. That is, the tax is the difference between social and private marginal cost, evaluated at the efficient output Q_1.

The tax t is paid on each unit of output produced up to Q_1. The total value of the revenue from the tax is $ABHE$.

The tax internalizes the externality. By paying the tax, producers are made to realize that their production has social costs in addition to the privately paid costs of production. The tax is paid in place of the payments that producers would make, if a market existed for the right to create environmental damage.

Rather than interpreting the tax as a punishment for creating the adverse environmental effects, we interpret the tax as changing incentives by making producers behave as if there were a market for the right to create environmental damage. Under the competitive conditions in Figure 4.5, an individual producer chooses the quantity of output to produce by setting price equal to marginal cost. When there is no public policy to correct the externality, output is chosen by setting price equal to private MC. After the corrective tax has been imposed, individual producers choose output by setting price equal to $(MC + t)$. When all producers revise their output decisions to include the cost of the tax, the supply function is $\sum(SOCIAL\ MC)$ and efficient output Q_1 is produced.

Instead of imposing a tax on production, the government could achieve the same contraction of output from Q_2 to Q_1 in Figure 4.5 by paying producers a per-unit output subsidy

$$s = \sum SOCIAL\ MC\ (Q_1) - \sum PRIVATE\ MC\ (Q_1). \tag{4.6}$$

The subsidy is paid on units of output between Q_2 and Q_1 that are *not* produced. That is, the subsidy is a payment to producers for not producing more than the efficient quantity Q_1. In Figure 4.5, the total amount of the subsidy paid to producers in the industry is the area $EJVH$.

We see from expressions (4.5) and (4.6) that the values of Pigovian tax and subsidy are equal: the subsidy on each unit of output not produced between output Q_2 and Q_1 is the same as the level of the tax per unit of output on each unit produced up to output Q_1. The equal tax and subsidy are both costs for producers. The tax is an explicit cost. The subsidy is also a cost, in the form of an *opportunity cost* of producing more than the efficient output. Producers receive the subsidy on the output $(Q_2 - Q_1)$ that is *not* produced. By choosing to produce more than the socially desired quantity Q_1, producers incur a cost through the subsidy that is lost.

The tax and subsidy have the same effect on producer incentives. Production decisions are made by setting market price equal to private marginal cost plus additional marginal cost imposed through payment of the tax. With m producers, individual production decisions are made according to

$$P = MC_j + t \qquad j = 1, \ldots, m, \tag{4.7}$$

where the tax t is an additional cost imposed by public policy. In the case of the subsidy, individual producers make production decisions according to

$$P = MC_j + s \qquad j = 1, \ldots, m, \tag{4.8}$$

where the subsidy s is likewise an additional cost imposed by public policy.

In expressions (4.7) and (4.8), MC_j indicates that different producers can have different costs of supply. The different costs are included in the summation of individual marginal costs, which defines the industry supply function. Although costs differ among producers, the corrective Pigovian tax or subsidy makes no distinction among producers and is applied equally to all producers.

Although the tax and subsidy are both means of achieving efficient output, producers prefer to receive the subsidy rather than to pay the tax. Whether the tax or subsidy is the appropriate public policy, however, depends on who has legal rights. When considering private resolution of externality problems through the Coase theorem, we saw that whether the polluter pays the victim or the victim pays the polluter depends on whether the polluter or the victim has legal rights. Similarly, if the public (the victim) has legal rights, the producer is taxed, and, if the producer has legal rights, the producer receives the subsidy. For example, a producer is taxed for polluting a river when the public has the legal right to a clean river. If, however, legal rights allow the factory to pollute and the public seeks a cleaner river, a subsidy provides compensation to the factory's owners for accommodating the public interest and decreasing production, and thereby reducing pollution.

Revenue from taxes and the financing of subsidies

When legal rights call for use of a corrective tax as the means of public policy, the tax revenue is not paid to the victims of environmental damage. The tax revenue becomes part of general government revenue. Corrective public policy requires only that polluters pay the tax in the same way that they would pay for "causing environmental damage" if such a market were to exist. The purpose of the tax is to change the behavior of producers. This does not require payments to persons who are harmed by the adverse externality. Transferring the tax revenue to adversely affected persons could indeed have undesirable efficiency effects, since it could be worthwhile for some people to respond to payment of tax revenue to victims by locating in a polluted area so as to become victims and so be eligible for the payments.

Yet when an externality problem is resolved privately through the Coase theorem, victims *are* paid when they have legal rights. The purpose of the payment to victims is then to provide incentives for the victims to agree to compromise their legal rights to allow an adverse externality at the efficient level. When government has taken responsibility for resolving the externality problem, the government is the agent of the victims and acts on their behalf. In acting on behalf of the victims, the government uses the tax to change producer incentives. The tax revenue is an *incidental consequence* of using the tax to change producer behavior and is kept by the government.

If the factory has legal rights, the persons harmed by pollution do not privately finance the corrective Pigovian subsidy. The subsidy is publicly financed by government, which is implementing public policy as an agent of the public. Taxpayers finance the subsidy, but the subsidy is financed through the government budget by taxpayers in general and not by the particular taxpayers who happen to be victims of the factory's pollution.

A double dividend?

A "polluter-pays principle" gives the public legal rights not to be subjected to pollution and places the burden of change in behavior on the originators of the environmental damage, who pay a tax. When a polluter-pays principle is adopted, there is a "double dividend." The first dividend is the beneficial corrective effect of the tax. The second dividend is the tax revenue, which can be used to rectify the *past* damage to the environment.

Use of tax revenue to rectify past damage does not create adverse incentives for people to locate in polluted areas to benefit from personal compensation. The second dividend provided by the tax revenue can be used to clean up the environment. For example, hazardous waste matter that was dumped in populated areas can be removed, and trees and foliage can be replanted where the landscape was made barren.

The case for use of the revenue from polluters' corrective taxes to rectify past damage is based on a conception of social justice. However, even though we may want polluters who caused damage in the past to pay to rectify the damage, past polluters cannot pay if they cannot be located or if they are bankrupt.

The presence of the second dividend from corrective taxes does not influence the desirability of public policy to rectify past environmental damage. Cost-benefit analysis establishes whether a clean-up project is socially worthwhile. Cost-benefit analysis is based on an efficiency criterion (we determine whether $W = B - C$ is positive). If the environmental clean-up project is socially worthwhile, independently of whether past polluters pay, the clean-up project should nonetheless be publicly financed from the government budget, just as for any project for which the cost-benefit criterion is satisfied.

Taxes and damage
In Figure 4.5, the area OEH is the total social cost of the environmental damage at the efficient quantity Q_1.[3] Could a corrective tax that results in producers paying total taxes equal to total social cost OEH be designed? The level of such a corrective tax varies with output and is equal to the difference between social and private marginal cost. With such a tax, producers would precisely pay, through the tax, the value of the marginal social damage for each unit of output. The tax based on marginal damage cannot be implemented. The different producers do not decide on output sequentially. It is therefore not possible to levy a tax that requires knowing the sequence in which producers cause the negative externality by producing additional output.

With a constant per-unit corrective tax, the total tax revenue $ABHE$ can be greater or less than OEH. The relation between total tax revenue and the value of total damage does not matter for efficiency. Efficiency requires the level of the tax *at the efficient output* to be equal to t as in expression (4.7). The corrective tax t that provides incentives for efficient producer behavior can therefore be constant per unit of output. The same applies to a corrective subsidy.[4]

Information and the choice between taxes and subsidies
Although legal rights indicate whether a corrective tax or subsidy is required, information problems can restrict the feasibility of using a tax or subsidy. It may be difficult to subsidize the activity of "not causing environmental damage," since, to use a subsidy, a government needs to know the output that would have been

---

[3] The area OEH is the difference between the areas under the social and private MC functions, evaluated from output of zero to the efficient quantify of output Q_1.

[4] If there were a monopoly or a single producer, it would be possible to associate the producer's decision to change output with marginal damage. A variable tax or subsidy (whichever is required) would in that case be feasible.

produced if there were no subsidy. That is, in Figure 4.5, the government needs to know the output Q_2 that determines the base for the subsidy. The output Q_2 is not observed if the efficient output Q_1 is being produced. When a tax is used as the means of implementing public policy, a problem of counterfactual information does not arise; the tax is based on output Q_1, which is observed, because this output is produced. The solution to the information problem justifies a polluter-pays principle on feasibility grounds.

Education as a positive externality

Figure 4.6 shows a positive externality associated with an individual's education. The externality is expressed as the difference between private and social MB. The source of the externality may be benefit from interacting and working together with better-informed people. Or more education may reduce crime, by increasing future incomes from legal income-earning activities or by simply keeping children in school and off the streets.

When schooling that provides the quality of education or period of education indicated by ($E_2 - E_1$) is not compulsory, a subsidy from government of GH (equal to the difference between social and private MB at E_2) increases the quality of education or the number of years of study from E_1 to E_2. The subsidy resolves the externality problem by ensuring that social benefits of education are precisely internalized in personal education decisions.

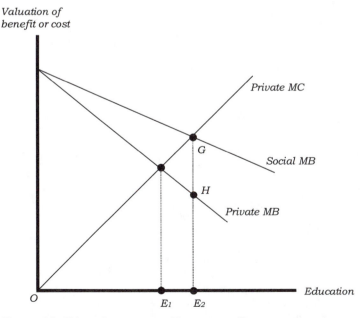

Figure 4.6. Education as a positive externality.

A subsidy to education or tax imposed for not going to school can correct a positive externality due to education. The corrective tax and the corrective subsidy are both equal to GH.

The Pigovian alternative to the subsidy is a tax on years of education between E_1 and E_2 that people do *not* undertake. The years of schooling ($E_2 - E_1$) are not compulsory because individuals can avoid these years of schooling by paying the tax.

In a choice between the subsidy and the tax, we might decide that the tax is inconsistent with social justice. Teenagers who are compelled to work because their parents are too poor to finance their education privately might pay the tax and continue working. Or a teenager who lacks the temperament or ability for formal study might have to pay the tax. Principles of social justice suggest that, in a choice between Pigovian taxes and subsidies to resolve education externalities, governments should subsidize education rather than tax "non-education."

Inputs that have adverse externalities

The principles involved in the design of Pigovian taxes and subsidies apply whether externalities are defined as being the result of production or the use of particular inputs. In Figure 4.7, a producer uses an environmentally damaging input V. The input is purchased at a competitive market price r. The output produced using the input is sold at the price p (in a competitive market). The net private benefit to the producer from using the environmentally harmful input is

$$MB = pMP_V - r, \tag{4.9}$$

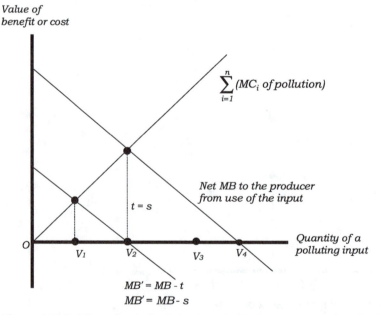

Figure 4.7. Public policy using a tax or subsidy to correct market decisions about use of an input.

which is shown in Figure 4.7. The producer will wish to use the quantity of the input V_4 where

$$pMP_V = r. \tag{4.10}$$

In choosing to use the quantity of input V_4, the producer is ignoring (or not internalizing) environmental costs of using the input.[5]

When n people are harmed by use of the input, the marginal social harm is

$$\sum_{i=1}^{n}(MC_i \ of \ pollution), \tag{4.11}$$

which is shown in Figure 4.7.

Efficient use of the environmentally damaging input is V_2, where the marginal social harm to the population is equal to marginal benefit MB to the producer from use of the input. That is, the use V_2 is efficient, since $W = B - C$ is maximized, where B is total benefit to the producer from production and C is the total social cost imposed on the public.

For example, the environmental damage might be pollution of a lake. When the public has legal rights to a nonpolluted lake, the Coase theorem suggests that the public will use the legal rights to extract payment from the factory owners in return for the factory owners being allowed limited production. The efficient use of the environmentally harmful input V_2 would then be established through private negotiation between the producer and the affected public. The public may not, however, be able to exercise legal rights effectively because of transactions costs and problems of organizing collective action, and government can be invited to enforce the public's legal rights through public policy.

In Figure 4.7, when the government has acted in the public interest and imposed a fixed per-unit tax t on use of the input, owners of the factory face the post-tax marginal benefit function

$$MB' = MB - t. \tag{4.12}$$

After the tax, the owners of the factory recompute their privately profitable use of the environmentally harmful input by setting $MB' = 0$, which results in private choice equal to the socially efficient use of the input at V_2.

---

[5] The input provides an addition to output given by its marginal product MP_V. The market value of this addition to output is pMP_V. The cost of purchasing a marginal quantity of the input is the market price of the input r. Expression (4.9) subtracts the cost r of purchasing an additional quantity of the input from the contribution of the additional input to the value of production, which gives the marginal benefit MB to the producer from marginal use of the environmentally harmful input. In Figure 4.7, the use of the input at V_4 is determined at $MB = 0$ where private profits from use of the input are maximized.

At V_2, private marginal benefit from use of the input equals the tax-inclusive cost of the input so that

$$pMP_v = r + t. \tag{4.13}$$

The tax makes the owners of the factory personally aware that they are imposing a cost on society. The tax substitutes for a market price that would exist in a market for "public health hazards due to the factory's environmental damage of the environment." The public policy of imposing the tax on the input makes the producer behave as if such a market existed.

For an alternative specification of legal rights, we can consider a factory that was built on the shores of a lake many years before anyone used the lake for recreational purposes, or before there was public awareness of the need to protect aquatic life in the lake. Standards of social acceptability and public awareness may have changed over time, and also over the years the area around the lake may have become inhabited. If the factory has the legal right to produce at its location and to use an environmentally harmful input, corrective public policy requires a subsidy to the factory's owners as compensation to the factory's owners for forgoing their legal rights. In Figure 4.7, payment of the efficient corrective subsidy s per unit of output changes private producer marginal benefit from use of the environmentally harmful input to

$$MB' = MB - s. \tag{4.14}$$

We see in Figure 4.7 that once more (as in Figure 4.5) the efficient per-unit corrective subsidy s is precisely equal to the efficient corrective per-unit tax t when the public has legal rights. The tax and the subsidy again have the same effect on producer behavior because the tax t is an explicit cost for factory owners and the subsidy is an equal opportunity cost, now through a loss of s for each unit of the input used in excess of V_2. Just as voluntary private resolution of an externality through the Coase theorem can result in the same efficient outcome independently of how legal rights are assigned, in Figure 4.7, corrective public policy by either a Pigovian tax or a subsidy similarly achieves the same efficient outcome.

Combinations of public policy and private resolution

A government may have used a Pigovian tax to achieve efficient use of the input at V_2 in Figure 4.7, and then the private negotiations of the Coase theorem take place. Beginning from V_2, the private negotiations are based on marginal benefit MB' after the corrective tax has been put into effect. The private Coase negotiations achieve mutual benefits for the producer and the victims of pollution by reducing the use of the input to V_1. The combination of public policy and private negotiation has resulted in inefficient use of the input because the socially efficient use of the input that maximizes $W = B - C$ is at V_2, not V_1.

A way of stating the Coase theorem is that public policy is not required to resolve externality problems when legal rights allow efficient private voluntary resolution. Stating the Coase theorem in this form emphasizes the significance of the sequencing of private resolution and public policy. Efficiency requires that attempts at private resolution take place first. The government then takes responsibility through public policy for resolving externality problems that remain after attempts at private resolution.

In Figure 4.7, private resolution may, for example, have reduced use of the environmentally harmful input to V_3. The responsibility remaining for government through public policy is to complete the reduction in use to the efficient level V_2.

With attempts at private resolution coming first, the Coase theorem implies that we should never see an externality for which public policy does not have a corrective role. This is because it will have been in the mutual interest of private parties to have voluntarily internalized all externalities by private negotiation to the extent that has been possible.

Innovation as a response to a Pigovian tax or subsidy

A Pigovian tax provides an incentive for producers to innovate to avoid the tax. Similarly, a Pigovian subsidy provides an incentive to innovate so as not to lose the subsidy. The incentive to innovate to reduce pollution can result in technologies that provide a cleaner environment than indicated by the Pigovian socially efficient solution.

Limitations of Pigovian taxes and subsidies

Use of Pigovian taxes and subsidies is subject to limitations.

(1) The use of Pigovian taxes and subsidies requires availability of information about market demand and supply, and about the differences between private and social benefits and costs. In the examples that we have used, we have taken for granted that this information is available.

(2) Public policy through Pigovian taxes and subsidies also requires an administrating government bureaucracy. The bureaucracy determines and levies the taxes and, if subsidies are required, sets and dispenses the subsidies. The presence of the administrating bureaucracy re-introduces the issues that were raised in Section 3.3 about principal-agent problems between the public and government bureaucracy.

(3) If public policy requires the use of subsidies, taxes are required to finance the subsidies. The taxes impose the excess burdens on taxpayers that we identified in Section 2.3.

(4) The idea that government can resolve externality problems through taxes or subsidies is based on the principle that appropriate public policy can always replicate the efficient market outcomes that would exist if externalities were internalized in actual market behavior of buyers

and sellers. As shown in Supplement 4B, a missing market need not have an equilibrium price, in which case duplication of the equilibrium price through public policy is impossible.[6]

4.2.3 Direct regulation

An alternative to Pigovian taxes and subsidies that requires less information and may require less bureaucratic administration is direct regulation of externalities. Direct regulation specifies allowable behavior and sets penalties for noncompliance. In the case of externalities associated with education, children are simply compelled to attend school up to a minimum age. Traffic lights are a means of direct regulation at intersections, as are requirements that automobiles use only unleaded fuel and that exhaust filters be used to reduce auto emissions. In hot climates, regulations sometimes require private cars to be air-conditioned to spare other drivers the negative externality of sharing the road with drivers who are aggravated by the summer heat. Emission of pollutants by factories can be directly regulated by requiring filtering devices and by limiting the types of technologies and inputs that can be used. There are direct regulations on permitted levels of noise and on where garbage can be dumped. Cigarette smoking is directly regulated through prohibition in specified locations.

The Coase theorem suggests that direct regulation is in general an inefficient response to externalities. For example, when regulations determine that smoking in a classroom is not permitted, non-smokers and smokers alike cannot gain through Coase negotiations that result in perhaps some limited smoking. Transactions and bargaining costs, and free-rider problems, can, however, be extensive when a number of smokers negotiate with a number of non-smokers. The time-consuming negotiations and possible turmoil before a class begins are avoided by prohibiting smoking in the classroom by direct regulation.

Changes in direct regulation reflect changes in legal rights. Direct regulation that allows smoking of cigarettes benefits smokers. A change in legal rights that prohibits smoking benefits non-smokers. Changes in direct regulation thus have distributional effects. A direct regulation that prohibits smoking in place of previously freely permitted smoking makes non-smokers better off. Similarly, a change in legal rights giving women the right of protection from sexual harassment in the workplace makes women better off and harassers worse off.

Direct regulation requires a clear unambiguous definition of the type of behavior that is to be restricted. Medical studies led to the banning of smoking on airplanes when statistics revealed high rates of cancer for flight attendants who inhaled passengers' smoke. In the case of sexual harassment, the definition of restricted behavior is more complex than the prohibition of smoking. Some

---

[6] If a market for clean air does not have an equilibrium price, points such as E in Figure 4.5 do not exist to allow corrective taxes and subsidies to be computed and applied. The Coase theorem confronts a similar problem. The Coase theorem is based on a market to resolve externality problems through private negotiation and takes for granted that an equilibrium price and quantity exist in the market that is created. For more explanation and detail, see Supplement 4B.

societies allow people to compliment one another on their appearance, whereas compliments about appearance in other societies might be viewed with suspicion and distrust, and as a preamble to harassment. Different societies have therefore adopted different interpretations of the sexual harassment externality. Public policy regarding direct regulation of smoking or industrial pollution is more uniform.

Reciprocal externalities and a prisoners' dilemma

Direct regulation need not make some people better off at the expense of others. When there are reciprocal externalities, direct regulation can make everybody better off. Reciprocal externalities occur, for example, though pollution from automobiles. Individual drivers might prefer that all *other* drivers use more expensive but more environmentally friendly unleaded fuel, while they themselves continue to use cheaper more polluting fuel, in the knowledge that one automobile using leaded fuel (their automobile) has a negligible adverse effect on the environment.

These circumstances define a prisoners' dilemma. The dominant strategy is to use cheaper leaded fuel (if other people use leaded fuel, the best personal response is also to use the leaded fuel; if other people use the more expensive unleaded fuel, the best personal response is again to use leaded fuel). Independently made personal decisions based on private self-interest therefore result in everyone choosing environmentally unfriendly leaded fuel, but everyone is better off when all drivers use only unleaded fuel. A public policy of direct regulation solves the free-rider problem of the prisoners' dilemma by prohibiting use of environmentally harmful unleaded fuel for everybody.

4.2.4 Quotas

We have now considered Pigovian taxes and subsidies and direct regulation as public-policy responses to the presence of externalities. A third (and final means) of using public policy to correct externality problems that we shall consider is through quotas. Quotas are a response to externalities by the setting of limitations on allowable output or use of inputs. For example, efficient total output Q_1 in Figure 4.5 or efficient use of an input V_2 in Figure 4.7 can be directly computed, and quotas can be set to limit maximum allowable output or maximum allowable use of the input to these levels.

Establishing the limit to allowable output or use of an input is the first stage of a public policy based on quotas. In a second stage, a public policy decision is made about how the quota will be distributed among individual producers. Possibilities for distribution of the quota are that (1) the quota rights are auctioned to a highest bidder, (2) the quota rights are sold through a competitive market, or (3) the quota rights are given away without payment.

Auction of quotas

When quota rights are auctioned or sold, the purchaser of the quota rights can have two intentions. One intention is to use the quota rights to produce output.

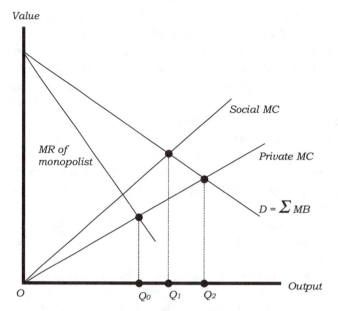

Figure 4.8. The use of a quota and monopoly.
The objective of public policy is to use a pollution quota that limits output to Q_1 to reduce output of the industry from Q_2. A firm that buys the entire quota to monopolize the industry produces output Q_0, which is less than the intended efficient output Q_1.

Each unit of allowable output obtained by a firm under a quota is a unit of output that other firms cannot produce, and so another intention can be to buy quota rights to exclude other firms from production.

Because having the entire quota excludes all competitors, a firm bidding for quota rights is willing to pay up to the value of monopoly profits to obtain the entire quota. The firm that has the rights to the entire quota becomes a monopoly through exclusive control over the right to produce, by having exclusive control over the right to pollute. A government obtains maximum revenue from auction of a quota when one producer buys the entire quota and uses the quota to monopolize the industry.

Figure 4.8 shows a firm that has been successful in monopolizing a market through exclusive purchase of quota rights. The profit-maximizing output of the monopolist is Q_0 where

$$MR = Private\ MC. \tag{4.15}$$

However, the intent of public policy is to use the quota to reduce industry output from Q_2 to Q_1. In Figure 4.8, a firm that has monopolized the industry through exclusive purchase of the quota uses only Q_0 units of the quota for production. The part $(Q_1 - Q_0)$ of the quota has not been acquired for the purpose of production, but to forestall production by competitors.

Monopolists and environmentalists as allies: The second best

A monopolist can be an environmentalist's ally. Some people may be dissatisfied with the government's quota of Q_1 in Figure 4.8 and may wish to have a more stringent environmental policy with less output. The successful monopolist in Figure 4.8, by producing output Q_0, imposes stricter environmental standards than were sought through public policy at output Q_1. The lower production at Q_0 may then be more satisfying for more stringent environmentalists.[7]

When there is no public policy at all to correct an externality, a monopolist can move an outcome in the direction of greater efficiency, compared to a competitive market. We see in Figure 4.8 that monopoly output Q_0 more closely approximates the efficient output Q_1 than the output Q_2 of a competitive industry.

Public policy in a "second-best" situation

The conclusion that, in the absence of a pro-environmental public policy, a monopolized industry can be socially preferable to a competitive industry is an example of the *theory of the second best*. The theory of the second best indicates that, if two sources of inefficiency are present, it may be better to leave both efficiency problems unresolved than to resolve just one of the problems. The two efficiency problems that we have here are that the industry is not competitive but rather monopolized, and that there is at the same time an environmental externality. Each of these efficiency problems calls for a public-policy response, first to replace the monopoly with competition, and second to implement an appropriate corrective public policy that results in internalization (in private decisions) of the negative environmental externality. The first-best outcome for the society is achieved when both problems are resolved through public policy (when these are the only sources of inefficiency in the society).

When the government does not apply corrective public policy to both sources of inefficiency but directs public policy toward solving either the problem of monopoly or the problem of the environmental externality, there is no assurance that public policy will improve efficiency. If one problem remains unattended to, we have a situation of second best, and not first best where public policy resolves both problems. We see an example of the second best in Figure 4.8 because, given the presence of both monopoly and the adverse externality, public policy to implement competition while not addressing the externality problem would result in a less efficient outcome at output Q_2 than the outcome when the monopoly is allowed to persist with its chosen output at Q_0.

---

[7] We now have to ask how the more stringent environmentalist determines that a more stringent environmental policy than limiting production to Q_1 is socially desirable. Perhaps the more stringent environmentalist has applied a lower discount rate than was used to determine public policy and so places more weight on the future and wishes to reduce the accumulated future effects of environmental damage. Or perhaps the more stringent environmentalist is simply more sensitive to environmental damage than indicated by social MC in Figure 4.8. Social MC may for example have been determined by majority voting, with the more stringent environmentalist among the minority.

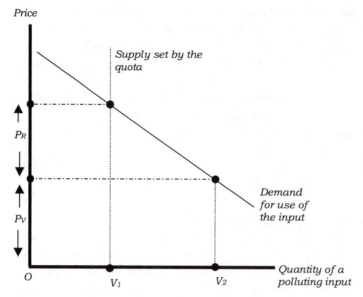

Figure 4.9. A competitive market for quota rights.
The objective of public policy is to reduce the use of the input from V_2 to V_1. Producers can buy the input at a market price of P_V, but they cannot use the input if they have not paid the market price P_R for the right to use a unit of the input. At the combined input price $(P_V + P_R)$, market demand for the input is precisely equal to the total permissible quantity V_1 set by the quota as the limit on use (per period of time).

Sale of quota rights in a competitive market

Quota rights can be sold and traded in competitive markets. Figure 4.9 shows a competitive market for the rights to use a polluting input. The rights could also be for emission of environmentally harmful substances. A government agency can act as supplier of quota rights to such a market. Producers can buy emission rights from the government agency. They can also trade rights among themselves. With many buyers and sellers (including the government agency), the market in emissions can be competitive.

In Figure 4.9, the government agency sets a limit to total supply of rights through a quota at the level V_1. The demand function for use of the input (or for emissions) is the sum of individual producers' demands. The competitive market price of the polluting input is P_V. When there is no public policy restricting use of the input, total demand for the input is V_2. When the price of the input is $(P_V + P_R)$, demand for the input equals the supply V_1 set as the allowable total quota.

The component P_R in the market price $(P_V + P_R)$ is the cost to a producer of buying the right to use a unit of the input in the competitive market for quota rights. Individual producers choose use of the input by setting marginal benefit from use (or the value of the marginal product of the input) equal to the combined cost of purchasing the input and the right to use the input:

$$pMP_V \equiv MB \text{ of use} = P_V + P_R. \tag{4.16}$$

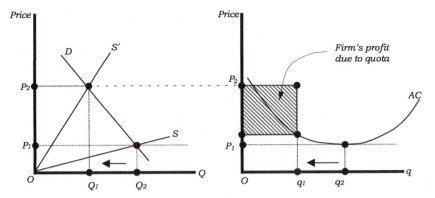

Figure 4.10. Assignment of a quota among producers.
The efficient quota Q_1 is assigned among preexisting producers, who profit from the correction of the externality.

A competitive market in the right to use environmentally damaging inputs therefore results in efficient use of the input. We see that, in expression (4.16), the condition for efficient use is satisfied because marginal benefit from use is equal to social marginal cost of using the input. Through the competitive market, those producers who can most profitably use the polluting inputs pay the price P_R for the right of use. The inputs and accompanying emission rights are thereby distributed to highest value users.[8]

By selling quota rights in a competitive market as in Figure 4.9, a government duplicates the outcome of using a Pigovian tax or subsidy. The price P_R in the competitive market for the right to use the input is equal to the efficient Pigovian tax or subsidy.

Distribution of the quota to existing producers

Rather than selling quota rights, a government could choose to give quota rights away free to existing producers. The decision to give away rights to pollute without payment to existing producers could be based on a sense of justice. Producers may have made investments in productive capacity when harm to the environment was not regarded as a social problem. Now, through no fault of their own, the producers confront changed social awareness of environmental problems.

The producers who receive the free quota rights are freed from the discipline of competition. Figure 4.10 shows a competitive industry in which, before recognition of the social cost of environmental damage, industry output is Q_2 and the

---

[8] In a competitive market for quota rights, the benefit to any one producer from using quota rights to forestall competing sales by other sellers is small, and rights to use an input (or emission rights) are purchased in order to produce and sell. Therefore, the limit set by the allowable quota determines how much is produced, and the public policy objective regarding use of inputs (or emissions) is achieved.

market price is P_1. An individual firm in the industry is at the same time shown as producing the average-cost-minimizing output q_2.

After society acknowledges the social cost of damage to the environment, the industry's true social market supply function is recognized to be $S' = \sum (Social\ MC)$, which determines the socially efficient outcome as Q_1 and the corresponding price as P_2. The government responds to awareness of the externality by setting Q_1 as the limit on total output (or use of inputs) for the industry. In the second step of the public policy decision, the quota Q_1 is distributed among the existing producers. The distribution might be in proportion to producers' original output before the quota was introduced. The quota of the representative individual producer in Figure 4.10 is q_1.

We see in Figure 4.10 that, after the free distribution of quota rights, individual firms are no longer producing at minimum average cost. The firms in the industry earn excess noncompetitive profits. The price P_2 at which the firm in Figure 4.10 sells is greater than average cost, and the firm earns excess profits given by the striped area.

Profits should attract entry of new firms into the industry. Entry in response to profits, however, cannot take place because new entrants do not have the right to produce. Potential new entrants cannot produce because they lack emission rights; they have no share of the allowable quota. In the absence of competitive entry, the firms that received shares of the quota can continue earning noncompetitive profits by producing levels of output such as q_1.

The firms that were assigned free shares of the quota can capitalize their profits by selling their quota rights to other firms or to new entrants into the industry. A new firm with a better product or a superior technology can thereby purchase rights to produce and offer its superior product to consumers.

A new firm with the same technology and costs of a preexisting firm can earn no more than competitive profits by buying quota rights that allow it to produce. The asset (the right to use the environmentally damaging input) that the firm has bought can yield no more than a rate of return equal to other risk-adjusted competitive returns available from other investments in the economy. The owners of the firms that received the free rights to use the input when the rights were originally distributed are the beneficiaries of all excess profits from the introduction of the quota.

4.2.5 Political decisions

We have now identified Pigovian tax and subsidy policies, direct regulation, and quotas as different ways of implementing public policy to correct externalities. When the quota is used, a further public-policy decision to determine whether to sell the quota rights or to distribute the rights without payment to producers is required.

Which of the different means of implementing public policy can we expect governments to choose? In considering this question, we shall consider legal rights to be with the public, so that from the tax-subsidy alternatives the appropriate form of public policy is a tax on the polluter.[9]

A Pigovian tax, direct regulation, and competitive sale or free distribution of quota rights are all means of achieving efficient levels of output or use of inputs when an externality is present. However, when the method of freely distributing a quota is used, production is not cost-efficient; as we saw in Figure 4.10, individual producers do not produce average-cost minimizing quantities.

Also, when the method of freely distributing a quota is used, producers earn above-competitive profits. When the other methods of solving externality problems are used, producers do not earn above-competitive profits. Direct regulation adds extra costs to production by requiring investment in pollution abatement equipment. When a Pigovian tax is the instrument of public policy, firms earn competitive profits before and after the tax; nevertheless, some firms will have been forced into bankruptcy or will have been compelled to leave the market.[10]

When public policy takes the form of free distribution of quota rights, producers do not incur short-run losses and do not face the threat of having to close down their production facilities. All producers who were in the industry when the pro-environmental policy was introduced earn the sustainable non-competitive excess profits that we have described.

A Pigovian tax or sale of quota rights provides a government with revenue. Free distribution of quota rights to producers provides no government revenue. When free distribution of quota rights is used as the method of implementing pro-environmental policy, a government loses revenue, and also production is not cost-efficient; at the same time, producers in the industry have gained from the pro-environmental policy.

Therefore, existing producers favor correcting externalities through free distribution of a quota over a corrective Pigovian tax because of the profits provided by the free quota rights. Producers also prefer free distribution of quota rights to a market where they have to pay for emission rights. As we have observed, Pigovian taxes and purchase of quota rights in competitive markets are equivalent for producers. Producers also favor free distribution of quota rights over direct regulation because of the additional costs imposed on producers by direct regulation.

James Buchanan (Nobel laureate, 1986) and his collaborator Gordon Tullock predicted (in 1975) that we can expect to see governments resolving problems

---

[9] Because subsidies are not required, the excess burden of taxation that would be associated with taxation to finance subsidies does not affect choice of the means of public policy.

[10] In Figure 4.10, if a government uses a corrective Pigovian tax to achieve efficient output Q_1, producers incur losses in the short run because the price received for output in the short run is less than average cost of production plus the tax. The losses by producers are a short-run phenomenon. The short run is defined with the number of producers given, and the long run is defined as enough time for some producers to close down their production facilities. In the long run, after some producers have closed down their production facilities, the industry will have adjusted to the tax with producers choosing output at minimum average cost plus the tax and earning no more than the normal competitive level of profit for the industry.

of adverse externalities by free distribution of quota rights to producers, even though this method of implementing public policy results in production that is not cost-efficient and also deprives governments of revenue that could be obtained from taxes or from sale of quota rights. The reason for using the method of free distribution of quota rights is political. By freely distributing quota rights, governments ensure that producers support pro-environmental policy. Indeed, by freely distributing the quota rights, governments ensure that producers are active proponents of pro-environmental policy. Producers have an interest in actively supporting a pro-environmental policy that gives them free quota rights because of the non-competitive profits that the producers thereby earn.

An example of a market for emission rights

Coal-burning electricity power stations emit sulfur dioxide (or SO_2). The emissions harm plants and trees, as well as aquatic life. In 1990, the U.S. government introduced a market for the right to emit sulfur dioxide. A maximum allowable quota on total emissions was set, and the quota of total allowable emissions was decreased over time. Rights to emit SO_2 were assigned free to existing electricity utility companies. Each electricity utility was obliged to present sufficient quota rights to cover emissions to the U.S. federal Environmental Protection Agency. Companies without quota rights to match emissions faced financial penalties and further reductions in their allowable emission levels. The quota rights were made tradable in a market.

The program establishing the market could have been initiated through competitive sale of quota rights rather than by distributing quota rights free to the preexisting producers. A Pigovian tax on emissions of SO_2 could also have been used, or direct regulation could have been used to set emission standards and to require investment in abatement.

By distributing the emission quota rights without charge to existing producers and establishing a market where emission rights could be traded, the government made the emission reduction program attractive to producers, in particular to producers who were effective in reducing emissions. The market rewarded electricity companies for reducing environmental damage, since unneeded quota rights could be sold in the market for emission rights.

The political decision whether to correct externalities

We have been considering choice of the method of public policy for resolving environmental externality problems. There is also a question of whether a government will adopt a corrective policy at all. Governments have not always acted spontaneously to resolve externality problems. Air quality has at times been permitted to deteriorate. Dumping of hazardous materials has been permitted. The quality of drinking water has sometimes been allowed to deteriorate through environmentally harmful run-offs from agriculture and industrial production. Recreational sites (beaches, rivers, and lakes) have become polluted, as has the atmosphere. Public policy to provide remedies for these environmental problems has often required public outcry and lobbying by environmental activists, or there has been a crisis of dimensions that could not be ignored.[11]

4.2.6 Global externalities and international agreements

There are significant types of externalities that extend across national boundaries. The release into the atmosphere of carbon dioxide, sulfur dioxide, methane, and nitrous oxide and the destruction of rain forests have been linked to global warming and climate change. When externalities extend across national boundaries, we cannot call upon a government to resolve the externality problems through public policy because no global government exists to implement the global policies required to protect the global environment.

Rain forests

A national government has sovereignty over its land, including in particular areas where rain forests are located. The continued presence of the rain forests is globally beneficial to all people, including people living outside the boundaries of the countries where rain forests are located. The global greenhouse effect when forests are cut down creates a negative externality that is an undesirable public good for the entire world, but a society, through its national government, can claim "the rain forests belong to us, which gives us the right to do as we wish with the trees." A world government with global authority could internalize the externality associated with the cutting down of rain forests, by paying people not to clear rain forests, or by buying and preserving rain forests.

Rather than allowing rain forests to be cleared for private profit from timber or farming and pasture, a country's government can sell the right to rain forests to foreign governments whose populations are more sensitive to the quality of the global environmental. Extensive free-rider problems can be expected in such a market because whoever pays to sustain a rain forest provides a public-good benefit to the global population.

Yet, although we anticipate that free-rider problems would preempt the creation of a market in the right to sustain a rain forest, the market has existed, even if on a small scale. For example, the government of the Central American state of Costa Rica successfully established an international market for "not cutting down" rain forests in the 1990s. Parts of its rain forests were sold to foreign governments. Only very few foreign governments participated in the market to buy and sustain part of a rain forest. Most of the world's governments, when confronting the prisoners' dilemma of whether to contribute, chose to free ride. The few foreign governments that participated in the market created by Costa Rica provided a free public good to the populations (and governments) of the many

---

[11] It may seem to be a puzzle why a government needs to be convinced that environmental problems require policy attention when a majority of voters favor public policy to resolve an externality problem. We shall return to the puzzle of a government that disregards the environment in Chapter 6, when we look more closely at how public-policy decisions can be influenced by political objectives.

other countries that chose not to participate but nonetheless enjoy the benefits of the global public good provided through preservation of rain forests.

Some individuals have also used parts of their personal wealth to buy and preserve rain forests. These individuals have privately provided the world with a public good.

Biodiversity and protection of wildlife

The preservation of biodiversity by protecting wildlife is another international externality. In some cases, this externality is also related to preservation of rain forests.

Elephants are hunted for the ivory from their tusks. Rhinos are hunted because, as we have previously noted, some people believe that their horns, when ground up and ingested, are aphrodisiacs. Some species of the world's largest mammals, the whales, have been hunted to near extinction. International agreements attempt to preserve wildlife and biodiversity, but not all countries' governments have the same will or incentive to comply.[12]

The ozone layer

Emissions of man-made chlorofluorocarbons and other substances (halons, carbon tetrachloride, and methyl chloroform) have been identified as the cause of a hole in the earth's ozone layer over the continent of Antarctica.[13] The ozone layer protects us from ultraviolet radiation from the rays of the sun. A diminished ozone layer increases the incidence of skin cancer and is also harmful to agricultural crops.

International agreement was reached on eliminating emissions of chlorofluorocarbons when the extent of the damage to the earth's ozone layer became known. Under the Montreal Protocol of 1987 on substances that deplete the ozone layer, governments of the world agreed to phase out emissions of ozone-depleting substances. The World Bank provided assistance. Under its Global Environmental Facility, the World Bank financed investments that enabled poorer countries to comply with the Montreal Protocol.[14]

The prisoners' dilemma and impediments to international agreement

The Montreal Protocol shows that international agreement is possible when the urgency is evident. Often, however, international agreement is difficult to reach.[15] Difficulties in reaching international agreement on environmental policies can be understood against the background of the prisoners' dilemma.

---

[12] Supplement 4C describes the protection of dolphins by the United States, in the face of opposition from other countries.

[13] Icy clouds in the stratospheric ozone layer result from stray chlorine atoms that emanate from chlorofluorocarbons and other substances. The ozone layer is destroyed when the stray chlorine atoms take oxygen atoms from ozone, which is a three-oxygen molecule.

[14] The World Bank is an international finance and development agency with headquarters in Washington, D.C. The Bank lends to poorer countries and also provides technical assistance and advice on economic policy.

[15] The path of implementation of the Montreal Protocol by different countries was also uneven.

TABLE 4.2. THE PRISONERS' DILEMMA IN INTERNATIONAL AGREEMENTS

	Government 2 agrees to reduce emissions	Government 2 refuses to reduce emissions
Government 1 agrees to reduce emissions	30, 30	10, 40
Government 1 refuses to reduce emissions	40, 10	20, 20

People in different countries are, at the same time, both polluters and victims. They benefit through consumption and production when they pollute, but they also adversely affect themselves and one another. That is, the externalities are reciprocal. We have observed how reciprocal externalities give rise to a prisoners' dilemma.

Emission reductions are public goods that benefit everyone globally. A government committing to a reduction in emissions by its population provides global benefits and imposes a cost on its own population through the need for adjustment to the stricter environmental standards. A prisoners' dilemma is present.

The prisoners' dilemma is shown in Table 4.2 for the governments of two countries, although the dilemma applies to agreement among many countries. The efficient outcome is (30, 30) where the countries' governments both agree to reduce emissions. The best outcome 40 for an individual government is achieved by free riding and not agreeing to reduce emissions when the government of the other country does. The worst outcome 10 is where a country reduces emissions and the other country does not.

The Nash equilibrium is at (20, 20) where neither government agrees to reduce emissions. If the government of the other country agrees to reduce emissions, the best response of a government is not to impose emission restrictions on its own citizens. If the other government does not agree to reduce emissions, the best response of a government is also not to impose emission restrictions on its own citizens. The dominant strategy for each government is therefore to attempt to free ride on reductions in emissions in other countries, which leads to the inefficient Nash equilibrium at (20, 20).

Cooperation to escape the inefficient Nash equilibrium at (20, 20) and to achieve the efficient outcome (30, 30) requires governments to agree on (1) the magnitude of a total reduction in global emissions and (2) assignment of obligations to reduce emissions among individual countries. In a further step, the government of each individual country assigns emission rights among local producers in accord with the country's emission quota.

The decision about the reduction required in global emissions is based on scientific information about the total emissions that the earth can bear. The assignment of obligations among countries to reduce emissions is an economic decision that affects the international distribution of income and wealth. As is characteristic of distributional questions, we can expect disagreement about how quotas of emission rights should be assigned among countries. Richer or more industrialized countries benefit from a rule that allocates the global emission quota in proportion to contemporary emissions. Poorer less industrialized countries benefit from a rule that assigns the global emission quota on the basis of population and so gives each person on earth the same legal rights to the global environment independently of contemporary contributions to global pollution.[16]

After the rule for assignment of national quotas for emissions has been decided, the emission rights can be traded in an international market. Tradability of emission rights ensures global efficiency, in the same way that a national market in emission rights ensures domestic efficiency. A global market in emission rights allows producers who can more profitably take advantage of emission rights to purchase rights from producers anywhere in the world who have lower demands for the right to emit pollutants.

The market for emission rights allows producers in the richer or more industrialized countries to use the majority of emission rights independently of whether richer or poorer countries are initially assigned a substantial share of rights. The assignment of legal rights does not affect efficient use, as we expect from the Coase theorem. The assignment of legal rights does, of course, affect income distribution in determining whether producers who wish to use the emission rights have the rights in the first place or need to buy emission rights.

Free riding in the prisoners' dilemma takes place at the stage where governments face the decision whether to agree to the rule for assignment of emission rights among countries. A government can decide to reject the quota it has been assigned and to free ride by continuing to permit its producers to emit pollutants at will.

Preconditions for the prisoners' dilemma

There are preconditions that must be satisfied in the assignment of a quota of emission rights among countries if escape from the prisoners' dilemma by international agreement is to be at all possible. The symmetric prisoners' dilemma in Table 4.2 describes benefits from different outcomes when both countries have received sufficient emission rights to make participation in an international agreement worthwhile. That is, when the conditions of the prisoners' dilemma are present as in Table 4.2, both countries individually prefer the globally efficient outcome (30, 30) to the noncooperative Nash equilibrium outcome (20, 20). A different situation is described in Table 4.3. Here a proposal for assignment of quota rights

---

[16] Agreement can also be difficult about the role of "sinks" in determining national emission quotas. Sinks are forests and foliage that increase the natural capacity to absorb greenhouse gasses. Governments of countries with large absorption capacity wish to have the capacity of sinks included as a credit against their obligations to reduce emissions. Governments of countries that do not have substantial natural sinks tend to object.

TABLE 4.3. A PROPOSED QUOTA ASSIGNMENT FAILS TO PROVIDE THE
GOVERNMENT OF COUNTRY 1 WITH AN INCENTIVE TO AGREE TO MUTUAL
EMISSION REDUCTION

	Government 2 agrees to reduce emissions	Government 2 refuses to reduce emissions
Government 1 agrees to reduce emissions	15, 45	10, 40
Government 1 refuses to reduce emissions	40, 10	20, 20

provides the government of country 2 with an interest in efficient global resolution of environmental externalities, but not so the government of country 1. Benefits for country 2 in Table 4.3 from different outcomes do not follow the ranking of the prisoners' dilemma. Nor do country 1's benefits follow the rankings of the prisoners' dilemma. For country 1, the best outcome (at 40) remains to free ride when the other country reduces emissions and the worst outcome (at 10) remains to reduce emissions when the other country does not. Contrary to the prisoners' dilemma, country 1 is, however, better off without an agreement (at 20) where no country reduces emissions than when there is agreement (at 15) to mutually reduce emissions.

The reason for the higher benefit for country 1 without an international agreement is the proposed division of quota rights to emissions. Country 1 is being offered too small a share of the global emissions quota for cooperation to reduce emissions to be attractive. The proposed division provides country 1 with less benefit than at (20, 20) where no agreement is reached and no country reduces emissions.

When emission rights are assigned and a market in emissions rights is introduced, the population in a country requires rights to do what could previously be freely done (i.e., pollute the environment). If a country is not given sufficient emissions rights, there is no incentive for the government of the country to agree to a cooperative outcome where all countries restrict emissions.

From the perspective of world efficiency, we see that the efficient outcome in Table 4.3 is an international agreement to reduce emissions, since total benefit is then a maximal $(15 + 45) = 60$. The worst global outcome is without an agreement where total benefit is a minimal $(20 + 20) = 40$. An intermediate outcome of global benefit of $(40 + 10) = 50$ would arise if one country were to unilaterally reduce emissions while the other does not.

In Table 4.3, the government of country 1 has a dominant strategy of not agreeing to reduce emissions. The government of country 2 does not have a dominant strategy. The Nash equilibrium is the outcome at (20, 20) where there is no agreement to reduce emissions.

A precondition for cooperation to achieve the global efficient outcome is that emission rights be allocated so that each country can be better off by cooperating to accept the allocation of rights. In Table 4.3, this precondition is not satisfied for country 1.

The precondition for cooperation is satisfied by the proposal in Table 4.2 that assigns emission rights so that the two countries share equally the global benefit of 60 available in the efficient emission-reduction outcome. With the incentive provided for the government of country 1 to participate in an international agreement to reduce global emissions, global agreement is feasible. In this case, global agreement makes the world better off and at the same time each country is individually better off.

Bargaining in international negotiations determines the division among countries of the global benefit from mutual agreement to reduce emissions. In Table 4.3, any alternative outcome that provides country 1 with a benefit exceeding 20 from on international agreement provides an incentive for country 1 to cooperate to reduce global emissions.

When in Table 4.3 the government of country 1 does not agree to participate in an international agreement to reduce emissions, it is not attempting to free ride in the sense of the prisoners' dilemma. Rather, with all goodwill to cooperate on its part, the government of country 1 has not been given an incentive to participate in an international agreement because of the proposed accompanying division of the global quota for emissions among countries.

Country 1 may be a poor country with little industry and with little present use for emission rights in its domestic production. Country 1 may however anticipate that in the future it will close the gap between its production and the production of presently richer countries. The ranking of benefits for country 1 from Table 4.3 can therefore be based on anticipation of future need for emissions rights compared to the division of global emission rights that is being proposed. Country 1 may alternatively be a presently rich country that has been offered too small a share in the proposed division of global emission rights.

The scope of the problem of international cooperation

The scope of the problem of international cooperation is that, even if, as in Table 4.2, the assignment of emission rights *can make* every country better off, the dominant strategy of each individual government remains to free ride.[17]

4.2.7 Differences in sensitivity to environmental problems

Environmental quality appears to be a "luxury" good for which demand is highest in wealthiest countries. In very poor societies, a large part of the population tends to

---

[17] In particular, governments of poorer countries that are sufficiently small might hope to be sufficiently insignificant for their nonparticipation in international agreements not to be noticed.

focus effort on satisfying basic needs of daily survival. Also, in those poor countries with limited or no democracy, the rulers might choose to focus on personal profit from clearing rain forests to sell the lumber from the trees rather than being concerned with environmental consequences of their business activities.

Differences in environmental standards can be a source of tension between richer and poorer countries. Environmentalists in richer countries can fear a race to the bottom in environmental standards. The race to the bottom occurs if local environmental standards in richer countries decline to keep local costs near foreign production costs. To avoid a race to the bottom in environmental standards that they believe will occur, environmentalists might support polices that restrict free international trade. The environmentalists reason that, if foreign goods do not compete against domestically produced goods, there will be no local political pressure to reduce domestic environmental standards for the purpose of competing with the foreign goods under equal conditions.

Because of the personal benefit from reduced foreign competition, local producers in the richer countries also have an interest in supporting protectionist restrictions on domestic sale of foreign goods. We previously observed that stringent environmentalists might support monopolization of markets. Because of the desire to preempt a race to the bottom in environmental standards, stringent environmentalists likewise might side with local import-competing producers in objecting to free international trade or globalization of markets.[18]

Environmental standards as a source of international comparative advantage

Lax environmental standards in poor countries allow producers to produce at lower cost than producers elsewhere who confront higher standards. The idea that a country's comparative advantage in international trade might be based on lax environmental standards is controversial because some people think that it is unjust or unfair that poorer countries should use production technologies that are harmful to their local environmental. The position taken might be that, being already poor and having low life expectancies, people in poor countries should not be made to suffer further from adverse environmental effects on their health. The concern in this case is about local environmental impacts in other countries, and not with global environmental consequences of foreign decisions.

In addition to the question of use of production technologies that are locally environmentally harmful, there is a question whether poorer countries should be permitted to profit by agreeing to import hazardous waste. Generally, countries pay for goods they import. In the case of hazardous waste, countries receive payments to accept the imports.

---

[18] Free trade is also called globalization because markets have become globalized by the liberalization of the international trade policies that separated national markets.

In 1992, there was controversy when the then head of economic research at the World Bank (U.S. economist Lawrence Summers, on leave from the department of economics at Harvard University) observed that lax environmental standards give poor countries a comparative advantage in producing environmentally un-friendly goods. Summers also raised the question whether poorer countries should import hazardous waste. These issues were raised in an internal note that was not intended for general release; nonetheless, the note reached the press. Ob-jections arose because of an interpretation that a proposal was being made that people in poor countries should be permitted to be environmentally victimized through international markets. Or environmentally victimized by their govern-ments. Governments in poorer countries (as elsewhere) choose environmental standards through public policy. However, in many poorer countries governments have not been democracies. There can be a concern that rulers who are not cho-sen democratically might not care all that much about harm to the health of the people, providing there is personal profit.[19]

When the question is asked whether lax environmental standards are an ap-propriate basis for comparative advantage in international trade for poorer coun-tries, the issue is also being raised whether poorer societies should be allowed to choose their own local environmental standards. That is, in the absence of cross-border or international externalities associated with a country's environmental standards, should richer countries interfere in public policy decisions in poorer countries?

The same question has arisen in regard to externalities from education in poorer countries, or rights to education. Child labor may be the norm in a foreign country so that children work and provide low-cost labor rather than go to school. Should child labor in poor countries be a concern of people in richer countries?

Issues of motives arise regarding positions that can be taken in answering the question whether foreign societies should be permitted to choose their own envi-ronmental and social standards. As we have noted, producers in richer countries have reason to care about lax local environmental and likewise about social stan-dards in poorer countries because of the lower costs of production facilitated by the lower foreign standards, independently of altruistic concern for the well-being of the people in foreign countries. The coalition that we have observed can arise between environmentalists and producers in seeking restrictions on free interna-tional trade or resisting globalization may be joined by labor in rich countries, which may fear a "loss of jobs" to foreign countries with low environmental or social standards.[20]

---

[19] In principle, the international transportation of hazardous waste is regulated by an international agreement (the Basel convention on transboundary movement of hazardous wastes and their dis-posal). The agreement requires that importing countries agree willingly to receive the hazardous waste and that exporting countries guarantee that the waste will not be disposed of or stored in a way that might be harmful to the environment.

[20] The case of the dolphins in Supplement 4C is another instance where environmentalists and domestic producers had common cause – but sought to protect the dolphins for different reasons.

When producers in rich countries ask for international harmonization of environmental and labor standards with the intent that foreign competitors face the same costs as they do, the argument is being made that differences in environmental standards should not be a source of comparative advantage in international trade. If the same producers ask for protectionist policies (import duties or prohibitions of imports) to counter low foreign costs that are due to lax foreign environmental and labor standards, the argument is the same; that is, if lax foreign standards cannot be changed, at least foreign standards should not be the basis for advantage for international trade.

A contrary position that can be taken is that markets should be allowed to provide benefits to buyers and sellers without judgments by others about whether people are harming themselves through their market decisions. The case made in Chapter 1, following Adam Smith, was that voluntary decisions in markets are beneficial, and that, in particular, in earning a living people should be allowed to use whatever advantages they have. Therefore, it would follow that, if people in poorer countries are voluntarily prepared to earn income by producing goods that locally degrade the environment or that involve child labor or by accepting to live with hazardous waste, they should be allowed to do so if this is what they want to do.

Yet lax standards toward the local environment and child labor are the consequence of decisions made by governments in poorer countries not to internalize externalities through any of the corrective methods that we have considered. Not only might local externalities be permitted to persist, but governments in the poorer countries might also invite and increase adverse externalities by accepting imports of hazardous waste in return for sufficient payment. NIMBYs (or people who take the view that locally adverse environmental effects should be "not in my backyard") can be expected to be pleased by such outcomes that direct adverse externalities elsewhere through voluntary market payments. People with broader sensitivities will be unhappy that markets direct adverse externalities to poorer countries, even though foreigners, or more specifically foreign rulers and governments, voluntarily accept the adverse externalities in return for sufficient payment.

Changes in foreign attitudes to externalities through income growth

When income and wealth reach sufficiently high levels, people begin to become more sensitive to the quality of the environment and seek improvements in environmental quality. By increasing incomes, competitive markets and free international trade increase a population's demand for improved environmental quality and for education for children to replace child labor.

Nonetheless, until the income gap between rich and poor societies is sufficiently reduced, a poor society may tend to have less regard for the environment and may be less concerned about child labor than a rich society. A consequence of the lax environmental and labor standards in poorer countries is that production facilities located in the poorer countries (but sometimes owned by firms or people in richer countries) will have a competitive advantage (or comparative advantage) in more environmentally unfriendly production, but we expect this situation to change as incomes in poorer countries grow.

Is the problem markets or governments?

We have observed that governments in poorer countries have often not been democratic, and that rulers may be more concerned with increasing their personal wealth than safeguarding the health and improving well-being of the people whom they rule. Foreign governments may then expose their people to harmful environmental effects or refrain from taking public-policy measures to end child labor. The same foreign rulers may deplete rain forests and may choose to free ride in not joining in international agreements to protect the global environment.

Protests at times take place against freedom to trade in international markets, or equivalently against globalization of markets. The protests have often been directed against the World Bank (which we recall funded the implementation in poorer countries of the Montreal Protocol to protect the ozone layer) or the International Monetary Fund and the World Trade Organization.[21] Yet it would appear that protests against environmental and social problems in poor countries should not be directed at international organizations that advocate free markets, but at those foreign governments and rulers who do not implement socially appropriate policies that would resolve environmental and educational externality problems in their countries.

4.2.8 Public health and private rights

Tuberculosis is an infectious disease of the lungs. The disease, which was once very prevalent, was often fatal but can generally be cured by antibiotics. An extended period of time is required for treatment: antibiotics have to be taken over a period of months. An infected person who begins treatment and does not complete the required course of antibiotics creates a negative externality for society, since partial treatment allows new strains of bacteria that are able to resist the antibiotics to develop. This externality is the basis of a case for infringement of private rights, by requiring internment of patients so that their intake of antibiotics can be monitored. Internment at the same time prevents the disease from spreading, so resolving another externality.

---

[21] The International Monetary Fund (IMF) is an international agency that, like the World Bank, has a financial and advisory role in assisting governments. Like the World Bank, the IMF is located in Washington, D.C. The World Bank focuses its assistance on poorer countries, while the IMF has a broader mandate. The World Trade Organization (WTO) has its headquarters in Geneva. The objectives of the WTO are to promote free international trade and to avoid discriminatory practices in international trade.

Internment resolves the externality problem by direct regulation. Pigovian taxes or subsidies are not used, no quotas are set, and no markets are created to internalize the externality. People are interred to protect the public from adverse health externalities.

A prominent case study in public health is the story of "Typhoid Mary." Mary Mallon, which was the true name of Typhoid Mary, was a carrier of typhoid but was herself immune to the disease. She worked as a cook in New York and, between 1900 and 1907, infected (in one case fatally) a number or people who ate her cakes and puddings. She was tracked down by the government and placed in confinement, where she spent the last 30 years of her life.

When awareness of AIDS became prominent in the 1980s, proposals were made that people identified to be carriers of the HIV virus that eventually leads to AIDS (with rare exceptions of apparent natural immunity) should be marked (or tattooed) with indelible ink. The marking was intended as a warning to others and not as a sign of personal rebuke. That is, the marking was proposed as a means of resolving an externality. The intention was to place the indelible mark on a part of the body where the mark would not be conspicuous (people walking in the street would not be identified). The idea was rejected, although the identification mark would have saved lives. The mark was regarded as an infringement of personal rights for people who tested HIV-positive and did not want the stigma of being marked. Proposals were also rejected that people who were HIV-positive should be interned for the safety of the public. The public policy response was therefore different to that of the case of people with tuberculosis and the case of Typhoid Mary.

4.2.9 Conclusions

The Coase theorem suggests a limited role for government in the resolution of externality problems. According to the Coase theorem, government need do no more to resolve externality problems than provide the legal system that allows legal rights to be defined so that private mutually beneficial negotiations can take place. The responsibility of government in resolution of externality problems expands when the Coase theorem is compromised by transactions and bargaining costs, unwillingness of people to participate in markets that would resolve externalities, and costs of organizing collective action. We have seen that, in the expanded domain of responsibility through public policy, externality problems can be resolved (1) by Pigovian taxes or subsidies, (2) by direct regulation, or (3) through quotas that set limits on permissible activities or emissions.

Whether a Pigovian tax or subsidy is the appropriate means of public policy depends on legal rights. We have seen however that feasibility and social justice can also influence the choice between Pigovian taxes and subsidies.

Direct regulation provides direct control over the source of an externality. Direct regulation also solves a prisoners' dilemma when people attempt to free ride by wishing to continue to create negative externalities when others no longer do so.

The use of quotas requires a further decision about how quota rights are to be distributed among producers. Auctioning quota rights can maximize government revenue but can create monopoly. A competitive market in quota rights replicates the Pigovian tax solution and ensures efficient distribution of quota rights among producers. A policy of giving quota rights free to preexisting producers creates noncompetitive profits, and production is not cost-efficient. Free distribution of quota rights however makes producers supporters of pro-environment policies. Producers would seek a quota accompanied by free distribution of quota rights independently of environmental policy.

We have also observed that governments have sometimes had to be convinced to adopt public policies that resolve environmental problems.

The solution of global environmental problems encounters difficulties because of incentives for governments to attempt to shift the burden of reduction in emissions to populations in other countries. We have seen that reaching global agreement on reductions in emissions is a problem of the type of the prisoners' dilemma. However, a precondition for being able to achieve the efficient cooperative solution to the prisoners' dilemma is that the division of a global emissions quota give each individual country reason to prefer participation in an international agreement to the outcome where there is no agreement.

Global environmental problems are compounded by different sensitivities of richer and poorer countries to the environment and to local externalities associated with schooling of children. The different sensitivities can give environmentalists and producers common cause in seeking to restrict international trade. The behavior of environmentalists depends on whether they are pleased that foreign countries have agreed to accept adverse externalities for payment or whether they think that it is unjust or immoral to shift adverse externalities to foreigners even if foreigners, or their governments, readily accept the externalities in exchange for profit or payment.

We have also noted that the underlying source of the problem of adverse foreign externalities is not international markets where goods produced in rich and poor countries are traded but attitudes of foreign governments and rulers to resolving externality problems in their countries.

When externalities affect health, we have seen that public policy decisions can involve a conflict between personal rights and the public interest.

We also noted at the beginning of this section the question of limits on rights to declare an externality. Externalities can be subjective, and societies set limits on the right or discretion to declare an externality.

We have also observed that externalities are often the underlying reason for the need for cost-benefit analysis; leaving externalities out of account or inappropriately valuing externalities can change the conclusions of cost-benefit valuations of public spending.

References and related literature

On the theory of externalities, see Pigou (1920/1962) and Cornes and Sandler (1996). On environmental policy, see Baumol and Oates (1988). On social benefits of education, see Behrman and Stacey (1997); on beneficial externalities through schooling reducing crime, see Donohue and Siegelman (1998). On the U.S. market in emission rights for SO_2, see Montero (1999) and Ellerman et al. (2000). On the effects of taxes and tradeable permits on incentives to innovate, see Requate (1998). On political considerations that affect public policy toward the environment, see Buchanan and Tullock (1975), Pashigan (1985), Maloney and McCormick (1992), Congleton (1996), Aidt (1998), and Lee (1999). For an analysis that takes an optimistic view of the state of the world environment, see Lomberg (2001). On international aspects of resolving externalities, see Rauscher (1990), Chander and Tulkens (1992), Schelling (1992), Grossman and Krueger (1993), Nordhaus and Yang (1996), Petrakis and Xepapadeas (1996), Hoel and Schneider (1997), Boadway and Hayashi (1999), Bommer and Schultze (1999), Schultze and Ursprung (2001), Wooders and Zissimos (2002) and Carraro (2003). On the Montreal Protocol for protecting the ozone layer, see Benedick (1991). On uneven implementation of the Montreal Protocol, see Murdoch and Sandler (1997). On the policy alliance between environmentalists and producer interests, see Hillman and Ursprung (1992). Hefeker and Wunner (2002) consider the producer interest in foreign labor standards. On health externalities, see Avery, Heymann, and Zeckhauser (1995) and Geoffard and Philipson (1997). On Typhoid Mary, see Leavitt (1995); on AIDS, see Philipson and Posner (1993). For a view of discrimination as personal internalization of an externality, see Becker (1971). On externalities in cost-benefit analysis of nuclear energy, see Young (1998).

Aidt, T. S., 1998. Political internalization of economic externalities and environmental policy. *Journal of Public Economics* 69, 1–16.

Avery, C., S. J. Heymann and R. Zeckhauser, 1995. Risks to selves, risks to others. *American Economic Review, Papers and Proceedings* 85, 61–6.

Baumol W. J. and W. F. Oates, 1988. *The Theory of Environmental Policy*. Cambridge University Press, New York.

Becker, G., 1971. *The Economics of Discrimination*. University of Chicago Press, Chicago.

Behrman, J. R. and N. Stacey (eds.), 1997. *The Social Benefits of Education*. The University of Michigan Press, Ann Arbor.

Benedick, R., 1991. *Ozone Diplomacy: New Directions in Safeguarding the Planet*. Harvard University Press, Cambridge, Massachusetts.

Boadway, R. and M. Hayashi, 1999. Country size and the voluntary provision of public goods. *European Journal of Political Economy* 15, 619–38.

Bommer, R. and G. G. Schultze, 1999. Environmental improvement with trade liberalization. *European Journal of Political Economy* 15, 639–61.

Buchanan, J. M. and G. Tullock, 1975. Polluters' profits and political response: Direct controls versus taxes. *American Economic Review* 65, 139–47.

Carraro, C. (ed.), 2003. *Governing the Global Commons*. Edward Elgar, Cheltenham, U.K.

Chander, P. and H. Tulkens, 1992. Theoretical foundations of negotiations and cost sharing in transfrontier environmental damage problems. *European Economic Review* 36, 288–99.

Congelton, R. D. (ed.), 1996. *The Political Economy of Environmental Protection*. University of Michigan Press, Ann Arbor.

Cornes, R. and T. Sandler, 1996. *The Theory of Externalities, Public Goods, and Club Goods*. Cambridge University Press, Cambridge, U.K.

Donohue, J. J., III and P. Siegelman, 1998. Allocating resources among prisons and social programs in the battle against crime. *Journal of Legal Studies* 27, 1–43.

Ellerman A. D., P. L. Joskow, R. Schmalensee, J-P. Montero and E. M. Bailey, 2000. *Markets for Clean Air: The U.S. Acid Rain Program.* Cambridge University Press, New York.

Geoffard, P-Y. and T. Philipson, 1997. Disease eradication: Private versus public vaccination. *American Economic Review* 87, 222–330.

Grossman, G. M. and A. B. Krueger, 1993. Environmental impacts of a North-American Free Trade Agreement. In *The Mexican-U.S. Free Trade Agreement*, P. Garber (ed.). MIT Press, Cambridge, Massachusetts, 13–56.

Hefeker, C. and N. Wunner, 2002. The producer interest in foreign labor standards. *European Journal of Political Economy* 18, 429–47.

Hillman, A. L. and H. W. Ursprung, 1992. The influence of environmental concerns on the political determination of trade policy. In *The Greening of World Trade Issues*, K. Anderson and R. Blackhurst (eds.). Harvester Wheatsheaf, New York, 195–220.

Hoel, M. and K. Schneider, 1997. Incentives to participate in international environmental agreements. *Environmental and Resource Economics* 9, 153–70.

Leavitt, J. W., 1995. Typhoid Mary strikes back: bacteriological theory and practice in early 20th century public health. *Isis* 86, 617–18.

Lee, D. R., 1999. Lowering the cost of pollution versus controlling pollution. *Public Choice* 100, 123–34.

Lomberg, B., 2001. *The Skeptical Environmentalist: Measuring the Real State of the World.* Cambridge University Press, New York.

Maloney, M. T. and R. E. McCormick, 1992. A positive theory of environmental quality regulation. *Journal of Law and Economics* 25, 99–123.

Montero, J-P., 1999. Voluntary compliance with market-based environmental policy: Evidence from the U.S. acid rain program. *Journal of Political Economy* 107, 998–1033.

Murdoch, J. C. and T. Sandler, 1997. The voluntary provision of a pure public good: The case of reduced CFC emissions and the Montreal Protocol. *Journal of Public Economics* 63, 331–49.

Nordhaus, W. D. and Z. Yang, 1996 . A regional dynamic general equilibrium model of alternative climate-change strategies. *American Economic Review* 86, 741–65.

Pashigan, P. B., 1985. Environmental regulation: Whose self-interests are being protected? *Economic Enquiry* 23, 551–84.

Petrakis, E. and A. Xepapadeas, 1996. Environmental consciousness and moral hazard in international agreements to protect the environment. *Journal of Public Economics* 60, 95–110.

Philipson, T. and R. Posner, 1993. *Private Choices and Public Health: The AIDS Epidemic in an Economic Perspective.* Harvard University Press, Cambridge, Massachusetts.

Pigou, A. C., 1962. *The Economics of Welfare*, Macmillan, London (4th edition, first published 1932; 1st edition 1920).

Rauscher, M., 1990. Can cartelization solve the problem of tropical deforestation? *Weltwirtschaftliches Archiv* 126, 378–87.

Requate, T., 1998. Incentives to innovate under emission taxes and tradeable permits. *European Journal of Political Economy*, 14, 139–65.

Schelling, T. C., 1992. Some economics of global warming. *American Economic Review* 82, 1–14.

Schultze, G. and H. W. Ursprung (eds.), 2001. *Globalization and the Environment.* Oxford University Press, Oxford.

Wooders, M. and B. Zissimos, 2002. The efficiency, equity and politics of emissions permit trading. In *Environmental Policy and the International Economy,* L. Marsiliani, M. Rauscher and C. Withagen (eds.). Kluwer Academic Publishers, Boston and Dordrecht, 203–19.

Young, W., 1998. *Atomic Energy Costing.* Kluwer Academic Publishers, Boston and Dordrecht.

Questions for discussion

1. When, or why, do we need to give government responsibility for resolving externality problems through public policy? Why is the order of public policy and private resolution of externalities important?

2. There are many possible externalities based on subjective likes and dislikes. How can we determine which externalities should be the target of resolution through public policy? Would you agree to a proposal that all people who leave their homes should be obliged to shower or take a bath once a day using soap and to wash their clothes at least three times a week, and that verified complaints about people in public places who have failed to do so should be punishable by law? Explain.

3. Find information on Love canal and on east Woburn. How did the adverse externalities arise in these cases? Why were the externalities allowed to persist? What was the role of government in these externalities?

4. Why are externalities a principal reason for cost-benefit analysis? Give an example where inappropriate recognition of externalities can change the result of a cost-benefit evaluation of public spending?

5. How do Pigovian taxes and subsidies internalize externalities? How do legal rights influence the choice between a Pigovian tax and a subsidy? Does whether an externality is negative or positive determine whether public policy should take the form of a tax or a subsidy? Explain.

6. Variable Pigovian taxes, if feasible, could be set so as to result in total tax revenue equal to the total value of damage from a negative externality. Why are such variable taxes in general not feasible? Why is it not necessary in any event for achieving efficiency that total taxes paid by polluters equal the total value of damage? Why is the revenue from a Pigovian tax not paid to victims of a negative externality? Is your answer also the reason why victims do not finance a Pigovian subsidy?

7. Pigovian taxes and subsidies and direct regulation through compulsory schooling are different ways of using public policy to account for positive externalities due to education. What are the merits and disadvantages of these different methods of responding to externalities due to education?

8. Why might governments prefer to resolve externality problems such as smoking and sexual harassment through direct regulation rather than through Pigovian taxes and subsidies?

9. What is the theory of the second best? How is this theory relevant when there are externalities in a monopolized industry?

10. Why is a competitive market in quota rights equivalent to a Pigovian tax as a means of internalizing externalities?

11. It is sometimes proposed that governments prefer to resolve externality problems by assigning quota rights without payment to existing producers. What are the

consequences of this public-policy decision compared to other means of resolving externality problems? Why might governments have a preference for free distribution of quota rights to existing producers?

12. "Failure to resolve international environmental externalities is a failure of governments to agree and not of markets." Why do you agree ar disagree? What are the difficulties that can stand in the way of international agreements to resolve externality problems?

13. Governments, and also people, in different countries often have different sensitivities to environmental problems. What underlies the different sensitivities? Find information about the Aral Sea. What do you conclude from the fate of the Aral Sea?

14. What are your views on whether lax foreign environmental standards should be permitted to be a source of a country's comparative advantage in international trade?

15. How do your views regarding the issue in question 14 change when the source of a cost advantage is foreign disregard for benefits of education as expressed in extensive child labor?

16. Why can producers and people expressing environmental concerns become allies in the quest for public policies that they want to see governments adopt? How does the relation between environmentalists' concerns and producer interests depend on whether environmentalists are NIMBYs or have broader social concerns that extend to local conditions in foreign countries?

17. "Protestors expressing concern about adverse externalities in foreign countries should not protest against the free trade of a global economy, but should direct their protests at foreign rulers and governments." Why do you agree or disagree?

18. In protecting dolphins from tuna fishers, the U.S. government acted unilaterally and was prepared to enter into international disputes. Why did the U.S. government act to help the dolphins? (See Supplement 4C.)

19. A person who has a contagious or infectious disease can be a source of a severe externality for others. What are the obstacles to seeking resolution of such externalities through the Coase theorem? Should a society rely on voluntary restrictions on contact with others by people who have a contagious or infectious illness? What is your opinion on the use of an indelible but inconspicuously placed marker that enables identification of people who are HIV-positive?

20. Supplement 4B demonstrates a technical impediment to replicating missing markets. After following through the logic of the case made in Supplement 4B, how would you react if a government claimed that it would like to, but cannot, adopt a public policy to correct an environmental externality and then justifies its inability to implement a corrective public policy by referring to the problem in Supplement 4B?

4.3

Prohibition of Markets

Restrictions are often imposed on the market decisions that children are permitted to make and on decisions that others (including parents) can make on behalf of children. For example, in the societies in which we live, parents are obliged to send their children to school (or provide an acceptable substitute for schools) and a market for child labor is not permitted. The sale of cigarettes and alcohol to children is also in general illegal. The public policies that we shall consider in this section concern restrictions through public policy on market transactions not particularly for children, but for adults. Public policy in such cases is referred to as paternalistic[1] because adults are not legally allowed to buy and sell according to their own preferences, but are subject to restrictions imposed by government. Paternalistic public policies are intended to prevent people harming themselves, whereas public policies associated with negative externalities are based on harm done by people to others.

4.3.1 Subjugation of personal preferences

Markets permit people to express their personal preferences for consumption. When the existence of a market is prohibited, public policy is subjugating personal preferences. In such cases, even though there are willing buyers and sellers, public policy views the voluntary transactions that people wish to undertake as undesirable because of the harm that people inflict on themselves. Harm to others (but including perhaps harm to oneself) is the basis for prohibition of a market on the grounds of externalities (e.g., the prohibition of markets in goods that emit chlorofluorocarbons because of damage to the earth's ozone layer or the prohibition of smoking in planes because of the harm to flight attendants and other passengers).

Convention, addiction, and taxes

Markets that result in people harming themselves can persist because of convention. Markets in tobacco products would not be legally allowed if tobacco were a newly introduced product that was required to satisfy contemporary health safety standards. Markets in tobacco products persist because of convention, and perhaps also because of political infeasibility of abolishing the markets since large numbers of voters smoke. Markets in tobacco products therefore continue to be legal despite incontrovertible evidence linking cigarette smoking to cancer, heart disease, and other health problems. Tobacco companies have however been required to pay compensation for harm that has arisen from the existence of markets that allow voluntary purchase of tobacco products. Tobacco purchases are not entirely voluntary because of addiction.

Taxes are often used to discourage the consumption of tobacco products. The intention of the taxation can be to reduce consumption, so as to reduce the harm that people do to themselves. There can, however, also be revenue motives for the taxes and the persistence of the markets. Taxation of addictive consumption provides a government with a secure revenue base for taxation.

---

[1] The term "paternalistic" comes from the Latin word *pater* for father. Policies that subjugate personal preferences have in general not been referred to as maternalistic.

Public policy regarding personal safety

Another category of paternalistic policy takes the form of compulsory purchases. Public policies require cars to be sold with seat belts and helmets are often legally required to be worn when riding motorbikes. Government safety regulations also require protective clothing and eye or ear protection in various occupations. Employers are often required to pay for compliance with the safety regulations. The cost of compliance is like a tax on employment, and, as with a tax, the burden of payment is determined not by who has the legal obligation to pay, but by substitution possibilities expressed in supply and demand elasticities in the labor market where the safety regulations apply. In these cases, public policy is paternalistic because people might be expected to be able to make personal decisions about their own safety.

Illegal markets and permitted free provision

Markets are in some cases illegal, but free provision is not. Markets for supply of body parts to people awaiting transplants are in general illegal, while donation of body parts is legal and is viewed as socially meritorious.

Blood is a special case. In some communities, there is market in blood, and blood donors are paid. In other communities, markets in blood are illegal, but while it is illegal to pay blood donors, voluntarily donating blood is encouraged and praised as socially responsible behavior.

People supply blood voluntarily for reasons of intrinsically motivated altruism. They derive personal satisfaction from their own behavior in helping others. When blood is a marketable commodity, the intrinsic motivation for supplying blood disappears, and voluntary supply in general ceases. The people who supply blood for money may moreover be using the market for blood as a last resort for earning income. Such people may impair their own health by selling too much of their blood. There is at the same time an externality present. If low income is correlated with bad health, the people selling blood may be providing blood that is more likely to be contaminated by disease than blood that is voluntarily supplied.

There are therefore different reasons why markets in blood are disallowed. One reason is paternalistic, that sellers may harm themselves. The second reason is an externality associated with the quality of blood when blood is a marketable commodity: we expect the quality of blood supplied in a market to be lower than the quality of blood provided through voluntary giving. Also, when a market in blood exists, people who would donate blood without payment may not be prepared to sell their blood; therefore, a market in blood may not increase supply but rather may reduce supply compared to blood supplied through voluntary donations.

A market for blood also introduces the possibility that unscrupulous suppliers might take blood from people against their will. When blood has no market value, this problem cannot be present.

Markets and sex

Sex is another case where markets may be illegal but voluntary free provision is not. The case against markets in sex is similar to the case against markets in blood. Supply can be a means of last resort for earning income, and suppliers, in particular teenagers, harm themselves. As with blood, there is an externality present, through disease transmission.

Markets in sex are therefore usually illegal. However, community standards determine tolerance for legal markets. Prostitution is usually made illegal even if enforcement is imperfect, so that the profession will not be an openly available choice when career options are being considered. The social stigma of illegality reduces supply beyond the disincentives due to legal penalties.

The potential for personal exploitation that we might fear when there is a market for blood is often present in markets for sex. Pimps may appropriate a large part of the income that is earned and may not allow women freedom of choice to leave the profession. Women can become objects that are traded and can be transported against their will between markets in different locations.

Although communities may prefer that markets for sex do not exist, supply is usually available illegally if not legally. The profession is often identified as the world's oldest.

Addiction

In the cases of blood, body parts, and sex, there are problems because of supply incentives associated with the existence of the markets. In the case of harmful drugs, there are problems because of addiction to the product itself, which debilitates and often eventually kills. Gambling can also become an addiction. When people gamble, they can lose their incomes and even their entire wealth. Prohibitions on gambling attempt to prevent such losses, which impoverish people and their dependents. There are also externalities present when people become addicted to drugs and gambling. Drug addicts may finance their habit through crime. Gamblers may also turn to crime to recoup losses. Both drug addicts and addicted gamblers can impose costs on society (including an excess burden of taxation; see Chapter 2) through the need to provide tax-financed income transfers to their dependants.

4.3.2 Time-inconsistent behavior

The case made for the market in Chapter 1 is that, for private (and not public) goods and in the absence of external costs or benefits, voluntary transactions between buyers and sellers result in efficient outcomes and preserve individual freedom. This case for voluntary transactions in markets does not make allowance for the possibility of time-inconsistent behavior. We noted in Chapter 2 when considering the choice of the discount rate for cost-benefit analysis that people can behave in a time-inconsistent way and come to regret past actions. They would not have behaved in the way they did, had they adopted a rule of minimizing future regret.

The source of the regret is a focus in behavior on immediate gratification. Because of the time-inconsistency problem, people become addicted to drugs and die of drug overdoses. They become HIV positive and eventually develop AIDS. They become pregnant (or make people pregnant) when they did not intend to. They delay giving up smoking or giving up hard drinking. They may delay, until it is too late, studying to pass exams. In such cases, benefit through immediate gratification overrides the self-discipline that would avoid the future regret of past decisions.

People should rationally be able to foresee the future consequences of their present behavior. Behaving in a time-inconsistent manner is irrational. The study of economics is based on rational behavior. How then are we to interpret people behaving in a time-inconsistent manner, that is, in ways that they know they will come to regret?

We can trace the problem of time-inconsistent behavior to short time horizons. We expect people rationally to give weight to their lives (or the quality of life) in the future. Short time horizons place zero weight on life beyond a particular date. Immediate gratification then prevails over future consequences beyond the time horizon. The short time horizons might be measured in months, days, hours, or even minutes.

Decisions made with a short time horizon can also be described as impulsive. Drug addiction results in impulsive behavior whereby addicts share needles. Studies also show that alcohol is associated with sexually transmitted diseases and pregnancy among teenagers.

Future benefits and costs need not be given zero weight for people to come to regret their past decisions. Time-inconsistent behavior also occurs when the future is given positive weight, but there is hyberbolic discounting of future benefits and costs. Under hyberbolic discounting, the discount rate people use to compare benefits and costs over time is not constant. Benefits and costs are more highly discounted (i.e., are given less present value), the further away in the future a cost or benefit will occur.

When in Chapter 2 we considered a government seeking to evaluate costs and benefits of a public investment, we took the discount rate to be constant over time. At any point in time, costs and benefits were therefore always compared over time applying the same constant discount to the future compared to the present. With hyberbolic discounting, the discount rate changes with time, with discount rates ever changing to value the present more highly than the future. The discount rate changes depending on the time distance from which an event is viewed. When the date of the event is far off, the benefit or cost associated with the event is given low weight. As the date of the event approaches, the weight given to the event through the discount rate increases. At the moment of the event, the weight on the benefit from the event is high while weights on future costs are low. The consequence is a decision of immediate gratification.

Thus, for example, people may place high benefit on smoking at any moment they are smoking, and health effects in the future are evaluated with increasingly higher discount rates (are given lower present value), the further into the future the health effects are due to take effect. The satisfaction is immediately felt and valued (not discounted), but costs incurred in 10 years or 20 years time are highly discounted, and are reduced by discounting more, the further in the future the costs arise. In such circumstances, people will tend to choose actions with high contemporary benefit. Then, when the future arrives and a high cost must be incurred, a high weight is placed on the cost at the time when the cost arises. It is, however, then too late to do anything to avoid the high present cost of the past action. The high cost could only have been avoided by forgoing the past benefit. However, the decision was made in the past to take the benefit.

We can consider people who know that they should give up drugs because of adverse effects in the future, or who know that they should begin a diet to lose weight, or who know that they should start studying for an exam, or who know that they should begin saving for their old age. Rationally, with a constant discount rate applied to compare benefits and costs over time, the beneficial action would be taken to stop drugs, begin the diet, start studying, or begin saving. With hyberbolic discounting, the high weight on immediate gratification leads to a decision rule of procrastination. That is, the rule at any time is always to wait one period before making the beneficial long-term decision. With this decision rule, past decisions are regretted in the future when drug addiction has taken hold, or personal costs are confronted through adverse health effects of obesity, failing exams, or being destitute in old age.

People would be better off had they been able to commit themselves to a nondiscretionary rule of "make the beneficial long-term decision today rather than always putting off the decision until tomorrow." Paternalistic public policy is a means of enforcing a nondiscretionary decision rule. For example, prohibiting a market for drugs, if effective, prevents a decision rule whereby people decide to stop taking drugs tomorrow (always). Prohibiting prostitution prevents decisions to start a new life tomorrow (always). Social security is a means of forcing people to save for their old age. Public policy in these cases is intended to prevent people from choosing "to live for today as if there is no tomorrow" when there will indeed be a tomorrow.

Public policies cannot be effective against all cases of time-inconsistency. Public policy cannot in general precommit people to choosing a healthy diet (it would be difficult for governments to prohibit markets for foods that make up an unhealthy diet). There is also no public policy that can make people precommit not to put off studying for exams.

4.3.3 Information

The source of the time-inconsistency problem is the changing weight people attach over time to benefits and costs. The time-inconsistency problem arises when people are informed about benefits and costs over time. People may, however, not be well informed about the future consequences of their decisions. They might base their personal decisions on subjective beliefs that are far removed from true information. The declaration "nothing bad will happen to me" indicates a subjective probability of zero of an adverse event occurring. When personal decisions are not based on objective probabilities, mistakes are made and people regret their decisions. Personal miscalculations can result, for example, in road fatalities due to alcohol, in sexually transmitted diseases, and in drug addiction and overdoses.

4.3.4 The libertarian view

The libertarian view is that people should be permitted to make their own mistakes and to consume (or do) anything they wish, provided that they harm no one but themselves. The libertarian view does not recognize the existence of victimless crimes. Time-inconsistency provides no justification, according to the libertarian view, for public policy that restrains people's market choices. Personal decisions are rather regarded as an expression of personal freedom in which government should not be involved. Therefore, a libertarian view would not have government intervene when people are seen to be harming themselves by taking hard drugs. Similarly, on a libertarian view, there are no acceptable grounds for censorship, and pornography becomes a matter of personal taste. Rather than prohibiting markets, the libertarian view is that public policy should be limited to providing a clear statement of known risks. People can then make their own decisions based on the information that is provided, and, if these decisions inflict self-harm, it is not one's business other than that of the people making the decisions.

4.3.5 Markets in people

Markets in which people are bought and sold are prohibited in civilized societies. Such markets, which allow slavery, contradict the basic right to individual freedom.

At some times in history, voluntary slavery was allowed. People who were impoverished and had no means of support, or had accumulated debts that they could not repay, could voluntarily sell themselves as slaves for a limited period of time. In return, they received prepayment of the income from their future services. After the period of time for which they had sold themselves had passed, they were obliged to return to freedom. If they had become accustomed to the life of a slave and refused to accept the freedom that was due to them, they were subject to humiliation, to increase their incentive to accept their freedom. The alternative to people selling themselves into slavery for a limited period might have been starvation. Slavery was in these circumstances a form of borrowing against future income. Becoming a slave was the way of providing assurance that the loan would be repaid, since work was not a discretionary decision while a slave.

People no longer have to sell themselves into slavery when they find themselves destitute or in debt. Government often provides assistance to people who earn no income, and bankruptcy laws protect debtors from destitution.

In civilized societies, markets in babies for adoption are illegal even though there are willing buyers and sellers. Markets for babies for adoption are replaced by government mediation in adoption procedures. If babies are not marketable commodities, having babies for supply to the adoption market cannot be a professional income-earning activity. The absence of a market also prevents unscrupulous people from buying babies and using the children as personal slaves and for nefarious purposes. The incentive to steal babies is also reduced.

Likewise, the absence of a market in people reduces the incentive to kidnap or steal people.

4.3.6 Illegal markets

When public policies prohibit markets, almost invariably illegal markets arise, for example, in babies for adoption, narcotics, prostitution, and gambling.[2] When a market is illegal, prices are higher than in legal markets, as in general are profits, because of more limited competition in illegal markets and the higher risk associated with illegal supply. The high profits based on illegality invite criminal elements into supply.

Large rewards relative to other income-earning opportunities can also attract young people into illegal supply. Individuals who have become wealthy through activities in illegal markets can become role models who set the standards for aspirations of young people.

The contests for control of illegal markets increase crime, as different suppliers seek to monopolize a market by eliminating one another. Innocent bystanders can suffer. At the same time, because restricted illegal supply increases prices, drug users can be drawn into theft and burglary to find the means to sustain their habits.

There is a logical inevitability to illegal markets. If legal markets are prohibited, individuals attempt to satisfy their private preferences in illegal markets. Where there is sufficient willingness to pay, there will usually be supply, even if supply is illegal.

Because prohibition of legal markets is an invitation to illegal supply, a society can confront a dilemma. The dilemma is that the markets that government is attempting to suppress continue to exist illegally, while the social costs of the illegal markets can be higher than the social costs of legal markets. If markets for drugs were legal, prices would be lower, and there would be less need for theft and prostitution to finance drug habits. We would expect that, with lower prices and legal supply, more people would, however, experiment with and take drugs.

A society may prefer illegal to legal markets, even if the illegal markets introduce or increase other social costs. For example, prostitution may be inevitable even if illegal, but, as we have observed, illegality adds a stigma that may deter choice of this means of earning an income. When declaring markets to be illegal, society is signaling that buying or selling in these markets is not consistent with values that the society views as having merit.

4.3.7 Legal rights and externalities

A case for prohibiting markets might be made in terms of externalities rather than self-harm to participants in a market. An externality is present when a market that

---

[2] Alcohol is usually illegally available during times of legal prohibition.

would allow someone to pay to achieve or to avoid an outcome does not exist. We might then want to define altruism (or caring about others) as an externality. That is, we might be prepared personally to pay to suppress markets that allow drug abuse and teenage prostitution, even though the markets involve buyers and sellers who are complete strangers; we do not know the persons harming themselves but, despite the anonymity, we care about the self-harm that is being done.

In a case where a market would allow activities that are contrary to our ethical values, there may be no price that could be paid that would lead us to agree to the presence of the market. The Coase theorem tells us that, when externalities are present, the same efficient outcome is obtained independently of who has legal rights. Legal rights however matter when finite prices do not exist. For example, if there is no finite price that we are prepared to accept to agree to allow a market in child pornography, Coase-type negotiations cannot establish a mutually beneficial outcome where we agree to be compensated for allowing supply of children to child pornographers. The inconsistency between allowing a market in child pornography and a society's ethical values is the justification for public policy that prohibits these markets.

Paternalistic prohibition of markets thus differs from usual externalities, in that we are not prepared to contemplate the assignment of legal rights that would presume that some markets could be allowed to exist. If the principles of the Coase theorem were to apply, child pornographers could have legal rights to create a market, and people who view child pornography as evil would pay the child pornographers not to supply the market. However, ethical societies do not regard child pornography as a case of an externality, where legal rights could in principle be on either side of a market. Society subjugates the preferences that would be expressed in the market that child pornographers would supply. The market is prohibited, and child pornographers and pedophiles are treated as criminals.

4.3.8 Community values and social norms

The markets that a society disallows are an expression of community values and social norms. Values and social norms differ among communities. In some communities, therefore, prostitution is legal and in others not. The legal age of alcohol consumption also varies, and in some communities it may be illegal to be seen drinking an alcoholic beverage in the streets. Sometimes gambling is legal for visitors but not for local residents. In some countries, markets in means of contraception have been illegal. Some communities allow more or less unrestricted markets in guns, whereas in other communities markets in guns are subject to severe restrictions. Communities take different attitudes toward abortion, with some people taking the position that whether or not to have a baby is a personal decision, and others taking the position that life, once created, cannot be arbitrarily terminated and that abortion clinics are not far removed from the supply side of a market for murder.

We previously observed in Chapters 2 and 3 how locational mobility among government jurisdictions allows personal choice in taxation and public spending similar to choice in markets. We saw how, through locational choice, information could be revealed about people's preferences for public goods, and how locational choice allowed people to sort themselves by similarities in demands for public goods to avoid majority voting outcomes where people with minority tastes are systematically disadvantaged. Decisions about community values usually reflect the majority view of which markets should be disallowed. Subjugation of preferences may therefore affect only a minority of people, who may, for example, favor legal markets in drugs or gambling and prostitution when the community in which they are located does not allow these markets. Locational choice, where available, allows people to choose communities where community values expressed in social norms are consistent with their individual personal preferences.

Locational decisions as a means of choosing community values or social norms are thus similar to locational decisions as a means for choosing taxation and public spending. Through choice of location, an individual can in either case substitute personally undesirable majority decisions for more personally favorable outcomes.

Decisions about community values thus determine the markets (and thereby the practices facilitated through payment) that are allowed or prohibited. The decisions have a public-good nature in affecting the entire population in a jurisdiction. When seeking a location with community values or social norms of behavior consistent with his or her personal values, an individual is, therefore, seeking the equivalent of a public good through the decision where to live. Usual public goods have market costs associated with supply through the purchase of the inputs required for public goods. Social norms or community values as public goods do not have these types of costs of supply. The collective question regarding community values is whether the community or the society wishes to have present markets that facilitate particular practices.

4.3.9 Practices in other locations

In making their collective decisions, communities set their own standards to determine the markets they wish to prohibit. However, a position in favor of paternalistic policies can also extend to practices in other locations. In Section 4.2, we considered externalities through foreign practices of child labor and degradation of the environment that affect costs of foreign goods that compete with domestic producton. We also noted that people might object as a matter principle to foreign child labor and to foreign degradation of the environment. When the objection to foreign practices is due to economic consequences in our own economy, a case of externalities is present. When the objection is based on principle, paternalistic preferences are being expressed about practices in other locations.

Various foreign practices might lead us to make judgments and express preferences based on principle rather on direct effects in our own society. For example, in some places women do not have basic human rights. Moreover, in some countries parents bring daughters to practitioners who mutilate the girls. The practice, which can cause long lasting wounds and has other lasting adverse effects on personal heath, takes place to enforce subservience of women to men.[3] Locational sorting of people facilitates diversity in the social norms that underlie community values. However, it appears that we may not always wish to applaude diversity.

4.3.10 Conclusions

A fundamental normative principle of economic analysis is that people should be allowed to judge their well-being according to their own preferences. This normative principle underlies the case for the efficiency of the market; that is, people making voluntary decisions in markets cannot be harming themselves. Yet we have noted in this section that time-inconsistent behavior and inadequate information (and inability to understand objective probabilities) can lead people to regret past decisions. Then, just as parents impose restraints on small children, there may be merit in public policies that similarly constrain adults. Yet, we are dealing with adults, not children. A libertarian view is that once information about consequences has been provided, an individual should be free to do as he or she pleases even if the consequences are self-damaging, provided that no one else is harmed. A counter to the libertarian view is that societies have norms of behavior, and that people who choose to be part of a community oblige themselves to conform to a community's social norms reflected in the types of markets that the community chooses to prohibit.

Legal prohibitions on markets do not ensure that illegal markets do not exist. We have observed that illegal markets can create social dilemmas by inviting criminal elements into supply and by turning buyers into criminals. High incomes from illegal supply also provide socially inappropriate role models for young people. Illegality of markets nonetheless signals behavior that a society wishes to discourage.

We have also observed that communities set their own standards regarding markets they wish to prohibit or suppress, and individuals can choose to locate in a community where social norms most closely reflect their own personal values. We have also raised the question whether we are obliged to accept as ethical or as socially meritorious or responsible all social norms expressed in behavior through markets that other communities might choose to allow.

---

[3] Barbara Crossette observed (2000, p. 184): "The practice has long served men by rendering the women they marry uninterested in sex or unappealing or inaccessible to any other man – a safe albeit damaged, piece of property. Next comes the rationalization/belief that no girl or woman will be marriageable unless she has submitted to this process."

References and related literature

Musgrave (1959) discussed paternalistic public policy using the terminology of merit wants. On goods or services that markets cannot or should not value, see Arrow (1997). On addiction, see Whinston (1980), Becker and Murphy (1988), and Epstein, Rapoport, and Weiss (1999). On time-inconsistent behavior and hyperbolic discounting, see Akerlof (1991), Laibson (1997), and Caillaud and Jullien (2000). On social customs that override markets, see Akerlof (1980); on the subjugation of personal values to social norms, see Kuran (1995); on stigma, see Rasmusen (1996). On child labor, see Landes and Solomon (1972), Basu and Van (1998), and Moehling (1999). On tobacco, see Harris (1980), Viscusi (1990), and Hu, Sung, and Keeler (1995); on blood, see Titmuss (1970) and Hamish (1992); on the connection between alcohol and sexually transmitted diseases, see Chesson, Harrison, and Kassler (2000). On values and public policy, see Aaron, Mann and Taylor (1994). On foreign customs, see Crossette (2000).

Aaron, H. J., T. E. Mann and T. Taylor, 1994. *Values and Public Policy*. Brookings Institution, Washington, D.C.

Akerlof, G. A., 1980. A theory of social custom, of which unemployment may be one consequence. *Quarterly Journal of Economics* 94, 749–75.

Akerlof, G. A., 1991. Procrastination and obedience. *American Economic Review* 81, 1–19.

Arrow, K. J., 1997. Invaluable goods. *Journal of Economic Literature* 35, 757–65.

Basu, K. and P. K. Van, 1998. The economics of child labor. *American Economic Review* 88, 412–27.

Becker, G. S. and K. Murphy, 1988. A theory of rational addiction. *Journal of Political Economy* 96, 675–700.

Caillaud, B. and B. Jullien, 2000. Modelling time-inconsistent preferences. *European Economic Review* 44, 1116–24.

Chesson, H., P. Harrison and W. J. Kassler, 2000. Sex under the influence: The effects of alcohol policy on sexually transmitted disease rates in the U.S. *Journal of Law and Economics* 43, 215–38.

Crossette, B., 2000. Culture, gender, and human rights. In *Culture Matters: How Values Shape Human Progress*, L. E. Harrison and S. P. Huntington (eds.). Basic Books, New York, 178–99.

Epstein, G. S., Rapoport and A. Weiss, 1999. Drug addiction and the economic rationalization of gun control. *Economics Letters* 65, 55–7.

Hamish, S., 1992. Rationality and the market for human blood. *Journal of Economic Behavior and Organization* 19, 125–43.

Harris, J. E., 1980. Taxing tar and nicotine. *American Economic Review* 90, 300–11.

Hu, T-W., H-Y. Sung and T. E. Keeler, 1995. The state anti-smoking campaign and the industry response: The effects of advertising on cigarette consumption in California. *American Economic Review, Papers and Proceedings* 85, 85–90.

Kuran, T., 1995. *Private Truths, Public Lies: The Social Consequences of Preference Falsification*. Harvard University Press, Cambridge, Massachusetts.

Laibson, D., 1997. Golden eggs and hyperbolic discounting. *Quarterly Journal of Economics* 112, 443–77.

Landes, W. M. and L. C. Solomon, 1972. Compulsory schooling legislation: An economic analysis of law and social change in the nineteenth century. *Journal of Economic History* 22, 54–91.

Moehling, C. M., 1999. State child labor laws and the decline of child labor. *Explorations in Economic History* 36, 72–106.

Musgrave, R., 1959. *The Theory of Public Finance*. McGraw Hill, New York.

Rasmusen, E., 1996. Stigma and self-fulfilling expectations of criminality. *Journal of Law and Economics* 39, 519–43.

Titmuss, R. M., 1970. *The Gift Relationship: From Human Blood to Social Policy*. George Allen and Unwin, London.

Viscusi, W. K., 1990. Do smokers underestimate risks? *Journals of Political Economy* 98, 1253–69.

Whinston, G. C., 1980. Addiction and backsliding: A theory of compulsive consumption. *Journal of Economic Behavior and Organization* 1, 295–324.

Questions for discussion

1. "In the case of paternalistic intervention, government is seeking to suppress markets. In the case of externalities government is seeking to replicate missing markets." How does this difference distinguish public policies regarding externalities from public policies that paternalistically prohibit markets?

2. How do short personal time horizons result in time-inconsistent personal decisions? Do you believe that short time horizons justify public policies that prohibit particular markets?

3. What is the relation between short time horizons and hyberbolic discounting? Explain how discount rates change under hyperbolic discounting? Why is the rule under hyperbolic discounting always to defer a beneficial long-term decision to the future?

4. Research has linked alcohol to sexually transmitted disease (see Chesson et al., 2000). In your view, what kind of responsibility does government have regarding public policy toward alcohol in the light of this study?

5. In your view, does addiction to gambling justify prohibition of gambling? Are policies restricting permissible locations of legal gambling casinos a reasonable compromise in dealing with the problem of addiction to gambling? Explain.

6. If tars and nicotine in tobacco are harmful and tobacco companies have been compelled to pay compensation based on harm done, why are markets in tobacco not prohibited?

7. Markets in blood and body organs are often prohibited, but there are no prohibitions on voluntary giving. Voluntary giving is regarded as virtuous at the same time as markets are illegal. How can this be justified or explained?

8. What should a society do about markets for sex? Why are these markets legal in some places and illegal elsewhere?

9. If individuals find themselves in government jurisdictions where community values have led to the prohibition of particular markets that provide substances or services that the individuals want, is asking people to relocate to a community where the standards and values they seek are the social norm a reasonable solution? Explain. Why are different social norms among communities similar to public goods? Are there differences between communities' social norms and usual tax-financed public goods available by location in a government jurisdiction?

10. Do you believe that markets for sale of babies for adoption should be legal? Should purchase of foreign babies be legal? Justify your answers.

11. What do you believe, if anything, should be done if people reveal through their market behavior that they do not understand objective probabilities?

12. Illegal markets are often the response to prohibition of legal markets. Should illegality be maintained even if prohibition is impossible, so as to stigmatize participation in markets that a society is seeking to repress?

13. Suggest a general rule for determining limits on prohibitions on markets when there are voluntary buyers and voluntary sellers. Explain why majority voting should/should not be the general rule for determining the markets that a society prohibits.

14. Governments act paternalistically in not allowing people to make investment decisions based on the advice of people who have not been certified as investment advisors. Yet certified investment advisors can give advice that results in financial losses for clients (since certified investment advisors cannot predict stock prices). Do you believe that allowing only certified investment advisors to give investment advice is justified? Would you approve of a policy allowing anyone to act as investment advisor, but past investment recommendations have to be publicly available on the internet? Do you think that all medical surgeons should be legally obliged to publish the successes and failures of their surgical procedures on the internet? In some places advertising by lawyers and medical practitioners is prohibited and in other places such advertising is allowed. What do you believe underlies the different public policies toward prohibiting or allowing markets for advertising by lawyers and medical practitioners?

15. Read the summary (available on the internet) of the paper by Ndu Eke and Kanu E.O. Nkanginieme in the *World Journal of Surgery,* 1999, volume 23, issue 10 pages 1082–7. The practices that Eke and Nkanginieme describe occur in foreign countries. What do you believe we should do, or do we have any responsibility, when we learn of these practices? When we learn that slavery exists in some countries, do you believe that this is something that we can or should ignore because the markets in which people are bought and sold are not in the area of jurisdiction of our government? How does your answer relate to the proposal that people should be permitted to choose social norms with which they are comfortable in the location where they have chosen to be?

16. Do you believe over all that there is a justifiable case for prohibiting markets that result in self-harm, and self-harm only? Or do you believe that that government has no responsibility beyond providing information, and that people should be left to make their own decisions (and their own mistakes)? Justify your position.

5

SOCIAL JUSTICE

We now turn to consider social justice. Public finance and public policy directed at social justice involve income distribution, and also opportunities for earning income. We shall begin with the relation between social justice and social insurance provided by government. We shall then consider how the entitlements associated with social insurance affect incentives and income distribution. We shall also consider whether social justice can be achieved without government.

5.1

Social Welfare and Social Insurance

Our focus until now has been on efficiency. We have sought to identify how to achieve efficient spending on public goods and how to correct market outcomes when externalities are present. We also looked at public policies that prohibit markets, where efficiency consequences are more ambiguous. Although our focus has been on efficiency, we have also encountered issues of income distribution. We have seen that spending on public goods affects income distribution through who pays and who benefits, and that voting on public spending on public goods has distributional effects through collective decisions that benefit a majority of voters at the expense of a minority, or through the voting rule that is used. The resolution of externality problems also has distributional effects: assignment of legal rights determines whether Pigovian taxes are paid or subsidies are received, and the means chosen to implement public policy that corrects an externality affects income distribution. Distributional aspects are also present when decisions are made to prohibit markets, by disallowing benefits to buyers or sellers.

Although we have encountered these distributional aspects of public finance and public policy, the questions we have asked have been about efficiency. We shall now ask questions about social justice and income distribution. We shall again find that we shall not be able to maintain a strict separation between the effects of public finance and public policy on social justice and efficiency.

We observed in Chapter 1 that social justice can be defined in different ways. We shall now define social justice with reference to insurance. People usually want insurance to protect themselves against personally adverse outcomes that would leave them with inadequate income. If the insurance that protects against having inadequate income could be provided through private insurance markets, nobody would require assistance from the government, since private insurance companies would provide income and assistance for those in need.

5.1.1 The private demand for insurance

People seek insurance because they wish to avoid risk, that is, because they are risk-averse. A way to measure a person's risk aversion is to ask how much he or she is prepared to pay to avoid a fair gamble.[1] The more a person is prepared to pay to avoid a fair gamble, the greater is the person's *risk aversion*. A person who is willing to pay nothing to avoid a fair gamble is *risk-neutral*.

---

[1] A fair gamble has an expected value of zero. We can for example ask someone: how much are you prepared to pay to avoid a gamble where you stand to lose $1,000 with 50 percent probability and to win $1,000 with 50 percent probability? Although the expected value of this gamble is zero, risk-averse persons are not indifferent between this fair gamble and having zero with certainty. They are prepared to pay a sum of money to avoid the fair gamble.

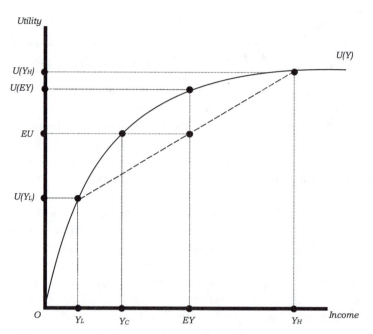

Figure 5.1. Risk aversion and the personal demand for insurance.

A risk-averse person values additions to income less than losses of income. Therefore, risk aversion is reflected in declining marginal utility of income. We see declining marginal utility of income in Figure 5.1, where a person's utility U increases with personal income Y. The slope of the utility function $U(Y)$ is the marginal utility of income (or marginal benefit from additional income). Since marginal utility (the slope of the utility function) declines as income increases, utility as shown in Figure 5.1 indicates risk aversion.[2]

The risk is with respect to income. In Figure 5.1, suppose that with 50 percent probability personal income determined by the market will be low at Y_L and with 50 percent probability will be high at Y_H. The expected (or average) value of these incomes is EY.[3] The utility of this expected income is $U(EY)$.

Income Y_L would provide utility $U(Y_L)$, and income Y_H would provide utility $U(Y_H)$. Expected utility EU in Figure 5.1 is the average of these utilities.[4]

Risk aversion is reflected in $U(EY) > EU$. If the marginal utility of income were not declining but were constant, the utility function $U(Y)$ would be a straight line. In that case, $U(EY)$ would equal EU, which would indicate an individual who is risk-neutral.

---

[2] We have previously referred to personal benefits received by individuals, but we shall now refer to an individual's utility. We shall use the terms "benefit" and "utility" interchangeably.

[3] For example, if low income Y_L is 10 and high income Y_H is 110, expected income EY is the average, which is 60.

[4] EU is found by joining the points of utility from low and high income on the utility function and finding the midpoint of the straight line that joins these two points.

We have observed that risk aversion can be measured by the amount of money that a person is prepared to pay to avoid a fair gamble. The fair gamble in Figure 5.1 is the chance of having low income Y_L with probability 50 percent and high income Y_H with probability 50 percent. The expected income provided by the fair gamble is EY. Expected utility provided by the fair gamble is EU.

Instead of being offered EU through a gamble, the person in Figure 5.1 could be offered the utility EU with certainty by being given the certainty-equivalent income Y_C. That is, the income Y_C provides utility EU with certainty.

Because of risk aversion, the person in Figure 5.1 is prepared to pay the sum of money $(EY - Y_C)$ to avoid the fair gamble that offers Y_L and Y_H with equal likelihood in return for receiving income Y_C with certainty. By paying $(EY - Y_C)$ and accepting the certainty equivalent income Y_C in place of the fair gamble, the individual eliminates all income risk. $(EY - Y_C)$ is the price of insurance, or the insurance premium, that the individual is willing to pay to receive Y_C with certainty and avoid the risk involved in accepting the fair gamble.

Risk pooling through insurance in a large population

Figure 5.1 shows one risk-averse person. Members of a large population can face the same income uncertainty as the person in Figure 5.1. The many people in the population might all have expected income EY before individual incomes are known and face the risk that income will be Y_L or Y_H with 50 percent probability after personal incomes have become known. To avoid the income risk, the people in the population can pool the risk through an insurance contract with an insurance company. Under the terms of the insurance contract, the insurance company bears all risk by paying everybody the certainty-equivalent income Y_C, independently of whether their personal incomes will be revealed to be Y_H or Y_L.

The personal incomes, when revealed, belong to the insurance company, which has taken risk away from individuals. The insurance company faces no risk. The risk of the population has been pooled. The insurance company knows that half of the population will have income Y_H and that half will have income Y_L. The insurance company also knows that it will receive EY per person on average with certainty. Therefore, the insurance company makes a profit by providing insurance to the population. On average, an individual has income EY, and the insurance company pays each person the certainty-equivalent income Y_C. The profit is $(EY - Y_C)$ per insured person.

The sum of money $(EY - Y_C)$ is the most an individual is prepared to pay for insurance. Competition in offering insurance decreases the price of insurance below $(EY - Y_C)$ and increases the income that individuals receive with certainty above Y_C. The utility that individuals achieve with certainty through the insurance market is then also greater than the utility of the fair gamble EU. Perfect competition in the insurance market would bid down the price of insurance to eliminate any above-competitive profits of insurance companies and would provide buyers of insurance with gains equal to $(EY - Y_C)$. Competitive insurance markets thus provide Pareto improvement for people seeking insurance, in the same way that other competitive markets provide Pareto efficiency.[5]

5.1.2 Social welfare and social justice

In response to the desire of risk-averse individuals for insurance against income risk, governments can act as an insurance company and provide social insurance. Social insurance is related to the idea of a social welfare function. A social welfare function measures the social (or total) welfare of the entire population of a society. Social welfare depends on the personal utilities of the members of the population. When there are n people in a population, we can express a social welfare function as

$$W = f(U_1, U_2, U_3, \ldots, U_n), \tag{5.1}$$

where W is the total welfare of the society and U_i is the personal utility of an individual i. We want all individuals to count in a positive way in the measurement of social welfare. When the personal utility of any one person increases, we therefore want social welfare to increase. That is, we want a social welfare function to have the characteristic that

$$\frac{\partial W}{\partial U_i} > 0 \qquad i = 1, \ldots, n. \tag{5.2}$$

An increase in any one person's utility U_i, leaving all other persons' utilities unchanged, therefore increases social welfare W. This ensures that a Pareto-improving change increases social welfare, since, when any person is better off, the measure of social welfare indicates that the society as a whole is better off. The opposite is, however, not true: social welfare can increase when some persons have been made worse off.

The violation of the Pareto criterion when social welfare increases is shown in Figure 5.2 for a society made up of two persons. Social welfare along the contours W_1 and W_2 is defined as constant. W_2 indicates higher social welfare than W_1. A move from point 1 to point 2 increases social welfare from W_1 to W_2 by making both people better off, and so satisfies the Pareto criterion for change. A move from point 1 to point 3 also increases social welfare, but fails to satisfy the Pareto criterion because person 2 is better off at the expense of person 1. A move from point 1 to point 4 keeps social welfare constant and also fails to satisfy the Pareto criterion because again person 2 is again better off at the expense of person 1. Social welfare can therefore increase or remain constant, even though the Pareto criterion is violated and some persons are made worse off.

Because (5.2) indicates by how much an increase in an individual's personal utility increases social welfare, we can interpret the information provided by (5.2)

---

[5] Insurance companies confront no risk when it is known that half of the population will have high incomes and half will have low incomes. Insurance companies may, however, confront unpredictable events that would require large payouts. Insurance companies might therefore reinsure, or spread risk among themselves, and also maintain reserves for contingencies. Insurance companies are sometimes regulated by government to ensure that reserves are adequate.

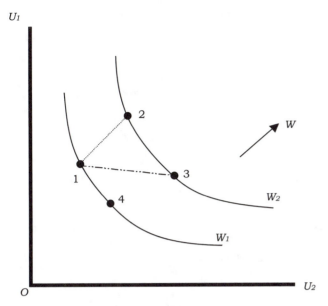

Figure 5.2. Social welfare and Pareto efficiency.

as indicating an individual's social weight in the measurement of social welfare. The social weight need not be constant, and in general is not. In Figure 5.2, the social weights of the two persons change along a social welfare contour. The slope of a contour at any point is defined by the ratio of the two individual's social weights. The slope indicates how much we can reduce the utility of one person and increase the utility of another person, and still regard social welfare as constant. That is, the slope indicates a society's willingness to trade off the utility of one person for the utility of another.

Let us regard individuals as identical so that they have the same utility functions and we can compare their utilities. In Figure 5.3, the utilities of persons 1 and 2 are equal along the 45° line. At point A, person 1 is better off than person 2. Suppose both persons are behind a veil of ignorance, and do not know whether they will be person 1 or person 2. They know however that the society might find itself at the point A. If the two people are risk-averse, they are willing to have person 1 (whoever this might eventually be) lose substantial utility around point A so that less well-off person 2 can have increased utility. In Figure 5.3, the two persons (not yet knowing who they will be) are willing to see person 1 give up AB of utility to provide BD of utility to person 2. The relatively large amount of utility they are prepared to take from high-utility person 1 to provide a smaller amount of utility for low-utility person 2 is a reflection of risk aversion, or in particular is the response to the risk that, at point A, either might be person 2.

The higher the social weight expressed by (5.2) for one person relative to another, the more sensitive social welfare is to a decline in that person's utility relative to a decline in the utility of the other person, and the more that person is protected by the social welfare function against a loss in personal utility. Consequently, we

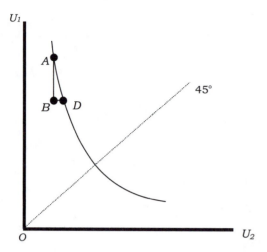

Figure 5.3. Social welfare contours and risk aversion.

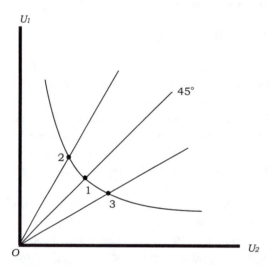

Figure 5.4. A symmetric social welfare contour.

might want to ask who chooses individuals' social weights in a social welfare function for a society. We ask this question because we want to ensure that the social
welfare function treats different people fairly and does not arbitrarily assign high
social weight (or high social importance) to some people relative to others.

The choice of a social welfare function behind a veil of ignorance where people
do not know who they are going to be ensures anonymity in the properties of the
social welfare. No person-specific individual self-interest enters into the choice of
individuals' social weights in the social welfare function because people do not
know who they are going to be.

Figure 5.4 shows a social welfare contour that is symmetric around the equal-
utility 45° line. The social welfare contour has the same symmetric shape whichever

direction we move from point 1 on the 45° line. Points 2 and 3 are the same distance from point 1 and are the same distance from the origin. This symmetry ensures that the shape of social welfare contours is independent of the identities of the persons whose utilities are measured on the axes. Along the contour indicating constant social welfare, only the distance from the equal-utility 45° line matters in determining the slope of the social welfare contour and so in determining the trade-off between personal utilities that keeps social welfare constant. Because of the symmetry of the social welfare contour around the 45° line, the social welfare function is anonymous, and, from behind the veil of ignorance, there is no scope for personal gain from being labeled "person 1" as against "person 2." Because a social welfare function that is symmetric around the 45° line is nondiscriminatory and anonymous with respect to personal identities, behind a veil of ignorance we expect people to agree that social welfare contours should be symmetric.

We can now consider a government that has a fixed amount of money Y available for distribution between person 1 and person 2. We shall not at this point ask about the source of the available income Y. The income is simply available for distribution. Person 1 will receive income y_1, and person 2 will receive income y_2, so that

$$Y = y_1 + y_2. \tag{5.3}$$

Person 1 and person 2 are behind a veil of ignorance, and are risk-averse as in Figure 5.1. Their utilities from income are

$$U_1 = U_1(y_1), \qquad U_2 = U_2(y_2). \tag{5.4}$$

We shall continue to view the two people (and all people) as having identical utility functions. We do not know people's utilities, so we treat people as alike.[6]

In Figure 5.5, SV shows the different outcomes possible in the two-person society for different distributions of the available amount of income Y. SV is the *utility-possibility frontier* for the distribution of the income Y.

Distributions of income along SV are Pareto-efficient because divisions of the income Y along SV result in outcomes where one person cannot be made better off without the other person being made worse off. Because the two people in Figure 5.5 have identical utilities, the utility-possibility frontier SV is symmetrically *concave* around the equal-utility 45° line.[7]

---

[6] We are now describing behavior that is similar to that of the social planners of maximal government in section 1.3. The social planners also did not know individuals' utilities (they could not) and so treated people as alike.

[7] If all income is given to person 1, the outcome in Figure 5.5 is at point S. If all income is given to person 2, the outcome is at point V. Because utility functions are identical, person 1's utility OS from the entire income Y is the same as the utility OV when person 2 is given the entire income Y. That is, $OS = OV$. Divisions where each person receives some part of Y result in outcomes along the utility-possibility curve SV between points S and V. The concavity of SV is due to declining

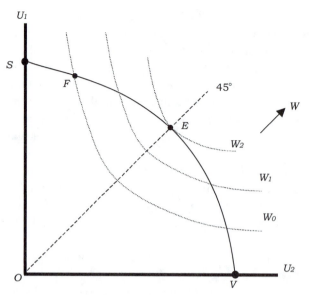

Figure 5.5. The utility possibility frontier and social welfare maximization.

In Figure 5.5, social welfare is maximized at the point E along the symmetric utility possibility frontier SV by dividing the income Y equally between the two persons. The equal division at the point E provides the highest attainable social welfare W_2. The equal division of income to maximize social welfare is not surprising. The two people have identical utilities and are equal before the distribution of income. A rule of "equal treatment of equals" results in the two persons having equal income and equal utility after the income Y has been distributed.

In Chapter 1, we described two persons in a desert with water available that would allow only one person to survive. Because the water was indivisible (the water provided no benefit to anyone if divided), achieving an equal outcome such as at point E in Figure 5.5 was impossible. No such indivisibility affects the income Y, which is perfectly divisible.[8] Therefore, an outcome of equality at point E is achievable.

For identical people who are behind a veil of ignorance and do not know who they will be, we can define an outcome of income equality as socially just. Social justice has accordingly been achieved through the equal distribution of available income Y that has maximized social welfare at point E. That is, achieving social justice and maximizing social welfare through equality are equivalent.

marginal utility (or benefit) from additional personal income. If the society is, for example, at point S where person 1 has the entire available income Y and person 2 has nothing, and some income is then given to person 2, because of diminishing marginal utility, person 1 loses less than person 2 gains. For example, the transfer of a given amount of income to person 2 at S moves the society to point F, and person 2 has gained more than person 1 has lost.

[8] The income Y available for distribution is large enough so that the indivisibility of the smallest coin is insignificant.

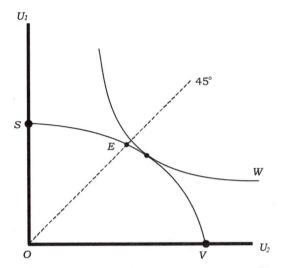

Figure 5.6. The utility-possibility frontier and maximization of social welfare when utilities differ.

Nonidentical utilities

Let us digress to consider what would happen if we did not view people as having identical utilities. Figure 5.6 shows a utility-possibility frontier when person 2 is defined as having greater capability for enjoyment of income (or of life) than person 1. Giving the entire income Y to person 2 provides that person with utility OV, which exceeds the utility OS of person 1 from the entire income Y. Because of the different personal utilities, social welfare is now not maximized at the equal utility point E; instead, maximizing social welfare requires giving more income to person 2 than to person 1. We see that the maximal social welfare contour W is tangential to the utility possibility frontier below the equal-utility 45° line, indicating that social welfare is maximized with a higher level of utility for person 2 than for person 1.

People perhaps do differ in capacities to enjoy income as implied by Figure 5.6. However, we face a problem in making the measurements that would allow us to conclude that one person has benefited more than another person from spending the same income. If we view people as having the same utility function, we can compare personal utilities through the common measure of utility that applies to both persons.[9]

Identical utilities also avoid problems that can arise when a social welfare function is not chosen behind a veil of ignorance. Choice not behind a veil of ignorance could take place if a society decided on the social welfare function that would be applied to income distribution decisions 100 years in the future. Personal self-interest

---

[9] When people are not viewed as identical and interpersonal comparisons between different people's utilities cannot be made, problems arise in defining a social welfare function as the aggregation of the preferences of all persons in a society. See Supplement 5A.

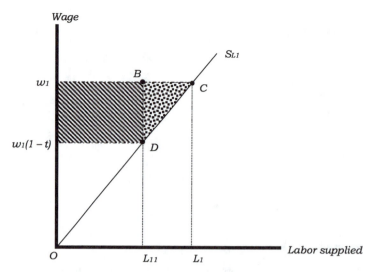

Figure 5.7a. The leaky bucket of income redistribution through taxation.

would then not influence the choice of the social welfare function because of the time distancing between the choice of the social welfare function and the use of the social welfare function to determine how income ought be distributed among the population.

If such time distancing between the choice and application of the social welfare function cannot be assured, preimposition of identical utilities in a social welfare function limits the scope for people deciding (perhaps by majority voting) that their utility from spending a sum of money is worth more than the utility of someone else.

A view of people as having identical utilities therefore has the same role as symmetry of social welfare contours. In each case, the purpose is to avoid self-interest and discrimination after people have appeared from behind the veil of ignorance (or have been born) and know who they are.

5.1.3 Efficiency and income redistribution

We shall now ask where the government has obtained the income Y that is available for distribution between person 1 and person 2. Governments *redistribute* rather than distribute income. Some people are taxed to provide income transfers to others.[10] Because of the excess burden of taxation, a government faces a "leaky bucket" of income redistribution.[11]

Suppose that person 1 pays taxes that finance income transfers to person 2. Figure 5.7a shows person 1's labor-supply function S_{L1}, which indicates the

---

[10] When a government obtains revenue by selling bonds, there is a need for future taxes (or more future borrowing) to repay the government's loans (see Chapter 2).

[11] Recall (from Chapter 2) that the presence of an excess burden of taxation is indicated by a taxpayer's willingness to pay more than the value of taxes that he or she has paid to avoid a tax or by the amount of compensation required in excess of the amount paid in taxes for having had to pay a tax.

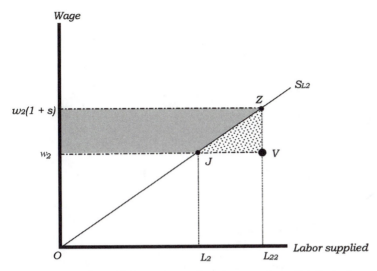

Figure 5.7b. The efficiency loss when income is redistributed.

substitution from income-earning activity to free time as the net-of-tax wage declines. Person 1's market-determined hourly wage is w_1. At the wage w_1, person 1 chooses to work L_1 hours a day. When the government sets an income tax at rate t, the post-tax wage is $w_1(1 - t)$. Person 1 responds to the lower take-home wage by a substitution response that reduces hours worked to L_{11}. The tax revenue paid by person 1 to the government is equal to the striped area in Figure 5.7a. The excess burden of this tax payment is BCD.[12]

The taxes paid by person 1 could simply be given to person 2 as a direct noncontingent income transfer.[13] Alternatively, the tax revenue paid by person 1 could also be used to subsidize person 2's market wage. In Figure 5.7b, S_{L2} is person 2's labor supply function. w_2 is person 2's market-determined wage without the subsidy. The tax revenue from person 1 is used to finance a subsidy of s for each hour that person 2 works. The subsidy increases person 2's post-transfer wage to $w_2(1 + s)$, and person 2's substitution response is to increase labor supply from L_2 to L_{22}. The total income transferred by the government to person 2 is the combined shaded and dotted rectangle in Figure 5.7b. The income transfer received by person 2 is equal to the tax revenue paid by person 1 (i.e., to the striped rectangle in Figure 5.7a). Person 2 values the income transfer less than the amount of money received. The reason is an efficiency loss in *receiving* the transfer. The efficiency loss is shown in Figure 5.7b as JVZ.[14]

---

[12] The revenue from the tax on person 1 might for example be $10,000, and the excess burden of the tax might be $2,000. Person 1 is then prepared to pay $12,000 to avoid paying a tax that yields the government revenue of $10,000.

[13] The income transfer is noncontingent, if the recipient has to behave in no particular way to receive the income transfer, for example, is not required to work, or is not required *not* to work.

[14] The transfer recipient's valuation of the income transfer in terms of free time is given by the area under the supply of labor function between w_2 and $w_2(1 + S)$. This valuation is less than the income

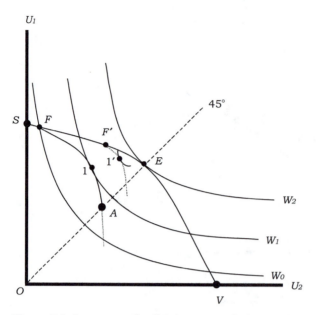

Figure 5.8. Income redistribution to maximize social welfare with a leaky bucket.

In Figure 5.7b, the recipient of the income transfer is working. Alternatively, a condition for receiving the income transfer might be that the recipient not earn income. In that case, there is an efficiency loss if, because of the income transfer, person 2 decides not to work. The income recipient might also receive the transfer as a subsidy for consumption. In particular, the taxes paid by person 1 might be used to finance an in-kind transfer to person 2, such as counseling from social workers, free or subsidized housing, education, health care, or vouchers that can be exchanged for free food. In that case, there is an efficiency loss similar to the loss when the income transfer is given as a subsidy for employment.

We have now seen that the "bucket of redistribution" has leaks, or that there are efficiency losses when taxes finance income redistribution. Let us look at how the efficiency losses affect income redistribution that maximizes social welfare. Point F in Figure 5.8 indicates market-determined incomes and, therefore, utilities, for person 1 and person 2 after they have emerged from behind a veil of ignorance. For example, person 1 is revealed to be a higher-ability person, which allows person 1 to earn higher income, and so person 1 has higher utility. The two persons agreed when behind the veil of ignorance that social welfare would be maximized after they have emerged from behind the veil of ignorance and know who they are (person 1 did not know behind the veil of ignorance that he or she would be person 1; person 2 did not know that he or she would be person 2). The two people find

transfer by JVZ because of the opportunity cost in terms of free time of supplying labor. If JVZ is \$1,000 and the income transfer received is \$10,000, person 2 values the transfer at \$9,000. The efficiency loss is \$1,000. Just as the excess burden of taxation is borne by the taxpayer, the efficiency loss from the income transfer is borne by the recipient of the transfer.

themselves at point F, with revealed identities as person 1 and person 2. Income redistribution is now required, according to the prior agreement behind the veil of ignorance, from person 1 to person 2. Because of efficiency losses, the bucket of income redistribution is leaky, and income redistribution beginning from point F (or any point along SV) is possible only to the interior of SV. Because of the leaky bucket, income redistribution from point F can accordingly only take place along FA. Outcomes along FA lie increasingly further inside SV as we leave the market-determined income distribution at F. Movement along FA requires more tax revenue to finance the greater income redistribution from person 1 to person 2, and we recall from Chapter 2 that efficiency losses increase when more tax revenue is required.

From among the income redistribution possibilities along FA, social welfare is maximized at the point 1. Redistribution from F to the point 1 increases social welfare from W_0 to W_1.

Although both persons are risk-averse, have identical utility functions, and are treated symmetrically by the social welfare function, social welfare is no longer maximized by achieving equality at a point on the 45° line. Equality is achieved by redistribution from the initial point F to point A. At point A, however, social welfare is less than W_1 at point 1.

If income redistribution were not costly because of efficiency losses, social welfare would be maximized by income redistribution to the equal-utility point E in Figure 5.8. Redistribution of income along the frontier SV could take place only if there were no efficiency losses from redistribution; that is, a redistribution of income along SV could take place only if people supplied labor (or worked) without regard for reward, or equivalently if market incentives did not affect personal decisions to work.[15]

The efficiency losses from redistribution introduce a trade-off between social justice defined as income equality and efficiency. Consequently, along FA, social welfare is not maximized at point A on the equal-utility 45° line, but rather at point 1 where utilities are unequal.

At point 1, person 1, who initially at point F before taxation and income redistribution had higher income and higher utility, still has higher income and higher utility after redistribution has taken place. Comparing the initial pre-redistribution point F to the post-redistribution point 1, the income distribution disparity has been reduced, but has not been completely closed.[16]

---

[15] That is, redistribution of income along SV would require behavior according to the principle of "contributing according to ability, not reward" (see Chapter 1). There would be no substitution responses and no efficiency losses, if people could be made to contribute according to their ability and not according to after-tax rewards received for productive effort.

[16] Figure 5.8 also shows that efficiency losses are smaller and social welfare is higher when there is greater initial equality in pre-tax or market-determined incomes. In Figure 5.8, we see an alternative initial market-determined income distribution point F' that is closer to the equality-utility point E than point F. Redistribution to maximize social welfare beginning from F' results in the post-redistribution outcome at point 1'. Social welfare is higher at 1' than at 1. Therefore, there is a social gain from the initially more equal income distribution. The social gain is due to the smaller amount

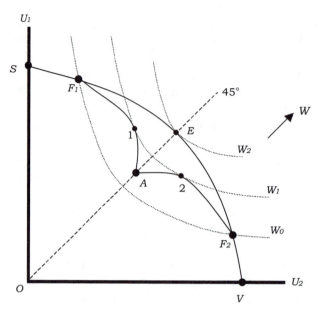

Figure 5.9. Income redistribution acts as social insurance.

5.1.4 Social insurance

A government that redistributes income to maximize social welfare is providing social insurance. Figure 5.9 extends Figure 5.8 to show two alternative possible market outcomes for income distribution at points F_1 and F_2. The outcome at point F_1 is more beneficial for person 1, and the outcome at point F_2 is more beneficial for person 2. The market outcomes at F_1 and F_2 are equally likely and are symmetric.[17]

Again, the two people have agreed behind the veil of ignorance to redistribute income to maximize social welfare. If the initial income distribution is at point F_1, income is redistributed along F_1A to point 1. If the initial market income distribution is at point F_2, income is redistributed along F_2A to point 2. In either case, income redistribution increases social welfare from W_0 to W_1. The income transfers that move the society to point 1 or point 2 provide insurance against the personally adverse outcomes for person 2 at point F_1 and for person 1 at point F_2.

Complete insurance would be provided by income redistribution from either F_1 or F_2 to a point along the equal-utility 45° line. At point 1 on F_1A and point 2 on F_2A, post-redistribution utilities are not equal, and therefore insurance is incomplete. However, the incomplete insurance maximizes social welfare.

---

of tax revenue required to finance the income redistribution that maximizes social welfare and the corresponding smaller efficiency loss from redistribution when the pre-tax outcome is at point F'.

[17] The symmetry is that F_1 is the same distance from the point S as F_2 is from the point V, so F_1 and F_2 are the same distance from the equal-utility point E. Feasible redistribution along F_1A or F_2A is also symmetrically inside SV.

We can now redefine social justice as requiring complete insurance, as would be achieved through income redistribution from either F_1 or F_2 to point A in Figure 5.9. The efficiency losses due to income redistribution are an impediment to complete insurance: the social welfare function indicates that gains from greater income equality beyond points 1 and 2 do not justify the efficiency losses from continuing to redistribute income to move closer to the complete-insurance point A.

The decision that efficiency losses do not justify redistribution of income beyond points 1 and 2 was made behind the veil of ignorance when the social welfare function was chosen.

The efficiency losses due to the leaky bucket of income redistribution are the cost of implementing insurance after exit from behind the veil of ignorance has revealed who people are and their market-determined incomes and utilities. The greater the cost of implementation of insurance is because of efficiency losses, the smaller is the redistribution that takes place.[18]

Rawls and the weakest link

Of the many (or unbounded) number of symmetric social welfare functions, which social welfare function can we expect people to choose when behind a veil of ignorance? The philosopher John Rawls (1921–2002), in his book *A Theory of Justice* (1971), proposed that people would want to choose a social welfare that focused on improving the well-being of the poorest or most unfortunate person in their society. After having done the best that is possible for the most unfortunate person, a society would then proceed to attend to the needs of the next most disadvantaged person, and so on, through the different people in the society. Throughout this procedure, no one's utility matters for the definition of social welfare other than the utility of the worst-off person. A society is then like a chain where the chain is as strong as its weakest link and the weakest link is the worst-off person in the society. All attention is directed at strengthening the weakest link.

Rawls's conception of social welfare implies a social welfare function of the form

$$W = \max\{\min U\}. \tag{5.5}$$

That is, the society should identify the person who has minimum utility and then maximize this person's utility – and having done this, a society should repeat the process consecutively through the population.[19]

Rawls's social welfare function therefore uses a maximin criterion to maximize the minimum utility in a society. Figure 5.10 shows the social welfare contours implied by Rawls's social welfare function. The social welfare contours are at

---

[18] Greater efficiency losses from redistribution than indicated in Figure 5.9 would move the frontiers F_1A and F_2A further inside SV, and, for a given social welfare function, at the new points 1 and 2 corresponding to the greater efficiency losses, less income redistribution would take place.

[19] To be able to identify the person with the minimum utility, the society must be able to compare utilities of different people, which we can do if all people have the same utility function that measures their utility.

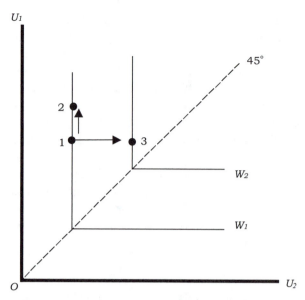

Figure 5.10. Social welfare contours for Rawls's social welfare function.

With Rawls's definition, only an improvement in the well-being of the least-well-off person increases social welfare.

right angles to the 45° line. The right angles indicate that there is no trade-off in social welfare between helping richer and poorer people. Only improvements in the well-being of the poorest person count as improving social welfare.

Above the 45° line in Figure 5.10, person 1 has higher utility than person 2, so social welfare cannot increase unless the utility of the less-well-off person 2 increases. Therefore, a move from point 1 to point 2 does not change social welfare because the utility of better-off person 1 increases but there is no change in the utility of less-well-off person 2. Yet this change is a Pareto improvement because person 1 is made better off and person 2 is no worse off. A Pareto improvement can therefore occur, but Rawls's social welfare function recognizes no social improvement if the person who has been made better off is not the "weakest link" in the society. Social welfare increases as the consequence of a change from point 1 to point 3 in Figure 5.10 because this change increases the utility of weakest-link person 2.

The preferences expressed in Rawls's social welfare function are lexographic. No trade-offs between people's utilities that would distract from maximizing the utility of the worst-off person are possible. Recalling the social weights of individuals in a social welfare function defined by expression (5.2), the worst-off person has positive social weight in Rawls's social welfare function, and all others have zero social weight.

Figure 5.11 shows social insurance with Rawls's social welfare function. Behind the veil of ignorance, the two people do not know whether the market-determined income distribution and utilities will be at F_1 or F_2. Independently of whether the market outcome is F_1 or F_2, Rawls's social welfare function maximizes social

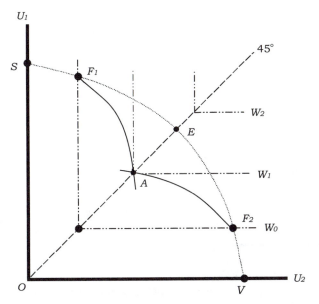

Figure 5.11. Social insurance with Rawls's definition of social welfare.

welfare by redistributing income to point A on the equal-utility $45°$ line. Rawls's social welfare criterion therefore provides complete insurance.

Since Rawls's concern is for the weakest link in society, efficiency costs of redistribution imposed on other people do not matter. Therefore, efficiency is not an impediment to achieving social justice defined as complete social insurance.[20]

Bentham

An alternative approach to defining social welfare is associated with the English political economist Jeremy Bentham (1748–1832). Bentham proposed that a society should follow the objective of seeking "the greatest good for the greatest number."[21] This social objective has been interpreted as implying that social

---

[20] There may be limitations due to indivisibilities on being able to achieve the complete insurance and complete income equality sought through Rawls's social welfare function. In the case of the water in the desert, the water has no value if shared and utilities cannot be equal. Equivalently, the feasible redistribution functions F_1A and F_2A in Figure 5.11 may stop before reaching point A. This would require, for example, a poor country where a king or ruler has a few very large palaces and the rest of the population lives in hovels. Like the water in the desert, the palaces are not divisible and so cannot be indivisibly assigned to people to achieve complete equality (since there are more people than palaces). We have also observed that part of the efficiency cost of redistribution can fall on recipients of income transfers. Efficiency costs incurred by the recipients of income transfers could only prevent complete income equality if the efficiency losses incurred by the recipients of income transfers were to exceed the value of the income transfer received. We see in Figure 5.7b that this can never be so.

[21] Bentham believed that it would be possible one day to measure individual capacities for enjoyment by designing machines that measure personal satisfaction, which would allow objectively comparable measurement of different utilities of different people. Bentham's expectations about objective measurement of utility have not been realized.

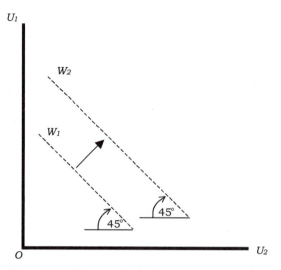

Figure 5.12. Bentham's social welfare function.
The straight lines with slopes of 45° indicate perfect substitutability in social welfare between the utility of one person and the utility of another.

welfare is defined by adding the utilities of everybody in society. For n people in a society, the social welfare function is, therefore,

$$W = U_1 + U_2 + U_3 + \cdots + U_n. \tag{5.6}$$

All n people have equal social weights (equal to one). When society consists of two people, social welfare is the sum of the utilities

$$W = U_1 + U_2. \tag{5.7}$$

The dashed lines with 45° slope in Figure 5.12 show the shape of Bentham's social welfare contours for a society of two people.[22]

The slope of $-45°$ of Bentham's social welfare contours indicates that, for the purpose of measuring social welfare, utilities of different people are perfectly substitutable or interchangeable. That is, in measuring social welfare, utility provided for one person is as good as utility for any other person. All that matters for social welfare is the sum of utilities. The distribution of utilities does not matter.

---

[22] A change in social welfare is the sum of changes in the two people's utilities,

$$dW = dU_1 + dU_2.$$

since, along a social welfare contour, social welfare is constant, along a social welfare contour

$$0 = dU_1 + dU_2.$$

The slope of a social welfare contour for Bentham's social welfare function is therefore

$$\frac{dU_1}{dU_2} = -1,$$

which is the slope indicated by the 45° lines in Figure 5.12.

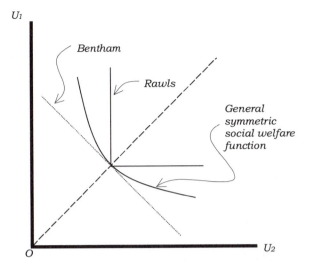

Figure 5.13. The social welfare functions of Rawls and Bentham.

The definitions of social welfare of Rawls and Bentham are limiting cases.

Rawls and Bentham are limiting cases of social welfare functions. Rawls cares only about distribution, and only about the worst-off person, and does not care about efficiency costs of redistribution imposed on taxpayers when taxes are levied to finance income transfers to the worst-off person. Bentham is indifferent to distribution and wants the sum of utilities to be maximized without regard for distribution.

Figure 5.13 shows how the social welfare criteria of Bentham and Rawls are limiting cases. The smooth-substitution symmetric social welfare contour lies between the social welfare contours of Rawls and Bentham.

Figure 5.14 shows social insurance using Bentham's social welfare function. Points F_1 and F_2 are again equally likely market outcomes on the efficient utility-possibility frontier (the efficient frontier is not shown in Figure 5.14). $F_1 A$ and $F_2 A$ reflect the leaky bucket of redistribution and lie inside the (not-drawn) efficient utility-possibility frontier. If the market income distribution is at F_1, social welfare is maximized by redistributing income (and utility) from person 1 to person 2 along $F_1 A$ to the point 1. If the market income distribution is at the point F_2, social welfare is maximized by redistributing income (and utility) from person 2 to person 1 along $F_2 A$ to the point 2. In either case, redistribution of income increases social welfare from W_0 to W_1. We see that social insurance provided through Bentham's social welfare criterion is incomplete. Complete insurance would have brought the society to the equal-utility 45° line at the point A.

Rawls or Bentham?

The choice of Rawls's social welfare function behind a veil of ignorance would indicate a population of people extremely concerned about being the worst-off in

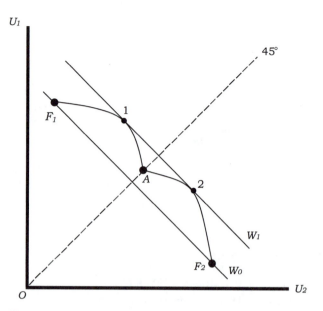

Figure 5.14. Social insurance with Bentham's definition of social welfare.

society. The concern is so intense, that, in maximizing social welfare and providing social insurance the population agrees that social welfare will be measured by the utility of whoever will happen to be revealed as the worst-off person when the population emerges from behind the veil of ignorance.

We can consider n people behind a veil of ignorance who know that a number n_1 persons will have high ability and earn high incomes and a number n_2 persons will have low ability and earn low incomes. A high-income person will have utility U^H and a low-income person will have utility U^L. Bentham's social welfare criterion adds the population's utilities so that social welfare is

$$W = n_1 U^H + n_2 U^L. \tag{5.8}$$

When we divide social welfare in (5.8) by the total population n, we have

$$\frac{W}{n} = p^H U^H + p^L U^L = EU. \tag{5.9}$$

Bentham's social welfare function expressed in the form (5.9) contains the probabilities of having high and low incomes or utilities. The probabilities are

$$\frac{n_1}{n} = p^H = \text{probability of having high income}$$

and

$$\frac{n_2}{n} = p^L = \text{probability of having low income.}$$

Bentham's social welfare function expressed in the form (5.9) is therefore precisely

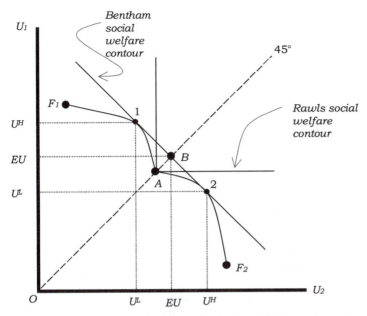

Figure 5.15. Comparison between social insurance using the definitions of social welfare of Rawls and Bentham.

equivalent to the expected utility of any member of the population behind the veil of ignorance.

Therefore, maximizing the expected utility of a member of the population behind a veil of ignorance is equivalent to agreeing to maximize Bentham's social welfare function after people have emerged from behind the veil of ignorance. The weights on high- and low-utility persons are objectively determined by the probability of each outcome.[23]

Rawls's social welfare function maximizes only the utility U^L of low-utility persons. The utility U^H does not appear in Rawls's social welfare function, nor do the probabilities of having high and low incomes.

Figure 5.15 compares social insurance based on the Rawls and Bentham definitions of social welfare. In Figure 5.15, we return to a population of two people, but the general principles apply to large populations. Rawls's social welfare function in Figure 5.15 provides complete social insurance at point A. Bentham's social welfare provides incomplete social insurance, with the outcome after income redistribution either at point 1 or point 2, depending on whether the market-determined income distribution is at point F_1 or point F_2. The expected utility EU provided to the population by Bentham is determined at point B as the average of U^H and U^L. Point B can never be achieved but is the equivalent of the value of a lottery ticket that offers equal chances of being at point 1 or point 2.

[23] If, for example, there is 60% chance of having high income and high utility, P^H is 0.6 and P^L is 0.4.

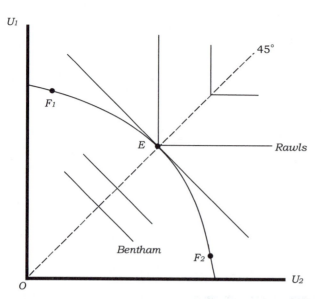

Figure 5.16. If there were no efficiency losses from redistributing income, Bentham and Rawls would both provide complete social insurance at E.

In Figure 5.16, we return to a hypothetical case where there is no efficiency loss when income redistribution takes place. Beginning from a market income distribution at either F_1 or F_2, the outcome with Bentham's or Rawls's social welfare function is complete insurance at point E.[24]

The equivalent outcomes in Figure 5.16 indicate that the difference between social insurance provided according to Rawls and Bentham is due to the effects of the leaky bucket of income redistribution. When efficiency losses of redistribution are present as in Figure 5.15, a society using Bentham's definition of social welfare cares about the efficiency losses that accompany redistribution of income, and responds to the trade-off between achieving efficiency and income equality by providing social insurance that is incomplete. The taxpayers who provide the revenue and who incur the efficiency cost of income redistribution through the excess burden of taxation have no weight in Rawls's definition of social welfare, and so, no matter how large the efficiency losses, income redistribution with Rawls continues until income equality is attained and insurance is complete.

The efficiency losses of redistribution could be very high, as in Figure 15.17 where $F_1 A$ and $F_2 A$ fall precipitously as redistribution takes place. In Figure 15.17, Bentham's social welfare function is now maximized with no redistribution at all (post-distribution points 1 and 2 in Figure 15.4 or Figure 15.5 coincide in Figure 15.17 with the initial market income-distribution points F_1 and F_2).

---

[24] Any symmetric social welfare function gives the same result of complete insurance when there are no efficiency losses from income distribution.

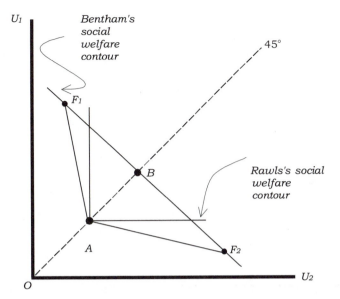

Figure 5.17. Comparison between Rawls and Bentham when efficiency losses of redistribution are high.

Although no income redistribution takes place, this outcome was agreed upon as the response to the high efficiency costs of redistribution when, behind the veil of ignorance, the decision was made to provide social insurance according to the Bentham social welfare function. On the other hand, high efficiency losses from redistribution do not deter complete equality and complete insurance if Rawls's social welfare function was chosen behind the veil of ignorance. No matter how close to the origin the complete-insurance point *A* in Figure 15.17 might be, Rawls's social welfare function calls for redistribution to that point to achieve equality. Rawls makes no compromise regarding complete equality and complete insurance because for Rawls complete equality and complete insurance are supreme values that cannot be compromised.

Social insurance with different attitudes toward risk

Figure 5.18 returns to the more general circumstances where redistribution takes place when Bentham's social welfare function has been chosen. The curved symmetric social welfare contour in Figure 5.18 provides more insurance (at the post-tax outcomes at points 3 and 4) than the straight-line social welfare contours of Bentham's social welfare function (at the post-tax points 1 and 2). When the social welfare contours have Rawls's shape, complete social insurance is provided at the point *A*. A society that chooses Rawls provides the utility U_c to everyone in the population with certainty. Such a society would have a comprehensive program of social insurance (or a comprehensive welfare state) with high taxes, as well as high excess burdens of taxation. Social insurance is more costly the more leaky the bucket of income redistribution is. Since equality is a supreme value for a society

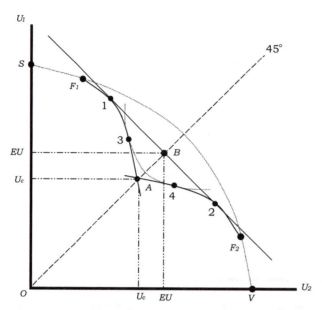

Figure 5.18. Social insurance with different social attitudes toward risk.

that uses Rawls's definition of social welfare, such a society is prepared to incur any efficiency cost in order to have the complete insurance that brings the society to a point such as A in Figure 5.18.

A society choosing Bentham in contrast offers a lottery in life. The value of the lottery in Figure 5.18 is expected utility EU offered through incomplete insurance. Income distribution after applying Bentham's social welfare function is unequal at point 1 or point 2, but the society has lower efficiency losses than a society that has chosen Rawls's definition of social welfare and provides complete insurance.

The expected utility EU offered by Bentham's lottery exceeds the utility U_c offered by Rawls. Rawls, however, offers U_c with certainty. Bentham's lottery in life confronts person 1 with the chance of a personally beneficial outcome at point 1 after emerging from behind the veil of ignorance, but also with the chance of being at the personally less beneficial outcome at point 2. Person 2 faces the same symmetric risk.

The intermediate case between Bentham and Rawls in Figure 5.18 also offers a lottery in life: the outcomes at points 3 and 4 are closer to equality than the outcomes of Bentham's lottery, and the efficiency losses of redistribution are correspondingly greater.

A society makes its choice of the social welfare function and consequent social insurance behind the veil of ignorance according to tolerance for income inequality. Or, equivalently, the social welfare function and social insurance are determined behind the veil of ignorance by tolerance for accepting inefficiency losses of income redistribution to achieve a more equal income distribution.

Comparing social welfare

We cannot compare the different levels of social welfare in Figure 15.8 as measured by different social welfare functions. The social welfare functions of Bentham and Rawls, and more generally all social welfare functions, rank social outcomes through their own distinct measures of social welfare.

We can, however, compare individuals' utilities obtained as a consequence of choice of a social welfare function, since utilities depend on individuals' incomes. Followers of Rawls might nonetheless propose that their definition of social welfare is based on broader visions of benefit to a society than personal utility derived from income alone because the social objectives expressed in Rawls's social welfare function define a *supreme value* of social equality that should under no circumstances be compromised.

We can notice that when a choice is made to use Rawls's social welfare function for guidance in providing social insurance, there is a problem of how to reconcile the preordained social (or income) equality with the will to work. Rawls's social welfare function requires that people be motivated to exert effort and work, although they know that their income after redistribution will, through complete social insurance, ultimately be determined not by their own efforts but as the average of everyone's efforts. With personal incentives to exert effort to earn income therefore absent, followers of Rawls must hope that people decide to (or can be made to) exert effort to contribute according to their ability.[25]

5.1.5 Private insurance

We have now set out a theory that explains why governments use taxation to redistribute income, or a theory that explains why governments should redistribute income through taxation. In the first case, we have a positive theory that explains income redistribution. In the second case, we have a normative theory that justifies income redistribution. The theory is based on risk-averse people who seek protection against personally adverse events that are beyond their control, and who view government as an insurance company that spreads risk among the population. By spreading risk through social insurance, the government increases personal utilities of the risk-averse population.

When we considered public goods and externalities, we first investigated the outcomes of private voluntary decisions without government. Thereafter we considered the scope for improvement through public finance and public policy. In considering social justice, our point of beginning has been responsibility taken by

---

[25] We are returned once more to section 1.3, where experiences of societies were described where a supreme uncompromising value of income equality was applied and where people were asked to contribute according to ability and not in response to personal rewards. We saw that problems of inefficiency arose in these societies because of reluctance to exert effort, and there were also problems of loss of personal freedom in the attempts to re-engineer society so that people would work without regard for reward. Peter Bernholz (1993) of the University of Basel studied societies with supreme values throughout history and confirmed that supreme values are inconsistent with personal freedom.

government in providing social insurance. We began with government because we identified social justice as an objective sought through social insurance, and we have interpreted the extent of social insurance chosen by a society in terms of choice of a social welfare function. Social welfare functions are in the domain of government. We therefore considered government as providing social insurance to maximize social welfare. However, is social insurance through government necessary? Why cannot private insurance markets provide the insurance that a government provides through social insurance?

What does social insurance protect against?

Before considering the alternative to social insurance of private insurance markets, let us look more closely at the nature of the adverse events against which social insurance provides protection. Primarily, social insurance protects against low incomes, or no income and deprivation. Where there is no social insurance, and the family or friends or private charity do not provide support, people can starve. Persons who in particular face prospects of low or no income are old people who cannot work, mothers who cannot work because they have to attend to their children, and people who are disabled from birth or incapacitated through accidents or bad health.

Also people capable of working may not be able to find a job. More precisely, because there is always a wage at which someone can find a job, the problem is that the income that the market offers a person is not sufficient to maintain living standards that a society regards as minimally acceptable. The minimal living standards are reflected in a legally determined minimum wage. Figure 5.19 shows an

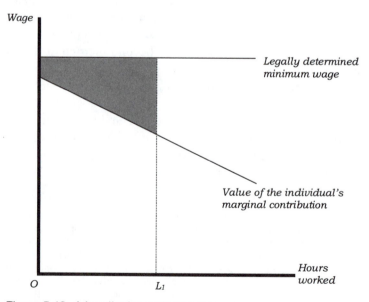

Figure 5.19. A legally determined minimum wage.

individual whose marginal contribution to the value of production never exceeds the legally determined minimum wage for any number of hours worked. An employer who gives this person a job loses. For example, if the person were employed at the minimum wage for L_1 hours, an employer would lose an amount of money equal to the shaded area.[26] Therefore, the individual in Figure 5.19 cannot earn income from a job. Or, people who cannot obtain job offers that pay at least the minimum wage cannot find a job because they are not legally allowed to work if they cannot earn the minimum wage.[27]

Private insurance markets cannot offer everyone personal insurance against having low income, or not being eligible to earn income at all because of an inability to earn the minimum wage. People who have established a reputation for being employed can usually buy private unemployment insurance, and private insurance is generally available for income lost through injury or bad health. Private life insurance provides protection against not having income when old and protects families against being deprived of income due to the untimely death of an income provider. Private insurance markets provide such insurance for people who have enough income to pay the insurance premium.

Private insurance cannot, however, provide insurance against all the types of risks insured by social insurance. We cannot buy private insurance against being born into unfortunate circumstances because we cannot buy insurance before we exist. Nor can parents enter into insurance contracts to guarantee future incomes of children. There are other types of insurance that private insurance companies are not willing to supply. For example, private insurance companies are unwilling to provide insurance that protects a female head of household from having inadequate income because of her need to care for increasing numbers of children or that protects her against low income because the male has left the household and provides no financial support. Private insurance companies are also unwilling to provide insurance that protects against (and compensates for) being consistently unemployed. In general, private insurance companies are unwilling to enter into insurance contracts that guarantee personal future incomes.

There are three broad reasons why private insurance companies refuse to provide insurance. The reasons are (1) adverse selection, (2) inability to verify the outcomes against which insurance is sought, and (3) moral hazard. Each of these reasons has to do with asymmetric information, that is, with some people knowing what others do not.

---

[26] A justification sometimes proposed for a legal minimum wage is to prevent competitive bidding for jobs at the low-wage end of the market so as to counter asymmetric bargaining power between employers and job seekers when more than one person applies for a job vacancy.

[27] Prohibition of working at less than a legally determined minimum wage is a case of the prohibited markets that we considered in Chapter 4. Employers and employees might choose to ignore the legal minimum wage. People who work illegally at less than the minimum wage remain eligible for income protection through social insurance because their incomes are not officially recorded. The people who work illegally at less than the minimum wage may be illegal immigrants, who are in any event illegal, and for whom the less-than-minimum wage provides a better life than incomes in their former locations.

Adverse selection

Adverse selection occurs when people know more about their own characteristics and personal risks than do suppliers of insurance. For example, people who very much enjoy leisure or who do not have the self-discipline required to have a job know that they will consistently require payments from insurance to maintain their incomes. When such people are in the same insurance group as people who consistently work for a living, they receive systematic and not random income transfers from the people who work for a living. The purpose of insurance is, however, not to provide systematic payments to particular people, but to provide random payments that are more or less equally likely to be received by anybody.

Adverse selection can lead people who know they are low-risk to underwrite their own risk, or to self-insure themselves. Low-risk people therefore leave the insurance pool of the general population, but high-risk people do not.

The exit of the low-risk people increases the average cost of financing insurance payouts for the people who remain. The higher expected payouts increase the insurance premium for people who remain in the insurance pool, and more people then choose self-insurance because of the higher costs of insurance. Sequential exit therefore takes place by the lower-risk people who know, after an increase in the premium, that the likelihood of their benefiting from insurance has decreased. Because of adverse selection, demand for private insurance therefore becomes restricted to high-risk people who believe that they have a high chance of not being successful in earning income, or who know that their life-styles are likely to impair their future income-earning abilities.

High-risk people thus select themselves as the ones who most need insurance, by staying in the market as the insurance premium increases. At the same time, to avoid systematic income losses, low-risk people exclude themselves from the private insurance market. The consequence is that adverse selection can lead private insurance markets to collapse.[28]

Private insurance markets can be sustained, if insurance companies have ways of identifying high- and low-risk people. The high-risk people then remain uninsured. For example, when employers provide health insurance for employees, the non-working population is outside the employer insurance pools and requires personal private-market health insurance contracts. If non-working persons have systematically higher demand for health care (they may be people who are unable to work because of chronic health problems), the private insurance market

---

[28] The idea of adverse selection was described by George Akerlof (1970) through the example of a market for used cars. Akerlof (from the University of California at Berkeley) received the Nobel Prize in economics in 2001 for his contributions to understanding behavior under asymmetric information. Akerlof supposed that sellers knew the true quality of their cars, whereas buyers did not, and that the market price was determined by average quality. Because the market price reflects average quality, owners of better-than-average quality cars withdraw from the market, which decreases the average quality of remaining cars and decreases price. After the fall in price, above-average quality cars among remaining cars in the market are withdrawn, and, in the end, only the worst quality cars are left in the market. There has been adverse selection in the determination of which cars remain in the market.

will respond with high health insurance premiums for these people. Or, since the required high insurance premiums might be regarded as "unfair," and would also in many cases be unaffordable, private insurance companies might prefer simply to decline to insure individuals who are not covered in the group insurance programs organized through employers. Because of adverse selection, some people are then not insured or are non-insurable.[29] The private insurance market has however been able to provide insurance, precisely because means have been available to distinguish high-risk from low-risk persons. If the means of identifying high- and low-risk persons were not available, the private health insurance market could face collapse through adverse selection.

Inability to verify outcomes

A second reason why private insurance markets can fail to provide insurance is that outcomes against which insurance is sought cannot be verified. For example, someone may want insurance against not being able to work because of emotional problems. However, verifying emotional impediments to having a job can be difficult. A person might want insurance against the random event occurring where one day he or she declares: "I cannot now emotionally cope with the stress of going to work and having to stay in one place all day and having to do what other people tell me. I am therefore leaving my job and I want compensating replacement income through insurance." Although such emotional impediments to work may arise randomly in the population, the observed behavior can be indistinguishable from laziness. Private insurance companies are therefore understandably reluctant to offer insurance that would provide compensating income payments when people declare that they cannot cope with the emotional stress of a commitment to go to work. As with adverse selection, there is a problem of asymmetric information. The insurance company does not know the true reason for a person's inability to work, while the person seeking insurance does.

Moral hazard

Moral hazard is a third reason why private insurance markets can fail to provide insurance. Insurance, as a matter of definition, is provided against random unpredictable outcomes that people cannot influence. Such a random event occurs when people become unemployed through no fault of their own, as when a new technology makes jobs redundant or people cannot work because of unforeseen health problems. An unforeseen family crisis may prevent people from completing their education, or a person may have been left with small children to care for after the partner has left or has died. Moral hazard describes personal behavior that influences the likelihood that such adverse outcomes arise.

[29] In the United States, the federal government's Medicaid and Medicare programs provide health care as publicly financed social insurance for poor people and for the elderly, but large parts of the population have been without health insurance.

The likelihood of an adverse outcome may depend on precautionary actions or efforts. If precautionary actions and effort are unobservable, private insurance companies can refuse to provide insurance because people through their behavior and decisions can contribute to bringing the adverse outcomes on themselves – for which they will be compensated through insurance.

Moral hazard is avoided if insurance contracts can be made contingent on effort to avoid adverse outcomes.[30] When personal effort cannot be observed, private insurance companies rationally refuse to provide insurance. The hazard for the insurance company is "moral," through the absence of due care or effort by the people who are insured. A person might, for example, prefer to spend the day with friends in a bar or on the beach rather than working for a living. When a private insurance contract makes income payments contingent on the observed outcome of not having a job, such a person might not look for a job, or might behave in a way that leads to dismissal from any job. Similarly, an insurance contract that fully compensates for income losses for not successfully completing studies might lead some people to decide not to study.

In such cases, a person's own actions and effort influence the likelihood of adverse outcomes. The outcomes are, however, no longer personally adverse if an insurance company pays full compensation for losses. With full compensation (or complete insurance), instead of working or studying, some people might enjoy themselves, while the insurance company provides personal income.

As with adverse selection and inability to verify outcomes, moral hazard involves asymmetric information. The asymmetric information is that people know their own efforts at taking precautions to avoid adverse outcomes, but the insurance company can only observe outcomes and not effort.[31]

5.1.6 Government as insurer of last resort

When private insurance markets fail to provide insurance, government can take the role of insurer of last resort and provide social insurance to substitute for the absent private insurance. Government then acts like an insurance company in the way that we have described by taxing some people and giving income transfers to others. When government or society takes the responsibility for providing insurance, government or society confronts the problems of adverse selection, nonverifiability of outcomes, and moral hazard.

Adverse selection and government

Government can address the problem of adverse selection by making participation in social insurance compulsory. Adverse selection occurs through low-risk persons

---

[30] For home insurance, for example, alarm systems and window and door locks may be required as a condition of insurance. The presence of the alarm and locks is verifiable. Whether the alarm has been set may also be verifiable.

[31] A solution to moral hazard is often participatory self-insurance under which people personally bear some of the costs of adverse outcomes. Damage that might be incurred in misjudging the size of a parking space is, for example, often not insurable.

exiting an insurance pool. Exit cannot take place if everyone in the population has no choice but to be in an all-inclusive social insurance pool.

A government can justify compulsory participation in a social insurance pool for redistribution of income by pointing to the idea of a social contract formulated behind the veil of ignorance. In seeking to opt out of social insurance that redistributes income, higher-income people are in a sense attempting to renege on the social contract that underlies social insurance. Once people already know who they are, and they know that their prospects in life are good, they have an incentive to select themselves out of the social insurance contract, whereas the social contract is based on uncertainty about prospects in life behind the veil of ignorance when people do not know who they will be.

Adverse selection is associated with a time-inconsistency problem. Behind the veil of ignorance, risk-averse people would want insurance as protection against possible adverse outcomes after they are born. People who subsequently discover that they are more likely to pay the taxes that finance income redistribution than to benefit from social insurance regret decisions made behind the veil of ignorance that there should be social insurance and want to exit from the insurance pool. The exit is sought because, after people know who they are, "social insurance" is no longer insurance. Social insurance has rather become systematic income redistribution that imposes losses on successful people. If exit from the population's insurance pool can take place, the time-inconsistency problem leads social insurance to collapse.

A means of exit is emigration. Relocation to another government jurisdiction where social insurance is less extensive and where taxes and the excess burden of taxation are lower offers people at low risk of having low incomes a means of escape from compulsory participation in social insurance. Emigration can unravel social insurance by leaving only the high-risk people who have high probabilities of benefiting from social insurance in a population's social insurance pool. Adverse selection can also occur through immigration, if people at high risk of having low incomes locate in a government jurisdiction with generous social security benefits.[32]

Inability to verify outcomes and government

Government cannot resolve the problem confronting private insurance markets of inability to verify outcomes. For example, a government faces the same difficulties as a private insurance company in verifying that a claimed emotional aversion to work is not laziness.

Moral hazard and government

Government has no advantage over private insurance markets in solving problems of moral hazard. Solving problems of moral hazard requires an ability to observe

---

[32] Just as locational choice is a means of choosing taxes and benefits from public goods, locational choice is also a means of choosing participation in social insurance.

effort. When government provides social insurance, the asymmetric information about effort that is the basis of moral hazard remains.

Some people might, for example, avail themselves of benefit from the government's social assistance, not because they have fallen on hard times for no reason of their own making, but because life with publicly financed personal income is a preferred and comfortable life-style. Social insurance provided by government will then be subject to the same moral hazard that deters private insurance markets from offering insurance for personal income protection.

If social insurance provides adequate personal income, and if self-respect and job satisfaction are not reasons to work, people may make no effort to find work, or may not work when they are directed to an employer who is looking for employees. A culture can develop of living off the state. Social insurance can therefore make a society less productive because of moral hazard.

Changes in social norms can combine with moral hazard to affect the demand for social insurance. Welfare stigma may deter some people from living off government transfers, but, when sufficient numbers of people receive income from the government, social norms may change and welfare stigma can disappear, leading people to regard living off the state as ethical and reasonable.

Changes in social norms about life-styles can also influence social insurance payments. When single motherhood is a social norm, the incidence of single motherhood increases. If social insurance did not provide income for single mothers, single motherhood would be less attractive. When the existence of social insurance influences the decision to be a single mother, moral hazard has increased the demand for social insurance.[33]

Separation and divorce may not be an option if social insurance is not available to provide income for a woman with children. A man may also have fewer qualms about leaving a family when he knows that government will provide for his family through social insurance.[34] Social insurance can therefore also affect decisions to continue a marriage, or to separate and divorce. Because social insurance affects behavior, we have another case of moral hazard.[35]

Moral hazard is a source of loss to society due to behavior of people who choose to become eligible for income transfers by reducing effort and being less productive and less self-reliant. Although these people personally benefit (they have made a voluntary decision based on the incentives that confront them), there is an efficiency loss through the increased excess burden of the higher taxes required to finance the income transfers that they receive.

---

[33] Social norms regarding single motherhood changed in the latter half of the twentieth century at the same time as benefits to single mothers in the United States from social security were declining. The change in social norms influenced behavior more than the decline in benefits through social insurance. Some women could afford to have children without the further accompaniment of men because of other changes in social norms that opened opportunities for high-income careers for women. For other women who were poorer, income transfers from government facilitated single motherhood. For the evidence, see Brinig and Buckely (1999).

[34] In principle, the man may be obliged by law to provide alimony payments.

[35] A person trapped in a bad marriage or relationship benefits when social insurance allows an escape.

We see that, when government provides social insurance, moral hazard results in subversion of social justice. Because of moral hazard, social insurance redistributes income in ways not justified by criteria of social justice.

5.1.7 Voting on social insurance

The view of social insurance as a social contract chosen behind a veil of ignorance where people do not know who they will be is not an actual representation of how the conditions of social insurance are decided. In practice, choice of a social insurance program is not made in a state of ignorance about personal benefits. Rather, the conditions of social insurance are determined through voting and political decisions by people who know who they are. Under majority voting, the median voter determines the scope of social insurance.[36] The social insurance program chosen by the median voter depends on the personal risk that the median voter confronts.[37]

In principle, people should vote on a definition of social justice and the extent of social insurance through choice of a social welfare function. However, because of the problems of asymmetric information (adverse selection, inability to verify outcomes, and moral hazard), the issue confronting voters can change from the design of social insurance to the willingness to pay taxes to finance income redistribution. Low-risk (or high-income) voters may wish to avoid paying taxes systematically to finance income transfers to low-income people. Such reluctance to finance social insurance is a reflection of the time-inconsistency problem that underlies adverse selection. High-income voters may have voted for extensive social insurance if the vote were actually to take place behind a veil of ignorance where they do not know who they are going to be, but, once they know they have high incomes, they have no incentive to vote for extensive social insurance. Voting on the extent of social insurance (or choice of the social welfare function) is therefore influenced by adverse selection.

At the same time, low-risk people who view themselves as diligently working to earn incomes may wish to avoid financing systematic income transfers to people

[36] We can envisage voters being asked whether they want to expand welfare benefits and increase taxes to finance the benefits. The procedure for determining the outcome of majority voting is the same as that we described for public spending on public goods in Chapter 3. When the median voter votes for less social insurance than high-risk people want, high-risk people could attempt to turn to the private insurance market for the insurance that they seek. For the reasons that have been described, the private market may not offer the insurance. If private insurance is offered, high insurance premiums will reflect the adverse selection that leads high-risk people to the private market.

[37] We can infer the risk confronting the median voter in a population by the social insurance contract that societies choose. For example, the U.S. social security scheme was introduced during the Great Depression in the 1930s, when there was widespread risk that people would starve in their advanced years because unfavorable economic conditions during their working lives had not allowed them to save for their old age. In Europe, governments in some countries were often consistently reelected on a platform of maintaining an extensive social insurance program of birth-to-death publicly financed entitlements to education, health care, old-age pensions, and housing, and income in general.

whom they perceive as not putting in enough effort to be self-reliant. Perceptions of moral hazard therefore also influence how people vote on social insurance.

Voters can also be influenced by the problem of inability to verify that people are truly in need of public assistance. Questions might be asked about whether family members could not help, whether people receiving welfare payments are truly not capable of working, and whether some people are in fact working and at the same time receiving public assistance.

If, because of asymmetric information, people who are deserving and non-deserving of public assistance are indistinguishable, the choice in a vote on the scope of social insurance is between two types of errors. The deserving poor can be assisted through extensive social insurance that unintentionally benefits non-deserving persons. Or alternatively a vote for modest social insurance will restrict unintentional benefits to nondeserving people but at the expense of assistance to deserving people.

5.1.8 Global social insurance

Global social insurance would provide compensating payments for adversity wherever in the world people happen to be born and wherever they happen to find themselves. The global social insurance contract would, for example, protect people from being born into poverty in a country where home is a hovel with a dirt floor with no electricity or running water and where the population does not have access to basic health services or basic education. The global social insurance contract would also protect people from being born in a country where a large part of the population is HIV-positive. Where the HIV-virus is prevalent, children's future incomes are reduced when the children do not go to school because they stay home to attend to parents and other family members with AIDS. In countries that are poor to begin with, incomes are reduced further when parents are disabled and die in the prime of their lives. Besides indignity and loss of personal freedom, women in some countries are disadvantaged by low-earning capabilities because of biases against educating girls and because of restricted employment opportunities that are the result of limitations on women's activities outside the household. The bias against educating girls may be the result of a society's norms but economic incentives to educate girls are also adversely affected by the restrictions on women's employment opportunities. Faced with such possibilities, people behind the veil of ignorance would want a global insurance contract to protect themselves against adverse conditions in any location.

The idea of global social insurance is reflected in foreign assistance programs of governments of richer countries and international agencies. The World Bank and the International Monetary Fund in particular seek to alleviate poverty by providing loans and development aid for poorer countries.

Insurance implies random compensating payments when adverse events take place. The assistance provided by the World Bank and the International Monetary

Fund has not tended not to be randomly distributed but rather has been given systematically for the most part to the same countries over the course of time. The international agencies, acting as if under the terms of a global insurance contract, appear to have confronted the moral-hazard problems that we have identified as associated with failure of insurance markets. The international agencies have provided resources to governments in poor countries to finance public investment and to provide health care and education so that the lives of the populations of the poor countries could be improved. Yet the substantial resources have, with few exceptions, not resulted in the sought improvements. After resources have been provided, more resources have additionally been required, and still more in a process that yielded little or no improvement in the lives of the poor.

Evidence on continued aid from the World Bank with little or no benefit or deterioration of living standards for poor people in poor countries has been provided by William Easterly (2001). Resources have been made available to governments of poor countries on condition that the governments adopt public policies that would allow the resources to be utilized effectively to improve the lives of the poor. Reporting from personal experience at the World Bank, Easterly describes behavior and outcomes that we recognize as moral hazard: "even if the conditions are not met, the donors want to alleviate the lot of the poor, and so they give the aid anyway. The recipients can anticipate this behavior of donors and thus sit tight without doing reforms or helping the poor. . . . The poor are held hostage to extract aid from the donors" (Easterly 2001, p. 116).

Another aspect of moral hazard arises through cancellation of debts. The governments of the poor countries are forgiven their debts when the debts become so high that it is evident that the debts cannot be repaid. People of course feel sorry for poor countries that have accumulated substantial debt that cannot be repaid. Canceling the debt provides the opportunity for a fresh start. Yet, after the debt has been canceled, new debt soon reaches levels where the only solution is again cancellation of the debt. Commenting on this cycle of indebtedness and debt cancellation, Easterly observed that "[t]he same mismanagement of funds that caused the high debt will prevent the aid sent through debt relief from reaching the truly poor" (Easterly, 2001, p. 136).

Governments in poor countries have often been under the control of local political elites. There is moral hazard because the political elites know that they will obtain no more resources from the World Bank and the International Monetary Fund that they can appropriate for themselves if the poor in their countries cease to be poor. Hence Easterly describes poor people in poor countries as *hostages*. The poor have remained hostages to allow ongoing transfers of resources from which the political elites benefit.

Moral hazard occurs when the presence of insurance increases the likelihood of benefit from insurance, or makes the benefits certain. We see that this has been the consequence of the global social insurance provided through the resource transfers of the World Bank and the International Monetary Fund.

The moral hazard is embedded in a principal-agent problem. The World Bank and the International Monetary Fund provide resources and should be the principals. Governments in poor countries should be agents who dispense the resources to help the poor as intended by the principals. However, governments in poor countries become the principals and divert the resources that are intended to help the poor. The moral hazard is through the behavior of the governments in ensuring that the poor in their countries stay poor so that aid resources will again be made available in the future with the intention of once more of helping the poor. Because of moral hazard, the attempt at implementing a global social insurance contract that encompasses the poor in poor countries (not all people in poor countries are poor) is therefore unsuccessful.

5.1.9 Summary

We began our investigation of social justice by considering why people want personal insurance. We defined social justice as an outcome of income equality for people who were equal behind a veil of ignorance. Alternatively, but equivalently, we defined social justice as complete insurance in the face of income uncertainty (and more generally other uncertainties) in life. Choice of a social welfare function implies the choice of the form of social insurance for a society. Rawls's social welfare criterion focuses on the weakest link in a society without regard for the inefficiency losses imposed on taxpayers and results in public policies that provide complete social insurance. A definition of social welfare based on Bentham is equivalent to maximizing the expected utility of a member of a population behind a veil of ignorance and results in incomplete insurance. Rawls and Bentham are limiting cases. While Rawls's social welfare function places all social weight on the person in a society who is worst-off after emergence from behind a veil of ignorance and, only after this person has been attended to, does Rawls proceed to attend to the next worse-off person, Bentham's social welfare function is unaffected by the distribution of utilities: only the sum of utilities in a population matters. The social welfare function chosen between Rawls and Bentham reflects tolerance for inequality, or willingness to incur the inefficiencies due to the leaky bucket of income redistribution. A society choosing Rawls's social welfare function confronts the problem of motivating people to exert productive effort, since with complete insurance ultimate personal well-being depends not on personal effort but on the average of everybody's productive contributions.

We identified reasons why private insurance markets fail to provide insurance. The reasons are adverse selection, nonverifiability of outcomes against which insurance is sought, and moral hazard. Government can address the problem of adverse selection by making participation in social insurance compulsory, although adverse selection can then occur through emigration (and also immigration). Government has no advantage over private insurance markets in solving the problems of inability to verify outcomes and moral hazard.

We also observed that social norms affect personal willingness to receive benefits from social insurance. Social norms can interact with moral hazard to increase the public spending required for social assistance payments. As a consequence of moral hazard, people can be led to manipulate social insurance for personal benefit. Social norms affect the inclination of people to take advantage of opportunities for such manipulation.

Our theory of social insurance views the social welfare function as chosen anonymously behind a veil of ignorance by people who do not know who they will be. Social insurance programs are, however, chosen and changed by voters who are not behind a veil of ignorance and who know who they are. Voters may decide to limit social insurance programs because of adverse selection, moral hazard, and the inability to verify whether beneficiaries of the programs are truly deserving of social assistance. Voting outcomes reflect the tolerance for errors that can leave some people who are deserving but unfortunate without the benefits of social assistance.

We noted that global social insurance could in principle provide insurance against being born into poverty in a poor country. The moral hazard that deters insurance through private markets and that confronts social insurance in separate government jurisdictions appears to be confronted by international agencies that act to implement a global social insurance contract.

References and related literature

For Bentham's original writings, see Bentham (1879), and for Rawls, see Rawls (1971). On social insurance, social welfare, and social justice, see Harsanyi (1955), Pattanaik (1968), Varian (1980), and Kolm (1998). For a statement of the case for interpersonal comparisons of utility, see Ng (1997). On adverse selection and moral hazard, see Friedman (1954), Akerlof (1970), Pauly (1974), and Schansberg (1996). For a view of moral hazard in terms of a concept of ethics of responsibility, see Fleubaey (1995). On social norms and moral hazard, see Brinig and Buckley (1999) and Lindbeck, Nyberg, and Weibull (1999). On voting and social insurance, see Anderberg (1999). On problems of attempting to implement global social insurance, see Easterly (2001); for a summary of Easterly's observations, see Hillman (2002).

Akerlof, G., 1970. The market for "lemons": Quality uncertainty and the market mechanism. *Quarterly Journal of Economics* 84, 488–500.

Anderberg, D., 1999. Determining the mix of public and private provision of insurance by majority rule. *European Journal of Political Economy* 15, 417–40.

Bentham, J., 1879. *An Introduction to the Principles of Morals and Legislation*. The Clarendon Press, Oxford.

Bernholz, P., 1993. Necessary conditions for totalitarianism, supreme values, power, and personal interest. In *Government: Servant or Master*, G. Radnitzky and H. Boullion (eds.). Rodopi, Amsterdam and Atlanta, 267–312.

Brinig, M. F. and F. H. Buckley, 1999. The price of virtue. *Public Choice* 98, 111–29.

Easterly, W., 2001. *The Elusive Quest for Growth: Economists' Adventures and Misadventures in the Tropics*. The MIT Press, Cambridge, Massachusetts.

Fleurbaey, M., 1995. Equality and responsibility. *European Economic Review* 39, 683–9.

Friedman, M., 1954. Choice, chance, and the personal distribution of income. *Journal of Political Economy* 61, 277–90.

Harsanyi, J. C. 1955. Cardinal welfare, individualistic ethics, and interpersonal comparisons of utility. *Journal of Political Economy* 63, 209–321.

Hillman, A. L., 2002. The World Bank and the persistence of poverty in poor countries. *European Journal of Political Economy* 18, 783–95.

Kolm, S-C., 1998. *Modern Theories of Justice*. Cambridge University Press, New York.

Lindbeck, A., S. Nyberg and J. W. Weibull, 1999. Social norms and economic incentives in the welfare state. *Quarterly Journal of Economics* 114, 1–35.

Ng, Y-K., 1997. A case for happiness, cardinalism, and interpersonal comparability. *Economic Journal* 107, 1848–58.

Pattanaik, P. K., 1968. Risk, impersonality, and the social welfare function. *Journal of Political Economy* 76, 1152–69.

Pauly, M., 1974. Overprovision and public provision of insurance: The roles of moral hazard and adverse selection. *Quarterly Journal of Economics* 88, 44–61.

Rawls, J. A., 1971. *A Theory of Justice*. Belknap Press, Cambridge, Massachusetts.

Schansberg, D. E., 1996. *Poor Policy: How Government Harms the Poor*. Westview Press, Boulder.

Varian, H. R., 1980. Redistributive taxation as social insurance. *Journal of Public Economics* 14, 49–68.

Questions for discussion

1. Why do individuals have a demand for insurance? In Figure 5.1, what is the relation between risk aversion and the difference in value between certainty-equivalent income and the expected value of income?

2. If you could decide on insurance for yourself behind a veil of ignorance, against which types of contingencies would you wish to insure yourself? Can you rank the different contingencies for which you would seek insurance by degree of risk aversion?

3. How does the social insurance contract that you would choose compare with the actual social insurance in the place where you live or study? Have there been any significant changes in public policy toward social insurance? If so, do these changes bring actual social insurance closer to the social insurance program that you would choose for yourself behind a veil of ignorance?

4. Suppose that people had somehow agreed on an insurance contract before they were born, and then, after being born, some people found that they had parents who valued education and encouraged study, and found that they had high ability and could expect to do well in life. Would these people now wish to change the conditions of the insurance contract specified before they were born? What changes would they want? How is adverse selection involved here? How is adverse selection related to a time-inconsistency problem?

5. Asymmetric information (someone knowing what someone else does not) is involved in all three reasons for failure of private insurance markets to offer insurance. How does asymmetric information arise in each case?

6. If private insurance markets fail to offer insurance, can government provide social insurance in a way that solves any of the problems that inhibit private insurance? Explain.

7. What is the relation between choice of a social welfare function and choice of social insurance for a society? In which respects are Rawls's and Bentham's social welfare functions limiting cases of social insurance?

8. If you had to choose between the social welfare function of Rawls or of Bentham, which would you choose, and for what reasons? Would following Rawls bring us close to the maximal-government societies that we described in Section 1.3?

9. What is the difference between efficiency losses incurred through the leaky bucket of redistribution and efficiency losses incurred through moral hazard? Why is moral hazard a case of a principal-agent problem?

10. Governments in poor countries in general provide limited or no social insurance. Why do you believe this is so?

11. Would you favor a global compulsory social insurance program that includes everybody in the world no matter where they were born or live? Does your answer depend on whether you are making this decision behind a veil of ignorance? If you could choose a social welfare function for global social insurance behind a veil of ignorance, would you choose the same social welfare function as when your decision is about social insurance limited to your own country or your community? Explain.

12. In what sense do international agencies that seek to substitute for a global social insurance contract confront the moral-hazard problem that we have associated with insurance? Are problems of adverse selection and inability to verify outcomes also present?

13. Suppose that all insurance contracts could be based on individuals' observed efforts rather than their observed incomes. Would social insurance still be required, or could private markets provide insurance? Explain.

14. How do social norms interact with moral hazard to affect social insurance payments?

15. What do you believe is the responsibility of society through social insurance to a woman with a number of children who has no source of personal income and is pregnant again? What you do believe is the responsibility of society through social insurance, if a person claims that he or she cannot cope emotionally with the discipline and commitment of a job and has no sources of personal income? More generally, can moral hazard subvert social justice?

16. People can take different positions on the extent to which government should be insurer of last resort. Some people might see the need for a significant role for government in providing social insurance, while others might point to the inefficiencies associated with social insurance through the leaky bucket, moral hazard, adverse selection, and inability to verify outcomes. Why do people take such different positions? How does tolerance for error appear in your answer? Is tolerance for error the only consideration in your answer?

17. We view a social welfare function as being chosen behind a veil of ignorance. Why do we refer to a social welfare function as being chosen in this way? Although the social welfare function that determines social insurance should in principle be chosen before people know who they are, social insurance is in fact influenced by voting when people already know who they are. How do you expect voting to influence the provisions of a society's social insurance contract?

18. The following quotation (abridged) is from Charles Krauthammer, Washington Post Writers' Group, July 2002:

> To understand American politics, you have to understand this fundamental law: Conservatives think liberals are stupid. Liberals think conservatives are evil.[38]

> Liberals tend to be nice, and they believe – here is where they go stupid – that almost everybody else is nice too. Deep down, that is. If only we could get social conditions right, eliminate poverty, everybody would be holding hands smiley faced. Liberals suffer incurably from naiveté, the stupidity of the good heart. Who else could run the puzzled headline: Crime keeps on falling but prisons keep on filling. *But?* How about this wild theory: If you lock up criminals, crime declines.

> Liberals think conservatives are mean. How can conservatives believe in the things they do – self-reliance, self-discipline, competition, military power – without being soulless? How to understand the conservative desire to actually abolish welfare, if not to punish the poor? The argument that it would increase self-reliance and thus ultimately *reduce* poverty is dismissed as meanness rationalized. Or as put more colorfully in a recent House debate on welfare reform: "a cold blooded grab for another pound of flesh from the demonized welfare mothers".

> Liberals who have no head believe that conservatives have no heart.

Do you agree with this characterization of the different views? Relate your answer to the public policy question concerning the extent to which government should provide social insurance given moral hazard and inability to verify whether people are in need of public support.
19. What does the "impossibility theorem" show to be impossible? (See Supplement 5A.)
20. We can compare two societies, one with a precisely equal distribution of income, and the other with an unequal distribution of income that Pareto dominates the equal incomes. The first society consists of five people who have incomes of 1,000 each, and the second society consists of five people with incomes of (1,200, 1,500, 2,000, 5,000, 10,000). What are the Gini coefficients of the two societies? Is there merit in the "better" Gini coefficient of the first society? Explain. (See Supplement 5B.)

---

[38] In the United Stated, the term "liberal" refers to a position favoring high taxes and extensive redistribution. In the Europe, the term "liberal" means the precise opposite: that is, liberal in Europe means preferring the market to public finance.

5.2

Entitlements and Incentives

The benefits provided by government through social insurance are called entitlements because people are entitled to the benefits under the society's social insurance contract. Entitlements can take the form of payments of money or *in-kind transfers*, for example of health care, education, housing, or food.

Entitlements provided through social insurance can have public-good and externality characteristics. Education and health-care entitlements are sources of beneficial collective (public-good) externalities, through a more educated and healthier population. Education and health care at the same time provide private benefits. Although public-good and externality attributes can be present, in this section we shall consider entitlements as providing only *private* benefit. In providing the entitlements, government is therefore using *public finance* to provide *private goods*.[1]

When entitlements are targeted to particular people, a restriction on income or wealth (known as a means test) or on age defines eligibility. To ensure that only targeted people receive entitlements, the quality of free or subsidized entitlements such as housing and health care may be deliberately kept lower than the quality provided through the private market. The low quality makes the government's entitlements unattractive to people who can afford the market alternatives available through private spending. Contact with the government bureaucracy that manages entitlement programs can also act as a deterrent to seeking to benefit from entitlements. Demeaning treatment by the government bureaucracy that administers the entitlements may be purposeful, so as to increase the personal cost of seeking entitlements and so increase the likelihood that only targeted people truly in need request the entitlements.

Entitlements are sometimes not targeted to particular people in need but are intended to be universally available. In some countries, health care is a universal entitlement. Schooling of children is a universal entitlement in most countries. Low-quality universal entitlements to government schools or health care can however lead people to privately pay for market alternatives. People who decide to forgo the free universal entitlements pay taxes to finance the entitlements that they do not use and pay again for private market supply.

5.2.1 Moral hazard and social assistance

We begin our consideration of entitlements by looking at the relation between moral hazard and targeted entitlements to income support. We saw in Section 5.1 that the conditions for receiving an entitlement can affect behavior of the beneficiaries of the entitlement and that moral hazard can arise due to incentives set in place by the way in which entitlements are delivered. The moral hazard associated with entitlements can affect personal decisions about employment, fertility, and marriage. When money is paid as income support on the condition that people do not earn income, the activity of "not earning income" is subsidized and encouraged, and the activity of "earning income" is discouraged. Similarly, when money is paid to women with children contingent on the absence of a man in the household, the absence of a man is subsidized, and the presence of a man is taxed. When money is paid contingent on being a single mother, being a single mother is subsidized (and being a married mother is taxed). Society in these cases confronts unintended consequences of public assistance. Moral hazard is the basis for a principal-agent problem between society and the beneficiaries of

---

[1] We have previously considered private spending on private goods in markets (Section 1.1), private spending on public goods (Section 2.1), and public spending on public goods (Section 2.3). We now complete the possibilities by considering public spending on private goods.

the entitlements, when the beneficiaries are led to act in ways that society did not intend. Principal-agent problems can be solved through incentives. That is, to solve principal-agent problems, entitlements need to be provided in ways that do not have unintentional effects on personal behavior through incentives tied to the conditions for receiving the entitlements.

Work and welfare

Entitlements can be linked to work by designing an income tax that encourages work at the low levels of earned income as an alternative to publicly financed income support. For example, tax credits can be given at the low levels of earned income. The tax credits can make initial marginal tax rates negative so that earning income is subsidized (and not taxed) through the income tax structure. As earned income increases, eventually, at high enough levels of income, the subsidy for earned income is eliminated, and marginal tax rates become positive.[2] An administrative advantage of subsidies for earned income through the income tax is that entitlements are determined through personal reporting of earned income, and a new government bureaucracy does not have to be set up to administer the entitlements.[3]

We can in particular consider an entitlement to a personal income of Y dollars (or euros, etc). Y dollars is a minimum entitlement to income. An individual will therefore always minimally have Y dollars, and the public policy question is how to provide the entitlement.

Figure 5.20 shows the supply of labor function S_L of a person receiving an income transfer of Y dollars who does not work. By choosing to work, this person can earn an hourly market wage w. The market wage w can be a legal minimum wage, but need not be. We see that in Figure 5.20 the individual's personal labor-supply function S_L is always above w. The disutility of work (indicated by S_L) is therefore above the personal benefit from work given by the wage w. When the individual faces the alternatives of receiving the income transfer Y without the need to work and working at the wage w, the choice is therefore not to work.[4]

---

[2] For example, the marginal tax rate might be minus 25 percent for the first $1,000 of income earned, in which case earning an income of $1,000 provides a total income of $1,250. In the United States, an earned-income tax credit that subsidizes earned income through the personal income tax was introduced in 1975, and subsequently underwent various modifications. On the history of the earned-income tax credit, see Holz and Scholz (2003).

[3] Low-income people can also be encouraged to work through government subsidies to employers who hire people who were previously on welfare or were unemployed. Employers then, however, have an incentive to substitute subsidized for nonsubsidized workers. Providing tax credits for earned income affects the wage at which the individuals are prepared to work and so can also lead to displacement of other workers, but the effects are less direct and not through the calculations of the employer.

[4] We have seen how a legal minimum wage, by preventing low-skilled people from working, can be a reason for a need for social insurance entitlements. Here the reason for not working is not a minimum wage when people want to work. The decision not to work is voluntary, given income transfers that are provided by government contingent on not working.

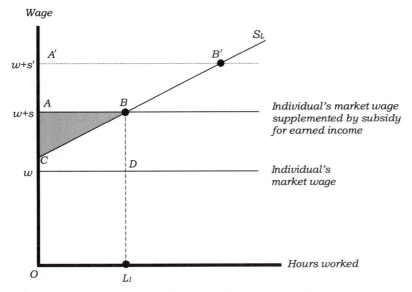

Figure 5.20. Welfare compared to workfare.

The government might now change public policy so that the individual in Figure 5.20 is no longer given the income transfer (or welfare payment) Y contingent on not earning income, but instead can receive a subsidy of s dollars for every hour worked. The return from working is now $(w + s)$ per hour. We see in Figure 5.20 that the individual then chooses to work for L_1 hours.

Since income of Y is a minimal entitlement, the subsidy s per hour of earned income is set so that the individual earns Y dollars from participation in the labor market. In Figure 5.20 earned plus subsidized income is therefore equal to Y. That is,

$$Y = (w + s)L_1. \tag{5.10}$$

The individual in Figure 5.20 is now receiving the entitlement to income Y through choosing to work. Previously the same income was provided as a direct income transfer from government and the individual did not work.

Although income is the same before and after the change in public policy, the individual in Figure 5.20 is now worse off with the new public policy. Previously, the entitlement Y was received without the need to exert effort and without the need to be subject to the discipline of a commitment to go to work. After the change in public policy, the income Y has an associated personal disutility of effort and discipline. The area CBL_1O under the labor-supply function S_L up to L_1 measures the disutility of working L_1 hours. The individual's net benefit from market participation to earn the income Y at a subsidized hourly wage $(w + s)$ is ABC. When income Y was provided without working, the individual's net benefit was the entire rectangle ABL_1O (which equals the entitlement Y).

The individual has therefore incurred a personal loss from the change in the means of ensuring the income entitlement Y. The loss is the disutility of the effort (given by CBL_1O) now required to earn the income Y.[5]

Taxpayers have gained from the change in public policy. When the income Y was provided as a transfer without the person in Figure 5.20 working, taxpayers paid taxes of ABL_1O to finance the direct income transfer and also incurred an accompanying loss due to the excess burden of the taxes that financed this income transfer. The subsidy for earned income requires lower taxes to finance the total subsidy payment $ABDw$ in Figure 5.20, and the excess burden of taxation is also correspondingly smaller.

The change in public policy does not satisfy the Pareto criterion because the person receiving the publicly financed income transfers has lost and taxpayers have gained. The loss and the gains have occurred against the background of a principal-agent problem. The objective of taxpayers or society as principal is to ensure that the individual has the entitlement of Y dollars of income. Society's objectives and society's evaluation of cost and benefit in this case do not include the disutility that the beneficiary of public policy feels because of the need to work for a living. From society's perspective, the public policy of subsidizing earned income is preferable to providing income transfers to people who do not work. The gain to society is the output (with value wDL_1O in Figure 5.20) produced when the individual works, and the lower taxes and excess burdens on taxpayers.

In choosing a public policy that requires work in order to receive government income transfers, a society is not making a social judgment that prevents people from choosing not to work for a living. Any person with adequate financial means that allow not working for a living can choose not to work, just as, by choosing how many hours they want to work, people voluntarily divide their day between free time and working. Society is making the judgment that taxpayers are under no obligation to support people who are without adequate income, but who are capable of working for a living and choose not to do so.[6]

In Figure 5.20, the public policy of providing a subsidy for earned income of s dollars per hour has changed incentives and has led the recipient of tax-financed income transfers to choose to work to earn the minimal entitlement income of Y dollars. The complaint by the beneficiary of public policy can only be that society has completely discounted (or not valued) the disutility of the effort that

---

[5] To compensate the individual for the change in public policy, the subsidy for earning income would have to be greater than s dollars per hour. A subsidy of s' dollars per hour in Figure 5.20 provides precise compensation for the change in public policy if the area $A'B'C$ is exactly equal to the rectangle ABL_1O. The area $A'B'C$ is the net benefit from participation in the labor market when the subsidy for earning income is s'. Precise compensation is provided when this benefit is equal to the income received when income transfers were given without working, which is the entitlement Y equal to ABL_1O.

[6] We can again compare this situation with a legal minimum wage, where low-skilled people want to work but are legally not allowed.

he or she must now exert in obtaining the minimum entitlement of Y dollars of income by having a job.[7]

Entitlements contingent on fertility and living arrangements

The purpose of entitlements provided by government is to allow escape from poverty. Society confronts another principal-agent problem, and also a dilemma, when entitlements contingent on fertility (the number of children) and living arrangements (presence or absence of a male in the household) create incentives that result in poverty. The purpose of an entitlement to a single mother in need is, for example, to assist the mother and the child, and not to encourage behavior that results in someone becoming a single mother without personal means of support.

Solving the principal-agent problems that arise in these circumstances is difficult. Incentives can be changed by making entitlements contingent on not having more children, or contingent on living with a partner. These conditions for entitlements are, however, difficult to verify if children can be hidden and if partners can always be found to move in for payment. Moreover, there are problems of ensuring justice for people who simply do not want to live with a partner or who happen to be without a partner who suits them. Government is intervening in life-style decisions of low-income people when limitations on fertility and having a partner in the house are conditions for income entitlements. On the other hand, there are adverse incentives when entitlements are contingent on having children or on not having a partner in the house, and this conditionality also affects life-style decisions. The dilemma is that the condition for receiving entitlements of being a mother without the presence of man who accepts responsibility for children is specifically designed to ensure targeted assistance when the mother is in need because she is unassisted by the father, but the same condition provides incentives for single-parent households for whom the source of income is publicly financed welfare payments.

Social norms and the response to incentives of public policy

A policy of subsidizing earned income can for example bring unskilled single mothers into the labor market, if affordable child care is available or if child care is provided through the extended family, and if jobs are available that are suitable for people who are low skilled and have limited experience. However, while effort can be put into changing incentives through public policy, retained personal values that influence behavior can make public policy ineffective. Personal values required for effectiveness of public policy include the discipline required to have a job. At the same time, social norms set expectations of personal behavior by someone

---

[7] The beneficiary of the government income transfers can propose, "I am part of society and therefore my utility is part of the welfare of society. My disutility from work should therefore be included when public-policy decisions are made about how I am to obtain the Y dollars of income that I need to live at an acceptable level in our society." This case is based on an entitlement to Y dollars of income independent of the effort and self-reliance (and work incentives) associated with the entitlement.

who has a job, such as punctuality and discipline in attending to assigned tasks
and following instructions. The changes in incentives sought through public policy
may require changes in norms of personal behavior. If people continue to behave
as they did in the past by perhaps conforming to the behavior of the people around
them, attempts to change incentives and solve principal-agent problems through
changes in the conditionality for eligibility for entitlements may be unsuccessful.[8]

5.2.2 Unemployment insurance

Unemployment insurance provides entitlements to income, conditional on first
having had a job and then becoming unemployed. The entitlements are generally
financed by payroll taxes paid by employers on behalf of employees, although
employees may also contribute.[9]

The three reasons that we identified in Section 5.1 for failure of private markets
to provide insurance apply to unemployment insurance.

   (1) There is adverse selection. Some people tend to lose their jobs more
       often than others, perhaps because they lack qualities that employers
       value (timeliness in arriving at work, consistency in coming to work,
       initiative, diligence, etc). Some people (perhaps the same people) also
       find it more difficult than others to receive a job offer. The adverse
       selection arises through the asymmetric information that people know
       their likelihood of losing their job and their likelihood of finding a job,
       but an insurance company does not.
   (2) There is moral hazard because the presence of unemployment insur-
       ance can affect the likelihood that someone will remain unemployed
       through unobservable effort that is put into looking for a job, and
       through reluctance to accept a job that is offered.
   (3) The problem of inability to verify the circumstances against which in-
       surance is sought is also present. Some people may claim to be un-
       employed when they are in fact employed in the unofficial or shadow
       economy, where they pay no taxes and their employment is not legally
       recognized or known.

Private insurance markets with some limited exceptions therefore fail to provide
unemployment insurance, and the insurance is provided through government.

In response to adverse selection, government can make unemployment insurance compulsory. With all people in the same insurance pool, income redistribution is then taking place from people less likely to be unemployed and less

---

[8] The role of personal values and social norms in countering incentives provided through public policy
has been emphasized by Glenn Loury (1996) of Boston University.

[9] We saw in Chapter 2 that the true shares of payments of taxes and also shares of the excess burden
of taxation depend on elasticities of supply and demand and not on the legal liability to pay a tax.
If supply of labor is quite inelastic, the true share of the cost of unemployment insurance paid by
the employee is high, even if nominally the employer is required to pay all or the greater part of
the tax.

likely to remain unemployed for extended periods of time, to people with greater likelihoods of losing their jobs and with greater likelihoods of being unemployed for considerable periods of time.

Moral hazard again results in a principal-agent problem: society wishes an unemployed person to accept a job offer, while an unemployed person may be content to continue to receive income transfers through payments from unemployment insurance. To address the moral hazard that underlies the principal-agent problem, unemployment insurance is usually provided for a limited period of time. An accompanying solution is a declining schedule of insurance payments over time that makes rejection of job offers costly and creates incentives for finding a job as soon as possible.[10]

Solving the asymmetric-information problem of inability to observe whether a person is truly unemployed requires investigating how recipients of benefits from unemployment insurance spend their time.

Observed durations of unemployment can provide information about moral hazard and adverse selection. The likelihood and expected duration of future unemployment can be inferred from an individual's past unemployment record and can be used to make judgments about the individual's expected insurance payouts in the future (adverse selection) and the individual's personal effort to find a job or willingness to accept a job offer (moral hazard). Because of remaining asymmetric information, people who have genuinely looked for jobs and have received no job offers would however be unfairly penalized, if duration of past unemployment were used as an indicator of adverse selection and moral hazard to determine eligibility for future unemployment insurance.

Another proposal may be that taxes to finance future unemployment insurance should increase with the duration of past unemployment. The case for future taxes that increase with the duration of unemployment is that individuals should repay the insurance fund if the duration of unemployment has required payment of excessive unemployment benefits. That is, the argument is that the primary purpose of unemployment insurance is averaging of income over time. Payments received while unemployed are therefore regarded as a loan, to be repaid from future income. Tying future taxes to the duration of unemployment can of course create disincentives for some unemployed persons ever to accept a job offer because of the accumulated tax liability from past unemployment. That is, the future tax liabilities can become an impediment to exit from unemployment.

In addition to allowing income averaging over time, a further benefit of unemployment insurance is increased length of time of job search. In the absence of unemployment insurance, the time spent looking for a job depends on personal assets and savings available to finance personal spending while unemployed and searching for a job. Job choices might then be made overly quickly. By

---

[10] Extended lower income transfers, not defined as payments through unemployment insurance but as welfare payments, are sometimes provided when the limited period of eligibility for unemployment payments has elapsed.

providing extended time to search for a job, unemployment insurance increases the likelihood that jobseekers will find jobs for which they are well suited, rather than having to accept unsuitable jobs that come along. Other jobseekers also benefit when jobseekers do not take jobs that are more suitable for other people. Unemployment insurance therefore improves matching between jobseekers and jobs.

Without compulsory unemployment insurance provided by government, people could voluntarily personally save the money they implicitly[11] pay in taxes to finance the government unemployment insurance program. Provision for the likelihood of unemployment, however, requires savings that need to be used only if unemployment should occur. That is, protection against the *risk* of becoming unemployed requires insurance that provides benefits *contingent* on the adverse outcome of being unemployed. Personal savings in anticipation of unemployment do not provide such contingent benefits. The contingent benefits are provided by unemployment insurance that pools risks and provides payouts if and when a person should become unemployed.

Without compulsory unemployment insurance, an unemployed person could attempt to borrow to finance living expenses and to repay the loan after finding a job. Private lenders, however, then face the same deterrents to lending as private insurance companies face when deciding whether to provide insurance. Because of adverse selection, moral hazard, and inability to verify employment or unemployment, private lenders have no assurance that jobseekers will find jobs, nor therefore that they will ever be repaid.

If people who are unemployed were obliged to mortgage their houses to provide collateral for loans while unemployed, they could end up both without a job and without a house if they were very unlucky. Unemployment insurance avoids the additional risks of having to mortgage assets for loans when people are already in adverse personal circumstances because of unemployment.

5.2.3 The choice between income and in-kind transfers

Entitlements can be provided either as income or as in-kind transfers. We now consider the choice between providing entitlements in these alternative forms. We shall see that the taxpayers who finance entitlements prefer that entitlements be provided in-kind rather than in money.

One reason for preferring transfers in-kind is to ensure that entitlements are delivered, in particular to children in the form of schooling, but also for health care, housing, and food. Taxpayers, however, prefer in-kind transfers because of lower taxes.

As an example of the choice between in-kind transfers and transfers of money, we shall consider two households that differ in their incomes but have the same preferences regarding spending on education. Both households have a school-aged

---

[11] The tax payments are implicit when it is the legal obligation of employers to deliver the taxes to government.

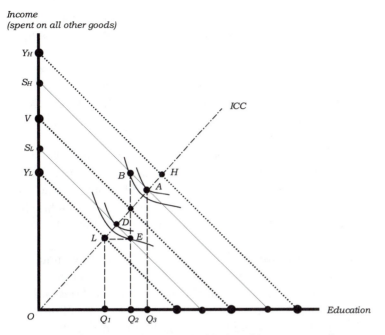

Figure 5.21. The choice between in-kind and income transfers.

child. Figure 5.21 shows spending on the quantity or quality of education. The two households have initial pre-tax incomes of Y_H and Y_L.

The line ICC in Figure 5.21 is an income-consumption curve or line that shows how demand for education of either household changes with income when the relative price of education remains unchanged. We shall not change the relative price of education. All voluntary spending choices for both households are therefore along the ICC line.

With the different personal incomes Y_H and Y_L and no involvement by government in private spending decisions, the two households respectively choose education in private markets at the points H and L on the income-consumption line ICC.

In a next step, a government sets Q_2 as a minimum and compulsory education entitlement for children. The market choice of the low-income household at point L is below the entitlement; the low-income household's voluntary spending at point L provides Q_1, which is less than the entitlement Q_2. The high-income household's voluntary spending at point H provides more than the entitlement.

The government can ensure the entitlement for everybody by providing education in government schools at level or quality Q_2. The low-income household is thereby provided with an in-kind transfer of education equal to $(Q_2 - Q_1)$. The low-income household then moves from point L_1 to point E. The low-income household continues to pay for Q_1 but now through a tax payment to the government. The additional education through the in-kind transfer is financed by a tax on the high-income household.

The cost of providing the in-kind transfer ($Q_2 - Q_1$) to the low-income household is ($S_L - Y_L$). The high-income household pays a tax ($Y_H - S_H$), which is equal to ($S_L - Y_L$), to finance the in-kind transfer to the low-income household.

After paying the tax, the high-income household has remaining income S_H. With this post-tax income, the high-income household would like to choose point A on the ICC line. The high-income household, however, cannot make the choice that it wishes but is required to receive (and through taxation pay for) the compulsory government-provided entitlement Q_2 at the point B.

As an alternative to being given the in-kind transfer ($Q_2 - Q_1$), the low-income household could be given the money that finances the in-kind transfer directly. The low-income household would then receive ($S_L - Y_L$) as additional income. With this additional income to spend as it wishes through private market spending (the government school that provides the in-kind transfer is gone), the low-income household would choose point D on the ICC line.

At point D, the low-income household is not voluntarily spending enough on the education of its child to achieve the entitlement Q_2. To voluntarily spend enough on education to reach the entitlement Q_2, the low-income household requires income V. The income V can be provided to the low-income household by taxing the high-income household and providing the low-income household with a direct income transfer of ($Y_H - V$) = ($V - Y_L$). After taxation and the income transfer that will lead the low-income family voluntarily to choose private spending at the level of the entitlement Q_2, we see in Figure 5.21 that the two households have the same income V.

With after-tax income V, the (former) high-income household also voluntarily spends to provide the entitlement Q_2. The income transfer that equalizes post-tax and post-transfer incomes is therefore a solution for achieving the compulsory entitlement for each child.

Given the objective of providing the entitlement Q_2 for the low-income household, the high-income household is better off paying the taxes that finance the in-kind transfer than paying the taxes that finance the income transfer that leads the low-income family voluntarily to choose to spend enough to reach the entitlement. To finance the in-kind transfer, the high-income household pays a tax of ($Y_H - S_H$) and incurs the associated excess burden of taxation. To finance the income transfer, the high-income family pays the higher tax of ($Y_H - V$) and incurs the associated higher excess burden of taxation.

As a general conclusion, income transfers to provide entitlements require higher tax payments and incur a greater excess burden of taxation than transfer-in-kind. Taxpayers therefore prefer in-kind transfers to direct income transfers as means of providing entitlements to beneficiaries.

As we previously noted, there are other reasons why taxpayers who finance entitlements might prefer to provide entitlements as in-kind transfers rather than through transfers of income. In-kind transfers are a more certain means of delivering entitlements than income transfers. In-kind transfers do not rely on personal decisions about how income is to be spent. We have taken for granted that, when income increases, demand for the quality of education of children increases. Some parents might not view their children's education in this way, and giving such parents more money need not result in greater spending on the education of their children. Extortion can also take place when parents declare, "pay me enough and I will send my children to school." In-kind transfers eliminate parental discretion and avoid such extortion.

In-kind transfers to preempt future income transfers

We have been viewing entitlements as the consequence of social insurance agreed upon behind a veil of ignorance. This perspective is backward-looking. An alternative view of the reason why taxpayers agree to finance entitlements is not compliance with a past social contract but is forward-looking and considers the financing of future entitlements. According to this view, compulsory in-kind transfers of entitlements to education and health care increase children's future incomes, and so reduce the likelihood that the children, when grown, will require future income transfers from social insurance. High-income households therefore have an interest in financing education entitlements for children from low-income households, or for children from all families, to preempt the need for future taxes to finance income transfers. The hope is that the compulsory in-kind transfer of schooling and health care will increase income-earning ability and will thereby reduce future taxes that would have been required to provide income transfers to low-income persons.

5.2.4 Rejected entitlements and income redistribution

Education of children is in general a universal and not a specifically targeted entitlement. After taxes have been paid to finance the entitlement, access to the entitlement is in general free.[12] The option is, however, often present to forgo a free entitlement, and to choose to obtain the types of benefits that an entitlement offers through private market spending. For example, when entitlements are provided for attendance at government schools, some children may attend private schools. Also, people eligible for entitlements may reject free public housing or free health care. We shall now investigate incentives to reject free entitlements, and the consequences when an entitlement is rejected.

We shall consider people with the same incomes, but who differ in evaluation of the types of benefits that entitlements provide. When we considered the choice between delivering entitlements through income or in-kind transfers, we compared people with the same preferences but with different incomes.

When high-income people pay for entitlements that low-income people value, high-income people lose and low-income people gain. When people, however, have the same incomes, how do free tax-financed entitlements affect incentives and people's welfare? Is everybody with the same income made better off by the free tax-financed entitlements?

---

[12] There may be a participatory payment, with the entitlements substantially subsidized.

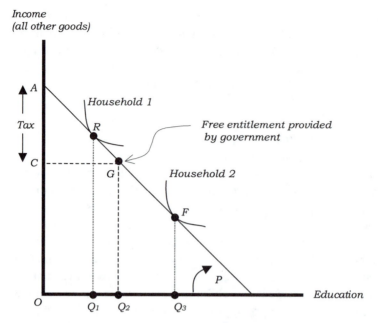

Figure 5.22. In-kind transfers when people have different preferences.

Market choices

To answer these questions, we begin with private benefits from private market spending. There are no taxes and no government. In Figure 5.22 the cost (or price) of a private service (we shall continue to use education for illustration) is given by the relative price P (which is the slope of the budget line). Two households have the same pre-tax income OA but differ in their preferences for education of children. For household 1, the preferred choice is at point R where quality of education is Q_1. For household 2, the preferred choice is at point F, where the quality of education is Q_3. These are private choices in a private market.

Government then appears and provides a compulsory in-kind entitlement through government schools at point G, with no private market option.[13] In Figure 5.22, the compulsory entitlement provides Q_2, which is more than household 1 wants and less than household 2 wants.

To finance the entitlement, both households pay income taxes AC. Taxes are equal because the families have the same incomes. The taxes have excess burdens (not shown in Figure 5.22). The tax AC is paid whether or not children attend government schools.[14]

We see in Figure 5.22 that each household was better off, by its own valuation of its own well-being, without the compulsory tax-financed government entitlement.

---

[13] Point G is on the same budget line as the choices made through private schooling. That is, in Figure 5.22 the cost for the same quality of education is the same for government schools as private education. This is in general not the case.

[14] Education in a government school is "free" because, after paying the tax AC, there are no additional private costs of attending a government school.

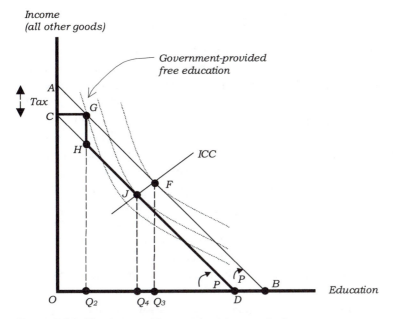

Figure 5.23. The free entitlement is not accepted.
A household forgoes the government's free entitlement to Q_2 at point G and chooses private spending to obtain Q_4 at point J, where utility is higher than at point G offered by the government. Without the entitlement, the choice through private spending is Q_3 at F. The household is prepared to forgo income equal to FJ for the government to withdraw its tax-financed free entitlement. FJ is precisely equal in value to the tax AC.

The entitlement lowers the well-being of both households because the entitlement Q_2 is either lower or higher than a household's preferred choice.

We now introduce the option to forgo the free government entitlement and to choose instead private spending, provided that through private spending at least Q_2 is chosen. That is, the government requires that all children minimally receive Q_2, but children are not required to attend government schools. With no tax credit when private spending is chosen in place of the entitlement supplied by government, and with the government not supporting private spending through subsidies, rejecting the entitlement supplied by government entails paying twice, once through taxes and again through private spending.

In Figure 5.23, the tax AC is paid to finance the entitlement program. OC is income remaining after payment of the tax AC. After payment of the tax AC, the choices are (1) to accept the free entitlement at the point G, or (2) to forgo the government entitlement and choose a point along HD through private spending.[15]

In Figure 5.23, point J with private spending on Q_4 provides a higher level of utility than accepting the free entitlement at G. Therefore, private spending

---

[15] The effective post-tax budget constraint is $CGHD$ in Figure 5.23, which allows for the alternatives of choosing or rejecting the entitlement at the point G. The entitlement at G is *Pareto-superior* to any point along CH. CH is not part of the effective relevant post-tax budget constraint. The choice is therefore between the entitlement at G and private spending along HD.

along *HD* (at point *J*) is preferred to accepting the free entitlement from the government.

The household in Figure 5.23 loses from the tax-financed free entitlement. We can determine the loss by asking how much the household is willing to pay for the government to end the free entitlement and to cancel the taxes that finance the entitlement. The answer is that the household is willing to pay *AC*, or equivalently is prepared to forgo income equal to *FJ*, to end the free (tax-financed) entitlement, plus the excess burden (not shown in Figure 5.23) of the tax *AC*.[16] The household's loss from the entitlement program is precisely equal to the taxes paid and the excess burden of taxation for the entitlement that the household chooses not to utilize.[17] Asking how much the household is prepared to pay for the government to end the free entitlement program is the same type of question that we asked to determine the efficiency loss due to the excess burden of taxation. The free entitlement has resulted in the household in Figure 5.23 paying the tax *AC*. The household does not utilize the government's entitlement so this tax payment provides no benefit. The total loss to the household from the entitlement is, therefore, the tax paid plus the excess burden associated with the tax.[18]

Figure 5.24 shows a household that pays the compulsory tax and accepts the free tax-financed entitlement. Utility at the entitlement point *G* for this household exceeds the utility attainable through after-tax private spending along *HD*. In Figure 5.23, the benefit attainable at entitlement point *G* is less than the benefit attainable from private spending along the line *HD*. In Figure 5.24 the benefit attainable at the entitlement point *G* dominates any personal benefit attainable along *HD* through private spending.

Although the household in Figure 5.24 accepts the entitlement, this household is also prepared to pay the government to withdraw the tax-financed free entitlement program. If we ask this household how much it is prepared to pay to end the entitlement, the answer is an amount of income equal to *FN*. By paying *FN*, the household would save the tax payment *AC* (and the excess burden). We see that the tax payment *AC* exceeds the payment *FN* that the household is prepared to make to end the entitlement. The presence of the entitlement compels the household to pay a tax *AC* (and to incur the additional excess burden of this tax) in order to receive a benefit from government that the household values at only *FN*.

---

[16] *FJ* is the amount of income by which the budget line *AB* exceeds the budget line *CD*. ICC in Figure 5.23 is again an income-consumption curve that shows how demand changes when income changes and relative price remains constant.

[17] The tax *AC* is equivalent in value to the income *FJ*. Either payment places the household on the budget line *HD*, and at point *J*, where Q_4 is obtained through private spending. When the entitlement program is in place, the household chooses private spending at point *J* after paying the tax *AC* and forgoing the entitlement. If the household paid *FJ* for the government to withdraw the free entitlement and not impose the tax *AC* (and leaving out effects through the excess burden of taxation), the choice through private spending would again be at *J*.

[18] We know that there is an excess burden of taxation in the labor market when taxes are levied on income. Each market has its own possible excess burden of taxation. There is an excess burden in the labor market because of the tax *AC*, but for the household that pays the tax *AC* and does not use the free entitlement there is no excess burden in the market for schooling.

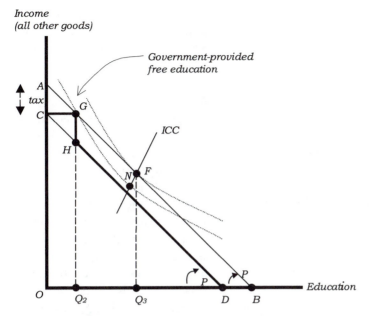

Figure 5.24. The free entitlement is accepted.

The household chooses the government's offer of free education at *G* in preference to private spending, since utility with the free entitlement at point *G* is greater than utility attainable through private spending at any point along *HD*. In the absence of the government entitlement, the family chooses Q_3 at *F* through private spending. The household is prepared to forgo income *FN* for the government to withdraw the tax-financed free entitlement, which the family has accepted. *FN* is less than the tax *AC* that the household pays to finance the free entitlement.

The two households shown in Figures 5.23 and 5.24 have the same incomes and pay the same taxes (and have the same excess burden of taxation) and would make the same private market decision Q_3 if the tax-financed government entitlement were not offered. The households, however, value the entitlement differently. Both households are prepared to pay to end the entitlement program, but the amounts they are prepared to pay differ, and one household avails itself of the government entitlement while the other rejects the entitlement and, after paying taxes, spends again in the private market.

The reason for the existence of the tax-financed entitlement is the behavior of household 1 in Figure 5.22. This household fails to reach the entitlement Q_2 through private spending when the entitlement program is not in place. The low priority this household places on education is indicated by the market choice without government at the point *R* in Figure 5.22. The compulsory entitlement increases education for the children of household 1, which pays more in taxes than it wishes to spend on education. We see that the source of the problem for households that give high priority to education is the government overriding the preferences of households that place low priority on education. The compulsory entitlement compels households for whom education is a low priority to increase spending on education. At the same time, the entitlement, whether accepted or not, reduces education in households where more than the entitlement would be provided through private spending if the publicly financed free entitlement program were not in place.

5.2.5 Supplemental private spending

We have been considering the government entitlement and private spending as exclusive alternatives. However, it may be possible to supplement an entitlement through private spending. Supplementary private spending is in general possible for education, health care, food, public housing (through internal renovation), and personal security. When private spending can supplement entitlements, and the quality of an entitlement is not a deterrent to accepting the entitlement, an entitlement is always accepted. For example, the budget line in Figures 5.23 and 5.24 is then CGB, and the household in both cases accepts the entitlement Q_2, which is supplemented through private spending on the additional quantity $(Q_3 - Q_2)$.

We now return to Figure 5.21 where incomes differ but preferences are the same. After the high-income household in Figure 5.21 has paid taxes to finance the in-kind transfer to the low-income household, it has remaining income S_H. The high-income family's preferred choice given this income is at point A where the quantity (or quality) is Q_3. When supplemental private spending is possible, the quantity Q_3 at point A can be attained by private spending that adds to the tax-financed entitlement Q_2.

The opportunity for supplemental private spending increases the number of households with more than the government entitlement. Access to the market through supplemental spending is Pareto-efficient; for example, in Figure 5.21, allowing the high-income household to choose point A rather than point B makes the high-income household better off without making the low-income household worse off. We expect that, since supplemental spending is a voluntary market decision, the consequence is necessarily a Pareto improvement.

5.2.6 Entitlements and locational choice

Often supplemental spending is not an adequate solution when tax-financed entitlements do not match personal spending preferences. Relocation to another government jurisdiction that offers an alternative more suitable entitlement may, however, be a solution. For example, the household in Figure 5.23 that rejects the entitlement can avoid the loss from the education entitlement by relocating to a school district where government schools provide the entitlement Q_3 at point F. The household would then pay the increased taxes that finance Q_3 but would benefit from the match between the entitlement and the household's own preferences (the excess burden of taxation is still incurred). The household in Figure 5.24, which accepts the entitlement, also benefits, although less so, from relocation to a government jurisdiction where the publicly financed entitlement is Q_3, since this household thereby also matches its spending preferences with the tax-financed entitlement. The household in Figure 5.22, whose low priority on spending for education instigated the entitlement program, also has an incentive to relocate but to a school district where educational objectives and taxes that finance entitlements are more modest.

Relocation is in these cases a quest of compatibility with preferences for tax-financed private goods. We previously considered locational choice when people seek personal compatibility with tax-financed public goods. Tax financing of free-access entitlements introduces collective elements and thereby locational incentives into choices about private goods.

Locational choice can also be disadvantageous for entitlement programs by limiting the scope of the entitlements that a jurisdiction provides. The example of an educational entitlement requires paying taxes for benefit, and the problem is to match taxes with benefit. In other cases, as we observed in Section 5.1, entitlements result in adverse selection. High-income people leave high-tax jurisdictions where they finance income transfers to others. At the same time, people who benefit from entitlements may enter the jurisdiction. A jurisdiction with generous public assistance to poor people may attract poor people, while health care entitlements may attract people in need of health care. People in need of housing may locate in a jurisdiction that is generous in providing public housing. Such adverse selection through people locating in a jurisdiction increases the burden on taxpayers in the jurisdiction, providing incentives for more high-income people to relocate to jurisdictions where social insurance benefits and taxes are lower. Adverse selection therefore takes place by people coming and by people leaving. The people arriving in the jurisdiction do so because the value of the entitlements exceeds their tax obligations. The people leaving the jurisdiction do so because their tax obligations exceed the value of their entitlements. Under these conditions, societies cannot choose entitlements without taking account of how entitlements affect locational decisions, and how locational decisions affect financing of entitlements.

5.2.7 Vouchers as means of delivering in-kind entitlements

In-kind entitlements can be delivered through vouchers. The vouchers can be spent like money, but only for the purpose designated by the voucher and for the sum indicated by the voucher.[19] Vouchers can deliver entitlements to schooling, food, housing, health insurance and care, and vocational training (or, retraining), and can also allow unemployment benefits to be converted voluntarily into employment subsidies.

If, for example, educational vouchers completely finance costs of schooling, the vouchers not only allow all schools, whether public and private, to compete for students but also allow parents to seek the best educational standards for their children without limitations imposed by location in a school district or parents' ability or willingness to pay for education.

The significant characteristic of vouchers is that public finance is separated from government supply in the delivery of entitlements. For example, when people receive vouchers for food, the government does not supply the food, but rather the

---

[19] Vouchers are also sometimes called stamps, as in the case of food stamps.

vouchers finance market purchases of food. Vouchers for education do the same in financing personal spending without the need for government involvement in supply. Delivery of housing entitlements through vouchers allows private choice from among alternatives offered in private housing markets, and vouchers for health insurance and health care similarly permit choices and supply through markets. In a limiting case, government could itself directly take responsibility for providing jobs (as did the maximal government described in Section 1.3), whereas subsidized employment vouchers allow people who have experienced difficulties finding jobs to seek employment based on market valuations of their outputs.

Vouchers eliminate the need for government procurement in providing entitlements. In government schools, for example, procurement ranges from purchase of pencils to the construction of school buildings. For public housing, government procures the housing. Government procurement requires government officials to make decisions about public spending. A dedicated government bureaucracy as described by Max Weber (see Chapter 3) would always choose least-cost private suppliers who satisfy requisite quality standards and would never accept personal benefits in exchange for choosing inflated bids from suppliers. When entitlements are delivered through vouchers, government bureaucracy is not, however, in any event required to make decisions about spending of tax revenue.[20]

5.2.8 Market responses and the value of entitlements

We saw in Chapter 2 that the identity of people paying a tax is not determined by the legal obligation to pay the tax. The identity of the beneficiary of an entitlement from government is similarly not determined by the legal right to receive the entitlement. An entitlement might, for example, take the form of a government subsidy for home ownership. The entitlement can be delivered through tax deductibility of interest payments on mortgages. The subsidy increases demand for home ownership. If demand increases in an area where the supply of housing is more or less fixed, the beneficiaries of the subsidy are the sellers of houses, not the buyers. If places available in private schools are more or less fixed and vouchers are for fixed values and do not necessarily finance the complete cost of schooling, the introduction of educational vouchers increases school fees, and so the delivery of the entitlement through vouchers acts as a subsidy to the private schools. Over time, in response to the higher school fees, we expect new private schools to appear, or existing private schools to expand, and the benefit from the vouchers is then transferred to students or parents.

A form of entitlement mandated by government may be maternity benefits. Benefits can be directly paid by government or can be mandated as payment of income by employers for periods of time after the birth of a child. If financed by government, the maternity benefits allow temporary withdrawal of a parent from the labor force while maintaining part or full income. When it is employers who pay, the benefits are from the perspective of employers equivalent to a tax on

---

[20] When entitlements through vouchers are targeted, the government bureaucracy still determines eligibility or social workers inform people of their entitlements.

employing people who are entitled to family benefits. Employers might therefore reduce demand for people whom they perceive as likely to become eligible for the benefits, and the wages of people perceived as potentially eligible for the benefits fall. Entitlements can then become eroded, with the beneficiaries of the entitlements themselves substantially financing the entitlements through reduced wages.

In the case of entitlements to employment subsidies, the benefits to one person may be at the expense of another. As we have previously observed, employers have incentives to replace an employee without a government-provided entitlement by a person who costs the employer less because of an entitlement to a contributing government payment. Such substitution of employees may be illegal. However, there can be problems of verifiability when employers claim that an employee has been negligent or incompetent, or that because of changes in the technology of production particular types of employees are no longer required.

5.2.9 Summary

In this section, we have investigated the relation between entitlements and incentives. We have considered entitlements targeted to people without means of earning income and benefits provided through unemployment insurance. We have seen that contingent targeted entitlements are subject to problems of moral hazard because of incentives for people to adapt their behavior to the conditions required to receive the entitlements. In some cases, targeted entitlement programs can be designed in ways that resolve or ameliorate moral hazard problems, for example, through the effects of tax credits for earned income on incentives to be self-reliant. In other cases, where entitlements affect decisions about fertility and living arrangements, designing incentives associated with eligibility for entitlements to overcome moral hazard is more difficult.

We have investigated the choice between entitlements provided in terms of income and in-kind, and have seen that taxpayers prefer that entitlements be delivered in-kind rather than as income transfers.

We also considered free tax-financed entitlements provided to people with the same incomes but with different preferences for spending. People are affected differently according to whether free entitlements are accepted. The different effects on people cannot be justified in terms of transfers between rich and poor or between high- and low-income people because incomes are equal.

We have considered the relation between locational choice and entitlements. People have incentives to locate in jurisdictions where tax-financed entitlements match their spending preferences. Locational choice therefore offers a means of achieving efficiency when private benefits are provided through tax-financed entitlements.

Without restrictions on eligibility to entitlements, adverse selection can occur, as low-income people enter and high-income people leave a jurisdiction. Adverse selection through locational choice can therefore make entitlements nonsustainable and deprive a population of the ability to choose entitlements for social insurance.

Vouchers allow the delivery of publicly financed entitlements to be separated from government supply. The entitlements provided through vouchers – to education, health care, housing, or food – do not require a government bureaucracy to undertake procurement and oversee and administer delivery of entitlements. Similarly, entitlements to subsidized employment allow jobs to be found through markets.

We also noted that persons at whom an entitlement is targeted do not necessarily receive the entire entitlement. This is an extension of our previous observation in Chapter 2 that taxes legally specified as payable by designated people do not imply that the designated people necessarily pay the taxes. Moreover, if governments provide entitlements to subsidized employment, the benefits from the entitlement may be at the expense of others who lack the entitlement.

References and related literature

On targeted transfers, see Le Grand (1982), Nichols and Zeckhauser (1982), and Munro (1992). On welfare stigma, see Moffit (1983) and Besley and Coate (1992). On incentives regarding marriage and fertility and income transfers, see Moffit (1998), Dickert-Conlin (1999), and Rosenzweig (1999). For a view that points out the roles of values and social norms as sources of resistance to changed incentives for ending poverty, see Loury (1996). On unemployment insurance and benefits, see Flemming (1978), Shavell and Weiss (1979), Albrecht and Axell (1984), Chiu and Karni (1998), and Marimon and Zilibotti (1999). On the choice between income and in-kind transfers, see Blackorby and Donaldson (1988), Bruce and Waldman (1991), Currie (1994), and Gavhari (1995). Musgrave (1959) used the term "merit wants" to describe goods and services that people were entitled to have; see also Sandmo (1983). On free public schools, see Sonstelie (1982). On adverse selection, locational choice, and entitlements, see Borjas (1999) and Dodson (2001). On identifying who pays for and who benefits from maternity entitlements, see Gruber (1994). On vouchers that allow entitlements to unemployment benefits to be used as personal employment subsidies, see Snower (1994).

Albrecht, J. and B. Axell, 1984. An equilibrium model of search unemployment. *Journal of Political Economy* 92, 824–40.

Besley, T. and S. Coate, 1992. Understanding welfare stigma: Taxpayer resentment and statistical discrimination. *Journal of Public Economics* 48, 165–83.

Blackorby, C. and D. Donaldson, 1988. Cash versus kind, self-selection, and efficient transfers. *American Economic Review* 78, 691–701.

Borjas, G., 1993. Immigration and welfare magnets. *Journal of Labor Economics* 17, 607–37.

Bruce N. and M. Waldman, 1991. Transfers in kind: Why they can be efficient and nonpaternalistic. *American Economic Review* 81, 1345–51.

Chiu, H. W. and E. Karni, 1998. Endogenous adverse selection and unemployment insurance. *Journal of Political Economy* 106, 806–27.

Currie, J., 1994. Welfare and the well-being of children: The relative effectiveness of cash vs. in-kind transfers. In *Tax Policy and the Economy*, J. Poterba (ed.). MIT Press, Cambridge, Massachusetts, 1–43.

Dickert-Conlin, S., 1999. Taxes and subsidies: Their effects on a decision to end a marriage. *Journal of Public Economics* 73, 217–40.

Dodson, M. E., 2001. Welfare generosity and locational choices among U.S. immigrants. *International Review of Law and Economics* 21, 47–67.

Flemming, J., 1978. Aspects of optimal unemployment insurance: Search, leisure, savings, and capital market imperfections. *Journal of Public Economics* 10, 403–25.

Gavhari, F., 1995. In-kind versus cash transfers in the presence of distortionary taxes. *Journal of Public Economics* 33, 45–53.

Gruber, J., 1994. The incidence of mandated maternity benefits. *American Economic Review* 84, 622–41.

Holz, V. J. and J. K. Scholz, 2003. The earned income tax credit. In *Means-Tested Transfer Programs in the U.S.*, R. A. Moffit (ed.). University of Chicago Press, Chicago, 141–97.

Le Grand, J., 1982. *The Strategy of Equality: Redistribution and Social Services*. Allen and Unwin, London.

Loury, G. L., 1996. A dissent from the incentive approach to reducing poverty. In *Reducing Poverty in America: Views and Approaches*, M. R. Darby (ed.). Sage Publications, Thousand Oaks, California, 111–20.

Marimon, R. and Z. Zilibotti, 1999. Unemployment vs. mismatch of talents: Reconsidering unemployment benefits. *Economic Journal* 109, 266–91.

Moffit, R. A., 1983. An economic model of welfare stigma. *American Economic Review* 73, 1023–35.

Moffit, R. A., 1998. The effect of welfare on marriage and fertility. In *Welfare, the Family, and Reproductive Behavior*, R. A. Moffit (ed.). National Academy Press, Washington, D.C., 50–97.

Munro, A., 1992. Self-selection and optimal in-kind transfers. *Economic Journal* 102, 1184–96.

Musgrave, R. 1959. *The Theory of Public Finance*, McGraw Hill, New York.

Nichols, A. and R. Zeckhauser, 1982. Targeting transfers through restrictions on recipients. *American Economic Review, Papers and Proceedings* 72, 372–7.

Rosenzweig, M. R., 1999. Welfare, marital prospects, and non-marital childbearing. *Journal of Political Economy* 107, S3–S32.

Sandmo, A., 1983. Ex-post welfare economics and the theory of merit goods. *Economica* 50, 19–33.

Shavell, S. and L. Weiss, 1979. The optimal payment of unemployment insurance over time. *Journal of Political Economy* 87, 1347–62.

Snower, D., 1994. Converting unemployment benefits into employment subsidies. *American Economic Review* 84, 65–70.

Sonstelie, J., 1982. The welfare cost of free public schools. *Journal of Political Economy* 90, 794–808.

Questions for discussion

1. Which entitlements does government provide in the place where you live or study? Which of the entitlements are targeted to specific groups? Are all the entitlements in your view justified? Which entitlements that do not exist would you add? When did the last comprehensive changes in entitlements take place? What were the features of the changes?

2. It is sometimes claimed that the way in which eligibility for entitlements is determined can create incentives that perpetuate poverty rather than alleviate poverty. What is your opinion? Do you believe that any existing entitlements have this characteristic? Explain.

3. Entitlements contingent on fertility or living arrangements selectively affect low-income people. Personal decisions of higher income people who are ineligible for entitlements are not influenced by public policy. In your view, what are the issues of fairness or justice involved in the selective effects of entitlements on personal decisions of low-income people? What efficiency issues are involved?

4. In a change of public policy in the mid 1990s, the U.S. federal government required that minimally 25 percent of welfare recipients in a state should be working. By the end of the 1990s, outcomes ranged from around 13 percent compliance in the state of Louisiana to around 97 percent in the state of Oregon. What explanations can you offer for such wide differences?

5. Do you support limitations on entitlements to welfare payments for any one person over the course of a lifetime? Explain. How can the limitations on time on welfare be credibly imposed?

6. Incentives to work can be provided by subsidizing employers who hire people who have been on welfare or by providing subsidies for work directly to recipients of entitlements, as through tax credits for earned income or through entitlements to unemployment benefits that are convertible to personal employment subsidies. What are the advantages and disadvantages of the different approaches?

7. Compare the different circumstances that underlie unemployment in Figure 5.19 in Section 5.1 and Figure 5.20 in this section. Why is a principal-agent problem present in the latter case but not the former? What are your views on the recipient's case that he or she is worse off in Figure 5.20 after the change in public policy?

8. What are the benefits of unemployment insurance? Are there also disadvantages? What can government do in the face of the information problems that prevent private insurance markets from providing unemployment insurance?

9. An alternative to unemployment insurance is for people to borrow money to tide them over a period of unemployment. Why is borrowing an inadequate solution? Is taxation of time spent unemployed through higher unemployment insurance payments after a new job has been found a good idea?

10. Why do taxpayers generally prefer that an entitlement be provided as an in-kind transfer rather than in terms of money?

11. Free tax-financed entitlements can affect differently people who have identical incomes but different preferences. Are the different ways in which people can be affected justified by social justice or efficiency? Why do the different effects take place?

12. Give examples where spending to supplement free government entitlements is possible. How does supplemental spending change your answer to question 11?

13. Consider household 1 in Figure 5.22. In what sense is this household a source of losses for household 2 in Figure 5.22, and for the households in Figures 5.23 and 5.24?

14. Public goods affect locational incentives because of the collective benefits provided by public goods. Why do entitlements to private goods, or private benefits also lead people to match their personal spending preferences with public spending through locational choice?

15. What are the costs and benefits of using vouchers to deliver in-kind entitlements?

16. Governments sometimes determine entitlements but require employers to pay for entitlements of employees, for example, to health insurance and maternity benefits. Employers might also pay taxes that in part or wholly finance entitlements to unemployment insurance. Can public policy that mandates compulsory payments by employers be assured to direct benefits to intended beneficiaries? Do in-kind transfers, as

opposed to transfers of money, ensure that people to whom entitlements are directed receive the entitlements in full?

17. Entitlements to public housing are in general targeted. Public housing is often an unsuccessful social experiment. Why do you believe that this is so? Is there a remedial public policy or change in public policy that you would recommend?

18. Through macroeconomic policy, governments accept responsibility for overall employment levels. What would you expect to happen if a government were to announce an entitlement to a job for everybody? How is the answer to this question related to the idea of "soft budgets" that we encountered in Section 1.3? Relate your answer here to your answer to question 6.

19. Recalling our study of bureaucracy in Chapter 3, what are the incentives that confront government bureaucracies that administer delivery of entitlements and monitor eligibility requirements for targeted entitlements? What is the relevance in this context of vouchers as a means of delivering personal entitlements?

20. Should entitlements of social insurance be available to everyone who arrives in a government jurisdiction? What is your view regarding locational adverse selection? Illegal immigrants in general do not pay taxes. Do you believe nonetheless that children of illegal immigrants should have free entitlements to tax-financed education? Should children of illegal immigrants have free entitlements for publicly financed immunization programs?

5.3
Social Justice without Government

Until now, we have viewed social justice as a responsibility of government. In this section, we shall consider social justice without government. We first investigate prospects for social justice without government through voluntary charitable redistribution of income. Then we shall consider prospects for achieving social justice through social mobility, that is, through opportunities for people to advance themselves without regard for their family backgrounds.

5.3.1 Voluntary charitable transfers

When income redistribution takes place through publicly financed spending, the source of finance is *compulsory* tax payments. Income redistribution can also take place through voluntary private charitable transfers. Income redistribution is then not based on a social insurance contract before people know how well-off they are going to be. The transfers are made after people know how well-off they are.

Private charity is consistent with self-interested behavior. Adam Smith observed, at the beginning of his book *Theory of Moral Sentiments* (1759), that the self-interest of people included a charitable concern for the well-being of others:

> *However selfish soever man may be supposed, there are evidently some principles in his nature, which interest him in the fortune of others, and render their happiness necessary to him, though he derives nothing from it, except the pleasure of seeing it.*

Adam Smith thereby observed that people feel sympathy or empathy for one another and can be expected to be charitable and to care about others. The degree of concern may depend upon the closeness of the personal relationship, with greater concern for immediate family and personal friends.

The idea that people have charitable inclinations can be expressed through interdependent utilities. That is, the utility or feeling of well-being of one person depends not only the person's own circumstances but as well on the well-being of others.

We can consider person 1 and person 2 and a given amount of income Y that can be allocated between the two people so that

$$Y = y_1 + y_2, \tag{5.11}$$

where y_i is the amount of income received by individual i. This is the same problem that confronted the government in Section 5.1 when we considered social welfare functions and social insurance. If the two people cared only about themselves, their utility functions would be

$$U_1 = U_1(y_1), \qquad U_2 = U_2(y_2), \tag{5.12}$$

and each would ideally want to have all the income. If the two people care about each other, their utility functions are

$$U_1 = U_1(y_1, y_2), \qquad U_2 = U_2(y_2, y_1). \tag{5.13}$$

That is, each person's well-being depends not only on how much he or she has but also on how much is available to the other person. With such charitable feelings, the utility of each individual increases with the amount of personal income he or she has, but also with the amount of income available to the other person.[1]

We have to be precise about why a person feels better off when the other has more. In the expressions for utility in (5.13), the personal gain from the other person having more is not due to satisfaction from the act of giving. The gain is in seeing that the other person has more, or, for example, in seeing that the other person is not destitute or hungry.

Figure 5.25 shows the utilities of the two people with the interdependent utilities in expression (5.13). At point A, person 1 has all available income ($Y = y_1$) and at point D person 2 has all available income ($Y = y_2$).

If we begin at point A, person 1 can improve his or her feeling of well-being by voluntarily transferring income to person 2, but only until point B is reached. After point B, the personal loss from giving exceeds the personal gain from seeing that person 2 is better off. After point B, person 1's utility begins to fall. The utility of person 2, who is the recipient, continues to increase along BC with increasing income transfers. Beginning from point A, we therefore expect person 1 to make

---

[1] The interdependence between utilities in expression (5.13) can also describe envy. In that case, a person's feeling of well-being decreases when the other person has more. We noted in Chapter 1 that envy is a source of inefficiency because people feel better off when they destroy the property of others. When the interdependence between utilities expresses a good feeling that others have more, there is never an incentive to destroy.

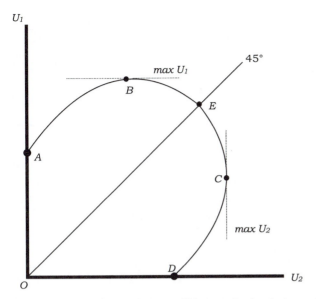

Figure 5.25. Interdependent utilities as the basis for voluntary income transfers.

voluntary income transfers to person 2 up to point B where person 1's utility U_1 is maximized.

We can begin the same process of voluntary transfers from point D where person 2 has everything and person 1 has nothing. Person 2 will make voluntary income transfers up to the point C, where person 2's utility U_2 is maximized.

Depending on whether the initial position is A or D, the society ends up at either B or C. In either case, income redistribution takes place through voluntary transfers without government. The income redistributions are Pareto-efficient because, with interdependent utilities, the redistributions make both the donor and the recipient better off.

A three-person society

Figure 5.25 and the interdependent utilities in expression (5.13) show a population of two people. Often, looking at two people is sufficient to establish a general principle for a society that consists of many people. In the case of voluntary income transfers, however, the situation changes substantially when we add a third person. Let us suppose that persons 1 and 2 are well off and that person 3 is poor or unfortunate. Persons 1 and 2 are aware that person 3 will suffer hunger and deprivation if not assisted and both will feel uncomfortable if person 3 is not helped. The utilities of persons 1 and 2 depend on their own incomes, and also on the income of the disadvantaged person 3, so that

$$U_1 = U_1(y_1, y_3) \qquad U_2 = U_2(y_2, y_3). \tag{5.14}$$

Person 3 is so unfortunate that he has in mind no one other than himself, and his utility is

$$U_3 = U_3(y_3). \tag{5.15}$$

TABLE 5.1. THE PRISONERS' DILEMMA OF PRIVATE INCOME TRANSFERS		
	Person 2 gives	Person 2 does not give
Person 1 gives	3, 3	1, 4
Person 1 does not give	4, 1	2, 2

Although persons 1 and 2 feel better when person 3 is better off, they nonetheless each prefer that the other help the unfortunate person. As we have noted, interdependence in utilities does not reflect a personal good feeling from giving but rather the satisfaction from seeing that unfortunate people have more.

The income of the unfortunate person y_3 appears in the utility functions of both persons 1 and 2 and has the characteristics of a public good. That is, persons 1 and 2 provide benefits to one another when either makes voluntary contributions that increase the income of person 3.

The public-good nature of the income transfers to person 3 introduces a free-riding problem. Person 1 and person 2 both have an incentive to act strategically, to attempt to place the burden of helping the unfortunate person on the other.

We can pose the question of helping the unfortunate person 3 as not how much to give but whether to give. We then have the prisoners' dilemma between the two potential donors that is set out in Table 5.1. The best outcome for each person is 4 where he or she does not give to person 3 and the other does. The next best outcome 3 is that both share the burden of helping person 3. The next best outcome 2 is that neither gives. The worst outcome 1 is where one person has the burden of helping the unfortunate person 3 without the participation of the other.

The dominant strategy is not to give income to the unfortunate person.[2] The Nash equilibrium is that neither person gives. Both persons are better off if they can move from the Nash equilibrium to the efficient outcome at (3, 3), where they share the burden of providing income for person 3. Government can enforce the efficient outcome by compelling persons 1 and 2 to pay taxes that finance income transfers to person 3.

We have therefore identified a justification based on the prisoners' dilemma for taxes to finance income redistribution. Higher-income people want to see income transfers made to unfortunate people, but because of the public-good nature of the income transfers and the prisoners' dilemma, they cannot achieve the transfers voluntarily and independently by themselves. Government resolves the prisoners' dilemma and the free-rider problem through taxation and publicly financed income transfers to the unfortunate in a society.

Table 5.1 describes a symmetric prisoners' dilemma. More generally, when donors differ, to answer a question about how much should be given to the

---

[2] If person 2 gives, the best response of person 1 is not to give. If person 2 does not give, the best response of person 1 is again not to give. Person 2 makes the same calculations.

TABLE 5.2. PLEASURE FROM GIVING

	Person 2 gives	Person 2 does not give
Person 1 gives	8, 8	10, 5
Person 1 does not give	5, 10	0, 0

unfortunate person, information is required about the benefit of each charitable donor from assistance to the unfortunate person. In the absence of this information, a government can only take a best guess about the taxes that should be levied to finance an income transfer.

Pleasure from giving

We can also consider people who derive pleasure from giving. The two donors whom we considered in the context of the prisoners' dilemma do not derive pleasure from giving. They have a social conscience and want the unfortunate to be cared for, but their personally best outcome is to free ride on the income transfers of others.

Table 5.2 shows two charitable persons who derive pleasure from giving. The best personal outcome 10 is achieved when a person is the sole donor, and therefore has the satisfaction that he or she alone is the source of the charitable transfer. The next best outcome 8 is obtained by giving in conjunction with the other person. The donors in Table 5.2 do not like to free ride: their benefit when they free ride on the charitable contributions of one other is 5. The worst outcome for both donors is (0, 0) when neither gives.

The dominant strategy in Table 5.2 is to give.[3] Persons 1 and 2 are identical and each therefore has the same dominant strategy. The Nash equilibrium is at (8, 8) where both voluntarily give. The Nash equilibrium is efficient: $(8 + 8) = 16$ is the maximum combined benefit for both donors.[4] The donors now have no reason to invite taxation by government. They both voluntarily give as their best personal strategies. They both accordingly save the excess burden of taxation.[5]

The two donors may alternatively experience pleasure from giving and prefer that they give together. In Table 5.3, the best outcome for both donors is that both give, at (10, 10). The next best outcome 8 is where one donor gives and the other does not. The donors do not like to free ride (which gives a donor a benefit of 5), and the worst outcome is that neither gives. The dominant strategy is again to

---

[3] If person 2 does not give, person 1 achieves 10 by giving. If person 2 does give, person 1 achieves 8 by giving. Symmetric circumstances apply to person 2.

[4] In Table 5.2, as in Table 5.1, we are looking at the desirability of outcomes from the perspective of the donors, not the recipient.

[5] Rather than deciding simultaneously, the two people in Table 5.2 could make their decisions sequentially. Because the dominant strategy is to give, the same efficient Nash equilibrium is achieved through sequential decisions.

TABLE 5.3. PLEASURE FROM GIVING TOGETHER

	Person 2 gives	Person 2 does not give
Person 1 gives	10, 10	8, 5
Person 1 does not give	5, 8	0, 0

give. The unfortunate are again helped without government imposing taxes and redistributing income.

Prospects for Voluntary Charitable Contributions

We see that the prospects for voluntary income redistribution without government depend on how social conscience is manifested or charitable feelings are expressed. If charitable feelings are expressed as caring about the unfortunate, but preferring that other donors give, society is in a prisoners' dilemma, and a responsibility is identified for government to resolve the prisoners' dilemma through taxation and income redistribution. Government is not required if charitable feelings are expressed in personal satisfaction of helping others who are less fortunate.

5.3.2 Fairness in ultimatum and dictatorship games

Fortunate people may feel that it is unfair that they have a lot and others have little. Unfortunate people of course may feel the same way. The voluntary decision whether to give is, however, made by the fortunate who are able to give.

A way to investigate the idea of a feeling of fairness is by observing behavior in two experimental situations known as the ultimatum game and the dictatorship game.

The ultimatum game

In the ultimatum game, a sum of money is available for division between two people. One person is chosen to act as the donor and the second as recipient. The identities of the two people can be hidden from one another.

The sum of money to be divided might, for example, be $100. The donor is asked to propose a division of the $100. The recipient can respond by accepting or rejecting the division of the $100 proposed by the donor. If the recipient accepts the proposal, the money is divided according to the donor's proposal. If the recipient rejects the proposal, no one receives anything – the $100 is taken away from both people, and they are both left with nothing.

Rational behavior in these circumstances is for the recipient to accept any offer from the donor that provides a positive sum of money. For example, if the donor offers the recipient one dollar out of the $100, the recipient should take the dollar. The offer is a take-it or leave-it ultimatum, and a dollar is better for the recipient than nothing.

By rejecting the offer, the recipient however ensures that the donor also receives nothing. Therefore, by rejecting the offer, the recipient can punish "unfair" offers. The recipient is then inflicting self-punishment as the cost of punishing perceived unfair behavior. The punishment is irrational by economic criteria for efficiency. The principle of Pareto efficiency is based on "more is better than less."

A donor who believes that the recipient will reject an unfair offer has of course reason to make "fair" offers or to offer a division that is too good to be refused. An ultimatum game therefore involves two questions:

(1) Will the recipient act rationally (by economic criteria) and accept any sum of money that the donor offers, or will the recipient reject offers that are felt to be unfair?
(2) Does the donor believe that the recipient will reject unfair offers?

It is enough for the donor to believe that the recipient will reject unfair offers for unfair offers not to be made. If the donor believes that the recipient will react to violation of an idea of fairness by not accepting a very unequal offer, we can expect offers of division to be reasonably fair.

The ultimatum game indicates how conceptions of fairness influence behavior in a society. When fairness is not an issue, the recipient accepts any positive offer of money, as efficiency would require. When fairness is felt to be important, the recipient is prepared to reject unfair offers and to incur a loss in order to punish for offers that are regarded as unfair. If a donor makes a fair offer, we do not know if this is because the donor is a generous person who believes in fair sharing, or if the donor fears the recipient's rejection of an unfair offer.

The dictatorship game

In the dictatorship game, a person is again given a sum of money and makes a decision about how to divide the money with another person. The decision of the prospective donor is, however, not strategic because the recipient has no decision to make. The recipient simply keeps any money that he or she is given. Only altruism, or a concept of fairness, would lead to an offer to share.

In experiments, the persons receiving the money (usually students) often give generous sums to the other person. By giving away money, donors confirm their self-image of themselves as generous and caring persons.

The decision about how much to give can be made collectively by a number of donors. A collective decision usually results in a more generous charitable transfer than an individual decision. The self-perception of being a caring and generous person that affects donors' behavior is now reinforced by the self-perception of being more caring and generous than others, where the people in the group of donors provide the reference point. That is, people in groups look at the behavior and proposals of others and attempt to make decisions that are more generous and more caring than the positions of others in the group. The outcome is that people tend to act more charitably in groups than as individuals.

TABLE 5.4. THE CHARITABLE PERSON'S DILEMMA		
	Lazy person (#2) works	Lazy person (#2) does not work
Donor (#1) does not give	2, 2	1, 1
Donor (#1) gives	4, 3	3, 4

Dividing earned and unearned money

In some ultimatum and dictatorship experiments, a distinction is made between the sharing of earned and unearned money. Unearned money is a gift, and the potential donor can decide how much of the gift to pass along to the recipient. Earned money is "won" in a preliminary contest, and reinforcement is provided that the donor has "earned" and somehow deserves the money. People are in general less generous in giving away money that they feel they have earned than money they have received as a gift.

5.3.3 Lazy people

James Buchanan (of George Mason University, who received the Nobel Prize in 1986) described the strategic interaction between a charitable person who derives pleasure from helping disadvantaged people and a lazy person who prefers not to work. The interaction between the charitable and lazy persons is set out in Table 5.4. The charitable person must decide whether to give money to the lazy person. The lazy person must decide whether to work for a living. The first number in Table 5.4 is the ranking (or benefit) of the donor, and the second number is the ranking (or benefit) of the lazy person.

The donor and the recipient both consider the worst outcome (1, 1) as occurring where the donor does not provide income support and the lazy person does not work. The lazy person then has no means of support and could starve to death, which is an outcome neither person wants.

The donor and the recipient also agree that the outcome where the donor does not provide income support and the recipient work's is the next worst outcome. This outcome, shown as (2, 2), is contrary to the nature of both people. The donor likes to give, but in this case does not give. The lazy recipient does not like to work, but works. For their own different reasons, neither the donor nor the lazy person likes this outcome.

The outcome preferred by the donor is (4, 3) where the donor provides income support and the lazy person also works. The donor wants to help but also wants the recipient to make an honest effort at self-reliance by working for a living.

The outcome preferred by the recipient is (3, 4), where the donor provides income support and the recipient does not work.

The recipient does not have a dominant strategy. If the donor does not give, the recipient's best response is to work for a living. If the donor gives, the recipient's best response is to not work.

TABLE 5.5. MISREPRESENTED PREFERENCES BY THE DONOR

	Lazy person (#2) works	Lazy person (#2) does not work
Donor (#1) does not give	2, 2	4, 1
Donor (#1) gives	3, 3	1, 4

The donor does, however, have a dominant strategy. Whether the lazy person works or does not work, the best response of the donor is to give, which assures either 3 or 4 for the donor, depending on whether the recipient works.

The recipient knows that the dominant strategy of the donor is to give. By not working for a living, the recipient therefore ensures the outcome (3, 4) where the donor gives and the recipient does not work. This outcome is a Nash equilibrium: neither the donor nor the recipient can do better by independently deciding to do something else. The recipient has the best outcome that he or she can achieve, and the donor loses by changing his or her decision and deciding not to give.

The donor is unhappy with the outcome at (3, 4), and would like the recipient to find a job, which would move the outcome to (4, 3) where the recipient works for a living. That is, even if the lazy person does not earn a high income, the donor wants the lazy person to make an effort to earn the personal income that is possible, while the donor provides supplementary income support.

A change in the behavior of the lazy person requires however a change in the benefits associated with the outcomes in Table 5.4. The donor could declare that he or she simply does not care whether the lazy person dies of hunger. This declaration changes the structure of benefits in Table 5.4. In Table 5.5, the donor's declared preferred outcome is at (4, 1) where the lazy person would die of hunger (since the lazy person has neither income from charitable transfers nor from work). The remaining order of preferences of the donor are 3 where the donor gives and the lazy person works, 2 where the donor does not give and the lazy person works, and the declared worst outcome for the donor is to give when the lazy person does not work. In Table 5.5, the preferences of the lazy person remain as in Table 5.4.

The lazy person now decides again whether or not to work, based on the following calculations. If I do not work, the donor will not give, and I will have nothing and will starve. However, if I do work, then the donor will give. The lazy person therefore decides to work. The outcome in Table 5.5 is then (3, 3), which, based on the donor's true preferences in Table 5.4, is the outcome that the donor wants.

For the change in outcomes from Table 5.4 to Table 5.5 to take place, the lazy person must believe that choosing not to work will truly result in the donor allowing him or her to die of hunger. This will not be credible if the lazy person knows that the donor is in fact kind and charitable. The lazy person may therefore decide to call the donor's bluff and to choose not to work, and, because Table 5.5 does not represent the donor's true preferences (which are set out in Table 5.4), the donor would not let the lazy person starve and would provide the income transfer.

The donor declaring not to care if the recipient starves may therefore not be effective. A government bureaucracy can, however, credibly mediate between the donor and the lazy person. The bureaucracy can be given the task of disbursing entitlements to income support by following strict rules. That is, the government bureaucracy is given no discretion with respect to the conditions under which income transfers are or are not provided. The government bureaucrat informs the lazy person that no income support will be provided unless the lazy person makes an effort to be self-reliant and earn income, and that this is a rule for which there are no exceptions. The government bureaucracy thereby enforces the outcome that is desired by the donor. The lazy person finds a job and receives supplementary income support, which is now provided through government and financed by taxes.

The government, by mediating between the donor and the recipient, saves benevolent charitable persons from the exploitative consequences of their own kind nature. The recipient might, however, now attempt to call society's bluff and decide not to work to see whether he or she is indeed left destitute and allowed to starve.

5.3.4 Voluntary charity as a solution for social inequality

Historically, with government not providing social insurance, unfortunate people could hope to receive private charity. The private charity was provided by religious and local community institutions. The personal behavior of donors was based on ethical precepts of the virtue of charity. People who were favored in life confronted the moral obligation to give to those who were less favored.

The safety net provided by private charity had many holes. People could find themselves in dire personal circumstances and be forced into lives of crime or prostitution to survive from day to day.

In more contemporary times, government is the provider of income of last resort, but people nonetheless make voluntary charitable contributions. The charitable contributions are made out of a sense of personally wishing to help the disadvantaged, and also because of personal discretion of the donor in determining whom the charitable contribution will help. The private charitable contributions are subsidized by government through tax deductions.

Private charitable contributors are often made anonymously by giving to a charitable organization. In that case, neither the donor nor the recipient is aware of the identity of the other. It is said that there are different degrees of charity, depending on whether the donor knows the identity of the recipient or the recipient knows the identity of the donor. The lowest degree of charity is where the donor knows the identity of the beneficiary, and the beneficiary knows the identity of the donor. The highest degree of charity is where the donor does not know the identity of the beneficiary, and the beneficiary does not know the identity of the donor.

Private charity and publicly financed income transfers

People may not see the need to contribute to the unfortunate twice, once through taxes that finance income transfers through government and again voluntarily. There may be a feeling that, once government has taken responsibility for helping the unfortunate, private charity is not necessary. A person seeking charity might then be directed to a social worker who can offer guidance on suitable programs of government assistance.

Declarations and actions

The success of private charity as a solution to social inequality depends on how close-knit a society is and on the sense of mutual obligation and moral responsibility among people.

The success of private charity also depends on how many people are prepared to actually give part of their personal incomes to the unfortunate rather than declaring that "someone should do something" to help the unfortunate. That is, private charity depends on the scope of the free-rider problem in voluntary private charitable transfers.

Behavior of the recipients

The scope for private charity replacing government social insurance also depends on the behavior of the beneficiaries of private charity. If recipients behave in the manner of the lazy person as described by Buchanan and take advantage of charitable inclinations, donors become disenchanted with the beneficiaries' responses to their private charitable transfers.

5.3.5 Economic and social mobility

Social justice without government can be achieved through social mobility. Social mobility offers opportunities for personal improvement over time. Through the opportunities for personal improvement, future personal income and wealth can be disconnected from income and wealth at birth (or from the income and wealth of parents).

Personal opportunities for self-improvement are provided in particular through the education system. Education allows people from low-income families to make the transition to high income. A society in which wealth and income are based on inherited ownership of land and which offers no educational opportunities for poorer families preserves the existing social order and offers no prospect of self-improvement for people born into poorer families.

Estimates of intergenerational social mobility

Studies of intergenerational social mobility estimate the relationship between children's incomes Y^{child} and the incomes of their parents Y^{parent}. An equation is estimated for

$$Y^{child} = a + bY^{parent} + \mu, \tag{5.16}$$

TABLE 5.6. INTERGENERATIONAL ECONOMIC CHARACTERISTICS

Economic characteristic	Range of estimates	Average
Years of schooling	0.14–0.45	0.29
Earnings, wages	0.11–0.59	0.34
Family income	0.14–0.65	0.43
Family wealth	0.27–0.76	0.50
Family consumption	0.59–0.77	0.68

Source: Mulligan (1999).

where μ is a random error term. If $b = 0$, there is complete social mobility because the income of children is completely uncorrelated with the income of parents. If $b = 1$, there is complete social immobility because the incomes of children and parents are perfectly correlated. When b is between zero and one, regression to the mean is taking place in incomes over generations because parents with high incomes do not necessarily have children who will have high incomes, and similarly parents with low incomes do not necessarily have children who will have low incomes. A negative b is also in principle possible; that is, income of children could be negatively correlated with the income of parents.

The estimated value for b depends of course on the sample of people who provide the data for the estimation. Studies based on data in the second half of the twentieth century have suggested correlations between children's and parents' incomes in the United States in the neighborhood of $b = 0.4$. Higher values of b, indicating lower social mobility, have been reported for the United Kingdom.

Table 5.6 shows the range of correlations and the average correlation across generations in the United States in the twentieth century for a number of personal economic characteristics. We see that the lowest correlation is for years of schooling and that the highest correlation is for consumption. Educated people therefore do not necessarily have educated children, but the children of the more educated tend to maintain the consumption levels of their more educated parents. Table 5.6 indicate that the identity of parents matters more in determining personal consumption than in determining personal income, wealth, or wages. Since high-consumption people tend to run down family wealth to maintain consumption at the standards to which they have become accustomed, a social equalizing process is taking place over time.

Table 5.6 shows a low correlation for wages between generations: wages are personally earned and related to education. The intergenerational correlation is higher for income than for wages because income includes the non-wage returns from family assets and wealth. The intergenerational correlation is in turn higher for wealth than for wages or income. Wealth is, however, run down by the high correlation across generations of consumption.

Reversion to the mean

An equalizing process, or reversion to the mean of the population, was predicted by Francis Galton (1822–1911) in his studies (Galton, 1989) of inherited human characteristics. If the characteristics of a child are the average of the characteristics of both parents, the child is closer to the mean of the population than at least one of the parents. For example, suppose that we could measure motivation to succeed in life, and that the average measure in a society is 100. A child of two parents who have respective measures of 120 and 140 has (on average) a measure of 130, which is closer to the mean than one of the parents. A child whose parents have measures of 90 and 110 has 100, and is closer to the mean than both parents. The averaging process indicates natural increasing equality over time.

High-wealth parents are more likely to leave their children with larger inheritances. It is sometimes observed, however, that transition from poverty to riches and back to poverty often takes no more than three or four generations. If the children do not consume (or lose) the wealth accumulated by the parents, the loss may occur in the following generation because of reversion to the mean in abilities. The estimates in Table 5.6 do not confirm such extremes; nonetheless, there is an equalizing tendency in social mobility. In different generations, different people from different family backgrounds do well.

On the other hand, tendencies for inequality arise, and reversion to the mean does not take place, if high-ability men disproportionately tend to marry high-ability women, and low-ability men disproportionately tend to marry low-ability women. The tendencies for inequality arise if traits are inherited and also if the home environment influences study habits and attitudes to succeeding in life through education (i.e., if there is cultural transmission of traits). There would then be reversion to the mean within subgroups. The tendencies for inequality in family incomes become greater if high-ability, high-income women have fewer children than low-ability, low-income women.

Social mobility and social stability

High social mobility is associated with social stability. The wealth of the hereditary rich has often been appropriated when there has been limited social mobility. The revolutions through which the wealth was appropriated did not take place in democracies with publicly financed education systems. In the Roman Empire of some 2,000 years ago, the rich (the patricians) provided the masses of the poor (the plebeians) with "bread and circuses," in the hope of distracting the masses' attention from the distribution of wealth and income. The distraction was successful, and the empire fell to external assault, which was, however, made easier by internal decline. In contrast, the queen of France, Marie Antoinette, is reported to have replied to a plea that the poor have no bread with the proposal, "let them eat cakes." Marie Antoinette may not have been serious in proposing her solution, but she did not survive the French revolution that soon followed (nor did her husband the king).

Social mobility and social insurance

Social mobility does not end the demand for social insurance. The time dimensions for social insurance and social mobility differ. Social insurance is provided for needs that tend to be immediate. Social mobility involves change over generations.

We noted in Sections 5.1 and 5.2 that there are moral hazard problems associated with social insurance. There are also moral hazard problems associated with social mobility. It may be impossible to determine whether the reason that people have not fared well and not progressed in life is limited social mobility or lack of effort to take advantage of the opportunities for social mobility that have been available.

5.3.6 Conclusions

We began our consideration of social justice in Section 5.1 with a view of income redistribution as social insurance, and with government making income redistribution decisions based on the choice of a social welfare function. According to this view, people face the uncertainty of not knowing who they will be or how well they will fare in life, and since the private market cannot provide the insurance that people seek, government acts as insurer of last resort and redistributes income from the more fortunate to the less fortunate. In this section, we looked at income redistribution that occurs through voluntary income transfers after people know who they are. The uncertainty that underlies demand for insurance is not present. The income transfers are made when people know their situations in life.

We have seen that the prospects for voluntary charity depend on whether people derive satisfaction from giving. If the satisfaction is not from giving, but from the assurance that people in need are helped, a prisoners' dilemma arises, and there is a case for government to take responsibility for income redistribution to solve the associated free-rider problem of private charity. The prisoners' dilemma is not present if people derive pleasure from giving. In that case, reliance on private charity can be successful as a means of providing for people in need.

If some recipients of voluntary income transfers, however, attempt to exploit the goodwill of charitable people, there is a further reason for giving government responsibility for income redistribution. A government bureaucracy that disburses entitlements can more credibly precommit not to give income transfers to people who do not make an attempt at self-reliance through gainful employment.

We have also considered social mobility as a means of providing social justice. Social mobility as a substitute for publicly financed income transfers requires patience. If people are very badly off, they may starve while waiting for their incomes to be improved through social mobility, or through the social mobility of their children. Social mobility is moreover not certain but probabilistic. There is no certainty that social mobility will increase any particular person's future income. Nonetheless, high social mobility allows people to improve themselves and underlies a culture of personal motivation to succeed as opposed to a culture of fatalism and reliance on government.

We have also noted how conceptions of social justice or fairness are expressed through outcomes of ultimatum and dictatorship games.

References and related literature

On voluntary income transfers, see Hochman and Rogers (1969), Sugden (1982), Magat (1989), Andreoni (1990), and Rosenzweig and Wolpin (1994). On conscience, see Frank (1987). On the dilemma of the charitable, see Buchanan (1975). On work obligations as an accompaniment of income transfers, see Besely and Coate (1992) and Meyer (2000). On ultimatum and dictatorship games, see Thaler (1988), Roth (1995), and Cason and Mui (1997). On crowding out of private charity, see Abrams and Schmitz (1978), Roberts (1984), and Kingma (1989). On social mobility, see Becker and Tomes (1979), Solon (1992), Zimmerman (1992), Dardanoni (1993), Picketty (1995), Deardon, Machin, and Reed (1997), Fields and Ok (1999), and Mulligan (1999). On sorting and inequality, see Ferdández and Rogerson (2001).

Abrams, B. A. and M. S. Schmitz, 1978. The crowding out effect of government transfers on private charitable contributions. *Public Choice* 33, 29–40.

Andreoni, J., 1990. Impure altruism and donations to public goods: A theory of warm-glow giving. *Economic Journal* 100, 464–77.

Becker, G. and N. Tomes, 1979. An equilibrium theory of the distribution of income and intergenerational mobility. *Journal of Political Economy* 87, 1153–89.

Besley, T. and S. Coate, 1992. Workfare vs. welfare: Incentive arguments for work requirements in poverty alleviation programs. *American Economic Review* 82, 249–61.

Buchanan, J. M., 1975. The Samaritan's dilemma. In *Altruism, Morality and Economic Theory*, E. Phelps (ed.). Russell Sage, New York, 71–85.

Cason, T. N. and V.-L. Mui, 1997. A laboratory study of group polarization in the team dictator game. *Economic Journal* 107, 1465–83.

Dardanoni, V., 1993. Measuring social mobility. *Journal of Economic Theory* 61, 372–94.

Deardon, L., S. Machin and H. Reed, 1997. Intergenerational mobility in Britain. *Economic Journal* 107, 47–66.

Fernández, R. and R. Rogerson, 2001. Sorting, education, and inequality. *Quarterly Journal of Economics* 116, 1305–41.

Frank, R., 1987. If homo economicus could choose his own utility function, would he want one with a conscience? *American Economic Review* 77, 593–604.

Fields, G. R. and E. A. Ok, 1999. The measurement of income mobility: An introduction to the literature. In *Handbook on Income Inequality*, J. Silver (Ed.). Kluwer Academic Publishers, Dordrecht, 557–98.

Galton, F., 1889. *Natural Inheritance*. Macmillan, London.

Hochman, H. M. and J. D. Rogers, 1969. Pareto optimal redistribution. *American Economic Review*, 59, 542–57.

Kingma, B. R., 1989. An accurate measure of the crowding out effect, income effect, and price effect for charitable contributions. *Journal of Political Economy* 97, 1197–1207.

Magat, R. (ed.), 1989. *Philanthropic Giving*. Oxford University Press, Oxford.

Meyer, B. D., 2000. Making single mothers work: Recent tax and welfare policy and its effects. *National Tax Journal* 53, 102–61.

Mulligan, C. B., 1999. Galton versus the human capital approach to inheritance. *Journal of Political Economy* 107, S184–S224.

Picketty, J., 1995. Social mobility and redistributive politics. *Quarterly Journal of Economics* 110, 551–84.

Roberts, R. D., 1984. A positive model of private charity and public transfers. *Journal of Political Economy* 92, 136–48.

Rosenzweig, M. R. and K. I. Wolpin, 1994. Parental and public transfers to young women and their children. *American Economic Review* 84, 1195–1212.

Roth, A. E., 1995. Bargaining experiments. In *Handbook of Experimental Economics*, J. Kagel and A. E. Roth (eds.). Princeton University Press, Princeton, New Jersey, 253–348.

Solon, G., 1992. Intergenerational income mobility in the U.S. *American Economic Review* 82, 393–408.

Sugden, R., 1982. On the economics of philanthropy. *Economic Journal* 92, 341–50.

Thaler, R., 1988. The ultimatum game. *Journal of Economic Perspectives* 2, 195–206.

Zimmerman, D. J., 1992. Regression toward mediocrity in economic stature. *American Economic Review* 82, 409–29.

Questions for discussion

1. In the place where you live or study, what proportion of income do people voluntarily give to charity? What are the largest private charities and what are the purposes of these charities?

2. Do you believe that private charity is reduced by public policies that provide tax-financed income transfers? If you have already paid taxes, part of which is intended to finance social insurance, and an anonymous stranger on the street asks you for money and explains that he has no income, would you give him money or direct him to the local office where social workers attempt to solve personal problems within the framework of publicly financed assistance programs? Where there are programs of publicly financed assistance in place, why might a person still give a stranger money?

3. Interdependent utilities are a way of formally expressing the idea of altruism, or that people care about the well-being of one another. Yet people do not appear to care equally about the well-being of others. People sometimes contribute differently to help friends and family, people in their own neighborhood or city, people in their own region, and people in far away countries. Do you believe that these differences reflect empathy based on the likelihood that the donors could have faced the same situation? Explain.

4. Do you believe that the "pleasure from giving" scenarios described in Tables 5.2, 5.3, and 5.4 are more accurate descriptions of how people commonly feel about helping others than the prisoners' dilemma? Explain.

5. If you were playing the ultimatum game with a person drawn at random from the people around you, what proportion of $10 would you offer the other person? What proportion of $100 or $1,000 would you offer. What considerations would enter into your decision? How would these considerations influence your decision about sharing in the dictatorship game? To what extent would your decisions be influenced by your own altruism and by your perception of the other person's attitudes to fairness?

6. In the ultimatum game, if you were the recipient, what percentage of $100 would you require to be offered in order to accept an offer of division? As the recipient, what percentage would you require if the amount were $1,000 or $10,000?

7. Suppose that, when the ultimatum game is played in two different societies, in one society the low offers that are made are generally accepted, and in the other society the low offers that are made are generally rejected. What does this tell us about the two societies?

8. In the dictatorship game, suppose that people in one society make generous divisions of the money, but that in a second society people choose to give nothing. Then the situation changes to the ultimatum game. In the ultimatum game, the people in the first society do not change their behavior, but the people in the second society now make generous offers. What can we infer about conceptions of fairness and attitudes toward private charity in the two societies?

9. In the charitable person's dilemma in Table 5.4, why does the charitable person care whether or not the lazy person makes an effort to be self-supporting?

10. Why can the interaction between the donor and the lazy person in Table 5.4 be described as a case of moral hazard and a case of a principal agent problem? How is the idea of "credible commitment" involved in the solution to the principal–agent problem through government bureaucracy?

11. In Table 5.4, the donor derives pleasure from giving, and giving is the donor's dominant strategy. In Figure 5.5, the outcomes are reformulated. Explain the basis for the reformulation. What is the outcome of interaction between the donor and the lazy person in this case?

12. What is social mobility, and how is it measured? Is social mobility a reasonable means of achieving "social justice" in a society? Explain. How is "social justice" defined when this question is asked?

13. Major elements of social mobility are access to educational opportunities and meritocracy in the job market (so that jobs are allocated not according to personal and family connections but according to individual merit). When social mobility is low, how can public policy increase social mobility? Who will object to public policies that increase social mobility?

14. How do demographic trends and associated changes in the value of women's time affect the tendency for reversion to the mean in incomes in a population?

15. How would you expect social mobility to affect the social insurance contract that people might want?

16. How does the quest for social status affect private charitable contributions? Do you believe that the quest to sustain social status is an impediment to redistribution of income through voluntary giving? Explain. (See Supplement 5C.)

6

POLITICS AND REDISTRIBUTION

In this chapter we shall look at how political processes can affect redistribution of income or wealth. We begin with direct voting. We shall then consider political decisions about public policy when, under representative democracy, political representatives and candidates for political office view winning elections as a primary personal objective. We shall also look at rent-seeking behavior, which takes place when political favors are sought from political decision makers.

6.1

Voting and Redistribution

6.1.1 Income redistribution through majority voting

Unless there are constraints, under majority voting, any 51 percent of voters can in principle vote to redistribute income or wealth to themselves from the other 49 percent of voters. Voting is therefore a means of redistributing income or wealth.

A redistribution of income or wealth that takes place through majority voting need not be justified on grounds of social justice. That is, the people making up the majority who benefit at the expense of the minority need not be deserving of assistance because they have had unfortunate personal experiences that do not allow them to earn incomes. All that matters for achieving a redistribution of income or wealth through majority voting is being in the majority. Since the majority determines the redistribution of income or wealth from the minority, the majority is like a dictator. When the majority votes to distribute income or wealth to itself from the minority, from the viewpoint of the minority, it is as if a dictator had ordered the minority to give up parts of their income or wealth.

In principle, the majority could be based on any attribute that 51 percent of voters have in common. For example, in a society where 51 percent of the population have blue eyes, the majority made up of voters with blue eyes could vote to distribute income to itself from the minority of voters who do not have blue eyes. Discrimination in income distribution based on personal attributes such as the color of people's eyes is unconstitutional or illegal. However, in a society where the majority of voters is old, the old could vote to distribute income to themselves from the young, by voting on the levels of social security taxes and benefits to social-security recipients, unless there are restraints on tax-financed income transfers from the young to the old.

6.1.2 Private benefits from public spending

Previously, in Chapter 3, we investigated majority voting as a means of making collective decisions about public spending on public goods. We saw that majority voting regarding public spending for public goods could affect income distribution. A majority could vote for public spending on public goods from which it benefited and for the public goods to be financed by taxes levied on the population at large. Some people might then pay taxes and not benefit at all from the spending on public goods chosen by the majority.

Public spending can also provide private benefits, rather than the collective benefits of a public good. To describe majority voting on publicly financed private benefits, we can consider an example due to Gordon Tullock (1959). A number of people (let us say 100) each have private access roads from their homes to a highway. The 100 people meet to make decisions through majority voting about financing the maintenance of their private access roads. At the meeting, a proposal is put forward that maintenance of the private access roads should be publicly financed. The proposal is accepted by a consensus vote, and the maintenance of each person's private road is financed by identical taxes levied on all 100 persons. Each access road provides private benefit for one person; therefore, a decision has been made to provide public finance for goods that provide private benefit.

We saw in Chapter 1 that private goods are efficiently provided through voluntary personal decisions in competitive markets. Since this is the case, why would the 100 people with the private access roads vote in favor of public finance to maintain the private roads? Each individual could just personally pay for his or her road maintenance through private market expenditures. The private spending would avoid the additional personal costs of public finance. The additional costs of public finance through the excess burden of taxation would be avoided, as would the cost to taxpayers of administering the government bureaucracy. Moreover, when the maintenance of the private access roads is publicly financed, individuals lose direct control over costs and the quality of the service they receive. In some societies, there could also be a problem of corruption: when a policy decision is made to use public finance, a government agency is engaged in procurement of the services of road maintenance from private contractors. Where there is corruption, people working for the government agency might ask for and receive bribes (also known as kick-backs) for choosing one private contractor over another and for agreeing to inflated prices for the services provided by the private contractor.

Why then should public spending ever be used to finance private benefits? In Chapter 5 where we considered social justice, we proposed that public spending might provide private benefits because income redistribution could be viewed as the outcome of a social contract that was agreed upon before people knew who they were going to be. People therefore had entitlements, which provided private benefit but were financed by the government. In these cases, the publicly financed private benefits were a social-insurance response to the consequence of previous uncertainty. In the case of public finance for the private access roads, there is no such uncertainty. The vote that we described provides publicly financed private benefits to all 100 people with access roads. We have also not introduced externalities that might possibly justify public spending on the maintenance of the private access roads. In these circumstances, the reason for majority voting to determine public spending is *neither* social injustice *nor* the existence of any externality to be corrected by public policy.

No income redistribution takes place when everybody pays equal taxes to finance the maintenance of everybody's roads because everybody benefits equally from the public spending that provides private benefits. However, with the convention established that decisions about private benefit (from maintenance of private roads) can be made collectively through majority voting, at the next meeting of the 100 users of the private access roads, a coalition of 51 voters can propose a different public policy. The 51-voter majority can propose that only their 51 roads be maintained through public finance, and that the other 49 persons pay the taxes that finance the roads. This proposal has majority support. The 51 persons thereby use taxation and public spending for their private advantage, through majority voting.

Two votes take place. In a first vote, the 51 percent majority proposes and votes in favor of a public policy of public finance for private benefit. In the second vote, the 51 percent majority votes to have the minority's taxes finance the majority's private benefits.[1]

6.1.3 Coalition size and coalition stability

The optimal size for members of the majority coalition to maximize their gains from public spending for private benefit is 51. If the majority coalition has 52 members, the benefits for the majority are smaller because then only 48 persons finance the benefits for 52.

A member of the minority wants to have as many people as possible sharing the costs of financing the benefits for the majority and, therefore, also wants there to be as few as possible people in the majority because the greater the number of people in the majority, the greater the financing burden on the minority will be. Therefore, a member of the minority also wants the division between majority and minority to be 51–49, and not, say, 52–48.

Because the majority gains at the expense of the minority, self-interest leads everybody to want to be in the majority. The 49 persons in the minority group therefore have an incentive to bribe two persons to leave the majority coalition, and instead to join them to make a new majority coalition. Through majority voting, private benefits can then be provided to the new majority at the expense of the new minority.

If two people can be bribed to switch coalitions to make a new majority coalition, the original majority coalition is unstable. The members of the new minority coalition have an incentive to bribe two members of the new majority to defect and join them, and, if two defectors can be found, the new majority coalition is also unstable.

The incentive is always present for people to leave a majority coalition to join a new majority coalition. For example, the 51 members of the majority might each gain 100 and the 49 members of the minority might each lose 130 (the loss consists of taxes paid plus the excess burden of taxation). The 49-member minority could then assure two members of the majority that they will receive more than 100 each for switching coalitions. By switching from being in the minority to being in the majority, the members of the original minority coalition gain (they have +100 instead of −130) before any payments has been made as a bribe to two defectors from the original majority coalition. The benefit per person from switching from being the minority to being the majority allows ample scope for payment to two defectors from the original majority.

Why might switching between coalitions not take place? People who can be bought too easily acquire a reputation of being opportunistic and unprincipled.

---

[1] In presenting the example of the publicly financed private access roads, Gordon Tullock (1959) thus proposed that a simple quest for private gain is the reason why majority voting is used to make public-finance decisions that provide private benefit.

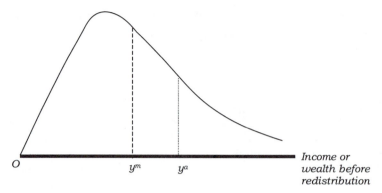

Figure 6.1. The distribution of income or wealth in a society.
Usually the distribution of personal income or wealth is skewed to the right, with the average y^a exceeding the median y^m. A majority therefore has below-average income or wealth.

Moreover, if one coalition can buy defectors from another coalition, then another coalition in the future can presumably buy the same people's votes. If fixed costs are incurred in forming coalitions, a commitment is therefore required that the persons whose votes are being bought become principled after the payment for joining the new coalition has been made. With fixed costs, the members of the new majority coalition would want a commitment that they will not be excluded from a winning coalition in the future.

The two persons who defect from a majority of 51 to form a new majority with the other 49 persons are also aware that their benefits in the new coalition depend on the new coalition holding together. They will therefore seek guarantees that the new coalition will not break up to leave them stranded outside the majority. If binding guarantees cannot be provided, defection will not take place, and the initial majority coalition may be stable.

6.1.4 Limits on redistribution through majority voting

Abilities in a population are usually normally distributed. However, income before redistribution, and more so wealth, is usually skewed as in Figure 6.1, with the median less than the mean (or average) of the population. The median in Figure 6.1 is y^m and the mean or average is y^a.[2]

When the mean or average exceeds the median, more people have income or wealth below the average than above the average. A majority coalition can then be made up of the median voter (whose income or wealth is y^m) and all voters with incomes or wealth less than y^m. With majority voting, the majority of voters with below-average income or wealth can then vote to redistribute income or wealth to themselves from the minority.

---

[2] Often the distribution of wealth or income among a population takes forms other than the distribution in Figure 6.1. The distribution is often consistently negatively sloped. As a general rule, the mean or average of the distribution exceeds the median, as in Figure 6.1.

Voting to redistribute wealth

If the majority were to vote to appropriate for their own benefit the wealth of the minority, a precedent would be set that people can lose all their wealth through majority voting. The precedent can be expected to affect adversely incentives to work and save and to take risks and make investments. When people know that their wealth can be appropriated in the future through majority voting, they may think that it is better not to exert too much effort and to wait (as a low-wealth person) for a vote that in the future will redistribute the wealth of the high-wealth minority to the low-wealth majority. Because of the adverse effect on incentives to be productive and to take risks, societies in general do not tax personal wealth, or only do so in limited ways.[3]

Voting to appropriate personal wealth is a violation of personal property rights. After income taxes have been paid, people can choose to consume or to invest their post-tax incomes; if saved, post-tax income is an addition to personal wealth. A tax on personal wealth is therefore a *retroactive tax* on personal income that was already taxed in the past. We observed in Chapter 1, when we considered the role of property rights as the foundation for markets, that retroactive laws are a violation of the rule of law. Had people known in the past that they were to be taxed on their wealth in the future, they may well have chosen to behave differently and to consume their past-tax incomes rather than accumulate wealth.

When income is redistributed through taxation and publicly financed transfers (of income or in-kind), there are efficiency losses through the excess burden of taxation. Taxation of wealth might be thought to have no excess burden because the minority whose wealth is appropriated can be surprised by the wealth appropriation. The surprise gives the minority who lose their wealth no opportunities for substitution responses (the minority cannot change their behavior to avoid the appropriation of their wealth), and so there is no excess burden, and also therefore no leaky bucket of redistribution. However, even though there is no efficiency loss through an excess burden at the time of redistribution of wealth, there are efficiency losses in the future. Taxation of wealth affects future personal behavior through unwillingness to exert effort or take risks. The precedent that the majority can appropriate the wealth of the minority therefore imposes future efficiency losses.[4]

---

[3] Governments in some countries do levy taxes on personal wealth. Also, local tax jurisdictions often raise revenue through property taxes, which are taxes on wealth held in the form of housing. The property tax is a tax on part of personal wealth. Property taxes are used to identify beneficiaries of spending by local government. The residents of the house benefit from the local public spending and pay the taxes (or if the house or apartment is rented, the owner may pay the property tax, but the people who rent the house pay indirectly through the rent). These property taxes are not what we mean by a tax on wealth. A tax on wealth is a tax on all wealth.

[4] An argument is sometimes made that wealth should be redistributed from a minority of very rich people to poorer people because the very rich have inherited their wealth and have done nothing to earn the wealth themselves. For this reason, governments impose estate taxes that tax personal wealth when the wealth is to be redistributed to heirs. We shall return to wealth and estate taxes in Section 7.2, where we consider the question of what to tax. At this point, we note that wealth

Voting to redistribute income

Redistribution of wealth is uncommon or limited, but income redistribution through taxation is pervasive. How much income redistribution can we expect to take place through self-interested majority voting if voters are able to choose taxation and redistribution of income to maximize their own utilities? The answer depends on the rules governing the forms of taxes that can be levied and on the efficiency losses (or equivalently the incentive effects or the excess burden) of taxation.

A 51 percent low-income majority could decide simply to redistribute income to themselves by appropriating the income of the 49 percent high-income minority (they might leave subsistence income for the taxed minority). Such appropriation would turn the former high-income minority into a destitute minority population. The redistribution is clearly unethical. Moreover, the members of the high-income minority have no incentive to work if they know that, through appropriation by the majority, their post-tax incomes are to be very low or zero. The circumstances are very similar to the game between the strong and the weak that we considered in Chapter 1 when we described the benefits to a society from the rule of law. The majority are the strong, and the minority are the weak.

Appropriative taxation of the incomes of the minority for the exclusive benefit of the majority is discriminatory. We can consider an alternative scheme for taxation and redistribution that is non-discriminatory, where the same rate of income tax is to be applied to all people in the population, and the proceeds of taxation are distributed equally among all the population. This is in contrast to the appropriation of the income of the minority by the majority, where the rate of taxation is zero for the majority and 100 percent (or a little less because of subsistence needs) for the minority, and the redistribution of income is only to members of the majority.[5] We denote by t the rate of taxation that is now to be applied to all pre-tax incomes no matter where the incomes are in the income distribution. With n persons earning different individual incomes y_i and paying taxes, the proportional tax rate t yields total revenue

$$R = t \sum_{i=1}^{n} y_i. \tag{6.1}$$

and estate taxes can often be avoided by means known as estate planning, and that these means of avoiding taxation (through payments to tax lawyers and accountants) are generally more readily available to the rich than to the poor.

[5] Under progressive taxation, the proportion of income paid in taxes increases with the level of income. Taxing a low-income majority at zero and a high-income minority at 100 percent is therefore an extreme form of progressive taxation. We shall proceed now to consider the choice of a single rate of taxation to finance income redistribution. We return to progressive income taxes in Chapter 7, where we shall see that a single rate of income taxation is also a progressive tax when combined with an income transfer financed by the tax revenue that is collected.

This tax revenue is redistributed equally to all the n taxpayers. Each taxpayer therefore receives an equal amount of redistributed tax revenue

$$S = t\left(\frac{\sum y}{n}\right) = ty^a. \tag{6.2}$$

That is, each taxpayer receives a share of the redistributed tax revenue equal to the rate of taxation multiplied by the average pre-tax income in the population.

Only to simplify matters, and not because we believe that reality has this feature, let us now proceed as if there were no excess burden of taxation. Therefore, taxation has no effect on incentives to work, and people contribute (or work and exert effort) according to their abilities and not according to the rewards they receive. In that case, the income available for redistribution is given independently of the tax rate that is chosen. The average income in the population y^a is also given as in the pre-tax income distribution in Figure 6.1. If work or effort decisions did respond to taxation (so that substitution effects away from work and effort and an excess burden of taxation are recognized to exist), the entire distribution of incomes available for redistribution would depend on the rate of taxation. People would take account of the rate of taxation when deciding on effort and the number of hours to work (or deciding whether to work), which would determine the incomes that they earn, and thereby determine the incomes that can be transferred to others.

Therefore, in Figure 6.1, the income distribution is invariant to the rate of income taxation t, as is the average income y^a in the population. The income transfer S that people receive from the redistribution of tax revenue thus depends on the choice of the rate of taxation t as in expression (6.2). Individuals' post-redistribution incomes also only depend on the choice of the tax rate t. For any individual, whom we label with i, the relation between pre-tax and post-tax income is

$$y^i_{after\ tax} = (1 - t)y_i + S. \tag{6.3}$$

Here y_i is the individual's earned income before taxes are paid, determined by the individual's location in the distribution of earned pre-tax incomes in Figure 6.1.

When we substitute the expression (6.2), which describes the equal income transfer S, into expression (6.3), the relationship between pre- and post-tax income becomes

$$y^i_{after\ tax} = (1 - t)y^i + ty^a. \tag{6.4}$$

Therefore,

$$y^i_{after\ tax} = y_i + t(y^a - y_i). \tag{6.5}$$

We now ask each person to vote on the rate of taxation t that is to be applied to all incomes. Each person votes for the rate of taxation t that maximizes his or her after-tax income as given by expression (6.5).

We see from expression (6.5) that the person whose pre-tax income is equal to the average income (i.e., the person for whom $y_i = y^a$) is indifferent to whichever tax rate is chosen.

All persons with incomes greater than the average would vote for zero taxation, which would leave them with their original pre-tax income y_i. That is, persons with greater than average pre-tax incomes would vote for no income redistribution.

On the other hand, all persons with incomes less than average would maximize their after-tax incomes by voting for appropriative taxation, that is, by voting for $t = 1$ or a tax rate of 100 percent. The appropriative tax rate combined with equal redistribution of tax revenue gives each person in the population the average income in the pre-tax income distribution. We see, substituting $t = 1$ into expression (6.5), that, after taxation and income redistribution, for each person denoted i,

$$y^i_{after\ tax} = y^a. \tag{6.6}$$

Because there are more people with below-average pre-tax income than above-average pre-tax income, majority voting results in the choice of appropriative taxation. After equal redistribution of the tax revenue, the outcome is equality of post-tax incomes.

The median voter

There is only one issue to be decided by majority voting, which is the proportional tax rate t. All voters have single-peaked preferences regarding their personal income-maximizing choice of the tax rate. Therefore, the conditions are satisfied for an equilibrium outcome of majority voting to exist.[6] The after-tax income of the median voter is

$$y^m_{after\ tax} = y^m + t(y^a - y^m). \tag{6.7}$$

Because the median income y^m in the income distribution is less than the average income y^a, the median voter votes for appropriative taxation (i.e., for $t = 1$) to maximize his or her after-tax income as given in expression (6.7). By voting for a tax rate of 100 percent, the median voter increases his or her income from y^m before taxation and income redistribution to the average income y^a after taxation and redistribution. After the 100 percent tax has been levied and the tax revenue has been equally redistributed, everyone in the population has the same income y^a. Therefore, majority voting results in post-redistribution income equality.[7]

The majority in favor of the outcome of appropriative taxation is greater than 51 percent. As we have observed, all voters with pre-tax incomes below the average y^a benefit from the full appropriation of all incomes and equal redistribution that gives them the average income y^a, and so they support appropriative taxation.

---

[6] Recall from Chapter 3 that, if there were more than a single issue to be decided, we could not be certain that majority voting would result in an equilibrium collective decision.

[7] Rather than the vote being on the rate of proportional income taxation t, the majority might alternatively vote for progressive taxes to finance income redistribution. With progressive taxes, higher-income individuals pay a larger share of their incomes in taxes than lower-income individuals. The median voter gains from the progressive taxes if the median voter pays less in taxes than the tax-financed income transfer he or she receives. However, if income equality is the objective, this objective can be achieved by a tax rate of 100 percent and equal redistribution.

More complex income taxes and redistribution programs

Income taxes and redistribution programs are in general more complex than the single proportional tax rate and equal redistribution of tax revenue that we have considered. In Chapter 7, we shall consider more general choices of taxes. Nevertheless, the case of a single rate of taxation shows us that, with no discrimination in the rate of income taxation and no discrimination in the distribution of tax revenue, the outcome of majority voting is complete appropriative taxation and post-redistribution income equality. We also see that if choices of taxes and redistribution are restricted so that the high-income minority cannot become worse off than the low-income majority, post-tax equality is the best that the low-income majority can achieve.

Equality through social insurance and social welfare maximization

The income equality through taxation and redistribution that is here the outcome of majority voting is the same as the outcome in Chapter 5 when we considered social insurance through maximizing a social welfare function under the same conditions of no excess burden of taxation, or no leaks in the bucket of redistribution. In that case incomes were also equalized after taxation and redistribution.[8] The idea of maximizing a social welfare function was based on social insurance with people not knowing who they are going to be, and therefore not knowing the incomes they will be earning. In contrast, the equality of post-redistribution incomes through majority voting takes place when people are not behind the veil of ignorance but rather they know their pre-distribution incomes and therefore their positions in the income distribution in Figure 6.1.

Incentives and the excess burden of taxation

We can now introduce the consideration, as we did when we viewed income redistribution as social insurance in chapter 5, that taxation has incentive effects that result in efficiency losses through the excess burden of taxation. We do not expect people to exert much effort when they know that the rate of income taxation is 100 percent, and that their personal incomes after taxation and redistribution will be determined as the average of the population. Under these conditions, people might be reluctant to work or exert effort at all.[9] The effect of the anticipated post-tax income equality on incentives to work and exert effort will be reflected in the shape of the pre-tax income distribution in Figure 6.1.

---

[8] When we considered social insurance in Chapter 5, the conditions that people had the same utility functions and that social welfare functions were symmetric were imposed. We proposed that having the same utility function was reasonable behind the veil of ignorance where people did not know who they were going to be, and that people behind a veil of ignorance would choose a symmetric social welfare function.

[9] We recall that the societies with collective property that we considered in Section 1.3 attempted to circumvent incentives by encouraging contributions according to ability and not reward.

We expect this distribution to collapse to zero incomes for the individuals in the population.[10]

When choosing the rate of income taxation that maximizes his or her post-redistribution income, the median voter is obliged to consider how taxation and redistribution affect incentives of people to work and exert effort, and in particular the effect on the average pre-tax income of the income distribution.[11] For this reason, we do not expect taxation chosen by majority voting to be completely appropriative as would be the case if there were no incentive effects of taxation on hours worked or effort exerted. Rather, as in the case of income redistribution chosen as social insurance to maximize social welfare, the determination of income redistribution through majority voting is subject to constraints imposed by efficiency.

Principles of socially just taxation

Principles of socially just taxation also constrain a majority (or the median voter) from arbitrarily discriminating against a minority. The principle of *horizontal equity* requires tax laws to treat equals equally. The principle of *vertical equity* requires just tax treatment of "unequal people" (people with unequal incomes or wealth). These principles of social justice in taxation, if followed, limit the redistribution that is possible through majority voting. In particular, the principle of horizontal equity prevents the application of extraneous criteria to the determination of personal taxation.[12] The principle of vertical equity imposes criteria of comparable loss for people with different incomes or sources of incomes, or for people who differ, for example, according to gender or the number of children they have or whether they are married or living as a part of the one household or living in separate households. The principles of horizontal and vertical equity thereby introduce considerations other than being in the majority or minority when majority voting determines taxation and redistribution.

Anticipation of future improvements

A low-income majority may not vote in favor of extensive income redistribution if because of high social mobility future improvement is anticipated in the positions of low-income or poorer persons. Prospects of future gain through social mobility lead people to wait for their personal fortunes to improve rather than vote to redistribute income from others. The patience is reflected in low discount rates and is based on not wanting to set a precedent for high taxation of high incomes because of the prospect of personally having high income in the future.

---

[10] The only reason people would work or exert effort is that satisfaction from work exceeds the value of free time.

[11] That is, from the median voter's perspective, the preferred rate of taxation takes into account the decline in the pre-tax average income y^a when the tax rate t increases.

[12] For example, extraneous criteria for taxation are race, ethnicity, or beliefs.

Nonetheless, if optimistic expectations are disappointed, people can become impatient and intolerant of inequality. Albert Hirschman (1973) used the analogy of people waiting in two lanes of stalled traffic to describe the disappointment due to lack of realization of optimistic expectations. When the traffic in one lane, but not the other, begins to move, the first reaction of the people in the lane that remains blocked is optimism. The traffic moving in the other lane is interpreted as a sign that the blocked lane will also soon begin to move. People in the blocked lane are therefore patient and do not attempt to force their way into the other lane where the traffic is moving. When, after some time has passed, the blocked lane is still not moving, feelings of people in the blocked lane change from optimism to envy, and they begin to force their way into the moving lane. Applied to attitudes toward income redistribution, the implication is that low-income people do not vote to appropriate the incomes of better-off people, as long as they continue to have optimistic expectations about eventual improvements in their own incomes. However, the persistence of optimistic expectations requires confirmation that social mobility is taking place.

Realized high social mobility is therefore a means of avoiding the disincentives and excess burdens of high redistributive taxation that a low-income majority might otherwise seek. The expectation of future progress, substantiated by realization of high-income possibilities for initially lower-income people or families, restrains incentives to vote for extensive present redistribution. How great do the prospects of social mobility, however, need to be to provide a basis for reasonable expectations of future improvement for the population with below-average income? Moreover, is the requisite social mobility that would make the present low-income majority beneficiaries of low taxation and redistribution in the future feasible? Everybody cannot move up in the income distribution at the same time. How then can future change be anticipated that gives members of a present low-income majority reasonable expectations that they will lose from high taxes and extensive redistribution in the future?

The anticipations about the future include expectations about the shape of the future income distribution. The present low-income majority may expect social mobility to reduce future incomes of present high-income earners and increase future incomes of present low-income earners. This change is equalizing and affects the likelihood that people who have below-average pre-tax incomes today will have above-average pre-tax incomes in the future. That is, the distribution of income in Figure 6.1 may be expected to become less dispersed without changing the average. Alternatively, people who are below the average in the income distribution today can be above the average in the future without necessarily moving in the income distribution, if the future average falls.[13] With such expectations, extensive income redistribution through majority voting will not take place.

---

[13] For an exposition of circumstances where anticipations of future change in the income distribution affect present incentives to support policies of high distribution, see Benabou and Ok (2001).

Present low-income voters may in particular be disinclined to vote for high taxation and extensive redistribution, if immigration is expected to change the future distribution of income. The new immigrants may on average be less skilled than the preexisting local population and so may take the lower-income jobs in the society. Or the immigrants may take the lower-income jobs because of initial language limitations, or because they lack the social networks and connections that may be required for some high-income jobs. The preexisting population may also upgrade its skills because of immigration. The preexisting population is then pushed up in the income distribution.[14] Low-income voters may also be disinclined to vote for high taxation and extensive income redistribution if redistributional income transfers attract low-income immigrants. After being pushed up in the income distribution by immigration, present low-income voters may be called upon to finance through taxes the income transfers to the immigrants who will have been attracted by the redistribution policy.

6.1.5 The right to vote

The right to vote in a population determines the composition of majority and minority voting coalitions. Richer people are protected from redistribution through majority voting if poorer people do not have the right to vote, or do not register to vote. It is also important who votes. Often people with lower incomes and less wealth appear to be less likely to vote than higher-income, wealthier, people.

Historically, when democracy was first introduced, the right to vote was based on ownership of property. The owners of property were concerned that the more numerous poor would vote to appropriate their property. Over time, the franchise was extended to all men, and then to women. The age at which the right to vote was given was also in time reduced (in general from 21 to 18).

6.1.6 Voting and gender

Women have tended to vote more so than men in favor of higher government spending. Increases in publicly financed income transfers are also correlated with extensions of the voting franchise to women.[15]

An explanation for this voting behavior is that women have been more vulnerable than men to adverse personal circumstances. In the traditional model of the family where the man earns the family income and the woman stays home and raises the children, the woman can become destitute if the man dies or leaves her. In the event of divorce, the woman might not be able to secure an adequate claim to the man's future income, or the man might renege on his obligations to pay alimony and support his children. Within the traditional family, the social insurance contract offered by government was therefore more important to women than to men.

---

[14] For a description of such circumstances, see Fuest and Thum (2001).
[15] See Lott and Kenny (1999).

When the traditional model of the family no longer applies, marriage and commitments by men are not prerequisites for women having children. Some single mothers may nonetheless require income support from government to support their children, in which case it is in the self-interest of single mothers to vote for political candidates who support larger publicly financed income transfers.

The greater vulnerability to income uncertainty that has systematically confronted women rather than men has therefore led women to tend to vote for greater income redistribution. The income vulnerability of women is also related to the proportion of men and women of marriageable age in the population. Usually the number of male children born is marginally more than the number of female children. Circumstances can, however, lead to substantial male-female imbalances. For example, in the American west in the nineteenth century, and particularly during the times of the gold rushes, there were substantially more men than women in the population. The response was that women were given great respect,[16] or placed "on a pedestal" by men. Although the fight for women's suffrage was fought in the eastern states, western states were the first to give women the right to vote.

When women have been in the minority, or with the ratio between men and women more or less balanced and with relationships and commitments defined within the traditional family, men have in general accepted responsibility for the support of their families. The need for publicly financed income redistribution to mothers with dependent children has then been limited. When men are in the minority, the situation can change. Because of the gender imbalance, not all women who seek stable partners for a traditional family with children can then find men willing to enter into long-term commitments. Depending on norms of behavior, available men may take advantage of the imbalance to forgo stable relationships and rather may have short-term relationships with many women. Women in turn are prepared to have these short-term relationships if only because of the lack of stable longer-lasting alternatives. If the women wish to have children, they therefore may have to do so without the commitment of support from the father (or fathers) of their children. The women who find themselves in these circumstances therefore have an incentive to vote for taxation and income redistribution that gives to government the responsibility of "father of last resort."[17]

Educational attainment also affects marriage opportunities for women. Highly educated women are in general reluctant to choose less-educated men as partners,

---

[16] It might be more precise to say that those women who were deemed to deserve respect according to the social norms of the time were given great respect.

[17] Gender imbalance has in particular affected African-Americans in the United States. Throughout the twentieth century, women in general outnumbered men: in 1970 the imbalance was two young women for every young male. The sustained gender imbalance, in particular in the latter decades of the twentieth century, has been attributed to a disproportionate number of young males in the armed services and also in prison and to a higher death rate for young males for different reasons including street violence, drug overdoses, and alcohol. For more information, see Wilson (2002).

whereas educated men do not necessarily have the same reluctance to choose less-educated women provided that the women have other attributes that the men find attractive or desirable. An imbalance can therefore arise where there are fewer unattached educated men than unattached educated women. In these circumstances, the educated woman does not in general need the government as father of last resort because of the woman's earning capabilities. Educated women are therefore less inclined to vote for extensive taxation and income redistribution.[18]

6.1.7 Intergenerational income redistribution

We saw in Chapter 2 that government borrowing can have intergenerational effects on income distribution. When public spending on public goods is financed through government borrowing, the costs extend over generations. When the benefits over time precisely match the burden of taxation on each generation, no intergenerational income redistribution takes place. If a present generation were, on the other hand, to vote to finance a highway system or a bridge using present taxes, income from the present generation would be redistributed to future generations.

A present generation might also vote to finance all of a public project by government through sale of government bonds, thereby imposing the entire burden of financing the public project on future generations. Future generations then inherit the obligation to repay both the government borrowing and interest payments, which are spread over time. A situation can then arise where a large part of the taxes paid by a generation of taxpayers is used to repay government loans and interest because past generations voted to finance past public spending through the sale of government bonds. A present generation has a ready majority to determine the form of financing of public spending (through taxation on the present generation or through bond financing), if the future taxpayers who will finance the bond and interest repayments are not yet born or are too young to have the right to vote.[19]

Voting can also take place on intergenerational redistribution that transfers income from younger generations, who are working and earning income, to older generations who have retired and cease to earn income. A present young generation can vote to receive tax-financed income transfers in the future and can specify the size of the future transfers that it will receive. When this generation retires, the generations that are still working find themselves paying taxes to honor the commitments for social security or pensions made in the past. The commitments were made by the now retired beneficiaries of the intergenerational income transfers, on their own behalf. Again, when the vote took place, the people due to pay

---

[18] We have observed that education and income tend to affect inclinations to register to vote, and then actually vote. More-educated women have correspondingly had a greater likelihood of registering and voting than less-educated women.

[19] The objective of balanced budget proposals is to restrain the ability of a present generation to vote to use bond financing to impose taxes on future generations.

the taxes that finance the future intergenerational transfers were not born or were too young to vote, so that the generation voting for future benefits for itself had a ready majority.[20]

6.1.8 Constitutional restraint

A society may want to limit the redistribution that can be decided by voting. The limitations can be specified in a constitution. The constitution may designate that, for particular issues, more support than 51 percent is required (including for changes in the constitution itself), and, for some issues, such as adherence to principles that protect basic rights to property and life, a majority is allowed to change nothing. As an alternative to a written constitution, conventions may be encoded in law based on past precedent, with the law limiting the changes that can take place by majority voting. Such constitutional or legal restraint formalizes the inhibitions that we previously considered on the use of voting to appropriate property or income.

Constitutional restraint on intergenerational redistribution can be applied through limitations on the size of the deficit in the government budget. A government has a budget deficit when government borrowing is used to finance benefits for a present generation at the expense of future generations.[21] Restrictions on allowable deficit financing limit the intergenerational redistribution that can take place. Another form of limitation on intergenerational redistribution is a maximal permissible ratio between accumulated government debt and the size of a country's national income.

6.1.9 Other majorities

A majority of 51 percent can be formed from different parts of an income distribution. The majority can take the form that we have thus far described and consist of all people with income below the median income y^m in Figure 6.1 plus the voter with the median income. A majority of 51 percent can also be made up of all persons with income above y^m and the voter with the median income. This majority could gain by voting to distribute income from the 49 percent of low-income voters to the 51 percent of high-income voters. The same 51 percent majority might vote simply not to tax the high-income population for the benefit of the low-income population.

The median voter is better off joining the low-income population to form a majority that votes to tax the high-income population – unless the high-income population could pay the median voter to join them. If the decision of the median

---

[20] We shall return to issues of income redistribution between young and old in Chapter 10, where we shall consider social security and old-age pensions.

[21] The deficit in a government budget is the amount by which current government expenditures exceed current tax receipts. The difference, or deficit, can be financed by the sale of bonds, to be repaid along with interest by future taxation (or by future borrowing).

voter whether to join the low- or high-income population is made according to who offers the largest payment, the high-income population has an advantage. Rather than the median voter, we might refer to the middle class. That is, the high-income population might pay the middle class to join it to make a 51 percent majority that does not distribute to the poor.

The voters making up the middle 51 percent of the income distribution (including the median voter) could also form a coalition against the poor and the rich in the tails of the income distribution.

A majority might also be formed without the voter with the median income, or without the middle class. The high-income population might form a majority of 51 percent by joining with the low-income population against the middle. This coalition is advantageous for the high-income population, which then redistributes income to the poor and not to the middle class. The 30 percent of voters with highest incomes might, for example, vote for income redistribution targeted to the 21 percent of voters with lowest incomes. The income redistribution is financed by the taxes paid by the 30 percent of voters with the highest incomes, together with taxes paid by the middle 49 percent of the population who are outside the majority coalition. The income transfers to the lowest 21 percent of the population are then financed by the taxes of 79 percent of the population. This outcome is preferred by both the low-income 21 percent and the high-income 30 percent to the alternative majority division based on the median voter and all voters with less than median income. Through the coalition formed at the two tails of the income distribution, the 21 percent lowest-income population can receive more, and the 30 percent highest-income population can pay less. That is, the coalition with low-income voters allows the high-income voters to preempt a majority vote that would have them transfer income to the 51 percent of the population with lowest incomes.[22]

6.1.10 Income redistribution in democratic societies

We shall now look at the evidence regarding who gains from income redistribution in democratic societies.[23] To determine the income redistribution that takes place in a society, we need to know the initial pre-tax market-determined income distribution, as shown by our example of the income distribution in Figure 6.1. We have noted that this initial income distribution is not exogenous (i.e., not independently determined) but rather depends on the level of taxes and the response of income earners to taxation. When the initial pre-tax income distribution as in Figure 6.1 is known, this distribution can be compared with the post-tax income redistribution outcome to see how income has been redistributed through taxation.

---

[22] A preemptive view of coalitions for income redistribution is provided by Friedrich Breyer and Heinrich Ursprung (1998).

[23] We ask this question recognizing that voting is in general delegated to elected representatives.

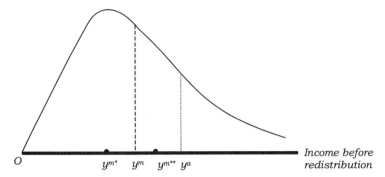

Figure 6.2. Voter participation and the median voter.

The results of such pre- and post-taxation comparisons reveal that, in democratic societies, income redistribution is more extensive when the initial inequality in market-determined incomes is greater. The person with the median income in the income distribution moreover tends consistently *not* to be a beneficiary of publicly financed income transfers.[24]

Voter participation

Voter participation affects the outcome of majority voting. Let us consider voting coalitions around either side of the median voter, when the median voter is in a coalition with lower-income voters.

The person with the median income in a population is the median voter only if everybody votes. Everyone may, however, not vote.

Voter participation could be the explanation for failure of the person with median income to benefit from redistribution, if higher-income people systematically participated less in voting than lower-income people. The participating median voter would then have less income than the person with the actual median income in the population. In Figure 6.2, the participating median voter would, for example, have an income of y^{m^*}, which is less than the median income y^m. Because only voters with incomes of y^{m^*} and less gain from redistribution determined by majority voting, the person with median income y^m would not gain, which would be consistent with the evidence on income redistribution.

Lower-income people are, however, in general less inclined to vote than higher-income people. In that case, in Figure 6.2, the income of the participating median voter $y^{m^{**}}$ is above the median income y^m in the population. Majority voting that benefits the participating median voter with income $y^{m^{**}}$ then also benefits the person with actual median income y^m.

---

[24] Branko Milanovic (2000) of the World Bank measured government income transfers in twenty-four democratic societies and found these results.

Alternative hypotheses about income redistribution

Since the evidence is that the person with median income does *not* benefit from income redistribution, voter participation in coalitions based on either side of a participating median voter cannot be the reason why persons around the median income in democratic societies do not gain from income redistribution. It does not appear therefore that median voters form majority coalitions based on pre-tax distributions of income and that self-interested majority voting is used to redistribute income to the median voter and to voters with pre-tax incomes less than the median voter.[25]

We can accordingly set aside voter participation as the reason why median voters do not gain from income redistribution.

We have alternative hypotheses about why the median voter does not benefit from income redistribution:

(1) Income redistribution can reflect a social insurance contract whereby society maximizes social welfare (the social welfare function is chosen behind a veil of ignorance) and, in the realization of the social-insurance contract, the poorer parts of the population receive income transfers financed by taxes paid by richer parts of the society.

(2) High-income voters have formed a coalition with low-income voters who benefit from publicly financed income transfers.

The evidence that median voters in democratic societies do not benefit from publicly financed income transfers is consistent with both hypotheses. That is, entitlements to income transfers to low-income persons are consistent with a social insurance contract, or, alternatively, the same entitlements to low-income persons can indicate a preemptive coalition by higher-income voters with low-income persons.

The median voter and public spending

Median voters do not benefit from publicly financed income transfers, but median voters (or the middle class) do appear to benefit disproportionately and systematically from public spending on goods or services.[26] For example:

(1) Wealthier people often tend to send their children to private schools and private universities, while the children of middle-income people are more likely to attend publicly financed schools and universities. If few children of poorer families attend college or university, government subsidies to higher education disproportionately benefit the middle class.

---

[25] In the case where majority voting determines a common tax rate for all incomes, we saw that the beneficiaries of the outcome of majority voting included voters with incomes greater than the median and less than the mean.

[26] This empirical regularity is known as Director's law of public income distribution. See Stigler (1970).

(2) Middle-income people benefit disproportionately from publicly financed police and security services. Poor people may have little property to defend, and very wealthy people often have their own private security guards.

(3) People who travel more benefit more from highways and airports. Poorer people tend to travel less. People who travel more also benefit from embassies and consulates in foreign locations. The people who travel are, for example, the ones who might need to have their passports renewed, or replaced if lost.

(4) Public housing provides housing for low-income people. Wealthy people might want and can afford housing locations that provide privacy. Middle-income people benefit from public housing for low-income people because lower-income people have a place to live and do not have to live on the streets or in neighborhood parks.[27]

Public spending on public goods and services therefore tends disproportionately to benefit the middle-income population. This pattern of evidence is consistent with public spending on public goods determined by majority voting for the benefit of the median voter as described in Chapter 3.

6.1.11 Different policies

We have viewed voters as self-interestedly choosing taxation and redistribution to maximize their own utility, and we have seen that self-interest can constrain a majority from imposing appropriative taxes on a minority. A majority of voters could, however, view equality as a supreme value for society that should not be compromised. Efficiency losses through effects on incentives to work and be productive would then not deter the majority from voting for appropriative taxation to achieve post-redistribution equality.[28] There are few instances where a majority of voters has voted in favor of income equality as a supreme value.[29] Rather, the inhibitions that restrain appropriative outcomes of majority voting have in general prevailed.

There are nonetheless different views that can be taken regarding restraint on redistribution. When the majority of voters is conservative, policies place a high value on protection of rights to property and the right to retain substantial personal income for personal spending, and modest redistribution is favored. If a majority emphasizes social equality, policies are observed where taxes are high and high government spending redistributes income. These are, broadly speaking,

---

[27] Public housing has, however, often become a problem rather than the source of a solution. The areas where public housing are located may not provide role models of people who have succeeded through education and social mobility.

[28] The outcome would then be the same as we observed in Chapter 5 when a social welfare function is defined according to Rawls. There would be complete equality after redistribution without regard for the incentive effects of taxation (i.e., without regard for the excess burden of taxation), and without regard for moral hazard.

[29] The exceptions have been in some states of India.

the views of the right and the left on the political spectrum. Voters on the right are conservative about redistribution, and voters on the left are less so.

6.1.12 Conclusions

Voting on redistribution of income and wealth introduces normative and positive questions. The normative question is whether a majority should be allowed to exercise its will for personal benefit at the expense of a minority. The positive question involves explaining the redistribution that is observed to take place through majority voting.

The normative question is about private property rights. Included in the conception of property are the incomes that people earn. Income earned in the last day or week or month belongs as much in principle to a person as past income that has been saved and invested and constitutes property.

Societies have made the normative judgment that property rights to past income that has been transformed to become personal wealth or property are more inviolate and more protected than property rights to presently earned personal income. This normative judgment, which is reflected in extensive taxation of income and more limited taxation of wealth and property, restrains the redistribution that a majority can impose on a minority.

In principle, however, majority voting can be used to redistribute income (and wealth) to benefit a majority of voters at the expense of the minority. The example of public finance of the maintenance of the roads showed how a majority could vote themselves publicly financed private benefits with no ethical foundation for the redistribution, which was arbitrarily based on having a majority. We have noted, however, stability problems of majority-voting coalitions.

We investigated the outcome of majority voting when public policy is required to be non-discriminatory in that the same rate of taxation applies to all incomes and the tax revenue is redistributed equally among the population. We saw that, in this case, with no incentive effects of taxation, majority voting results in appropriative taxation and equal post-tax incomes. Incentive effects of taxation, however, compromise the interest of the majority, or the median voter, in choosing post-tax equality. Because of incentive effects, a society that allowed the majority to appropriate the wealth of the minority or to impose appropriative income taxes for redistribution would be poor because there would be no reason for people to be productive. Social mobility also limits the self-interest of low-income present-day voters to support high taxation and extensive redistribution.

Allowing a majority to vote to appropriate the income or wealth of the minority would be like anarchy, in that rights of ownership would not be protected. Under anarchy, people can take defensive measures to protect themselves from appropriation. There is no protection for the minority when majority voting is the means of appropriation. A vote takes place, and if the majority defines legality and illegality, the minority has a legal obligation to abide by the vote of the majority.

Considerations other than having a majority should therefore bind upon redistribution. Principles of fair taxation through horizontal and vertical equity constrain the scope of redistribution through majority voting.

We have observed that voting coalitions need not be based on a majority of lower-income voters. The rich may preemptively redistribute income to allow them to form a coalition that protects their incomes from greater taxation or their wealth from appropriation.

Gender appears to affect voting on income redistribution. Women traditionally have preferred more income redistribution through government than men.

Voting also affects intergenerational income distribution. Present generations can vote to provide themselves with favorable income redistribution through intergenerational transfers, by voting for bond financing for public projects so as to place the burden of financing on future generations, by voting for bond financing of their own present consumption, or by voting for intergenerational income transfers that provide them with future consumption. In these cases, the problems of majority voting can be compounded by the absence, when voting takes place, of the generations who will be called upon to pay the future taxes.

A society may wish to impose constitutional or legal restraint on redistribution by voting. The restraint can affect redistribution within the same generation, but may more particularly be directed at limiting possibilities for redistribution between generations.

We have noted that the evidence supports the conclusion that publicly financed income transfers in democratic societies are not consistent with self-interested benefits to a majority that includes the voter with median income. Publicly financed income transfers therefore reflect an implicit social insurance that provides assistance to poorer people or a coalition between higher-income voters and poorer voters. On the other hand, public spending on public goods and services appears disproportionately to benefit median or middle-income voters, which is consistent with self-interested majority voting on public spending.

References and related literature

On redistribution through voting, see Tullock (1959), Roberts (1977), Meltzer and Richard (1981), Bowles and Jones (1991), Buchanan and Yoon (1995), Husted and Kenny (1997), Breyer and Ursprung (1998), and Roemer (1998). On the limits to redistribution, see Harms and Zink (2003). On the tendency for the likelihood of voting to increase with income, see Greene and Nikolaev (1999). On issues of stability of voting coalitions, see Tullock (1981). On social mobility and voting on income redistribution, see Benabou and Oks (2001). On how migration and income distribution, see Fuest and Thum (2001) and Hansen (2003). On the distribution of benefits from public spending and the median voter, see Stigler (1970). On gender and voting, see Abrams and Settle (1999), Lott and Kenny (1999). On gender imbalances, see Wilson (2002). Our evidence on income redistribution and the median voter came from Milanovic (2000).

Abrams, B. A. and R. F. Settle, 1999. Women's suffrage and the growth of the welfare state. *Public Choice* 100, 289–300.

Benabou, R. and E. A. Ok, 2001. Social mobility and the demand for redistribution: The POUM (prospect of upward mobility) hypothesis. *Quarterly Journal of Economics* 116, 447–87.

Bowles, R. and P. Jones, 1991. Political participation and the limits to redistribution. *European Journal of Political Economy* 7, 127–39.

Breyer, F. and H. W. Ursprung, 1998. Are the rich too rich to be appropriated? Economic power and the feasibility of constitutional limits to redistribution. *Public Choice* 94, 135–56.

Buchanan, J. M. and Y. J. Yoon, 1995. Rational majoritarian taxation of the rich: With increasing returns and capital accumulation. *Southern Economic Journal* 61, 923–35.

Fuest, C. and M. Thum, 2001. Immigration and skill formation in unionized markets. *European Journal of Political Economy* 17, 557–73.

Greene, K. V. and O. Nikolaev, 1999. Voter participation in the redistributive state. *Public Choice* 98, 213–26.

Hansen, J. D., 2003. Immigration and income redistribution in welfare states. *European Journal of Political Economy* 19.

Harms, P. and S. Zink, 2003. Limits to redistribution: A survey. *European Journal of Political Economy* 19.

Hirschman, A. O., 1973. The changing tolerance for income inequality in the course of economic development. *Quarterly Journal of Economics* 87, 544–66.

Husted T. A. and L. W. Kenny, 1997. The effect of the expansion of the franchise on the size of government. *Journal of Political Economy* 105, 54–82.

Lott, J. R. and L. W. Kenny, 1999. Did women's suffrage change the size and scope of government? *Journal of Political Economy* 107, 1163–98.

Meltzer, A. H. and S. F. Richard, 1981. A rational theory of the size of government. *Journal of Political Economy* 89, 914–27.

Milanovic, B., 2000. The median-voter hypothesis, income inequality, and income distribution: An empirical test with the required data. *European Journal of Political Economy*, 16, 367–410.

Mueller, D., 2003. Interest groups, redistribution and the size of government. In *Political Economy and Public Finance*, S. L. Winer and H. Shibata (eds.). Edward Elgar, Cheltenham, U.K., 123–44.

Roberts, K., 1977. Voting over income tax schedules. *Journal of Public Economics* 7, 127–33.

Roemer, J. E., 1998. Why the poor do not appropriate the rich: An old argument in new garb. *Journal of Public Economics* 70, 399–424.

Stigler, G., 1970. Director's Law of public income distribution. *Journal of Law and Economics* 13, 1–10.

Tullock, G., 1959. Problems of majority voting. *Journal of Political Economy* 67, 571–9. Reprinted 1969 in *Readings in Welfare Economics*, K. J. Arrow and T. Scitovsky (eds.). Richard D. Irwin, Homewood, Illinois, 169–78.

Tullock, G., 1981. Why so much stability? *Public Choice* 37, 189–202.

Wilson, J. Q., 2002. *The Marriage Problem: How Our Culture Has Weakened Families*. HarperCollins, New York.

Questions for discussion

1. What are the major differences between transfer of property and income through majority voting and the appropriation of property and income by force under anarchy, which we studied in Chapter 1?

2. What general conclusions about majority voting and public finance emerge from the example of voting on the financing of the maintenance of the roads?

3. It is sometimes proposed that, when voting takes place to determine the size of income transfers to redistribute income, only people whose taxes will finance the income transfers should have the right to vote, while people benefiting from the income transfers should not have the right to vote (for such a proposal, see Dennis Mueller, 2003). Do you agree with such a restriction on the right to vote on issues of income redistribution? Explain.

4. Why does the poor majority in general not vote to appropriate the *wealth* of the richer minority? Why do societies in general tax income rather than personal wealth?

5. Show that, when the vote is on the rate of income taxation, and all tax revenue is to be equally redistributed, and there are no efficiency losses from taxation (there are no incentive effects of taxation and so no excess burden), the median voter will maximize utility by choosing appropriative taxation. How large will the majority in favor of appropriative taxation actually be?

6. How do incentive effects of taxation change the self-interested outcome of majority voting on taxation and income redistribution?

7. What are the principles of horizontal and vertical equity, and how do these principles affect the outcome of majority voting? How would application of one or the other of these principles affect the outcome of majority voting on the maintenance of the roads?

8. How does social mobility affect incentives to vote for income redistribution?

9. How can majority coalitions on voting for income redistribution form without the inclusion of the voter who has the median income in the population? Which particular coalition is suggested by the presence of tax-financed entitlements for the poor?

10. Historically the right to vote when democracy was introduced was often based on ownership of property, and then the franchise was expanded. How would you explain the initial focus on property ownership and the subsequent extension of the franchise to one-person one-vote?

11. In past elections where you study or live, has there been a discernible gender bias in voting for and against political candidates who have favored greater taxation and income redistribution? How can gender differences in voting on income distribution be explained?

12. How can majority voting affect intergenerational income redistribution? What are the special characteristics of voting coalitions in the case of intergenerational income distribution? Are there economic or ethical justifications for intergenerational income transfers determined by majority voting?

13. What is the basis for a case for constitutional constraints on redistribution through voting? Should constitutional constraints be placed on how much a government can borrow?

14. What are the conclusions from the evidence in democratic societies about benefits to median voters from majority voting? What reasons would you propose for the conclusions provided by the evidence? Why do outcomes of majority voting appear to differ for income transfers and benefits from public goods and services?

15. Issues concerning voting and redistribution raise normative and positive questions. What are the different types of questions? Are the normative and positive questions related?

16. Right and left, or conservatives and liberals (using the U.S. definition, see footnote 38, page 350), vote differently on the extent of redistribution that should take place. Can we judge the different positions in terms of which view is correct? Explain.

6.2

Political Behavior and Public Policy

In this section, we consider the principal-agent problem that can arise between voters and political decision makers and examine how the principal-agent problem affects public policy.

6.2.1 The public interest and special interests

A principal-agent problem between voters and political representatives is present if the personal objectives of political decision makers differ from the public policies sought by voters. The personal interest of politicians is to win elections. There is no point in being a politician who does not win elections. By definition, a politician has to win elections. Otherwise he or she is an 'unemployed politician,' which may not be a politician at all. To win elections, politicians require both support from voters and money. The money is needed to finance the expenses of political campaigns. There are telephone bills and mail expenses to be paid. Staffers have to be paid (unless they volunteer, but volunteers still must be fed and provided with accommodation on the campaign trail). Political advertising must be financed. Money also must be available for opinion polls to evaluate the effectiveness of the political campaign. If journalists and reporters accompany the candidate on the campaign trail, the candidate may need money to pay for transportation of the accompanying entourage who provide valuable press coverage. Money may also be required for meals and other personal expenses of the entourage of journalists and reporters. The personal interest of the politician is to have enough money to pay these expenses. The need for money can lead political candidates to accept campaign contributions from special interest groups who seek public policies that are not in the public interest.

What is the public interest?

How is the "public interest" to be defined? A definition of the public interest is not straightforward because individuals have different personal interests. We could ask a population to vote on determining the public interest. Under a majority-voting rule, there are majority interests and minority interests. The outcome of majority voting reflects the median voter's interest, but the interest of the median voter may not be a good proxy for the public interest because all voters other than the median voter may prefer other outcomes.[1] The public interest can be unambiguously defined when there is consensus among voters. Consensus for collective decisions about spending on public goods is provided through the

---

[1] We have also observed that decisions made by majority voting need not result in public spending that is efficient in satisfying cost-benefit valuation (Chapter 3), and majority voting does not assure distributional outcomes that are socially just (Section 6.1).

Lindahl solution, but informational problems stand in the way of implementing this solution.[2]

We can also attempt to define the public interest through the idea of a social welfare function.[3] The choice of the social welfare function that defines the public interest would have to be made by consensus. Otherwise, if the decision were by majority voting, the decision would again reflect the majority interest or the median voter's interest, and not the public interest. The basis for consensus about a social welfare function is choice behind a veil of ignorance, before people know who they are going to be in life. After people know who they are, there can be disagreements about choice of the social welfare function because of the different income redistribution implied by different choices.[4]

Although there are difficulties in defining the public interest (as opposed to the majority's interest), we nonetheless need a definition of the public interest because we want to be able to compare the public interest with the self-interest of political decision makers. We can approach an understanding of the public interest by considering what is *not* in the public interest. It is *not* in the public interest for political decision makers to provide discriminatory special benefits for groups in society that have no moral or ethical case for benefit through public policy, and when at the same time (as is usually the case) the policies that benefit the interest group impose losses on society-at-large.[5]

Objectives of interest groups

Interest groups in general have narrow self-interested objectives. An interest group could nonetheless have broad social objectives. For example, an interest group might want public finance for medical research into diseases that affect populations too small to warrant commercial development of cures, or an interest group may want government to direct more attention to environmental problems. The objectives of interest groups in these cases have social merit and also are uncontroversial.

In other cases, interest groups may be seeking social objectives, but the objectives can be controversial. For example, a pro-gun lobby of voters (in tandem with the weapons manufacturing industry) might wish to protect the right of individuals to buy and own arms, on the grounds that weapons allow citizens to defend

---

[2] We noted these problems in Chapter 2 when looking for ways to finance public goods efficiently.

[3] We investigated socially just income redistribution based on the idea of a social contract to provide social insurance in Chapter 5 and saw how redistribution differs according to the social welfare function that is chosen.

[4] In Chapter 5, we identified such disagreement about redistribution after people know who they are with adverse selection. That is, when people know that they will most likely be taxed to provide income transfers to others, they may want to withdraw from the insurance pool, which however they entered voluntarily (although implicitly) before they were born, or before they had information about their prospects in life.

[5] We would have no objection to politically provided special-interest benefits, if the Pareto criterion is satisfied that members of a special-interest group are made better off when no one in the population is made worse off. In general, however, special interests are made better off at the expense of others in society – or at the expense of the public interest.

themselves when confronting people who wish to harm them. Other people may be concerned about the effects of access to guns on public safety.

Abortion (or the right of a woman to choose whether to complete the full term of a pregnancy) is a social issue on which people take different positions. The public-policy question can be whether to provide public finance for clinics that offer information about how to terminate unwanted pregnancies, or alternatively whether to fund centers that offer contraception advice or provide prenatal care and offer assistance with adoption procedures.[6]

Interest groups with broad social objectives are not seeking narrowly based personal gains for themselves. Industry interests seeking to influence public policy do however generally have narrow objectives of personal gain. A narrowly based special-interest group might, for example, want to forestall legislation that would require an industry to invest in pollution abatement. A trucking industry may seek public investment in expanding highway networks. Industries might seek protection against foreign imports, or might seek favorable tax treatment or subsidies from government. Agricultural and logging interests may oppose national parks and flora and fauna preservation policies. Tobacco companies might wish to preempt or repeal legislation that prohibits smoking in public places. Pharmaceutical companies might seek extended terms for patents on medicines and drugs or try to influence the government agency that grants permission for marketing of new drugs (the Food and Drug Administration in the United States) not to approve new medications that would compete with their own products. A firm supplying chickens for market might seek lax standards from a government regulatory agency for the conditions under which the chickens are kept while being fed and grown. A financial investment firm that has made inopportune bets in financial markets might seek a bailout financed by public money. A country's mortgage banking industry (savings and loans in the United States) might seek public money to prevent financial collapse. The continued list of such benefits that special interests can seek from political decision makers is long. The general principle is that narrow benefits are sought at the expense of the broad public interest.

Special interests need not be in the private sector. A teachers' union might, for example, object to proposals that would open a government school system to competition by giving parents vouchers that can be used for choosing among alternative schools for their children's education. Or employees in government bureaucracies can have a private interest in seeking large government budgets (that require corresponding high taxation).[7]

Collective action

Interest groups, whatever their objective might be, are engaged in collective action and are therefore subject to free-riding behavior in contributions by group

---

[6] Compromise on this issue can only come in terms of exceptional circumstances that people are prepared to allow to influence their positions.

[7] We considered self-interest in government bureaucracies in chapter 3.

members to achieving the group's objectives.[8] Interest groups with broadly defined social objectives can usually offer political support for political candidates
through votes, although sometimes money is given as well.[9] Narrowly based interest groups that are too small for their votes to matter can only offer money or
personal favors. In either case, whether an interest group offers votes or money
and personal favors, political effectiveness of the interest group depends on its
ability to overcome the free-riding problems that are present because of the public-
good benefit for all members of the group from achieving the group's objective.

Political decisions as the source of rents

The term "rents" can be used to describe benefits for a narrow special-interest
group from political decisions.[10] The incentive to obtain and protect rents by
influencing public policy is known as rent seeking. The term "rent seekers" is
applied to people who seek (or are looking for) rents. Rents can be provided as
a gift within the family.[11] A good friend might also provide rents. Beyond family
and friends, rents are most prominently provided by political favors.

An implicit contract

Special-interest groups seek rents from political favors and pay for the rents with
contributions of the money that politicians need to win elections. The politicians
who accept special-interest money enter into an implicit contract to provide the
special-interest benefits or rents.

Because the interests of the special-interest group in general differ from the
broad public interest, by accepting special-interest money, politicians compromise
the public interest. This compromise of the public interest underlies the existence
of a principal-agent problem between political decision makers and voters.

---

[8] Voluntary contributors to public goods have a self-interest component because the people making
the voluntary contributions benefit themselves, as well as others. For example, an interest group
seeking increased public finance for medical research into diseases that afflict small parts of a
population may also be seeking something for themselves (they or their relatives or friends may
have the disease, or have a high likelihood of being inflicted because of genetic disposition). At
the same time, the interest group is trying to expand the scope of society's implicit social-insurance
contract. Anyone who has the disease, or who faces the risk of having the disease, benefits if the
activities of the interest group are successful.

[9] In the late 1990s, for example, in the United Kingdom, an interest group made up of animal lovers
gave money to politicians to win support for a ban on fox hunting with hounds.

[10] We previously encountered rents as due to monopoly, in particularly the monopoly of a government bureaucracy in Chapter 3. Another source of rents is income from industry-specific capital.
Such capital cannot be redirected to alternative uses outside of its industry. Incomes earned from
industry-specific capital are therefore rents because of the lack of an alternative means for the
capital to earn a return. Because rents that people receive from ownership of industry-specific
capital or from their skills and knowledge specific to an industry are not replaceable in alternative employment, people are sensitive about their rents. Consequently, rents are guarded with
vigilance.

[11] A family provides rents when a son or daughter employed in a family business is paid more than
the income that he or she would receive in a job outside the family business.

6.2.2 Voters

A principal-agent problem can be solved if the principal (the voter) can design an incentive mechanism that leads the agent (the political representative) to internalize the interests of the principal perfectly when the agent makes his or her decisions. Voters face various problems in solving their principal-agent problem with political representatives.

The size of the group and collective action

When issues are decided by direct voting, it is advantageous to be in a large group because the number of votes matters. Under representative democracy, smaller groups can, however, be more effective politically than larger groups because of the superior ability of the smaller group to organize for collective action to influence public policy. The smaller group can be more effective in overcoming free-rider problems in raising money for political contributions. People in small groups cannot hide behind anonymity and are subject to peer pressure to contribute to the common objective. Under representative democracy, voters or the public at large can conversely be disadvantaged in being too large a group.[12]

Group size and the size of the stake

Overcoming free-rider problems is one source of advantage of small special-interest groups over voters in influencing public policy. A second source of advantage of special-interest groups over voters is the size of the stakes that group members have in the outcome of policy decisions. Members of special-interest groups tend to have large stakes in the outcome of political decisions because their personal incomes (or rents) are at stake. Individual taxpayers or voters face numerous special-interest groups and have small stakes in whether any one of the many interest groups succeeds in influencing public policy to obtain the outcome that it seeks. The stakes are small for voters because the public policy sought by any one special-interest group deprives voters of a small part of their incomes or adds a small part to the excess burden of taxation, or to voters' overall losses from political accommodation to special-interest public polices.

Because individual voters have many small stakes in many political decisions, whereas members of special-interest groups have large stakes in one political decision, special-interest groups are more focused in political action. The attention of individual voters in resisting special-interest groups is more dispersed and diffuse. The relative size of the stake, and the focus on the outcome of one particular public-policy decision, therefore gives the special-interest group a political advantage over voters in influencing public-policy decisions.

---

[12] Supplement 2B formally shows how the size of a group affects the group's total voluntary contributions to financing or achieving a collective objective.

Disciplining through elections

Voters can use elections to discipline politicians. Political incumbents can be re-placed in elections by political opponents.

A view of elections as a disciplining device for voters changes our previous perspective of the purpose of voting. Previously, in Chapter 3, we viewed voters as choosing between political candidates based on the policies that political candidates announce that they intend to implement if they are elected. We therefore viewed voters as being forward-looking in their evaluation of politicians because voters judged political candidates on the basis of future policies.

If elections are used to discipline politicians, voters take a retroactive or backward-looking view. Voters look back at the past performance of a politician seeking reelection and ask questions such as: Did the politician honor past election promises made to voters? Did the politician dutifully attend to constituents' needs when constituents faced problems with the government bureaucracy or with interpretations of policy or regulations? Did the politician cater to special interests? Was political office used for personal advantage by dispensing personal favors and receiving personal favors in return? Did the politician act in inopportune ways that exposed him or her to the possibility of blackmail? Does the politician have a pleasant demeanor that compensates for indiscretions? Answers to these questions determine whether voters support the incumbent for reelection.

Voting is, however, a disciplining mechanism that is available only every few years.[13]

Rational ignorance

Information about political behavior is often costly to acquire. The idea of rational ignorance, which we noted in Chapter 1, expresses the personal incentive to invest in acquiring only the information for which the personal benefit exceeds the cost. Because of rational ignorance, individual voters may not be well informed about the behavior of their elected representatives.

Free-riding in monitoring politicians

Monitoring political behavior is a public good because the benefits are freely available to the public-at-large. A free-rider problem is present if individuals rely on other taxpayers to take the time and make the effort to provide the public-good benefit of investigating political behavior and monitoring politicians.

Hidden political benefits

Public policies can purposefully hide political benefits that are provided to special interests. Voters' ignorance is then increased. For example, legislators can

---

[13] Impeachment is an additional disciplining device that allows politicians to be removed from office in mid term by other politicians, not by voters. Where impeachment procedures do not exist, public pressure can in some cases compel disgraced politicians to resign.

add a provision for special-interest benefit to legislation that has little or nothing to do with the special interests receiving the benefits. Terminology is also often changed.[14] Or, for example, instead of directly giving out public money to political beneficiaries, special tax concessions or depreciation allowances can be provided to an industry. The tax concessions or depreciation allowances can result in inefficient investment decisions, to take advantage of the special benefits provided through the tax code. These actions attract less voter attention than if the same special-interest benefits were to be provided through a direct income transfer financed through the government budget. Direct income transfers would appear as expenditure items in the government budget. Selective tax concessions or depreciation allowances are hidden in the copious pages of the tax laws.

The number of policy issues and the number of candidates

There are generally more policy questions than there are political candidates. Voters may therefore be unable to find a candidate who reflects their preferences on every policy question.[15] In elections, one or two issues generally become focal points for attention of voters. These become *the* issues for the choice between political candidates. The remaining issues introduce opportunities for exchanges between political decision makers and special-interest groups. The political candidate may need money, and providing money (not votes) is in particular the way that special-interest groups may hope to be able to influence political decisions.[16] Voters are therefore disadvantaged when seeking to counter special-interest groups by the relation between the number of political candidates and the number of policy questions.

The decision whether to vote

The likelihood of any one person's vote making a difference in an election is small when there are many thousands or millions of voters. One individual vote in general does not matter. Because the personal benefit from voting, measured as the likelihood of influencing the outcome of an election, can be expected to be less than the personal cost of taking the time to vote, the act of voting has been described as paradoxical or irrational.

The idea that voting is irrational is based on people having a positive value of time. If the value of time is positive, people should not be expected to use time in an activity (voting) that has zero anticipated benefit. Yet high-income people, whose time is presumably worth more than the time of low-income people, tend to

---

[14] Import taxes can, for example, become import tariffs or import duties (so in the latter case reminding taxpayers of their duty to pay). In Europe, some protective import taxes were named variable levies. Some protectionist instruments instigated and monitored by governments have been named voluntary export restraints.

[15] We also saw in Ostrogorski's paradox in Chapter 3 that a political representative elected by a majority vote can be against every proposal that would have majority support if voters could vote directly on each separate issue.

[16] If only votes mattered, special-interest groups would lose every time to the public interest.

vote in proportionately greater numbers than low-income people. Personal values, rather than a cost-benefit calculation, appear to explain why people vote. People vote because they have been educated to understand that it is their obligation to exercise their right to vote. Peer pressure also affects a person's decision to vote. Family, friends, and acquaintances may ask whether a person has been dutiful in voting. Voters may also see their vote as part of group identification. Voting may thus be participatory behavior of the sort that leads people to identify their personal well-being with the success of a sports team.

There are also strategic considerations. The number of people who vote depends upon the number of people who are expected to vote. In the limiting case, a person who believes that no one else is going to bother to vote has a strong incentive to vote. As a sole voter, he or she is assured of being decisive in determining the outcome. In a population of voters, therefore, if everybody believes that no one else will vote, perhaps everybody will vote, because of the greater perceived likelihood of being the decisive voter.

The disinclination of people to take the time to vote can be an impediment to voters' disciplining politicians. Interest groups provide money to political candidates, and voters counter with votes. Reluctance of voters to vote diminishes the source of political advantage of voters.

Term limits

Term limits are a way in which voters can hope to exercise discipline over politicians. Term limits set bounds on the time a politician can spend in office. The principle underlying term limits is that new political representatives often idealistically seek the public interest. That is, the Thomas-à-Beckett effect makes newly elected politicians sensitive to voter interests.[17] After some time in office, the Thomas-à-Beckett effect can wear off, as politicians' time in office provides more seniority and more influence over public spending and public policy, and as relationships develop with special interests. Term limits on political office are intended to ensure that the Thomas-à-Beckett effect does not have time to wear off and that relationships with special interests do not have time to develop.

The press

Voters are assisted in monitoring political representatives by an objectively informative press. In seeking to sell newspapers or offer attractive television viewing, the press focuses on people in the public eye, and can report indiscretions and opportunistic behavior of politicians. The rational ignorance of voters about political decision makers is thereby reduced.

The socially valuable task of providing information to the public is not performed when the press is subservient to a particular political viewpoint, or if the

---

[17] The idea underlying the Thomas-à-Beckett effect is that newly elected politicians will change from their self-interested behavior as private individuals to seek the public interest after achieving political office. We introduced the Thomas-à-Beckett effect in Chapter 3 when describing prospects for change in behavior of people beginning employment in government bureaucracy.

press has a predetermined prejudicial view of some politicians and some groups of citizens. A biased press lacks credibility among voters and, therefore, cannot perform the task of providing low-cost information that voters can rely upon to make informed voting decisions.

Special-interest groups benefit when selective reporting of a biased press exposes the political opportunism of one political party and not another. By not reporting the relationships between special-interest groups and the political party of its choice, a biased press facilitates special-interest influence over public policy.

Reporters are obliged to prepare "stories" that have short lives after publication in newspapers or appearance on television. One issue of a newspaper or one news-cast quickly follows the next. With the effort of preparing a story quickly buried in yesterday's newspaper and yesterday's newscast, journalists and reporters can become cynical about the worth of their reporting efforts. The accuracy of the in-formation that is presented can accordingly be compromised.[18] Depth of content is also compromised when information is measured in sound bits.

In principle, the press can help voters to overcome information problems, but there can also be problems with the press.[19]

Political spin

Politicians often need to be flexible in stating policy positions, if they are to be able to announce diverse public policies required to obtain campaign contributions from different special interests and also attract the support of voters at large. On some issues, politicians may have little policy flexibility. They take a position early in life by joining a political party, argue the case for the party, and rarely switch parties in the course of their political careers. While there are voters who might think through and evaluate policy positions, and then change their political sup-port based on candidates' positions, politicians tend to be more adamant in their policy positions. A problem facing a politician can therefore be how to reconcile this association with policy positions with the policy flexibility required to accom-modate special-interest policies. Credibility with voters can be lost when evidence points to a politician having abandoned principle to support special-interest poli-cies that are not in the public interest. With extensive rational ignorance by voters, admission of catering to special interests may be unnecessary self-confirmation of disregard for the public interest. Rather than relating to the evidence, the response to suggestions that a politician has exercised bad judgment or has accommodated special interests can be "spin."[20] When an unbiased press and a perceptive elec-torate can detect spin, voters can make more informed choices when candidates present themselves for reelection.

[18] There is perhaps nothing as dated as yesterday's newspaper or yesterday's newscast.

[19] The financial press in general provides more qualified, in-depth, and credible analysis. The infor-mation in these cases affects people's investment decisions and wealth.

[20] "Spin" is a term that describes deliberate intent to hide facts by creating confusion.

How resolving one principal-agent problem creates another

As noted in Chapter 1, a principal-agent problem arises between managers and shareholders in firms when managers' personal objectives are not consistent with maximization of shareholder value, and managerial stock options are an attempt to resolve this principal-agent problem. The right to purchase stock at preferential share prices in the future ties the future personal wealth of managers to future profits of the firm. The incentive for managerial performance benefits shareholders. Such stock option schemes, or close alternatives, are not available to solve the political principal-agent problem between voters and political decision makers.

A stock option scheme is designed to make managers' interests coincide with shareholders' interests in any one firm. The general population tends, on the other hand, to own diversified stock in a broad range of firms throughout the economy. The interest of the population of shareholders, as well as the public interest, is served by public policies that promote broad economy-wide efficiency. Stock options, however, give managers incentives to seek policies that increase the profits of their particular firm. Stock options and other management remuneration schemes might resolve the principal-agent problem between shareholders and managers. Nonetheless, at the same time, stock options lead management to become advocates of special-interest policy positions. Management is provided with incentives to contribute corporate and personal funds to political candidates in return for special-interest policies that increase the value of stock options (and the value of stock). Stock options therefore resolve one principal-agent problem, that between management and shareholders, but at the expense of creating another, between political decision makers and taxpayers.[21] For political decision makers may respond to the campaign contributions of management by making decisions that are not in the public interest.

6.2.3 Politicians

We now leave the principal-agent problem that voters confront to consider problems that politicians face.

Voter support and special-interest money

Well-wishers, family, and friends may provide a politician with money to finance an election contest "with no strings attached."[22] The politician may also have personal wealth that he or she is prepared to spend in winning election. If money from these personal sources is not enough to ensure electoral success, special-interest money may be the only way to finance an election campaign with a reasonable chance of electoral success.

We observed that political candidates in particular need money for political advertising. Political advertising may be substantive in communicating to voters a candidate's position on different issues. Political advertising can also be aimed

---

[21] The relation between these two principal-agent problems was pointed out by James Cassing (1996).

[22] The strings apparently refer to the strings attached to a puppet.

at ensuring voter recognition of the candidate's name or face. Without adequate political advertising, a candidate's electoral prospects are in general not good – and hence the compulsion of the political candidate for money.

Money spent on political advertising introduces an anomaly into the relation between voters and politicians. The principal-agent structure of representative democracy is inverted if money spent on political advertising convinces voters how they should vote. Voters should be the principals; that is, voters should express their preferences about taxation and public spending through the political process. Political advertising suggests that voters' perceptions of their own self-interests are subject to persuasion.

The duration of political benefits

Politicians face problems caused by the duration of benefits from political decisions. The time horizon of politicians when considering political support may not extend beyond the time of the next election. Politicians might correspondingly prefer that the benefits from political decisions not extend much beyond the next election. If the benefits are sufficiently durable to extend beyond the next election and then the following elections, there may be no need for the beneficiaries to return in the future to seek political favors. On the other hand, if the benefits of past favors are gone when the time is reached for another election, the politician can benefit politically by again having something to give. Ideally, the politician would like, for example, to hand out ice cream. Building highways creates a problem for the politician because, once the highway is built, another highway may not be needed. The problem confronting the politician is that gratitude or obligation may be based on the answer to the question: what have you done for me lately?

The compulsions of political life and lame ducks

Because of the compulsions of political life, politicians may not consider themselves as corrupt when they accept special-interest money. Instead, they may view the necessities of political success as *compelling* them to accept special-interest money. A politician may therefore stress the distinction between personal corruption where public policies are chosen opportunistically for private benefit, and the necessities of political life that require accommodating and benefiting from the campaign contributions of special interests.

Politicians who have decided that they are not seeking reelection do not need money from special interests to finance political campaigns. Comparison between politicians not seeking reelection (who are sometimes called lame ducks because they will not "fly" again) and politicians who are seeking reelection reveals a systematic difference in voting behavior. The lame ducks are more likely to take positions in the public interest than political incumbents seeking reelection.[23]

---

[23] A study of the voting behavior of lame ducks was undertaken by Mark Zupan (1990).

TABLE 6.1. THE PRISONERS' DILEMMA FACING PRINCIPLED
POLITICAL CANDIDATES

	Candidate 2 refuses special-interest money	Candidate 2 accepts special-interest Money
Candidate 1 refuses Special-interest money	3, 3	1, 4
Candidate 1 accepts special-interest money	4, 1	2, 2

The principled politician's dilemma

The circumstances that make campaign contributions a necessity of political life define a prisoners' dilemma. The dilemma confronts principled politicians who prefer to contest political office without accepting money from special interests. Table 6.1 shows the prisoners' dilemma. Principled politicians would wish to enter into a binding agreement with political opponents that no candidate will accept special-interest money, which gives the outcome (3, 3). A candidate who secretly fails to honor such an agreement and takes special-interest money when political opponents honor the agreement has an advantage in the political contest, indicated by a benefit of 4 compared to the benefit of 1 for the candidate who has not accepted special-interest money. If there are no credible means of enforcing an agreement not to accept money from special interests, both candidates accept special-interest money and are in the Nash equilibrium at (2, 2).

Legal restrictions on permissible political contributions are attempts to resolve the prisoners' dilemma facing political candidates and to avoid political influence by special interests. However, enforcing legal restrictions on political contributions is difficult. The restrictions can be circumvented in various ways. A legal limit on the maximum value of the campaign contribution that one donor can give can be circumvented by channeling excess contributions from a single donor through other donors who are conduits for the large donor and who offer their names as sources of contributions. Limitations on individual private contributions, but not on contributions by public bodies, can be circumvented by setting up organizations for the purpose of channeling contributions to political candidates or parties. If foreign interests are prohibited from contributing to a country's politicians, domestic conduits for the money can be found. Special-interest money can thereby remain prominent despite legal restrictions – although, because of the restrictions, additional ingenuity may be required to channel campaign contributions to the candidates.

The symmetric prisoners' dilemma in Table 6.1, where people involved in the dilemma are identical, may not be an appropriate description of political candidates' interests and campaign contributions. An asymmetry is present when candidates' sources of political support differ. A politician whose support is primarily from the general population of voters has greater reason to favor legal restrictions on maximal allowable campaign contributions by any contributor than a politician whose major support is from wealthier voters. Politicians whose support comes from wealthier voters depend more on money received as campaign contributions for political success, and so will have reason to oppose limitations on total allowable contributions that any one political candidate can receive. Politicians whose basis for political success is campaign contributions from wealthier voters may believe that is unfair that their political advantage is undermined by restrictions on the amount of money that any one individual political donor can give, or on how much can be given in total to any one candidate.

Since voters dislike donations of special-interest money to politicians, a politician can benefit politically by making public declarations of opposition to special-interest money. A majority of politicians might publicly declare their support for restrictions on political contributions. Nonetheless, legislation to enact the restrictions may not have majority support among elected representatives.

Contradictory policies

A politician who has accepted special-interest money is obligated by an implicit contract with the interest group that has provided the money. After a successful political campaign, the elected political representative must decide whether to honor the promises made to special-interest groups when special-interest money was accepted.

The private promises made to special interests may contradict the public promises that the politician made to voters when seeking election. The politician may therefore have to choose between reneging on promises to special-interest groups or promises to voters.

This can be a difficult decision for an elected representative. With more elections to take place in the future, the politician requires credibility with both voters and special-interest contributors. The decision in the end might be based on the politicians' beliefs about who has the shorter memory. The political spin that we previously considered may also be involved.

Public finance for political expenses

Political candidates or parties are often provided with publicly financed grants to cover political expenses. If public finance is the only source of political funds, the prisoners' dilemma of the principled politician is resolved.[24]

Rules for publicly financing political expenses differ in different countries. One form of public finance for political expenses is matching public grants for private money received.[25] The matching grants subsidize private political contributions. Public finance is contingent on receiving private political contributions, and every dollar of private money is effectively worth more through the publicly financed

---

[24] Public finance is the only source of financing of political expenses when no candidate cheats by secretly accepting private money.

[25] This has been the case in the United States.

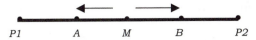

Figure 6.3. The effect of matching public funding.
Without public funding and with no special-interest groups, the two candidates choose the public-interest policy at the point M. With special-interest groups giving political contributions and seeking respective policies at *P1* and *P2*, the candidates diverge from the common policy at *M* and announce policies at the points *A* and *B*, respectively. When publicly financed political funds are based on matching of private contributions, the candidates move further to the extremes from *A* and *B*, since a dollar of private money is now worth more than a dollar because of the government subsidy to private contributions.

matching grant. Public finance has then not been the sole source of finance for political expenses. On the contrary, private money is necessary for receiving public money, through the matching grants.

In Chapter 3, we considered two candidates competing for political support based only on votes, with no financial contributions, and we saw that candidates duplicated their policies and proposed the policy sought by the median voter. In Figure 6.3, we interpret the point *M* not as the preferred position of the median voter, but as the policy position that reflects the public interest. *P1* and *P2* are policy positions of two private interest groups. Under the policy of public financing of political expenses where public money is given as a matching grant for private money, candidates have an incentive to depart from the public interest policy at *M*, and to move their respective policy positions toward the special interest positions at *P1* and *P2* to obtain special-interest money for their political campaigns. Candidate 1 moves toward the special-interest position *P1* and candidate 2 moves toward the special-interest position *P2*. If the candidates did not move from the public interest point *M*, they would obtain no special-interest money because their policies would be indistinguishable.

We can suppose that a candidate receives more money from a special-interest group, the closer the candidate moves to the special-interest group's preferred position, and loses support from voters, the further the candidate's policy position is from the public-interest position at *M*. Without public finance of political contributions, each candidate chooses a policy that trades off the political gain in money against loss of voter support. The candidates might, for example, choose policies *A* and *B*. Publicly financed matching grants make approaching the special-interest groups' positions more valuable. Candidates then choose policies closer to the special-interests groups' preferred positions than points *A* and *B*.

An alternative policy for public funding of political expenses is to provide public finance based on votes received in the last election.[26] Larger political parties, for whom more people have voted, then receive more public funding than smaller parties. Because votes are the means of expression of political support of voters,

---

[26] This has been the procedure in Europe and elsewhere.

this form of public finance of political expenses reinforces the benefits of appealing to voters.

However, if money buys votes through political advertising, there is a political incentive to take special-interest money to increase political advertising, so as to win more votes and secure more public funding.

Public funding of political expenses based on votes received benefits larger parties that received more votes in the last election. Public funding based on past votes is therefore a barrier to new political parties or to new candidates contesting elections. We expect large disciplined parties to vote for public funding based on party size or the number of votes received. In contrast, in a more individualistic political system as that of the United States, we expect a policy of publicly financed subsidies for private contributions. The barriers to entry of new candidates seeking elected office are correspondingly lower.

6.2.4 Compromises

Political candidates need political support from voters, and also need money that special interests can provide. Politicians may therefore find that they need to compromise between the public interest and special interests. The compromises can be expressed as choice of public policy to maximize political support, defined by

$$S = f(U_1, \ U_2, \ U_3, \ldots, \ U_n).$$ (6.8)

Political support S in expression (6.8) depends on the utilities (or benefits) of n groups in the population. The higher the benefit for a group from a candidate's policies, the greater is the group's political support. That is,

$$\frac{\partial S}{\partial U_i} > 0.$$ (6.9)

Expression (6.8) defines political support but looks very much like a social welfare function as introduced in Chapter 5. Social welfare, like political support, also depends on individuals' utilities. We cannot presume that, in choosing policies to maximize political support, political decision makers will maximize social welfare. Politicians wish to win elections, and electoral success requires accommodating the trade-off between the public interest and benefits to special-interest groups.

A trade-off between the public interest and support from special interests arises when a special-interest group (an industry) wants lax environmental regulation. Social welfare is maximized when the environmental externality is efficiently resolved. A political decision maker might however choose to allow laxer environmental standards than are in the public interest, in order to receive special-interest money. The political decision maker will then have chosen a socially inefficient policy to maximize political support.

Figure 6.4 shows the trade-off between environmental standards and benefits (or rents) to a special-interest group. Along each of the contours S_1, S_2, and S_3, political support is constant. Political support S increases when the level of pollution declines because this pleases voters.

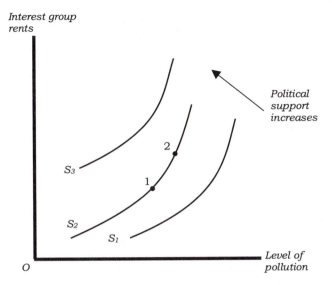

Figure 6.4. The trade-off in political support.
Political support from the public is greater when the level of pollution is lower, and political support from the industry is greater when industry rents (or profits) are greater. Along contours S_1, S_2, and S_3, political support is constant because of the trade-off between political support from the public (through votes) and political support from the industry (through campaign contributions).

Political support also increases when industry rents increase because this pleases the special-interest group. In a move from point 1 to point 2 on contour S_2, political support from voters declines because of increased pollution; however, at the same time, there is a compensating increase in political support from the special-interest group because of increased industry rents. Political support along the contour therefore remains constant.

The objective of the political decision maker is to maximize political support by achieving the highest political-support contour. The constraint on feasible choice of public policy is shown in Figure 6.5 as OC. Along OC, as the level of allowable pollution increases, the rents of the special-interest group increase. The political decision maker can choose environmental policy anywhere along OC. The policy decision determines the level of pollution and interest-group rents.

We define the public interest along OC in Figure 6.5 to be at the point 1. That is, L_1 at point 1 is the efficient outcome that would result from the Coase theorem if negotiations took place between the public and the industry. Industry profits in the efficient outcome are R_1.

When legal rights to a clean environment are with the public, the public nevertheless may need to rely on government to enforce the rights.[27] Society then faces

---

[27] In Chapter 4, we considered various reasons why the Coase theorem might not allow private resolution of externality problems, and why public policy might therefore be required.

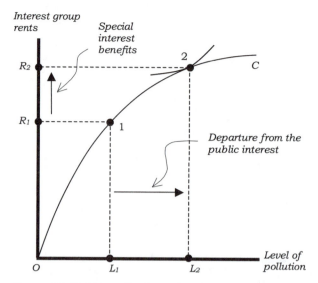

Figure 6.5. Public policy based on political support.
Higher levels of pollution allow greater industry rents (or profits). The point 1 and pollution L_1 define the public interest. The political compromise between the public interest and the interest of the industry is at the point 2 where the pollution level is L_2 and industry rents are R_2. The benefit to the industry from the political compromise is $(R_2 - R_1)$.

a political principal-agent problem, and political decision makers may choose not to enforce the public's rights, but rather to seek political support from the special-interest group by setting lax environmental standards.

The political compromise between the public interest and special interests that maximizes political support is shown in Figure 6.5 at point 2, where a political-support contour is tangential to the constraint OC. The level of pollution L_2 at point 2 is greater than is in the public interest. The interest group receives benefits or rents of $(R_2 - R_1)$ from the compromise of the public interest.

The public interest and political support

Political support in Figure 6.5 is determined by deviations of public policy from the public interest at point 1. Voters express their political dissatisfaction by looking at how environmental standards deviate from the public-interest standard at the point 1. The special interest group also values its politically assigned benefits as the deviation from the public interest at point 1. The deviation from the public interest at point 1 indicates the extent of political favor that the special-interest group has received. In Figure 6.5, political support is therefore determined by the deviations $(L - L_1)$ and $(R - R_1)$ from point 1. That is, political support is measured as

$$S = S(L - L_1, R - R_1). \tag{6.10}$$

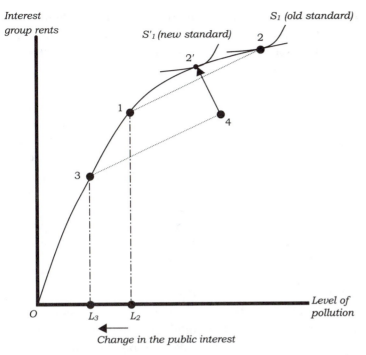

Figure 6.6. *Change in public policy when the public interest changes.*

The environmental standard defined as the public interest changes from point 1 to point 3. If public policy were determined in the public interest, the environmental policy would be at the point 3. Point 3 becomes the new origin for measurement of political support. The political compromise policy changes with the change to the more stringent public-interest environmental standards, from point 2 to point 2′. In the new political compromise, the public gains from an improved environment (less pollution). Relative to the new more stringent standard, the industry has also gained, by being permitted a larger deviation from the new standard.

More stringent standards in the public interest

Suppose now that environmental standards change and become more stringent because the extent of environmental damage was not previously properly understood. The new standards move the public interest in Figure 6.6 to point 3. The origin for the measurement of political support is now point 3 and is no longer point 1, and political support is measured in terms of the deviation from point 3 as

$$S = S(L - L_3, R - R_3). \tag{6.11}$$

A new political compromise now maximizes political support. The new compromise is shown at point 2′ in Figure 6.6. Political support at point 2′ is S_1', measured with reference to the new public interest at the point 3.

We see that, in the new political-support compromise, environmental standards have become more stringent, and the public is better off, with less pollution at 2′ than at 2.

At the same time, the rents of the special-interest group have fallen. Interest group rents were higher at point 2 than at point 2'. With the more stringent public-interest environmental standards as the reference point, the industry has nonetheless gained.

How did the industry gain?

The gain to the industry is revealed in the greater deviation in industry benefits from the public interest. When the public interest was defined at point 1, the distance between point 2 and point 1 measured the deviation in environmental standards from the public interest. This is the same distance as between point 3 and point 4 in Figure 6.6. The move from point 4 to the new point 2' where political support is maximized increases the industry's rents. Comparing point 2 and point 2', industry rents have fallen. The political decision maker is, however, more generous to the industry at 2' than at 2, by allowing the industry a greater deviation from the public interest.

Something for everybody

The political response to the change in the public interest in environmental standards therefore provides "something for everybody." The public interest is better served by the more-stringent environmental standards at point 3 compared with the original standards at point 1. At the same time, the industry is treated more leniently by being allowed a greater deviation from the public interest.

The political response to the changed environmental standards therefore leaves both voters and special interests with reason to feel *more* grateful to policy makers.

Political importance

The political importance of a group is formally measured by the group's political weight in the political-support function given previously as

$$\frac{\partial S}{\partial U_i} > 0.$$

The political weight measures the sensitivity of the political decision maker to an increase in a group's well-being or utility.

If the political decision maker cares a lot about support from a group, the group's political weight is high. When a political decision maker regards the group as politically irrelevant or marginal for determining political support, the group's political weight is low.

In Chapter 5, we viewed a social welfare function as treating all people equally when social weights for different people or groups are chosen behind a veil of ignorance. We did this to avoid discrimination that would give some people more social weight than others. Discrimination among different people in a population is, however, a characteristic of public policies based on political support. Special interests are purposefully seeking discriminately favorable treatment through political contributions. The privilege sought by special interests is precisely the

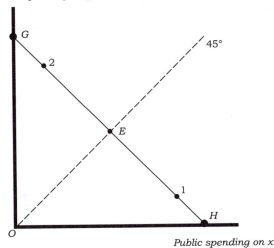

Public spending on y

G

2

45°

E

1

H

O

Public spending on x

Figure 6.7. Probabilistic voting.
The *probability* that a voter will vote for one candidate rather than the other depends on the difference in the voter's personal benefit from the two candidates' policy proposals.

contrary of the principle of equal treatment of equals that underlies equal social weights of the social welfare function. The equal weights for individuals or groups in the social welfare function are intended to reflect equality in a situation behind the veil of ignorance where people do not know who they will be; however, the weights in the political support are purposefully influenced through political contributions by people who know who they are (and know what they want).[28]

6.2.5 Probabilistic voting

Politicians may not be certain about how people will vote. Politicians are then obliged to assign probabilities to the voting decisions of different groups of voters. As far as politicians are concerned, voters' behavior is then probabilistic, and an increase in political support then takes the form of an increase in the likelihood that a voter will vote for a politician. Figure 6.7 shows an example of political choice of a public policy when voting is probabilistic. In Figure 6.7, line *GH* indicates how a sum of public money *E* can be divided between two purposes *x* and *y*. Along *GH*,

$$E = x + y. \tag{6.12}$$

We shall look at only two voters 1 and 2. Along line *GH* in Figure 6.7, voter 1 wants the outcome at point 1, and voter 2 wants the outcome at point 2. Two political

---

[28] We have used environmental policy as an example to describe political choice of public policy that can depart from the public interest. We could have used other public policies as examples. Restrictions on international trade provide another example of public policy that departs from the public interest to benefit special-interest groups. The benefits to industry special-interest groups from protectionist policies have been described by Ronald Jones (1971) of the University of Rochester.

candidates, whom we identify as candidate C and candidate D, choose policies for division of public spending along line GH. Voters judge the candidates in terms of their policy announcements and not in terms of past performance of an incumbent candidate.

When we previously considered a similar situation of voting and political competition in Chapter 3, we proposed that a voter would support a candidate whose policy was closest to the voter's preferred policy. Now, however, the probability that the voter 1 will vote for candidate C rather than candidate D depends on the difference in the voter's personal benefit from the two candidates' policy proposals.

That is, the probability that voter 1 will vote for candidate C is

$$P_1^C = f(B_1^C - B_1^D) = f(\Delta B_1), \tag{6.13}$$

where the B_1's indicate the benefits to voter 1 from the policies of candidates C and D and

$$\Delta B_1 \equiv B_1^C - B_1^D. \tag{6.14}$$

Voter 1 votes for either candidate C or candidate D (we do not consider abstentions), so

$$P_1^C + P_1^D = 1. \tag{6.15}$$

The probability that voter 2 will vote for candidate C is correspondingly

$$P_2^C = f(\Delta B_2). \tag{6.16}$$

Each candidate chooses a policy to maximize the probability of being elected. Therefore, candidate C chooses a point (a policy position) on line GH to maximize the sum of the probabilities in (6.13) and (6.16):

$$P_1^C + P_2^C. \tag{6.17}$$

In Figure 6.8, candidate C's choice of policy is at point 3 where the condition is satisfied that

$$a_{C1} ML_1^C = a_{C2} ML_2^C, \tag{6.18}$$

where ML^C indicates the marginal loss of a voter from the candidate not choosing the voter's preferred policy, and a_{C1} and a_{C2} indicate the political importance of the two voters to the candidate.[29]

If the policy chosen were at point 1, which is the preferred point of voter 1, the marginal loss ML_1^C to voter 1 would be zero. If the policy chosen were at point 2, which is the preferred point of voter 2, the marginal loss to voter 2 ML_2^C would be zero.

---

[29] In Figure 6.8 the functions showing weighted marginal loss are shown as straight lines. The functions are more generally not linear.

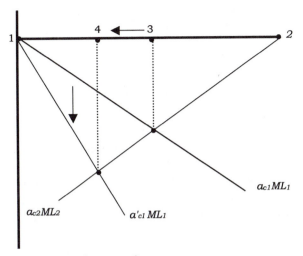

Marginal loss due to departure from the voter's preferred policy

Figure 6.8. Public policy with probabilistic voting.
Points correspond to the same points in Figure 6.7. Voter 1 prefers point 1 and voter 2 prefers point 2. Candidates choosing policies based on probabilistic voting choose the policy at 3 as a compromise where weighted marginal losses of departures from voters' preferred points are equalized. When the political weight of voter 1 increases, this voter's marginal loss function shifts, and the new compromise policy is at point 4, which is an improvement for voter 1 but is worse for voter 2.

With departures in Figure 6.8 from point 1 toward point 2, voter 2 is better off at the expense of voter 1. Conversely, with departures from point 2 toward point 1, voter 1 is better off at the expense of voter 2.

The policy at point 3 in Figure 6.8 equalizes the marginal losses to the two voters from the deviations from their preferred policies, corrected for the political weights, which are defined as (see Supplement 6A)

$$a_{C1} \equiv \frac{\partial P_1^C}{\partial \Delta B_1}, \qquad a_{C2} \equiv \frac{\partial P_2^C}{\partial \Delta B_2}. \tag{6.19}$$

That is, the political weights reflect how differences in a voter's benefits from the policies of the two candidates affect the likelihood that the voter will vote for one candidate or the other. A higher political weight for a voter implies higher political sensitivity of the candidate to the voter's losses. When a voter's weight is higher, a candidate is more reluctant to move away from the voter's preferred point.

Voters' political weights in expression (6.19) are in general not constant, just as we saw in Chapter 5 that individuals' weights in a social welfare function are in general not constant. This allows us to consider the consequences of a change in political weights. For example, in Figure 6.8, an increase in the political weight of voter 1 from a_{C1} to a'_{C1} changes the policy position of candidate C from the point 3 to the point 4, which is a preferable policy for voter 1.

An egalitarian outcome

The point E on the 45° line in Figure 6.7 is a symmetric deviation from the preferred policies of the two voters. We can place the voters behind a veil of ignorance so that they do not know which person (or voter) they will be. Each voter therefore has a 50 percent probability of being voter 1, who prefers the outcome at point 1, and a 50 percent probability of being voter 2, who prefers the outcome at point 2. Choice by candidate C of the policy at point E in Figure 6.7 is then equivalent to maximizing a symmetric social welfare function.

Candidate C chooses point E as a policy if the following conditions are simultaneously satisfied:

(1) The political weights a_{C1} and a_{C2} are the same for both voters.
(2) Points 1 and 2 are symmetrically distant from the 45° line.
(3) The voters' losses from departure from their preferred points 1 and 2 are symmetric (and measurable and comparable).

We have been looking at the policy decision of candidate C. Candidate D has the same objective of winning the election. In a symmetric situation, both candidates choose the same policy at E.

The idea of probabilistic voting is therefore a way of interpreting the choice of policies that maximize a social welfare function chosen behind a veil of ignorance as described in Chapter 5. At the same time, probabilistic voting is a way of looking at policies chosen to maximize political support when the politicians choosing the policies and voters are not behind a veil of ignorance. The objective of choosing policies to maximize political support that we previously considered is transformed to maximizing the probability of a candidate winning an election.

6.2.6 Political auctions

Probabilistic voting is based on political support expressed through voting. However, special-interest groups in general hope to increase their political influence not by offering votes, but by giving money to politicians.

Let us now consider a political decision maker, who wishes to maximize the amount of money received from special-interest groups, but who also cares about support from the voters who will ultimately determine the electoral outcome. The politician faces the trade-off that we have described between support from voters by catering to the public interest and political benefit from catering to the policy wishes of special interests.

Many different special-interest groups usually seek personally beneficial public policies from a political decision maker, and the political decision maker cannot afford to alienate voters too much. The benefits that the political decision maker can provide to interest groups are therefore limited.

The political decision maker could invite representatives of the different special-interest groups to an auction. At the auction, the political decision maker could announce that he or she is open to offers of payment from special-interest groups, in return for public policies that depart from the public interest. That is, the political decision maker can make clear that a limited amount of political influence or departure from the public interest is available for sale.

The representatives of the different special-interest groups then bid the amounts of money they are prepared to pay for special-interest policies and, based on the bids, the political decision maker chooses the special-interest policies to implement. The bids by the representatives of the special-interest groups determine the weights (or political importance) of a special-interest group in the political decision maker's political-support function.

Such open auctions of special-interest policies do not literally take place. However, the idea of representatives of different interest groups participating in an auction arranged by political decision makers illustrates how political accommodation to special interests and departure from the public interest would be seen to take place, if the process were openly and forthrightly displayed in a market for political influence. For such a view of political behavior, see Gene Grossman and Elhanan Helpman (1994).

6.2.7 Political corruption

We can define corruption as the abuse of the authority of public office for illicit personal gain. The politicians whose behavior we have been describing are not corrupt in seeking personal monetary gain. They face the compulsion of requiring money to finance election campaigns, and the only illegal activity that they may have undertaken is violation of campaign contribution laws. The special-interest public policies are not illegal.

On the other hand, when a politician accepts money (or a personal service or gift) not as a campaign contribution, but for personal gain, in return for helping to obtain a favorable policy, political behavior is quite explicitly personally corrupt.

Political culture

We have been describing societies where political culture is inconsistent with political corruption, and where corruption is consequently uncommon and evokes public outrage.

In societies where a culture and tradition of honesty and public service have been lacking, government has often been endemically corrupt. In such societies, the political culture often presupposes that political office will be used for personal benefit and for dispensing privilege. Political contests in these societies determine who will obtain the personal benefits that are available through corrupt government.[30]

Because of the personal benefits from corruption, rulers in corrupt societies are reluctant to step down. Corrupt societies are usually not democratic, and the means of change of government is usually by death or dementia of the ruler, or by military coup.

The risk in offering a bribe

Where bribes are part of the political culture, there is little risk in offering a bribe to a political decision maker. In the honest societies that we have been studying, offering a bribe is unwise (as well as dishonest) because the likelihood of acceptance of the bribe is small and the penalty for offering the bribe is high. In corrupt societies where political decision makers can be presumed to be seeking bribes, not offering and paying a bribe can be unwise.[31]

Arbitrary rules and corruption

A corrupt government could ban the import of particular medications, and people wishing to gain access to the medications may have no choice but to bribe the minister of health to allow illegal imports. Arbitrary restrictive rules have then been imposed by the corrupt government to provide a source of income for government officials.

Corruption and the composition of public spending

Studies have revealed that corruption affects the composition of public spending. When government is corrupt, there is a tendency for greater public spending on defense equipment, highways, bridges, dams, and physical projects in general, at the expense of public spending for example on salaries of teachers or public health officials. The preference of corrupt governments for spending on physical projects (such as the highway, or absent highway, in footnote 30) is explained by the greater

---

[30] An anecdote describes a young ruler on an official foreign visit seeking advice about how to govern from an older, longer-established ruler. The young visitor observes that the population is quite poor but that his host lives quite well. The visitor asks how so much personal wealth could be accumulated in such a poor country. To illustrate the source of the personal wealth, the host takes the visitor to a highway and declares, "We received international-agency financing to construct this highway, and I took 30 percent." Some years later the older ruler reciprocates the visit, and the now more-mature host says to the guest: "We were also given international-agency financing to build a highway." The visitor replies, "I have seen no highways in your country." To which the now not-so-young ruler replies proudly, "Yes, I have been more successful than you were. I took 100 percent." The anecdote illustrates a political culture where pride is expressed in success in appropriating public funds rather than serving the public interest.

[31] A dilemma arises in attempting to do business in societies where the political culture allows corrupt politicians. The only way to win a bid for a government project in these countries may be to bribe the local political decision makers. Yet bribes are not only unethical but also illegal by home-country laws.

ease of obtaining kickbacks than when public spending is on services such as on education or health.

Scandal as an indicator of political culture

Political culture cannot be directly measured. However, an indicator of political culture is the activities that are "scandals." In societies with socially beneficial political cultures, a political scandal might be a sexual episode by a president or cabinet minister. In other societies, political scandals may involve abuse of public office for personal financial benefit. When the political culture is tolerant or supportive of political corruption, nothing that a political ruler or politician does for personal self-benefit is a scandal. The political culture takes for granted that political office will be used for personal gain.

6.2.8 Summary

Inconsistency between objectives of taxpayers (or voters) and the politicians who should be the taxpayers' agents creates a principal-agent problem for voters because of voters' inability to monitor and discipline political decision makers effectively. Even though political support ultimately takes the form of political support from voters, money is also required to win elections. In particular, money is required for political advertising that can influence how voters decide to vote. Money can be provided by broadly based interest groups seeking social objectives (that not everyone may agree with), but more usually political contributions are provided by special-interest groups that have advantages in organizing for voluntary collective action to influence policy decisions for personal benefit.

Voters are at a disadvantage in influencing public policy because of incentives for rational ignorance. Free-riding is also a problem for voters because of the public-good nature of benefits from monitoring and acquiring information about politicians' behavior. Voters' abilities to express their preferences through voting can be hindered by difficulties in finding political candidates whose positions reflect voters' own positions on all issues. The focal issues that dominate an election provide discretion for political decision makers to cater to special-interest groups on issues that are not the focus of voter attention. The problems facing voters in influencing public policy are compounded by the disinclination of some people to vote. A comparison of costs and benefits might lead people to decide not to take the time to vote because the likelihood that one individual vote will decide the outcome is small. Term limits on political tenure might help voters counter political advantages from political entrenchment. A vigilant, honest, and bipartisan press (a press that is not the consistent agent of a particular political party or of a particular ideology) assists voters by countering rational ignorance and disciplining political behavior.

Politicians also face problems. The objectives sought by special interests are generally contrary to the public interest; consequently, by accepting special-interest money, politicians are implicitly agreeing to act against the public interest. Political circumstances may make it difficult for politicians to change policy positions, and politicians may find themselves resorting to spin to explain changes in behavior to support special-interest policies.

Principled politicians may confront a prisoners' dilemma because of the need for money to finance their political campaigns. The dilemma can be resolved by legal restrictions on private contributions to political candidates, if the restrictions can be enforced.

We have also looked at public finance for political expenses as a means of escape from the dilemma of whether to accept special-interest campaign contributions. We have seen that the effect of public funding on public policy depends on the rule that determines how public funding of political expenses takes place.

An investigation of the trade-off that politicians face between catering to special interests and seeking broad voter support has revealed how public policies can reflect political compromise of the public interest. We have also examined how political decisions can be expected to change when the definition of the public interest changes, and we have seen that the political response tends to provide something for everybody.

The idea of probabilistic voting allows maximizing political support to be reinterpreted as maximizing the probability of electoral success of a political candidate. We have also seen how political weights of special-interest groups who pursue their interests through financial contributions can be thought of as being determined in a political auction.

We have also considered political corruption. Politicians may take the view that accepting money from special interests is not corrupt behavior, but rather a necessity of success in political life. If we choose to accept this view, we can confine the use of the term "corruption" to descriptions of use of authority of government for self-serving personal benefit. Whether such personal corruption is widespread is a reflection of the political culture, which determines norms of political behavior. We have noted that political corruption in particular affects the composition of public spending.

The distinction between normative and positive propositions is important for understanding political behavior.[32] In Chapter 5, we applied the normative concept of a social welfare function to consider how societies might resolve problems that arise because of personal uncertainties in life, and we interpreted income transfers as social insurance that benevolently replaces missing private insurance markets. We have now looked at income distribution from the perspective of positive economics by considering how voting and political decisions can affect income distribution. We have seen that we cannot predict that income redistribution that takes place through political processes will always satisfy normative criteria of merit for assistance to the unfortunate or the disadvantaged. The political determinants of income redistribution complement our conclusion in Chapter 5 that,

---

[32] Recall that normative propositions describe desirable public policies, while positive propositions explain and predict but do not judge (at least not explicitly).

because of moral hazard, we cannot be assured that income redistribution motivated by normative social-insurance criteria for assistance will necessarily benefit the deserving unfortunate or disadvantaged.

References and related literature

On the voting behavior of politicians, see Peltzman (1985) and Zupan (1990). On the effects of political advertising on voters, see Holbrook (1996). On political contributions and interest groups, see Baron (1989), Morton and Cameron (1992), Snyder (1992), Sorauf (1992), Stratmann (1992), Potters and Sloof (1996), Austin-Smith (1997) and Grossman and Helpman (2001). On term limits, see Lopez (2003). On agriculture, see Abler (1991) and Lopez (2001). On the formation of lobbying groups, see Damania and Fredriksson (2000) and Hillman, Long, and Soubeyran (2001). On the trade-off in policy support between votes and serving special interests, see Peltzman (1976) and Hillman (1982). On political influence and environmental policy, which we have used as an example, see Congelton (1996) and Dijkstra (1999). On probabilistic voting, see Coughlin and Nitzan (1981); for an application, see Mayer and Li (1994). On political auctions, see Bernheim and Whinston (1986) and Grossman and Helpman (1994). On management interests and political principal-agent problems, see Cassing (1996). On purposeful obfuscation of public policy, see Lindbeck (1985) and Magee, Brock, and Young (1989). On the decision whether to vote, see Silberman and Durden (1975), Chamberlain and Rothschild (1981), and Matsusaka and Palda (1999). On political culture, see Hillman and Swank (2000). On corruption and the composition of public spending, see Mauro (1998) and Gupta, de Melo, and Sharan (2001). For an overview of corruption in government, see Rose-Ackerman (1999). On scandal, see Holler (1999). On reluctance of politicians to change policy decisions, see Dur (2001).

Abler, D. G., 1991. Campaign contributions and house voting on sugar and dairy legislation. *American Journal of Agricultural Economics* 73, 11–17.

Austin-Smith, D., 1997. Interest groups: Money, information, and influence. In *Perspectives on Public Choice: A Handbook*, D. C. Mueller (ed.). Cambridge University Press, New York, 296–321.

Baron, D. P., 1989. Service-induced campaign contributions and the electoral equilibrium. *Quarterly Journal of Economics* 104, 45–72.

Bernheim, B. D. and M. D. Whinston, 1986. Menu auctions, resource allocation, and economic influence. *Quarterly Journal of Economics* 101, 1–31.

Cassing, J. H., 1996. Protectionist mutual funds. *European Journal of Political Economy* 12, 1–18.

Chamberlain, G. and M. Rothschild, 1981. A note on the probability of casting a decisive vote. *Journal of Economic Theory* 25, 152–62.

Congelton, R. D. (ed.), 1996. *The Political Economy of Environmental Protection*. University of Michigan Press, Ann Arbor.

Coughlin, P. and S. Nitzan, 1981. Electoral outcomes with probabilistic voting and Nash social welfare maxima. *Journal of Public Economics* 15, 113–22.

Damania, R. and P. G. Fredriksson, 2000. On the formation of industry lobby groups. *Journal of Economic Behavior and Organization* 41, 315–35.

Dijkstra, B. R., 1999. *The Political Economy of Environmental Policy*. Edward Elgar, Cheltenham, U.K.

Dur, R. A. J., 2001. Why do policy makers stick to inefficient decisions. *Public Choice* 107, 221–34.

Grossman, G. M. and E. Helpman, 1994. Protection for sale. *American Economic Review* 84, 833–50.

Grossman, G. M. and E. Helpman, 2001. *Special Interest Politics*. MIT Press, Cambridge, Massachusetts.

Gupta, S., L. de Melo and R. Sharan, 2001. Corruption and military spending. *European Journal of Political Economy* 17, 749–77.

Hillman, A. L., 1982. Declining industries and political-support protectionist motives. *American Economic Review* 72, 1180–7.

Hillman, A. L. and O. Swank, 2000. Why political culture should be in the lexicon of economics. *European Journal of Political Economy* 16, 1–4.

Hillman, A. L., N. V. Long and A. Soubeyran, 2001. Protection, lobbying, and market structure. *Journal of International Economics* 54, 383–409.

Holbrook, T. M., 1996. *Do Campaigns Matter?* Sage Publications, Thousand Oaks, California.

Holler, M., 1999. (Ed.) *Scandal and Its Theory*. Homo Oeconomicus, volume 16.

Jones, R. W., 1971. A three factor model in theory, trade and history. In *Trade, Growth and the Balance of Payments: Essays in Honor of C. B. Kindleberger*, J. N. Bhagwati et al. (eds.). North-Holland, Amsterdam, 3–21.

Lindbeck, A., 1985. Redistribution policy and the expansion of the public sector. *Journal of Public Economics* 28, 309–28.

Lopez, E. J., 2003. Term limits: causes and consequences. *Public Choice* 114, 1–56.

Lopez, R. A., 2001. Campaign contributions and agricultural subsidies. *Economics and Politics* 13, 257–79.

Magee, S., W. A. Brock and L. Young, 1989. *Black Hole Tariffs and Endogenous Policy Theory*. Cambridge University Press, New York.

Mayer, W. and Li-Jun, 1994. Interest groups, electoral competition and probabilistic voting. *Economics and Politics* 6, 59–77.

Matsusaka, J. C. and F. Palda, 1999. Voter turnout: How much can we explain. *Public Choice* 98, 431–46.

Mauro, P., 1998. Corruption and the composition of government expenditure. *Journal of Public Economics* 69, 263–79.

Morton, R. and C. Cameron, 1992. Elections and the theory of campaign contributions: A survey and critical analysis. *Economics and Politics* 4, 79–108.

Peltzman, S., 1976. Toward a more general theory of regulation. *Journal of Law and Economics* 19, 171–240.

Peltzman, S., 1985. An economic interpretation of the history of congressional voting in the twentieth century. *American Economic Review* 75, 656–75.

Potters, J. and R. Sloof, 1996. Interest groups: A survey of empirical models that try to assess their influence. *European Journal of Political Economy* 12, 403–42.

Rose-Ackerman, S., 1999. *Corruption and Government: Causes, Consequences and Reform*. Cambridge University Press, New York.

Silberman, J. and G. Durden, 1975. The rational behavior theory of voter participation. *Public Choice* 23, 101–8.

Snyder, J. M., 1992. Long term investing in politicians; or give early, give often. *Journal of Law and Economics* 35, 15–43.

Sorauf, F. J., 1992. *Inside Campaign Finance*. Yale University Press, New Haven, Connecticut.

Stern, P. M., 1988. *The Best Congress Money Can Buy*. Pantheon Books, New York.

Stratmann, T., 1992. Are contributors rational?: Untangling strategies of political action committees. *Journal of Political Economy* 100, 647–64.

Zupan, M., 1990. The last period problem in politics: Do congressional representatives not subject to a reelection constraint alter their voting behavior? *Public Choice* 65, 167–80.

Questions for discussion

1. What are the sources of the principal-agent problem between voters and elected political representatives?
2. What problems arise in defining the public interest? Interest groups can seek public policies that have broad social objectives that are controversial. How are such interest groups different from interest groups that have narrow self-interest objectives that privately benefit smaller numbers of people?
3. Interest groups that seek narrow personal benefit need not be in the private sector but rather can also be found among people employed by government. What might these interest groups seek? What is a rent? How are rents related to political favors?
4. How does group size affect ability to organize for collective action? (See also Supplement 2B). Conclusions about the effect of group size on political effectiveness under representative democracy are based on individual Nash-equilibrium contributions to a collective objective, but peer pressure can lead to cooperative behavior. How does peer pressure to cooperate affect small groups relative to large groups? Compare the effect group size has on political effectiveness under direct democracy and under representative democracy.
5. How does the size of the stake in a political decision provide an advantage for special-interest groups in influencing public policy?
6. What problems deter voters from solving the principal-agent problem with political representatives? What would a solution to the principal-agent problem require? Resolving the principal-agent problem between shareholders and management creates a principal-agent problem between shareholders and political decision makers. Why is this so?
7. How would you reply when someone declares: "How dare you talk about principal-agent problems between voters and politicians. My aunt is a politician and she is one of the nicest people that I know"? Someone else declares: "I can see that money is an essential ingredient of political success when running for election. My uncle is, however, independently wealthy, and, while he spent millions, he used only his own personal money to win the election." How would you reply? How do you think the person making this statement would reply if you asked why his or her uncle chose to spend millions to win a political election?
8. How do different forms of public finance for political expenses affect political candidates' policy positions? Do you believe that political candidates should receive publicly financed subsidies for political expenses? If so, how should the public money be distributed?
9. What is the relation between a biased press and special-interest campaign contributions?
10. How does the duration of benefits to voters from public policies affect political decision makers?
11. Why do politicians tend to be adamant in their policy positions?

12. Why does political advertising introduce an anomaly into the principal-agent relationship between voters and politicians? What does evidence from the voting behavior of lame-duck politicians indicate about principal-agent problems between voters and elected representatives?

13. In the place where you live or study, are elected representatives subject to term limits? At what levels of political representation do the term limits apply? Do you favor term limits for politicians? Explain.

14. In recent elections in the place where you live or study, what proportion of voters voted? Why do you think people do not exercise their right to vote? Do you believe that voting should be an obligation rather than a right? That is, should voting be compulsory, with fines levied on people who do not vote? Explain.

15. What problems confront a principled political candidate? Why might it be difficult for political candidates to come to an agreement to set limits on campaign spending? The following is a statement by Thomas Eagleton, former U.S. senator for the state of Missouri, explaining why he did not seek re-election: "I just did not want to go through what I called the tin-cup routine – that is, begging for money.... Every PAC has its special interest or special interests. If I take x thousands of dollars from a dairy PAC, I know what it is the dairy boys are interested in. If I take x thousands of dollars from a tobacco or trucking PAC, I know what it is those fellows are interested in, because I have been around them. So the minute you accept their money, you are tacitly acknowledging that you are part of their philosophical orientation" (Stern, 1988, p. 108). (PAC refers to a political action committee.) How is this above statement related to the dilemma of a principled politician?

16. How do political support and social welfare functions differ? Why does public policy tend to provide "something for everybody" when political decision makers are concerned with political support?

17. What is probabilistic voting? How are outcomes of probabilistic voting related both to public policy that maximizes political support and to public policy that maximizes social welfare?

18. The political decision-making process can be described as political decision makers choosing public policies in response to bids by different interest groups seeking special-interest policies, subject to politicians maintaining sufficient broad political support from voters. Do you believe that this is an accurate description of how public policies are influenced by special interests? Explain.

19. Are politicians "corrupt" when they compromise the public interest in taking money from special interests? What actions of politicians would you regard as explicitly corrupt? What do you understand by "political culture"? How does corruption affect the composition of public spending? How does a society's attitude to "what is scandal" provide an indication of political culture? Supplement 6B describes an extreme example of personal political corruption. Could corruption on the same scale take place in the place where you live or study? What are the impediments to extensive personal political corruption in the place where you study and live? Have there been prominent cases of personal political corruption?

20. In the place where you live or study, are there identifiable special-interest groups that benefit from tax-financed transfer payments or public policies? In particular, is agriculture subsidized? If so, can you find data on the value of the subsidies received by agriculture? Are the recipients of the subsidies mainly small farmers or large agricultural firms? Do you believe the agricultural subsidies are justified or partly justified? If the beneficiaries are many small farmers rather than large agricultural conglomerates, can you still explain the benefits as the consequence of political activity by special-interest groups?

6.3

Public Policy and Rent-Seeking Behavior

A "rent" is a personal benefit that a person receives beyond that necessary to provide incentives to perform particular tasks. We have encountered rents in connection with benefits obtained within government bureaucracy in Chapter 3 and benefits provided through public policies by political decision makers in Section 6.2. The term "rent seeking", as the name implies, describes the behavior of seeking rents. We shall now study the relation between rent seeking and public-policy decisions.

6.3.1 Rents and rent seeking

Rent seekers do not set themselves the challenge "what productive activity can I undertake today to earn income?" Rather they ask themselves the question "what can I convince someone to do for me today?" The use of resources (time, effort, initiative) in rent seeking is socially wasteful. Resources that could be productively used are directed toward trying to influence distribution rather than to produce goods or services.

Resources are also used in a socially wasteful way in appropriative activity under anarchy where there is no government present to provide the protection of the rule of law and people do not abide by principles of respect for ownership. However, rent seeking does not arise in response to the absence of government; instead, rent seeking is the consequence of the presence of government. Rent seeking takes place when people feel that people in government are amenable to persuasion to provide privileged personal benefits (i.e., to provide rents). If it were known that public policy and public finance were exclusively determined by normative principles that define the public interest, there would be no private incentive to seek personal gains from influencing political decisions, and resources would not be wastefully used in rent-seeking activities. Rent seeking is therefore a response to the perceived inclination of political decision makers to respond positively to requests for favors.

Socially beneficial and socially wasteful competition

The social loss through rent seeking arises when rents are contestable through persuasion or lobbying of political decision makers. That is, the social loss due to rent seeking arises because of the use of time and other resources in competition for rents.

We can therefore identify two types of competition – one socially beneficial and the other not. Socially beneficial competition is competition in markets to provide goods, whereas socially wasteful competition takes place to determine winners of rent-seeking contests.

The form of government and rent seeking

Rent seeking is competition for privilege. The form of government affects the extent of rent seeking that takes place.

In a hereditary absolute monarchy, there is a designated successor by birth, and privilege due to being the ruler is not contestable. Hereditary monarchies were thus intended to avoid socially costly rent seeking in seeking to become the king or queen. There were, however, wars where succession was disputed, and resources were then used in the rent-seeking activity of contesting the right to be the king or queen. Monarchies were also bastions of rent seeking through the quest for privileges bestowed by the monarch. Palace intrigues influenced royal decisions such as who should have the right to be an exclusive importer of spices or colonize different locations.

Rent seeking has also been the primary means of seeking personal gain in forms of government other than monarchies. In the maximal government described in Chapter 1, political decisions determined who benefited from collective property; therefore, there were private incentives to influence political decisions, or better still to become the political decision maker.

In general, whenever personal benefits depend on decisions made by other people, life can become a quest for personal favors, and people spend time and effort in rent-seeking activity.

6.3.2 Rent dissipation

We are interested in rent-seeking behavior when we study public finance and public policy because rent seeking is a social cost of political discretion. The objective in an investigation of rent-seeking behavior is to measure the cost to society of rent seeking.

When a benefit or rent is politically assigned, the social loss due to the political discretion in assigning the rent is measured by the value of the resources that are attracted into the competition to determine who receives the rent. That is, a rent is a benefit, but resources used in contesting the rent dissipate the benefit.

When the competition for a rent attracts resources equal to the value of the rent, rent dissipation is complete. With complete dissipation, we can measure the social cost of rent seeking by the value of the rent that was the "prize" in the rent-seeking contest. There is an advantage to being able to use the value of the prize as the measure of rent dissipation because rent seeking is not usually an openly observed activity and so resources used in rent-seeking behavior are generally not observable and measurable. It is therefore computationally very useful if an observed rent-seeking prize of $1,000 could be associated with unobserved resources with a value of $1,000 used in rent seeking.

The conditions determining the extent of dissipation of a rent in a rent-seeking contest depend on many factors. Supplement 6C describes influences on rent dissipation.[1] The important point is that rent seeking is socially costly through the rent dissipation that takes place.

6.3.3 Rent seeking and social norms

Whether rent seeking is dishonorable, or how dishonorable, depends on social norms. A political culture may view rent seeking as the social norm. The purpose of seeking political office is then openly acknowledged to be to dispense favors. People who have attained positions in government and who do not assign rents for personal benefit may, in these societies, be considered aberrant in their behavior. In such societies where the social norm allows open rent seeking, personal fortunes depend less on self-application to effort and hard work and more on political persuasion and lobbying. Achieving privileged benefit through successful rent seeking may be unfair. The problem with rent seeking is, however, not only unfairness but also inefficiency due to the socially wasteful use of resources. Since time, initiative, and other resources are diverted away from productive activities by rent-seeking behavior, societies with social norms that allow prevalent rent seeking are poorer than societies where the social norm is that government does not dispense personal favors through public finance and public policy.

In a society where rent seeking is contrary to social norms, both rent seekers and the providers of political favors have reason to go out of their way to hide rent seeking, and both have reason to deny that rent seeking has occurred. If challenged, successful rent seekers might present their gains as deserved achievement through productive effort, or as morally and ethically justified, and they might deny that their gains are privileged rents from success in developing personal connections with political decision makers.

Political decision makers will claim that their decisions to provide private benefits through public policies are the outcome of objective deliberations.

6.3.4 The ambiguities of rent-seeking behavior

A note of caution is required in applying the concept of rent seeking. When too broadly and indiscriminately applied, rent seeking can make for an excessively cynical picture of personal behavior. Consider a personal example. Someone offers to buy you a cup of coffee or a drink or pays for your dinner because the person wants to talk to you and feels that you are pleasant company. Applying the concept of rent seeking would, however, lead to the view that the offer to pay for your

---

[1] In general, the more competitive rent seeking is, the greater rent dissipation is. In one case, rent dissipation is complete in an average sense when as few as two rent seekers are active in contesting a rent. This occurs when the rule for winning a rent-seeking contest is that the person spending the most money in seeking the rent is the successful rent seeker. Supplement 6C provides more details.

drink or dinner is necessarily a prepayment made in anticipation of the request for a return favor.

The idea of rent seeking imparts a distrusting attitude to personal favors.[2] If someone has been observed to benefit from a privileged favor, rent seeking suggests a hidden side of the exchange that gave rise to the privileged favor. On the other hand, the idea of rent seeking also leads to the question why some people benefit from favors while others do not, or why some people must pay for benefits that are provided as favors to others.

6.3.5 Rent seeking and transfers

Let us now consider ten thieves who are aware that you have $100 in your pocket. Suppose each thief has an equal chance of stealing the money from you. If each thief is risk-neutral,[3] each thief will invest $10 in terms of time and resources in an attempt to steal the $100, since $10 is a thief's expected benefit from participating in the contest to steal your money (10 percent of $100).

Before the theft takes place, the thieves will have made investments valued at a total of $100 of resources in their attempts to steal $100. Before the identity of the successful thief has been determined, a social loss of $100 has therefore been incurred through socially wasteful activities in positioning to be the successful thief. The social loss is precisely the $100 that will be the "prize" for the ultimately successful thief.

In this example, there is complete dissipation of the rent-seeking prize, because the value of the resources used in contesting the prize is precisely equal to the value of the prize.

After one of the thieves has been successful in stealing the $100, a transfer of money will have taken place, from our pockets to the pocket of the successful thief. This transfer is an act of involuntary income redistribution, from us to the thief.

No social loss is incurred in the transfer of money. The efficiency loss is incurred before the identity of the successful thief is known and before the transfer of income to the thief takes place. The social loss consists of the resources used by all the aspiring thieves in their attempts to be the successful thief. Rather than spending their time preparing their attempts at theft and acquiring implements (e.g., a weapon or tools to be used in forced entry), the aspiring thieves could have used their time and resources in socially productive ways.

In considering rent seeking, we emphasize the distinction between the rent-seeking prize secured by the successful rent seeker, and the resources used in rent seeking before the successful rent seeker receives the prize. The assignment of the prize redistributes income. The inefficiency due to rent seeking is incurred before the transfer of the income takes place.

---

[2] Adam Smith had a similar distrusting attitude to personal favors in markets, as we recall from chapter 1.

[3] Each thief is therefore prepared to accept a fair gamble as described in Chapter 5.

The social cost of monopoly and rent seeking

A number of rent seekers who are aware of the opportunity for monopoly privilege might contest the privilege to be the monopolist. The rent seekers will use resources to influence who will be the monopolist before political decision makers determine the identity of the successful monopolist. As in the case of the aspiring thieves, aspiring monopolists use time and resources and initiative in their efforts to become the ultimately successful monopolist before the identity of the successful rent seeker is determined. The successful rent seeker who becomes the monopolist and the successful thief are both stealing. The thief steals directly and is punished if caught and convicted. The theft of the monopolist is more devious and consists of the monopoly profits earned from the public. If competitive supply were to replace the monopolist, the public would not need to make the payments that provide the monopoly profits.[4]

Therefore, there are two social losses due to monopoly. There is an efficiency loss because the competitive market outcome is not achieved.[5] There is an additional efficiency loss through resources used in seeking the position of a monopolist, that is, in influencing who the monopolist will be.

While both the thief and the monopolist steal from the public in their different ways, there is a difference between the rent contested by thieves and the rent contested by aspiring monopolists. The rent sought by the aspiring monopolists is created through a public-policy decision that preserves monopoly privilege. The rent sought by the thieves is not created by public policy but is simply present in the form of the money in our pockets.

In modern democratic societies, political decision makers do not openly create and assign monopoly rents.[6] Rents are, however, sometimes assigned by policies that provide protection for domestic producers against foreign competition, by concessionary treatment in tax laws, and through public spending decisions.[7]

Private rationality and social losses

Although rent seeking is socially costly behavior, from an individual perspective, rent seeking is privately rational. Rent seeking takes place when a person compares personal benefits expected from alternative use of time and resources and finds that a rent-seeking opportunity yields the highest personal return.

---

[4] The profits are an unnecessary benefit for supply to take place, which is an attribute of a rent.

[5] These inefficiencies due to monopoly power, and also restrictions on imports, are similar to the inefficiencies due to the excess burden of taxation.

[6] There are also socially productive ways to become a monopolist. A pharmaceutical company that develops new medications is protected by patent laws and has a monopoly until the patent expires. Monopoly through a patent provides social benefit though incentives to innovate. An operating system for computers can provide market dominance if everybody decides that the operating system is superior to alternatives. We noted in Chapter 1 that monopoly is defined by barriers to entry of potential competitors rather than by the presence of a single supplier.

[7] Supplement 6D shows how rents arise through a quota restriction on permissible imports. Two categories of rents are created. There are rents for the privileged importers, as well as rents for domestic producers who benefit from the reduced foreign competition.

Of course, people who find rent seeking ethically objectionable will, as a matter of principle, not include returns from rent-seeking activities when considering alternative uses for their resources and time.

6.3.6 Rent creation

A form of rent seeking occurs when people change their behavior in order to benefit from social insurance entitlements from government. That is, the behavior that we described as moral hazard can have a social cost through rent seeking. For example, when government provides entitlements of income transfers to single parents, a person who has limited opportunities for earning market income might decide to have a baby. The act of rent seeking is the personal effort and time to have the child that, in the absence of the conditional government entitlement, the parent would not choose to have. Or we can consider unemployment insurance. Income entitlements through government-provided unemployment insurance provide assistance to people who are making an effort to find a job. At the same time, some people might respond to availability of payments from unemployment insurance by not diligently looking for a job. A social cost of rent seeking is incurred in the output lost because of the change in behavior due to the entitlement to unemployment benefits.[8]

In these preceding cases, public policy has created rents that have resulted in rent seeking, although the intention of government was socially beneficial social insurance. On other occasions, rents can be created purposefully for political assignment. The public policies that create such rents impose inefficiencies on a society. Yet the purpose of public policy should be to correct market inefficiencies and not to create market inefficiencies in order to create rents. We have noted that political decision makers might nonetheless choose inefficient policies that depart from the public interest in order to benefit from money provided by special interests.[9]

Suppose that a public policy can create a rent (or private benefit) of $100 million, that the rent is contestable, and that $60 million is spent in time and other resources in seeking to influence the political decision makers who will decide who will have the rent. At the same time, $40 million is given in political contributions in attempts to influence the political decision about who will receive the rent. Since only $60 million has been spent on resources used in rent seeking, the rent of $100 million has not been fully dissipated through rent seeking. The sum of $40 million was paid as a transfer of money, which is not a social waste (because no resources were wastefully used, but rather money changed hands, albeit unethically or not in the public interest).

If political decision makers personally benefit from the $40 million transfer from special interests who seek the public policy that creates the $100 million

---

[8] There is, in addition, a social loss through the excess burden of the taxes that finance the entitlement.

[9] We saw in Section 6.2 how political support might be maximized (or, the probability of winning the next election maximized) by trading off voter support against special-interest money.

rent, the sum of $40 million has become a prize in a second rent-seeking contest. The second rent-seeking contest is to determine who will benefit from the $40 million dollars of political contributions. Political candidates have incentives to use time and resources to attain political office in order to benefit from the $40 million available through the political discretion to make decisions about public policy.

The rent of $100 million is therefore dissipated in two separate contests. One contest is to influence political decisions about the assignment of the rent, and the other contest is to determine who will win political office and so who will receive the transfer payments made to political decision makers. Private-sector rent seekers spend $60 million in resources and pay $40 million to political decision makers. If the contest to be the political decision makers is competitive, $40 million of resources are used in political competition in this contest. Rent dissipation is then complete.[10] A total of $100 million of resources has been used in contests to obtain rents of $100 million.

We thus see that, when money changes hands, computation of the social cost of rent seeking requires following through the process of the transfer of money to establish whether the money is a prize for a further rent-seeking contest. If so, rent dissipation includes the resources used in the further contest where potential beneficiaries contest the transfers.

We can also envisage rents being created and contests being designed to provide maximal benefit to the political decision makers who have created the rents. Supplement 6C refers to studies of optimal contest design.

Rent seeking can also be associated with explicit corruption. Cases of rent creation through multiple-level rent-seeking contests arise in bureaucratic hierarchies when lower-level bureaucrats are obliged to pay a proportion of a bribe that they have received to their superiors in the hierarchy. In turn, the superiors may be obliged to pay a share to their superiors, and so on. At each level of the hierarchy, the value of a bureaucratic position is determined by the rents created for the position in the hierarchy. Because hierarchies tend to be pyramids, more rents flow through to higher levels of the hierarchy, making rent seeking and rent defense more strident the further up in the hierarchy the rent-seeking contests take place.

6.3.7 The social loss from unsuccessful rent seeking

Rent seekers may be unsuccessful in their attempts at political persuasion to create rents. The social cost of rent seeking is nonetheless incurred through the resources that were used in the unsuccessful attempt to create the rents.

Rent seeking may have been unsuccessful because of countervailing opposition by groups seeking to preempt the intentions of the rent seekers. Resources

---

[10] We have provided no explanation for the 60/40 division in our example between resources used in rent seeking to influence political decision makers' decisions and the transfer of money to influence decisions. The division might be an optimal decision for special interests between use of resources (e.g., lobbyists) and money in seeking to influence political decisions.

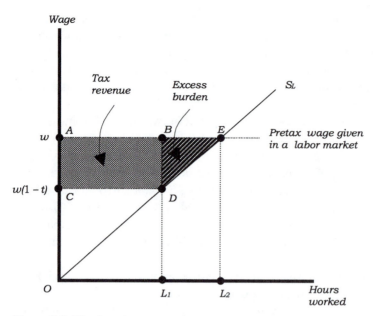

Figure 6.9. The loss to person 1.

will then also have been used in resisting the activities of rent-seeking interests. In that case, part of the social cost of rent seeking is the resources used in such countervailing activity. (See Supplement 6C.)

6.3.8 Excess burdens and rent-seeking incentives

Excess burdens and losses from use of resources in rent seeking are different sources of social loss. Excess burdens and rent seeking are also related. Let us consider a policy proposal to levy a tax of $1,000 on person 1 to finance a subsidy on consumption of a good by person 2. Figure 6.9 shows the labor supply function of person 1. A tax levied at a rate t reduces the wage received by person 1 from the market wage w to the post-tax wage $w(1-t)$, and hours worked contract from L_2 to L_1. The tax revenue paid by person 1 is $ABDC$, which is the $1,000 that is to be used to subsidize person 2's consumption. The excess burden of the tax is the area BDE. The excess burden might be $300. Person 1 stands to lose altogether $1,300 from the policy proposal. This is the value to person 1 of the prize in the rent-seeking contest to influence the policy decision. Person 1 is prepared to spend maximally $1,300 to preempt the policy.

Figure 6.10 shows the demand by person 2 for the good that is to be subsidized. The subsidy reduces person 2's price from P to $(P-S)$ and increases the quantity purchased from q_1 to q_2. The subsidy received is $AFEC$, which is the $1,000 paid in taxes by person 1. Person 2's valuation of the subsidy is $ABEC$. The difference between the value of the subsidy and person 2's valuation of the subsidy is FBE,

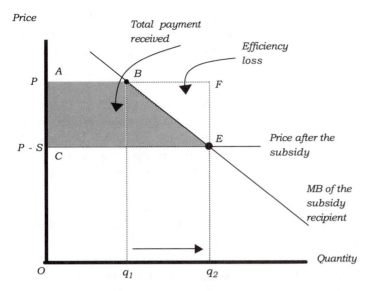

Figure 6.10. The gain to the subsidy recipient.

which is an efficiency loss. *FBE* might be $200. Person 2 then values the subsidy of $1,000 as $800.

Person 2 is therefore prepared to spend $800 to encourage adoption of the policy, and person 1 is prepared to spend $1,300 to forestall the policy. Resources of $1,300 opposing the policy are then matched against resources of $800 in favor of the policy. The political advantage is therefore with person 1 who opposes the policy. In this type of contest, the values of the prizes differ for different participants and the advantage in the contest is with those who have more to lose, or whose prize from success is greater.[11]

6.3.9 Political efficiency

If political decision makers decide to proceed with the policy that taxes person 1 in Figure 6.9 for the benefit of person 2 in Figure 6.10, their incentive is to make the transfer in a way that minimizes the efficiency loss of the transfer policy. The sum of *BDE* in Figure 6.9 and *BFE* in Figure 6.10 might be the minimal efficiency loss possible for making the transfer. It is in everybody's interest to minimize inefficiency because the smaller the efficiency losses are, the more there is to be shared among everybody. The idea of sharing efficiency gains was the foundation for the Coase theorem in Chapter 4 about private incentives for voluntary resolution of externalities. The resolution of the externalities provided the efficiency gains to be shared. Political decision makers similarly have an incentive to choose the most efficient means of creating and delivering rents to rent seekers.[12]

---

[11] See Supplement 6C on models of rent-seeking contests with asymmetric valuation of prizes.

[12] The case that political decisions are efficient has been made by Gary Becker (1983) of the University of Chicago and Donald Wittman (1995) of the University of California at Santa Cruz.

Political efficiency can be compared with market efficiency. We described market efficiency in Chapter 1 as arising through the invisible hand. Political efficiency is about efficiency when departures from the invisible hand take place through public policies.

When creating rents, political decision makers would in general also like to have an invisible hand because political decision makers do not want voters to observe the creation and assignment of rents through public policy. Obtuse means of making income transfers or creating and assigning rents may be available, although such means may also be less efficient in incurring greater excess burdens (i.e., greater values than BDE in Figure 6.9 combined with BFE in Figure 6.10). There is an incentive for political decision makers to choose the less efficient means of public policy, if the political creation of rents is thereby made less obvious to voters. For example, a direct handout of public money may be the most efficient means of providing a rent. However, the rent would then be part of the visible statement of a government budget.[13] A monopoly rent or a rent from a restriction on foreign competition does not appear as an item in the government budget. The rent does not pass through the hands of government in its passage to a successful rent seeker, but is transferred to the rent seeker through higher market prices that buyers pay. When rents are not recorded in the government budget, political decision makers can hope to give the appearance of not having been responsive to rent-seeking approaches. Political efficiency, which would involve choice of public policies with the least amount of social loss, can therefore be compromised by political benefits from using obtuse means of creating and assigning rents.

In other cases political efficiency is compromised because rents can only be provided through public spending. We observed in Chapter 3 that logrolling may allow a political representative to obtain majority support from fellow representatives for public spending on a project that benefits the representative's constituency, but the project need not pass the test of cost-benefit analysis and so need not be efficient. When a project does not pass the test of cost-benefit analysis, the people in the representative's constituency would prefer to receive the public money directly for private spending rather than have the money finance the public project. A direct transfer of public money for private spending to a politician's constituency is in general not feasible. If the rent is to be delivered to the constituency at all, the delivery may only be politically feasible through public spending on the inefficient project.

It appears that political efficiency in public policies that deliver rents cannot be ensured. Less efficient means of delivering rents that are less visible can be preferred, to avoid rents passing through public hands on the way to beneficiaries and so to avoid the payments being recorded in the government budget. Inefficient public spending may also be the only politically feasible means of delivering rents.

---

[13] The rent could perhaps be effectively hidden within the many items of the government budget; nonetheless, the rent passes through the hands of government on its way to the successful rent seeker.

6.3.10 Locational choice

If locational choice among government jurisdictions has resulted in a population of individuals seeking identical public finance and public policy decisions, there would be no rent seeking because no one would want anything other than the policies that voters will have chosen by consensus.

However, rent seeking might still take place if politicians had the means to provide special favors for individuals. More usually, rent seeking takes place by groups. If one group has chosen a location because of common interests in public spending and public policy, there is no rent seeking by groups.

Populations in different jurisdictions are in general not entirely uniform in their requirements regarding public-finance and public-policy decisions, in particular when sufficiently diverse locational options do not exist to allow substantial locational sorting. Locational choice nonetheless reduces rent-seeking incentives to the extent that populations have formed with more similar requirements for political decision making.

6.3.11 A comparison between two societies

We can compare two societies. In one society, all competition takes place beneficially through markets. In another society, there is substantial competition for politically created rents. The latter rent-seeking society will be more unfortunate and poorer because of the personal efforts and initiative directed at rent seeking. We may also see in the latter rent-seeking society successful rent seekers who have amassed considerable wealth.

The two societies have different political cultures. The different political cultures are reflected in the reasons people choose to go into public life and seek political office or a position in the government bureaucracy. In the society without rent seeking, a person may choose to enter politics because of a desire to improve the welfare of society, and perhaps also because of egotistical personal objectives that are satisfied through public office. In the rent-seeking society, people are more likely to choose a career in politics so that they can dispense favors through public policy with the intention of enhancing their personal wealth.

In the rent-seeking society, there will also be more discontent and envy because personal success and benefit will be attributed to successful rent seeking. Self-improvement through personal effort and merit will be undermined because people will perceive that influence over political decisions offers better private rewards than productive effort.

Rent seeking takes place because of the perception that political decision makers can be influenced to create and assign rents. If political decision makers are perceived in this way, then, whether the political response to rent seeking is ultimately favorable or not, the incentives are present to use resources in socially wasteful rent-seeking activities. The incentives to use resources in rent seeking are conversely not present when it is known that decisions about public policies cannot be influenced for privileged personal benefit. In the final analysis, therefore, rent seeking is determined more by the political culture that determines the behavior of political decision makers than by the behavior of private rent seekers. Where the behavior of political decision makers does not provide incentives for rent seeking, rent seeking does not take place.

References and related literature

On rent seeking behavior, see Tullock (1967, 1988). On rent extraction, see McChesney (1997). On rent seeking under monarchy, see Baysinger, Ekelund, and Tollison (1980), and on rent seeking under collective property, see Gelb, Hillman, and Ursprung (1998) and Hillman and Ursprung (2000). On rent seeking and the social cost of monopoly, see Posner (1975). On rent seeking to benefit from import quotas, see Krueger (1974). On rent seeking and protectionist polices, see Hillman (1989). On political efficiency, see Becker (1983), Coate and Morris (1995) and Wittman (1995). On rent seeking and similarity of preferences in a population, see Fafchamps, de Janvry, and Sadoulet (1999). For collected readings and surveys of rent seeking, see Buchanan, Tollison, and Tullock (1980), Rowley, Tollison, and Tullock (1988), Nitzan (1994, 1998), and Congleton and Tollison (1995). On how the form of rent-seeking contents affects rent dissipation, see Supplement 6C.

Baysinger, B., R. B. Ekelund and R. D. Tollison, 1980. Mercantilism as a rent seeking society. In *Toward a Theory of the Rent Seeking Society*, J. M. Buchanan, R. D. Tollison, and G. Tullock (eds.). Texas A&M Press, College Station, 235–68.

Becker, G., 1983. A theory of competition among pressure groups for political influence. *Quarterly Journal of Economics* 98, 371–99.

Buchanan, J. M., R. D. Tollison and G. Tullock (eds.), 1980. *Toward a Theory of the Rent Seeking Society*. Texas A&M Press, College Station.

Coate, S. and S. Morris, 1995. On the form of transfers to special interests. *Journal of Political Economy* 103, 1210–35.

Congleton, R. and R. Tollison (eds.), 1995. *The Economic Analysis of Rent Seeking*. Edward Elgar, Oxford.

Fafchamps, M., A. de Janvry and E. Sadoulet (1999). Social heterogeneity and wasteful lobbying. *Public Choice* 98, 5–27.

Gelb, A., A. L. Hillman and H. W. Ursprung, 1998. Rents as distractions: Why the exit from transition is prolonged. In *Economic Interdependence and Cooperation in Europe*, N. C. Baltas, G. Demopoulos, and J. Hassid (eds.). Springer, Berlin, 1998, 21–38.

Hillman, A. L., 1989. *The Political Economy of Protection*. Harwood Academic Publishers, Chur. Reprinted 2001, Routledge, London.

Hillman, A. L. and H. W. Ursprung, 2000. Political culture and economic decline. *European Journal of Political Economy* 16, 189–213.

Krueger, A. O., 1974. The political economy of the rent seeking society. *American Economic Review* 64, 291–303.

McChesney, F. S., 1997. *Money for Nothing*. Harvard University Press, Cambridge, Massachusetts.

Nitzan, S. I., 1994. Modeling rent seeking contests. *European Journal of Political Economy* 10, 41–60.

Nitzan, S. I. (ed.), 1998. *Contest Theory*. Special issue, *European Journal of Political Economy* 14 (4).

Posner, R., 1975. The social costs of monopoly and regulation. *Journal of Political Economy* 83, 807–27.

Rowley, C., R. D. Tollison and G. Tullock (eds.), 1988. *The Political Economy of Rent-Seeking*, Kluwer Academic Publishers, Boston and Dordrecht.

Tullock, G., 1967. The welfare costs of tariffs, monopoly, and theft. *Western Economic Journal* 5, 224–32.

Tullock, G., 1988. *The Economics of Rent-Seeking and Privilege*. Kluwer Academic Publishers, Boston and Dordrecht.

Wittman, D. A., 1995. *The Myth of Democratic Failure: Why Political Institutions Are Efficient*. University of Chicago Press, Chicago.

Questions for discussion

1. What is the definition of a rent? Why is a contestable rent a source of private gain but social loss? A medical device can be patented, but medical procedures cannot be patented. Suppose that a medical surgeon who has devised a new medical procedure spends two years trying to change public policy to allow medical procedures to be patented. How has society incurred a social loss through rent seeking? Does the social loss depend on whether the attempt to change public policy was successful?

2. Are professional tennis players competing in a tennis tournament engaged in rent seeking? Explain.

3. There is a similarity between social loss from rent seeking and the social loss under conditions of anarchy when people use resources to appropriate the property or output of others. Yet the social losses due to rent seeking and the social loss due to appropriation under anarchy have different institutional backgrounds. What is the difference in institutional backgrounds? How is this difference related to government?

4. Hereditary monarchy based on absolute power was often justified as preempting rent seeking. Yet absolute hereditary monarchies were also bastions of rent seeking. What privileges could the monarch offer that people could seek? In present times, do hereditary absolute monarchies still exist? Can you identify countries that are not official hereditary monarchies but where children of the ruler have more or less automatically succeeded the ruler? If these countries exist, is the mass of the population rich or poor? How is whether the population is rich or poor affected by incentives for rent seeking?

5. In 1967, Gordon Tullock proposed the idea that rent seeking is a source of social loss by observing common elements of import taxes (or tariffs), monopoly, and theft. Tullock could have based the common elements of import taxes, monopoly, and theft on the observation that import duties and monopoly are both like theft because of the extra unnecessary costs imposed on buyers by import duties and monopoly. However, Tullock based the common relation on rent seeking. Why is rent seeking a characteristic that import tariffs, monopoly, and theft have in common?

6. Rent-seeking activities are usually hidden and so are not directly observable, but quite often the value of the rent-seeking prize can be observed. Economic models of rational behavior when prizes are available from successful rent seeking provide relationships between the unobserved value of resources used in rent seeking by people aspiring to obtain the rents and the value of the rents available. How does the specification of the "contest-success function" affect the relation between the observed rent that

is contested by rent seekers and the total value of all resources used in rent seeking by rent seekers? (See Supplement 6C.) What are the other principal influences on the relation between a rent and the resources used in contesting the rent?

7. How do social norms affect the prevalence of rent seeking?

8. "Rent seeking is privately rational but socially (or collectively) irrational." Can you explain why this is so using the relationships of the prisoners' dilemma? In the context of the prisoners' dilemma, in a society when people in government are responsive to rent seeking, why are ethical people who refuse to participate in rent seeking disadvantaged?

9. People whose success has been due to rent seeking will in general deny that rent seeking has been the basis of their personal success and will in general put forward alternative explanations for their success based on their abilities and personal merit. Yet there are also societies where people are openly proud of their rent-seeking successes? Could this happen in the society where you live? What would you predict about a society where open pride in rent-seeking successes is common?

10. How can social losses from rent seeking arise in connection with social insurance entitlements provided by government? How are such losses related to the problems of moral hazard that can affect social insurance?

11. When computing the efficiency losses to a society of a quota on imports, why does account have to be taken of both excess burdens and rent seeking? Why is a quota like a tax that has an excess burden of taxation? (See Supplement 6D.) How is the social cost of monopoly similar to the social cost of an import quota?

12. Why would political decisions makers ever choose public policies that create rather than correct inefficiencies?

13. How do efficiency losses through excess burdens affect incentives to use resources in political contests to influence policy decisions about redistribution? How do such efficiency losses affect the prospects of success in such political contests?

14. In a society where government officials are corrupt, how are bribes transformed into contestable rents? That is, how does the social cost of rent seeking become a component of the social cost of corruption?

15. "Everyone has an interest in using the most efficient public policy means to achieve an income redistribution objective, because efficiency losses benefit nobody and efficiency gains can be shared to make everyone better off. Therefore political decision makers will be sure to choose the most efficient policy means of catering to rent seeking." Do you agree? Explain.

16. Why is rent seeking taking place when a student who has not studied for an exam and has consequently received a low grade tries to improve his or her grade by persuading the instructor that a higher grade is merited? What is the form of the social loss of rent seeking in this case? Who bears the social loss?

17. Suppose that a student offers a personal favor to the instructor in return for a higher grade. Why would the student believe that the instructor could be approached with such an offer? Rather than a student seeking to persuade an instructor to change a grade, is there any difference in principle if a special-interest group is attempting to persuade a political decision maker to choose a public policy that is not in the public interest?

18. How can we guard against the excessive cynicism of viewing rent seeking as being involved in all offers of personal favors and all special privileges that people seem to have been given?

19. Why is a social loss incurred through unsuccessful rent seeking? When rent seeking has been unsuccessful in creating a rent, what have rent seekers misjudged?

20. How is rent seeking related to political culture? How is rent seeking related to envy?

7

TAXATION

Governments require revenue from taxation to finance public spending. We have encountered taxation many times in previous chapters. This chapter focuses on issues specific to the design of taxation. We begin with personal taxation. We shall then look at the different forms of taxation that a government can choose. Finally, we shall consider refusal to pay taxes, or tax evasion and the informal economy.

7.1

Personal Taxation

7.1.1 The Ramsey rule for efficient taxation

We shall now be concerned with two objectives, choosing taxes that are efficient and choosing taxes that result in or are consistent with social justice. We begin with taxation that is efficient. For this purpose, we consider a government that has decided that it requires a particular amount of tax revenue. The reason the government requires the tax revenue is for now not important: the tax revenue might be required for spending on public goods (as in Chapter 2) or for financing income transfers to people in need (as in Chapter 5).[1] Efficient taxation is defined as taxation that minimizes the efficiency losses incurred through the excess burden of taxation when collecting the specified amount of tax revenue. The solution for efficient taxation is known as the Ramsey rule, named for the British scholar Frank Ramsey (1903–1930), who derived the rule in 1927.

For example, suppose that sales taxes can be levied on two goods A and B. A rate of tax t_A will be levied on good A and a rate of tax t_B will be levied on good B, and a government is looking for the efficient combination of taxes on the two goods.[2] Let us add the information that the markets for the goods A and B are competitive, and that, as in the case shown in Figure 7.1, supply is at constant costs. With ε_{Di} denoting the market demand elasticity of good i, the Ramsey rule for efficient taxation is that the tax rates should be set in the two markets so that

$$\frac{t_A}{t_B} = \frac{\varepsilon_{DB}}{\varepsilon_{DA}}. \tag{7.1}$$

Expression (7.1) indicates that the tax rates on the two goods should be inversely related to the demand elasticities of the two goods. The tax rate should therefore be higher on the good that has the lower price elasticity of demand. It follows in particular from expression (7.1) that, if there exists a market in which the demand elasticity is zero, taxes should only be imposed in that market.[3]

---

[1] Governments levy taxes to finance public spending on public goods and to finance income redistribution, but taxation is also part of the Pigovian solution for externality problems and can also be used to discourage consumption when there is a perception that people are harming themselves. In these cases, which we considered in Chapter 4, the purpose of taxation is to affect incentives and not to provide revenue for public spending. In this chapter, we shall consider taxation only for the purpose of financing public spending.

[2] These sales taxes set in percentage terms are called ad valorem taxes. The taxes could also be specific, which are taxes set in value terms. Whether taxes are set in ad valorem or specific terms matters when there is inflation (inflation erodes the value of specific taxes) or when there is uncertainty about market prices (the lower a market price is, the higher the rate of tax when the tax is specific, whereas an ad valorem tax by definition always maintains the same rate of taxation).

[3] The expression for the Ramsey rule in (7.1) is based on (1) constant costs of supply for the two goods A and B (as in Figure 7.1) and (2) a tax in one market not affecting tax revenue in other markets (i.e., cross-price elasticities are zero). The expression for the Ramsey rule is more complex when these conditions are not satisfied. The basic principle of the Ramsey rule is, however, retained in these

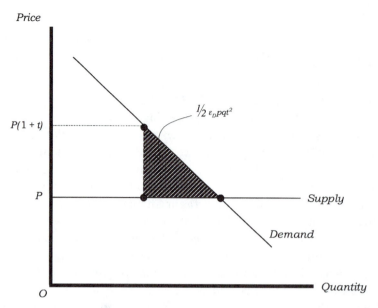

Figure 7.1. The efficiency loss or excess burden in a single market.

Expression (7.1) shows the Ramsey rule for efficient taxation when a government chooses taxes on two goods. The Ramsey rule extends generally to any number of taxes on different goods. The Ramsey rule applies for taxes levied on different components or sources of income that a person might have, and also applies to different people earning incomes from the same source. We shall presently consider the implications of the Ramsey rule in these cases. First, however, we shall see how the Ramsey rule for efficient taxation is derived, and we shall consider in more detail the logic underlying the Ramsey rule. We shall then see how the Ramsey rule is applied in the different circumstances when the purpose of taxation is to finance public spending on public goods and to finance income transfers.

How is the Ramsey rule derived?
We derived the expression for the excess burden of a tax in Chapter 2 as

$$\frac{1}{2}\varepsilon_D p q t^2. \tag{7.2}$$

Figure 7.1 shows the excess burden in a competitive market.[4] With no tax, the market determines the price in Figure 7.1 as P. A tax at rate t increases the price to $P(1+t)$. The excess burden of the tax is given by expression (7.2).

With markets for two goods A and B, we have two figures like Figure 7.1, one for each good, and two tax rates t_A and t_B. Taxation is efficient when the

---

more complex situations: efficient taxation requires tax rates to be lower where market elasticities are higher.

[4] Again, expression (7.2) for the excess burden of a tax is based on constant costs and presupposes that a tax in one market has no effects in other markets.

combination of the two taxes t_A and t_B minimizes the combined excess burden in the two markets of raising a target sum of revenue R.

Efficient values of the taxes t_A and t_B therefore minimize the sum of excess burdens in the two markets

$$\frac{1}{2}\varepsilon_{D1}p_A q_A t_A^2 + \frac{1}{2}\varepsilon_{D2}p_B q_B t_B^2 \tag{7.3}$$

subject to satisfying the revenue target of the government

$$R = t_A P_A Q_A + t_B P_B Q_B, \tag{7.4}$$

where $Q_i (i = A, B)$ are the quantities sold in the market. The solution to this problem is the Ramsey rule as expressed in (7.1).[5]

Expression (7.1) gives the ratio between the tax rates t_A and t_B. When we know the ratio, substitution into expression (7.4) provides the absolute values of the tax rates t_A and t_B that minimize the excess burden of taxation *and* provide sufficient combined revenue to meet the government's revenue target R.

Efficient taxation of personal incomes

Expression (7.1) shows the Ramsey rule for taxation of goods. That is, the taxes are paid when people spend their incomes. The Ramsey rule similarly applies to taxes that people pay when income is earned (i.e., to personal income taxes). In that case, we envisage a government as again having a tax revenue target of R. The government chooses different constant (proportional) income tax rates t_1 and t_2 for two persons.[6] With ε_1 and ε_2 denoting the individual labor supply elasticities (which reflect substitution responses between work and leisure), the Ramsey rule for efficient proportional income taxes levied on the two people is

$$\frac{t_1}{t_2} = \frac{\varepsilon_{S2}}{\varepsilon_{S1}}. \tag{7.5}$$

That is, the two individuals' personal income tax rates should be inversely related to their personal labor-market supply elasticities.

The logic of the Ramsey rule for efficient taxation

Let us now consider the logic of the Ramsey rule. The source of the excess burden of taxation is a substitution response between work (or effort) and free time, and the magnitude of a substitution response is measured by a supply or demand

---

[5] The Ramsey rule follows from forming the Lagrangean function from (7.3) and (7.4). Differentiating with respect to the tax rates t_A and t_B establishes that $t_A \varepsilon_{DA} = t_B \varepsilon_{DB}$, which implies the expression (7.1). If, for some reason, with many goods, a particular good cannot be taxed or a tax on a good cannot be changed, the Lagrangean function includes an additional constraint. In this framework, which is known as "second-best" because the first-best efficient outcome is not attainable (see also Chapter 4), the Ramsey rule accommodates the inability to adjust one of the taxes.

[6] We are here not looking at the structure of an income tax schedule. One tax rate characterizes the income tax for each person. We shall investigate the structure of an income tax schedule with variable tax rates later in this section.

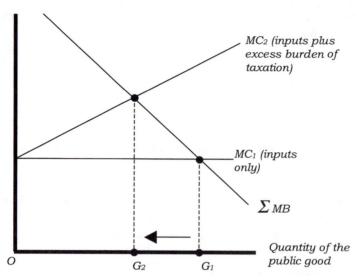

Valuation and cost

Figure 7.2. The Ramsey rule and efficient public spending on public goods.
The Ramsey rule ensures that efficient supply of public goods is financed by efficient taxation.

elasticity. When elasticities are low, substitution responses are low, and the excess burden of taxation is low.

When a tax is increased, a marginal increase takes place in the loss imposed on the taxpayer through the excess burden of taxation.[7] The increased loss occurs through the substitution response as individuals change their spending or income-earning behavior because of the increased tax. The logic of the Ramsey rule for efficient taxation is that the marginal losses due to excess burdens of increases in different taxes should be equal. Thus, in expression (7.1), the greater the demand elasticity is, the greater the substitution response to the taxes; therefore, to keep the combined excess burden of taxation low, lower taxes should be levied on goods with greater demand elasticities. To minimize combined excess burdens, the tax rates should be inversely proportional to the elasticities.

The Ramsey rule and public spending on public goods

Let us now look at how the Ramsey rule is applied when the purpose of taxation is to finance public spending on public goods. Figure 7.2, which is reproduced from Chapter 2, shows how efficient spending on a public good is determined. The rule for efficient public spending on public goods is that $\sum MB$ of the population should equal the MC of providing the public good, where costs consist of public spending plus the excess burden of taxes that finance the public spending. MC_1 in

---

[7] We see in expression (7.1) that the excess burden is increasing with the square of the tax rate. See also Chapter 2.

Figure 7.2 is the constant market cost of the inputs required for the public good. MC_2 is the marginal cost of supplying the public good through public spending when the excess burden of taxation is included as part of the cost. If there were no excess burden of taxation, efficient public spending on the public good would provide the quantity G_1. Because of the excess burden of taxation, efficient public spending provides the smaller quantity G_2.

To find the efficient quantity G_2, a government proceeds through the following steps.

(1) The government uses cost-benefit analysis to determine the total marginal benefits $\sum MB$ of the population. The government may know MC_1 from market costs of the inputs required to supply the public good; otherwise, cost-benefit analysis is also required to compute the costs of the inputs for the public good.[8]

(2) For every amount of tax revenue R that the government might possibly require to finance public spending, the government uses the Ramsey rule to identify the efficient combination of taxes that raise this revenue. The government thereby identifies the function MC_2 in Figure 7.2. After the function MC_2 is known, the government equates $\sum MB$ and MC_2 to determine the efficient quantity G_2.

The Ramsey rule is thus part of the procedure for determining efficient public spending on public goods. The rule ensures that efficient quantities of public goods are financed by efficient taxation.[9] We note the two aspects of efficiency that are involved: (1) choice of the efficient quantity of the public good and (2) choice of efficient taxes to finance supply of the efficient quantity of the public good.

The Ramsey rule and the financing of income transfers

Now let us look at the role of the Ramsey rule when the purpose of taxation is to finance public spending on income transfers. In Chapter 5, we considered taxation as the means of implementing a social insurance contract. The social insurance contract was chosen before people knew who they were going to be and was reflected in the choice of a social welfare function. The social insurance contract specified that government would levy taxes on people with high incomes who have had fortunate outcomes in life and would transfer the tax revenue to people with low incomes whose outcomes had been more unfortunate. Figure 7.3 returns us to circumstances we considered in Chapter 5, where two people face alternative market-determined outcomes for income distribution and consequent personal utilities at points F_1 and F_2. If the market outcome at F_1 arises, person 1 is taxed, and the revenue is transferred to person 2 to move the society to the point 1. The policy of tax-financed income redistribution increases social welfare from W_0 to W_1.

---

[8] There could be negative externalities as part of costs (see Chapter 4). There could also be positive externalities.

[9] That is, the efficient taxes minimize the distance between MC_1 and MC_2 in Figure 7.2.

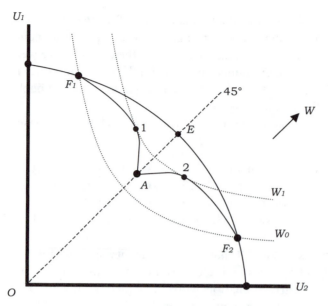

Figure 7.3. The Ramsey rule and taxation to finance income redistribution.

The Ramsey rule ensures that efficient taxation is used to redistribute income along F_1A or F_2A.

Similarly, should the market outcome be at point F_2, taxation and income redistribution move the society to point 2, and again social welfare increases from W_0 to W_1.

Higher rates of taxation increase the loss incurred through the excess burden of taxation.[10] The more tax revenue required for redistribution, the lower the levels of utility that are therefore available along the frontiers F_1A and F_2A in Figure 7.2 along which tax-financed income redistribution takes place. When a government has a number of different possible tax bases, the Ramsey rule indicates the efficient combination of the different taxes for providing tax revenue for redistribution. The Ramsey rule therefore identifies the location of the efficient transfer frontiers F_1A and F_2A in Figure 7.3.

In Figure 7.3, suppose that the market pre-tax outcome is at point F_1. Person 1 will then be taxed to finance the income transfer to person 2. Person 1 personally pays the tax and personally bears the excess burden of the tax. Therefore, person 1 wants the excess burden of taxation to be minimized. At the same time, except for the case of social welfare defined according to Rawls, the amount of the income transfer received by person 2 decreases with the excess burden of the tax levied on person 1.[11] Because the income transfer received by person 2 is greater, the

---

[10] If there were no excess burden of taxation, income redistribution in Figure 7.3 would be from F_1 or F_2 to point E.

[11] We saw in Chapter 5 that Rawls cares only about the utility of the worst-off person and not about the efficiency losses incurred through the excess burden of taxation in providing the least-well-off person with tax-financed income transfers.

lower the excess burden of taxation (the less leaky is the redistributive bucket) is, person 2 also wants taxation to be efficient in accord with the Ramsey rule. There is consensus between the taxpayer and the transfer recipient that taxation should be efficient.

7.1.2 Social justice and the Ramsey rule

In principle, everybody should favor efficiency. Everybody should therefore favor using the Ramsey rule to find the efficient combination of taxes for raising government tax revenue, whether the revenue is to be used to finance public spending on public goods or to finance the income transfers of a social insurance contract.

The focus of the Ramsey rule is on achieving efficiency. We should not necessarily expect the Ramsey rule to provide social justice. Indeed, the Ramsey rule seems to contradict ideas of social justice.

Efficient taxation according to the Ramsey rule requires tax rates to be high for goods that have no close substitutes because demand elasticities for such goods are low. The Ramsey rule accordingly calls for high tax rates on goods such as food and housing, spectacles and contact lenses, toothbrushes, soap, wheelchairs, and baby cereal. Tax rates should, on the other hand, according to the Ramsey rule, be low on designer clothes, dining in luxury restaurants, jewelry, yachts, private planes, and luxury houses because demand elasticities (and substitution opportunities) for these goods are high.

Efficiency requires keeping substitution responses to a minimum. Therefore the Ramsey rule proposes high tax rates for goods and services that people continue to purchase (or still need to buy) after taxation has increased the price to buyers. With taxation of goods based on the Ramsey rule, the poor whose spending is principally on necessities of life bear a relatively greater burden of taxation for the sake of efficiency. Placing higher tax burdens on necessities that are more important components of poorer (or lower-income) people's spending contradicts conceptions of social justice.

Similarly, the recommendations of the Ramsey rule regarding taxation of personal incomes also contradict ideas of social justice. Let us consider two people. Person 1 is independently wealthy but is prepared to work if paid enough. Person 2 has no source of income other than from work and has no choice but to work for a living. The richer person's labor supply elasticity is higher because of the alternative of not working, while the poorer person's labor supply elasticity is lower because of the need to earn income from work to survive. Hence, in expression (7.5), $\varepsilon_{S1} > \varepsilon_{S2}$. The Ramsey rule therefore proposes that the wealthier person should be taxed at a lower rate than the poorer person who has less flexibility when making labor supply decisions.

In Figure 7.3, we considered income transfers between two people, one a taxpayer and the other the recipient of the tax-financed transfers. Suppose that there are three people – two taxpayers and one recipient of an income transfer. One of the two taxpayers might have higher pre-tax income than the other. The injustices of the Ramsey rule arise when higher taxes are levied on goods that are necessities on which the lower-income person spends a larger share of income, and when the lower-income person faces a higher rate of income tax because of more limited possibilities for substitution away from work.

Efficient taxation and gender differences

Let us now consider how the Ramsey rule affects proposals for taxing the incomes of men and women. In the traditional model of society based on the institution of the family and children, a man and woman marry and have children. When the children are young, the woman might reduce labor-market participation. The post-tax income available to the woman determines when she reenters the labor force or how much she works. Under these circumstances, the woman's labor-supply elasticity is greater than that of the man. The Ramsey rule then calls for higher tax rates on the income of men than on income earned by women on efficiency grounds because women's substitution possibilities include caring for their young children at home. The woman's greater substitution possibilities (or higher labor-supply elasticity) are also reflected in the decision to have a child.

This conclusion derived from the Ramsey rule regarding taxation of incomes of men and women is specific to the traditional model of the family and as such does not apply when there is equality between men and women in labor-market behavior and in home and income responsibilities. In that case, when the woman has decided on a career unencumbered by family responsibilities or when (subject to biological limitations) the man shares all responsibilities, the Ramsey rule calls for equal personal tax treatment of men and women.

The family and gender equality therefore affect efficient income taxation of men and women. When or where the traditional family prevails, efficiency calls for more favorable tax treatment for women, but not when gender distinctions have become unimportant in the labor market.

Seeking efficiency by taxing ability and personal attributes

The excess burden of taxation is zero if there are no substitution responses to taxes. Therefore, as we previously observed in interpreting the Ramsey rule, if a tax base could be found with no substitution responses, the Ramsey rule would advise levying all taxes on that tax base because taxation would then be efficient with no excess burden.

Payment of income taxes can be reduced by choosing to earn less income, that is, by substituting free time for work. There is an excess burden of taxation through the substitution effect. However, if innate personal abilities could be taxed, substitution responses could not take place. People cannot make substitution decisions that change their innate ability. Taxes based on personal innate abilities are therefore efficient according to the Ramsey rule.

We recall from Chapter 1 the principle of proposed behavior that was part of the ideology of collective property. This principle would have people contribute according to their ability and not according to the personal rewards they receive.[12] We also noted the observations of Hayek and others that this principle contradicts human nature. The Ramsey rule indicates that, if people can nonetheless be found who have been convinced that they should contribute according to their abilities and not their personal rewards, governments should tax these people highly because such people will continue working and producing according to their abilities without regard for their post-tax incomes. That is, taxation of these people will result in no substitution responses.

If innate abilities could be identified and taxed, there would also be no substitution responses because innate abilities are given and not subject to change. We see that there is a relationship between the idea that people should contribute according to their ability, and the conclusion from the Ramsey rule that personal innate ability should be taxed.

Innate ability is difficult to measure. Suppose however that measurement were possible. Would we want to follow the recommendation of the Ramsey rule that people should be taxed according to their ability to earn income – and not according to the incomes they actually earn? People with high innate ability might have different preferences about combining a traditional family with a career. With taxation based on innate ability to earn income, people who choose a lifestyle that includes a family would face the same obligation to pay taxes as people who have decided to focus on career goals and have high incomes. Taxing ability then corresponds to taxing personal preferences of those people who voluntarily wish to forgo high income for other sources of personal satisfaction. Taxing ability as proposed by the Ramsey rule would be an intrusion in people's personal lives and their personal choices.

Taxation based on innate ability would also provide incentives for people to hide their true abilities by pretending to have low abilities. Parents might train their children to avoid revealing true ability. Taxes based on ability would then have high excess burdens because of the acts undertaken in pretense to show low ability.

The Ramsey rule and taxing beauty

Innate beauty is like innate ability. The role of beauty has been studied as a personal innate attribute that determines income in the labor market. The results revealed that "better-looking" people choose the types of jobs where beauty yields a higher return, but also that beauty increases personal income across occupations.[13] If beauty is innate, so that a market return to beauty is similar to a market return to innate ability, the Ramsey rule would propose that people should be taxed according to their beauty, on the grounds that since substitution away from beauty is impossible, beauty can be taxed without an excess burden. That is, taxing

---

[12] The principle is consistent with limitations on people being personally rewarded when output and property are collective and, therefore, cannot be personal property.

[13] The study was by Daniel Hamermesh and Jeff Biddle (1994).

innate beauty is efficient. If beauty can however be manipulated or hidden, there are substitution effects. Excess burdens would therefore arise from personal taxes on beauty. Like the pretense of low ability, parents might train their children to make themselves appear personally unattractive.

7.1.3 Progressivity and regressivity in an income tax

Social justice in taxation is often associated with progressivity in personal income taxation. We define progressivity through the share of income that an individual pays in taxes,

$$\frac{\text{Income paid in taxes}}{\text{Income earned}} = \frac{R}{Y}, \tag{7.6}$$

where R is the total personal income tax the person pays and Y is the person's pre-tax income. For a progressive tax, the share of income paid in taxes indicated in expression (7.6) increases with income. An income tax is regressive when the share of income paid in taxes declines with income. With proportional taxation, the share of income paid in taxes remains constant.

The Ramsey rule appears to suggest that income taxes need to be regressive. We have seen that the Ramsey rule requires higher rates of taxation on lower incomes, if free-time or leisure substitution possibilities for a low-income person are more restricted than for a high-income person.

Principles of socially just taxation

Let us now set aside the Ramsey rule. We shall proceed as if there were no excess burden of taxation and therefore no efficiency losses from taxation. With no efficiency losses from taxation, we can focus on the objective of socially just taxation.

Two principles of social justice in taxation are horizontal and vertical equity. Horizontal equity requires that people with the same incomes and same attributes (family status, dependents) pay the same taxes. Vertical equity requires that people with different incomes make equal sacrifices when paying taxes.[14] Horizontal equity requires "equal treatment for equal people" and so rules out arbitrary discrimination in taxation. Vertical equity requires equal treatment of unequal people.

To obtain a perspective on vertical equity, we can begin by considering a person who earns $2,000 a month. This income can be divided into the first $1,000 and the second $1,000. A government can levy a tax rate of t_1 percent on the first $1,000 of income and a tax rate of t_2 percent on the second $1,000. The government wants to treat the two parts of income "equally" for purposes of taxation. Because of diminishing marginal benefit (or utility) from income, the personal benefit from the first $1,000 of income is greater than the benefit from the second $1,000 of income. If the same rate of taxation is applied to both parts of income, the taxpayer therefore loses more from the tax on the first $1,000 of income than from the tax on the second $1,000 of income.

---

[14] In Chapter 6, we observed that these principles of social justice limit the redistribution that can take place from a majority to a minority through majority voting.

It follows then that, to equalize the losses due to the taxes on the two parts of income, the rate of taxation should be lower on the first $1,000 than on the second $1,000. That is, the income tax structure should be progressive.

Now consider two different people, one of whom earns $1,000 a month and another who earns $2,000 a month. The two people benefit equally when spending the same income. Because the two people have different incomes, we require a rule for "equal treatment of unequals" or vertical equity to determine the taxes that each person pays. Vertical equity calls for a tax structure that is progressive. Both people pay the same rate of taxation t_1 on the first $1,000 earned, and the person who earns the additional $1,000 of income pays a higher rate of taxation t_2 on the second $1,000. There are two "tax brackets." The same principle of progressivity in rates of taxation applies to further higher incomes, for which there are further tax brackets. The progressivity of income taxes is achieved through the increasing marginal rates of taxation that apply to different tax brackets as personal income increases.

A more formal statement of the vertical equity of progressive taxation

Another way of reaching the conclusion that vertical equity implies progressive taxation is to begin by observing that the intention of an income tax is to tax the benefit (or utility) that a person derives from spending income. We again divide income into two parts. Let the personal benefit from the first part of income be $B(Y_1)$ and the benefit from the second part of income be $B(Y_2)$. That is, Y_1 is the first $1,000 of income, and Y_2 is the second $1,000. The total tax revenue received by the government from taxes on the two parts of income is

$$R = t_1 B(Y_1) + t_2 B(Y_2). \tag{7.7}$$

For any given amount of tax revenue R,

$$dR = 0 = t_1 MB_1 dY_1 + t_2 MB_2 dY_2, \tag{7.8}$$

where

$$\frac{\partial B(Y_1)}{\partial Y_1} \equiv MB(Y_1), \qquad \frac{\partial B(Y_2)}{\partial Y_2} \equiv MB(Y_2).$$

When income is kept constant in expression (7.8), $dY_1 = -dY_2$. Then it follows from (7.8) that

$$\frac{t_1}{t_2} = \frac{MB(Y_2)}{MB(Y_1)}. \tag{7.9}$$

Because the marginal benefit (or utility) of income declines as income increases,

$$MB(Y_1) > MB(Y_2). \tag{7.10}$$

For any given amount of tax revenue collected from given personal income, it follows from (7.9) and (7.10) that

$$t_1 < t_2. \tag{7.11}$$

That is, rates of taxation should be higher for higher levels of income, and so the tax structure should be progressive.

A conflict between efficient and socially just taxation

We have arrived at the conclusion that income taxes should be progressive by not accounting for efficiency losses through the excess burden of taxation. The social desirability of progressive taxation has followed from an "equal-sacrifice principle" of vertical equity. That is, in setting out the case for progressive taxation, we did not allow for changes in work effort and in personal incomes in response to taxes. Rather, we defined vertical equity taking personal income and work effort as given.

We have seen that if higher-income people are more responsive to marginal tax increases in reducing productive effort than lower-income people, efficiency according to the Ramsey rule requires regressive income taxation and not progressive income taxation. There is therefore a conflict between social justice and efficiency. If we want efficiency, we need regressive income taxes. If we want social justice, we need progressive income taxes.

Regressive taxes and the tax base

The efficiency case for regressive taxes based on the Ramsey rule presupposes a given amount of tax revenue. An additional aspect of the case for regressive taxation looks to the effects of taxation on the tax base and on the amount of tax revenue that can be collected for redistribution.

Because taxes reduce taxable incomes by encouraging substitution of leisure and free time in place of productive effort, the tax base changes because of taxation.[15] Changes in the tax base affect the people who stand to benefit from income transfers financed by tax revenue.

The following example illustrates how problems of the tax base affect recipients of income transfers. Let us consider how a dentist who likes to play golf responds to progressive and regressive income taxation in the course of a day. If the tax structure is progressive, the dentist is, for example, taxed at 10 percent for the first hour's income, at 20 percent for the second hour's income, and so on. After eight hours of work, the dentist may be paying taxes that are 80 percent on the last hour's income. At this point or before, the dentist may decide to stop taking patients and to head for the golf course.

With a regressive tax, incentives are reversed. The dentist pays, for example, 80 percent tax on the first hour's income, and the tax rate falls on income earned in subsequent hours. The dentist might then confront a 10 percent tax rate on income earned in the eighth hour of the day. The regressive tax structure gives the dentist an incentive to keep working longer in the course of the day by encouraging substitution of hours worked for benefit from playing golf. That is, the regressive

---

[15] The tax base for a personal income tax is the pre-tax income on which income taxes are levied.

income tax structure has a substitution effect that is the opposite of that of the progressive income tax structure.

The tax revenue paid by the dentist to the government can be used to finance an income transfer to a low-income person. The dentist's utility from playing golf cannot be transferred to another person. Income earned from work can, however, be transferred through taxation. The regressive tax provides more tax revenue that can be transferred to the low-income person, through the greater incentive for the dentist to keep working and to keep earning taxable income during the course of the day.

There are nonetheless qualifications regarding the description of the behavior of the dentist. We cannot be certain that the dentist will work more and earn more taxable income under regressive taxation. The conclusion that the dentist will work more with the regressive tax is based on a substitution effect: that is, in each successive hour, the regressive taxes provide a greater incentive to work and not head for the golf course. An income effect, which affects the dentist's incentives in the opposite way, is also present: after a few hours work, the dentist may feel that he or she now has earned enough income (after paying taxes) from the day's patients and may still head for the golf course at 2 P.M. The dentist will work longer hours and provide more tax revenue with regressive taxation, only if the substitution effect outweighs this income effect. See Supplement 2E.

When the income tax is regressive, low-income people may also not earn sufficient income to escape the high initial tax rates. The low-income people can receive income transfers financed by the tax revenue received from the higher-income population. The income transfers do not, however, resolve the problem of the disincentive of low-income people to work under regressive taxation. The choice is therefore between the disincentive for low-income people to work under regressive taxation and the disincentive for high-income people to work under progressive taxation.

7.1.4 Negative income taxes and the decision whether to accept a job offer

A personal income tax structure should take into account the incentives affecting the decision whether to work. We noted previously in Chapter 5 that the form of delivery of social-insurance entitlements affects work incentives through moral hazard, and that a solution to moral hazard is to subsidize rather than tax the decisions of welfare recipients to accept job offers.

Suppose, for example, that a welfare recipient is receiving $1,000 a month in income and entitlements from the government, and that the law stipulates that the entire $1,000 is lost if the welfare recipient finds a job. The welfare recipient then faces a tax of $1,000 on finding a job. With the preference that the welfare recipient work for a living rather than live at taxpayer expense,[16] the tax on finding a job is undesirable.

---

[16] We can recall the charitable person's dilemma in Table 5.4.

A welfare recipient who can do no better than find a job that pays less than $1,000 a month will not accept the job, because of the decline in personal income after losing the welfare payment – unless the satisfaction from being self-reliant compensates for the income loss due to accepting the job. The welfare recipient will also not accept a job that pays $1,300, if the extra $300 of income is insufficient compensation for having to go to work.

An income tax structure that provides incentives for the welfare recipient to accept a job does not tax a decision to accept a job to the extent that accepting a job offer is not worthwhile. To encourage welfare recipients to accept job offers, the government could for example continue to pay $700 a month as an income supplement to a welfare recipient who accepts a job that pays a $1,000 a month: the former welfare recipient then has an income of $1,700 when working. Alternatively, if the welfare recipient accepts a job paying $1,300, the government might continue to provide an income supplement of $600, so that total income is $1,900. Rather than paying taxes, the former welfare recipients who take these jobs continue to receive income subsidies from the government. The income subsidies are negative income taxes, and decline as market income increases. At a sufficiently high market income, the income subsidies can be phased out.[17]

7.1.5 A linear income tax

When subsidies for earned income are provided at low incomes, the complete structure of personal income taxation includes the component of negative income taxation at low levels of earned income. A particular way of introducing such negative income taxes is through a linear income tax. We previously considered a linear income tax when, in Chapter 6, we investigated the outcome of majority voting regarding income redistribution. We shall now look at a linear income tax more closely.

Figure 7.4 shows a linear personal income tax. Y measures an individual's market-determined income. R is the value of total tax revenue that the individual pays to the government. S (or the distance OS) is an income subsidy that everyone in the population receives from the government. Earned income is taxed at a constant flat or proportional rate t. Total taxes that an individual pays are accordingly

$$R = -S + tY. \tag{7.12}$$

The slope of the linear income tax schedule in Figure 7.4 indicates the fixed tax rate t. All individuals in the population receive the same sum S as an income transfer from the government, and everybody also faces the same constant marginal income tax rate t. People have different incomes, and each person pays a different amount of taxes R_i as determined by expression (7.12) according to personal earned income Y_i.

---

[17] We noted in Chapter 5 that tax credits that vary with earned income and blend into a progressive tax structure are a means of subsidizing the decision to accept a job offer and earn income.

R = tax paid

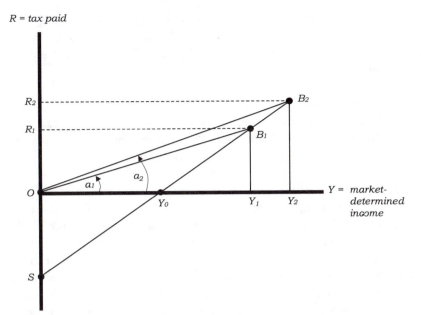

Figure 7.4. A linear income tax.
A linear income tax has a constant marginal tax t that finances an equal income transfer S for the entire population and is progressive.

We see in Figure 7.4 that a person earning the pre-tax income Y_0 pays zero net taxes. The taxes tY_0 that this person pays to the government are exactly equal to the income transfer S received from the government. People with pre-tax incomes in excess of Y_0 pay positive taxes to the government. People with pre-tax market incomes below Y_0 receive net income transfers from the government (i.e., they pay negative income taxes).

The linear income tax provides social insurance. People with pre-tax earned incomes less than Y_0 receive income support through the tax system, and those with pre-tax incomes higher than Y_0 pay taxes to finance the income-support payments to the low-income population. The pre-tax market income Y_0 is the dividing income between people who receive income support and people who pay taxes to finance income support for others.[18]

The progressivity of the linear income tax structure

With progressive taxation, people with higher pre-tax incomes pay higher shares of their incomes as taxes. We see in Figure 7.4 that a person with market income Y_1 pays total taxes R_1 and has average tax liability of

$$a_1 = \frac{R_1}{Y_1}, \tag{7.13}$$

[18] For example, if the government provides a basic income support of $1,000 a month and the tax rate is 20 percent, the break-even income Y_0 is $5,000 a month.

where a_1 is the slope of the line OB_1. A person with higher pre-tax income Y_2 pays higher total taxes R_2 and has the higher average tax liability a_2 given by the slope of the line OB_2. The tax structure is therefore progressive, although the marginal tax rate is constant.

The effect on incentives to work

Although the tax structure is progressive, the flat rate of income taxation provides favorable incentives to work. The disincentive to work when progressive taxation takes the form of increasing marginal tax rates is not present.

The choice of the optimal linear tax

The choice of the optimal linear tax is made simple by the need to choose only one rate of taxation. The rate of taxation determines the income transfer S paid to everybody in the population, by determining the tax revenue that is available for redistribution. The value of the income support S reflects the extent of social insurance in the tax structure. A higher value of S provides more social insurance by providing more income support for the low-income population but, at the same time, also requires higher tax revenue. More tax revenue in turn implies a higher excess burden of taxation. Choice of the income subsidy S is linked to the choice of the tax rate t through the government's budget constraint. Total tax revenue finances total transfer payments. With a population of n people, the government has a budget constraint,

$$nS = t \sum_{i=1}^{n} Y_i. \tag{7.14}$$

Because all n persons in the population receive the transfer S from the government, the government pays out nS. The tax rate t is levied on the total market income of the n people in the population and provides the revenue to allow the payout nS to take place.

A complexity that a government faces in choosing the rate of taxation t is that pre-tax market incomes Y_i in Figure 7.4 and in expression (7.14) depend on the tax rate and on the income subsidy S that is provided (where S in turn depends on t).

In principle, a government can choose the tax rate to maximize a social welfare function subject to the budget constraint (7.14) and other characteristics of the economy including individuals' labor supply responses (which determine how pre-tax incomes Y_i depend on the income subsidy S and the tax rate t).

The choice of the rate of taxation, and through expression (7.14) the consequent subsidy S that can be financed, varies with the social welfare function that has been chosen. For example, a society that chose Rawls's social welfare function would require more income redistribution than a society that chose Bentham's social welfare function. Because Rawls's social welfare function focuses on the well being of the people who are worst off in having lowest pre-tax incomes, a higher value of S is required for income support at low-income levels. A higher value of the tax rate t is correspondingly required to finance the larger income transfers.

There is then also a greater loss from the higher excess burden of taxation because of the higher tax rates.

7.1.6 Optimal income taxation

A linear income tax schedule is one possibility for choosing an income tax. More generally, however, the structure of personal income taxation need not be linear with a constant rate of taxation as in Figure 7.4, but rather marginal tax rates can vary with different levels of income. This is the case in practice. Usually marginal tax rates increase with income.

Suppose that we set out to determine the general optimal income tax structure that maximizes a social welfare function. We are then looking for a relationship between the tax rate and earned income that could in principle be progressive or regressive. If the rate of taxation were to change with every change in income, we would be looking for an optimal income schedule

$$t = f(Y). \tag{7.15}$$

If a linear income tax schedule as in Figure 7.4 were to maximize social welfare, this would be revealed as the solution to the general problem of optimal personal income taxation.

We can expect the quest to identify a general structure of optimal income taxation as expressed by (7.15) to be complicated. In the case of the linear income tax, we had to find values for S and t related through the government budget. In the case of the tax schedule (7.15), we are looking for a relationship between the tax rate and income that maximizes social welfare. That is, the solution to the general optimal taxation problem is a function that tells us how to set the tax rate t for all values of income Y. We have seen that there are cases for both progressive and regressive taxes, and we therefore do not know beforehand whether the relationship expressed in (7.15) will indicate progressive or regressive taxation. We do know that finding an optimal income tax schedule requires a compromise between the progressive taxation sought for reasons of social justice (through the equal-sacrifice principle) and the efficiency and tax-base benefits of regressive taxation.

Through the substitution effect between work (and effort) and leisure, progressive taxation increases the leaks in the redistributive bucket. We can return to our example of the dentist who responds to increasingly greater marginal tax rates by stopping work and heading for the golf course. The substitution effect places an excess burden of taxation on the dentist, but also we saw that the dentist is led by progressive taxes to take personal utility in the form of leisure rather in the form of earned income. Because leisure cannot be taxed, the beneficiaries of the income transfers financed by the dentist's taxes have reason to want the dentist to keep working and earning taxable income. In deciding on a tax schedule, an important question is therefore, how do taxpayers respond in their work and leisure decisions to the degree of progressivity or regressivity in the income tax schedule? The answer to this question determines the efficiency losses (through the excess burden of taxation) that are required to be incurred for the sake of social justice defined as a more equal post-tax income distribution. Going back to Figure 7.3, the answer tells us how far inside the efficient frontier a society has to go to approach greater post-tax income equality.

In a choosing a social welfare function, a society can stress efficiency or social justice (expressed as a preference for post-tax equality). We have seen that a society's choice of social welfare function correspondingly expresses the society's aversion to risk and determines whether social insurance is complete (with Rawls) or incomplete (with Bentham and other formulations of social welfare).

The extent of inefficiency, or the leak in the bucket of redistribution through the response of taxpayers to progressivity or regressivity in the income tax schedule, is an empirical matter. We need to be able to observe labor-supply behavior to determine how people respond to taxes. The choice of the social welfare function to be maximized is an ideological issue. Some economists and political decision makers stress the desirability of social justice with little concern for efficiency (they are followers of Rawls) and want highly progressive income taxes. Others (who are closer to Bentham) stress the desirability of efficiency and want low marginal income tax rates or flat tax rates.

Although labor-supply behavior is empirically determined, different people often have different views or priorities about how labor-supply decisions respond to taxes. For economists and political decision makers who take the view that people more or less "contribute according to their ability," work and effort substitution responses to taxes are low, and efficiency losses through excess burdens of taxation are not a deterrent to highly progressive income taxes. Such economists and political decision makers might then see their way free to choose a social welfare function close to Rawls, with resulting high tax rates and high progressivity in the tax schedule. Economists and political decision makers who interpret the evidence as an indication that incentives to work and exert effort are important stress the efficiency losses from taxation and recommend income tax structures with low tax rates and low levels of progressivity. In particular, the latter group of economists and political decision makers often recommends a linear income tax schedule, or a schedule with a small number of tax brackets with low rates of taxation and low progressivity.

The Mirrlees problem

In formal economic analysis, economists derive an optimal income tax schedule by maximizing a social welfare function after choosing a utility function that represents the preferences of the population for work (or consumption) and leisure. Individuals are generally viewed as having the same preferences or utility functions regarding work and leisure but as having different abilities to earn income. The income tax affects how individuals apply their different abilities to productive effort, and so determines the value of the output that people produce.

James A. Mirrlees (of the University of Cambridge, who received the Nobel Prize in economics in 1996) pointed out (1971) that, although a government might want to maximize a social welfare function by taxing individuals' abilities to earn income, individuals' abilities are not observable.[19] Governments therefore confront a problem of asymmetric information when seeking to tax ability: the information is asymmetric because individuals know their personal abilities, but governments do not. A government can therefore only observe personal incomes earned through the application of personal ability and can only tax personal incomes. Mirrlees solved the optimal income tax problem by maximizing social welfare when all people have the same utility function but differ in their unobserved abilities to earn income.[20] The government in Mirrlees's optimal income tax problem also could not observe how many hours a person worked or how much effort a person put into work. The government did, however, know the distribution of abilities in the population.

The question posed by Mirrlees is therefore: if a government were to know the common utility function of the population and the distribution of taxpayers' abilities but could only observe the incomes that people earn yet wished to maximize social welfare, how progressive or regressive a personal income tax would the goverment wish to choose? When this question is answered, much hinges on the choice of the utility function proposed to describe the labor supply behavior of the population. The trade-off between efficiency and social justice depends on the efficiency losses through the excess burden of taxation, which through the substitution effect depends on the utility function that is chosen to represent the labor-market behavior of the population. A utility function could be chosen according to which free time or leisure is little valued. Taxes then do not much affect efficiency, and the optimal income tax can focus on achieving equality in post-tax income distribution and can be quite progressive. If a utility function is chosen for which people do significantly value free time or leisure and respond to high marginal taxes by significantly reducing work hours or work effort, the optimal income tax will not be all that progressive and may be regressive. Mirrlees found this ambiguity: no generally valid answer could be given to the question whether income taxes should be progressive or regressive at different levels of income.

Mirrlees's optimal income tax solution does however have some definitive attributes. The income tax should provide incentives for higher-ability people to work at least as much as lower-ability people. We can see this by considering the behavior of one person with high ability and another with lower ability. The higher-ability person can always copy the work behavior of the lower-ability person, thereby earning the same pre-tax income and paying the same taxes as the lower-ability person. The higher-ability person who is behaving in a way that makes him or her seem to be a lower-ability person earns the same (observable) income

[19] If individuals' abilities are innate (and are not acquired or enhanced through personal decisions to invest in education), the taxation of ability would provide a tax base with no efficiency loss through an excess burden of taxation because, as we have noted, there are no substitution responses available to individuals to avoid a tax on innate ability. We have also observed that a tax on ability would be unfair, by taxing a personal life-style decision not to use ability to earn market income.

[20] An additional incentive-compatibility constraint ensures that individual decisions to work maximize personal utility for the structure of taxes that a government chooses.

as the lower-ability person but works fewer (non-observable) hours or exerts less (non-observable) effort than the lower-ability person. To avoid this outcome, and to induce higher-ability people to exert more effort, the optimal income tax should provide the higher-ability person with a higher level of post-tax utility than a person who has less ability. That is, it is efficient to give the higher-ability person an incentive through the tax structure to earn more income than a lower-ability person. The tax structure should not therefore discourage more able people from working more than less able people. That is, the optimal income structure should provide an incentive for high-ability people to reveal their superior ability through the greater pre-tax incomes they earn.[21]

Simulations

The inconclusiveness of the solution to the general problem formulated by Mirrlees had led to emphasis on attempts to identify the ideal structure of an income tax from simulations of a model of an economy. As we expect, simulations that presuppose high substitution between free time and income-earning activity show that society is better off with income tax structures that have low income tax rates and low progressivity. The simulations also sometimes reveal that a flat tax (a constant marginal tax rate as in the linear income tax) is the preferred way of taxing income because of the minimal disincentives for productive activity.

When simulations are based on low substitution between free time and hours worked or work effort, the simulation results, on the other hand, show that high progressivity in income taxes does not significantly impede work effort, and that social welfare is maximized by marginal tax rates that can be quite high at higher incomes.[22] Mirrlees's own simulations suggested that the ideal income tax structure is not very progressive and that the highest marginal rate should not exceed 30 to 35 percent.

The different results and views leave us to make a personal choice about how we view the relation between taxes and incentives to earn income and about the importance we assign to efficiency compared to social equality when choosing an income tax. We may believe that personal incentives are important in determining how hard people work and the time they put into work. In that case, we would not accept that highly progressive income tax rates and high rates of taxation are in the best interests of a society. An emphasis on efficiency and the effects of taxation on the tax base would lead us to want to choose low and moderately progressive

---

[21] The analysis of optimal income taxation has also provided conclusions about marginal tax rates at the bottom and top of the income distribution. A zero marginal tax rate at the highest income is optimal because this does not deter the highest-income person from working more. If this person is deterred from working because of a positive marginal tax rate, the income tax structure cannot be efficient because, when the highest-ability person works more (by free choice), he or she is better off. At the same time, no tax revenue is lost to the government by the decision to work more. If everybody is working, the marginal tax rate is also zero for the lowest-ability person in the population (but, if some people are not working, the marginal tax rate at the bottom can be positive).

[22] For example, Emmanuel Saez (2001) suggested top marginal tax rates between 50 and 80 percent.

personal income taxes or the linear income tax with an ammendment that adds one or two low-tax brackets.

High rates of taxation appear to be associated with tax evasion. We shall return to consider tax evasion in Section 7.3.

Social mobility and the structure of the income tax

In Chapter 5, we considered social mobility as an approach to social justice. A society with high social mobility places no impediments to people born into low-income families progressing to the upper end of the income distribution. Income tax structures with high tax rates and high progressivity obstruct social mobility by impeding the accumulation of wealth of people born into poor families. The traditionally wealthy families pay the same high and progressive income taxes, but these families have income from their endowed personal wealth. High tax rates and high progressivity in the income tax structure therefore favor preservation of the status of the traditional wealthy families. That is, high tax rates and high progressivity in income taxes preserve social inequality over time by stopping low-income people from becoming rich because of the high taxes that are paid and the disincentives to exert the effort that is required to achieve upward social mobility. The desire not to impede social mobility is another reason for moderate taxation in an income tax schedule.

7.1.7 A government that maximizes tax revenue

The Mirrlees problem of finding the optimal personal income tax is based on a view of government that seeks only to serve citizens and taxpayers and that has no self-interest in revenue from taxation. Consequently, in the Mirrlees optimal income tax problem, the government maximizes social welfare when deciding on taxation.

We have noted in previous chapters that a principal-agent problem can exist between taxpayers and government. A manifestation of the principal-agent problem is that political decision makers do not necessarily use tax revenue to maximize social welfare.

Tax revenue might rather be used for the personal benefit of people in government. We saw in Chapter 3 that a self-interested government bureaucracy benefits from more public spending than taxpayers want. In Chapter 6, we saw that elected representatives can benefit by making politically motivated public-spending decisions.

A view of government that recognizes the principal-agent problem between government and taxpayers leads to proposals that governments should have only limited authority to tax, including taxing future generations by borrowing. Government can be restrained in taxation and borrowing by constitutional limitations. Governments in need of such constitutional restraint have been described by the term "leviathan." The leviathan government does not seek optimal taxation to maximize social welfare but rather seeks to maximize tax revenue for its own benefit.[23] That is, with m tax bases (or activities or goods and services) that can be

---

[23] "Leviathan" is in the Hebrew word for whale.

Tax revenue

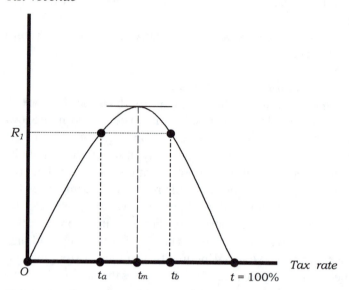

Figure 7.5. *The relation between the tax rate and tax revenue.*

taxed, a leviathan government would set a tax t_i on each tax base L_i to maximize total tax revenue given by

$$R = \sum_{j=1}^{m} t_j L_j. \tag{7.16}$$

We have previously observed that pre-tax incomes depend on taxes, through substitution effects. A tax base L_j, in expression (7.16), which may, for example, be supply of labor in terms of hours worked, thus itself depends on the size of the tax, since people respond to a tax by the substitution response of earning less income by working less.

In Figure 7.5, we see the relation between total tax revenue and the rate of income taxation. No tax revenue is provided when the tax rate is 100 percent. Nor is any tax revenue provided when the tax rate is zero. Between zero and 100 percent, there exists a tax rate t_m that provides maximum revenue.[24] This is the tax rate that a leviathan government would set.

---

[24] The tax rate t_m in Figure 7.5 is established from

$$\frac{\partial R}{\partial t_j} = L_j(1 + \varepsilon_{tL}) = 0,$$

where ε_{tL} is the elasticity of the tax base with respect to the tax. Therefore, tax revenue is maximized for taxes for which $\varepsilon_{tL} = -1$. This is so when a tax in one market does not affect behavior and so revenue from taxes in other markets. The more general problem of determining revenue-maximizing taxes requires accounting for interdependencies among markets. The same interdependencies affect the Ramsey rule, which we also derived using the simplification that a tax in one market has no effect on revenue from taxes in other markets.

The Ramsey rule and a self-serving government

An objective of uncompromising revenue maximization makes no allowance for the excess burden of taxation. Because of the excess burden of taxation, a self-serving government may not wish simply to set taxes that maximize tax revenue. The government might rather wish to maximize revenue, subject to an upper bound on the efficiency losses imposed through the excess burden of taxation. The structure of taxes that a leviathan government would choose is then precisely given by the Ramsey rule. That is, tax rates would vary inversely with the elasticities that indicate taxpayers' substitution opportunities. The Ramsey rule therefore applies to a leviathan government that places a bound on the excess burden of taxes in an economy.

The government could equivalently set a revenue target and choose tax rates according to the Ramsey rule to minimize the excess burden of taxation incurred in achieving the revenue target. The problem of maximizing revenue subject to a given total excess burden of taxation is the dual of the problem of minimizing the excess burden of taxation subject to achieving a specified tax revenue target.[25]

Locational mobility and escape from the leviathan

When government is a leviathan, locational mobility can restrain the government from using its legal monopoly power to tax for its own benefit. Rents (or personal profits) of governments from monopoly power to tax are eliminated by the competition among governments offering people different combinations of taxation and benefits from public spending. When people move to avoid a leviathan government, the leviathan government loses its tax base.

Escape from leviathan government is, however, not possible when the government levies taxes on immobile tax bases. Local government jurisdictions often use property taxes to raise revenue. Property is an immobile tax base that cannot leave the tax jurisdiction of the government.[26]

Let us consider a leviathan government that decides to increase taxes on immobile property with no benefits to taxpayers from increased public spending. The leviathan government is simply taking advantage of its legal right to tax. After the increased taxes have been announced, house owners cannot escape the higher taxes by selling their houses and moving to another government jurisdiction because the higher taxes are capitalized into the value of houses and reduce property values.

The decline in a property value is equal to the present value of the obligation of the owner of the house to pay the increased taxes. If home-owners were to sell their houses, they would pay the entire future tax increase through the reduced price received for their houses.

---

[25] Dual problems give the same solution as the original problem.

[26] Depreciation allowances in tax codes make improved commercial property mobile between tax jurisdictions over the course of time. Personally owned houses usually cannot be depreciated; however, residential rental properties can usually be depreciated against earnings.

The people to whom houses are sold after the tax increase is announced correspondingly do not pay the tax. The buyers of houses after the tax increase has been announced transfer money to the government in the future when they pay property taxes. The buyers have however been compensated for these future taxes by the reduced price they have paid for the house.

When a tax base is mobile, the legal monopoly of governments to tax can be escaped (e.g., by people moving). When taxes are levied on an immobile tax base such as property, there is no escape. A tax on property cannot be escaped by selling the property.

We should note that governments that use property taxes to finance spending are not necessarily leviathans. The Ramsey rule for efficient taxation advises any government to set high taxes on immobile tax bases. The identifying characteristic of a leviathan government is that maximal tax revenue is sought in the absence of taxpayer benefit from taxes paid.

7.1.8 Excessive taxation: the Laffer curve

Tax rates can be so high that they reduce the total tax revenue. In Figure 7.5, we see that increasing tax rates beyond the rate of taxation t_m decreases total tax revenue. The tax in Figure 7.5 could be an income tax, or a sales tax, or any tax when substitution possibilities are present that reduce the tax base (e.g., by substitution in response to a tax by working less or buying less of a good).

The relation in Figure 7.5 between tax rates and total tax revenue is known as a Laffer curve (so named because of its introduction into popular discussion in the United States by Arthur Laffer). If the tax rate exceeds t_m, taxation is excessive, and the government is on the "wrong side" of the Laffer curve. This is to the detriment of both the taxpayer and the government.

When taxpayers are on the wrong side of the Laffer curve, they have responded to the high rate of taxation by substituting non-taxable free time or leisure for taxable income to the extent that total tax revenue has declined. For example, we see in Figure 7.5 that the tax revenue R_1 can be achieved by the government setting the tax rate at either t_a or t_b. At the smaller tax t_a, there is a smaller excess burden of taxation, while the government receives the same revenue.

Tax evasion and the Laffer curve

The fall in tax revenue when the tax rate is increased beyond t_m can be due to the substitution effects we have described, but the reason for the decline in tax revenue can also be tax evasion. When tax rates are too high, people may also decide to find covert ways of conducting their income-earning activities so as to escape payment of taxes.

Such "black" or "shadow" market activities introduce inefficiencies into the economy. Resources and effort are used in hiding and misconstruing taxable income. A form of rent seeking is therefore taking place. When excessive taxation leads people to move their income-earning activities into the shadow economy, artificial restraints are placed on the expansion of successful businesses because of the decreased opportunities for evading taxation when businesses are too large and visible (and too successful).

The Laffer curve in the short run and long run

Reducing taxes and observing the change in tax revenue will reveal whether rates of taxation are so high as to have reached the wrong side of the Laffer curve. There are, however, shorter-run and longer-run aspects of a revenue response on the Laffer curve. It takes time for people to respond to lower taxes. How people respond to the reduced taxes also depends on the long-run credibility of the government's reduction in taxes. There will be a reluctance to make new investments or to bring business activities out of the shadow economy if people believe that taxes will be increased again in the future.

7.1.9 Political objectives

Political objectives can affect the taxes that governments choose. There are political-support limitations to applying the Ramsey rule. Because the Ramsey rule for efficient taxation calls for high tax rates on the necessities of life (i.e., goods for which price elasticities, or substitution responses, are low), we can expect the taxes that are indicated as efficient by the Ramsey rule to be politically unpopular. Because of the political consequences, high taxes on food, clothing, and medications can lead to electoral defeat for a government that has sought efficient taxation through the Ramsey rule.

Desirable personal income tax structures tend to be simple, with few marginal tax rates and with limited progressivity, limited exemptions from payment of taxes, and limited tax deductions. Tax structures are, however, on the contrary, often complex, with many exceptions and deductions.[27] Moreover, the exemptions and deductions appear selectively targeted. The selectiveness has been interpreted as reflecting political objectives sought through discrimination among different categories of taxpayers.[28]

It is also sometimes suggested that complex tax codes benefit accountants and tax lawyers, who earn their incomes by providing professional advice on tax matters.

7.1.10 Tax reform

Changes to simplify complex income tax schedules sometimes take place. The changes are known as tax reforms. The purpose of a tax reform is generally to remove inefficiencies and undue complexities from a tax system. By eliminating

---

[27] A tax exemption refers to income that is exempt from payment of income tax. A tax deduction refers to expenses that can be deducted from taxes due to the government.

[28] Walter Hettich and Stanley Winer (1999) proposed that political objectives underlie complex tax structures and suggested a framework of political decision making based on probabilistic voting to explain the different tax treatment of different classes of taxpayers.

inefficiencies, a tax reform might result in Pareto-improving change (i.e., everyone is made better off or no one loses from the tax reform). When this is possible, there will be consensus among voters for change (since the change is Pareto-improving).

Change need not, however, be Pareto-improving. Rather tax reforms can affect post-tax income distribution, with some people gaining and others losing. If the tax reform is efficient, the gainers could in principle compensate the losers and be better off.

The distributional effects of a tax reform might set constraints on the type of tax reform that a society regards as acceptable. One distributional constraint on tax reforms is that a reform satisfy the condition of being Dalton-improving: this condition, set out by Hugh Dalton in 1920, requires that a tax reform redistribute income from high- to low-income households with no change in the ranking of households in the income distribution. That is, the reform cannot result in higher-income households being displaced in the income distribution by lower-income households. If this condition is not satisfied, lower-income households benefit from the tax reform while new lower-income households are created. It then becomes difficult to judge whether the tax reform has increased social welfare (specified as a particular social welfare function).

Tax reforms often appear, however, to be associated with political objectives rather than social welfare. After a tax reform has taken place, complexity in the tax laws often returns. Dispensations that once more provide tax deductions and exemptions for different groups of taxpayers are legislated. Tax revenue falls because of the newly introduced exemptions and deductions, and tax rates tend to increase to compensate for the fall in tax revenue.

When once more the inefficiencies and injustice of the complex tax structure become evident, another tax reform takes place. A simplier, more efficient, and more uniform tax structure is again introduced – and the tax code is again made sufficiently complicated by exemptions and deductions, and eventually a new reform is warranted. A clean slate on tax exemptions and deductions after a substantive simplifying reform opens new opportunities for selective changes in tax laws that increase political support. Also, before a tax reform, the political benefits through the exemptions and deductions of the tax code may have been provided by a previous generation of political decision makers.

7.1.11 Summary

The optimal design of taxes involves efficiency and social justice. We began in this section with the Ramsey rule for efficient taxation. The Ramsey rule has a role in efficient public spending on public goods and in efficient taxation to finance income redistribution. We observed, however, that taxes based on the Ramsey rule can contradict fairness or justice.

Our focus has been on income taxes. The Ramsey rule can imply regressive income taxes. Responses to taxation that diminish the tax base for income taxation also suggest a case for regressive taxes. On the other hand, a progressive income tax structure is suggested by a rule for socially just taxation based on the principle of vertical equity or equal sacrifice in taxation.

We have observed that income tax structures should make allowance for the effects of taxation on willingness to accept job offers.

Optimal income taxes combine objectives of efficiency and social justice in taxation. An optimal linear income tax is progressive and provides income transfers to low-income people.

A more general representation of optimal income taxation comes to more ambiguous conclusions. The tax schedule could be progressive or regressive. Recommendations about optimal income taxes depend on evaluations of how taxes affect personal effort decisions and the willingness to work and on the choice of the social welfare function, which will reflect the relative importance assigned to efficiency and social justice. Views on how incentives affect work and effort affect the choice of the social welfare function. Economists and political decision makers who feel that taxes do not affect work and effort incentives very much can feel comfortable suggesting a social welfare function that stresses social equality through high taxation and extensive income redistribution. On the other hand, economists and political decision makers who regard incentives as being important in influencing work and effort decisions in general tend to recommend income tax schedules with low tax rates and low progressivity.

We have also noted that high rates of income taxation encourage tax evasion and are an impediment to social mobility.

The principal-agent problem between governments and taxpayers suggests that some governments might not be interested in choosing optimal income taxes that maximize social welfare but rather might choose tax rates that maximize tax revenue for the benefit of persons in government. If such a leviathan government cares about the inefficiencies that arise through the excess burden of taxation, there is a role for the Ramsey rule for efficient taxation. Locational mobility provides a means of escape from a leviathan government: people can leave for another government and another tax jurisdiction. When a tax base cannot move out of the government's tax jurisdiction, escape is not possible: high property taxes cannot be escaped by selling a house because the value of the taxes is capitalized into the value of the house when the intention to introduce higher taxes with no associated benefit becomes known.

We also saw that excessively high taxes bring an economy to the wrong side of the Laffer curve. The fall in revenue on the wrong side of the Laffer curve can be a result of substitution away from earning income because of high tax rates, or the consequence of moving economic activity into the shadow economy to evade payment of high taxes. A reduction in taxation on the wrong side of the Laffer curve can benefit both taxpayers and government; however, the time dimension matters because taxpayers will want to be convinced that the tax reduction is not temporary.

We have noted that applying the Ramsey rule to determine taxes can also be inconsistent with political objectives of electoral support because of the social injustice that can be associated with the efficient Ramsey taxes.

The usual recommendation is that income tax structures should be simple, with low tax rates, low progressivity, few tax brackets, and minimal deductions or exemptions; nonetheless, income tax structures are often complex and discriminatory across different classes of taxpayers, with tax deductions and tax exemptions that appear to have little economic or social justification. Studies of the complex tax structures suggest relationships to political support (which we considered in Chapter 6). We have also observed that accountants and tax lawyers benefit from complex tax structures.

Tax reforms can be motivated by efficiency and can have distributional objectives or be subject to distributional constraints. The reforms usually change complex high-tax, highly progressive tax structures to more simple tax structures with lower tax rates, lower progressivity, and limited exemptions and deductions. Over time the tax structure tends to become complex again as exemptions and deductions are reintroduced, and taxes increase because of the consequent declines in tax revenue. Cycles of tax reform can therefore take place.

References and related literature

On the Ramsey rule, see Ramsey (1927) and Diamond (1975). On women and the labor market, see Grossbard-Shechtman and Neuman (2003). On progressive taxation, see Young (1990) and Ok (1995). On optimal income taxation, see Mirrlees (1971, 1997), Stern (1976), and Kanbur and Tuomala (1994). See Sadka (1976) and Seade (1977) for the case for zero tax rates at the extremes of the income distribution. On the case for high progressivity at high incomes, see Diamond (1998) and Saez (2001). Saez (2001) also provides a simple presentation of the Mirrlees model. On the case for simple low-tax structures, see Hall and Rabushka (1995) and Boskin (1996). On the Laffer curve, see Laffer (1981) and Fullerton (1982). On leviathan government, see Brennan and Buchanan (1980). On capitalization of taxes, see Caplan (2001). On taxes as the outcome of political processes, see Snyder and Kramer (1988) and Hettich and Winer (1999). On the theory of Pareto-improving tax reform, see Guesnerie (1995). On the Dalton criterion for tax reform, see Dalton (1920); for an application of the Dalton criterion, see Mayshar and Yitzhaki (1995).

Boskin, M. J. (ed.), 1996. *Frontiers of Tax Reform*. Hoover Institution Press, Stanford, California.

Brennan, G. and J. M. Buchanan, 1980. *The Power to Tax*. Cambridge University Press, Cambridge, U.K.

Caplan, B., 2001. Standing Tiebout on his head: Tax capitalization and the monopoly power of local governments. *Public Choice* 108, 101–22.

Dalton, H., 1920. The measurement of the inequality of income. *Economic Journal* 30, 348–61.

Diamond, P. A., 1975. A many-person Ramsey tax rule. *Journal of Public Economics* 4, 227–44.

Diamond, P. A., 1998. Optimal income taxation: An example with a U-shaped pattern of optimal marginal tax rates. *American Economic Review* 88, 83–95.

Fullerton, D., 1982. On the possibility of an inverse relationship between tax rates and government revenues. *Journal of Public Economics* 19, 3–22.

Grossbard-Shechtman, S. and S. Neuman, 2003. Marriage and work for pay. In *Marriage and the Economy: Theory and Evidence from Advanced Industrial Societies*, S. Grossbard-Shechtman (ed.). Cambridge University Press, New York, 222–47.

Guesnerie, R., 1995. *A Contribution to the Pure Theory of Taxation*. Cambridge University Press, Cambridge, U.K.

Hall, R. E. and A. Rabushka, 1995. *The Flat Tax*, 2nd ed. Hoover Institution Press, Stanford, California.

Hamermesh, D. S. and J. E. Biddle, 1994. Beauty and the labor market. *American Economic Review* 84, 1174–94.

Hettich, W. and S. L. Winer, 1999. *Democratic Choice and Taxation: A Theoretical and Empirical Analysis*. Cambridge University Press, New York.

Kanbur, R. and M. Tuomala, 1994. Inherent inequality and the optimal graduation of marginal income tax rates. *Scandinavian Journal of Economics* 96, 275–82.

Laffer, A. B., 1981. Government extractions and revenue deficiencies. *Cato Journal* 1, 1–21.

Mayshar, J. and S. Yitzhaki, 1995. Dalton-improving indirect tax reform. *American Economic Review* 85, 793–807.

Mirrlees, J. A., 1971. An exploration in the theory of optimal income taxation. *Review of Economic Studies* 38, 175–208.

Mirrlees, J. A., 1997. Information and incentives: The economics of carrots and sticks. Nobel Prize Lecture. *Economic Journal* 107, 1311–29.

Ok, E. A., 1995. On the principle of equal sacrifice in income taxation. *Journal of Public Economics* 58, 453–68.

Ramsey, F. P., 1927. A contribution to the theory of taxation. *Economic Journal* 37, 47–61.

Sadka, E., 1976. On income distribution incentive effects and optimal income taxation. *Review of Economic Studies* 43, 261–8.

Saez, E., 2001. Using elasticities to derive optimal income tax rates. *Review of Economic Studies* 68, 205–29.

Seade, J., 1977. On the shape of optimal tax schedules. *Review of Economic Studies* 7, 203–36.

Snyder, J. M. and G. H. Kramer, 1988. Fairness, self-interest, and the politics of the progressive income tax. *Journal of Public Economics* 36, 197–230.

Stern, N. H., 1976. On the specification of models of optimum income taxation. *Journal of Public Economics* 6, 123–62.

Young, H. P., 1990. Progressive taxation and equal sacrifice. *American Economic Review* 80, 253–66.

Questions for discussion

1. What is the Ramsey rule for efficient taxation? How is the rule derived? What is the logic underlying the rule?

2. What is the role of the Ramsey rule in the determination of efficient public spending on public goods?

3. What is the role of the Ramsey rule in the determination of efficient tax-financed income redistribution?

4. What is the basis of a case for regressive personal income taxes?

5. What is the basis of a case for progressive personal income taxes?

6. If finding a job means losing publicly financed benefits, the marginal tax rate for low incomes can be very high. The loss of the publicly financed benefits is moreover like a tax on finding a job. How can a personal income tax schedule address this problem? Does the personal income tax in the place where you live or study address the problem? Explain.

7. How does the linear income tax provide a solution to the problem in question 6? Why is the linear income tax progressive? What is the relationship between the policy variables of the linear tax system, and what are the trade-offs that enter into choice of the parameters?

8. What information is required to set up and solve the general problem of an optimal structure of a personal income tax? Why are the recommendations that emerge from the solution to the general problem inconclusive?

9. We observe progressive income taxes but rarely, if ever, regressive income taxes. Why are political representatives reluctant to propose regressive taxes to voters?

10. How is social mobility affected by the structure of an income tax?

11. What is the meaning of leviathan government? Would a leviathan government ever want to use the Ramsey rule?

12. "The monopoly power of the leviathan to tax can be escaped by locational mobility." To what extent, or in what circumstances, is this so?

13. What determines the shape of the Laffer curve? Why might different views on the desirability of high taxation and high public spending make the idea of the Laffer curve controversial?

14. Personal income tax structures are often complex, with concessions and exemptions for different groups of taxpayers and for different types of income. What reasons have been proposed for the complexity?

15. Why does the complexity of taxation at times give way to tax reforms that simplify the income tax structure, but then over time the complexity returns?

16. Provide a brief description of the structure of the personal income tax in the place where you live or study. If it were up to you, would you change the existing minimum income at which taxes become payable? Would you change the structure of marginal tax rates? Would you change the tax structure that affects persons facing a choice between taking a job and continuing to receive income transfers from government? Explain.

17. What are the main tax deductions and tax exemptions in the principal personal income tax in the location where you live or study? In your view, are all the deductions and exemptions justified? What are the deductions and exemptions subsidizing? Would you add deductions or exemptions that are not present?

18. Does the personal income tax in the place where you live or study discriminate in favor of or against couples living together in the same household? Is there any justification that you can see for discrimination one way or another? Explain.

19. In general, what would you regard as an ideal personal income tax structure?

20. When did the last substantial changes take place in the structure of the personal income tax? Who was principally affected by the changes? Did the changes decrease or increase tax progressivity? Do you approve of the changes that were made? Explain. If no substantial changes in the income tax structure have taken place over the last few decades, is that because the personal income tax structure is ideal? Does the personal income tax structure tend to change with electoral results that favor one political party over another? Do the constituencies of the main political parties have different views of the ideal personal income tax structure? Cite any differences.

7.2

What to Tax?

In Section 7.1, we considered personal taxation and focused on the characteristics of personal income taxes. Various taxes are available to governments. The different possible taxes raise questions about what to tax and how.

For example, should income from capital (interest and dividends, capital gains, income from ownership of rental properties) be taxed at the same rate as personal income from wages and salaries? Also, corporations are legal entities that are in general subject to tax rates and tax laws that differ from personal taxation, although the income earned by corporations ultimately belongs to the individuals who own stock or shares in a corporation. This raises the question, why are corporate profits taxed separately and not as part of taxation of individuals' personal incomes?

The terms "direct taxes" and "indirect taxes" distinguish between taxes that are levied when income is earned and when income is spent. Sales taxes, import taxes, and value-added taxes are different forms of indirect taxation. We shall compare these different indirect taxes and also consider whether there is a case for using indirect taxes when personal income taxes have already been optimally set.

We shall look at the properties of lotteries, inflation, and financial repression as a means of taxation. We shall ask whether personal wealth should be taxed, during life or in the form of an estate tax. We shall also investigate the desirability of lump sum or head taxes. Direct taxation can take the form of taxes on personal spending rather than on personal income, and we shall consider the case for a direct tax on personal spending rather than on personal income.

7.2.1 Taxation of income from capital

The Ramsey rule for efficient taxation provides a justification for taxing income from capital differently from income from labor, since governments are advised to set tax rates inversely proportional to supply elasticities. That is, with t_L the rate of taxation of labor income and t_K the rate of taxation of income from capital, the Ramsey rule proposes that tax rates be set so that

$$\frac{t_L}{t_K} = \frac{\varepsilon_{SK}}{\varepsilon_{SL}},\tag{7.17}$$

where ε_{Si} $(i = L, K)$ is the supply elasticity.[1] The supply elasticities in expression (7.17) reflect opportunities to leave a tax jurisdiction. If capital can readily leave, the elasticity of supply of capital ε_{SK} is high. Conversely, if labor cannot leave, the elasticity of supply of labor ε_{SL} is low. The Ramsey rule therefore implies that the rate of taxation on income from capital should be lower than the rate of taxation

---

[1] As we noted in Section 7.1, this statement of the Ramsey rule is based on infinite elasticities on the other side of the market (here demand elasticities) and independence between markets so that a tax in one market does not affect tax revenue in other markets.

on income from labor.[2] If capital in a tax jurisdiction is part of a broader capital market and can simply leave in response to a tax on income from capital, the tax rate on capital indicated by the Ramsey rule is zero.[3]

The home bias in investment

Possibilities for taxing capital depend on the willingness of investors to hold assets outside their tax jurisdiction. Investors often seem reluctant to hold foreign assets, which results in a "home bias" in asset holdings. The home bias may be due to investors' believing that they are better informed about investments in their home markets. Investors may also trust their own government more than foreign governments to protect their ownership rights. The home bias reduces the supply elasticity of capital and, through the Ramsey rule, increases the efficient tax on income from capital relative to income from labor.

Social justice

A government may believe that social justice requires taxing income from capital at a higher rate than income from labor. The presence of capital markets that extend beyond the government's tax jurisdiction, however, limits the scope for taxing income from capital. If capital can leave the jurisdiction to escape the tax, a government has no choice but to set low taxes on income from capital and high taxes on income from labor because, by attempting to tax income from capital, the government ends up with little or no capital to tax.

Portfolio investment and real assets

When people choose to save rather than consume, resources can be invested to create capital. The capital can be human capital invested in the skills, ability, and knowledge of a person or can take the form of physical capital. When we refer to movement of capital out of a tax jurisdiction, we may mean physical capital, and also human capital. Machinery and equipment move as firms relocate their operations to other tax jurisdictions, and high human-capital people might also move to escape taxes.

People are also described as investing when they buy stocks or shares in a company, or when they buy government or corporate bonds. Such portfolio investment changes the ownership of assets but does not create new assets. Where people hold their personal investment portfolios affects their tax obligations, through the different taxes that different government levy in their jurisdictions.

---

[2] Personal income taxes usually have more than one rate. In expression (7.17) for the Ramsey rule, there is one rate of taxation for income depending on the source of income. That is, we are not now asking questions about the structure of taxation for different levels of income. Nor are we asking questions about different rates of taxation for different people implied by the Ramsey rule. We considered these questions in Section 7.1.

[3] If the broader market, for example, offers a return of 5 percent, any attempt to tax capital to reduce the local return below 5 percent will lead investors to move their capital outside the jurisdiction where they can obtain the 5 percent return.

Where people "hold" their asset portfolios is a legal fiction. For example, a portfolio of shares in U.S., European, and Japanese companies can be "held" in a Caribbean island where low taxes (or no taxes) are levied on income from portfolio investments of nonresidents. The government of the Caribbean island gains tax revenue by attracting offices of "off-share" portfolio management companies and through legal fees.

Locations with low or no taxes on nonresidents' income from portfolio investment are known as tax havens.[4] The presence of tax havens limits other governments' abilities to tax income from ownership of capital. When taxes on income from capital increase, no actual capital may leave the tax jurisdiction, but an asset "portfolio" may leave, by the transfer of the location of ownership of the asset portfolio to a tax haven.

We therefore need to distinguish between investment as financial capital and investment as physical capital. In both cases, capital can be mobile. However, portfolio investment is more mobile than physical investment.

Residence-based taxation

To avoid loss of tax revenue by transfer of assets to foreign locations, governments may define tax liability based on the location of residence of the taxpayer and not on the location of the office of the investment company that holds assets in the name of the taxpayer. However, even with residence-based taxation, assets can be held abroad beyond the reach of the taxation authorities, if foreign banks maintain a policy of confidentiality regarding identities of account holders. Taxpayers are then engaging in tax evasion by holding asset portfolios in foreign tax havens.

Dynamic inconsistency

Taxation of income from capital is subject to the problem of dynamic inconsistency. To explain this problem, we observe that, even though financial capital is in general very mobile, the physical capital in place after an investment has been made is less mobile. Often, after an investment in physical capital has been made (a factory has been built), the capital cannot readily move elsewhere. The supply elasticity of capital after the investment has been made is then zero. The supply elasticity of capital before the investment is made, may however be, quite high because of alternative locations where the investment can be made and also because of the option not to make the investment at all.

Therefore, the supply elasticity of capital before the investment decision has been made is in general greater than after the investment has been made. A government that wishes to apply the Ramsey rule for efficient taxation could announce a low rate of taxation of income from capital before an investment is made, to reflect the high supply elasticity of capital. However, after the investment has been made, the Ramsey rule calls for a high rate of taxation on income from the investment because of the subsequent low (or zero) supply elasticity of capital.

---

[4] The financial press lists information about the values of shares in investment companies in tax havens.

Announcement by a government of a low rate of taxation on income from capital is therefore *dynamically inconsistent*. The low tax announced today will not be the tax rate that the government will wish to apply tomorrow. The announcement of a low tax rate before the investment has been made will therefore not be credible to investors because investors know that it is in the interest of the government to increase the tax rate after an investment has been made. If the announcement of a low tax rate is not credible, investments will not be made, because of the anticipation by investors of high taxes in the future.

There is a saying that the best tax is an old tax. That is, it is wise for government not to change taxes. Stable taxes allow investment decisions to be made without the uncertainty of having to predict future government tax policy. Investment is by nature subject to uncertainty. Uncertainty about taxes increases the uncertainty that firms face when deciding whether to invest. A reputation for stable taxes is a way of establishing and confirming a commitment not to take advantage of capital that becomes immobile after an investment has been made.

Therefore, there are benefits from maintaining an unchanged rate of taxation on income from capital. When tax rates on income from capital are increased, the credibility that tax rates will not be changed again in the future is lost, and investors can become reluctant to invest.

Similar considerations affect taxation of natural resources. After an exploration company has discovered an oil deposit, the income earned from the oil is a rent because there is no way to use the asset other than to extract oil. The Ramsey rule calls for appropriative taxes on rents because rents are returns from investments for which supply elasticities are zero. We see the time-inconsistency problem about taxation intentions that confronts an oil exploration company. The elasticity of supply of capital for oil exploration is high, which by the Ramsey rule calls for low tax rates on future income from successful exploration. However, after oil is found, the Ramsey rule calls for high taxes. Because of the time-inconsistency problem, the rule that an old (stable) tax is a good tax also applies to incentives for oil exploration, and exploration for other natural resources.

7.2.2 Corporate or company taxation

The corporate or company tax is a tax on the profits of firms. After wages and salaries of employees and other expenses have been paid and interest has been paid on money that has been borrowed, the residual or profit is a return to the owners of equity or shares in the company.

The corporate tax allows governments to discriminate in their tax treatment of profits (and losses) of corporations and personal incomes. Tax structures, as well as tax rates, often differ between individuals and corporations. Whereas personal income taxes tend to be progressive, corporate taxes tend to have flat rates.

Income earned by a corporation belongs in principle to the corporation's individual shareholders. If adjustments are not made for the taxes paid by individuals through personal taxation, the corporate income tax results in individuals' incomes from ownership of shares in corporations being taxed twice. An individual's income from ownership of a share of the corporation is taxed through the corporate income tax, and then, when the income is distributed as a dividend to shareholders, the same income from capital ownership is taxed again at the rate of personal income taxation applicable when the individual receives the dividends.[5]

Because the profits earned by corporations ultimately belong to individuals, it should be sufficient to have only a personal income tax. It appears that there is no need for a separate corporate income tax. Or, if there is to be a corporate profits tax, individuals should receive tax credits for taxes paid on corporate profits.[6]

The corporation as an independent legal entity

The corporation is an independent legal entity that retains its identity when ownership changes (through the buying and selling of shares) and when management changes. Also, under the principle of limited liability, owners of the capital of the cooperation are liable for losses only up to the level of their investments (or in some cases callable but not yet contributed investments). That is, limited liability ensures that the bankruptcy of a firm does not bring with it the bankruptcy of shareholders, who are limited in their personal obligations to cover losses by the corporation.

The corporation therefore facilitates individual participation in risky investments, by permitting people to avoid losing their other personal assets should the corporation incur high losses or become bankrupt. The corporation or firm can, however, be a separate legal entity without having a separate tax liability. The tax liability of the corporation can be computed and distributed among the individuals who own the firm. In the event of losses or bankruptcy, the liability of taxpayers to participate in the losses remains limited to the personal investment made in the firm.[7]

Selective policies

Perhaps the corporate tax is justified as a means for facilitating government policies that encourage or discourage the economic activity undertaken by a firm? We saw, for example, when considering externalities in Chapter 4, that corrective taxes or subsidies on production activities might be required to achieve efficiency. We did not, however, identify the corporate profits tax as a necessary means of achieving efficiency.[8]

---

[5] Identifying the individuals who ultimately pay a corporate income tax necessitates tracing the effects of the tax through the entire economy (or in a global world economy, through the entire world). See Chapter 2. Here we are identifying tax liability with ownership of stock in the corporation.

[6] Personal tax rates could differ for income earned from labor and capital according to the source of the income.

[7] We are using the terms "corporation," "company," and "firm" interchangeably. The terms have the same meaning.

[8] For example, the profits of tobacco companies could be taxed to discourage the production and sale of cigarettes. Returns to investments in cigarette production and sales could be taxed, but the cigarette externality problem can be solved by imposing taxes on consumption or production in the market for cigarettes. Policies in the market for cigarettes solve externality problems, without the need to impose taxes on the supply of investment capital to the cigarette industry.

The corporate profits tax and risk

Income from wages and salaries is in general risk-free because individuals receive predetermined wages and salaries (although they may receive bonuses). Risk in general falls upon the owners of the capital. The corporate profits tax affects investment behavior in the face of risk.

If there are losses, the losses can be offset against tax liabilities from future profits. Even if future profits are never made and the capital provided by investors is all lost, the accumulated losses have value as tax offsets for profitable firms. A profitable firm can buy the firm with the accumulated losses, and use the losses to reduce its own tax liabilities. Risk is therefore shared with the government through a firm's ability to use losses to reduce its tax liability.

The provisions of the corporate profits tax permit special accommodations to risk to be made. For example, oil and natural gas exploration companies can be given special allowances in writing off exploration costs. Research and development expenses, which can be substantial for pharmaceutical and other knowledge-based industries, can also be written off against corporate profits. Depreciation allowances written off against corporate profits can also be selectively determined to reflect different risks of investment in plant and machinery in different industries.

The special industry accommodations of the tax system to risk do not require a separate corporate profits tax. After the tax concessions and allowances have been taken into account, profits can be distributed to shareholders, and personal tax obligations can be determined according to the personal incomes of the individual owners.

Capital gains

A means of avoiding double taxation of corporate profits is to provide individual tax credits for taxes that corporations have paid. In the absence of such personal tax credits for corporate profit payments, there are incentives not to distribute corporate profits as dividends but to keep the profits within the company for further investment so to avoid personal taxes. The profits not distributed to shareholders are added to the capital value of the firm and are available as means of financing investment that is tax-free from the perspective of the individual shareholder. If the profits passed through the hands of individual shareholders before being reinvested, the government would take a further part of the profits through the personal income tax paid by individuals.

Therefore, by retaining rather than paying out profits to shareholders, the corporation provides individual shareholders with the benefit of a capital gain because the value of individuals' shareholdings in the firm increases. A capital gains tax, however, imposes tax obligations when an individual sells the assets or shares of the firm. The capital gains tax is usually applied at a flat rate that is lower than the highest marginal personal income tax rate. Individual taxpayers with high incomes therefore benefit when corporate profits are converted to increased share values, although they do not benefit as much as they might if there were no capital gains tax.[9] There is no such gain if personal liability to pay a capital gains tax is based on the personal marginal income tax rate.

Why are dividends ever paid?

If there is no individual tax credit for the taxes paid through the corporate profits tax, and there is a tax advantage to shareholders from conversion of corporate profits to capital gains, why are corporate profits ever distributed as dividends? The reason for dividend payments appears to be related to information and signaling to investors.

A dividend demonstrates the ability of management to provide a cash payout from the firm's activities. Not paying dividends and instead retaining profits is beneficial for management of a firm because capital financing is made available internally within the firm without the need to persuade investors to contribute new capital. Paying dividends can oblige the corporation to raise new capital for its investment activities. The willingness of new investors to provide new capital to the firm provides investors with information about the confidence of the market in the firm's future prospects. Managers then can signal or provide information about the confidence that the capital market has in their abilities. The cost of providing this information is the more costly means of raising revenue through external market financing.

Payment of dividends also sets a lower bound to share prices. If the share price falls and the dividend is kept constant, the return from purchasing and holding the stock increases. When the yield reaches the approximate level of the market rate of interest, investors will purchase the stock for the return provided by the dividend payout. Therefore, the dividend payout (if sustainable) acts as insurance for the stock price.

External financing

The corporate profits tax imparts a bias toward bond financing (i.e., borrowing) for new external financing rather than issuing new equity because the interest that the firm pays to bondholders is a tax-deductible expense. For example, a firm might issue bonds for a million dollars and pay annual interest of 7 percent. The $70,000 interest payment on the bonds is an expense deducted from the firm's profits. The firm could increase its capital by selling one million dollars of new capital equity to shareholders. A $70,000 return received by the firm on this capital investment is taxable income. By using bond financing rather than equity financing as much as possible, the firm minimizes corporate taxes.

However, bond financing exposes the firm to increased risk. The $70,000 interest on bonds is due every year, even when the cash flow to finance the bond payment is

---

[9] Capital gains taxes can have different characteristics. Tax liability may depend on how long assets have been held. There can be (or should be) provision for portfolio realignment (i.e., for sales of assets for the purpose of changing the asset composition of an investment portfolio). There should be an allowance for increases in value due to inflation.

not available. In the choice between bond and equity financing, there is a trade-off between tax advantages of bond financing and the risk resulting from the need to pay the interest on the bonds independently of corporate earnings.[10]

Why is there a corporate profits tax?

We are still left looking for a justification for a separate corporate profits tax. We have identified no efficiency reason for a corporate profits tax. Nor have we identified a social-justice reason for the tax. And considerations regarding tax deductions and exemptions, effects of risk, withholding of profits within the firm, and incentives regarding bond and equity financing do not suggest a justification for a corporate profits tax.

   We can conclude that, with a cooperate profits tax in existence, the individual taxpayers who are shareholders in a firm should receive a tax credit for the personal taxes that have been paid on their behalf through the corporate profits tax. When individual shareholders in the company are not provided with such tax credits, the corporate profits tax results in taxation of the same income twice. There is then a simple revenue motive for the corporate profits tax. The corporate profits tax provides revenue for the government, by allowing the government to tax income earned by corporations twice.

7.2.3 Indirect taxes: sales taxes, import duties, and the value-added tax

Governments use various indirect taxes (taxes levied when income is spent) to raise revenue: sales taxes, excise taxes, import duties, and value-added taxes (also called generalized sales taxes in some locations). Let us begin with a comparison of sales taxes and import duties. A sales tax is a tax on all sales and purchases in a particular market. An import tax (or tariff or duty) is a tax on domestic sales of foreign imports. Therefore, an import tax is a discriminatory tax that makes foreign goods more expensive than domestically produced goods. A sales tax provides a wider tax base than an import tariff because the import tariff provides revenue only from domestic sale of imported goods, whereas a sales tax provides revenue from sale of all goods irrespective of where the goods have been produced. When tax revenue is the objective, we expect to observe the use of a sales tax, with the broader tax base and more revenue.

The effects of an import duty

Figure 7.6 shows domestic supply and demand of a good in a home market and a price P^{world} at which the good can be bought in a world market. If there is neither a sales tax nor an import duty, the world price P^{world} is also the domestic price.

---

[10] Without taxes, and under some further conditions, it can be shown that shareholders should be indifferent regarding the choice between equity and bond financing. This result is known as the Modigliani-Miller theorem (1958). Franco Modigliani of MIT received the Nobel Prize in economics in 1985.

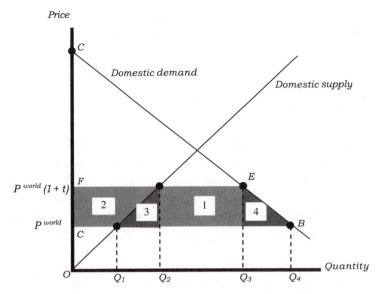

Figure 7.6. Comparison between an import duty and a sales tax as sources of government revenue.

Domestic demand is then Q_4, and domestic supply is Q_1. The difference between domestic demand and domestic supply is imports of $(Q_4 - Q_1)$.

An import duty of t percent increases the domestic price to $P^{world}(1+t)$. Sellers of imported goods receive this price, but pay the import duty $t \cdot P^{world}$ to the government. Domestic producers receive and keep the entire higher price. At the higher price, domestic producers supply the increased output Q_2, and domestic buyers buy the reduced quantity Q_3. The quantity of imports has been reduced to $(Q_3 - Q_2)$. The import duty has selectively taxed imports, and imports have decreased.

Before the import duty, when consumption was at Q_4, consumer benefit was ABC. After the tariff, consumption at Q_3 provides consumer benefit of CFE. Therefore, the tariff has reduced consumer benefit by the combined areas $(1 + 2 + 3 + 4)$.

Area 1 is tariff revenue received by the government. Area 2 is the benefit from the tariff to domestic producers.[11] Area 3 is a loss to society because of inefficient domestic production resulting from the tariff.[12] Area 4 is the benefit

---

[11] Producers receive post-tariff revenue from sales of $P^{world}(1+T) \cdot Q_2$ and have a total cost of production given by the area under the market supply function up to the quantity Q_2. Before the tariff was imposed, producers received revenue from sales $P^{world} \cdot Q_1$, and total costs were the area under the supply function up to Q_1. The difference is area 2.

[12] Because of the tariff, domestic production has increased by $(Q_2 - Q_1)$. The cost of producing this output domestically is the area under the supply function between Q_2 and Q_1. Before the tariff was imposed this same output $(Q_2 - Q_1)$ was provided to consumers at a cost of $P^{world}(Q_2 - Q_1)$. The excess cost of domestic production compared with supply through imports is area 3.

lost to consumers from contraction of consumption by $(Q_4 - Q_3)$.[13] Combined areas 3 and 4 indicate the efficiency loss or excess burden of the government securing the tariff revenue given by area 1.[14]

A sales tax at the same rate as the import duty

Rather than imposing the import tariff, a government could set a sales tax at the same rate of t percent. The sales tax increases the price paid by consumers to $P^{world}(1 + t)$ but leaves the price received by producers at P^{world}.

Because the price to consumers is the same, there is no difference for consumers between the sales tax and the import tax. That is, consumers pay the same post-tax price $P^{world}(1 + t)$, and have the same post-tax demand Q_3 whether there is a sales tax or import duty. The decrease in consumption from Q_4 to Q_3 results in the same efficiency loss to consumers due to the excess burden of taxation given by the area 4.

With the sales tax, producers continue to receive the price P^{world} for their sales and continue to produce the quantity Q_2. Producers have the option to sell in either the domestic or world market,[15] and so the entire excess burden of the sales tax falls on consumers. Producers therefore escape an excess burden of the sales tax, while consumers do not tax. The full incidence of the sales tax thus falls on consumers, who also have the only excess burden.[16]

The sales tax is levied uniformly on the output Q_1 supplied by domestic producers and the imported goods $(Q_3 - Q_1)$ that are domestically sold. The revenue to the government from the sales tax is the area $(1 + 2 + 3)$. The sales tax therefore converts areas 2 and 3 to government revenue.

Comparing the import duty and the sales tax

When we compare the import duty with the sales tax, we see that (1) tax revenue is higher with the sales tax, (2) the excess burden of taxation is lower with the sales tax, (3) consumers are indifferent between the import tariff and the sales tax, and (4) domestic producers are better off with the import tariff.

If a government chooses a tariff instead of the sales tax, the government (1) decreases its tax revenue, (2) increases the excess burden of taxation, and (3) provides additional benefit to domestic producers.

---

[13] EBQ_4Q_3, which is the total loss, is the area under the demand function, and the cost of previously supplying this consumption through imports was $P^{world} \cdot (Q_4 - Q_3)$; the difference is area 4.

[14] The revenue obtained from an import tax can be obtained equivalently from an import quota, through competitive auctioning of the right to import allowed by the quota. In Figure 7.6, competitive bidding for the right to import the quantity of goods $(Q_3 - Q_2)$ provides the revenue given by area 1. More often than not, import quotas have been assigned rather than auctioned. We saw in Chapter 6 that import quotas have been associated with rent seeking. Rents from quotas have sometimes been assigned to foreign exporters through policies known as voluntary export restraints.

[15] That is, the demand elasticity facing domestic producers in the world market is infinite.

[16] We considered the relation between tax incidence (who pays a tax) and the excess burden of taxation in Chapter 2.

An advantage of an import tariff is low administrative costs of collection of revenue. An import tariff is a tax on goods that pass through a specific location. Government revenue collectors need only position themselves on a wharf or at an airport and wait for the goods to arrive. Because of the simplicity of placing a few people at border crossings to collect the taxes, an import tariff was often historically the first source of tax revenue.[17]

A value-added tax

A value-added tax is an indirect tax that is paid on the value that is added at different stages of production. For example, suppose a person buys a table from carpenter for $300 plus a 15 percent value-added tax. The price paid for the table is $345 of which $45 is the tax. The carpenter may have paid $100 for the wood used to produce the table. When buying the wood, the carpenter also paid 15 percent tax on the wood, or a tax of $15. After the table is sold, the carpenter pays a tax $30 = ($45 − $15) to the government, after providing proof, through receipts, of the payment of $15 in taxes that the carpenter paid when the wood was bought that was used to make the table. The tax of $30 paid by the carpenter is levied on the value added to the wood by the carpenter's productive activity. In producing the table, the carpenter added $200 to the value of the wood (which was bought for $100). The carpenter pays $30, 15 percent of $200, as value-added tax.

The virtue of the value-added tax compared to a sales tax is that the value-added tax does not depend on the structure of ownership of productive activities. A uniform sales tax of 15 percent would be paid every time a market transaction took place on the full value of the product. It might then be worthwhile for carpenters to own sawmills, to save the round of taxation in the sale of the wood. The value-added tax makes such considerations of ownership of the stages of production irrelevant in determining tax payments. Given the scale of efficient production of tables by carpenters and the scale of efficient production of lumber from logs, it may not be efficient for a carpenter to own a sawmill. Or the carpenter may be skilled in making a table but may have no advantage in managing a sawmill. The value-added tax provides no incentive for the carpenter to own a sawmill.

7.2.4 Should indirect taxes accompany the optimal income tax?

The optimal personal income tax that we considered in Section 7.1 balances efficiency against social justice. Although we have observed that it is difficult to identify precisely the characteristics of the tax schedule for the optimal personal income tax, suppose that a government has been successful in designing an optimal income tax that maximizes social welfare. A question then arises whether there is a need for indirect taxes to accompany the optimal personal income tax.

We might think that there is no need for additional indirect taxes if the optimal balance between efficiency and social justice has been achieved through direct

---

[17] The opposition to the British import tax on tea was a precursor to the American war of independence.

taxation of personal income. In 1976, Anthony Atkinson and Joseph Stiglitz (Stiglitz, of Columbia University, received the Nobel Prize in economics in 2001) confirmed that indirect taxes are unnecessary, provided some conditions were satisfied. The conditions were that all taxpayers have the same preferences for spending income and differ only in abilities to earn income (recall these were the conditions Mirrlees imposed when setting out the optimal income tax problem). Also, the common preferences of the population had to be separable between labor supply and utility from consumption of goods.[18]

People do not, of course, have identical consumption preferences.[19] When consumption preferences differ, indirect taxes affect people in different ways. Indirect taxes can then be used to target people who have particular preferences.

For example, indirect taxes on tobacco products target smokers, in addition to the personal income taxes that smokers pay. If a government has identified cigarette smokers as a group of people that it wishes to tax, this group of people can be taxed through a tax on tobacco because only these people spend on tobacco products.

Thus, the income tax taxes incomes, but indirect taxes also allow goods to be selectively taxed. In Chapter 4, we saw how governments impose indirect taxes for paternalistic reasons. Such paternalism underlies the use of indirect taxes together with an optimal income tax.

Additional taxation of high-income people

Let us now consider two people who have the same utility function (the same preferences) and different abilities. We have therefore returned to the conditions of the original Mirrlees optimal tax problem. We define social welfare for two people, whom we identify as H for high-ability or high-income and L for low-ability or low-income, in the Bentham form as

$$W = U^H + U^L. \tag{7.18}$$

---

[18] Identical separable utility and different income-earning abilities allow Bentham's social welfare function for a population of n persons to be expressed as

$$W = \sum_{i=1}^{n} v(\ell^i) + \sum_{i=1}^{n} u(c_1^i, c_2^i, \ldots, c_m^i),$$

where ℓ^i is leisure and c^i is consumption of individual i. The income of individual i after the leisure/labor supply decision is $y^i = w^i \gamma^i L^i$, where w is a market wage, L^i is labor supply, and γ^i is the individual's ability. The larger γ^i is, the more income a person earns from any given number of hours worked. The optimal income tax maximizes the sum of utilities based on the different leisure choices, which have determined different incomes from different individual labor-supply decisions and different personal abilities. The second part of social welfare is the sum of utilities from consumption of goods. With the optimal income tax already trading off efficiency and social justice, indirect taxes would impose excess burdens of taxation with no gain from social justice. Much depends on the structure of preferences. Common homothetic consumption preferences ensure that expenditure shares are the same for all people independently of their incomes, and that indirect taxes therefore symmetrically affect all people in terms of relative excess burdens.

[19] James Mirrlees (1976) considered the broader class of consumption tastes consistent with a personal income tax that required no additional indirect taxes.

Person H has utility U^H, and person L has utility U^L. We saw in Chapter 5 that when the social welfare function defined by (7.18) is chosen behind a veil of ignorance, maximizing this social welfare function also maximizes the expected utility of each person, when the two people do not know who they are going to be.

In expression (7.18), the two people have equal personal social weights (equal to one). The low- and high-ability individuals can also be given different social weights. Let the different weights be a and b, where $(a + b) = 1$. Social welfare is then

$$W = aU^H + bU^L. \tag{7.19}$$

When $a = 0$ and $b = 1$, only the utility of the low-ability person matters for determining social welfare, and we have a social welfare function defined according to Rawls.

Although they have the same preferences, the different incomes of the low- and high-ability people can lead them to consume different goods. As a limiting case, the high-ability person might only consume good A (eating out in gourmet restaurants), while the low-ability person might only consume good B (groceries used for cooking at home). An indirect tax on good A imposes a utility loss on person H through taxes paid and the excess burden of taxation. Social welfare defined according to Rawls places no weight on the high-ability person's utility loss. It is socially efficient in that case to impose an indirect tax on the good A that is exclusively consumed by the high-ability person.[20] The revenue from the tax can be transferred to person L, and society defined according to Rawls's social welfare function is better off. More generally, the optimal structure of combined direct and indirect taxation can include indirect taxes on goods that are large components of high-ability (or high-income) people's personal spending and small components of low-ability (or low-income) people's spending.

Can we however necessarily associate income levels with particular spending patterns? Some people whose pre-tax incomes are not all that high may be prepared to live without owning a car or without going to football games in order to afford gourmet meals because good food is very important for the quality of their lives. Similarly, people with low-income earning ability may wish to attend operas rather than go to the movies, although tickets to the opera cost many times more than movie tickets. High indirect taxes on gourmet meals and on opera tickets then change the spending pattern of lower-income people, who, because of indirect taxes, may no longer be able to afford gourmet meals or going to the opera. An excess burden of taxation is imposed on low-income lovers of opera and gourmet meals because of the substitution in their spending. A case for indirect taxes to accompany optimally designed income taxes requires an assurance that only

---

[20] For example, the social weights could also be $a = 0.2$ and $b = 0.8$. Taking utility from the low-ability person is then four times more costly in terms of social welfare than taking utility from the high-ability person.

high-income people spend on good food and the opera, so as to allow the indirect taxes to target high-income people who have been given a low social weight.

A case for indirect taxes to accompany optimal income taxes therefore stereotypes people. In a society with diverse tastes, high-income people might like to go to the movies, and lower-income people might like to go to the opera. High taxes on opera tickets then stratify the society through a self-fulfilling prediction of segmentation. The indirect taxes make already expensive opera tickets more expensive still, and low-income people go the movies although they would prefer to be at the opera. Taxation of opera tickets is quite different from paternalistic taxation (e.g., taxation of tobacco products on the grounds that tobacco is harmful). If opera tickets were taxed, low-income people who enjoy opera may be denied the opera without any social justification.[21]

The indirect taxes would be imposed in conjunction with direct taxes that we can suppose have made the post-tax income distribution more equal. Because direct taxes have reduced the variation in post-income-tax incomes, direct taxes have also diminished the scope for using indirect taxes to target people by spending patterns.

We might therefore have reservations about the idea that categorizing people by incomes also allows a division into classes of people by spending preferences. Rather, in a population with a broad range of spending preferences, indirect taxes cannot be targeted. Indirect taxes then become unwarranted intrusions into people's personal lives when an optimal income tax has already been designed.

Revenue maximization and political calculation

A leviathan government that wants to maximize revenue from taxation will wish to use both indirect taxes and income taxes. If we see a government levying a personal income tax accompanied by a plethora of different indirect taxes, we may therefore be observing a leviathan government with no concern for social optimality.

A government observed to be selecting different rates of indirect taxation may also be setting taxes with an objective of providing political favors (and disfavors). For example, owners of video rental stores might like to see high taxes on movie tickets. Supermarket owners might like to see high taxes on eating out in restaurants. Bus companies might like to see high taxes on parking for cars and on taxi fares.

Uniform taxes limit such political discretion in choice of indirect taxes.[22] Indirect taxes (sales taxes and value-added taxes) are usually uniform, with some small numbers of exemptions. On the other hand, import taxes have usually not been uniform and have often been identified as politicized taxes set to benefit special interests.

---

[21] Rather than imposing taxes, governments tend to subsidize opera companies and other forms of the arts.

[22] Agnar Sandmo (1974) showed how, under special conditions on individual preferences, uniform taxes could be efficient in satisfying the Ramsey rule.

7.2.5 Lotteries

Lotteries offer a means by which governments can obtain revenue. The revenue might be collected by a government agency that directly manages a lottery or might be provided by selling the right to operate legal lotteries to private firms.

A lottery is a gamble. The gamble is moreover an unfair gamble because, through the taxation component, the government takes a share of the lottery revenue. That is, the implicit tax in the lottery reduces the value of prizes below the value of the revenue from the sale of lottery tickets. The unfair gamble can only be sustained when the lottery is a government monopoly. If there were competition, competitors would announce increased percentage payouts from lotteries until, through competition, the value of the payout in prizes would approach the value of the revenue from sale of lottery tickets.

Adam Smith made the following observations about lotteries (in the *Wealth of Nations*, 1776, Chapter 10):

> *In state lotteries, the tickets are not really worth the price. There is not a more certain proposition in mathematics than the more tickets you adventure upon, the more likely you are to be a loser. Adventure on all the tickets in the lottery and you lose for certain; and the greater the number of your tickets, the nearer you approach this certainty.*

Adam Smith also noted that the sole source of demand for lottery tickets is the "vain hope of gaining some of the great prizes." Low-income people tend to spend more on lottery tickets; consequently, taxation through a lottery tends to be regressive.

7.2.6 Taxation through inflation and financial repression

Governments have resorted to satisfying revenue needs by printing money. Financial repression has also been used to provide governments with revenue. In both cases, a government obtains revenue by being a monopoly.

Government has a monopoly on printing the domestic currency. Printing money without accompanying increases in availability of goods or assets increases nominal prices. The government pays the increased nominal prices when spending the money that it is printing. The government gains, however, from the reduced real value of nominal assets in the economy. For example, if there has been overnight inflation of 20 percent, a $100 bill placed under a pillow before going to sleep is worth only $80 in the morning. The $100 bill now buys only $80 worth of goods or assets, and a tax of 20 percent has therefore been imposed overnight. This is the inflation tax.

For inflation to be a tax, people must be surprised by the inflation. Otherwise domestic financial markets will account for inflation by including the expected rate of inflation in the nominal interest rate. For example, suppose that the rate of interest is 3 percent per year when there is no inflation. That is, the real (inflation-free) rate of interest is 3 percent. Then, suppose that inflation of 4 percent per year is anticipated. The nominal rate of interest now increases to 7 percent because people who lend money will want the 3 percent real return plus additional 4 percent compensation for the expected inflation.[23]

Unanticipated inflation also reduces the real value of government debt, and thereby reduces the real value of the payments that a government makes to redeem its bonds. The beneficiaries when unanticipated inflation reduces the future value of government bonds are future taxpayers, for whom taxes for redeeming the bonds are reduced. Therefore, unanticipated inflation causes an intergenerational transfer of income, from present holders of government bonds to future taxpayers.

Financial repression provides government revenue by restricting the rights of people to invest abroad. For example, the interest rate available to investors in the global capital market might be 5 percent, but a government may not allow its citizens to invest abroad and may set a domestic interest rate of 2 percent. By borrowing from its citizens at 2 percent, the government then gains compared to the 5 percent interest that the government would be obliged to pay for its borrowing if people had access to the global capital market.[24] Revenue from repression of domestic financial markets requires a government to legislate for itself a monopoly position in domestic financial markets and to make investment by the population outside the country illegal.

Inflation and financial repression as a means of providing government revenue have been primarily used by governments in poorer countries.

7.2.7 Wealth and estate taxes

A tax on land or property is a tax on a part of personal wealth. Some governments have imposed more broad wealth taxes on personal assets. Wealth is past accumulated income that was taxed when the income was earned. Taxing wealth is a retroactive tax, which taxes the same income twice.

More common than wealth taxes are estate or inheritance taxes.[25] Payment of these taxes can often be avoided through trusts and other means of transferring wealth when alive. Wealthier persons can be expected to have better access to legal advice and to be better informed about means of avoiding taxes on wealth than poorer people. The wealthy will know about trusts and about offshore tax havens where wealth can be stored away from tax authorities.

---

[23] If inflation turns out to be higher than the anticipated 4 percent, lenders will have lost. Lenders gain if inflation is lower than the anticipated 4 percent.

[24] The government could also gain by borrowing from its citizens at 2 percent and lending the same funds at 5 percent in the global capital market. Another means of gain for a government through financial repression is to require that the country's financial institutions hold some part of their assets in its low-yielding bonds.

[25] An estate tax is levied on the estate. An inheritance tax is levied on the beneficiary of the inheritance. The difference between estate and inheritance taxes arises when taxes are progressively graduated according the value of the estate or individual inheritance. That is, with graduated taxes, an inheritance tax makes allowance for the number of people who share the estate when tax liability is computed.

When holdings of wealth are concentrated in the one asset, payment of a wealth tax or estate tax can require sale of the asset. For example, it may be necessary to sell the family house or the family farm to provide the money to pay the tax to the government.

From a property rights perspective, a tax on income deprives people of parts of current additions to personal wealth but leaves past after-tax income free of appropriation by further taxation. A wealth or estate tax opens all of a person's assets to potential loss by taxation.

7.2.8 Lump-sum taxes

Lump-sum taxes by definition have no excess burden of taxation. An example of a lump-sum tax is a head tax, which people pay because they exist. Applying the Ramsey rule, the head tax is efficient because the tax cannot be escaped. However, there is no assurance that a head tax will be used in a way that is socially just. Head taxes in principle allow political decision makers to discriminate among people in setting personal taxes.[26] A head tax can take away a person's entire income or property. A head tax is like a wealth tax because the only limitation on what a government can ask for in taxes is individual wealth. In contrast, an income tax or an indirect tax is based on anonymous market activities. An income tax does not usually depend on the identity of the person who has earned the income, and an indirect tax does not depend on the identity of a buyer or seller.[27] The income tax is based on how much income has been earned, and the indirect tax is based on how income has been spent. Personal freedom is preserved through income taxes and indirect taxes through the right to avoid taxation by choosing to work less or spend less. Head taxes offer no such guarantee of personal freedom. We expect that head taxes will not be used.

A head tax levied when people are free to leave (and enter) a local government tax jurisdiction does not, however, compromise personal freedom. If the tax can be escaped by exit from the tax jurisdiction, payment of the tax is by choice, and the tax is a voluntary price that is paid for the benefits offered by location in a jurisdiction. Local government jurisdictions do not use head taxes to finance public spending. As we previously observed, taxes in local government jurisdictions are usually levied on land or property that cannot leave the jurisdiction.

7.2.9 A direct tax on personal expenditure

We have taken for granted that direct taxation is taxation of personal income. An alternative to a direct tax on personal income is a direct tax on personal expenditure. A personal expenditure tax is not a sales tax that is levied on separate purchases of goods or services. The personal expenditure tax is similar to a personal

---

[26] We noted this problem in Chapter 2 when we asked whether taxes without an excess burden of taxation that governments can use to finance public spending on public goods exist.

[27] Where there is discrimination in an income tax, the discrimination is over classes of people with general attributes (e.g., all people filing a tax return together or all people filing separately).

income tax in that individuals report the value of their annual spending to the government and pay taxes on an annual basis. The tax structure can be progressive, just as with a personal income tax. To comply with a personal expenditure tax, a taxpayer reports (1) personal wealth at the beginning of the year, (2) personal wealth at the end of the year, and (3) personal income during the year. Personal income includes returns from investment of capital, income from ownership of stock or shares in companies, capital gains, and income from ownership of property (i.e., income from all sources).

Suppose a taxpayer reports personal wealth of $100,000 at the beginning of the year and $120,000 at the end of the year, with personal income of $50,000 during the year. The taxpayer therefore spent $30,000 during the year and is taxed on this $30,000. No taxes are paid on the $20,000 that was added to savings.

As another example, consider a person who has no income from a wage or salary and lives off a family inheritance. The person reports having $500,000 at the beginning of the year, $450,000 at the end of the year, and income from interest during the year of $30,000. Personal expenditure during the year is therefore $80,000, and he or she is taxed on this amount.

With an income tax, the first person with income of $50,000 pays more tax than the second person, who pays tax on income of $30,000. The expenditure tax, however, determines tax liability based on money spent. The source of a person's income, or the source of the money spent, is of no importance for the expenditure tax. The money spent may have been earned as income as in the case of person 1, or may be the return from an investment as in the case of person 2, or alternatively the money spent may have been provided as a gift. Or the source of the money spent may be capital gains or corporate dividends. The personal expenditure tax thus eliminates separate taxes for different sources of income.

The social justice of the expenditure tax is that people are taxed according to their spending, and not according to the value of their contribution to production. Productive persons who are frugal are taxed less than less-productive people who are extravagant in their spending (to the extent that they have money to spend).[28]

Problems with a personal expenditure tax

Except for bequests and gifts, the present value of a person's lifetime income is equal to the present value of lifetime spending and tax payments. The difference between the income tax and the expenditure tax is the timing of taxation. With the income tax, taxation occurs when income is earned; with the expenditure tax, taxation takes place when income is spent.

Spending is often more concentrated in time than income. The personal largest expenditure most people make is buying a house. A progressive tax structure for the expenditure tax would make buying a house unattractive because of the high

---

[28] With an expenditure tax, personal savings are not taxed. With an income tax, income is taxed whether it is spent or saved.

tax liability incurred in the year that the house is bought.[29] Similar considerations apply to cars and other consumer durables for which expenditure is at a point in time and the benefits are over time. An expenditure tax would have to accommodate the timing of spending by allowing taxes to be spread over time to match the benefits over time.

To avoid high taxes of a progressive expenditure tax, high-expenditure people could give tax-free gifts to low-expenditure people and send them shopping on their behalf. If gifts within the family were tax-free, the "family" would have to be defined. We can imagine disagreement on who is, or is not, part of the same family or the same household.

Expenditures often provide shared benefits (e.g., a number of people might use the same refrigerator). A personal expenditure tax has to make allowance for shared spending.

A problem arises in transition from an income tax to an expenditure tax. If an expenditure tax were to replace an income tax, people who have paid taxes all their working lives according to the incomes they earned would be asked to pay taxes during retirement years according to what they spend. The change to an expenditure tax from an income tax would therefore be unjust for retired people and also for other people still working and earning income who have paid income taxes over the years and are approaching the stage of their lives where they will spend but not earn income. Compensation could be provided through exemptions to the expenditure tax based on age, but then care would have to be taken to avoid transfers of money to people exempt from the expenditure tax who could spend on behalf of nonexempt people.

7.2.10 Summary

In this section, we have proceeded beyond the personal income taxes and sales taxes that people pay to consider the broader ranger of taxes that governments can or do use to collect revenue. We have considered whether different tax rates should be applied to income from capital as distinct from income from labor or personal effort and have investigated the implications of the Ramsey rule for efficient taxation when investment and capital are mobile among tax jurisdictions but property and labor are not. We have observed that issues of social justice as well as efficiency arise. Tax havens allow taxation of income from capital to be avoided, although people also move in response to taxes. We have considered taxation of corporate profits and have sought reasons why corporate profits are taxed independently rather than the profits being regarded for tax purposes as part of the incomes of the owners of the firms.

We have compared sales taxes and import duties as sources of government revenue. We have seen that sales taxes are superior to import duties as a means

---

[29] The incentive would be to rent to spread housing expenditures over time. A person or firm that bought the house for rental would, however, face the same problem of large expenditures in a single year. A mortgage allows the cost of buying a house to be spread over time.

for governments to obtain revenue from indirect taxes. Sales taxes are generally more uniform than import duties. The diversity in import duties or tariffs suggests protectionist objectives. Since, compared with an import duty, a sales tax converts returns to domestic producers and an excess burden of taxation to government revenue, the motive for import duties cannot be for revenue when a corresponding sales tax is feasible. We have also considered the value-added tax (or generalized sales) tax as a form of indirect taxation for raising revenue and have seen that such a tax has advantages over indirect taxes such as a sales tax that is levied irrespective of value added. We investigated the question whether, if an optimal (direct) income tax has been successfully designed and implemented, indirect taxes are needed at all.

Lotteries are a form of taxation. Lotteries require government monopoly; otherwise, competition would increase the payout. As Adam Smith remarked, lotteries are not rational for participants but depend on optimism not objectively justified. Inflation is a tax that relies on the government's monopoly in printing money, although the inflation must be unanticipated for the inflation tax to provide tax revenue. Financial repression is another means for government to collect tax revenue through monopoly, in this case by preventing access by residents to competitive returns in international capital markets.

We have also considered wealth and estate taxes and lump-sum taxes as sources of government revenue. Wealth and estate taxes raise issues of incentives and justice. We have noted that governments rarely tax wealth in general, although wealth in the form of property is taxed, in particular by local tax jurisdictions to finance locally provided public goods and services. Estate taxes, or inheritance taxes, are more common, although such taxes can often be avoided by estate planning. Lump-sum taxes raise the problem of arbitrariness and discrimination, since the taxes need not be anonymous.

We considered the case for a direct tax on personal spending as a substitute for a direct tax on personal income. We saw that a direct tax on spending has advantages compared to the income tax, but there are also problems associated with large expenditures at a point in time and shared expenditures. A difficulty in implementing a personal expenditure tax is the problem of transition from an income tax. Injustices would arise if people who have paid taxes on income all their lives were required to pay taxes according to personal expenditure when they reach a stage of life where they cease earning income.

References and related literature

On different tax systems, see Sandford (2000). On the basis for the income tax, see Haig (1921) and Simons (1938). On who pays the corporate income tax, see Harberger (1962). On excess burdens and the corporate income tax, see Gordon (1985); on the relation between personal taxation and corporate financing decisions, see Graham (1999); for an overview of the corporate income tax, see Mintz (1995); on dividends as a signal, see Bernheim and Wantz (1995). On the bias toward home investment, see Feldstein and Horiaka (1980) and Gordon and Bovenberg (1996), and on foreign investment and taxation of capital, see Huizinga and Nielsen (1997). On the use of import duties to provide political benefits, see Hillman (1989). On different types of value-added taxes, see Tait (1988). On indirect taxes as an accompaniment of direct taxation, see Atkinson and Stiglitz (1976), Mirrlees (1976), Christiansen (1984), and Saez (2002). On the ethics of estate and gift taxes, see Erreygers and Vandevelde (1997), and on responses to these taxes, see Poterba (2001). On lotteries as taxation, see Gully and Scott (1993), Walker (1998), and Beenstock, Goldin, and Haitovsky (2000). On inflation as a tax, see Phelps (1973). On taxation through financial repression, see Fry (1982) and Giovannini and de Melo (1993). On the income tax and the expenditure tax, see Pechman (1990).

Atkinson, A. B. and J. Stiglitz, 1976. The design of tax structure: Direct versus indirect taxation. *Journal of Public Economics* 6, 55–75.

Beenstock, M., E. Goldin and Y. Haitovsky, 2000. What jackpot? The optimal lottery tax. *European Journal of Political Economy* 16, 655–71.

Bernheim, D. B. and A. Wantz, 1995. A tax-based test of the dividend signalling hypothesis. *American Economic Review* 85, 532–51.

Christiansen, V. A., 1984. Which commodity taxes should supplement the income tax? *Journal of Public Economics* 24, 195–220.

Erreygers, G. and T. Vandevelde, 1997. *Is Inheritance Legitimate?: Ethical and Economic Aspects of Wealth Transfers*. Springer, Heidelberg.

Feldstein, M. S. and C. Horiaka, 1980. Domestic savings and international capital flows. *Economic Journal* 90, 314–29.

Fry, M., 1982. Models of financially repressed developing economies. *World Development* 10, 731–50.

Giovannini, A. and M. de Melo, 1993. Government revenue from financial repression. *American Economic Review* 83, 953–63.

Gordon, R. H., 1985. Taxation of corporate capital income. Tax revenues versus tax distortions. *Quarterly Journal of Economics* 100, 1–27.

Gordon, R. H. and A. L. Bovenberg, 1996. Why is capital so immobile internationally? Possible explanations and implications for capital income taxation. *American Economic Review* 86, 1057–75.

Graham, J. R., 1999. Do personal taxes affect corporate financing decisions? *Journal of Public Economics* 73, 147–85.

Gully, O. D. and F. A. Scott, 1993. The demand for wagering on state operated lotto games. *National Tax Journal* 46, 13–22.

Haig, R. M., 1921. *The Federal Income Tax*. Columbia University Press, New York.

Harberger, A. B., 1962. The incidence of the corporation income tax. *Journal of Political Economy* 70, 215–40.

Hillman, A. L., 1989. *The Political Economy of Protection*. Harwood Academic Publishers, Chur. Reprinted 2001, Routledge, London.

Huizinga, H. and S. B. Nielsen, 1997. Capital income and profit taxation with foreign ownership of firms. *Journal of International Economics* 42, 149–65.

Mintz, J., 1995. The corporation tax: A survey. *Fiscal Studies* 16, 23–68.

Mirrlees, J. A., 1976. Optimal tax theory: A synthesis. *Journal of Public Economics* 6, 327–58.

Modigliani, F. and M. Miller, 1958. The cost of capital, corporation finance, and the theory of investment. *American Economic Review* 48, 261–97.

Pechman, J. E., 1990. The future of the income tax. *American Economic Review* 80, 1–20.

Phelps, E. S., 1973. Inflation in the theory of public finance. *Swedish Journal of Economics* 75, 67–82.

Poterba, J. M., 2001. Estate and gift taxes and inter vivos giving in the U.S., *Journal of Public Economics* 79, 237–64.

Saez, E., 2002. The desirability of commodity taxation under non-linear income taxation and heterogeneous tastes. *Journal of Public Economics* 83, 217–30.

Sandford, C., 2000. *Why Tax Systems Differ: A Comparative Study of the Political Economy of Taxation*. Fiscal Publications, Bath, ME.

Sandmo, A., 1974. A note on the structure of optimal taxation. *American Economic Review* 64, 701–6.

Simons, H. C., 1938. *Personal Income Taxation*, University of Chicago Press, Chicago.

Tait, A. A., 1988. *Value-Added Taxation: International Practice and Problems*. International Monetary Fund, Washington, D.C.

Walker, I., 1998. The economic analysis of lotteries. *Economic Policy* 27, 357–402.

Questions for discussion

1. Is there a case for taxing income from capital at different rates from income earned from labor and personal effort? Explain.

2. How is income from capital (interest and dividends from ownership of stocks and shares, and capital gains) taxed in the place where you live or study? Is income from capital taxed differently from income from labor and personal effort?

3. What does the Ramsey rule for efficient taxation imply about the structure of taxes on income from capital and income from labor and personal effort? How does the mobility of capital between tax jurisdictions affect the taxes indicated by the Ramsey rule?

4. Studies show that there is a home bias in asset portfolios expressed as a preference for investment in assets in the country where people live. What are the consequences of this home bias for taxation indicated by the Ramsey rule? What do you believe are the reasons for the home bias?

5. How is taxation of income from capital affected by a time inconsistency problem?

6. How do issues of social justice become involved with supply elasticities of locationally mobile capital?

7. What is the rate of taxation on corporations or companies in the place where you live or study? Is the rate of corporate taxation higher or lower than the highest marginal tax rate on personal income? How does the relation between the corporate tax rate and the highest marginal personal income tax rate affect economic decisions?

8. Is there a justification for a separate tax on corporate profits? Should taxes paid by a company be tax credits deducted from the personal taxes paid by individual shareholders in the company? Explain.

9. How does a corporate profits tax affect firms' decisions between using issue of new share capital and sale of bonds to raise new capital? Why do firms pay dividends? How is the answer to this question related to the case for a capital gains tax? Do you believe that there should be a tax on capital gains? Explain.

10. "We should not try to explain taxation of imports by government revenue motives. A government seeking tax revenue can always obtain more revenue from a sales tax than a tax on imports." Do you agree? Explain.

11. What are the advantages of a value-added tax over a sales tax? Are there disadvantages of a value-added tax?

12. If income taxes have been optimally set, are there justifications for also using indirect taxes?

13. Lotteries provide tax revenue that people pay voluntarily. Given Adam Smith's observations about lotteries, how do governments succeed in raising revenue through lotteries?

14. What is the tax base for inflation as a tax? Why, if inflation is to be a tax, does the inflation have to be unanticipated by the public? Why would a government use inflation as a tax?

15. How can financial repression be used as a form of taxation? Why would a government ever wish to raise revenue in this way?

16. Would you support a wealth tax? Explain. Is there an ethical or economic case for taxing wealth at the end of life through inheritance or estate taxes?

17. "Because of the different forms of taxation, the same personal income is taxed over and over again in different ways using different taxes, and this is unfair." Do you agree? Explain.

18. What are the main differences between direct taxes based on personal income and on personal spending? Which tax do you believe to be the more justified, and on what grounds?

19. If a change were proposed from a personal income tax to a personal expenditure tax, what would be the impediments to implementing the change? Do you believe that the impediments to change explain why governments tax personal income and not personal expenditure? Explain.

20. Why do different governments use different types of taxes to raise revenue rather than simply taxing personal incomes?

7.3

Refusal to Pay Taxes

7.3.1 Policies to deter tax evasion

When payment of taxes is based on self-assessment and self-reporting by taxpayers, tax compliance requires taxpayer honesty. Governments do not rely on taxpayer honesty alone. Policies are adopted that attempt to ensure taxpayer compliance.

Tax authorities could maximize the likelihood that taxes are paid in full by meticulously auditing every tax return. The cost of such complete systematic audits might exceed the benefits obtained through additional tax revenue. Tax returns are therefore more usually randomly audited. The random auditing introduces a probability of detection for taxpayers who understate taxable income.

Random auditing is accompanied by penalties. The combination of the likelihood of detection and the penalty if detected is intended to deter tax evasion. Increasing the probability of detection is costly because of the additional personnel required for auditing of tax returns. Increasing the penalty may be less costly: the costs of increased penalties consist of public spending for additional time in prison and the output lost because a person has been imprisoned (e.g., imprisonment of a skilled surgeon deprives society of the surgeon's skills). If penalties are fines and not imprisonment, these costs are avoided, and also revenue increases when a tax evader is detected.[1]

Since tax evasion is illegal, people who evade taxes believe they will be successful in underpaying or not paying taxes. Otherwise the threat of the penalty for tax evasion would deter them from evading tax payments.

7.3.2 Social norms and tax evasion

Tax evasion can reflect to a feeling of injustice that taxes are too high.[2] People might feel that they are paying taxes to a leviathan government that cares little for them and maximizes tax revenue for its own self-interested purposes. That is, people might feel that they work hard for their money and that taxes take up too much of their earned incomes and deliver too little in return. The consequence can be a social norm of tax evasion. The social norm can override an individual's personal values that would lead to honest payment of taxes.

When the social norm is to evade taxes, people who admit to honestly paying taxes may find themselves socially ostracized. Self-assessment of tax obligations by taxpayers relies on a social norm of honesty in payment of taxes. When the social norm is honesty, there is a cost of personal embarrassment in being found to be evading taxes in addition to the cost through penalties and fines. Where the social norm is not to pay taxes, there is not the same personal stigma of being found out to be a tax evader.

The threat of punishment is ineffective in deterring tax evasion when tax compliance is low because the social norm is not to pay taxes. If the social norm is to evade taxes, punishment of someone whom the government has accused of evading taxes is seen as arbitrary and unfair because the tax evader is being accused of behaving in a way that conforms to the social norm of behavior. Punishment is therefore politically unpopular. Persons in government may, consistently with the social norm, also be evading taxes, and they may not wish to act hypocritically in penalizing others who behave as they do.

Social norms are therefore important in determining the extent to which a government can rely on accurate taxpayer self-assessment of tax obligations. Social norms also determine the effectiveness of actions to deter tax evasion.

---

[1] To enforce tax compliance, penalties could be set extremely high. However, the principle of penalties commensurate with acts committed deters extreme penalties.

[2] We tend to associate higher tax rates with increased tax evasion. Shlomo Yitzhaki (1974) pointed out that economic theory can also predict a decline in tax evasion when tax rates increase. When tax rates increase, if there is no change in hours worked and income earned, a taxpayer's after-tax income falls. If risk aversion decreases with income, the lower after-tax income makes the taxpayer more risk averse. Tax evasion is risky. A taxpayer who is evading taxes will then reduce taxes evaded when the tax rate increases. This suggests that a way to discourage tax evasion is to set high taxes, to take advantage of the risk averse behavior of taxpayers. Since higher taxes appear to encourage tax evasion, we conclude that the reason why people respond to higher taxes by increasing tax evasion is that their degree of risk aversion does not decline with increased income, or they act out of a feeling of injustice when high taxes are accompanied by little perceived personal gain from the taxes paid.

7.3.3 Opportunities for tax evasion

Opportunities for tax evasion are not equally present. Some people have greater opportunities to evade taxes than others. When employers transfer income taxes, and payroll and social security taxes, directly to the government, there is little opportunity for employees to evade taxes. Self-employed persons and employers or owners of businesses have, on the other hand, means for evading taxes by finding ways to understate revenues and overstate expenses. Sellers who deal directly with final purchasers have the most extensive opportunities for tax evasion because final purchasers in general receive no tax deduction or credit for expenses and so do not have a reason to ask for a receipt that documents the seller's revenue. A plumber or electrician may, for example, offer a less expensive quote if the customer requires no receipt, as may a lawyer or accountant or dentist. Social norms determine whether the offer is made and whether the offer is accepted. Tax evasion can also take the form of exchanges of services. A dentist may do "free" dental work for a lawyer who in return provides "free" legal services.

Some taxes are also more difficult to evade than others. It is, for example, difficult to evade a property tax. The tax base, which is the property or house, is very visible, and ownership is usually well-defined.

7.3.4 Guilt feelings and tax amnesties

People who have evaded payment of taxes sometimes have guilt feelings. Or they may not feel guilty, but cannot sleep at night because of anxiety about detection.

Guilt feeling and anxiety can be used to increase tax revenue by announcing a tax amnesty. A declaration can be made that people who voluntarily come forth and pay the taxes they have evaded in the past will not have to pay penalties. Besides providing past unpaid revenue, a tax amnesty has the advantage for the government of opening the evading taxpayer's future income to taxation.

7.3.5 The behavior of the tax authorities

Benjamin Franklin wrote about the unpleasant treatment received by taxpayers from tax-enforcement agents of the British Crown before the American Revolution of 1776. He described the principles of behavior of the tax-enforcement authorities as:

> If any revenue officers are suspected of the least tenderness for the people, discard them. If others are justly complained of, protect and reward them. If any of the under officers behave so as to provoke the people to drub them, promote those to better office.

Benjamin Franklin viewed the principles of behavior of tax-enforcement authorities as part of the "rules by which a great empire may be reduced to a small one." That is, he attributed the American Revolution in part to the behavior of the British tax officials.[3] Centuries after these words were written, treatment of taxpayers at the hands of tax-enforcement officials has also been criticized.

The behavior of tax-collection agents is influenced by incentives. Employees of the government tax authority are sometimes paid a personal bonus for increasing tax revenue. To increase revenue, tax officials can apply presumptive taxation, which is based on a presumption of ability to earn income. For example, the tax inspector may know more or less the average income of a category of taxpayers (e.g., lawyers or plumbers or taxi drivers). Every taxpayer who is audited might, however, be given a presumptive tax assessment above the average income.

Presumptive tax assessments above the average of the distribution of true incomes for all taxpayers increase the prospects of a bonus for the employee of the tax administration. Those taxpayers whose true tax obligations are below average can be expected to protest more strenuously about the tax assessment and are in general prepared to provide evidence confirming their claims of lower than assessed taxable incomes. Taxpayers who cannot provide confirmatory evidence may have to pay the above-average assessment whether or not the assessment reflects their true incomes.

Some taxpayers for whom the assessment is excessive compared to their true tax liability might pay taxes that they do not owe. They may not be able to cope with the emotional stress of ongoing communication with the tax administration. Or they may pay the unjustified taxes to avoid personal expenses on tax lawyers and accountants.[4]

There is a further question whether the audits of tax inspectors are random or rather follow a systematic pattern that suggests bias in the choice of taxpayers to audit. In Chapter 3 where we considered the behavior of bureaucracy, we noted that bureaucrats can be independent of political decision makers, but also, depending on the institutional mechanism for control over the budgets of bureaucracies, political decision makers can exercise control over bureaucracies. In particular, political decision makers may wish to control the auditing decisions of the income tax authorities. Such control could be used (illegally) against political adversaries.

Political decision makers may want to increase tax revenue but are sensitive to the adverse effects on political support and campaign contributions because of the harassment felt by constituents and political supporters when tax audits are aggressively carried out. If possible, political decision makers might wish to have the best of both worlds by increasing tax revenue collection through aggressive

---

[3] A cry of the Revolution was "no taxation without representation." Although the American colonies were obliged to pay taxes to England, the colonies had no representation in the English parliament.

[4] In some countries, tax evasion takes place with the complicity and cooperation of officials of the tax administration. Corrupt tax inspectors who extort income from taxpayers by harassment can be instrumental in increasing tax evasion, by combining the harassment with solicitation of bribes in exchange for offers of cooperation in nonpayment of taxes. Corruption also affects the penalties that can be set for tax evasion. If tax officials can be bribed, high penalties increase the personal gains available to a tax administration official from cooperating with a tax evader and increase the incentive for corruption.

auditing but, at the same time, by having the audits carried out in the constituencies of political opponents, or in constituencies other than theirs.

Evidence suggests that during the 1990s the tax audits of U.S. Internal Revenue Service (IRS) were subject to political influence. The incidence of audits of individuals' income tax returns was systematically lower in constituencies of politicians who, through membership of congressional committees, had oversight roles regarding the IRS. Likewise, the incidence of auditing of returns was found to be systematically lower in districts that were politically important to the U.S. president.[5]

7.3.6 The shadow economy

In the shadow economy, tax evasion is complete. Incomes are not reported to the government. Income taxes are not paid nor are the payroll or social security taxes that finance employees' social benefits.

Welfare fraud also occurs through the shadow economy. People employed in the shadow economy are not officially employed, so they retain entitlements to unemployment benefits or welfare payments. Such people are fraudulently taking money from the government (i.e., from taxpayers), while at the same time they are evading taxes on their incomes.

The size of the shadow economy cannot be directly observed, and indirect approaches to measurement are therefore used. Supplement 7A describes indirect approaches to measurement of the shadow economy.

One approach looks at the demand for cash. Cash payments are not equally used in legal and shadow-economy activities. Transactions in the shadow economy are disproportionately financed through untraceable cash payments. The extent of shadow economy activity can therefore be estimated by looking at the relation between cash in circulation and total economy activity. Economic activity implied by cash in circulation can be compared with reported national income. The difference is an estimate of the size of the shadow economy. When taxes increase, more economic activity tends to move into the shadow economy, and the demand for cash or banknotes increases to finance the greater nonreported transactions. The increased demand for cash can be observed. If the relation between demand for cash and the value of national income is known, an estimate can be made of the increase in output in the shadow economy associated with the increased demand for cash. Such indirect approaches to measurement cannot, of course, ensure complete accuracy in computations of the size of the shadow economy.

Table 7.1 shows estimates, made by Friedrich Schneider in conjunction with associates, of the size of the shadow economy for a number of countries. The numbers show the estimated size of the shadow economy relative to reported national income. We see that there are substantial differences in the size of the

---

[5] The evidence is from a study by Marilyn Young, Michael Reksulak, and William F. Shughart II (2001). The researchers noted the qualification that the data used were principally for a period of time when one person (Bill Clinton) was president of the United States and the favorable audit treatment of districts politically important to the president may therefore apply only to this president. On his last day in office, this president also pardoned people under indictment for income tax evasion.

TABLE 7.1. THE SIZE OF THE SHADOW ECONOMY AS A PROPORTION
OF REPORTED OFFICIAL GROSS NATIONAL PRODUCT

	1970	1980	1997
Greece	No information	No information	29[a]
Italy	11	17	27
Portugal	No information	No information	23
Spain	10	17	23
Belgium	10	16	22
Sweden	7	12	20
Norway	7	11	19
Denmark	7	8	18
Germany	3	11	15
France	4	7	15
Netherlands	5	9	14
Canada	No information	11	14
Australia	No information	No information	14
United Kingdom	2	8	13
United States	3	5	9
Austria	2	3	9
Switzerland	4	7	8

[a] 1996

Source: Schneider and Enste (2000). Numbers are rounded up and averaged.

shadow economy among countries, and that the size of the shadow economy has tended to increase over time.

We expect the shadow economy to be larger where people do not trust their government to spend tax revenue in socially beneficial ways. In the societies shown in Table 7.1, with perhaps some possible exceptions, voters and taxpayers do not in general perceive government as extensively corrupt, and public spending is viewed as generally benefiting the population rather than specifically benefiting people in government.[6]

Where government is for the most part trusted, high rates of taxation can nonetheless be inducements for large shadow economies. For example, the Scandinavian countries in Table 7.1 had high taxation, extensive social insurance, and relatively large shadow economies. The southern European countries, however, lead in the size of the shadow economy. Belgium ranks with the southern European and the Scandinavian countries in the size of its shadow economy and has a significantly larger shadow economy than its neighbors Germany, France, and the Netherlands. The United Kingdom, Australia, and Canada had smaller shadow economies than the latter countries. The smallest shadow economies were in the United States, Austria, and Switzerland.

[6] Tax compliance decisions can nonetheless be influenced by inconsistencies between the objectives that taxpayers seek from public spending and the decisions made through political processes, and by perceived excess spending by government for its own benefit.

We might wonder why in every case the size of the shadow economy increased over time. Perhaps personal attitudes to paying taxes changed, or opportunities for tax evasion changed.

There was also illegal migration into the countries in Table 7.1. The illegal immigrants do not work in the formal economy, and so the increased presence of the illegal immigrants might explain the expanding shadow economies. If immigrants moreover come from countries where the social norm is not to pay taxes, it may take time to adapt to the new social norm of voluntary self-assessment and compliance in paying taxes.

7.3.7 The social costs of tax evasion

People who regard taxation as excessive face the alternatives of not working or working and evading taxes. Choosing tax evasion is then a means of personal escape from the burden of taxation and also from the accompanying excess burden of taxation. Tax evasion is a decision to keep working rather than to respond to high taxes by taking more free time and leisure.

The decision to work and not pay taxes is efficient from a personal and social perspective. The individual is better off, and the government would in any event receive no tax revenue if the individual chose the alternative of responding to high taxes of not working.

The individual refusing to pay taxes is, however, subject to the personal risk of being discovered and having to pay the penalty for tax evasion, as well as to the social stigma of being a tax evader in a society where the social norm is to pay taxes.

Limitations on applying abilities

There are reasons besides driving a person into illegal activity why tax evasion and a shadow economy are socially undesirable. As we noted previously in Section 7.2 when looking at the Laffer curve, the shadow economy limits the scope of economic activity undertaken by an individual person or firm. Too much success compromises the ability to remain invisible to tax authorities inside the shadow economy. Successful persons in the shadow economy are therefore limited in applying their abilities.

Competitive advantages in the informal sector

Activity in the shadow economy provides an artificial cost advantage. Producers and sellers who pay taxes can find themselves at a cost disadvantage relative to competitors in the shadow economy. Honesty is therefore penalized. Tax evasion increases if honest producers move to the shadow economy in order to match the lower costs of competitors who do not pay taxes.

Anarchy and principle in the informal sector

In a civil society, disputes are settled through the legal system. People look to the courts and law enforcement authorities for enforcement of contracts and protection of their property. Illegality of the shadow economy limits recourse to the courts and appeal to law enforcement authorities. Disputes in the shadow economy are therefore settled privately, and protection is private. The shadow economy can be a place of inefficient anarchy of the sort that we described in Chapter 1. Social norms of the same sort that dictate honor among thieves can, however, set principles of orderly behavior for the shadow economy.

Rent seeking

We have identified rent seeking as an activity that wastefully uses resources to increase personal income or personal benefit. Tax evasion is a form of social loss through rent seeking because of the resources and time used to evade taxes. Higher-income people have greater benefit from tax evasion, and so can be expected to engage more in this form of rent seeking than lower-income people. Part of the social loss from rent seeking associated with tax evasion is a government's use of resources and personnel to detect tax evasion.

7.3.8 Evasion of indirect taxes

We have been focusing on evasion of personal income taxes. Evasion can also take place of indirect taxes. Sales taxes, import duties, or value-added taxes are evaded when goods are smuggled across borders from low-tax locations. Harmonization (or equalization) of indirect taxes among government jurisdictions eliminates such incentives for tax evasion by smuggling. Rent seeking as wasteful use of resources is particularly evident when indirect taxes are evaded: resources are used in devious ways to smuggle goods across the boundaries of government jurisdictions.

7.3.9 Tax evasion through transfer prices

Tax evasion can take the form of moving tax liabilities from high to low tax jurisdictions. Individuals usually have limited access to opportunities for such tax shifting. Corporations with offices and operations in different countries do, however, have such opportunities. When different components of a good are produced in different locations, different units or subsidiaries of a corporation engage in internal transactions when the components are shipped for assembly. A subsidiary producing components charges the subsidiary that assembles the components a price, but the price is not a market price, since no market transactions have taken place. The price rather is an internal accounting valuation within the corporation. Because determination of a price for the transfer of components or goods within the corporation is an internal decision, the corporation has the opportunity to set the price.

The corporation can charge a low price when components or goods are shipped from a high-tax to low-tax location, which shifts profits to the low-tax location and so reduces taxes. Conversely, when components or goods are shipped from a low-tax location to a high-tax location, high internal prices can be charged for the internal transfer, which reduces profits in the receiving high-tax location and reduces total taxes paid by retaining profits in the low-tax location.

Such internal pricing designed to minimize taxes is known as transfer pricing. Transfer pricing is a form of smuggling. To counter transfer pricing, governments in high-tax jurisdictions may insist on their own valuations rather than accept the internal prices that corporations set for shipments of components and goods among their international operations.

7.3.10 The prisoners' dilemma and tax evasion

There is inefficiency as well as social injustice where some people refuse to pay taxes and others behave honestly and pay. In terms of the prisoners' dilemma, the people not paying taxes achieve their most preferred outcome of not contributing to the financing of public spending while benefiting from public spending. People who are honest in paying taxes are in the worst outcome of the prisoners' dilemma because they finance public spending without the contributions of others who benefit from the public spending.

7.3.11 Tax avoidance and tax evasion

The term "tax avoidance" is used to distinguish legal methods of not paying taxes from tax evasion, which is illegal. Tax avoidance takes place by taking advantage of opportunities offered by tax laws to reduce tax payments.

For example, it may be beneficial for tax purposes for an individual to form a corporation with family members and close friends as shareholders, since expenses incurred by the corporation can be the source of benefit for individuals.[7] Also, depending on the corporate tax rate and personal income tax rates, tax payments might be reduced. Trusts that save on payment of taxes might be set up. Although trusts are legal entities independent of a taxpayer, a trust can remain effectively controlled by the taxpayer. Income-earning assets might be transferred to offshore companies in foreign tax havens. Special tax deductions or exemptions might be available if individuals can define themselves for tax purposes as farmers or natural-resource explorers. Converting income to capital gains is another form of tax avoidance. As long as such activities are legal, tax evasion has not taken place.

Tax avoidance usually requires the services of skilled tax accountants or tax lawyers. Only high-income taxpayers may be able to afford or find worthwhile hiring the accountants and lawyers. Therefore, tax avoidance is generally undertaken by high-income or wealthier people who can afford to pay for professional advice (and for whom it is worthwhile). Poorer or low-income people may choose tax evasion, which does not require the professional expenses of tax avoidance, but which is illegal and subject to penalties if detected.

7.3.12 Summary

Levying taxes does not imply that the taxes due will necessarily be paid. Because people can refuse to pay taxes, governments require public policies to counter tax evasion. The policies can affect incentives to evade taxes through the probability of being detected in tax audits or through the penalties set for tax evasion.

---

[7] See Supplement 7C on expense accounts.

Social norms affect tax evasion. When the social norm is to evade taxes, enforcement of tax compliance becomes difficult, in particular because enforcement can seem arbitrary. A social norm of honest voluntary self-assessment and compliance reduces tax evasion.

We have noted that opportunities for tax evasion differ according to the source of personal income. It is also more difficult to evade a property tax than an income tax.

A government can use a tax amnesty to take advantage of guilt feelings and anxiety of tax evaders to collect past unpaid tax revenue. We have also considered the behavior of the tax authorities, who are required to follow standards that ensure just treatment of taxpayers. The principle of just treatment can be compromised when presumptive taxation is applied. We have also observed that there is evidence that tax auditing has been selectively applied on the basis of political objectives.

The shadow economy is outside of the domain of taxation. Measurement of the size of the shadow economy is necessarily indirect because the activities are not observed or reported. While a number of means of measurement are possible, a popular procedure uses the predominance of cash transactions in the shadow economy. We have reviewed data on the size of the shadow economy over time for different countries. The size of the shadow economy varies considerably across countries but in all cases there have been increases in the relative size of the shadow economy over time.

We have considered social costs of the shadow economy or tax evasion through impediments to growth and consequences for competition when some producers or sellers pay taxes and others evade taxes and do not incur this cost.

Indirect taxes can also be evaded, and tax evasion can take place internationally through transfer prices.

We noted the relation between the prisoners' dilemma and tax evasion. Also there is a difference between tax evasion and tax avoidance. Tax avoidance is legal, but usually requires expert advice that is not available to lower-income persons.

References and related literature

On the personal decision whether to attempt to evade taxes, see Allingham and Sandmo (1972), Yitzhaki (1974), Alm (1988), Gordon (1989), Myles and Naylor (1996), and Reinganum and Wilde (1988). For a comparison of methods of countering tax evasion, see Tzur and Yaari (2000). On tax evasion and the cost of public finance, see Usher (1986). On the relation between evasion of income taxes and value-added taxes, see Fideli and Forte (1999). On choice of occupation and tax evasion, see Pestieau and Posen (1991). On measuring the size of the shadow economy, see Tanzi (1999), Thomas (1999), and Schneider and Enste (2000). On tax evasion more generally, see Feige (1989), Cowell (1990), and

Slemrod (1992). On illegal immigration and illegal income, see Djajić (1997) and Hillman and Weiss (1999). On tax amnesties, see Malic and Swab (1991) and Graetz and Wilde (1993). On the problem of corruption in tax administration, see Sanyal, Gang, and Goswami (2000). The quote from Benjamin Franklin is noted by Adams (1993). On political influence on tax inspections, in addition to the study by Young, Reksulak and Shughart (2001), see Hunter and Nelson (1995).

Adams, C., 1993. *For Good or Evil: The Impact of Taxes on the Course of Civilization.* Madison Books, London.

Allingham, M. G. and A. Sandmo, 1972. Income tax evasion: A theoretical analysis. *Journal of Public Economics* 1, 323–38.

Alm, J., 1988. Uncertain tax policies, individual behavior and welfare. *American Economic Review* 78, 237–45.

Cowell, F. A., 1990. *Cheating the Government: The Economics of Evasion.* MIT Press, Cambridge, Massachusetts.

Djajić, S., 1997. Illegal immigration and resource allocation. *International Economic Review* 38, 97–117.

Feige, E. L. (ed.), 1989. *The Underground Economies: Tax Evasion and Information Distortion.* Cambridge University Press, Cambridge, 133–49.

Fideli S. and F. Forte, 1999. Joint income tax and VAT-chain evasion. *European Journal of Political Economy* 15, 391–415.

Gordon, J. P. F., 1989. Individual morality and reputation costs as deterrents to tax evasion. *European Economic Review* 33, 797–805.

Graetz, M. and L. L. Wilde, 1993. The decision by strategic non-filers to participate in tax amnesties. *International Review of Law and Economics* 13, 271–83.

Hillman, A. L. and A. Weiss, 1999. A theory of permissible illegal immigration. *European Journal of Political Economy*, 15, 585–604.

Hunter, W. J. and M. A. Nelson, 1995. Tax enforcement: A public choice perspective. *Public Choice* 82, 53–67.

Malic, A. and R. Swab, 1991. The economics of tax amnesties. *Journal of Public Economics* 46, 29–49.

Myles, G. D. and R. A. Naylor, 1996. A model of tax evasion with group conformity and social customs. *European Journal of Political Economy* 12, 181–96.

Pestieau, P. and U. M. Posen, 1991. Tax evasion and occupational choice. *Journal of Public Economics* 45, 107–25.

Reinganum, J. F. and L. Wilde, 1988. A note on enforcement uncertainty and taxpayer compliance. *Quarterly Journal of Economics* 103, 793–8.

Sanyal, A., I. Gang and O. Goswami, 2000. Corruption, tax evasion, and the Laffer curve. *Public Choice* 105, 61–78.

Schneider, F. and D. Enste, 2000. Shadow economies around the world: Size, causes and consequences. IMF working paper 00/26, Washington D.C. and *Journal of Economic Literature* 38, 77–114.

Slemrod, J. (ed.), 1992. *Why People Pay Taxes: Tax Compliance and Enforcement.* University of Michigan Press, Ann Arbor.

Tanzi, V., 1999. Uses and abuses of estimates of the underground economy. *Economic Journal* 109, 338–40.

Thomas, J. J., 1999. Quantifying the black economy: "Measurement without theory" yet again? *Economic Journal* 109, 381–9.

Tzur, J. and V. Yaari, 2000. Tax evasion as the outcome of organizational design. *Journal of Accounting, Auditing, and Finance* 15, 47–72.

Usher, D., 1986. Tax evasion and the marginal cost of public funds. *Economic Enquiry* 24, 563–86.

Yitzhaki, S., 1974. Income tax evasion: A theoretical analysis. *Journal of Public Economics*
    3, 201–2.
Young, M., M. Reksulak and W. F. Shughart II, 2001. The political economy of the IRS.
    Economics and Politics 13, 201–20.

Questions for discussion

1. Self-assessment of tax obligations nonetheless requires governments to monitor tax
   returns. What are the ways that governments can provide incentives for truthful reporting of taxable incomes? What are the considerations that enter into the choice of
   the means of controlling tax evasion?
2. Governments could attempt to ensure tax compliance through sufficiently high penalties. Why are the high penalties not imposed?
3. How do social norms affect taxpayer compliance? Why might social norms about
   honest voluntary self-assessment and compliance with tax-payment obligations differ
   in different locations?
4. Why do governments sometimes declare tax amnesties?
5. What underlies the different opportunities of self-employed persons and employees
   to evade personal income taxes?
6. Explain why some taxes are more difficult to evade than others.
7. How do personal incentives of tax collectors affect taxpayers? Why might tax collectors choose to base tax assessments on presumptive taxation? Do you believe that
   presumptive taxation assessment is a reasonable approach to solving the problem of
   tax evasion? Explain.
8. Do you believe that it is plausible that increases in tax rates could reduce tax evasion?
   Explain. (See footnote 1.)
9. Table 7.1 shows significant differences in the sizes of countries' shadow economies.
   What explanations would you propose for the differences?
10. Table 7.1 also shows changes over time in the sizes of countries' shadow economies.
    What explanations would you offer for these changes?
11. Why is a shadow economy undesirable? Are there circumstances where nonpayment
    of taxes can be beneficial to a society? Explain.
12. How is the prisoners' dilemma related to tax evasion?
13. Which of the different approaches that can be used to measure the size of the shadow
    economy do you believe is most accurate? (See Supplement 7A.)
14. What is the relation between evasion of value-added taxes and evasion of income
    taxes? How does a value-added tax provide a means of monitoring income tax com-
    pliance? (See Supplement 7B.)
15. What is the difference between tax avoidance and tax evasion? Who has opportunities
    for tax avoidance? How can expense accounts facilitate tax avoidance? What social
    losses arise when expense accounts are used for tax avoidance? (See Supplement 7C.)

8

USER PRICES

In this chapter, we shall consider user prices as an alternative to taxes and public finance. User prices restore a direct link between personal payment and personal benefit that is absent when taxes finance public goods. We shall first consider user prices as a means of financing noncongestible, or noncongested, public goods. User prices in these cases can inefficiently exclude and can be inconsistent with social justice. We shall then consider user prices when there is crowding or congestion in use of public goods. In these cases, the purpose of user prices is to exclude. Thereafter, we shall consider user prices for private goods that are natural monopolies.

8.1

User Prices for Public Goods

8.1.1 Attributes of user prices

User prices are voluntary payments for public services. User prices can nonetheless involve payments through taxes. A tax on gasoline is, for example, a tax on use of roads. A tax on automobiles is a tax on the option to use a road. A tax on tennis racquets is a tax on the use of free-access public tennis courts. In these cases, user prices through taxes on private goods are complementary to use of free-access publicly financed facilities. Although set as taxes, the user prices can be avoided by not buying gasoline or not buying a car or not buying a tennis racquet. Therefore, in these cases, user prices remain voluntary payments, in contrast to taxes, which are compulsory.

User prices are, on the other hand, not voluntary when set as compulsory payments for compulsory services. For example, if a government were to decide to finance compulsory schooling through user prices, the user prices would in effect be taxes, because of the absence of an option of not paying. The compulsory taxes are then regressive (payment is per child independent of income, and so the ratio between taxes paid and income falls as income increases). User prices are of course also regressive when payments are voluntary. All prices are regressive.

The case against user prices

A case against user prices is that a public service should be financed (a normative statement) through progressive taxation and not through a regressive user price. For example, the judgment might be made that schools should be financed through progressive taxation rather than through the regressive payments of user prices. We would then need to ensure that the local property taxes that often finance government schools are progressive.

The case against user prices for schools can alternatively be based on the judgment that taxes (without regard for progression) should finance schools because schooling is compulsory. That is, the requirement of compulsory school attendance should be accompanied by free access. Otherwise compulsory schooling cannot be truly compulsory, since some parents may not be willing or able to pay user prices.

A further normative case against user prices for schools is that the education of a child should not depend on the willingness or ability of parents to pay user prices. That is, children should not be excluded from school because of parents' income or preferences.

The case against user prices for schools generalizes to all entitlements provided through a social insurance contract. Delivery of entitlements cannot be assured if user prices are required for access to the entitlements.

The choice of user prices

User prices are sometimes partial and arise in combination with tax financing of public services. Parents with children in government schools might be required to pay for books or for school uniforms or to contribute to improving school facilities. School fees for higher education are a form of user price; the user price is incomplete when higher education is subsidized. User prices also arise in health care.

A health-care system may be completely based on user prices. Or where governments provide tax-financed health services, small user charges are sometimes imposed, to restrict demand for access to people whose complaints are serious enough to warrant attention.

Road and bridge tolls are another form of user price. In different locations, highways and bridges may be free or subject to tolls. Similarly, access to zoos and museums may be free or require payment.

The case for user prices

Individual taxpayers usually have little influence on the taxation and public spending decisions of public finance. Individuals and households can affect the taxes they pay and the benefits they receive from public spending, if locational choice allows them to choose among governments. Within a government jurisdiction, rational ignorance of taxpayers and the political principal-agent problem, and the insignificance of a single vote, leave taxpayers with little scope for discretion regarding the taxes they pay and the publicly financed benefits that they are eligible to receive. User prices restore the direct link between personal spending and personal benefit by allowing individuals to make a personal choice about paying for and benefiting from a public good or service.

User prices introduce transparency and accountability into the relation between taxpayers and providers of collective services. The transparency is through the explicit link between payment and the objective for which the revenue is used. The accountability is through the benefits that are implicitly promised when payments are made.

Government schools, for example, generally require only limited parental participation in costs. We observed, however, in Chapter 5, when considering entitlements provided by government, that households can choose to forgo a free-access government entitlement and choose to pay for private education. In that case, the household chooses to pay user prices. The reason is ostensibly that better-quality education is provided because of the accountability that accompanies user prices. When people pay directly, they tend to be more attentive to the benefits that they receive from the payments they make.

User prices when public finance is ineffective

User prices can be a private response to ineffective or absent public finance. For example, a government with inadequate tax resources may not be able to finance adequate schooling for children, or the quality of schooling a government is able to finance may be lower than parents in a community want. In such cases, user prices may be the only way that children can be provided with schooling at all, or with schooling of adequate quality, until governments are better able to fulfill their responsibilities through public finance.

User prices for schools are therefore a voluntary response when, for example, poor areas have inadequate tax bases, or where governments choose priorities for public spending that leave parents dissatisfied with the quality of schools. However, all parents may not be prepared to pay the voluntary user price. The user prices finance a public good (the presence of any one child in a classroom has a negligible effect on the quality of schooling in the class), and the problems of free-riding behavior for public goods reappear if children are permitted to attend school without their parents paying. Yet if the children of parents who do not pay do not attend school, inefficient exclusion is taking place. Besides efficiency, we can also apply criteria of social justice to the exclusion.

User prices and the inequality of the market
User prices therefore introduce a tension between allowing people to pay collectively for what they want and excluding others who are not prepared to pay or cannot pay. The tension arises when sufficient numbers of parents are dissatisfied with government schools and pay user prices for private education. The tension also arises when some people are prepared to pay user prices for superior health care. That is, user prices for collective services (or public goods) introduce the inequality and the exclusion of the market.

User prices and congestion
A reason for user prices is sometimes not to finance public goods but to alleviate congestion or overuse. In that case, the purpose of user prices is to ensure exclusion. In Section 8.2, we shall look at the role of user prices when collectively used facilities become congested.

Natural monopoly and user prices
User prices are not entirely voluntary when we face a natural monopoly that provides a "necessity" such as electricity or water, or when we have no choice but to cross a particular bridge or to use a particular highway. User prices are generally levied for electricity and water. In Section 8.3, we shall consider user prices and natural monopoly.

Public goods that are not congested or not congestible
We shall now proceed to consider user prices as a means of financing public goods that are not congested or congestible. That is, the public goods are "pure" as described in Chapter 2, so that allowing an additional person to benefit does not reduce the benefit to anyone else.

8.1.2 A market for use of public goods

A market in benefits from public goods makes willingness to pay a requirement for benefit. The market solves the free-rider problem of voluntary payments for public goods because a person who does not pay is excluded from benefit.

We considered a market for public goods in Chapter 2 through the Lindahl mechanism for voluntary financing of public goods. The Lindahl mechanism is based on free access to public goods: everybody benefits from the personal spending on public goods of everybody else. Free riding is thus part of the efficient Lindahl market solution for public goods. Free riding through the incentive to rely on others to pay prevents the Lindahl voluntary payments mechanism from being applied.

Free riding can be avoided if a person who does not pay is excluded from benefit. When payment is required as a precondition for use of public goods, a person cannot claim low or no benefit and pay little or nothing and still benefit by free riding on public goods financed by others.

Moreover, without excluding people who do not pay, there cannot be user prices. That is, avoidance of free riding requires that people who do not pay be excluded from benefits. Voluntary user prices cannot be applied without such exclusion.

When a gasoline tax is used to finance roads, the exclusion is automatic in that people who do not buy gasoline cannot use the roads. Or a person who does not buy a tennis racket cannot use the public courts.

In all cases, because of the need to exclude people who do not pay, user financing can be applied only where exclusion is possible at low cost. Therefore, not all public goods are candidates for user pricing. No one can, for example, be excluded from the benefits of a public-health program that eliminates an infectious disease, from the benefits of a public-safety program that reduces road accidents, from national security, or from expenses in maintaining foreign embassies (whether there is a personal benefit or not). Exclusion is possible from collectively used facilities such as a highway or road, a bridge, a tunnel, a national park, a zoo, and a museum, as well as from personal security provided by on-call response, education provided at a school, the options to use an ambulance or medical services, and more.

In Chapter 2, when we introduced taxation for financing public goods, we observed that in principle police protection could be financed through user pricing, with people paying whenever they called on the police for assistance. We noted, however, that it is unethical to make victims pay, and that user payments for police would deter reporting of crime, which is advantageous to criminals. We also noted that the police provide a pure public good of deterrence from which exclusion is not possible, and which cannot be financed through user pricing.

While financing of police protection is not based on user pricing, user pricing does support the court system when defendants pay court expenses and obtain private legal advice and defense (although the state will appoint a public defender if a defendant cannot afford private legal counsel). Relying on user pricing has the consequence that people receive the legal advice and legal defense that they can afford.[1]

Sometimes user prices are not possible, and sometimes we might have qualms about user prices. Therefore, user prices cannot be always used in place of taxes.

When user prices are used, the objective is, in principle, to duplicate the efficient Lindahl voluntary pricing solution by having people reveal their benefits through their willingness to pay the user price. However, as we have noted, the Lindahl market does not exclude those who do not pay, whereas user pricing is based on the market principle that payment is necessary for benefit.

There may be no exclusion with user pricing because everyone might choose to pay. Still, user pricing differs from the Lindahl voluntary-payment market because user pricing takes place in a market for use. A market for *use* requires people to pay for access and not for the public facility itself. For example, people who pay for admittance to a zoo do not pay directly for the cost of feeding and housing the animals. They pay to see the animals. Or, people who visit an art museum are not being asked to contribute to the construction of the building that houses the museum or to the cost of the art collection. They pay to enter the museum and see the works of art. In the case of both the zoo and the museum, people who do not pay do not benefit.

The Lindahl market is not a market for use. In the Lindahl market, people would make contributions to financing supply of the public good (the works of art in the museum, the feeding and housing of the animals in the zoo), and there is free access to the benefits for everybody. There is no user-price in the Lindahl voluntary payment solution.

A further illustration of the difference between a market for use and the Lindahl voluntary-financing solution is the financing of traffic lights at a road intersection. Information technology can identify all cars that pass through an intersection and owners of vehicles can be charged for use of the traffic lights, so allowing traffic lights to be financed on a user-pays basis. The market that would be created through user pricing is a market for use of the traffic light and payment would be for use. The market would not require drivers to pay directly for the cost of installing traffic lights. The Lindahl mechanism, on the other hand, would have users finance the cost of installing the traffic lights, and then use of the traffic lights would be free.

We can also consider a beach with lifeguards. Under the user-pays principle, people pay for access to the beach. An efficient Lindahl market would determine the number of lifeguards by consensus. People on the beach would pay personal shares of lifeguards' salaries based on their personal benefits from the presence of the lifeguards (their ability to swim and their inclination to enter the water). Access to the beach (and to the benefits of the presence of the lifeguards), if the Lindahl mechanism could be applied, would be free.

---

[1] In injury and compensation cases where lawyers take a proportion of the damages awarded, legal representation is independent of personal wealth or ability to pay for legal services.

When education is financed through user payments, parents or students pay school fees, but they are not involved in the Lindahl process of choosing total spending for the school.

8.1.3 Efficient pricing for use

Let us now consider efficient pricing in the market for use of a public good. Efficient pricing for any good or service requires that

$$MB_i = P_i = MC_i, \tag{8.1}$$

where MB_i and MC_i are marginal benefits and costs for person i and P_i is the price paid by person i. For private goods, competitive markets ensure efficient prices consistent with the efficient pricing principle (8.1). In making decisions about purchases of private goods, individuals set the market price P_i equal to their marginal benefit from consumption MB_i. At the same time, competitive supply ensures that the market price is equal to marginal cost of supply MC_i.

For a noncongested (or noncongestible) public good, the MC of use is zero because use by one person does not decrease benefit for anyone else. The efficient pricing rule for use of public goods is therefore that access should be free, that is,

$$P_{use} = MC_{use} = 0. \tag{8.2a}$$

Also, people should be permitted to use the public good as much as they want because their use affects no one else. That is,

$$P_{use} = MB_{use} = 0. \tag{8.2b}$$

People should therefore have unlimited free access.

Unlimited free access is clearly Pareto-efficient. Unlimited free access makes people better off, while, by the nature of a pure or noncongested public good, no one is made worse off.

We can consider a child who wishes to look at an elephant in a zoo. The MC of the child's viewing the elephant (other than the child's time) is zero. Therefore, the child should not have to pay a positive price for looking at the elephant. The child should be permitted to continue looking at the elephant until his or her marginal benefit falls to zero, after which time the child will voluntarily move on to view another animal in the zoo or go home.

Or we can consider a bridge. The cost of constructing a bridge is not zero, but the MC of use for a person crossing a bridge *is* zero. Efficient pricing of use therefore requires that a person who wishes to cross a river over a bridge should be permitted to do so free of charge because a positive price may deter someone who can benefit from using the bridge. A person without money might have to detour to a part of the river where the water is shallow enough to drive – or wade or swim – across.

These examples of exclusion from public goods because of user prices indicate problems of efficiency and not social justice. In the case of the child who wishes to see the elephant, we are not saying that it is unfair that the child cannot see the elephant because he or she (or the family) cannot afford to pay the price of admission to the zoo. It is inefficient that the child be excluded from seeing the elephant because the child derives positive benefit from seeing the elephant, while the cost of allowing the child to see the elephant is zero.

Demand for use

Different users in general value access to public goods or services differently. For a population of n people, the efficient scale G of a public-good facility is determined by the condition that we established in Chapter 2:

$$\sum_{j=1}^{n} MB_j(G) = MC(G). \tag{8.3}$$

Condition (8.3) is satisfied at the quantity G^* in Figure 8.1.

We know the relation (8.3) only as a matter of principle. We do not know the individual MB's that are required to be summed in expression (8.3). That is, applying expression (8.3) is subject to the public-good information problem that we considered in Chapter 2.

In applying user pricing, we are not asking people to provide personal valuations for $MB_i(G)$. That is, we have not set the objective of establishing (as the Lindahl mechanism would require) G^* in Figure 8.1. When user pricing is applied, all that we can do is to see how much each of the n people in the population is prepared to pay to use a facility of given size. That is, the size of the public facility G is given when we present people with the option of paying for use of the facility.

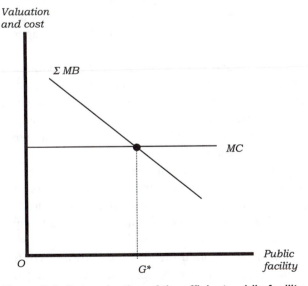

Figure 8.1. Determination of the efficient public facility.

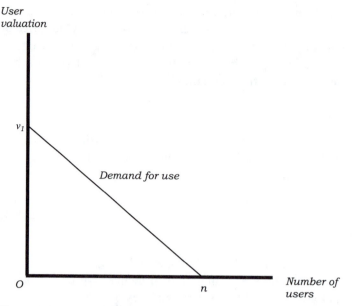

*User
valuation*

v_1

Demand for use

O n

*Number of
users*

Figure 8.2. The demand function for use of a public facility.
The population of users is ranked by willingness-to-pay for use down the demand function.
The area under the demand function is the total willingness of the population to pay for use,
or the total benefit from use to the population.

An estimate of the size of the efficient facility G^* in Figure 8.1 can be made
through cost-benefit calculations. This will require estimates of the combined
benefits $\sum MB$ of the population. The benefits will be revealed only when the
facility exists and people start indicating their willingness to pay for use. User
prices that people are willing to pay will reveal whether the estimates used
for cost-benefit analysis were reasonable approximations for true willingness
to pay.

To establish the demand for use in a market for use, we can rank the population
by personal willingness to pay for access to the public good facility of size G^* that
was determined through cost-benefit analysis. The demand for use is shown in
Figure 8.2. The population is ranked along the demand function according to
willingness to pay for use, from the highest user valuation v_1 to the lowest (zero)
valuation of person n. There are n prospective users.

Demand is not here measured in terms of quantity demanded. The decision
underlying demand is whether or not to use the facility. This is a dichotomous
yes–no decision. A user-price payment is made every time the facility is used or
accessed. The use could be traveling on a highway, crossing a bridge, attending
school for a year, or visiting a zoo or museum.

As an approximation, the demand function in Figure 8.2 is shown as continuous. In fact, people are not measured continuously but in discrete terms. The
continuous function is a reasonable approximation for a large population.

We cannot actually rank people along the demand-for-use function in Figure 8.2 because the information on personal benefits is not available to us. However, the demand-for-use function exists as a ranking of people's willingness to pay for use and is revealed through people's willingness to pay.

All users pay the same user price. We want the user price to be self-financing. The unit cost of the public good is P_G. The total cost of the public good facility G^* is a fixed cost

$$C = P_G G^*. \tag{8.4}$$

To be self-financing, the total user prices paid by the different users must cover this fixed cost. Therefore, a self-financing user-price is equal to the average cost per user

$$AC = \frac{C}{n}. \tag{8.5}$$

This average cost is shown in Figure 8.3. At any point on AC, the fixed cost of the public-good facility is self-financed by different numbers of users. For example, n_1 users paying the user price P_1^{use} finance the fixed cost C, as do n_2 users paying the user price P_2^{use}. That is, the AC function is a rectangular hyperbola: the area

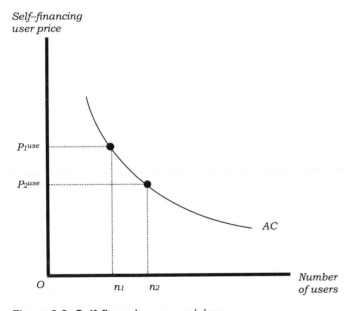

Figure 8.3. Self-financing user pricing.
The quantity of the public good that is to be supplied has been determined by cost-benefit analysis. There is a fixed cost C of supplying the public good. The public good can be self-financed through user pricing by setting the user price equal to the average cost for any number of users. The average cost function is a rectangular hyperbola. Any point along the average cost function is a self-financing solution.

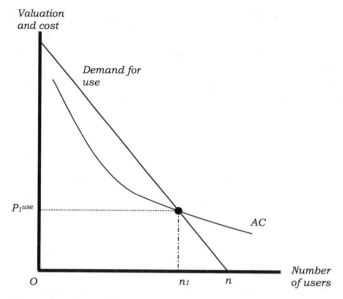

Figure 8.4. A self-financing user-pricing solution.
The self-financing user-payment solution is to charge the user price P_1^{use}. The n_1 people who are willing to pay this price for use provide revenue that finances the public good. There is inefficient exclusion from access to the public good. The $(n - n_1)$ people who do not pay for access could use the public good without imposing any cost on others because the public good is not congested.

under the function is always the same, reflecting the fixed cost of providing the public good facility.

8.1.4 Self-financing user-price solutions

All user prices along AC in Figure 8.3 or 8.4 allow self-financing, by different numbers of users. A self-financing solution requires that willingness to pay for use be equal to a self-financing user price.

We see such a self-financing solution in Figure 8.4, where demand for use intersects AC. The self-financing solution is that n_1 users pay a price of use P_1^{use}.

This self-financing solution results in inefficient exclusion: $(n - n_1)$ potential users are excluded, or have excluded themselves, by not being willing (or able) to pay a user price that covers average cost.

Allowing access to the $(n - n_1)$ excluded persons is costless and harms no one because the cost of the public-good facility is a fixed cost C. Therefore, the exclusion is a violation of Pareto-efficiency because through inclusion some people can be made better off when no one is made worse off.

Moving down the demand-for-use function to decrease the user price below P_1^{use} in Figure 8.4 results in people with a lower willingness-to-pay paying for use but reduces revenue from user payments below the total cost C. Reducing the user price to the level required for everybody to choose to use the public facility (i.e., reducing the user price to the valuation of the nth person) requires a use price of zero and provides no revenue at all.

We conclude that, at least in the case shown in Figure 8.4, user financing is inconsistent with efficient use of a public facility. Efficient use requires allowing free access for all n potential users. In that case, however, no revenue is provided to finance the public facility.

Although self-financing user prices inefficiently exclude, the benefit of user pricing is that there is no taxation and so no efficiency loss takes place through the excess burden of taxation. At the same time, the project is justified by willingness of users to pay for the benefits that the project provides.

Figure 8.5 shows another user-pricing solution. Demand-for-use intersects AC twice. The points of intersection 1 and 2 are both self-financing solutions. At point 1, n_1 people are willing to pay the user price P_1^{use}. At point 2, a larger number of people n_2 is willing to pay the user price P_2^{use}. The second solution, where the user price is lower and more people benefit from the public good, is preferred. Again, however, the self-financing solution inefficiently excludes some users. The inefficient exclusion would be avoided if the project were publicly financed and access to users were freely provided.

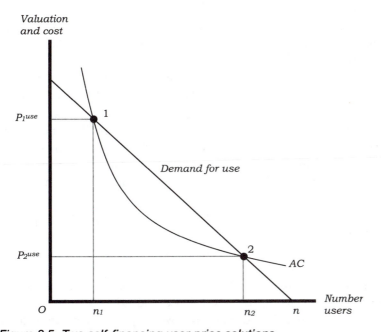

Figure 8.5. Two self-financing user-price solutions.

Two user-payment solutions self-finance the public good, at points 1 and 2. The preferred solution is at point 2 where more people benefit from using the public good (fewer are excluded) and the user price is lower.

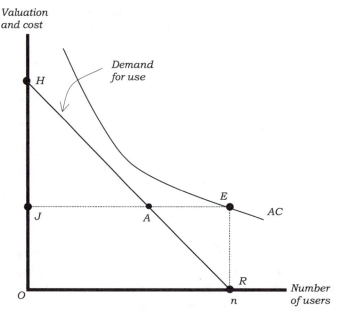

Figure 8.6. No self-financing user-payments solution exists, but the project satisfies the test of cost-benefit analysis.

8.1.5 Public facilities that cannot be self-financed

Figure 8.6 shows a public project that has no self-financing user-pricing solution. Willingness to pay, as expressed through demand for use, never reaches *AC* for any number of users.

In this case, for example, a community could not support a self-financing art gallery, archeological museum, or perhaps zoo because people do not value these facilities sufficiently.

The total benefit from the project in Figure 8.6 when all n persons benefit from the facility is *OHR*. The total cost is *OJER*. Since *HJA > REA*, total benefit exceeds total cost based on valuations of use at a point in time. The project therefore satisfies the test of cost-benefit analysis but cannot be self-financed through user pricing.

Figure 8.7 is another example where there is no self-financing user-pays solution when the public project satisfies the cost-benefit test.[2]

In the case shown in Figure 8.7, the reason that there is no self-financing user-price solution is that the population of users n_m is too small. If the population of users were sufficiently larger than n_m, the demand function could cross the *AC* function, and a self-financing user-pricing solution would exist.

Since the project in Figure 8.7 is socially worthwhile for n_m users, the project should be publicly financed through taxation.

---

[2] Total willingness to pay for use by n_m users in Figure 8.7 is *HRSO* and total cost is *OJES*. Total benefit exceeds total cost if *HJA* exceeds *REA*.

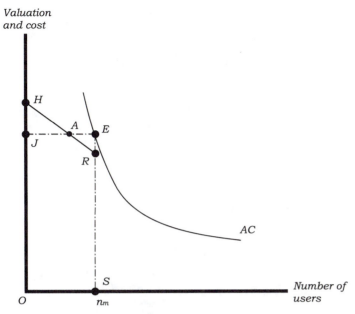

Figure 8.7. A user-payment self-financing solution does not exist because the maximum population of potential users is too small.

In the cases shown in Figures 8.6 and 8.7, insistence on self-financing user prices would block a socially worthwhile public project.

Private supply

A project that can be self-financed through user payments can be provided by private supply. In Figure 8.8, a population of n_m users paying a user price of P_m^{use} provides revenue that results in a profit given by the striped area.

The project in Figure 8.8 is socially worthwhile because users are willing to pay more than the cost. If government is the provider, the profits can be added to government revenue. A private supplier would, however, be willing to supply the good or service.

Private supply raises questions about how to deal with private natural monopoly. Natural monopoly is present because average cost per user declines as the number of users increases, and so it is not cost-effective to replicate the public facility. Least-cost supply is always by a single supplier. All noncongested public goods are natural monopolies. When additional users can be added without diminishing the benefit to preexisting users, duplication is of course wasteful, and it is cost-efficient that there be only one supplier. We shall return to natural monopoly later in this chapter.

Externalities and user pricing

Exclusion because of user pricing can be the source of undesirable externalities not only for schools. When entry to the museum, art gallery, or zoo is free, people

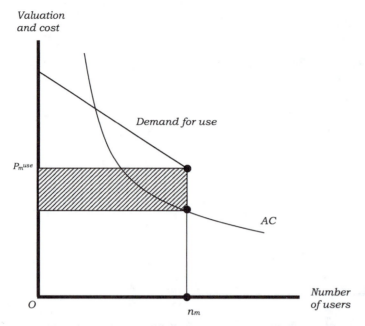

Figure 8.8. Profits from user pricing.
Supply through user pricing at the price P_m^{use} to the n_m users is profitable. The striped area indicates profits. A private supplier would be willing to supply the public good.

do not have to make a monetary calculation when deciding whether to go to the museum, art gallery, or zoo. In particular, children and teenagers have free options for spending time that may be self-improving and socially desirable compared to alternatives.

8.1.6 User pricing as an escape from leviathan government

In Chapter 7, we defined a leviathan government as being composed of people who have a self-interested objective of maximizing taxes for their own benefit. Voluntary user prices in place of taxes allow an escape from the public finance of leviathan government.

Rather than referring to a leviathan government, we could refer to corrupt government. User prices then allow escape from the public finance of corrupt government.

With voluntary user pricing, the personal option exists not to pay and not to use. People are not legally compelled to pay taxes to finance public goods that they may not want.

8.1.7 Summary

Taxes and voluntary user prices are alternative responses to the free-rider problem for financing public goods. Taxes solve the free-rider problem by making payment compulsory. Voluntary user prices solve the free-rider problem by excluding those who do not pay.

The ideal solution for financing public goods is the voluntary Lindahl pricing mechanism. The ideal Lindahl mechanism is not feasible. Therefore we are left facing the choice between user pricing and tax financing of public goods. The choice is between two imperfect alternatives.

Tax financing breaks the direct link between payment and benefit. Financing through taxation also introduces inefficiencies through excess burdens of taxation, and there are also costs of government tax administration and costs of tax compliance.

There are no excess burdens of taxation, no costs of tax administration, and no costs of taxpayer compliance when user prices create markets for voluntary self-financing of public goods. We also noted the possibility of escape from self-serving or corrupt government when voluntary user prices replace compulsory taxes.

We have seen, however, that user pricing can result in inefficient exclusion, and that a self-financing user price solution may not exist.

User prices involve issues of both efficiency and fairness or social justice. Self-financing according to the user-pays principle can be considered fair because only those people pay who reveal that they benefit from a public good. Tax financing can be considered unfair because people are compelled to pay for public goods from which they may never benefit. At the same time, however, tax financing allows low-income or poor people who cannot afford a user charge free (and efficient) access to public goods.

With user prices, people "exclude themselves" by not being willing to pay, but also exclusion takes place when people cannot afford to pay. For example, we can consider two people who do not go to a zoo that charges admission. One person can afford the price of admission but sees no point in looking at animals. The second person likes to look at animals but cannot afford the price of admission. The user-pays principle ensures that the first person does not pay taxes to finance a zoo that he or she will never visit but excludes the second person who would benefit from visiting the zoo and whose presence at the zoo would impose a cost on no one.

In the world around us, we observe different decisions regarding user prices. In some places, all highways and roads are free-access and tax-financed; in other places, user prices are applied and highways are toll roads. Similarly, a toll is sometimes required to cross a bridge or use a tunnel. Museums and zoos are free in some cities, but not in others. In general, access to local parks is free, but there is often a charge to enter a national park.

The different decisions reflect different attitudes to advantages and disadvantages of user financing compared to taxation. When exclusion is feasible and a self-financing user price does exist, a society may not wish to apply user pricing because of a judgment that exclusion is socially undesirable. A society may not wish to inefficiently exclude children from schools, or inefficiently exclude vehicles from (noncongested) roads and bridges, or to exclude individuals from local parks and beaches. When exclusion is not desirable, user payments can be supplemented by government subsidies. For example, tax-financed subsidies may supplement fees for financing state universities and colleges. When no exclusion at all is desired, the tax-financed subsidy might be complete. That is, taxes and not user prices are then the source of finance for public goods.

References and related literature

For theoretical analyses of exclusion with public goods, see Brito and Oakland (1980), Drèze (1980), Burns and Walsh (1981), and Fraser (1996). On user prices as a means of financing education and health in poorer countries, see Jimenez (1987). For an evaluation of the role of user prices for basic education in poor countries when there are limitations on publicly financed spending, see Hillman and Jenkner (2002).

Brito, D. L. and W. H. Oakland, 1980. On the monopolistic provision of excludable public goods. *American Economic Review* 70, 691–704.

Burns, M. E. and C. Walsh, 1981. Market provision of price excludable public goods: A general analysis. *Journal of Political Economy* 89, 166–91.

Drèze, J. H., 1980. Public goods with exclusion. *Journal of Public Economics* 13, 5–24.

Fraser, C. D., 1996. On the provision of excludable public goods. *Journal of Public Economics* 60, 111–30.

Hillman, A. L. and E. Jenkner, 2002. User prices for basic education in low-income countries. International Monetary Fund, Fiscal Affairs Department, working paper WP/02/182, Washington, D.C.

Jimenez, E. 1987. *Pricing Policy in the Social Sectors: Cost Recovery for Education and Health in Developing Countries.* Johns Hopkins University Press for the World Bank, Baltimore.

Questions for discussion

1. What is the general case against user prices for schooling of children? Given this case, why do some parents choose to pay user prices to private schools?
2. Do you agree that user prices create tensions in society? Explain.
3. How is an efficient user price determined?
4. How do efficient user prices differ from efficient Lindahl prices? What are the different types of efficiency sought through user prices and Lindahl prices?
5. Under what conditions is self-financing of a public good through user prices efficient?
6. Can we be assured that a self-financing user-price solution necessarily exists for a public good? Explain.
7. "The choice between user pricing and tax financing of public goods is a choice between two imperfect alternatives." Why is this so?
8. In principle, all cars could be equipped with measuring devices that calculate user prices for *all road travel*. Do you think this is a good idea? Explain.

9. As long as zoos, museums, and art galleries are not congested, should entrance be free or should user prices be charged? How are externalities involved in the answer to this question?
10. Is it fair that people who have no children pay taxes to finance schools? Explain.
11. Could user prices be applied to police protection? Explain.
12. What is the relation between user prices and leviathan government?
13. Should individuals be allowed to buy supplementary services on a user-pays basis from the local police? (See Supplement 8C.)
14. Would you like to live in a society where taxation is minimized by applying user prices wherever possible? Explain.
15. Table S8.1 in Supplement 8A shows shares of tax-financed government supply and user pricing for different services. Can you explain the differences between tax and user-price financing in the different cases?
16. Homes for the elderly can be financed through user pricing. Should prisons similarly be financed through user prices paid by prison inmates? (See Supplement 8B.)

8.2
User Pricing and Crowding

In Section 8.1, we considered user pricing when collective facilities are not congested. Public facilities can, however, often only comfortably accommodate a limited number of people at the same time. After some number of people has been admitted, congestion sets in. Congestion caused by capacity constraints affects roads, rail lines, bridges, tunnels, airports, and public transportation. An internet site can also become congested when the number of people seeking access to the site strains the capacity of the server. Educational facilities can become congested when the number of students in a class becomes too large for effective teaching. The option to use health services becomes congested when too many people at a time rely on the one ambulance or the one hospital. In this section, we consider user pricing for such public goods that can become congested.

8.2.1 Efficient user pricing with crowding

When collectively used facilities become congested, the efficient user price is no longer zero. The efficient user price rather reflects the cost through congestion imposed on other users. Suppose that there are n preexisting users and that one additional user wishes to use a collective facility. The efficient user price for the additional use is equal to the cost imposed on the n preexisting users by the access of the additional user to the facility. That is, the efficient user price when there is congestion is

$$P_{use} = MB \text{ of access for an additional user}$$
$$= \sum_{i=1}^{n} MC \text{ of congestion.} \tag{8.6}$$

The efficient user price reflects the Pareto efficiency of allowing access. A person who is admitted to the congested facility gains from access, but others lose because of congestion. Access of a new user is efficient if the new user is willing to pay enough for use to compensate all the losers from the congestion attributable to the new user.

For the noncongested public goods that we considered in Section 8.1, there was a problem that user prices could inefficiently deter use. When a public good is congestible, the purpose of the user price is explicitly to deter use. The user price is designed to resolve the negative externality problem that arises because of congestion. By paying the user price, users internalize the congestion externality.[1]

User prices for congestible public goods provide revenue. However, the revenue is unrelated to the cost of the public good. The user price defined in expression (8.6) is determined by congestion and not by the cost of providing the public good.

8.2.2 Private supply

Replication of congestible facilities, where possible, allows congestion to be avoided. With sufficient replication, an outcome can be achieved that approximates competitive supply. Moreover, there can be private ownership. Different competing private owners can offer the same public good under competitive conditions. For example, we see competitive duplication with portals (entry points) for the internet, gyms, entertainment facilities, transportation, and movie theaters. Many congestible public goods are provided through access to facilities that can be replicated. The combination of congestion and replication takes us away from a role for government that might be associated with natural monopoly. Replication is desirable because of congestion, and replication also offers the possibility of competing private suppliers.

Figure 8.9 shows an average cost function AC that is minimized with n^* users. Average cost AC in Figure 8.9 is defined for a given level of service or benefit. AC at first declines because of the gains from sharing collective costs, and then eventually increases because of congestion costs. For example, if AC represents the average cost of lifeguards providing a given standard of safety on a beach, an additional user imposes a cost on people already on the beach through crowding but also provides the benefit that there is an additional person to share the costs of paying the lifeguards. In Figure 8.9, the cost-efficient number of people in the sharing group n^* balances benefits from cost sharing against the inconvenience of increased congestion.

Suppose that 1,000 people seek access to a beach and that $n^* = 100$. Then ten replicated facilities allow least-cost provision, with groups of 100 users. In this example, no one is excluded.

---

[1] In the 1990s, the government of Singapore introduced a user charge for use of roads. Each car by law has an electronic detection devise that automatically deducts money from the stored value of a debit card at different locations, depending on the congestion on the road. Any one who has been caught in a traffic jam where no car moves for a considerable period of time can appreciate the efficiency of such user charges for congestible roads.

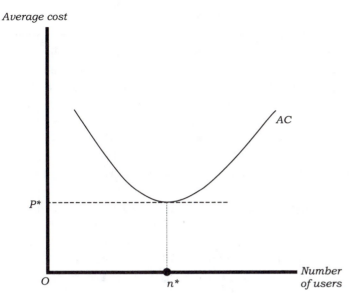

Average cost

Figure 8.9. Efficient group size for a congestible public good.
The average cost function *AC* reflects two off-setting effects of increases in the number of users. When the number of users increases, the cost per user of financing the public good declines. At the same time, crowding reduces the benefit to users. When the number of users is *n**, the benefit from an additional person sharing in financing the public good is equal to the cost imposed through additional crowding. *n** is the cost-efficient number of users. With sufficient replication and competition, private competitive suppliers admit *n** users and charge the user price *P**.

Suppose that there are 1,001 people and again $n^* = 100$. The one person excluded from one of the efficient sharing groups would be in an unfortunate situation. This person is denied participation in a cost-sharing arrangement. With large enough numbers of people, we can hope for sufficient replication so that exclusion does not occur.

When enough private suppliers offer access to the cost-minimizing number of users n^*, we have the conditions for a competitive market. The competitively determined user-price in Figure 8.9 is P^*, which is equal to minimized average cost. For example, private suppliers can offer access to patrolled beaches, and if there is free entry into making such offers (through the opportunity to add new segments of patrolled beach), the conditions for competitive supply are satisfied. Each owner chooses the profit-maximizing supply of the public good (the number of lifeguards patrolling the beach), and each owner admits the number of users that minimizes average cost of use. There is no difference from the conditions of supply in competitive markets for private goods. Just as competition minimizes the average cost of supply for private goods, so does competition minimize the average cost of supply for congestible public goods. Each private owner earns a competitive return and provides a self-financed service through a market based on the user prices.

8.2.3 User pricing through location

The locational mechanism for choice of public goods is based on user pricing. People pay for the public goods that are available for use in the jurisdictions in which they choose to live. To illustrate the locational user-pays mechanism for financing local public goods, we can return to the example of a beach. The beach is subject to crowding, and there is an efficient cost-minimizing number of users on any stretch of beach. People go to a beach for different reasons. People who want only a suntan do not wish to pay for lifeguards. Parents who have come with children might, on the other hand, want very good lifeguard surveillance. Some people might want to avoid the presence of children. Some people might like to wear swimsuits that others find inhibiting or unduly immodest and some people might want a beach to be segregated by gender. When a beach can be divided to cater to the different preferences, people can choose the part of the beach with the attributes that best suit them. They then pay user prices for different public goods, and they receive the particular type of benefit they seek. On each stretch of beach, people sort themselves and pay user prices according to their preferences.

More generally, each part of the beach is like a separate tax jurisdiction. Although taxes in different tax jurisdictions are compulsory for people living in a jurisdiction, the taxes are voluntary user prices because people choose to pay through location and have the option to leave one jurisdiction for another.

Locational rents

More people may wish to live in a jurisdiction to obtain the public goods provided than a jurisdiction can accommodate. When expansion or replication of the jurisdiction is impossible, we will observe the presence of locational rents. A locational "rent" is an excess payment, like a monopoly rent, that reflects the value of access to a sought-after jurisdiction. When people are prepared to pay the locational rent for the right to receive the public goods by satisfying the residence requirement, the value of a house in a sought-after jurisdiction will include the capitalized value of the locational rent.

As an example, Beverly Hills is a small independent local-government jurisdiction bordered by the city of Los Angeles. By locating in Beverly Hills, people have access to the services that the Beverly Hills local government provides to its residents. In general, these services are provided at a higher level of quality than the corresponding services provided by the surrounding city of Los Angeles. Housing prices in Beverly Hills tend to be higher than housing prices in Los Angeles because more people want the services that are provided by payment of taxes in Beverly Hills than Beverly Hills can accommodate. The excess demand to live and pay taxes in Beverly Hills increases housing prices, making the same houses in Beverly Hills more expensive than in Los Angeles.

If not for such excess demand, housing prices for similar houses would be the same in the two jurisdictions. Without the excess demand, the higher taxes paid in Beverly Hills would precisely match the higher costs of providing the superior public goods financed in and supplied to Beverly Hills residents.

The price of housing in Beverly Hills would fall if replication could take place to provide other communities with the same combination and quality of public goods as provided in Beverly Hills. Without such replication, higher-income people, who can afford to (and are willing to) pay the locational rents, choose to live in Beverly Hills. Beverly Hills is exclusive because lower-income people who would be prepared to pay the taxes and receive the superior public goods are excluded by the locational rents that have increased housing prices.

Zoning regulations may allow only expensive houses in a jurisdiction. Zoning is then another exclusion devise. Not everyone may be able to afford the minimal housing expenditure required by the zoning regulations.

Because of differences in incomes, not all people confront the same locational alternatives even when there are no zoning restrictions that increase housing prices because some people cannot afford the taxes that finance expensive local public-good supply in a jurisdiction. The same type of limitation on ability-to-pay is present in any market and not just locational markets. People buy in markets according to their preferences but are limited by their incomes in the choices they can make. The locational market for public goods is in this sense no different from other markets.

8.2.4 Not-for-profit clubs

A self-financing not-for-profit club can provide the same collective service or benefit as is provided by a for-profit private supplier or through location in a tax jurisdiction. Supply through not-for-profit clubs is similar to a locational market for local public goods. The difference is that, in the case of self-financing not-for-profit clubs, people who share the collective costs of public goods need not live in the same tax jurisdiction.

A self-financing user-pays principle can, for example, be applied to a country club that provides access to sports facilities. There are many types of "clubs" besides country clubs where people with common interests voluntarily come together for their private benefit – including chess, flower arrangement, specialty cooking, weight reduction and control, choral singing, avoiding drug or alcohol dependence, childbirth preparation, study groups, and common beliefs.

The club can identify the efficient number of members by balancing benefits of cost sharing against costs of congestion and can set self-financing user payments for members that finance efficient supply of the public good for its members.

Voluntary self-financing through clubs and private supply are both alternatives to taxation and public spending. However, why should a not-for-profit club be chosen in preference to private for-profit supply?

The alternative to a not-for-profit club may be a profit-maximizing local monopoly. One reason for a not-fot-profit club is to avoid such monopoly. There may also be a feeling that "self-ownership" is more pleasant than dealing with a private firm. That is, there may be a feeling of satisfaction from being "masters in one's own house."

The not-for-profit club is, however, subject to the same types of incentive problems that we identified in Chapter 3 as affecting government bureaucracies. Because the club does not seek profits, employed officials of the club have incentives to increase their salaries and benefits to match income received by the club. Club members should monitor costs and spending, but the benefits of any individual's monitoring are a public good for all members. Problems of rational ignorance and free riding can therefore intrude to prevent effective monitoring of costs and expenditures. Private owners would, of course, be very concerned about monitoring and controlling costs because of the consequences for profits. The attention of private owners to costs can be the basis for lower prices for users.

8.2.5 Summary

In Section 8.1, we considered user prices as a means of financing public goods when there is no crowding or congestion. Inefficient exclusion was a problem. The presence of crowding or congestion changes the role of user prices from financing public goods to ensuring efficient use through exclusion.

User prices that are set with the intention of deterring congestion also provide revenue, although the purpose of the revenue is not to finance the public good. However, when replication allows cost-minimizing supply, the user price precisely finances a congestible public good.

Congestion changes the cost structure for public goods. Through cost sharing, there are benefits when the number of users increases, but there are also congestion costs. The efficient number of users is determined through a trade-off between reduced personal benefit due to increased congestion and the increased personal benefit due to the presence of more people with whom to share the financing of the public good.

Replication of congestible public goods under separate private ownership introduces the possibility of competitive private supply, as we observe for movie theaters, concert halls, and sports events, as well as transportation and also schools, colleges, and universities.

When the locational choice mechanism is the means of choosing public goods, taxes are paid to finance public goods, but the taxes nonetheless are like voluntary user prices, By locating in a jurisdiction, people have indicated their willingness to pay the taxes that finance public spending.

Congestible public goods can also be provided through not-for-profit clubs. A not-for-profit club might be a response to private monopoly. Not-for-profit clubs confront the principal-agent problem of bureaucracies. Managers and salaried employees have incentives to increase expenses to match revenue from the user prices paid by club members. In contrast, private owners will attempt to minimize costs.

References and related literature

See Oakland (1974) and Arnott and Kraus (1998) on congestion and pricing of use of public goods. On the theory of voluntary collective grouping of people into "clubs," see for example Buchanan (1965), Hillman and Swan (1983), and Scotchmer and Wooders (1987).

Arnott, R. and M. Kraus, 1998. When are anonymous congestion charges consistent with marginal cost pricing? *Journal of Public Economics* 67, 45–64.
Buchanan, J. M., 1965. An economic theory of clubs. *Economica* 32, 1–14.
Hillman, A. L. and P. L. Swan, 1983. Participation rules for Pareto-optimal clubs. *Journal of Public Economics* 20, 55–76.
Oakland, W. H., 1974. Congestion, public goods, and welfare. *Journal of Public Economics* 1, 339–57.
Scotchmer, S. and M. Wooders, 1987. Competitive equilibrium and the core in club economies with anonymous crowding. *Journal of Public Economics* 34, 159–73.

Questions for discussion

1. How is an efficient user price determined when there is crowding? How does the efficient user price reflect the principle of Pareto efficiency?
2. Under what conditions does private supply result in an the efficient user price for benefits provided by a congestible facility?
3. Why do the taxes that are paid as the consequence of locational choice have the attributes of user prices? Are the locational user prices efficient? What different dimensions or types of efficiency are involved in an answer to this question?
4. Sometimes we see clubs owning collective facilities and providing benefits through user payments to members. For what reason would we expect such a cooperative form of organization rather than private ownership and private supply?
5. Would you like to see congestion payments introduced for road use through debit cards? Explain.
6. Of the activities that you engage in that have a user price and involve benefit to a number of people simultaneously, how many cases are there of private ownership, not-for-profit clubs, and supply through government? Are there common characteristics that provide a guide to establishing which of the three forms of supply apply?
7. Summarize the role or responsibility of government regarding benefits provided by collective facilities that are subject to congestion.

8.3
User Pricing and Natural Monopoly

8.3.1 Natural monopoly and private goods

All pure public goods (or noncongestible public goods) are natural monopolies because benefits to users are independent of the number of users. The same spending on a public good can benefit all users, so it is wasteful to duplicate a pure public good. In Chapter 2, we used the example of the lighthouse to illustrate the inefficiency of two lighthouses at a location.

Goods that provide private benefit can also be natural monopolies when costs of supply are predominantly fixed (or only fixed). The fixed costs are shared costs that are incurred independently of the supply to any user. The fixed costs are generally incurred in infrastructure investment that serves a population of users.

Electricity supply is a private good that is a natural monopoly. The fixed costs are incurred in the infrastructure that brings the electricity to users. Electricity production is, on the other hand, not a natural monopoly. There can be many competitive producers of electricity. The natural monopoly is in the delivery of the electricity to users. Delivery of water through pipelines is also a natural monopoly. As in the case of electricity, natural monopoly arises through the infrastructure of supply. Dumping of waste and garbage can be a regional natural monopoly because of fixed costs incurred in using a dumping site. Railroad tracks may be a natural monopoly, but transportation and freight services on the tracks are not a natural monopoly. Different suppliers might competitively use the tracks. The natural monopoly that owns the tracks is responsible for maintenance and for orderly use by different providers. Bus and air transportation can be a natural monopoly on routes where demand is sufficiently low. Schools can for the same reason be natural monopolies. That is, the presence of a natural monopoly can also be due to insufficient demand to warrant duplicative competitive supply.

When technology changes, a service or good can cease to be a natural monopoly. When telephone communication was exclusively through wires, the telephone company was a natural monopoly that installed the infrastructure, maintained network conformity, and owned the communications infrastructure that physically connected users to one another. Competition was introduced into long-distance communication by requiring regional telephone companies to act as conduits for competing long-distance companies. Cellular phones introduced competition into local as well as long-distance communication. The internet also allowed voice communication through personal computers.

Mail and parcels sent through the post used to be regarded as a natural monopoly. The cost of sorting and delivering mail was regarded as warranting a single supplier. Also, why should two persons make deliveries over the same route? Mail, however, eventually became competitively supplied through private courier and express services. The advent of the fax also provided competition for hand-delivered mail. E-mail became a substitute for letters written on paper. In many countries government mail service was preserved as a monopoly by law, until fax and the encroachment of private courier and express-service competition made it clear that the government mail service was not a natural monopoly, but rather just a simple monopoly.[1]

8.3.2 Financing solutions for natural monopoly

The common feature of natural monopolies for public and private goods is that in both cases, because of a fixed or sunk cost, there is a shared cost that is common to all users and is incurred independently of individual benefit. For a private good, average cost declines with output provided. For a public good, average cost of use declines with the number of users. Figure 8.10 shows the characteristic declining average cost of natural monopoly. Average cost AC is declining because a fixed cost F is divided among increasingly greater quantities supplied.[2]

In Figure 8.10, we focus on private goods. In addition to the fixed cost, there is a constant cost c for each unit of a privately consumed output delivered to the buyer. That is, c is the personal cost associated with connection to the infrastructure that has a fixed cost F.

Total cost of supply C is the sum of the fixed cost F and the additional cost c of delivering the total quantity supplied Q to users:

$$C = F + cQ. \tag{8.7}$$

Average cost is

$$AC = \frac{F}{Q} + c, \tag{8.8}$$

which is declining in the quantity supplied Q. The declining AC confirms that we have a natural monopoly.

We see in Figure 8.10 that AC is always greater than marginal cost of personal supply c, and that AC approaches the constant marginal cost c as the quantity supplied increases.

---

[1] As we have noted, natural monopoly can be the result of demand limitations. Natural monopoly can therefore arise in small towns and villages. There may be insufficient demand to support more than one grocery store, more than one doctor, more than one dentist, more than one plumber, and so on. In a small population, there can be many such natural monopolies. The problem can be more serious if, because of insufficient demand, there is no grocery store, no doctor, no dentist, no plumber. There is a question of how a small population accommodates itself to broad natural monopoly. The means of resolution can sometimes be through social custom and self-regulation. Members of a small community may not wish to have a reputation for taking advantage of their natural monopoly position.

[2] The source of natural monopoly can be a sunk cost rather than a fixed cost. A sunk cost is a cost that is incurred once and for always (e.g., communication cables or railway tracks or electricity lines or natural gas pipelines). A fixed cost is a recurring per-period cost that is independent of the number of users or the extent of use (e.g., maintenance of communication cables, railway tracks, electricity lines, or natural gas pipelines). If we think in terms of one time period, sunk and fixed costs are the same.

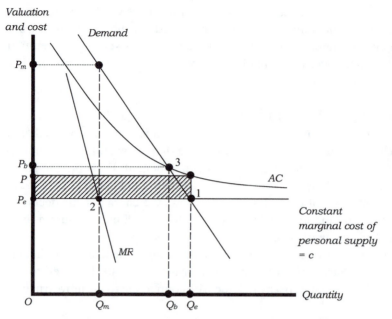

Figure 8.10. Solutions for natural monopoly.
For natural monopoly for a private good, the source of natural monopoly is shared or collective cost that results in declining average cost *AC*. The constant cost *c* is a private
cost of supply from the shared infrastructure. There are three alternative solutions: (1) At
point 1, the user price is efficient, and the efficient quantity is supplied. Efficiency requires
a subsidy from the government to the private supplier equal to the striped area. (2) At
point 2, private profits are maximized. (3) The user price at 3 can be achieved through competitive bidding where prospective suppliers declare the price at which they are willing to
supply.

Figure 8.10 shows three alternative financing possibilities for supply, at the
points 1, 2, and 3.

Efficient supply
The efficient solution is at point 1. Efficiency requires achieving maximal total
net benefit $W = B - C$ from supplying the good or service. Total net benefit is
maximized at point 1, where market demand intersects the MC function and
where

$$MB = P_e = MC, \qquad (8.9)$$

where P_e is the efficient user price.[3]
If the natural monopoly is under private ownership, the private owners would
make losses by charging the efficient user price P_e, since, at the corresponding

---

[3] As we saw in Section 8.1, for a pure public good, this price is zero.

quantity supplied Q_e, average cost of supply exceeds price. Profits (or losses) are given by

$$\text{Profits} = Q(P - AC).$$

The shaded area in Figure 8.10 is the loss to a private supplier from efficient user pricing. Therefore, efficient user pricing with private ownership requires government to provide subsidies equal to the value of this loss.

Maximal profits

The private interest of the natural monopoly is to maximize profits at point 2, where the user price is P_m and output is Q_m. The profit-maximizing outcome is inefficient because, at output Q_m, MB exceeds MC.

The self-financing user price

Figure 8.10 shows a self-financing user price at point 3, where the user price P_b is equal to average cost. The output that is supplied Q_b is then again inefficiently small but is closer to the efficient output Q_e than the monopoly profit-maximizing supply Q_m.

The case against government subsidies

The size of the government subsidy required for efficient user pricing depends on the monopolist's average cost of production. Cost, in turn, depends on the effort of managers of the natural monopoly, which is in general not perfectly observable.

Because of the subsidy, the natural monopolist faces a "soft budget." Under a soft budget (see Section 1.3), losses are automatically covered.

In the case of natural monopoly, the subsidy is specifically intended to cover losses. Low effort by managers is automatically compensated for by increased subsidies. Therefore, there is no personal incentive to exert effort to reduce costs. Greater losses are not a personal problem for the private owners and managers of the natural monopoly. The soft budget covers all losses through the subsidy.

The task of determining the subsidy at point 1 in Figure 8.10 is in general assigned to a government regulatory authority. Because of non-observable effort of managers and the soft budget, the regulatory agency confronts a principal-agent problem. Management in the natural monopoly determines costs through its unobservable effort and thereby determines the magnitude of the subsidy, which should be determined not by the producer but by the regulatory agency. The principal-agent problem is solved when the government regulatory agency can design and implement an incentive scheme that brings the actions of the producer into line with the objectives of the regulator. Because managers' actions are not observable to the regulator, the regulator is obliged to look for indirect financial incentives, which require public spending. For example, the natural monopoly can be rewarded for cost reductions.

There is a second problem in determining the value of the subsidy. Independently of effort, if the regulatory agency relies on self-reporting of information about the location of the AC function by the natural monopolist, the natural monopolist can report AC strategically. That is, the natural monopolist can misrepresent costs (within bounds of credibility). A natural monopolist can sometimes increase gain by reporting higher than true AC, and sometimes gain by reporting lower than true AC. Therefore, regulators do not know in advance the direction of strategic misrepresentation of costs.[4]

This is a distinctly different problem from the previous principal-agent problem, which is the result of unobservable effort. The problem of misrepresentation of costs arises when costs are predetermined (and not subject to manipulation by effort) but are unknown to the regulator. The supplier knows the true costs, and the government regulatory agency does not. In the previous principal-agent problem, the regulator can observe costs but not effort.

There is a third problem when a natural monopoly is subsidized, known as "capture."[5] Capture occurs when the producer being regulated succeeds in subverting the objective of the regulating authority so that the regulatory authority does not pursue the public interest but accommodates public policy to the interest of the regulated producer. This is not "capture" against one's will, but voluntary capture. The "capture" clearly must be in the interest of the persons in the regulatory authority who are captured.

In its most explicit form, capture is achieved through bribery. Bribery is illegal, and more subtle means of capture than outright bribery are possible. For example, employees in a government regulatory agency might be provided with advantageous conditions of employment in the regulated firm after they leave employment in the regulatory agency. This is, of course, also a form of bribery.

Capture can also occur because of political objectives. The regulatory authority may be accountable to political supervisors, who can benefit from campaign contributions and other expressions of political gratitude from the regulated producer.[6]

Competitive bidding

Because of the above problems, it can be desirable to avoid government subsidies to privately owned natural monopolies. The subsidies can be avoided by choosing the self-financing outcome at point 3 in Figure 8.10. Implementation is through competitive bidding. When prospective suppliers engage in competitive bidding

---

[4] The subsidy in Figure 8.10 depends on the claim regarding marginal cost of supply c. A lower than true value of c expands the quantity on which the subsidy is paid but reduces the value of the per-unit subsidy. A higher than true value for c reduces the quantity on which the subsidy is paid but increases the value of the per-unit subsidy. Therefore, the value of the total subsidy payment can sometimes be increased by higher claims of cost than true costs and sometimes by lower claims.

[5] The problem of capture was pointed out (in 1971) by George Stigler (1911–91), who was a professor at the University of Chicago. Stigler received the Nobel Prize in economics 1982.

[6] We saw in Chapter 6 how policies chosen by political decision makers can be the outcome of a trade-off between political support through campaign contributions and political support through votes.

for the right to be the monopolist, and the bidding is in terms of the user price that will be charged, the winning bid is the self-financing user price P_b.

The winning competitive bid P_b leaves zero surplus profits. The supplier bidding this price wins the right of exclusive supply for a given period of time – after which a new round of competitive bidding determines whether the same supplier will continue or will be replaced by a new supplier.

The competitive bidding outcome is not efficient. Harold Demsetz (1968) of UCLA made the case that competitive bidding is nonetheless justified to delink the revenue of a natural monopolist from the government budget.

The government is not looking for maximal revenue from the winning competitive bid. Maximal revenue is achieved by inviting bids for the right to be an unconstrained monopolist. The right of exclusive discretionary supply without a restriction on price allows the successful bidder to earn monopoly profits at point 2 in Figure 8.10 (where price is P_m and output is Q_m). The winning competitive bid is the value of these profits. By inviting bids for the right to be the monopolist and leaving open the choice of the price that the winning bidder can set, the government transfers monopoly profits to itself and leaves the public to confront the unregulated monopolist.

An objective by government of maximal revenue is therefore inconsistent with the self-financing user-price solution at point 3. The competitive bidding that leads to the user-price outcome at point 3 is in terms of the price that the supplier offers to users.

The user price established through competitive bidding avoids payment of government revenue to the private producer but introduces new problems. Suppose that the right to provide water or electricity or cable television is to be determined by competitive bidding, with the winning bidder having the right of supply for 10 years. During these 10 years, technology and quality standards will in all likelihood change. The contract for supply needs to encompass contingencies for such change, but the types of changes that will take place are often not known before the changes actually occur. It may not be possible to accommodate all contingencies regarding new technologies, changes in demand, and the quality of service in the contract designating conditions of supply. In that case, the supply contract is incomplete.

Other problems arise if, in a round of bidding, the incumbent supplier loses the bid. There is then a need to transfer ownership or use of the infrastructure to the new winning bidder. Suppose, for example, that a firm has invested in the infrastructure to provide cable television services. Then, after some designated number of years, competitive bidding takes place to determine the future supplier for another number of years, and the initial supplier loses the bid. The initial supplier owns the infrastructure but, after losing the bid, no longer has the right to use the infrastructure that it owns to provide cable services. It is socially inefficient for the new supplier to duplicate the infrastructure (unless there have been technological advances that justify new investments). Duplication would defeat the purpose of competitive bidding, which has been to allow supply under conditions of fixed or sunk costs of natural monopoly. The new supplier will wish to purchase the infrastructure, but at a cost below the cost of laying down new cables. Reaching an agreement on price for the transfer of ownership of the infrastructure can involve complex bargaining and can delay the transfer of the right to supply. Government involvement, or compulsory arbitration, may be necessary for orderly transfer of ownership of the infrastructure. Because the transfer is compulsory, property rights are being compromised.

An alternative is for government to own the infrastructure and to lease the infrastructure to winning bidders. The government is then responsible for maintaining the infrastructure.

When the infrastructure is leased to the supplier, the uncertainty of the outcome of future competitive bidding diminishes incentives of the supplier to maintain the infrastructure. A contract between government and the supplier using the government-owned infrastructure can stipulate maintenance requirements. However, it may be difficult for the contract to completely cover all contingencies and specify all maintenance precautions that should be taken, as well as enumerate all the responsibilities involved in taking the precautions.

The problem due to infrastructure ownership can also be addressed by a legal requirement of open access to use by all potential suppliers. That is, by law, any private owner of infrastructure might be obliged to allow any competitor to use the infrastructure. For example, cable companies might be obliged to allow other suppliers to offer internet access through their cable system. The right of access can apply to use of electricity supply grids, rail lines, gas pipelines, and telephone lines. In these cases, property rights are again compromised. The initial natural monopolist made the investments and owns the infrastructure. Then, subsequently, a public policy decision has been made to compel the owner of the infrastructure to allow competitors to use the infrastructure.

User prices established through competitive bidding therefore do not necessarily allow government to depart the scene after the winning bid for supply has been determined. Government responsibilities may remain to address problems of incomplete contracts and problems of transfer of ownership and use of infrastructure.

Waste management

A special case of natural monopoly is the storage of waste, in particular hazardous waste. The case is special because waste must be brought to the disposal site and a payment must be made for delivering the waste. Usually payment is made by a seller to a supplier. However, in the case of delivery of waste, the supplier makes the payment.

The payment is not voluntary, and motives of private profit provide incentives for illegal disposal of waste to avoid the cost of transporting the waste and the compulsory payment to the operator of the site. The incentive to dump waste illegally is reduced if no payment is required when delivering waste to the disposal site.

The socially preferred policy might require paying for waste delivered to the disposal site (although never paying enough to justify generating waste for delivery). Payments for waste delivered require government subsidies to the private owners of the disposal sites. A private owner could, of course, never make a profit without a subsidy, if the owner is obliged to pay when waste is delivered to the site.

Competitive bidding could still establish a least-cost operator of the site. The bids are now for negative prices, that is, for how much the government has to pay the waste operator.

8.3.3 Ownership by government and privatization

Decisions have sometimes been made to avoid problems that result from the relationship between government and a privately owned natural monopolist by making government the owner and operator of the natural monopoly. Government ownership is intended to solve the problem of determining values of government subsidies to private owners because the government is the direct supplier. The government as natural monopolist knows the losses that accompany efficient supply. The losses can be directly financed through the government budget. Problems of incomplete contracts in competitive bidding solutions do not arise because there is no need for contracts when the government is itself the supplier. Problems of transfer of ownership or use of infrastructure do not arise because no transfer of ownership takes place.

Throughout the major part of the twentieth century, the solution of government ownership and supply was prominent almost everywhere, with the exception of the United States. Outside of the United States, there was a presumption that the appropriate public policy for natural monopoly was to give government the responsibility of being the natural monopolist.[7] A natural monopoly under government control was often referred to as a state-owned firm. The natural monopoly was, however, effectively a department of government, and appointments to senior management and to the board of directors were often political decisions.

In the latter part of the twentieth century, governments in Europe and elsewhere embarked on a process of privatization, or conversion of natural monopolies to private ownership. Privatization reflected recognition of advantages of private ownership over government bureaucracy. The change from supply by an agency of government to private supply introduced cost-containment incentives. The privatized firm was also taken out of the domain of politicized decision making.

There was often resistance to privatization by employees of the state-owned firms. Employment in state-owned firms could often provide employees with

---

[7] Whereas outside of the United States natural monopolies tended to be government owned, in the United States electricity generation and supply were privately owned, as were the firms that shipped and marketed natural gas and producers of defense equipment. Among natural monopolies, only water supply has in general been provided in the United States by public bodies. In the United States, the natural-monopoly telephone company AT&T was privately owned. When technology changed, AT&T local services were divided among regional firms, and AT&T became a long-distance carrier subject to competition from other firms.

incomes and job conditions that were not available in private-sector employment. That is, employment in state-owned firms provided rents. The size of the rents is revealed by how vociferous employees are in resisting privatization, and by the value of the payments required to compensate employees for agreeing to privatization. After privatization has taken place, the magnitude of the previous rents enjoyed by the employees in the state firm is revealed in the profits of the firm under private ownership.[8]

The revenue from privatization

The amount of revenue received by a government from privatization depends on the permissible pricing behavior of the natural monopoly under private ownership. A government that sought to maximize revenue from privatization will have sold the natural monopoly as an unregulated monopoly that can set price as it wishes to maximize profits. Therefore, maximizing revenue from privatization exposes society to an unencumbered monopolist. The outcome is inconsistent with efficiency.

Back to the beginning

When a natural monopoly is privatized, the issues that we have considered in this section reappear. That is, a society faces the need to decide public policy toward natural monopoly.

8.3.4 Cost-sharing coalitions and natural monopoly

We conclude our investigation of natural monopoly with a perspective that is somewhat different from that which we have adopted so far. We can look at natural monopoly in terms of the benefits to different coalitions of users who share fixed costs. Consider three communities 1, 2, and 3. The communities can share fixed costs of a water supply system. Each community has a given demand for water supply. We shall not consider the responsiveness of demand to price. The question is how to satisfy given demands at least cost. The cost of supply for a community depends on whether the community chooses to make the infrastructure investment itself or joins with another community, or other communities, in sharing the cost.

Consider the following cost structure. If a community chooses to provide its own infrastructure, the total cost for each community is

$$C(1) = C(2) = C(3) = 150.$$

If any two communities join to share the cost of providing the infrastructure, the total cost is

$$C(1, 2) = C(2, 3) = (3, 1) = 180.$$

---

[8] Supplement 8D provides a case study.

If all three communities join to share the costs, the total cost is

$$C(1, 2, 3) = 300.$$

Therefore, costs for any individual community are minimized by a coalition of two communities. We see that:

(1) The cost of supply for a community supplying alone is 150.
(2) The cost of supply for a community in a coalition of two is 90.
(3) The cost of supply to a community when all three communities combine to organize supply is 100.

Two communities therefore have an incentive to form a coalition to provide the infrastructure. They thereby provide water supply to their residents at a cost per community of 90. Communities 1 and 2 might therefore form a coalition for supplying water. The total cost of providing water for all three communities is then

$$C(1, 2) + C(3) = 180 + 150 = 330 > 300 = C(1, 2, 3).$$

That is, when two communities form a coalition, the total cost for all three communities is greater than the all-inclusive supply coalition of the three communities.

The supply coalition for all three communities minimizes total costs of supply, and so the supply of water is a natural monopoly. The natural monopoly is, however, not *sustainable* by *voluntary* decision making because a coalition of two communities can achieve a lower cost per community than when all communities join to provide the service together.

The definition of natural monopoly

We previously defined natural monopoly as occurring when average cost is continually declining with output provided to users. Average cost in the preceding three-community example does not continually decline with the number of users. Average cost is *minimized* by two users. Continuous declining average cost indicates the presence of conditions of natural monopoly. However, all cases of natural monopoly need not involve continuously declining average cost.

Voluntary cooperation for Pareto improvement

Continuing with our example, the excluded community can approach the coalition of two and ask that an all-inclusive coalition supply water, and offer to pay 120. By paying 120 instead of the 150 that it is obliged to pay as a lone supplier, the excluded community saves 30, while the communities in the coalition of two are no worse off. When there is a possibility of Pareto-improving change, we expect the change to be implemented voluntarily. The Pareto-improving change here is the change from the coalition of two to a coalition of three.

If the previously excluded community pays 120 in the all-inclusive coalition, this community secures all the gains from the Pareto-improving change. The other two communities might, however, negotiate a share of the gains. As a limiting case, they could ask the excluded community to pay 149, which gives the excluded community a gain of 1 from an all-inclusive coalition, and leaves the two communities in the original coalition with 29 to share.

Problems of coalition instability

When natural monopoly takes the form of these above circumstances, there are problems of coalition instability of the sort we have encountered when considering majority voting (in Chapters 3 and 6). A coalition of two communities is not stable because the excluded third community can offer a payment that will make defection of one of the coalition members to form a new coalition worthwhile. For example, the excluded community can offer to reduce the cost of one of the included communities to below 90, in return for joining it in a new coalition. If the excluded community offers to pay 100 of the two-commumity shared cost of 180, it is better off than being excluded and paying 150. The new coalition partner that it has enticed pays 80 in the new two-community coalition and saves 10. The new two-community coalition formed after the break-up of the previous coalition is, of course, also unstable. The same incentives exist for the new excluded outsider to break up the new coalition. A higher government authority prevents instability by enforcing the all-inclusive natural-monopoly coalition. The efficient outcome is then sustained where the total cost of supply to residents of all three communities is minimized.

8.3.5 Summary

In this section, we have considered the role of user prices and the responsibility of government when there is a natural monopoly. All pure public goods are natural monopolies. We saw in Section 8.1 that the efficient user price for pure public goods is zero. To ensure that there is no inefficient exclusion, government is then required to finance a public good completely. When the natural monopoly is for a private good, the efficient user price is positive, but a supplementary subsidy is required if a private firm is to provide efficient supply. Principal-agent problems and other problems of asymmetric information that arise when government subsidizes a private supplier led us to consider competitive bidding as the solution for natural monopoly. Supply is then not efficient according to the usual criterion of equality of marginal benefit and marginal cost. Nonetheless there can be more than offsetting benefits because government does not pay the private supplier. We saw that competitive bidding introduces problems through incomplete contracts and issues related to transfer of ownership and maintenance of infrastructure.

A solution to natural monopoly in some countries has been government ownership. Problems when natural monopoly is part of government bureaucracy led to privatization. After privatization, if technology has not changed to transform natural monopoly to allow competition to be the means of least cost supply, the question returns of appropriate public policy toward privately owned natural monopoly.

We have also considered a case where natural monopoly minimizes total cost of supply, but not average cost of supply. Problems of coalition instability then introduce a responsibility for government to sustain efficient all-inclusive natural monopoly supply.

References and related literature

On price regulation, see Bös (1994). On the incentive problems that arise in regulating natural monopoly, see Laffont and Tirole (1993). On capture theory, see Stigler (1971). On the case for self-financing user pricing, see Demsetz (1968). On privatization, see Bishop, Kay, and Mayer (1994).

Bishop, M., J. Kay and C. Mayer (eds.), 1994. *Privatization and Economic Performance.* Oxford University Press, Oxford.

Bös, D., 1994. *Pricing and Price Regulation.* Elsevier North Holland, Amsterdam.

Demsetz, H., 1968. Why regulate utilities? *Journal of Law and Economics* 11, 55–65.

Laffont, J. J. and J. Tirole, 1993. *A Theory of Incentives in Procurement and Regulation.* MIT Press, Cambridge, Massachusetts.

Stigler, G. J., 1971. The theory of economic regulation. *Bell Journal of Economics and Management Science* 2, 3–21.

Questions for discussion

1. What is the definition of natural monopoly? Are different definitions required for private and public goods, and for different circumstances of demand and costs?
2. Why are all pure public goods natural monopolies? What are the fundamental differences between public-policy options for natural monopolies for public and private goods? Or, are there fundamental differences?
3. Besides supply of water, electricity, and cable television and internet connection, are there other natural monopolies that provide private and not collective benefit? Why does you answer depend on the size of the market (see footnote 1)?
4. Why might the "efficient solution" for natural monopoly based on user prices equal to *MC* supplemented by subsidies from government not be desirable for taxpayers?
5. Competitive bidding for the right to be the natural monopolist can be in terms of price or in terms of the amount to money that a bidder is prepared to pay to be the monopolist. What is the difference between the outcomes of the two types of bids?
6. When a cable company or a natural gas company has invested in infrastructure to supply customers, should the government compel the firms to allow competitors to use its infrastructure? Explain.
7. One solution to natural monopoly is for government to own the natural monopoly. Yet many countries that adopted the state-ownership solution to natural monopoly subsequently privatized the natural monopolies. Why were the decisions made to privatize?

8. Who can we expect to resist privatization? What are the reasons for the resistance?
9. Does the responsibility of government end when a natural monopoly has been privatized?
10. How can natural monopoly arise through costs of serving different groups of users? What is the responsibility of government in this case?
11. Is issuing a passport or driver's license a natural monopoly? Why do government agencies exclusively perform these tasks? Is it appropriate to charge for passports and driver's licenses?
12. One of the services offered by consular staff in foreign locations is to provide information about local business conditions in the foreign country. Should user prices be charged when a firm or business person seeks information about foreign market conditions from the commercial section of a consulate or an embassy? Are consulates or embassies in foreign locations that provide such information natural monopolies?

9

HOW MUCH GOVERNMENT?

The question "how much government" has a normative aspect that is expressed in how much government there should be, and in the desirable levels and structure of government. A positive aspect of the same question is concerned with explaining the size and the growth of government. In this chapter, we consider both the normative and positive aspects of the structure and size of government. We begin with the structure of government through the consequences of the existence of many governments. We then consider the extent to which cooperation and trust in a society can reduce the need for government. Finally, we review trends in the growth of government and consider the role of constitutional restraint on government.

9.1

Multiple Government

9.1.1 The benefits of choice among governments

We have a number of times during the course of previous chapters described individuals as choosing government by location. When people have the opportunity to choose among governments, a government no longer has a legal monopoly on public finance and public policy. Sufficient choice among governments makes paying taxes similar to paying prices in competitive markets. We can draw upon a number of previous conclusions regarding the consequences of multiple government through possibilities for choice of government through location.

Choice among governments is a means of choosing public goods, similar to choices in a market, by allowing matching of personal preferences with public spending on public goods. Choice among governments is sometimes described as people voting with their feet. Through choice of government, collective decisions about taxation, public spending, and public policy are transformed to become personal decisions. Compulsory taxes become voluntary user prices when, by choosing where to live, people can choose the taxes they wish to pay and the benefits they wish to receive.

By allowing grouping of populations with similar preferences for public spending, locational choice is also a means of escape from persistently being in the minority when public spending is determined by majority voting. When local public goods are subject to crowding, locational choice also allows the formation of cost-efficient sharing groups. More homogeneous groups of voters also reduce rent-seeking incentives; there are no special interests to seek political favors through public spending and public policy when all residents in a jurisdiction have the same requirements of government (although some groups in a government jurisdiction may still seek special tax concessions or preferential private benefits).

As with public goods, publicly financed entitlements of private goods provided as social insurance benefits provide incentives for people to match location with personal tax and spending preferences. That is, choice among governments allows choice of entitlements and taxes, just as locational choices are made for public goods. Choice of government also allows personal choice of communities when social norms and public policies are consistent with personal values.

Local government can also provide enhanced accountability to voters. Proximity to political decision makers and the bureaucracy can overcome rational ignorance by reducing the personal costs of being informed about taxation and public spending. Local government is closer to home. Proximity allows greater ease of access to persons in government, while smaller numbers of participating citizens and voters are required at the local level of government for effective expressions of dissatisfaction with the behavior of politicians and the officials in the bureaucracy.[1]

9.1.2 An ideal structure of government

An ideal structure of government has roles for hierarchical (vertical) and horizontal (replicated) government. The vertical structure of government allows public goods to be provided to cost-efficient sharing groups. The ideal hierarchical structure of government for public goods provided through locational choice is a pyramid. At the apex of the pyramid is the level of government that provides pure public goods. Down the hierarchy of government, smaller tax jurisdictions provide local congestible public goods. At each level of the pyramid, the horizontal structure of government would ideally provide sufficient locational choice to approximate supply in a competitive market.

9.1.3 Impediments to an efficient locational mechanism

There are various impediments to the existence of an ideal structure of government. Because pure public goods are natural monopolies, replication of supply through alternative government jurisdictions to approximate supply in a competitive market is not cost-efficient.[2] There are more alternative locations for choosing public goods at lower than at higher levels of government. Because of restrictions on migration between countries, higher levels of governments (federal or national governments) tend to be legal monopolies.[3]

Inflexibility in change of government jurisdictions is an impediment to an ideal structure of government. Existing vertical or horizontal structures of government do not necessarily correspond to the ideal pyramid for providing public goods. The geographic boundaries of the jurisdictions of different governments are usually predetermined by history and politics rather than designed as efficient configurations of government for public spending on public goods. The inflexibilities in boundaries of government jurisdictions do not allow adjustments when changes in technology or preferences change ideal sizes of sharing groups for different public goods.

The locational choice mechanism is based on willingness to relocate. For personal reasons, people might not wish to relocate. Personal relationships may

[1] Countering the proposal that it is preferable that collective decisions be made locally is the possibility that local government may respond more favorably to rent-seeking behavior and that it may be easier for special interests to obtain favorable political decisions in smaller government jurisdictions. For example, changes in zoning regulations for land use can be a source of private profit that attracts rent seeking.

[2] Besides the wasteful duplication, it would for example be impossible to determine to whom taxes should be paid if two governments were to provide defense to the same population. We previously made the same observation with reference to two lighthouses.

[3] A location can provide public goods in the form of culture and ambiance that cannot be readily duplicated elsewhere. With alternative competitive locations not available, local public goods are then also natural monopolies.

require joint decisions about location or relocation, or people may have become accustomed to friends and surroundings. Locational choice as a mechanism for competitively providing public goods is more effective when a society is individualistic and less based on personal relationships and commitments.

Public goods provided through public spending come in bundles and there may be insufficient jurisdictions to provide competitive supply offers for every bundle of public goods that people want. Problems of bundling do not arise for private goods, which can be separately purchased through personal market decisions. Because of bundling of public goods, compromises may be necessary in locational choice. For example, in jurisdictions with high spending on government schools, the majority of taxpayers may have high incomes. People with lower incomes may have chosen to locate in the jurisdiction because of the high quality of government schools.[4] Because of bundling of public goods, lower-income people can find themselves paying taxes to finance components of public spending that are sought by the high-income majority but are not appropriate for them (e.g., high spending on police appropriate for people who have substantial property to protect). Bundling then results in unwanted spending on public goods because of the inability to unbundle public spending on schools from public spending on the police department. Alternatively, the problem may be that the lower-income people attracted to a jurisdiction by the quality of the schools want more public spending to provide services that higher-income people prefer to finance privately, such as public parks or tennis courts.

Unbundling could take place if each public good had its own separate supply authority. Where feasible, just as payments are made to the local electricity company, tax payments could be made to an authority responsible for education, public health, police protection, and so on. With each separate authority independently and separately charging for each public good, taxpayers would know how much they are paying for each public good. There would be accountability, and people would have the means to compare personal benefit with personal cost through taxes.[5] The information would allow taxpayers to assert that costs exceed benefits for some categories of public spending. Collectively, voters could, where required, ask for a reevaluation of the merits of public spending. Although the problem of bundling of public spending would then be resolved, the problems of making efficient collective decisions about total spending on a public good and sharing of costs would remain, although the problems are ameliorated when local public goods are provided to populations with similar preferences.

---

[4] Zoning regulations can prevent mixing of low- and high-income people in the same local jurisdiction. Zoning regulations can favor expensive houses by specifying high minimal-sized building lots or by prohibiting or restricting apartment buildings and duplexes.

[5] Ideally we should be billed our Lindahl prices by each public authority responsible for financing each public good. No one, however, knows our Lindahl prices, and we cannot verify our claimed Lindahl prices.

9.1.4 Externalities among jurisdictions

We have reviewed the benefits provided by choice when there is multiple government. Norms and public policies in neighboring communities when there is multiple government can, however, also create disadvantageous externalities. For example, if a community has strict gun control laws and a neighboring community does not, criminals can buy their guns in one community and commit their crimes in the community where they know that honest people will not be armed. Or if a community has lax environmental standards and a neighboring community has strict standards, the community with strict environmental laws can suffer environmental damage from effluent and deterioration in air quality that originates in the neighboring community.

The presence of externalities that cross boundaries of different governments is, therefore, the basis of a case against multiple government and in favor of larger government jurisdictions that internalize and solve externality problems. We have seen that problems of the global environment can remain unsolved because of externalities that arise in the jurisdictions of different national governments.

9.1.5 Social insurance and migration

We have contemplated the idea of a global social insurance contract and asked what sort of social welfare function we would choose behind a veil of ignorance if we did not know where in the world we are going to be born, and since we also observed that, in the absence of a global social insurance contract, social insurance can be undermined by adverse selection through locational mobility. That is, poorer people benefit from relocating to jurisdictions that provide generous entitlements to low-income persons. While, at the same time, high-income people benefit from leaving such tax jurisdictions. A community may believe that its social insurance contract was chosen to apply to risks that people in the local population confront. If new arrivals systematically require benefits through the entitlements of local social insurance, insurance is not being provided, but rather systematic income transfers take place. When all new arrivals are eligible for entitlements of social insurance, locational mobility can thus limit the generosity of the social insurance that a jurisdiction is able to provide. Generous social insurance entitlements that people may have wanted (they may believe in social welfare defined according to Rawls) become impractical.

Illegal immigrants are in general not eligible for the entitlements of social insurance. Illegal immigrants also do not in general pay taxes. However, illegal immigrants are often visibly present and are allowed to continue working and living in a country. The permissible illegality often appears to restrict immigrants to jobs in which the immigrants do not compete with local workers. At the same time, the illegality also does not allow immigrants access to the entitlements of social insurance. Illegal immigrants can, however, have children who require education and also health care. Societies are in general unwilling to exclude children from schooling or from medical treatment.

Governments might decide from time to time to grant amnesties that allow illegal immigrants to apply for legal residence. Legal residence brings the incomes of the formerly illegal immigrants out of the shadow economy. The incomes can be taxed to match the public spending required because of the immigrants' presence.

People who emigrate need not be poor. We have noted that high-income people have incentives to emigrate to avoid generous social insurance entitlements financed by high taxes. High-income people, in particular tennis and golf players and Grand Prix drivers, might move to tax havens where rates of tax on personal incomes are low.[6]

9.1.6 Income redistribution in a federal structure

Taxes are often levied by government at the federal or national level and are redistributed among regions and localities. Such pooling and redistribution of tax revenue spreads risk among different regions. For example, if the price of oil falls, the regional economies of Texas, Alaska, and other oil-producing states in the United States contract, but the regional economies of other states that are users of oil and oil-based products expand. A common tax base through federal taxation and sharing of tax revenues thus provides insurance against changes in oil prices by allowing the states that gain and lose to pool their risks. Federal or central government tax revenues can therefore be viewed as provided from a portfolio of tax bases that are shared assets and spread risk.

Centralized taxation and redistribution of tax revenue to local or regional governments is not part of the locational model of choice of taxes and public spending. The locational choice model views individuals as financing local public spending by paying taxes that are equivalent to user prices for the services that are locally provided. By centrally taxing and redistributing tax revenue, a federal or national government imposes taxes that do not have the attributes of user prices, and rather subsidizes user prices in the locations that receive net transfers of tax revenue through the redistribution decisions that are made.

Political support calculations might influence regional or local tax-revenue distribution decisions. Tax-revenue redistribution among regions or localities motivated by political support at the federal or national level of government would not take place if regional or local governments were solely responsible for their own taxation and spending policies.

9.1.7 Migration and the quality of government

People who relocate or emigrate substitute the authority of one government for that of another. The reason for emigration may be arbitrary taxation and small personal benefits from public spending. Favors from government might be directed

---

[6] A popular tax haven is, for example, the small independent principality of Monte Carlo on the Mediterranean coast. While taxes in Monte Carlo are low, housing prices are high. The low taxes are capitalized into the housing prices. Taxes in the United States have generally been lower than in European welfare states, which has often led high-ability people to relocate to the United States.

to successful rent seekers. The people who emigrate will tend not to be the successful rents seekers but rather will tend to be people whose personal advantage is in working hard in productive activity. People may emigrate whether their arrival in another country is legal or not. The immigrants are seeking better incomes, but they are also seeking better government.

Sometimes two cities are located side by side on different sides of a national border. The people on the two sides of the border can have the same abilities. On one side of the border, there is respect for private property rights, taxes are reasonable and just, and tax revenue finances beneficial public spending. On the other side of the border, property rights may not be protected, public spending may not be socially beneficial and in particular may not be directed at improving social mobility through education, and government may be a means for the strong to exercise authority over the weak. The levels of incomes and also income distribution can be expected to differ on the two sides of the border. On one side of the border, the mass of the people will be poor, but there will also be some exceedingly rich people. We can then expect unrelenting effort by people on one side of the border to cross the border to the other side, again to substitute good government for bad government.

9.1.8 Yardstick competition

In democratic societies, voters change governments through elections. We have noted that voters can be rationally ignorant and may not have the information necessary for identifying self-interested political and bureaucratic behavior that is not in the public interest. Random events that make it difficult for voters to judge the reasons for inadequate government performance can also occur.

The presence of multiple governments provides information for voters, who can judge their own government against levels of taxes and benefits from public spending in neighboring government jurisdictions. That is, multiple governments allows yardstick competition. In one jurisdiction, local public goods may be of a high standard and taxes may be low, whereas in a neighboring jurisdiction taxes might be high and benefits from public spending might be low. The visibility of taxes and benefits to residents of different jurisdictions provides a comparative reference point or yardstick for identifying types of political decision makers in different government jurisdictions. The comparative information allows voters to make decisions about whether to support political incumbents or to support challengers when elections take place.

Without a basis for comparison provided by outcomes in different tax jurisdictions, voters in a government jurisdiction might conclude "all politicians and government bureaucrats are self-interested and self-serving, and enter into government to seek personal power to satisfy their egos." However, when voters observe better political and bureaucratic performance in other jurisdictions, they can conclude that better government is possible, and they can improve their situation by voting for candidates opposing inadequate incumbent politicians in their own jurisdictions.

At the same time, the incumbent politicians become aware that voters are judging their performance against the performance of their counterparts elsewhere. The consequence can be competitive discipline that leads to more conscientious and socially responsible political behavior.

Differences in the quality of government affect land and housing prices. With the quality of government capitalized into the value of land and houses, there is little to be gained from relocation. Bad government will have reduced the price of the house that a person who wishes to relocate is seeking to sell, and good government will have increased housing prices elsewhere. The election of a good government to replace the bad government will increase housing prices. Therefore prospects for personal improvement are better by using comparative observations on government to identify and replace bad government rather than seeking to escape bad government by choosing to relocate.[7]

9.1.9 Property taxes and poll taxes

We have previously observed that local governments tend to tax property because property is immobile between regions. Because property cannot escape a jurisdiction, the property tax is efficient, by the Ramsey rule.[8]

The general rule that we apply to determine efficient pricing is that, for any individual i, price should equal marginal benefit,

$$P = MB_i. \tag{9.1}$$

When in particular people choose local public goods through locational decisions, efficient pricing requires that the tax paid to a local government per unit of a public good be equal to marginal benefit so that

$$T = MB_i. \tag{9.2}$$

That is, the tax T should act like a user price to guide people to personally efficient locational choice.

The tax T establishes a price per person for benefits from public spending on local public goods. A price per person is a head tax. That is, every person pays for benefits from the public goods provided, because of his or her presence in the government jurisdiction. When people face locational options, a head tax is not a lump-sum tax because the tax can be escaped by relocation. The tax is therefore chosen by individuals or households from among alternative head taxes in different locational options. If a head tax is based on the right to vote, the head tax becomes a poll tax.

A head tax, or poll tax, is consequently the means for efficient pricing when public goods are chosen through locational choice. A head tax or poll tax corresponds

---

[7] People who rent housing do not gain from the change to a good government. Rents reflect the value of the services available in the jurisdiction through the taxes that are paid. Rents will therefore be low when a bad government is in office and will be high when a good government is in office.

[8] More specifically, a tax on unimproved property or land has no excess burden. A tax on improved property has an excess burden because of substitution responses in the quality of housing.

to a price per person for the individual benefits provided by public goods in a jurisdiction.

Nonetheless, property taxes, and not poll taxes, are in general used to finance local government spending. A property tax ties the taxes paid to finance public goods to the value of land or housing.

We can consider two houses for which property taxes are the same in the same jurisdiction. Two people live in one of the houses. In the other house, six people live together (the difference in numbers is not because of children). With property taxes financing local public goods, the couple pays three times more for the same services from local government than the six people sharing the house.

We can now ask whether the difference in taxes paid for the same benefits is justified by principles of socially just taxation, through either horizontal or vertical equity.[9] The property tax allows individual tax payments can be reduced by increasing the number of people living in a house because the tax is levied not according to the number of occupants but according to the value of the property.

A person who can afford to live alone might also be able to afford to pay more taxes. That is, such a person might have greater "ability to pay." The sole occupant of a house can, however, also be a widow, who has a small income and wishes to remain in the house in which she has lived for many years. She may be choosing to spend the greater part of her potential income (she could rent or sell the house) on staying in the house.

The property tax is a progressive tax based on ability to pay through the premise that wealthier or higher-income people can afford better housing. At the same time, the property tax discriminates against the widow. A claim that "the widow should not be living alone" is a paternalistic judgment about the right of the widow to choose to remain in the familiar surroundings of her own home.

The widow might be exempted from part or all of the property tax. The widow then has an incentive to rent out rooms in her house because location in her house to benefit from public spending is subsidized.

With the property tax, small numbers in a house subsidize larger groups in another house. The more people of voting age who live in a house, the more votes there are in the house. Therefore, when decisions are made by majority voting about choice of the means of financing public spending, a property tax may be favored over an individual user price paid as a poll tax.

The choice between a property tax and a poll tax also affects income distribution through private ownership of houses and public housing. If property taxes were to be replaced by poll taxes, private ownership of a house would no longer be accompanied by an obligation to pay taxes based on property values. The replacement of property taxes by poll taxes would be capitalized into private housing values, and private housing prices would increase. At the same time, people living in public housing projects may not pay a property tax at all. They do not own the

---

[9] We recall that horizontal equity refers to equal tax treatment of equals and vertical equity refers to just tax treatment of people who are different, in particular in having different incomes.

houses in which they live but live in subsidized rental housing because of their inability to pay market prices for private housing. However, when a poll tax replaces a property tax, residents of public housing confront the obligation to pay the poll tax.

Change from a property tax to a poll tax is change from an ability-to-pay principle for local government financing to a user-pays principle. The poll tax reflects the user-pays principle because all people in a location who benefit from public spending are obliged to pay the same taxes as all others in the same location. The property tax depends on the value of a house, and not on the number of persons who, by living in a house in the jurisdiction, benefit from the tax-financed public goods that are provided to the jurisdiction's residents.

An unsuccessful attempt at changing from a property tax to a poll tax
In 1988, a poll tax replaced property taxes as a means of financing local public services in the United Kingdom. The attempt at changing the tax base was unsuccessful, and the property tax was restored in 1991.

The repeal of the poll tax and the return to the property tax followed widespread public protest and noncompliance with the poll tax. The user-pays principle introduced through the poll tax increased tax obligations for people who lived in public housing and for people who lived in houses where there were more than average numbers of occupants. Taxes also increased for occupants of less expensive houses. Significant numbers of people refused to pay the poll tax. No change of government was involved in the return to the property tax. The poll tax was repealed, and the property tax was reintroduced, by the same government that had introduced the poll tax. The British poll-tax experiment was a case of successful popular resistance to the user-pays principle for local public goods.

9.1.10 Mobile tax bases and tax competition
In Chapter 7, we observed that some tax bases are more locationally mobile than others. Capital is particularly mobile and can be moved and reinvested. With no taxes, competitive markets, and adjustments for any differences in risk, we expect capital to provide the same return in two tax jurisdictions. If one government imposes a tax on capital, the net-of-tax return to capital in that jurisdiction falls, and capital leaves the jurisdiction until after-tax returns are equalized across tax jurisdictions.

Figure 9.1 shows this process. A fixed amount of capital (given by $O_1 O_2$) is allocated through a competitive market between two tax jurisdictions. A quantity K_1 is located in jurisdiction 1 and a quantity K_2 is located in jurisdiction 2 so that

$$K = K_1 + K_2. \tag{9.3}$$

O_1 is the origin for measurement of capital in region 1, and O_2 is the origin for region 2. With no taxes on capital in either jurisdiction, the market allocation of capital between the two jurisdictions is at point A. At A, the marginal product of

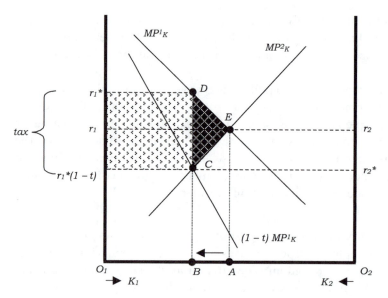

Figure 9.1. A mobile tax base.

O_1 is the origin for the amount of mobile capital K_1 in tax jurisdiction 1, and O_2 is the origin for mobile capital K_2 in tax jurisdiction 2. When jurisdiction 1 levies a tax at rate t on income from capital, a quantity of capital AB leaves jurisdiction 1 for jurisdiction 2. After capital has moved in response to the tax, the allocation of capital between the two tax jurisdictions is no longer efficient. The efficiency loss is the area CED.

capital is equal in each region, and the return to capital is also equal between the two regions, with

$$r_1 = r_2. \tag{9.4}$$

The government of region 1 then takes the decision to impose a tax at the rate t on income earned from capital in its region. The tax is levied independently of the residence or citizenship of the owner of capital. Because of the tax, capital leaves region 1 for region 2, and the new post-tax market allocation between the two regions is established where the post-tax rates of return from capital in the two regions are equalized, which is at point B. At B, we see that returns to capital are once more equal, after taking account of taxes paid on income from capital in region 1. After the tax,

$$(1 - t)MP_K^1 = MP_K^2. \tag{9.5}$$

That is, since capital is allocated so that returns after tax payments are equal,

$$r_1^*(1 - t) = r_2^*. \tag{9.6}$$

In response to the tax, the quantity of capital AB moves from region 1 to region 2. The tax base has contracted in region 1 where the tax was imposed, and has increased in region 2.

The tax on capital income in region 1 has reduced the private return to capital in both regions, from the return given by expression (9.4) to the return given by expression (9.6). The shaded area shows the excess burden of the tax DEC.[10]

Figure 9.1 illustrates the principle that a tax on a mobile factor in a region contracts the tax base for the tax through the exit of the mobile factor from the tax jurisdiction. Efficient spending on public goods is determined by including the effect of taxes that finance local public goods on the local tax base. In Chapter 2, we saw that the excess burden of a tax reduces efficient public spending on public goods below efficient voluntary private spending. We arrive at the same conclusion of reduced efficient public spending when the tax base used to finance public goods is mobile. The additional cost of financing public goods by taxing mobile capital is due to the "escape" of capital from the tax base of the jurisdiction.

In Figure 9.1, the government in region 1 obtains tax revenue equal to the dotted area. The revenue is determined as

$$R = tr_1^* K_1. \tag{9.7}$$

If the quantity of capital K_1 that remains in the region is very responsive to the tax, revenue from the tax declines. The decline in revenue can be precipitous if sufficient capital exits the region.

Figure 9.2 shows the rate of return to capital r^* available in a competitive global capital market. An investor can always obtain the rate of return r^*. Taxes do not affect this rate of return. In Figure 9.2, the imposition of a tax by the government in region 1 results in exit of capital AB from the region. Further increases in the tax lead to more exit of capital, and a sufficiently high rate of taxation can result in the disappearance of the domestic tax base for mobile capital.

A mobile tax base therefore limits public spending, whether on public goods or income transfers and entitlements of social insurance. A government may be left with little choice other than to tax the immobile people in its jurisdiction because mobile factors will respond to the announcement of a tax by simply moving away beyond the reaches of the intended tax.

Residence and source principles of taxation

Obligations to pay taxes can be determined according to residence of the taxpayer or the location where income is earned. Under the *source* principle of taxation, the owner of capital pays taxes to the government in the location where the income from capital was earned. Decisions about where to locate capital are then made by comparing *post-tax* returns in different locations. Therefore, the investment decision is sensitive to taxes in different jurisdictions. This is the case we have been considering.

---

[10] Before the tax was imposed, the quantity of capital AB was producing a quantity of output $BAED$ (the area under the marginal product of capital function for region 1). After the tax is imposed, the relocated capital produces the smaller output $ECBA$ (the area under the marginal product of capital function for region 2). The loss in output because of the relocation of capital in response to the tax is the difference between these areas, which is the shaded area DEC.

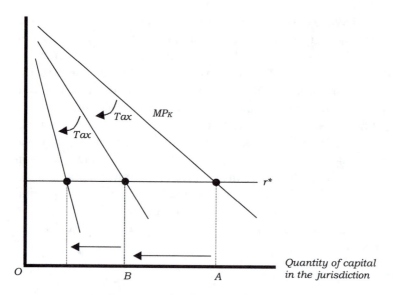

Figure 9.2. The change in the domestic tax base with a competitive global capital market.

The return to capital r^* is given in the global market. The tax base shrinks from *OA* to *OB*, and then further, when the government in the jurisdiction taxes income from mobile capital.

Under the *residence* principle of taxation, a recipient of income from capital pays taxes to his or her home government no matter where the capital is located. Therefore, owners of capital seek the highest return available anywhere in the world, after payment of any foreign taxes. If taxes everywhere are levied on a residence basis, all taxes are determined according to where a taxpayer lives, and not according to where capital is invested. A tax on capital imposed by the government of the investor's home location cannot now be escaped by moving the capital abroad. The investor would have to move to another tax jurisdiction to escape the tax.

Double-tax agreements

If both residence and source-based taxes are levied, investors pay taxes on income earned from capital invested in an outside tax jurisdiction, and they pay taxes again on the same income to the home government of their tax jurisdiction. Double-tax agreements between governments avoid this double burden of taxation. A double-tax agreement allows taxes paid in one tax jurisdiction to be deducted from tax obligations in another. Without a double-tax agreement, it is unattractive to invest in another region because both the government in the region where the capital is invested and the investor's home government levy taxes on the return from the same investment. Double-tax agreements provide compensating tax offsets for taxes paid to another government.

TABLE 9.1. TAX COMPETITION AS A PRISONERS' DILEMMA

	No change in tax in region 2	The tax in region 2 is reduced
No change in tax in region 1	3, 3	1, 4
Tax in region 1 is reduced	4, 1	2, 2

Tax competition and tax coordination

Higher taxes drive mobile capital away. Lower taxes attract capital and expand the local tax base. Governments can perceive, correctly, that they are in competition for tax bases, and that, by reducing taxes, they can hope to attract new capital to add to their tax base.

The end result of competition among governments to attract mobile capital can be that capital is not taxed, and perhaps is subsidized. The "race to the bottom" in taxes on mobile capital can be avoided if governments agree on tax coordination whereby each government agrees not to reduce taxes unilaterally on mobile factors.

A prisoners' dilemma is present when governments seek such tax coordination. A government is best off when it lowers taxes and governments in other jurisdictions do not. The Nash equilibrium is where each government reduces taxes. In Table 9.1, if the government in jurisdiction 2 decides not to change taxes, the best response of the government in jurisdiction 1 is to reduce taxes. If the government in jurisdiction 2 reduces taxes, the best response of the government in jurisdiction 1 is also to reduce taxes. The dominant strategy is to reduce taxes. The Nash equilibrium is that each government reduces taxes. However, tax coordination not to change taxes is the best outcome for each government.

A way to ensure tax coordination is to centralize the right to tax. The central or federal government levies taxes and redistributes the proceeds to lower-level governments.[11] We therefore have another explanation for the phenomenon of a central government levying and redistributing tax revenue among state and local governments. Our previous explanations were risk sharing through pooled (or collective) tax bases and political support calculations of political decision makers in the central government. To these explanations, we add the gains to governments from tax coordination.

Indirect taxes

A tax coordination problem between governments also arises with indirect taxes. When a neighboring jurisdiction has a lower sales tax on liquor, some people might drive to the neighboring jurisdiction to drink. They might then also drive

---

[11] If a federal government does not exist, then it can be created, as in the case of the European Union.

home drunk. Or they might succumb to the temptation to transport liquor illegally, so subjecting themselves to the risk of fines. Tax coordination changes these
incentives.

Tax competition and the nature of government

Resolving the tax coordination problem that confronts governments need not be
beneficial for taxpayers. The benefits in Table 9.1 refer to governments, not to taxpayers. Whether tax competition is harmful or beneficial for taxpayers depends
on whether taxpayers face principal-agent problems with political representatives
and government bureaucracy. Principal-agent problems make the Nash equilibrium of the prisoners' dilemma where there is tax competition advantageous
for taxpayers, by keeping taxes low. Tax cooperation is correspondingly disadvantageous for taxpayers by allowing high taxes from which taxpayers do not
benefit.

Therefore, whether tax competition is advantageous or disadvantageous to
taxpayers and citizens depends on the nature of government. When there is no
principal-agent problem between taxpayers and government, tax competition
can be harmful to government and to residents of a tax jurisdiction. When
the principal-agent problem is present, tax competition harms the government
but benefits the population. That is, tax competition can help tame a leviathan
government.[12]

9.1.11 Summary

This chapter is concerned with the size of government. In this section we have
considered the size of government from the perspective of multiple government,
or the existence of many governments. Multiple government offers benefits from
various sources. Multiple government counters the monopoly in its jurisdiction
of any single government over taxation and public spending; within available options, people can choose the government to which they pay taxes and from which
they receive benefits from public spending, and compulsory taxes become similar
to voluntary user prices. Multiple governments also allow personal choices to be
made about tax-financed entitlements and about social norms and standards. The
populations with more similar preferences made possible by multiple government
resolve or ameliorate problems of majority voting; as well, rent-seeking incentives
are reduced. There can also be gains from risk pooling among regional and local governments by sharing tax bases. A decentralized structure of government
provided through multiple government increases accountability for taxpayers and
citizens; local government is closer, more approachable, and more readily monitored than a distant central government.

---

[12] Tax competition cannot, of course, deter a leviathan government from taxing locationally immobile
factors. There is no competition for locationally immobile tax bases.

We have also observed possible offsetting disadvantages of multiple government. Duplication of government is not cost-efficient for supplying a population with pure public goods, which are a natural monopoly. Federal structures of government allow politically determined redistribution of tax revenue to lower levels of government. Negative externalities can arise that cross government boundaries. Adverse selection through locational mobility in response to entitlements and taxation can compromise the viability of social insurance programs.

We have noted that, although property taxes are often used for financing local government spending, the tax that corresponds to the user price in a locational market is a poll tax or tax per person. Property taxes and poll taxes have different distributional consequences. The property tax is based on ability to pay reflected in the price of houses, and the poll tax is a user price. Also the property tax is not paid by people who live in public housing and is independent of the number of people who live in a house. Therefore, we expect a property tax to be more popular politically than a poll tax. The unpopularity of a poll tax was confirmed by evidence from an attempt in the United Kingdom to replace property taxes with poll taxes for financing local public goods.

We have noted that the quality of government influences relocation decisions. People emigrate to escape bad government.

We have also seen that multiple government is beneficial in allowing voters to make yardstick comparisons of political performance. The information provided to voters from such comparisons assists in resolving the political principal-agent problem by allowing voters to discipline politicians when elections take place. Politicians in turn know that voters have standards for comparison for their political performance, and political behavior can thereby change. Therefore, by facilitating yardstick comparisons, multiple government provides benefits from other governments without the need for people to relocate.

We have noted that relocation is not an escape from incompetent or leviathan government for property owners because the quality of government is capitalized into property values. Changing the government increases property values.

We have seen that the type of government determines whether tax competition is advantageous or disadvantageous for taxpayers. When there is no principal-agent problem between taxpayers and government, tax competition among governments can restrict revenue from mobile tax bases and lead to the burden of taxation being borne by immobile factors – which the Ramsey rule recommends for efficiency, but which may not be consistent with socially just sharing of tax burdens. Tax competition, however, beneficially tames or constrains taxation when a leviathan government seeks tax revenue without regard for welfare of the population.

Overall, we conclude that multiple government is advantageous. There are qualifications. Subject to the qualifications, the more choice available among governments, the better the outcomes that individuals and households can expect from public finance and accompanying public policy.

References and related literature

On locational choice as a substitute for markets for public goods, see Tiebout (1956), and on limits of the locational mechanism, see Pestieau (1977) and Bewley (1981). For a proposal for geographically flexible jurisdictions, see Casella and Frey (1992). On capitalization, see Oates (1969) and Caplan (2001). For a survey of the empirical evidence on locational choice, see Dowding, John, and Biggs (1994). On comparing political performance, see Salmon (1987), Besley and Case (1995), and Wrede (2001). On taxes and income distribution within federal systems, see Buchanan (1950), Brown and Oates (1987), and Inman and Rubinfeld (1996). On risk sharing, see Asdrubali, Sørensen, and Yosha (1996) and Goldberg and Levi (2000). On accountability and level of government, see Seabright (1996). On public policy toward illegal migration, see Ethier (1986). On social insurance and immigration, see Wellisch and Waltz (1998). On emigration as a response to self-serving government, see Epstein, Hillman, and Ursprung (1999). On mobile tax bases and tax coordination and tax competition, see Wilson (1986), Oates and Swab (1988), Genser (1992), Edwards and Keem (1996), Eichenberger and Frey (1996), Mueller (1998), Rauscher (1998), Dhillon, Perroni, Scharf (1999), Sørensen (2000), and Eggert (2001).

Asdrubali, P., B. E. Sørensen and O. Yosha, 1996. Channels of interstate risk sharing: United States 1963–1990. *Quarterly Journal of Economics* 111, 1081–1110.

Besley, T. and A. Case, 1995. Incumbent behavior: Vote-seeking, tax-setting and yardstick competition. *American Economic Review* 85, 25–45.

Bewley, T. F., 1981. A critique of Tiebout's theory of local public expenditures. *Econometrica* 49, 713–40.

Brown, C. C. and W. E. Oates, 1987. Assistance to the poor in a federal system. *Journal of Public Economics* 32, 307–30.

Buchanan, J. M., 1950. Federalism and fiscal equity. *American Economic Review* 40, 583–99.

Caplan, B., 2001. Standing Tiebout on his head: Tax capitalization and the monopoly power of local governments. *Public Choice* 108, 101–22.

Casella, A. and B. Frey, 1992. Federalism and clubs: Toward an economic theory of overlapping political jurisdictions. *European Economic Review* 36, 639–46.

Dhillon, A., C. Perroni and K. Scharf, 1999. Implementing tax coordination. *Journal of Public Economics* 72, 243–68.

Dowding, K., P. John and S. Biggs, 1994. Tiebout: A survey of the empirical literature. *Urban Studies* 31, 767–97.

Edwards, J. and M. Keem, 1996. Tax competition and Leviathan. *European Economic Review* 40, 113–34.

Eggert, W., 2001. Capital tax competition with socially wasteful government consumption. *European Journal of Political Economy* 17, 517–29.

Eichenberger, R. and B. Frey, 1996. To harmonize or to compete? That's not the question. *Journal of Public Economics* 60, 335–49.

Epple, D. and T. Romer, 1991. Mobility and redistribution. *Journal of Political Economy* 99, 828–58.

Epstein, G. S., A. L. Hillman and H. W. Ursprung, 1999. The king never emigrates. *Review of Development Economics* 3, 107–21.

Ethier, W. J., 1986. Illegal immigration: The host-country problem. *American Economic Review* 76, 56–71.

Genser, B., 1992. Tax competition and harmonization in federal economies. In *European Integration in the World Economy*, H-J. Viscera (ed.). Springer, Heidelberg, 184–205.

Goldberg, M. A. and M. D. Levi, 2000. The European Union as a country portfolio. *European Journal of Political Economy* 16, 411–27.

Inman, R. P. and D. L. Rubinfield, 1996. Designing tax policy in federalist economies: An overview. *Journal of Public Economics* 60, 307–34.

Mueller, D. C., 1998. Constitutional constraints on governments in a global economy. *Constitutional Political Economy* 9, 171–86.

Oates, W. E., 1969. The effects of property taxes and local government spending on property values: An empirical study of tax capitalization and the Tiebout hypothesis. *Journal of Political Economy* 77, 957–71.

Oates, W. E. and R. M. Swab, 1988. Economic competition among jurisdictions: Efficiency enhancing or distortion inducing? *Journal of Public Economics* 35, 333–54.

Pestieau, P., 1977. The optimality limits of the Tiebout model. In *The Political Economy of Fiscal Federalism*, W. Oates (ed.). Lexington Books, Lexington, Massachusetts 173–86.

Rauscher, M., 1998. Leviathan and competition among jurisdictions: The case of benefit taxation. *Journal of Urban Economics* 44, 59–67.

Salmon, P., 1987. Decentralization as an incentive scheme. *Oxford Review of Economic Policy* 3, 24–34.

Seabright, P., 1996. Accountability and decentralization in government: An incomplete contracts model. *European Economic Review* 40, 61–89.

Sørensen, P. B., 2000. Tax coordination: Its desirability and redistribution implications. *Economic Policy* #31, 431–72.

Tiebout, C. M., 1956. A pure theory of local expenditures. *Journal of Political Economy* 64, 416–24.

Wellisch, D. and U. Waltz, 1998. Why do rich countries prefer free trade over free migration?: The role of the welfare state. *European Economic Review* 42, 1595–1612.

Wilson, J. D., 1986. A theory of interregional tax competition. *Journal of Urban Economics* 19, 296–315.

Wrede, M., 2001. Yardstick competition to tame the Leviathan. *European Journal of Political Economy* 17, 705–21.

Questions for discussion

1. Do you live under the jurisdiction of a number of governments? If so, outline the responsibilities of each level of government.
2. Are the responsibilities of the different levels of government financed by taxes that are levied by the same levels of government, or are taxes levied and spent at different levels of government? If taxation and spending are by different levels of government, why does each level of government not simply levy the taxes that are required to finance its particular spending responsibilities?
3. Which level of government is responsible for providing entitlements of social insurance? For example, which level of government provides public housing, and who decides on how much is paid to people receiving publicly financed income transfers? If local levels of government are responsible for these tasks, are there disparities in the entitlements provided in different government jurisdictions? Are people observed to make location decisions based on the disparities? Are there consequences for the ability or willingness of governments to provide welfare entitlements in their jurisdictions?

4. Do differences in taxes among government jurisdictions in the area where you live or study necessarily match differences in publicly financed benefits?

5. In the place where you live or study, do different government jurisdictions offer a wide range of choice for paying taxes and benefiting from public goods? That is, does the presence of multiple government provide a reasonable approximation to market choices? What are the limitations on choice among governments offering choices similar to that in competitive markets?

6. Do the choices that different jurisdictions offer primarily reflect differences in preferences for spending on public goods or differences in incomes and wealth? Explain.

7. If poll taxes provide better approximations than property taxes to efficient user prices for locally provided public goods, why are property taxes extensively used to finance local government spending? What are the conclusions of the failed experiment in the United Kingdom of replacing a property tax by a poll tax?

8. "Multiple government solves problems of majority voting (where the majority impose their will on a minority) by allowing sorting of people into ideal sharing groups." What are the conditions required to be satisfied for this statement to be true?

9. "An advantage of multiple government is that voters are presented with standards against which to judge their own local politicians. This advantage can be just as important as the competition through locational choice introduced into public-good supply by the presence of multiple government." Do you agree? Explain.

10. What is the role of risk sharing in explanations for federal governmental structures? Do you believe that this explanation is in practice important?

11. "The lower the level of government, the greater the accountability of government to taxpayers." Do you agree? Explain.

12. Why does the federal or central government usually redistribute income among regional and local governments in federal systems? Does such income redistribution affect the locational choice mechanism as a means of efficiently providing public goods? Explain.

13. Epple and Romer (1991) conclude that, when there are many jurisdictions among which people can move, the outcome of voting on income redistribution within a jurisdiction depends on the number of voters living in their own houses and the number of voters renting houses. Why do you think this is so?

14. Is the presence of a prisoners' dilemma in tax competition among governments beneficial to taxpayers or disadvantageous? Explain.

15. Why is tax competition based on source-based taxation of income from capital and not residence-based taxation? What are the reasons why governments enter into double-tax agreements?

16. A disadvantage of multiple government is that externalities can cross boundaries of government jurisdictions. Is presence of externalities an explanation for the structure of government that you observe in a hierarchical or federal system? Are other reasons more important for explaining the structure of multiple government? Explain.

17. What answers would you offer if asked to explain differences in incomes of populations that live in close proximity to one another but under the authority of different governments? Provide examples where incomes differ substantially on different sides of a border. What do you think would happen to people's incomes if the border moved one way and then the other way?

18. The question "how much government" has normative aspects (relating to how much government there should be) and positive aspects (relating to how much government there in fact is). Distinguish the normative and positive aspects that have arisen in considering "how much government" with reference to multiple government.

9.2

Cooperation and Trust as a Substitute for Government

9.2.1 The nature of people and of government

In the previous section, we considered the question of "how much government" in the context of multiple government. We shall now consider the nature of the relation between people and government. The question we ask is whether a society requires a government that exercises authority over the people or a government over which people exercise authority? Opposing answers to this question are provided in the writings of Thomas Hobbes (1588–1679) and John Locke (1632–1704). The different answers are based on different views of the nature of people.

Hobbes's case for imposed order

In his book *Leviathan*, which was published in 1651, Thomas Hobbes made a case for government that has absolute authority over all people. Hobbes proposed that men and women are by nature cruel and disrespectful to one another. To control the base instincts of men and women, Hobbes called for the controlling hand of a "leviathan."[1]

Hobbes declared that, without the order imposed by the leviathan, there would be anarchy. People would murder one another for each other's property. Life would be "brutish" and "short," there would be no rule of law and no private property rights, and all people would contest all things.

Hobbes's view of humanity was that all people could be categorized as either greedy or lazy. He viewed all people, regardless of whether they are greedy or lazy, as seeking power over other people. Peace and tranquility in a society only arose because people feared the retaliation of others. Hobbes viewed peace as not due to goodwill among people, but as the consequence of investments in defense and security that people make to protect themselves from the designs of others on their property and person.

Hobbes's absolute ruler or leviathan would ensure a civilized society through a monopoly on power over people. The leviathan would also own all property. The power of the leviathan would be permanent and hereditary, and, because power was not contestable, people would not use resources in rent-seeking contests to become the leviathan. The untrustworthy nature of people made surrender to the leviathan, according to Hobbes, the only rational response if individuals wished to live in a secure civilized society.

---

[1] The term "leviathan" appears in the biblical Book of Job to describe a sea-animal (whale) with power that has no equal on earth. As in Chapter 7, in more contemporary times, the term "leviathan" has been used to describe a self-interested revenue-maximizing government.

Hobbes was writing centuries before the prisoners' dilemma had been formally set out. However, he was stating the idea that, left to their own independent decisions, people would not cooperate and would harm one another, whereas voluntarily imposed coercive authority would improve everybody's life.

Although Hobbes was justifying government by absolute hereditary monarchy, his position also applies when people are called on to be subservient to decisions made by majority voting. Just as people would be subject to the leviathan, so, under majority voting, the will of the minority is subjugated to the decisions of the majority. Whether under absolute authority of the leviathan or under democratic majority voting, individuals are subject to the authority of others.

Locke's case for government that respects natural freedom

In his book *Two Treatises of Government*, published in 1690, John Locke made the case for government that is accountable to the people. Locke proposed that the natural state of men and women was personal freedom, and that every person was entitled by natural law to be free of the imposed order of others, including Hobbes's leviathan.

As did Hobbes, Locke also appealed to human reason to justify his position. Locke proposed that the exercise of reason led men and women to understand that the state of nature was civilized, and that nature was not anarchic and murderous as Hobbes proposed. Through their abilities to reason, men and women would understand that the lives and property of others should be respected. People would naturally understand that if they failed to respect the life and property of others, they could not expect others to respect their own lives and property. Locke thus proposed that the inefficient outcome of the prisoners' dilemma of anarchy would be avoided by mutual consent based on reason, although, like Hobbes, he did not formally set out the prisoners' dilemma.

For Locke, the natural right of a man and a woman to freedom superseded the authority of any government. Government was the creation of the people and should be subservient to the people, and not the other way around. Therefore, the authority of government rests in the people. Locke declared that "no government can have a right to obedience from a people that have not freely consented to it" (Locke, 1690/1960, II, paragraph 192). Political decision makers are therefore accountable to the people, and the people can remove and change their political decision makers at will, should the politicians "be so foolish, or so wicked, as to lay and carry on decisions against the liberties and the properties of the subject."[2]

---

[2] Locke did not propose one-person, one-vote democracy. He viewed owners of property as electing the government. In a society with concentrated wealth (and where wealth was for the most part land), one-person, one-vote democracy could result in appropriation of the property of the landed rich by the landless poor (see Chapter 6). Locke viewed the limitation of the right to vote to the landed classes as a means of protecting property rights. Locke believed that the landed rich would, by reason, ensure a benign and enlightened government that did not abuse individual freedom and that protected all people's rights of ownership.

A choice between order and freedom

Hobbes and Locke had different objectives in setting out their views of government. Hobbes viewed society as positioned on a scale from anarchy to order. Anarchy was undesirable, and authoritarian government would bring order. Locke viewed society on a scale from individual freedom to repression. The objective was freedom. The authority of government was therefore subjugated to the natural right of freedom of the individual, and ultimate authority rested with the individual, not with government.

Locke was correct if people cooperate spontaneously by natural reason to escape the prisoners' dilemma. Hobbes was correct if people do not cooperate voluntarily and cannot escape anarchy without government. If a broad basis for trust and cooperation can be established in a society, we have the means of substantiating Locke's position that collectively rational outcomes can be attained through individual reason without the coercion of government. Our question "how much government" is then answered with less government, in terms of the authority exercised by government.

9.2.2 Cooperation without government

The background for the contrasting positions of Hobbes and Locke is the anarchy that we considered in Chapter 1. We saw that a prisoners' dilemma can arise under conditions of anarchy, and that individual rationality does not solve the prisoners' dilemma; on the contrary, individual rationality gives rise to the dilemma.

The circumstances of the prisoners' dilemma extend beyond anarchy. We have seen that the prisoners' dilemma is involved in voluntary financing of public goods. Because many or most externalities have a public good nature, the prisoners' dilemma is also involved in the voluntary resolution of externalities. Voluntary income redistribution also has a public good dimension that involves the prisoners' dilemma. The problem facing political candidates who seek to win elections and do not wish to take money from special interests is also a case of the prisoners' dilemma.

Voluntary cooperation under the conditions of the prisoners' dilemma would accordingly resolve problems of anarchy, public goods, externalities, social justice, and political deviations from the public interest. There are a number of approaches to seeking voluntary cooperation to solve the prisoners' dilemma.

Credible commitment

Voluntary cooperation can be achieved in the prisoners' dilemma if people can make a credible commitment to cooperate.[3] A promise to cooperate can be made credible by introducing an additional benefit or cost that makes cooperation the best personal choice. An example of such an additionally imposed benefit or cost is

---

[3] It is not enough to promise to cooperate because cooperation is not rational behavior for an individual who confronts the prisoners' dilemma. A rational person will promise to cooperate, and then, when the time comes to act, will behave rationally to maximize personal benefit by not cooperating.

a penalty for not cooperating imposed by government, as we considered for solving the problem of anarchy in Chapter 1. Another solution to the prisoners' dilemma is enforcement by government of cooperation, as we considered for solving the problem of financing public goods through taxation in Chapter 2. Now, however, we are not looking to government to resolve the prisoners' dilemma. We are looking for voluntary cooperation without government.

A credible commitment to cooperate can take the form of individuals depositing a sum of money with an outside party. Any person who subsequently fails to keep the promise to cooperate loses the deposit. The amount of money deposited with the outside party needs, of course, to be greater than the gain that an individual has from not cooperating. In former times, cooperative outcomes were sustained along these lines by exchange of hostages or by strategic marriages. The hostages were in general never harmed. The purpose of the hostages was to introduce the potential for loss, so as to change incentives to make cooperation individually rational behavior.

"Exchange of hostages" or the holding of money by outside parties is not a practical means of enforcing voluntary cooperation among individuals in a modern society. Social interactions are too anonymous to be resolved by these types of schemes. Too many people are interacting with too many other people. Every person in a society would have to find a way of making a credible commitment to cooperate with every other person. The "outside party" required for this complex arrangement is suggestive of a government, and we are looking for alternatives to government.

Repeated encounters

Another approach to seeking voluntary cooperation is to recognize that the circumstances of the prisoners' dilemma may be recurring or repeated. We observed in Chapter 1 that, when interactions are continuously repeated over time, cooperation can be individually rational behavior. For example, consider two people who are obliged every day to make a decision whether to make personal contributions to finance supply of a public good. In this repeated game, the prisoners' dilemma game is played over and over again. Let us add the following conditions to the interaction between the two persons:

(1) The interaction is indefinitely repeated into the future.
(2) Individuals do not discount the future too much; that is, the future is relatively important for both persons.
(3) The identity of the persons who are involved in the interaction will forever remain the same, and the persons interacting under the conditions of the prisoners' dilemma know this.

Under these circumstances, rational individuals will cooperate. The escape from the prisoners' dilemma occurs because it is in the private self-interest of both individuals to have a reputation for cooperating. If each person knows that the other is a person who always cooperates, and if each person knows that the other person knows of his or her reputation for cooperating, then the reputation of each individual as cooperating leads the other to likewise cooperate. The outcome is mutual cooperation, and the prisoners' dilemma is solved.

The simultaneous presence of these three conditions is required to provide rational escape from the prisoners' dilemma. If conditions (1), (2), and (3) are not simultaneously satisfied, the quest to achieve a cooperative equilibrium entails each person setting out to convince the other that he or she is irrational. For it is irrational to cooperate under the conditions of the single-interaction prisoners' dilemma. Each of the three conditions has a role in ensuring cooperation in a repeated prisoners' dilemma.

We noted in Chapter 1 when the prisoners' dilemma was introduced in the context of anarchy that, if the number of interactions is finite, there is no value to reputation in the last interaction because there is no future interaction for which the reputation of being a person who cooperates is valuable. Therefore, cooperation does not take place in the last round of interaction. There is then no value to cooperation in the second last interaction, and so on, back to the first interaction. If people do not know the number of times interaction is to be repeated, the uncertainty about whether reputation has value reintroduces tendencies to cooperate because reputation may have future value.

The second condition for cooperation is that people sufficiently value benefits in the future relative to the present. An individual who sufficiently discounts the future does not care too much about the future consequence of present decisions. Because the gain from cooperation today is the reputation that has value tomorrow, a person for whom the future is not important has no reason to cooperate today to establish a reputation that provides benefits tomorrow. Thus "impatient" people who seek immediate gratification will not cooperate.

The third condition is that people know with whom they are interacting. If interactions are anonymous, there is no value to reputation from cooperating.

Incentives for cooperation to allow voluntary escape from the inefficient outcome of the prisoners' dilemma thus require a small group of people who know one another, who know that they know one another, and who know that they will meet one another in indefinite future interactions. However, a society consists of large numbers of anonymous people. It is the requirement that interactions not be anonymous that appears to be the main impediment to an outcome of voluntary cooperation.

Retaliation and reciprocity

Rational people who know one other and who care about the future should cooperate in an infinitely repeated nonanonymous prisoners' dilemma. Nonetheless, in interaction between two persons, one person might choose to behave opportunistically to benefit by free riding. A way of deterring such opportunistic behavior is a preannounced strategy known as tit-for-tat. This is a strategy where behavior is based on reciprocity. People continue to cooperate when others cooperate, but they retaliate by not cooperating if others behave opportunistically and choose to free ride. The retaliation can continue for a given number of future interactions. A preannouncement of tit-for-tat thus entails declaring: "If you behave opportunistically, I will do likewise, and for some time in the future." With future benefits sufficiently valued, the losses imposed by tit-for-tat make sustained cooperation an individually rational response.[4]

If tit-for-tat is to be an effective deterrent, individuals must know with whom they are interacting. Otherwise the threat of future punishment through tit-for-tat has no value. The enforcement of cooperation through tit-for-tat is thus based on the condition of nonanonymity in repeated interactions. The same people have to be involved because the retaliation has to be personal. Enforcement of voluntary cooperation through tit-for-tat thus appears appropriate for personal interactions but not for social interactions among a population of anonymous people. At the level of society, tit-for-tat therefore cannot solve the prisoners' dilemma.

Self-esteem

Contrary to Hobbes's view of the nature of men and women and contrary to the predictions of the prisoners' dilemma, anonymous people are observed to cooperate and to behave benevolently and in socially responsible ways. For example, people contribute to charity. They donate money to public radio and television. They do not litter. They do not exploit the weak and disadvantaged, even where exploitation would be anonymous and subject to neither punishment nor social chastisement. People vote. They join collective action groups that have broad social objectives such as protection of the environment. People overall appear to free ride less than the prisoners' dilemma predicts.

When independently choosing to cooperate in large anonymous populations, people are not attempting to acquire personal reputations nor are they seeking to impress others. We thus confront the puzzle that people act cooperatively in anonymous prisoners' dilemma encounters, whereas rationality suggests they should never choose to cooperate.

We might wish to explain such cooperative behavior as decisions by people who do not know what they are doing because they have not worked out the response that is in their best interest. There is indeed evidence that, in experiments conducted with students, those students who have been taught the elements of the prisoners' dilemma tend to cooperate less and free ride more than students to whom the prisoners' dilemma has not been explained. Nonetheless, with repeated encounters, we expect people to learn the response that is in their best personal interest, if they do not already know the rationally best response. So why are

---

[4] The purpose of tit-for-tat is to enforce cooperation. Nonetheless, suppose that one person at some point does not cooperate. After a response of noncooperation, the person who has been harmed by the opportunistic behavior might return to a strategy of cooperation. The return to cooperation signals a wish to attempt to try again to establish a cooperative relationship based on trust. The hope is that, in the course of the ongoing repeated interactions, the other person will come to understand that the best response is cooperation. A further opportunistic response by the other person should understandably diminish hopes of cooperative behavior.

rational informed people led to cooperate when the dominant strategy is to free ride? And, also, why do people need to have it explained to them that noncooperation is the best strategy?

One answer is that people choose not to free ride because of personal values and self-esteem. They may gain personal utility from being the type of people who cooperate and who do not take pleasure from personal gain at the expense of others, as was the case in Chapter 1 when we introduced personal ethical restraint as an alternative to the self-interest of the prisoners' dilemma. We saw that ethical restraint or self-esteem changes the structure of rewards so that maximal personal benefit is no longer obtained through free riding at the expense of others but is obtained by cooperating with others.[5]

Social approval

When personal values and self-esteem influence behavior, people may cooperate because of their feelings of self-esteem and honor *about* themselves. Cooperation can also result from people caring about how *others* perceive them because of social rewards from having a reputation as a cooperative or good-hearted person. People might then voluntarily and visibly contribute to public goods and to charity because of social approval.[6] Social rewards through the esteem of others also affect behavior in externality situations. People who care about social approval do not impose negative externalities on others.[7] Social approval and social rewards therefore foster voluntary cooperation when personal reputation matters. If social approval and social rewards are to be the basis for cooperative behavior, people cannot live in anonymous societies where no one knows who they are, or cares.

9.2.3 Reciprocating behavior

Independent Nash behavior supposes that people make decisions given the decisions made by others. Under Nash behavior, one person's decision does not influence other people's decisions within any one encounter (we saw that people can be influenced by each other's decisions over time in repeated encounters through reputation and through retaliation and reciprocity). Nash behavior underlies the Nash equilibrium of the prisoners' dilemma.

While Nash behavior supposes that individuals make personal decisions independently of the decisions of others, people might not act in this way and might

---

[5] Such a personal reward structure was present in Chapter 5 when we described people facing the decision whether to give charity for the needy. We saw that personal gratification from voluntary charity avoided the inefficiency that otherwise arose through free riding in the prisoners' dilemma.

[6] Social approval also changes the personal reward structure from that of the prisoners' dilemma. People derive benefit from being viewed favorably by others.

[7] See Chapter 4. People are sometimes embarrassed when they have been revealed to be the source of a negative externality. The embarrassment reflects concern for how others perceive them. If self-esteem were present, they would, however, have gone out of their way not to impose the negative externality on others in the first place.

rather consider how their decisions affect the behavior of others. That is, people might form an opinion about how others will react to their decisions and incorporate this *conjecture* about the behavior of others into their own calculations of how to behave. This departure from independent Nash behavior imputes a higher level of rationality to people. The high level of rationality takes the form of thinking about how others will respond to decisions and so not taking the decisions of others as given as in the Nash equilibrium.

When deciding whether or how to contribute to paying for a public good, a person might think along the following lines: "When I contribute, I subsidize the cost of a public good for others, who will themselves spend more on the public good, since their personal price has been reduced by my contribution." When each person conjectures in this way that an increase in his or her personal contributions will be matched by increased contributions of others, we can envisage the process of subsidization and reduction in cost shares continuing until the Lindahl efficient personal cost shares are attained and the efficient consensus Lindahl equilibrium is achieved. Even if the Lindahl outcome is not precisely achieved, the belief that others will match increased contributions, and the behavior of others in confirming this belief, increases voluntary cooperation.

9.2.4 Social norms and trust

The preceding matching-type behavior requires a substantiated belief that others respond to our increased personal contributions by giving more. We would want to be certain that others will respond to our increased contributions by matching our increased contributions. Otherwise, we are paying more through our increased contributions for the benefit of free riders. We will have placed ourselves in a position of subsidizing others who do not reciprocally subsidize us as we thought they would, or as we trusted them to do.

It is important that people believe that their trust will be substantiated. Whether trust is substantiated depends on the expectations that people have of one another. The expectations are part of social norms of behavior. If the social norm is benevolent reciprocity and people follow the social norm, trust is substantiated.[8]

When social norms substantiate trust, it makes no difference with whom a person interacts. Cooperation can then be sustained in large anonymous populations. A cooperative outcome occurs without reliance on personal reputation. The social norm has replaced personal reputation as the basis for cooperation.

People do not like to feel that they have been exploited or made fools of. A person who cooperates because of personal values and a belief that social norms will result in reciprocal cooperation can be expected to cease behaving cooperatively, if the behavior of others is opportunistic and exploitative. We can consider an individual who has moved from a society where the social norm is to cooperate

---

[8] That is, if people follow the rule in their personal behavior of not behaving toward others in ways that that they would not want others to behave toward them, they cooperate rather than seek to behave opportunistically.

to a society where the social norm is to be opportunistic. Such an individual will have become accustomed to cooperating but can be expected quickly to cease to trust others and to cease to cooperate in the society where behavior with the intent of exploitation is the social norm.

In other circumstances, an individual from a society where free riding and intent of exploitation are part of the social norm of behavior can arrive in a society where benevolent cooperation is the social norm. The new arrival may then adapt personal behavior to the new benevolent social norm.

The new arrival could, however, maintain old habits of noncooperative opportunistic behavior. With enough new arrivals, a population might become divided with significant numbers of opportunistic individuals as well as persons who are trustworthy and trusting. What can we expect to be the outcome when the two types of people meet and interact with each other randomly over time and there are no means of identifying people as benevolent or opportunistic?

Opportunistic individuals benefit whenever they encounter a trusting person because they exploit the trusting person. After a sufficient number of bad experiences, the trusting person might cease to be trusting and, for example, might no longer believe promises or accept credit cards or personal checks in payment. The cost of economic activity in markets then increases because the *public good* of trust dissipates, and distrust displaces trust.

Personal feelings of self-esteem about being a cooperative person can consequently be overtaken by personal feelings of exasperation and exploitation. When sufficient numbers of people who formerly had a trusting nature cease trusting others, new social norms of opportunistic behavior can replace the former norms of trust and trustworthiness. The rule of reciprocity of "do unto others" is applied in personal behavior under the new social norm of opportunism. If the number of exploitative people is small, the social norm of benevolent cooperation may persist, with disappointments for those trusting people who are unlucky enough to encounter exploitative persons.

A society with a social norm of trust and trustworthiness will be better off than a society where the social norm is distrust and opportunism. The population of trustworthy people will benefit from the benevolent cooperative outcomes of voluntary actions. The population in a society with social norms of distrust and opportunism lives, on the other hand, in a milieu of cynicism and mutual suspicion.

An experiment with trust

Evidence on trust in a population is available from the following experiment. Two mutually anonymous people are placed in two separate rooms. Neither one knows who the other is, nor will they ever know.

Person 1 is given a sum of money, say $100. Person 1 can either keep the money or give the money to person 2. Any transfer of money takes place through an intermediary to preserve anonymity.

If person 1 transfers the $100 to person 2, the $100 is multiplied to become $300 in the hands of person 2.

Person 2 who has received the money can decide to keep the entire $300 or to give some money back to person 1. Both persons know the rules of the game.

The transfer by person 1 to person 2 increases the mutual wealth of the two persons. A redistribution of the $300 can make both persons better off.

Whether person 1 decides to make the initial wealth-increasing transfer will reflect whether there are expectations of reciprocating behavior. The expectations derive from the social norms of the society. If person 1 believes that it is reasonable that person 2 will reciprocate, he or she will make the transfer. If person 1 believes that it is reasonable that person 2 will not make a reciprocal transfer, the initial wealth-increasing transfer will not take place.

Person 1's beliefs will reflect the experiences that he or she has had. In a society where social norms are consistent with a belief in reciprocal benevolent behavior, person 1 will make the transfer to person 2, and, if the expectation of reciprocity is substantiated, person 2 will act benevolently and cooperatively (even though anonymously) and share the gains with person 1.[9]

Person 2 has no strategic decision to make because person 2's decision evokes no response and concludes the game. Nonetheless, person 2 has an ethical decision to make if he or she receives the $300. Person 2 can decide to take the entire $300 and leave the scene (anonymously) or return money to person 1.

If person 2's actions are influenced by a conception of fairness, we would expect person 2 to give at least $100 to person 1. Person 2 might give person 1 $150, which is an equal sharing of the $300 now available in total. Or perhaps person 2 might give $200, keeping $100, in which case person 2 returns the original $100, and equally shares the $200 increase in mutual wealth from person 1's decision to trust him or her.

Person 1 is in a situation of having to decide whether to trust an anonymous stranger. Whether person 2 behaves in a trustworthy or in an opportunistic way affects person 1's perceptions of social norms and affects future behavior.

A society in which there is sufficient trust for the wealth-increasing transfer to be made will be better off than a society where the initial transfer is not made. Trust is substantiated and reinforced if the transfer is made and person 2 returns a reasonable sum of money to person 1.

Distrust and the segmentation of society

We have observed that when opportunistic people dominate a population, people who are trusting by nature and are themselves trustworthy will tend to cease trusting others (and perhaps cease being trustworthy) in anonymous interactions. Trust

---

[9] Person 1 makes his or her decision by comparing the utility of $100, which is obtained with certainty by not making the transfer to person 2, with the expected utility from transferring the $100 to person 2. This expected utility is based on the amount R that person 1 believes that person 2 will return, where R is a value between zero and $300. Person 1's decision will also depend upon aversion to risk. The more averse he or she is to risk, the greater the expected value of R that will be required for person 1 to decide in favor of making the transfer to person 2.

TABLE 9.2. TRUST		
	Person 2 trusts	Person 2 does not trust
Person 1 trusts	10, 10	−8, 8
Person 1 does not trust	8, −8	0, 0

can, however, be sustained in small groups where reputations can be established and disciplining can take place. Trust may then not extend beyond the immediate or extended family. Secret (or not so secret) subsocieties may form with members who have special bonds or ties that ensure cooperation, and among whom the means exist for discipline or punishment for opportunistic behavior. The special bond that underlies cooperation within the group may be common original location or common ethnic background. Society then becomes segmented. Moreover, the segmentation is into groups that do not trust one another.

In these circumstances, groups of mutually trusting people will tend to become wealthier than the general population that is caught in a milieu of distrust. The persons within the groups where there is mutual trust will have lower transactions costs of doing business with one another. Their "word" will carry weight to allow business transactions to be completed without costly precautions against opportunistic behavior. The people whose norms permit sustained mutual trust provide economic benefits for the whole of society because their lower transactions costs reduce costs of supply. Without the presence of the mutually trusting group, transactions costs may be too high to permit markets to operate.[10]

Table 9.2 shows the strategic interaction between two people who face a decision whether or nor to trust one other in a market transaction. With mutual trust, the transaction goes ahead, and the efficient outcome is achieved with a benefit of 10 for each person. With mutual distrust, the transaction does not take place, and each person has zero.

If one person trusts the other, but the trust is not reciprocated, the person who has been trusting loses 8, which is the gain to the distrusting person. The interaction is in that case zero-sum, that is, one person's gain is the other person's loss (the sum of 8 and minus 8 is zero).

When there is mutual trust, the interaction is positive-sum (the interaction provides mutual benefit of 10 and a positive total benefit of 20). The best outcomes for both persons are obtained when there is mutual trust.[11]

---

[10] History provides examples where the mutually trusting and therefore successful group is expelled or suffers appropriation or destruction of property. When this has happened, markets have often ceased to function with the remaining society going into decline.

[11] In contrast, in the prisoners' dilemma, personally best outcomes are obtained by free riding when the other person acts benevolently.

TABLE 9.3. TRUST AND HONESTY		
	Person 2 transacts	Person 2 does not transact
Person 1 acts honestly	10, 10	0, 0
Person 1 acts dishonestly	x, −200	0, 0

There are two Nash equilibria in Table 9.2, at (10, 10) and (0,0). In the first Nash equilibrium, there is mutual trust; in the second, there is mutual distrust.[12]

A Nash equilibrium supposes that decisions are made taking the decisions of others as given. Higher rationality might lead both people in Table 9.2 to trust one another. Higher rationality could lead the two people, both making independent decisions, to coordinate their actions based on the common knowledge of mutual gain from mutual trust.

Lack of trust when people can identify one another
The interaction described in Table 9.2 takes place once and is anonymous. The people do not know one another, and there is no role for personal reputation.

Let us change the circumstances to a situation where person 1 and person 2 can identify one another. They may not know one another personally, but they know the group identity of the other.

Suppose that, if the two people are from the same group, they mutually trust one another, but, if from different groups, they mutually distrust one another. When the two people are from the same group, the outcome is therefore the "good" equilibrium with mutual benefit. When the two people are not from the same group, the outcome is the "bad" equilibrium with zero benefit to both. The mutual distrust has prevented both persons from gaining from cooperation.

Trust and honesty
Table 9.3 shows a situation where person 2 faces a decision whether or not to transact with person 1. By not transacting, person 2 loses nothing and gains nothing. Person 1 also then has no gain or loss.

Person 2 believes that person 1 will act dishonestly, if acting dishonestly will provide greater gains to person 1 than acting honestly. If person 2 transacts and person 1 acts dishonestly, person 2 loses 200.

Person 2's decision whether to transact depends on person 2's belief about the gain x to person 1 if person 1 acts dishonestly and the transaction takes place. Person 2 does not know the value of x, but person 1 does (there is asymmetric

---

[12] When there is mutual distrust, a change of mind by one person to trust the other results in a loss of 8, and so staying at (0,0) is a Nash equilibrium. (10.10) is a Nash equilibrium because both persons receive their highest returns.

information). Person 1 cannot credibly communicate the value of x to person 2, nor credibly misconstrue the value of x.

Person 2 however knows his or her own loss if the transaction takes place and person 1 acts dishonestly (i.e., 200). Person 2 might judge the value of the gain x to person 1 if the transaction takes place and person 1 is dishonest as also around 200. It is sufficient for person 2 to believe that x exceeds 10 for the transaction not to take place.

If person 2 believes that person 1 will act dishonestly if it is in person 1's interest to do so, person 2 does not trust person 1. Person 2 may not trust person 1 because of previous unfortunate experiences when person 2 did trust person 1. In that case, person 1 and person 2 know one another. Alternatively, person 1 and person 2 may belong to identifiable groups that have a history of mistrust. Whichever is the case, with the transaction not taking place, the benefits of market exchange are lost, just as the benefits of market exchange are lost when the rule of law does not exist to certify property rights. The benefits of market exchange require trust to have been established.

We can make two final observations on trust and honesty. It is difficult or impossible to establish trust so long as there is no history of transactions with honest behavior. As long as person 2 decides not to transact, there will no transactions on which to base trust, if person 1 is trustworthy. Second, Hobbes might have been right, if not about human nature in general, then at least about the nature of some people. There may be a history of prior transactions between person 2 and person 1. If person 2 has had a history of bad experiences when seeking to transact with person 1 (person 2 may have unsuccessfully tried tit-for-tat as a means of establishing repeated cooperation), person 2 will look for other people with whom to transact.

9.2.5 Conclusions

We began this section by noting the different positions taken by Hobbes and Locke about the nature of people and the consequences for the nature of government. Hobbes was pessimistic about the ability of a society to function in a civilized way without the imposed order of government and proposed that people should rationally forgo their individual freedom to achieve security and protection from anarchy through imposed order. Locke viewed government as accountable to the people, and the source of authority as residing in the people themselves. Locke's position was based on a view that people naturally understand the benefits from cooperation, and that, as rational beings, people therefore act benevolently and honestly toward one another without imposed order.

We have compared the positions taken by Hobbes and Locke by looking at the prospects for voluntary cooperation in the prisoners' dilemma. Different approaches to seeking rational voluntary cooperation in the prisoners' dilemma are (1) the possibility of credible personal commitment, (2) incentives in repeated interactions, and (3) matching-type behavior that is based on reciprocity. These means of achieving voluntary cooperation all require that individuals value their personal reputations in future interactions with the same people, which cannot be the basis for voluntary cooperation in large anonymous populations.

We have considered social norms as the basis for cooperation and trust in large anonymous populations. Cooperation takes place when behavior is guided by social norms that reflect underlying personal values of self-esteem in not being the type of person who takes pleasure in exploiting or disappointing others. However, if a population contains sufficient numbers of opportunistic people whose self-esteem is not based on the self-perception of being a cooperating benevolent and honest person, social norms of trust and cooperation can be displaced by norms of distrust and failure to cooperate. We also considered an experiment designed to reveal the extent of trust and cooperation in a society. We looked at types of interactions involving trust and saw that the presence of trust determines whether the benefits from cooperation are realized.

Trust is a substitute for government. When Locke is correct, less government is required then when Hobbes is correct.

We can conclude that, where trust is lacking in a society, Hobbes was correct in his predictions about the inability of people to cooperate for their own good and the need for the authority of government that imposes order on the population. Locke's prediction about the ability of people to cooperate for mutual benefit is correct when people in an anonymous population are trusting when, at the same time, social norms result in reciprocating behavior that confirms others are worthy of trust. Of course, if Hobbes were correct that, because of the nature of people, trust cannot be relied upon and the imposed order of government is required, government itself needs to be honest and trustworthy.

References and related literature

On Hobbes and Locke, see Hobbs (1651/1962), Locke (1690/1960), and Rowley (2001). On voluntary cooperation, see Axelrod (1984), Kreps et al. (1982), Hollander (1990), Ockenfels (1993), Fehr and Gächter (2000), Guttman (2000), and Shilony (2000). On cooperation and common identity, see Grief (1994). On self-identity and behavior, see Akerlof and Kranton (2000). Experimental evidence on voluntary supply of public goods is reviewed by Ledyard (1995).

Akerlof, G. A. and R. E. Kranton, 2000. Economics and identity. *Quarterly Journal of Economics* 115, 715–53.
Axelrod, R., 1984. *The Evolution of Cooperation*. Basic Books, New York.
Fehr, E. and S. Gächter, 2000. Fairness and retaliation: The economics of reciprocity. *Journal of Economic Perspectives* 14, 159–81.
Grief, A., 1994. Cultural beliefs and the organization of society: A historical and theoretical reflection on collectivist and individualistic societies. *Journal of Political Economy* 102, 912–50.

Guttman, J. M., 2000. On the evolutionary stability of preferences for reciprocity. *European Journal of Political Economy* 16, 31–50.

Hobbs, T., (1651) 1962. *Leviathan (or the Matter, Forme and Power of a Commonwealth Ecclesiastical and Civil)*. Collier Books, New York.

Hollander, H., 1990. A social exchange approach to voluntary cooperation. *American Economic Review* 80, 1157–67.

Kreps, D., P. Milgrom, J. Roberts and R. Wilson, 1982. Rational cooperation in the finitely repeated prisoners' dilemma. *Journal of Economic Theory* 27, 245–52.

Ledyard, J., 1995. Public goods: A survey of experimental research. In *Handbook of Experimental Economics*, A. Roth and J. Kagel (eds.). Princeton University Press, Princeton, New Jersey, 111–94.

Locke, J., 1960 (1690). *Two Treatises of Government*, P. Lazlett (ed.). Cambridge University Press, Cambridge.

Ockenfels, P., 1993. Cooperation in prisoners' dilemma. *European Journal of Political Economy* 9, 567–79.

Rowley, C. K., 2001. Constitutional political economy and civil society. In *Rules and Reason: Perspectives on Constitutional Political Economy*, R. Mudambi, P. Navarra, and G. Sobbrio (eds.). Cambridge University Press, New York, 69–96.

Shilony, Y., 2000. Diversity and ingenuity in voluntary collective action. *European Journal of Political Economy* 16, 429–43.

Questions for discussion

1. How do the views of Thomas Hobbes and John Locke indicate opposing conceptions of the nature of people? How do the views of the nature of people affect views regarding the required nature of government?

2. Where does majority voting fall in the categorization of the alternative views presented by Hobbes and Locke?

3. With which view do you have more sympathy, that of Hobbes or Locke? Is your answer consistent with the view you would prefer were correct? Explain.

4. In repeated interactions of the prisoners' dilemma, under what conditions can cooperation emerge without government? What are the limitations on such cooperation emerging spontaneously in a large society of anonymous people?

5. How does the idea of reciprocating behavior differ from the idea of Nash behavior?

6. How can self-esteem and social approval diminish or eliminate the need for government to act to enforce socially beneficial outcomes?

7. What do you expect to be the outcome when people who behave opportunistically for personal gain whenever possible join a population of people that has behaved according to a social (and ethical) norm of trust and cooperation?

8. In the circumstances described in question 7, what do you expect to happen if the new arrivals are trustworthy but have become accustomed through experiences elsewhere to not trusting other people?

9. Recall the experiment about trust. Suppose that you knew that you were "playing" the game with one of the twenty people you know best (but you do not know with which one.) If you were the person initially receiving the money, would you transfer the money you have received to the anonymous other person? Why? If your role in

the game was to await possible transfer of the money, do you believe that the money would be given to you? Why?

10. In the situation in question 9, if you were to receive the money, would you return some part (remember that your behavior is completely anonymous)? How much money would you return? Suppose that you were playing the game with an anonymous stranger whom you have never met and not with one of the twenty people whom you know best. Would your decision about returning part of the money change? Explain. How do your answers reflect self-esteem and social norms?

11. Look again at Table 9.2. There are mutual benefits in this game from coordination where both people trust one another. There are two Nash equilibria, one where people trust one another and another where neither trusts the other. What is the difference between this game and the prisoners' dilemma in terms of incentives for cooperation? If decisions were made sequentially in Table 9.2 and person 1 decided first, what would you expect person 2 to do? Why?

12. In Table 9.2, would you expect social norms to sustain the efficient outcome of mutual trust in large anonymous populations? Explain.

13. In Table 9.2, what is the outcome if person 1 trusts person 2, but person 2 does not trust person 1, and person 1 knows that he or she is not trusted by person 2?

14. How does Table 9.3 explain social segmentation?

15. How do social norms and attitudes toward cooperation and trust affect the scope of the responsibilities of government, or the answer to the question "how much government"?

9.3

Growth of Government and Constitutional Restraint

9.3.1 Autocratic societies

At the beginning of the nineteenth century, public finance and public policy played a small and insignificant role in most people's lives. By the beginning of the twenty-first century, public-finance and public-policy decisions of government had an extensive influence on individuals' lives.

Let us return in time to a society with no taxation. There is then also no government borrowing from the public because no future taxes can be imposed to repay government borrowing. Without taxation or government borrowing, what sort of society would we expect?

Income sources for the rulers

If a society is agrarian, income comes primarily from agriculture. A king or queen, or a few noble families, might own most of the land. With no taxes available, the ruler might obtain revenue by selling the right to be a monopolist in different goods and services to private persons. The ruler would restrict entry of foreign goods into the country because the foreign goods might compromise not just the ruler's monopoly on produce from land but also the value of the monopoly rights that the ruler is selling.

The ruler might want to sell part of his produce to foreigners in exchange for gold or silver. The gold or silver would provide the ruler with revenue, which could be used to pay for external and internal security. The gold or silver could also be used to feed, clothe, and provide weapons for an army, which could attack neighboring rulers to take their land and thereby increase the income available from the ruler's ownership of land. The ruler might borrow from private bankers to finance wars, with the repayments of the debt anticipated to be financed from successful acquisition of new assets (if the ruler loses the war, the banker might experience difficulty in obtaining repayment of the debt).[1]

The system of thinking wherein exports provide increased wealth, whereas imports are a waste of wealth through payments made to foreigners, is known as *mercantilism*. When all rulers want to sell and no ruler wants to buy, market exchange does not take place, and the gains from market exchange are lost. Mercantilism was the economic ideology that Adam Smith sought to displace in his focus on markets and the invisible hand in his reinterpretation of the sources that provide the "wealth of nations." Adam Smith proposed the invisible hand of the market as a preferred alternative to the hand of the ruler and explained how the spontaneous order of the market was more effective in providing benefit to a population than the attempts of the ruler to horde gold and silver by selling and not buying. In a market, personal benefit comes from buying, not selling.

The only taxes that the ruler might be able to levy are import duties, which can provide revenue but could be intended to keep foreign goods out of the country. Excise taxes might also be levied on tea, sugar, and salt and other spices.

The mercantilist ruler might establish foreign colonies to expand the scope of control over land and resources. The colonies can be taxed. The American Revolution against colonial rule began with the principle of "no taxation without representation" and with the dumping into Boston harbor of tea that the foreign ruler of the colony wished to tax.

Spending

The rulers have personal incentives to provide the public good of defense to protect themselves and their property against external threat. The rulers also have incentives to provide internal security to protect their property. Public goods are, for the ruler, private goods. The ruler needs roads to move not just produce but also soldiers in the event of revolt or foreign invasion. The ruler would be expected to

---

[1] There is also the risk that, because the ruler is sovereign and above the law (there is the rule of man or woman, and not the rule of law), the ruler might simply decide not to repay. With the ruler in control without the rule of law, the ruler might then experience difficulty in obtaining voluntary loans.

internalize all externalities. A ruler who is charitable would also provide income to people who are incapacitated or old and cannot work. Efficiency and social justice are personal problems for the ruler. Such an all-encompassing ruler who is benevolent and for whom social problems are personal problems is perhaps the ruler that Hobbes had in mind when he recommended voluntary subjugation to his proposed leviathan.

9.3.2 The growth of government

After democratic government displaces absolute rulers, decisions about taxation and public finance became collective decisions, in principle made by taxpayers and in practice, where there is not direct democracy, made by elected representatives.

When the mercantilist rulers first departed, the size of government as measured by taxation and public finance was small. Long-distance roads and canals were principally private, with access to use requiring payment of user prices. The private roads and canals to transport goods were supplemented by private railroads (or railways). Travel by sea was the main means of long-distance travel and took place in privately owned ships. As we noted when considering public goods, lighthouses were also privately constructed.

The industrial revolution and the new middle class

The industrial revolution ended the idea that the source of wealth is primarily land. Energy from steam replaced animal, human, and natural energy (wind in windmills and sails of ships) in production and transportation. Wealth became dispersed among a nouveau-rich middle-income population. The new middle-class population demanded the right to vote if they were going to be taxed. The industrial revolution and the expansion of the right to vote (first to men, and in most cases only later to women) began a process of growth of government and public finance.

Increasing incomes and the demand for public goods

As incomes increased, people wanted more publicly financed public goods, as well as public policies to resolve externalities with public-good components. Publicly financed law and order were provided. Public roads were built. Children were sent to school in publicly financed schools. Government attended to environmental and public-health externalities. For considerable periods of time, gullible people could be sold snake oil and other "medications" as the cure for all their ailments, but government eventually intervened to regulate pharmaceuticals, medicines, and drugs (but not all drugs, and for some time not the nicotine of cigarettes).

Government grew when people sought social insurance. Higher incomes and wealth meant that there was more to insure against because of the greater relative personal loss of having little or nothing in a wealthy society. We have seen that income transfers to the poor and disadvantaged can be viewed as a public good, and perhaps government grew because people wanted more social equality (a public good) as society became richer.[2]

Demographics and health

The growth of government was also influenced by demographics and health. Improvements in medicine resulted in people living longer. Alzheimer's disease and cancer were less of a problem when people died of infections from a small scratch or as the result of a complication from a throat infection because antiseptics and antibiotics were yet not available. The increasing numbers of people who survived to reach retirement placed demands on government to ensure that old people could live with dignity. Health costs also increased as people lived longer, increasing demands for public finance for health-care entitlements for older people.

The extension of the franchise to women

We observed in Chapter 6 that studies show the right to vote by women increased the size of government. Women in general sought more social insurance than men because of the risk that through either death or desertion they would be left without their partners to care for children.

Expanded taxation opportunities

Expanded taxation opportunities contributed to the growth of government. The growth of incomes provided new and expanding forms of taxation. With economic growth taking place, lower-income people came to have above-subsistence income surpluses that could be taxed.

Increased market activity also expanded tax bases. Whereas previously people had lived self-sufficient lives, they now provided for themselves and their families through extensive taxable market transactions.

Advances in transportation and communication expanded tax revenue by allowing people to be taxed who had previously been out of reach or sight of the government's tax collectors.

Majority voting

Majority voting itself affected the growth of government. When a minority pays a substantial part of the taxes, the majority that can decide on public spending has an incentive to vote for more public finance, and taxation and public sending increase.

Political principal-agent problems

Political principal-agent problems also affect growth of government. With growth of incomes, people became more specialized in how they earned their incomes. Individuals no longer are self-sufficient on isolated farms and in isolated villages.

---

[2] Government grew the most where the paternalistic entitlements were greatest, as in welfare states of Europe that provided life-long "social protection."

Through markets, they specialize in doing what they do best to earn incomes, which in turn are spent through markets to diversify consumption. Adam Smith called this increased specialization "the division of labor." The personal specialization or division of labor was the basis for formation of special-interest groups seeking favors from political decision makers. As specialization grew, the demand and the ability to influence government increased as more special-interest groups appeared with common specialized incomes that could be increased by public policy. At the same time, because of the need for political financing, politicians and political candidates were willing to accept special-interest money.[3]

The principal-agent problem between taxpayers and government bureaucracies also introduced tendencies for increases in the size of government, through personal benefit in government bureaucracies from increases in public spending.[4]

9.3.3 Measuring the size of government

There are a number of approaches to measuring the size of government. One approach looks at the share of taxes or public spending in national income. However, such a measure provides only a lower bound to the size of government. Tax revenue and public spending do not fully indicate the involvement of government in a society. For example, a high tax can decrease economic activity in a market and provide little tax revenue.

A more accurate measure of government involvement than tax revenue and public spending is the excess burden of taxation. The excess burden of taxation remains positive and increases, even as increased taxes reduce or eventually eliminate tax revenue. The excess burden of taxation is, however, not readily observable. As we have previously noted, the excess burden is invisible, and there are measurement problems in evaluating excess burdens of taxation.

A measure of the size of government includes the value of the national debt (or government bonds outstanding). By including the national debt in the size of government, we account for past government spending for which taxation was deferred to the future.

A measure of the size of government includes public policies, as well as public ownership. A measure of the size of government should include indicators of personal freedom. Indicators are also required that reveal political and bureaucratic culture that in turn determine the scope of rent-seeking activity and the social losses due to rent seeking. Where there is corruption in government, a measure of the size of government should include the consequences of corrupt government.

---

[3] A counter to demand for special-interest benefits because of specialization in personal income sources is increased diversification in sources of personal income. As societies become wealthier, people diversify their income sources through asset diversification. If all individuals' sources of income were diversified to match the sources of a society's total income, everyone would only want the efficient policies from government that maximize a society's total income or wealth.

[4] We can think about taxation and public spending in a society where the majority of voters are government employees who derive their salaries and incomes from tax-financed public spending.

The different ways in which government affects economic activity and economic decisions make designing a comprehensive and inclusive measure of the size of government a complex undertaking. Because of the complexities, an approximation that is often used for measurement of the size of government is the relation between national income and public spending or taxation.

9.3.4 Social benefit and the growth of government

Table 9.4 shows public spending in the years 1960 and 1990 as a proportion of gross national product for three groups of countries that respectively had large, medium, and small sizes of government in 1990. For each group of countries, the size of government increased between 1960 and 1990.

Values for consumption in Table 9.4 show government spending on itself. Included is the financing of the government bureaucracy and the general expenses of government. We see that consumption by government increased for all groups of countries (as a proportion of gross national product).

Transfers and subsidies in Table 9.4 are publicly financed payments made by governments to redistribute income. We see that government spending on transfers and subsidies increased substantially (as a proportion of gross national product) in all three groups of countries.

Interest in Table 9.4 is the payment made by government to meet spending obligations due to government borrowing (or bond financing of government spending). We see that interest payments increased substantially.

TABLE 9.4. SIZE OF GOVERNMENT AND SPENDING

	Large governments[a]		Medium governments[b]		Small governments[c]	
	1960	1990	1960	1990	1960	1990
Government spending	31.0	55.1	29.3	44.9	23.0	34.6
Consumption	13.2	18.9	12.2	17.4	12.2	17.4
Transfers and subsidies	11.9	30.6	10.4	21.5	6.9	14.0
Interest	1.5	6.4	1.3	4.2	1.3	2.9
Investment	3.1	2.4	3.2	2.0	2.2	2.2

[a] Large governments are those for which public spending was more than 50 percent of gross national product in 1990 (Belgium, Italy, the Netherlands, Norway, Sweden).
[b] Medium-sized governments had public spending between 40 and 50 percent of gross national product in 1990 (Austria, Canada, France, Germany, Ireland, New Zealand, Spain).
[c] Small governments had public spending less than 40 percent of gross national product in 1990 (Australia, Switzerland, United Kingdom, United States).
Source: Tanzi and Schuknecht (2000).

Public investment in Table 9.4 indicates spending for infrastructure and projects that we associate with public goods. We see that public investment was a relatively small part of public spending. This category of spending declined for large and medium-sized governments and remained constant for small governments.

We conclude from Table 9.4 that substantial increases took place in the size of government in the latter half of the twentieth century, and that the primary components of these increases were government spending on itself (government consumption), spending for the purposes of income redistribution (transfers and subsidies), and interest payments on government debt. The public investment that we would associate with public goods was small and declined rather than grew.

The small and declining public investment for public goods and infrastructure indicates that the increased interest payments were for borrowing to finance public consumption, transfers and subsidies, and intergenerational transfers and not for financing increased public investment.

Government consumption can grow without benefit to taxpayers. Transfers and subsidies are part of a social insurance contract; however, because social-insurance payments can be subject to moral hazard, adverse selection, and inability to observe or verify outcomes, not all transfer payments need be socially beneficial. Publicly financed transfer payments and subsidies can also be the consequence of public policies introduced for reasons of political benefit from responding to special-interest groups rather than broad social benefit. Major parts of the growth of government do not appear to have any particular social benefit.[5]

Zero-based government budgets

To evaluate the benefits from the growth of government, we should conduct detailed cost-benefit analysis of all taxation and public spending. Obtaining the information for cost-benefit analysis requires zero-based government budgeting. Under zero-based budgeting, the costs and benefits of government spending are evaluated beginning with the first dollar of spending.[6]

The benefits from the growth of government and the nature of government

The nature of government affects the benefits from the growth of government. When political decision makers choose only policies in the public interest, and

---

[5] Table 9.4 provides general indications of how government has grown. More in-depth statistical evidence is available. See the comprehensive study by Tanzi and Schuknecht (2000) from which Table 9.4 is taken.

[6] Such zero-based procedures are generally not used to justify public spending. If cost-benefit calculations are made at all for government spending, the calculations are often for justification for a proposed increase in the budget of a government department or agency. For example, if a government department wants another deputy director and four additional secretarial staff, the cost-benefit calculation focuses on whether the benefits of the increased number of government employees exceed the costs, and not on whether the ongoing public financing of the preexisting government employees is justified. Under zero-based budgeting, justifications for public finance are made inclusive of all taxation and spending whenever a new government budget is proposed.

when government officials behave as the dedicated bureaucrats described by Max Weber, we have cause for optimism about benefits from the growth of government. Growth of government then can reflect additional beneficial government responsibilities. Principal-agent problems between politicians and taxpayers, and between government bureaucracy and taxpayers, introduce caution in attributing social benefits from growth of government.

9.3.5 Constitutional restraint on government

Political principal-agent problems return us to Hobbes and Locke. We left the comparison between Hobbes and Locke at the end of Section 9.2 noting that Hobbes's case for rule through imposed order requires an assurance that the authority of government will be in the hands of benevolent persons who seek the best for society. If people are, as Hobbes believed, in need of protection from one other, a problem arises when people in government are drawn from the same population whom Hobbes viewed as self-serving and untrustworthy. The people in government may have the same "base and evil instincts" as the rest of the population.

A solution to Hobbes' problem is the Thomas-à-Beckett effect. That is, as did Thomas-à-Beckett, the people who enter government leave their personal self-interest behind and become altruistic and pursue only the public interest. On the other hand, the Thomas-à-Beckett effect may not offer protection from personal self-interest exercised through the authority of government.

Hobbes's absolute ruler who owns everything and everybody has an incentive to ensure that society's resources are efficiently used, and so, by self-interest, would seek to make efficient decisions. Markets would, however, need to be present to reveal the information on which efficient decisions are based. The decisions in markets are made by individual buyers and sellers, and are not centralized. Markets require and provide individual freedom that will not be consistent with absolute rule. Markets also require private ownership, which contradicts the absolute ruler's owning everything. It is doubtful that Hobbes' absolute ruler could preside over an efficient society. There is also no assurance that Hobbes' leviathan ruler (whose authority cannot be challenged) will be socially just. Historical precedents, as well as more contemporary examples, provide cases where people exercising absolute authority of government have cared little for social justice and personal freedom of the population.

Since, in the end, the imposed order on which Hobbes would rely can only be provided by members of the same population of people whose self-serving instincts society is seeking to escape, how can a society ensure that government will be benevolent? This question applies to government under the conception not only of Hobbes but also of Locke.

Locke's government, which represents the people and can be recalled by the will of the people, is subject to the principal-agent problems between voters and elected representatives and bureaucracy. The principal-agent problems restrict the accountability of government to the people. That is, while government is in principle accountable to the people as Locke wished, society still confronts the question of how in practice to ensure accountability of government. In particular, if growth of government is not beneficial for society, how can society protect itself from growth of government?

A constitution

Restraint on growth of government, and on the decisions of government, is provided by a constitution. The constitution defines what people in government can and cannot do. Most fundamentally, a constitution protects people from the monopoly on legal coercion through the ability to tax that is in the hands of government. A constitution also protects the rights of a minority by limiting adverse outcomes allowable through majority voting. The constitution overrides the authority of government by subjecting people in government to rules of behavior, just as government itself sets rules of behavior for the population. A field of political economy known as *constitutional economics* studies the design and choice of mechanisms of constitutional restraint on government.

A constitution is the first part of a two-stage collective decision-making process. The rules that restrain the actions and decisions of government are designated in the constitutional or first stage of collective decision making. After the scope of permissible behavior of governments has been designated by the constitution, political decision makers can in the second stage choose from among alternatives allowed by the constitution. The constitution is intended to ensure benevolent and honest government by disallowing opportunistic behavior by bureaucratic and political decision makers in the second stage of government decision making.

The requirements for changing constitutions are more stringent than for changing the second-stage government decisions and laws. There is greater permanence or stability in the constitutional phase of decision making. The constitution protects people from government, and the constitution is itself protected from government. Constitutional amendments are made when new circumstances arise or fundamental values of a society change.[7]

Time-distancing of constitutional choice

A constitution should be free of personal self-interest. Yet, because a constitution is designed by people, a society confronts the same dilemma that would confront Hobbes regarding the honesty and integrity of his absolute leviathan ruler. How can a society ensure that the designers of the constitution will be forthright and honest and place the public interest before their personal self-interest?

A solution is time-distancing of constitutional choice. That is, the constitution should not come into effect until some distant time in the future. The distancing in time before implementation of a constitution is intended to ensure that present self-interest of the designers of the constitution does not enter into the

---

[7] For example, the U.S. constitution as originally formulated permitted slavery.

constitution. The expectation is that people who self-interestedly control present government will recognize the benefits to future generations from the limitations on political discretion imposed by the constitution and will agree to the introduction of the constitution to restrain government in the future. The same people may not be willing to support implementation of the constitution during their own period of tenure in government office or during any future period when they might conceivably be in office. Separation in time between the formulation and application of the constitution thus protects the virtue of the constitution, by separating the constitution in time from present-day personal and political interests.

The constitution will bind on future generations, for whom the constitution is predetermined (including rules for making amendments to the constitution). Ideally, a constitution should have the characteristic that, if unborn generations could have participated in the formulation of the constitution, they would have agreed to adopt the constitution. The virtue of the constitution is precisely that it comes bequeathed from a past point of time so that contemporary special interests, who may wish to change the constitution for their own advantage, are unable to manipulate the constitution.

We observed in Chapter 6 how, under representative democracy, candidates for political office can face a prisoners' dilemma when campaign contributions are offered by special interests, and that a political candidate might prefer to follow a code of personal behavior that is more forthright and socially responsible than is possible when political success requires catering to special-interest groups. If the constitution binds all political candidates not to provide benefits to special-interest groups, no special favors will be granted and rent seeking will not take place because there are no politically assigned discriminatory benefits to be sought. The way is then clear for politicians to choose to behave in forthright and socially responsible ways. Politicians thereby benefit from the constitutional restraint placed on their own behavior because the constitution permits the honest politician to be honest. The constitution can therefore "tie" the hands of politicians for their own benefit.

An analogy is provided in Greek mythology by the legend of Ulysses and the sirens. The sirens are nymphs who live on a island and whose songs charmed to the extent that mariners felt compelled to throw themselves into the sea. The solution adopted by Ulysses was to have himself tied to the mast of the ship. This allowed successful nondiscretionary resistance to the temptation of the songs of the sirens. The sailors placed wax in their ears so that they would not hear the calls of the sirens. That is, government imposes voluntary restraint upon itself. It does not matter so much whether Ulysses was motivated by a concern for his own life or for the lives of the sailors. Ulysses and the sailors were literally in the same boat. In voluntarily constraining himself and seeing to it that the sailors were likewise constrained, Ulysses used his authority to save his own life and the lives of the sailors.

By acting as he did, Ulysses resolved a *time-consistency problem*. He knew that, if the songs of the sirens were heard, he (and the sailors) would be drawn to the sirens, and thereby to collective misfortune. By constraining himself, Ulysses avoided the behavior that would provide present benefit but which he knew he would ultimately regret. The analogy is that politicians may likewise wish to save their souls by agreeing to be bound, or perhaps by placing wax in their ears when approached by special interests.

In other circumstances, Ulysses and the sailors may not be in the same boat, and the sirens may have special gifts for Ulysses. The constitution will then require time separation between design and implementation. Even though Ulysses may not agree to bind himself, he may agree to a constitution that binds a future ruler.

The constitution is an insurance policy for society. People seeking election to public office may be intrinsically motivated to do good for society and may succeed in their objectives. A person who succeeds in being elected to public office may, however, treat politics as a means of personal gain at the expense of the public interest, without doing anything overtly illegal (e.g., by catering to special interest groups). The constitution defines the limits of the exercise of self-interest in political decisions.

9.3.6 Summary

In Section 9.1, we asked the question how much government is desirable from the perspective of multiple government. In Section 9.2 we considered the need for government from the perspective of trust as a substitute for government. In this section, we viewed the question of how much government from the perspective of the growth of government and restraint that might be required on government.

We began with a brief historical account describing public finance in autocratic societies, and we noted the attributes of mercantilism as a way of thinking about public finance and public policy. We observed how the industrial revolution diversified private wealth away from the land-based wealth of an agrarian society, and how democracy came to replace autocratic regimes. Democracy brought growth of government. We considered various reasons why government grew: the demand for public goods, demographics and health, the extension of the franchise to women, expanded taxation opportunities, majority voting, and the political principal-agent problems when interest groups based on common specialized sources of income seek special-interest public policies.

We considered how the size and growth of government should be measured and noted that the information required for inclusive measurement is not in general available. Hence measurement is often based on taxation and public spending relative to national income. Evidence from the second half of the twentieth century decomposing the sources of growth of government by public spending suggests that significant parts of the growth of government may not have been socially beneficial. The evidence indicates that growth of government has been predominantly served to finance government consumption, finance income transfers, and pay for past borrowing without increases in public investment. We noted that the benefits from government could be more accurately measured if zero-based budgets were used.

The political principal-agent problems that suggest that growth of government is not beneficial for a society have led us to the case for constitutional restraint on political decision making. We noted that political principal-agent problems can be present whether government imposes order as proposed by Hobbes or whether government is in principle accountable to the people as proposed by Locke. Hobbes would face the dilemma that the people in government are drawn from the same population that requires protection from itself. It may not be enough to hope to rely on the Thomas-à-Beckett effect to solve this problem. The representative government of Locke requires constitutional restraint because of the principal-agent problems that taxpayers and citizens (or residents) face when confronting persons in government. We have noted that the design of a constitution requires time-distancing, to separate the people choosing the constitution from personal benefits and in particular because the people choosing the constitution may be reluctant to impose limitations on their own discretion in using political power and making political decisions.

This chapter concludes our investigation of the principles of the responsibilities and limitations of government through public finance and public policy. In the final chapter that follows, we draw upon the principles we have considered to look at public finance and public policies toward health, education, and provision for old age. A postscript will summarize the general theme of our investigation of public finance and public policy.

References and related literature

On types of autocratic government, see Wintrobe (1998). For data on the size and growth of government, see Hughes (1977) and Tanzi and Schuknecht (2000). On aspects of the growth of government, see Peltzman (1980), Demsetz (1982), Borcherding, (1985), North (1985), Bernholz (1986), Lybeck and Henrekson (1988), and Paldam (1991). On the relation between economic freedom and economic growth, see de Haan and Sturm (2000). On preferences of government employees regarding the size of government, see Gemmell (1990). On constitutional restraint, see Buchanan (1975), Elster (1984), Brennan and Buchanan (1985), Sass (1992), Mueller (1996), and Voigt (1996). On lagged implementation of a constitution, see Buchanan (1994). For an alternative view of a constitution as counterproductive, see Frey (1997).

Bernholz, P., 1986. The growth of government, economic growth, and individual freedom. *Journal of Institutional and Theoretical Economics* 142, 661–83.
Borcherding, T. E., 1985. The causes of government expenditure growth: A survey of the U.S. evidence. *Journal of Public Economics* 28, 359–82.
Buchanan, J. M., 1975. *The Limits of Liberty: Between Anarchy and Leviathan.* University of Chicago Press, Chicago.

Brennan, G. and J. M. Buchanan, 1985. *The Reason of Rules*. Cambridge University Press, New York.

Buchanan, J. M., 1994. Lagged implementation as an element in constitutional strategy. *European Journal of Political Economy* 10, 11–26.

de Haan, J. and J-E. Sturm, 2000. On the relationship between economic freedom and economic growth. *European Journal of Political Economy* 16, 215–41.

Demsetz, H., 1982. The growth of government. In *Economic, Legal, and Political Dimensions of Competition*. North-Holland, Amsterdam, 99–125.

Elster, J., 1984. *Ulysses and the Sirens*. Cambridge University Press, New York.

Frey, B., 1997. A constitution for knaves crowds out civic virtues. *Economic Journal* 107, 1043–53.

Gemmel, N., 1990. Public employees' preferences and the size of the public sector. *Journal of Economic Behavior and Organization* 14, 393–402.

Hughes, J. R. T., 1977. *The Government Habit: Economic Controls from Colonial Times to the Present*. Basic Books, New York.

Lybeck, J. A. and M. Henrekson (eds.), 1988. *Explaining the Growth of Government*. North-Holland, Amsterdam.

Mueller, D. C., 1996. *Constitutional Democracy*. Oxford University Press, Oxford.

North, D. C., 1985. The growth of government in the United States: An economic historian's perspective. *Journal of Public Economics* 28, 383–99.

Paldam, M, 1991. The development of the rich welfare state of Denmark. In *Diverging Paths: A Century of Scandinavian and Latin American Development*, M. Blomström and P. Meller (eds.). John Hopkins University Press, Baltimore, 67–98.

Peltzman, S., 1980. The growth of government. *Journal of Law and Economics* 23, 209–88.

Sass, T. R., 1992. Constitutional choice in representative democracies. *Public Choice* 74, 405–24.

Tanzi, V. and L. Schuknecht, 2000. *Public Spending in the 20th Century*. Cambridge University Press, New York.

Voigt, S., 1996. Positive constitutional economics: A survey. *Public Choice* 89, 1–43.

Wintrobe, R., 1998. *The Political Economy of Dictatorship*. Cambridge University Press, New York.

Questions for discussion

1. Suppose that you observed a society with an autocratic ruler who, like Hobbes's leviathan, owns everything. What form would public finance take in such a society?

2. What is mercantilism? Is there a connection between mercantilism and the American Revolution? Explain.

3. How did the industrial revolution and democracy affect taxation and public spending?

4. How have demographics and health affected the size of government?

5. "The size of government has grown because personal incomes have grown. With higher personal incomes, people want increasing shares of a society's income to be spent on public goods, which increases the size of government." Do you agree with this explanation for growth in the size of government? Explain.

6. "As societies have become richer, they have been able to implement more extensive social insurance programs, which has increased the size of government." Do you agree with this explanation? Explain.

7. "As societies have become richer, they have become more sensitive to negative externalities such as environmental damage, and more sensitive to positive externalities such as education, and the size of government has increased, as government public-policy responds to address the externality problems." Do you agree with this explanation? Explain.

8. "As societies have become richer, people have become more specialized in the sources of their incomes, providing the basis for collective action by special interest groups seeking political favors." Does this explanation for the growth of government seem reasonable to you? Explain.

9. What information is required to provide a precise measure of the size of government? Why is information on the proportion of income paid to the government in taxes a limited, and perhaps inaccurate, measure of the size of government, or the growth of government?

10. Table 9.4 shows the sources of the growth of government in the second half of the twentieth century. From the evidence in Table 9.4, what are the main reasons why government grew? Do you agree that the evidence appears to suggest that much of the growth of government may not have been socially beneficial? Explain.

11. What is zero-based budgeting? How would such budgeting aid in the evaluation of benefits from the growth of public spending?

12. How does the idea of constitutional restraint on government affect the decisions that government can make? Is time-distancing of decisions about the constitution an effective solution to finding means of limiting growth of government? Explain.

13. How is the concept of time-inconsistency relevant to the story of Ulysses and the sirens? What is the relevance for the design of constitutions?

14. "Markets allow free choices about how to earn and spend incomes. Sometimes, however, markets do not give us the outcomes that we want, and government can then be given responsibilities through public finance and public policy. Government introduces the legal obligation to pay taxes, and government spends taxes in accord with collective and political decisions." From this beginning, write a short essay on public policy, public finance, and the responsibilities and limitations of government. In your essay, relate in particular to the question whether defining the responsibilities of government ensures that government will resolve the problems that markets have left unresolved.

10

HEALTH, EDUCATION, AND RETIREMENT

We have considered various public policies as the response to inadequate outcomes of markets, including policies that provide the rule of law, protect the environment and resolve other externality problems, allow for financing and supply of different public goods, preempt personal time-inconsistency problems, and finance and provide the entitlements of social insurance. In this final chapter, we consider in more detail public policy toward health insurance and health care, education, and provision for retirement years when people have ceased earning incomes. In each of these cases, markets allow private individuals to make decisions without a role for government, but there is generally involvement of government through public finance and public policy.

10.1

Health Insurance and Health Care

10.1.1 Markets and government

Markets can provide health care and health insurance without government. Let us examine how the different considerations raised in past chapters affect the choice between markets and the public finance and public policies of government regarding health care and health insurance.

User prices can be charged when, because of collectively used facilities of hospitals and clinics, health care is a public good. Personal health care also has a public-good dimension through option demand: user prices can be charged for the option to use health-care facilities, through private health insurance. User prices allow markets to function.

Health care can involve externalities. Externalities are involved because some diseases are contagious and other diseases are infectious. There is consequently a broad social (or collective) incentive to ensure that other people are healthy so that we all remain healthy. Preventive medicine, through inoculation and research, provides public-health benefits by eliminating the negative externalities of contagious and infectious diseases. We benefit personally from a healthy population including the people with whom we come into repeated contact in the normal course of our daily lives, as well as the people with whom we come into contact randomly, for example, on public transportation and in classrooms. Government regulation of public safety and the safety of work conditions addresses health-related externalities.

Health concerns can underlie the prohibition of markets, and government can have a role in disseminating information about health consequences of personal decisions. Markets in various substances are prohibited for health reasons. Information about cigarette smoking, excessive alcohol consumption, unsafe sex, unhealthy diets, and so on, is a public service (public good) that involves government.

Through public finance, government can ensure an entitlement to basic health care that reliance on private spending cannot. The entitlements can provide protection against unforeseen adversity. The adversity can be the consequence of health problems from the time of birth, or unfortunate illnesses and accidents in the course of life that are debilitating and do not allow people to be self-reliant. Basic health care as an entitlement may be provided to everybody (as in Europe and elsewhere), or, as in the United States, the entitlements may be targeted to the poor (who cannot pay) and to the elderly (whose expenses are high because of physical changes as people become older).[1] Governments also enforce and often subsidize preventative inoculations for babies and small children.

---

[1] The entitlements protect the old who are vulnerable because of their increased demand for health care due to deterioration of health with age. The poor are vulnerable because they lack the means to provide themselves with health insurance. The elderly poor are doubly vulnerable.

Health care can also involve natural monopoly. When urgent emergency treatment is required, the closest emergency room of a hospital is a natural monopoly. Natural monopoly may be present in the form of specialized medical knowledge. The local hospital may be a natural monopoly, or a population in a town or region may require only one specialist in a particular field.

Political considerations can also affect health care. Government can subsidize medical research that is aimed at benefiting particular groups who may offer political support in return for the policies and public finance that they seek.

10.1.2 The special nature of health care

Health care is special because we may not want a person to have to make market decisions about medical treatment when ill or injured. A person who is sick or injured cannot be expected to have the state of mind to deal with health-care decisions under market conditions. We cannot expect sick or injured persons to have the time and composure, or mind set, to evaluate alternative market supply offers for treatment; the stress of circumstances of ill health or injury may not allow a reasoned consideration of alternative supply offers. People who are ill or injured simply wish to be treated to alleviate or cure their condition. It would be disconcerting if an injured or sick person had to negotiate with different doctors over the costs of treatment in an emergency room of a hospital.

Another reason why a person who requires medical care should not be obliged to make market decisions is that an ill or injured person is in general prepared to pay large sums of money for medical care. Demand for urgently required health care is in general not responsive to price. Ill or injured people may be prepared to pay their entire wealth for the prospect of preserving their lives. Because of the compulsion to be cured, a market transaction exposes a person seeking immediate medical treatment to the potential for extortion.

There is also asymmetric information regarding the quality of treatment. It may be difficult for an ill or injured person to judge the merits of alternative market offers of medical care. The health-care system diagnoses and treats people with illnesses or ailments. People decide that they need advice or treatment when they discern symptoms that suggest to them that they require medical care. At the same time, people may take their health for granted until indications appear that health care is required. When they are ill, people may not know how to identify the reason why they are ill, and hence they seek medical advice. They also may not know the most effective treatment for their medical problem, so that they must rely on the advice of the providers of medical services. The asymmetric information that is present in these circumstances introduces the possibility of opportunistic behavior, or even deception or fraud by medical practitioners. People may be offered treatment that is ineffective or detrimental rather than beneficial to their health. Because of asymmetric information and possibilities of extortion, or deception and fraud, health care is regulated by government. Regulation takes the form of certification of who is permitted to provide medical treatment, and certification of the effectiveness of drugs and medicines. There is also self-regulation by medical practitioners themselves, through professional associations.

Regulation is made complicated by medical treatment often being an inexact science. Information may not be asymmetric with the medical practitioner knowing and the patient not knowing. Rather, the medical practitioner may also not know the reason for the patient's medical problem. Particular symptoms can be consistent with many different ailments. A sore throat is, for example, consistent with a multitude of different medical problems that call for different treatments. Mistakes can be made in diagnosis and in laboratory testing. The problem in regulation and self-regulation is to distinguish reasonable error from incompetence and negligence.

The problem of containing health costs

The special nature of health care makes cost containment difficult and can lead to cost escalation over time. Medical research produces new medicines, new machines, and new procedures that require costly investments. Over time, the new costly procedures become commonplace and more familiar to medical practitioners, and new medical equipment is introduced into hospitals and clinics. The population that benefits from the new procedures and new equipment expands, and medical costs increase correspondingly. Medical practitioners' familiarization with, and standardization of, new techniques allows new procedures to be used, for example, on elderly people and on babies, or even fetuses, who were previously regarded as too high-risk for the procedures. As the range of the population to which the new procedures can be applied increases, so do health-care costs. Attempts to contain costs by limiting the use of new procedures or by limiting access to new medicines encounter ethical objections.

There are also impediments to containing the costs of the health-administration bureaucracy. Attempts at reducing administrative expenses of providing health care can be deflected to reduced care for patients. When proposals for budget cuts for health care are made, the cost reductions can be presented as taking away life-preserving medications from children rather than reducing bureaucratic salaries.

Medical practitioners purchase insurance themselves against the financial consequences of their mistakes. Health-care costs increase because of legal claims of negligence and high insurance costs for medical practitioners.

Demographic changes in the population increase health-care costs. When people live longer and elderly people make up a larger part of the population, the share of health costs in national income increases. Economic and moral dilemmas of health care and health costs tend in particular to arise toward the end of life. A large part of lifetime health costs tends to be incurred in the last months of life. Denying the chronically and incurably ill the last months of their life could substantially reduce health-care costs. Some societies allow euthanasia when suffering has become intolerable by reasonable conditions of what a person might be expected to have to endure. There are evident ethical considerations because of the sanctity of life.

Do increased expenses indicate increased benefits?

Increased spending does not always imply increased benefits. Benefits in general increase with spending when people make personal informed expenditure decisions in markets: when in such circumstances we voluntarily spend more, we generally receive more. In the case of health care, asymmetric information can make unclear what we are buying.

Studies have investigated whether greater spending on health care, through additional medical procedures (not higher salaries or incomes of medical practitioners), increase the quality of health care. The conclusion is that increased spending does not necessarily improve the quality of health care. The following summary is by David Cutler (2000, p. 52):

> Medicare spending (publicly financed spending for elderly retired persons in the U.S.) . . . varies by a factor of two between different regions of the country (the U.S.), with the gap typically associated with differential use of very expensive procedures. But people appear no healthier in regions that spend more compared to regions that spend less. . . .
>
> International comparisons reach the same conclusion. Patients who live closer to a high-tech hospital are more likely to receive high-tech health care than are patients who live farther away from such a hospital, and yet outcomes for the two groups of patients are relatively similar. . . .
>
> [D]irect examinations comparing when treatments are provided with clinical guidelines for when they are appropriate indicate that up to one-third of the use of many common procedures is either inappropriate or of equivocal value. . . .
>
> In other circumstances, particularly outpatient use of prescription drugs, many people receive too little care.

10.1.3 The market for health insurance

In order to allow a separation between medical treatment and the immediacy of market transactions, health care usually involves the purchase of health insurance. With insurance, monetary considerations of a market are not primary when health care is required. Sick and injured people do not have to worry about whether they can afford treatment, and the health-care system that supplies medical treatment can focus on providing the necessary care rather than waiting before treatment is given to ensure that people needing attention have the means to pay. Insurance also spreads risk by providing protection against large unforeseen medical expenses.

Private insurance markets may not provide the means for individuals to protect themselves against the costs of adverse health for the reasons for failure of private insurance that we noted in Chapter 5.

Verification

Some medical ailments are difficult to verify (e.g., a backache or hallucinations). There are recorded cases of people who are hypochondriacs, and of people who compulsively have a need to undergo surgery. These people artificially increase the costs imposed on health-insurance companies. However, the verification problem seems to be sufficiently minor not to provide a cause for concern that private markets for health insurance might collapse.

Moral hazard

Moral hazard affects health insurance, if health insurance changes personal behavior so that insured people to take more health-related risks. For example, there is a moral-hazard effect if health insurance increases the likelihood that a skier will attempt a particularly dangerous downhill run. Similarly, moral hazard is present when, because of health insurance, drivers of automobiles increase the speed at which they attempt to maneuver around sharp curves. The consequences of moral hazard for health-care costs appear to be small. Other than perhaps professional stunt men and stunt women, people do not normally increase their exposure to injury or illness because they have health insurance.

Adverse selection

The more important problem for health-insurance markets is adverse selection. Adverse selection occurs in markets for health insurance because of asymmetric information about personal health. People who know in advance that they have a higher than average likelihood of requiring medical care have a greater incentive to seek insurance. Such people systematically impose costs on others who know that they have a lower than average likelihood of requiring medical care. The people who expect to be healthier than average wish to avoid being in the same insurance group as the people who expect to be in need of medical care. The people who believe that their health will be good prefer to form an insurance pool with people in their own low-risk category, or if that is not possible they may prefer self-insurance (i.e., no health insurance).

For example, individuals with life-styles that increase the probability of becoming infected with HIV or hepatitis know that they face higher risks of future bad health than the population at large. The people whose life-styles place them at lower risk will not wish to be in the same insurance group with people who, because of their life-styles, have systematically higher probabilities of becoming ill with these diseases.

Adverse selection can be avoided by making private health insurance compulsory and by government providing health insurance as an entitlement to the entire population. Low-risk people are then unable to select themselves out of the insurance pool containing high-risk persons. Low-risk people then systematically subsidize health costs of high-risk people.

The scope for adverse selection increased when in the year 2000 a near-complete mapping of the human genetic structure was completed. Information about the human genome can allow predictions of future personal health. The purpose of insurance is to pool *risk* due to events that affect people randomly. With genetic dispositions known, randomness is eliminated for many health problems. People can have themselves tested for genetic predispositions. If the results indicate the likelihood of good health, they will make the information known to private health insurance companies, and they will seek lower health insurance premiums because of their lower health risk. Or they will seek to form insurance groups together with people who have similar low genetically predetermined probabilities of need for particular types of health care. An insurance company can infer that people who do not make the results of their personal tests public have reason to keep the results to themselves because of revealed genetic predisposition to high future health-care costs. Private insurance companies would then not offer to insure people who do not disclose their genetic health predisposition. Availability of information about personal genetic characteristics thus limits the scope of private insurance markets.

A means of overcoming the problem of adverse selection is personal discrimination in health insurance payments. High-risk people pay more or are grouped in insurance pools with other people with similar high risk. Private health insurers can screen applicants for insurance according to life-style, prior health records, age, gender, and genetic information, and set personal insurance payments accordingly. In the case of automobile insurance, discrimination in insurance costs is legal and takes place based on age and safe driving records. Injustice in this case occurs when discrimination in costs of insurance does *not* take place so that cautious and reckless drivers pay the same for insurance. Should people with a higher likelihood of requiring health care similarly be required to pay more for health insurance?

Discrimination in health insurance sometimes takes place against women, who, independently of medical expenses associated with pregnancy and childbirth, have systematically higher lifetime health costs than men. Discrimination also sometimes takes place against the elderly, whose medical expenses in general exceed the average of the population. Reckless drivers have a choice not to be reckless, but people do not choose their genetic predispositions to become ill, for example, with a disease such as diabetes. Nor do the old choose to become old and more prone to diseases of advanced age. Yet discrimination in insurance payments among people with different risks may be the only way to prevent the collapse of a private insurance market due to adverse selection.

10.1.4 Health care as social insurance

We have been considering health care and health insurance provided through markets. An alternative to markets is the provision of publicly financed health care as an entitlement of social insurance. We observed in Chapter 2 that public finance of public goods does not imply the need for government to be responsible for supply. Private medical practitioners and private hospitals can supply health care, which can be publicly financed as an entitlement of social insurance. Health-care facilities can be privately or publicly owned. Whether supply is private or through public ownership, publicly financed free health care protects people unable to pay for adequate care in private markets.

When health care is free, access to medical treatment usually involves queuing and waiting to receive treatment. Medical treatment also tends to be uniform. Higher-income or wealthier people, who wish to avoid the queues and waiting time, often seek market alternatives where treatment is more immediate and more personalized and of better quality than the uniform health care provided as an entitlement of social insurance. When people seek medical care through the private market, free health care is a form of income redistribution, since some people pay the taxes that finance public health care but choose to forgo the availability of free tax-financed medical care. That is, we can have an instance of the case that we considered in Chapter 5 where different preferences can lead people with the same incomes to accept or reject a free entitlement. More usually, income differences and ability to pay may underlie the decision to forgo a free entitlement.

10.1.5 Health and markets

We now leave government and return to the private market for health insurance and health care. Market alternatives can take different forms, depending on whether the insurer and the health provider are the same private entity or are different private entities.

When different private firms provide health insurance and health care separately, the providers of health care and the patient know that the insurance company is obliged to pay for costs of treatment. The effective cost to the physician or hospital and the cost to the patient of additional procedures or medicines is therefore zero. In that case, the insurance company is exposed to the risk of excessive health outlays because the true marginal cost is not zero. To avoid excessive costs, the insurance company in general issues directives about how much can be charged for different procedures and which medications can be prescribed.

In setting guidelines for physician behavior and patient treatment, the private insurance company is attempting to solve a principal-agent problem. If monitoring by the insurance company is to take place and directives are to be set to control costs, the insurance company might wish to address the principal-agent problem by being the health-care provider, employing the physician, and owning the hospital.

When the insurance company is the health-care provider, another type of incentive problem arises. To maximize profits, the combined private health-insurance and health-care company (HMO, or health management organization) has an incentive to provide minimal service. The public then relies on competition among health management organizations to provide health care that is not focused on maximal profits through cost containment. Imperfect information by the public can make personal evaluation of comparative offers of health care difficult. A patient is told only what treatments and medications are permitted and may not know about alternatives disallowed because of cost-containment measures.

The alternatives are either that the private insurance company and the private health provider are one and the same or are separate. Whichever is the case, adverse incentives are present. If the insurance provider and the health-care provider are separate commercial entities, the insurance company confronts problems of cost containment because the people making the decisions about health-care expenses are not the people paying the costs. A joint insurance health-care provider

can specify allowable treatments and has an incentive to limit allowable procedures and medications. Yet these are the alternatives: either insurance and health
care are provided separately, or they are provided by one private firm.

Responses to adverse selection by private insurance providers

Private health-insurance providers take measures to attempt to counter adverse
selection. To deal with the adverse selection problem, a private insurance provider
seeks to keep high-risk people out of the private company's insured population.
Personal risk may be known through past health records or personal behavior,
or risk can be judged by broad indicators, most prominently age. Or rather than
being excluded, high-risk people can be confronted with higher insurance payments. Indirect methods can also be used to counter adverse selection. Because
families with children are better health risks than older populations, the health
management organization can choose to have pediatricians on hand but few doctors specializing in geriatric medicine. Gatekeeper general practitioners can also
be instructed to be sparing in referrals to specialist doctors. These approaches to
solving the adverse selection problem contain health costs and can prevent the
collapse of private health-insurance markets due to adverse selection. The private market then, however, fails to provide adequate health care for the entire
population.

10.1.6 Universal health coverage through markets

A private market for health insurance can leave people without health coverage.
In the United States, for example, at the beginning of the twenty-first century, one
in six people in the population did not have health insurance. What is to be done
about the uninsured, and the uninsurable?

We can look at an attempt in the United States to introduce nationwide universal health insurance through private provision of health care by the Clinton
administration in the 1990s. The attempt failed. Universal compulsory health insurance would have involved government in the provision of health care in specifying payments to health-care providers. Physicians and other medical practitioners
would have lost income from the regulation by government. Medical practitioners
made past personal investments in education based on the anticipation of earning
market-determined incomes, and they could claim that government regulation of
their incomes was equivalent to retroactive taxation. There was no offer to provide compensation for the retroactive taxation. The government would also need
to become involved in the pharmaceutical market. Containing health-care costs
requires designating permissible medicines and setting maximum prices at which
pharmaceutical companies are permitted to sell their products. A consequence
however is that pharmaceutical companies face reduced incentives to develop
new medications. At the same time, the regulation of the pharmaceutical industry
imposes financial losses on people who owned stock in pharmaceutical companies
because lower profits (or the expectation of lower profits) depress stock prices.
Owners of stock in pharmaceutical companies would not be compensated for these

losses. The owners of stock in pharmaceutical companies are not necessarily the wealthier people in society who can "afford the loss." People own stock in pharmaceutical companies directly, or indirectly through ownership of mutual funds or through personal retirement savings programs.

Compulsory universal health coverage redistributes income to people who cannot afford private health insurance or who do not have health coverage provided by their employer (see Supplement 10A). Universal and compulsory health insurance requires a source of finance. If some people cannot pay for their coverage, others pay for them.

Mandatory universal health coverage also introduces personal loss through the restricted choice of quality of health care. The reduced choice of quality falls on those people who lack the financial means to seek health care outside of the allowable procedures and treatments covered by the universal mandatory insurance.

A broad coalition can thus be expected to oppose government-mandated universal compulsory health insurance. The people who benefit from universal compulsory health coverage are those who are too poor to afford health insurance in a private market and would be provided with free or highly subsidized medical services under universal coverage.[2] The consent of a majority of voters, or of representatives of the voters, is required to introduce a mandatory universal program of health care. In the Unites States in the 1990s, the majority was not to be found, despite the support of the prestige and political patronage of the office of the president.

Private competition with universal compulsory coverage

Let us suppose that universal mandatory health insurance is nonetheless introduced into a private market for health care. The government then determines a list of health-care services and medications that are the entitlement of each citizen, sets allowable prices and treatments, and allows market competition among private providers in offering the designated health-care services. The health-care providers cannot refuse insurance to people with chronic illnesses, old people, or people with life-styles that have higher than average expected health costs; if they did, there would not be the designated universal coverage. Elements of a market have now become minimal. Insurance companies do not decide on the services that are covered by insurance and do not decide who their clients are because they are obliged to accept everybody who applies. Health-care providers do not decide on the price for coverage because insurance payments are regulated. For the population, participation is compulsory, and payment is through the compulsory regulated health-insurance payments.

---

[2] Self-interest may not the sole consideration in determining a person's position on the desirability of government-mandated universal health coverage. People may support a basic entitlement to health care through universal coverage as a matter of principle. People without health insurance are joined in their support for universal health coverage by others whose support derives not from self-interest but from conceptions of basic entitlements and social justice.

Even where participation in health insurance is compulsory and coverage is in principle universal, there is nonetheless no assurance that everyone will take advantage of their entitlements. Evidence shows that, with universal free-access health care available, lower-income people can be less aware of their health needs and be less inclined to seek medical advice.[3]

When health insurance is compulsory, health-insurance companies and health-care providers can make a case that, because they are compelled to accept all applicants for health care, government has a responsibility to finance any losses that might arise. The government is then assigned the role of financer of last resort. In these circumstances, health-insurance companies and health-care providers confront a soft-budget constraint (see Section 1.3). That is, they know in advance that any losses will be covered, which reduces incentives to contain costs. Incentives are present for opportunistic cost enhancement to take place through increased spending on administrative salaries. If government attempts to enforce cost containment by refusing to finance the deficits of the providers, the providers can initiate a health-care crisis by not providing treatment. The objective of government in containing medical expenses and not subsidizing health providers is then undermined. As long as the circumstances continue, the inefficiency of the soft budget can be expected to continue as well.

10.1.7 Socialized medicine

When government socializes health insurance and health care, people receive tax-financed free treatment directly from the government. With the health-care system run by government, medical-care providers become government employees. The government is financer of last resort, now directly through the government budget. Again there is a soft budget constraint, in the face of a social value of saving life and returning people to good health. The soft budget becomes a particularly difficult problem if health care becomes politicized because of the direct responsibility of government to provide health care. All failures of the health-care system become directly attributable to government, and politicians become directly involved in health care. The administration of health-care spending becomes part of the government bureaucracy; spending on health care consequently becomes subject to the incentives of government bureaucracy. The soft budget of health-care spending is compounded by the soft budget of government bureaucracy.

Attempts to contain costs of socialized medicine in general result in either low-quality health care or long waiting times for treatment that may be beneficial if the treatment is received in time. The objective of socialized medicine is to provide equal health care for everybody, and in principle an accompanying private market should be unnecessary. Long waiting times for consultations and treatment, and impersonal medical attention, can, however, lead people to forgo free publicly financed socialized medicine in favor of the private market. There are then two levels of medical care: an inferior level of care for those who use government

---

[3] See Katz and Hofer (1994).

health care and a superior level of care for those people who can afford to or are willing to pay for private treatment.

Socialized medicine has adverse incentives if the medical practitioners who are employed in the government system also have private practices. In that case, low quality and long waiting times for free treatment within the socialized system of health care can be an opportunistic response of the medical practitioners, who gain from the demand that is created for the better quality and more immediate attention provided through their own parallel private practices. If patients do not seek treatment in parallel private practices, there are incentives for corruption in the bureaucracy that administers the socialized government health system, to provide queue-jumping possibilities when waiting for treatment. Personal contacts in the administering bureaucracy can also help in reducing waiting times.

10.1.8 Conclusions

In this section we have described roles of markets and governments in providing health care and health insurance. Expense is not the primary concern when a person is trying to regain good health. Yet health care involves resources and money. A contradiction thus arises between the principle of doing everything possible to save a life or return people to good health and the limitations of available resources.

A case against personal supply of health care through markets is based on the principle that all people have a basic entitlement to health care. The private market also has limitations in providing health coverage because of adverse selection, and because of exclusion of some people who cannot afford health insurance. The private market has adverse incentives that differ depending on whether the insurance company and the health-care provider are one and the same entity.

Attempting to enforce universal private insurance coverage introduces redistributional and incentive problems, including adverse selection and also soft budgets because government (or rather the taxpayer) becomes financer of last resort.

Cost-containment problems are intrinsically present in health-care provision because of the value placed on saving and sustaining life. Costs are also affected by problems of asymmetric information, with patients relying on the recommendations of medical practitioners. The additional disincentive for cost containment through government as financer of last resort to ensure universal health insurance coverage adds to these problems.

In some countries, health care is socialized and provided directly by government-paid medical practitioners and administrative staff as a free tax-financed entitlement. The government bureaucracy that administers health care spending adds a further dimension to the soft budget of spending on health care. Attempts to contain costs in socialized medicine can result in low-quality health care or in extended waiting times for treatment. The long waiting times can be opportunistically manipulated through offers of immediate private medical attention. Opportunities for corruption also arise through benefits to patients from avoiding the long waiting times that tend to be characteristic of socialized medicine.

Yet reliance on private markets alone leaves some people without health insurance. Private insurance companies attempt to solve adverse selection problems by denying health insurance to people with high expected health costs. The noninsured may in particular be those people who will tend to need health care the most. Government can attempt to target the vulnerable groups through selective publicly financed health insurance. Nonetheless people fall though the government's intended safety net.

Identifying socially desirable health-care provision therefore presents dilemmas. The failures of private market provision, particularly exclusion of parts of the population, point in the direction of forgoing markets and turning to government to take responsibility for ensuring universal health-care coverage. The introduction of government into health insurance and health care leads to soft-budget problems because of the compounded difficulty of containing health-care costs when the public finance of government is the source of finance of last resort.

Societies make different decisions about how to provide health care. Some societies choose to rely principally on the voluntary decisions of the market, while others choose considerable involvement of government. Where health care is provided through government, the criticisms are about inefficiencies, waiting times and quality of treatment, and insufficient allowance for individual choice; low salaries when health care is part of government bureaucracy also provide incentives for medical practitioners to emigrate. Where health care is through private markets, the criticisms are about social injustices because of exclusion from health insurance and sometimes unnecessary procedures that increase costs but do not benefit patients. The dilemmas of the choice between market and government are perhaps nowhere so revealed as in health insurance and health care.

References and related literature

On health-care systems in different locations, see Roemer (1991) and Hsiao (1992). On uncertainty and health care, see Arrow (1963) and Cutler and Reber (1998). On the demand for health, see Grossman (1972). On public and private provision of health services, see Culyer and Jönsson (1988). On managed health care and competition, see van de Ven (1995), Newhouse (1996), and Encinosa and Sappington (1997). On old age and publicly financed medical care, see Feldstein (1999). On mental health, see Machnes (1996). On spending and the quality of health care, see Weisbrod (1991), Cutler (2000), and Skinner and Wennberg (2000). On limitations that prevent effective universal coverage, see Katz and Hofer (1994). On the relation between government-administered health care and markets, see Olivella (2002). Many colleges and universities offer courses or complete programs on the economics of health care. The *Journal of Health Economics, Health Affairs, Health Care Financing Review*, and other journals provide specialized investigations of health care issues.

Arrow, K. J., 1963. Uncertainty and the welfare economics of medical care. *American Economic Review* 53, 941–69.
Culyer, A. J. and B. Jönsson, 1988. *Public and Private Health Services: Complementarities and Conflicts*. Blackwell, Oxford.

Cutler, D. M., 2000. Walking the tightrope of medicare reform. *Journal of Economic Perspectives* 14, 45–56.

Cutler, D. M. and S. Reber, 1998. Paying for health insurance: The trade-off between competition and adverse selection. *Quarterly Journal of Economics* 113, 433–66.

Encinosa, W. E. and D. E. M. Sappington, 1997. Competition among health maintenance organizations. *Journal of Economics and Management Strategy* 6, 129–50.

Feldstein, M., 1999. Prefunding Medicare. *American Economic Review* 89, 222–7.

Grossman, M., 1972. On the concept of health capital and the demand for health. *Journal of Political Economy* 80, 223–55.

Hsiao, W. C., 1992. Comparing health care systems: What nations can learn from one another. *Journal of Health Politics, Policy, and Law* 17, 613–36.

Katz, S. and T. Hofer, 1994. Socio-economic disparities in preventive care persist despite universal coverage. *Journal of the American Medical Association* 27, 530–4.

Machnes, Y., 1996. Incentives and production of mental health services. *European Journal of Political Economy* 12, 459–66.

Newhouse, J. P., 1996. Reimbursing health plans and health providers: Efficiency in production versus selection. *Journal of Economic Literature,* 34, 1236–63.

Olivella, P., 2002. Shifting public-health-sector waiting lists to the private sector. *European Journal of Political Economy* 19, 103–132.

Roemer, M. I., 1991. *National Health Systems of the World, volume 1, The Countries.* Oxford University Press, New York.

Skinner, J. and J. Wennberg, 2000. How much is enough? Efficiency and Medicare spending in the last six months of life. In D. Cutler (ed.), *The Changing Hospital Industry.* University of Chicago Press, Chicago, 169–93.

van de Ven, M., 1995. Regulated competition in health care: With or without a global budget. *European Economic Review* 39, 786–94.

Weisbrod, B. A., 1991. The health care quadrilemma: An essay on technological change, quality of care, and cost containment. *Journal of Economic Literature* 29, 523–52.

Questions for discussion

1. Health insurance and health care involve considerations regarding public goods, externalities, prohibition of markets, social justice and entitlements, user prices, and natural monopoly raised in previous chapters. Briefly list how the considerations are involved.

2. What are the special characteristics of personal demand for health care? How do these characteristics influence markets for health care (as contrasted with markets for health insurance)? How do the special characteristics of health care make cost containment difficult?

3. Evidence shows that increased spending on health care does not ensure improved health care. Why do you believe that this is so?

4. How do the reasons for problems with private insurance markets (adverse selection, moral hazard, inability to verify the circumstances against which insurance is sought) affect the private market for health insurance?

5. How does the mapping of the human genome affect health insurance?

6. Because women have higher health costs on average than men, health insurance payments are sometimes higher for women. Do you believe this is justified?

7. What are the advantages and disadvantages of "health management organizations" compared to health-care providers and health-insurance companies as separate providers?

8. In Chapter 2, we concluded that the legal obligation to pay a tax does not imply actual payment, and that actual payments are determined by the conditions of supply and demand in a market. How does this conclusion affect the outcome of a legal requirement that employers pay for the health insurance of employees? (See also Supplement 10A.)

9. In the place where you live or study, does the government provide special health insurance assistance for people for who cannot afford health insurance and for elderly people? What are the eligibility characteristics for entitlement to government benefits? Are the benefits justified for the elderly?

10. A proposal for containing health costs of people who are provided with publicly financed health insurance can be to allow market competition. Government can pay the health insurance costs, and individuals can choose their private health provider. Why might such a proposal not be successful? (See Supplement 10B.)

11. Why might you expect people who do not have health insurance to be either very poor or very rich? Would you make participation in health insurance compulsory for the poor as well as the rich? What happens if the poor cannot pay? Should the government (i.e., taxpayers) pay for them?

12. Would you except opposition to a compulsory universal insurance scheme based on private insurance and private health care? If such a scheme were introduced, would you expect the scheme to solve problems of cost escalation?

13. Some countries have socialized medicine where equal access for everybody is directly provided through employees of government to publicly financed medical care. Are you in favor of this solution for ensuring that everybody receives medical care? Explain.

14. In a country that provides socialized medical care, the government is the primary employer of medical practitioners and nursing staff, and salaries are in general lower than when health care is provided through private markets. The costs of medical school in a country with socialized medicine also tend to be lower, to match the lower salaries available locally after graduation. What do you expect to be the consequences when emigration can freely take place? (See Supplement 10C.)

15. Trade-offs are required between different objectives when choosing a system of health insurance and health care. Given that the trade-offs are necessary, what do you believe is the ideal means of providing health insurance and health care?

16. On the scale between complete reliance on private markets and complete government control, how are personal health care and health insurance provided where you live or study? Do you believe that there should be more government involvement or less?

17. What proportion of national income is spent on health in the location where you live or study? How has this proportion changed over time?

18. Compare the proportion of national income spent on health care in your location with other countries that have different systems of health insurance and health care. What do you believe are the reasons for the differences?

10.2

Education

As is the case with health care, education can be privately provided. In this section we consider the roles of public finance and public policy in education.

10.2.1 From private education to government schools

Historically, education of children was a privately financed luxury of wealthier families or nobility. In societies without a middle class population, people are either quite rich or extremely poor. The rich can afford to pay for education as a private good, while reliance on private finance often leaves children of the poor without educational opportunities.[1]

At levels of higher education, education was not privately and individually provided within the family but was a collective or public good. Early universities in Europe catered to students who had the necessary background (literacy in Latin), which required the prior privileged benefit of private education by home tutors.

Demand for literacy and education became more widespread with the end of feudal society, and education was offered outside of the home. The term "public school" in England refers to these original external schools. The schools were "public" in providing education outside of the home, but they were (and remain) private schools. Only wealthy families could afford to send their children to the public schools. The public schools were also "boarding schools" where children lived as well as learned. The boarding schools shaped preferences and values through childhood and adolescence, and beyond.

In a next step, government involvement made education a publicly financed *entitlement* for children, independently of the willingness or ability of parents to pay. Schooling became compulsory up to designated ages. Correspondingly, child labor was made illegal. Government provided schools and teachers and determined the subject matter of studies.

Government thus used its authority to make schooling compulsory in publicly financed schools and government determined the subject matter or curriculum of children's education. The extensive involvement of government in education is related to the reasons we have considered for responsibilities of government.

Collective benefits

Because efficient class size is more than one student in a class, education is a public good with the characteristics of collective benefit and shared costs. When increases in class size begin to decrease educational effectiveness, education becomes a congestible public good. Education as public good can be publicly financed with free access, or it can be provided through a market with private financing and user prices. As we have observed, the first schools were private and provided education under the user-pays principle.

User prices can, however, exclude children from education because of inability or unwillingness of parents to pay. That is, a case against the user prices is, as we saw in Chapter 8, inefficient exclusion from collective benefits.

---

[1] In many cases, poorer families also have educated their children, in particular when tradition and social norms placed education of children at the forefront of family obligations.

Still, when public goods are congestible and facilities can be readily replicated, private provision and user prices can approximate efficiency. For example, just as movie theatres are privately owned and operated on a user-pays basis, so schools can be private and financed through user payments. This is after all historically how public schools began.

Because schooling can be privately provided through exclusion and the private financing of user prices, the public good nature of education does not appear to be the reason why education is publicly financed and provided in government schools. When supply is private, children from poorer families can be given access to education by government providing parents with vouchers that allow public finance for private school fees.[2]

Natural and enforced monopoly

In looking for reasons for government involvement in children's schooling, we can consider whether schools are natural monopolies.[3] Education is a local natural monopoly when the objective is that children attend the school closest to their house. Neighborhood schools can be positioned to satisfy requirements that children live in close proximity to school rather than travel extended distances to and from school every day. If schooling is a natural monopoly because of a least-distance requirement, government can solve the natural-monopoly problem by providing publicly financed free-access education for each child in a government school in proximity to a child's home.

An alternative to a government-owned natural monopoly is a private provider determined through a process of competitive bidding. The government could own the school and could pay the private provider, who has successfully bid to provide education in the school facility.[4]

To ensure that educational standards are satisfied, government can regulate a private natural-monopoly supplier of children's schooling. However, there are various problems in regulating educational quality.

Grade inflation can be a problem. The private operator could give inflated grades to students in an attempt to give the impression of high educational achievement. To address problems of grade inflation, examinations could be externally set in common for all schools.

Moral hazard is another problem. If the effort of the private educational provider is not observable, poor student performance can be the consequence of inadequate teaching or inadequacies of pupils. Moral hazard through unobservable teaching effort introduces a principal-agent problem between government and the natural-monopoly private provider of education. Parents might tend to blame the government for poor educational results from the private-education

---

[2] We considered educational vouchers that allow public finance to be combined with competitive private supply in Chapter 5.

[3] Recall that natural monopoly arises when least-cost supply is by a single provider. See Chapter 8.

[4] We considered such competitive bidding procedures for supply under conditions of natural monopoly in Chapter 8.

contractor. In an attempt to overcome the moral hazard that underlies the principal-agent problem, government might itself wish to be the provider of education. Government then monitors the behavior of its own employees (administrators, teachers, janitors) in its schools.

Also, government administrators do not have an incentive to skimp in providing resources, as might a private contractor who administers a natural-monopoly school for private profit. On the contrary, we have seen that a government bureaucracy has an incentive to overspend. There is consequently also a principal-agent problem when government owns the school and directly pays the administrators and teachers. The school bureaucracy and teachers' organizations can "capture" education policy. A bureaucracy that administers a school system might also resist change that would increase competition by allowing students access to schools outside of its control. Competition would have adverse effects on administering bureaucracy's rents.[5] The school system's bureaucracy may favor the idea that schools should be natural monopolies, and that children ought to have no choice but to attend the designated natural-monopoly school to which they are assigned.

In small towns, the school is indeed often a natural monopoly. However, in larger towns and cities, populations of children are often sufficiently large to allow choice among alternative schools within reasonable bounds of travel time. Schools preassigned without choice when choice is feasible are not natural monopolies, but rather are administratively enforced monopolies. The enforcement of monopoly takes place through the denial of choice through insistence by government (or the administration of the school district) that children are obliged to attend the school to which they have been preassigned.

Externalities and education

When we introduced the idea of externalities in Chapter 4, we used education as an example of a beneficial "externality." We observed that social benefits arise from more educated fellow citizens when we interact in our professional and social lives with people who are more knowledgeable and educated. Knowledge and education are also foundations for economic growth through externalities over time; better teachers make better students, who make better teachers, and so on, which expands the knowledge base of society.

These social benefits are the basis of a justification for government subsidies to education or for providing free publicly financed education. At the same time, there are circumstances where education has negative externalities (i.e., where the private benefits from education exceed the social benefits). Negative externalities are present when education screens people for employment but provides no benefits through enhanced understanding or personal productiveness. That is, negative externalities arise when people study only to obtain the certification that

---

[5] The rents are the surplus benefit that would not be available if the bureaucracy were to confront competition in administering and providing education.

they have studied. Education is then a form of rent seeking.[6] The rents are available from the privileged employment obtained by graduates of good schools, but the process of study itself is socially unproductive with no long-lasting benefits. The social return from education is then low, but the private returns are high, and resources are used in socially unproductive schooling.

Government paternalism

Public policy with regard to schooling is paternalistic because preferences of parents who do wish to educate their children are overridden by the requirement of compulsory schooling. Parents may be unwilling or unable to make investments in the education of their children. They may not have the financial means to send their children to school, or they may prefer to send children to work to add to family income. A public policy of compulsory schooling paternalistically takes over the education decision from the child's parents.

A paternalistic case for compulsory education differs from the case for compulsory education based on social benefits of a more educated society. The paternalistic case for compulsory education is that every child has an entitlement to an education because of the personal and private benefits to the children. The compulsory education is free, to enable children to benefit from their entitlement. Parents have no choice but to comply with the legal obligation of sending their children to school and thereby to allow the children to benefit from the entitlement to education.

Some children may find school boring and onerous and may attempt to convince parents that school is a waste of time. Compulsory education places the decision of the child to go to school outside the domain of argument with the parent. Schooling becomes a legal obligation subject to truancy laws.

Moral hazard and social insurance

Paternalistic provision of education as a private entitlement also solves a moral-hazard problem associated with social insurance. By providing education as an entitlement, society hopes to make people self-supporting from their own productive activities and employment, and not dependent on future government income transfers for existence. If education were a private decision, moral hazard would arise when some children and teenagers chose not to study (or their parents might make this decision for them) with the awareness that the social insurance contract of the society will provide future protection from low incomes.

Why government schools?

Collective benefits, natural monopoly, externalities, paternalism, entitlements, and social insurance all enter into an answer to the question why there are government schools. In particular, with an educational entitlement part of the implicit social

---

[6] See Chapter 6.

insurance contract, direct control over education through government schools is a way of guaranteeing children's entitlements. The case for natural monopoly through government schools is then not based on proximity of children to schools, but principally on paternalistic and regulatory concerns. For example, there might be a concern that parents could pay private owners of schools to record their children as present in school when the children are being sent to work. Or there might be a fear that private owners of schools will abuse children. Parents might be viewed as inadequately informed about school quality, or as simply incapable of making competent education decisions for their children from among choices available in private markets. Or there might be a fear that unscrupulous and undocumented advertising about educational achievements will influence parents' decisions about their children's schooling.

10.2.2 Determinants of the quality of education

Different schools provide different qualities of education. Resources and class size can be expected to affect the quality of education. Also, however, interaction with fellow students is based on established norms of behavior, including attitudes about study and the merits of academic success. In some school peer groups, personal achievements may be judged not in terms of learning, but in terms of popularity, personal appearance, and originality and flare in choice of clothing. In extreme cases, children in a neighborhood school may not know anybody who has achieved success in life as a result of studying.

The home environment and attitudes of parents also influence children's attitudes about study. Children from homes where education is valued and encouraged set the norms for good schools. Children in good schools then have an advantage over children in schools where the student population is disproportionately from homes where parents do not encourage success in life through study.

Social norms about how conflicts or disagreements are resolved can also differ among schools. Conflicts and disagreements among students can be resolved through compromise and flexibility, or through violence accompanied by unforgiving memories.

Good schools have better administrators and better-qualified and motivated teachers. Teachers in good schools in general enjoy teaching more because they teach better-motivated students. The teachers are less prone to the fatigue and indifference that can arise from the repetition over the years of more or less the same basic material.[7]

In good schools, teachers also benefit from interaction with more concerned parents. When teachers in good schools wish to discuss students' performance or behavior, parents are interested in their children's scholastic performance and behavior at school.

---

[7] The enthusiasm of good students to learn and understand overcomes the tendencies for fatigue and indifference of teachers.

Good schools can be government schools. Often, however, good schools are private schools. Because a child's friends and fellow students are important in determining motivation for educational achievement, parents may prefer to send their children to private schools where, for extra payment, the children can be with other children whose parents are also willing to pay money for a better education.[8]

Good schooling, and perhaps a reputation for educational achievement, is what a private school is selling. The reputation of a private school can have value in itself, through superior prospects for job placement after graduation. The reputation of the private school is more valuable when a student is a relatively poor academic performer. More significant than the grades on the student transcript may be the identification on the transcript indicating where the student studied. Attendance at the private school can provide personal connections that can be used for future professional advancement or for political careers.

Does additional spending necessarily improve quality of education?
Private schools may have more resources per child than government schools, but not necessarily. Additional resources do not necessarily improve the quality of education. Objective measures of inputs into education include the size of the education budget, the number of computers per child, the class size, and the formal qualifications of the teachers. While we expect the relation between educational quality and these variables to be positive, there are adverse influences on the quality of education that money alone cannot rectify. Increased salaries for an overstaffed school district administration or for inadequate and indifferent teachers increase spending, but do not improve the quality of schooling.[9] If students do not develop habits of study and learning, more money spent on schools may do little to improve student achievement.

While teachers can become apathetic and indifferent if they feel that society rewards them inadequately, more money may not overcome the problems of inadequate motivation of teachers. The motivation to teach may be overwhelmed by student norms of immediate gratification and little regard for longer-term benefits of study. Because of satisfaction from teaching in classrooms where norms encourage learning and respect for the teacher, good schools can often attract and keep good teachers while paying lower salaries than in government schools.

More money spent on education, therefore, does not necessarily result in increased quality of schooling. Rather, the relation between spending and quality of schooling can be negative, in particular because of the need to compensate teachers for teaching in bad schools.

---

[8] In the United States, teachers in government schools have disproportionately sent their children to private schools. In the late twentieth century, 10 percent of children in the United States attended private schools, but 22 percent of children of teachers attended private schools (D. Eric Schansberg, 1996, p. 82).

[9] In New York City, for example, the government schools at the end of the twentieth century had 10 times more employees per student and more than 60 times the number of administrators per student than Catholic schools (D. Eric Schansberg, 1996, p. 85).

10.2.3 Locational choice and education

The quality of schooling can be chosen by location. We expect competition through locational choice to improve the quality of schooling offered in government schools.

Locational choice is, however, limited by income. Good government schools are capitalized into the price of housing in a school district, as are bad government schools. People living in a district with bad schools may not be able to sell their homes and move to a district with good schools because of the difference between the price they receive for their house and the price they must pay for a house in the district with good schools. Similarly, differences in apartment or housing rentals (which reflect different prices of housing) are obstacles to locational choice. Additionally, people may have the option of moving, but they may not be prepared to accept the more expensive but inferior quality housing that they can afford in the district with the better schools. Because of zoning laws in the districts with good government schools, there may be no modest housing that lower-income people can afford. Locational choice is therefore not an automatic escape from bad-quality schools. When locational choice is the means of access to schools, education can be expected to be unequal. At the same time, locational decisions among school districts will have been made against the background of the unequal educational standards.

Changes in locational rules for school assignment

A response to locational inequality can be to change locational rules for school assignment. Children can be re-sorted within a school district, or school districts can be merged.

Re-sorting children among government schools through changes in locational rules redistributes income or wealth among homeowners. Because of the capitalization of the quality of schools into housing values, a cost is imposed on owners of houses where government schools were good, and a benefit is provided to homeowners where schools were inferior. A wealth transfer therefore takes place.

In response to the wealth transfer, we can expect counter-claims of social justice. Parents in school districts where schools were good can make the case that "I worked hard and paid a lot of money to buy a house in a neighborhood where government schools are good. Because of the change in locational criteria for school assignment, my child is no longer permitted to attend the local school, and the value of my house has fallen." Parents in a neighborhood or school district where schools were bad can make the case that "all children should receive equal educational opportunities, and our children deserve the same opportunities as children elsewhere."

Because homeowners in districts that had inferior schools gain and homeowners in districts that had good schools lose, re-sorting by changes in locational rules for assignment to schools is not justifiable by the criterion of Pareto efficiency. If gainers have gained more than losers have lost, the gainers could in principle compensate the losers and still be better off.

However, the gainers may not be able to compensate the losers in practice. The benefits to the gainers will come in the future, through the higher incomes of children who were given improved educational opportunities.

We cannot expect the parents of the children whose educational opportunities have improved to be able to borrow against future increased incomes of their children to compensate voluntarily the parents of the children who have lost. Moral hazard problems keep the parents from receiving loans. Moreover, parents may not wish to take such loans because they also confront a moral hazard problem if they envisage their children repaying them.

Taxes could be imposed on the gainers to compensate the losers. The taxes would have to be imposed on lower-income people living in the areas that had bad schools, for transfer to higher income persons living in the areas that had good schools.

With neither voluntary compensation nor compensation through taxation feasible, a redistribution of wealth takes place. In Chapter 1 when we introduced Pareto efficiency as a justification for a change in public policy, we observed that efficiency can be interpreted as total benefits exceeding total losses without requiring actual compensation to ensure that no one loses.

Social justice based on social insurance can justify policies that equalize educational opportunities. In Chapter 5, we viewed educational opportunities as part of the entitlements of social insurance. Social insurance applies to a society. Determining eligibility for entitlements under social insurance requires defining the limits of the society. If the society extends beyond school districts, equalized educational opportunities through changes in locational criteria for school assignment have a social-insurance justification. The social contract that underlies social insurance includes insurance against the risk of having parents who could only provide inferior education if the ability or willingness to pay of parents were to determine children's educational opportunities.

As is the case when wealth transfers take place through capitalization, changes in wealth through housing prices affect only the people owning houses at the time of the announcement of change in public policy that merges school districts or makes choice of schools independent of the location of housing. After the change in policy, housing prices are de-linked from schools, and people who buy houses pay the new more-equal housing prices (because unequal educational opportunities are no longer capitalized in housing prices). The owners of houses in previous good-school areas lose when they sell, and the sellers of houses in previous bad-school areas realize their gains.

Changes in the quality of the schools

Attitudes toward study, the use of violence to settle disputes, the criteria for student popularity, attitudes toward teenage pregnancy, the topics of general conversation, the inclination to do homework, and students' extracurricular activities are included in social norms. Because the social norms of the school environment can determine prospects for future success in life, parents who care about their children's futures may be sensitive to the norms in the schools that their children attend.

Parents can also be sensitive to the behavior of other parents in the schools that their children attend. Parents who contribute time to monitoring and improving school activities provide a public-good benefit to all children. Because the contribution of parents is a case of private provision of a public good, there can be a free-riding problem. The behavior of different parents determines the scope of the free-riding problem.

When children attend schools without regard for location of parents' housing, a question arises about what has happened to the quality of schools. Schools might have the average quality of the previous locationally sorted schools. However, changes in social norms can result in school quality that is not the average of previous qualities. Social norms affect behavior because of a feeling of being ill at ease by not following the norms. The social norm may be to study and do well academically, but the social norm may also be to ostracize and socially exclude those children who emphasize scholastic achievement. Therefore, social norms introduce dynamics that affect personal behavior, through the incentive not to deviate too much from what others are doing and how they behave.

When government schools provide a quality of education that some parents and children regard as inadequate, decisions may be made to leave government schools for private schools. Families switching to private schools in that case lose twice from the change in the rule for attending government schools. They lose when the values of their houses declined, and they lose again because they now pay for private education.[10]

10.2.4 Private schools and adverse selection

The presence of private schools introduces adverse selection into schooling. Adverse selection takes place when exit from government schools to private schools reduces the average quality of input of parents and adversely affects social norms of children who remain in government schools. Successive exit to private schools then continually reduces quality of government schools and induces additional exit. A classic adverse-selection response is taking place. Only children whose parents cannot afford to pay for private schools, or children whose parents are satisfied with inferior-quality education, in the end remain in government schools. The objective of equalizing educational opportunities by changing the rule for school attendance has then not been achieved because of adverse selection. Social integration that may have been the objective of public policy has also not been achieved.

---

[10] We investigated the response of forgoing the government entitlement of free-access education in Chapter 5.

Voting and political decisions on public spending

When children exit government schools through adverse selection, fewer voters benefit from government schools. If government schools no longer serve middle-income parents because these parents have moved their children to private schools, the median voter may not favor more than minimal spending on government schools. Voting and political decisions on public spending can then result in reduced public spending on government schools. Voting is another path of adverse selection. As more children exit government schools, public spending falls, and, to the extent that spending does affect quality, there is a further decline in quality. More children are then taken out of government schools, and public spending and quality decline further.

Neglect of government schools by the median voter or middle-income voters can be short sighted. We have previously observed that a motive for providing educational entitlements is to avoid future claims on social insurance by people who have had an inadequate education. Decreased present public spending on government schools can then result in the need for increased future taxation to finance income transfers to people who in their youth received an inadequate education in public schools.

10.2.5 Education and income distribution

In Chapter 6, we noted that abilities are generally normally distributed among a population, but that the distribution of income and wealth are skewed. From behind a veil of ignorance, a person is more likely to emerge as high-ability and low-income than high-ability and high-income. When high-ability low-income children are denied equal access to educational opportunities with high-ability high-income persons, family income disparities are perpetuated, and social mobility does not take place.

Educational vouchers de-link quality of education from parents' ability or willingness to pay for private schools, or from the location of housing.[11] Sorting children among schools is then determined by a school's willingness to accept a child, and not by ability of parents to pay. With some schools better than others, there will be competition to attend the better schools. If admission to schools is according to academic merit, vouchers tend to result in sorting of students into better and inferior achievers. Vouchers then result in a meritocracy independent of family income. The meritocracy is based on personal educational achievement and replaces sorting among schools based on parents' abilities to afford payment for private schools or location in school districts with good or bad government schools based on household income or wealth.

---

[11] Access to equal educational opportunities requires that vouchers cover full or substantial parts of the fees at any school. At least in the short run, market competition facilitated by vouchers will result in excess demand for good schools and vacancies in bad schools. Under the market conditions, good schools might ask for school fees above the entitlement offered through the government vouchers. If the value of a voucher reflects a minimal entitlement, then the voucher system does not guarantee educational equality because not all parents may be able to afford additional payments.

If family background affects achievement, the sorting by scholastic achievement that takes place through vouchers may deny children from families where education is not valued the opportunity to learn at school from high-ability or high-motivation peers. Social segmentation then still occurs, and there is social immobility if children's scholastic achievements are correlated with those of their parents and if low-income parents have had low scholastic achievements. However, access to education no longer depends on parents' willingness or ability to pay. Through educational vouchers, good students from low-income households are provided with the benefits of an education that is consistent with their motivation and abilities.

Diversity in preferences

Some parents may have distinct preferences about the type of education they wish their children to receive. Government schools may not provide the education that these parents seek, and the parents may choose private education. Such parents need not be particularly wealthy. They might claim that it is an infringement on their liberties when they must pay taxes to finance government schools from which they do not benefit. Vouchers solve the problem of double-payment for children's schooling for these parents by combining market choice of nongovernment schools with publicly financed education.

While educational vouchers introduce free choice and competition into schooling, questions nonetheless arise about allowable educational preferences. What if, for example, some parents want their children to be taught that the earth is flat or that the sun revolves around the earth. Some parents could also wish their children to be taught that terror can be justified or that some people are superior by virtue of birth or belief? Publicly financed vouchers for private schools were validated by the United States Supreme Court in summer 2002 (in the case of *Zelman v. Simmons-Harris*, the Court ruled that the vouchers do not contradict the First Amendment to the U.S. Constitution). However, schools that participate in the voucher program cannot discriminate in accepting students based on ethnicity or religion and cannot teach hatred or demean the qualities or rights of anybody in society.

Property values and vouchers

A change in public policy that introduces educational vouchers to replace locational assignment to government schools has similar effects on property values as a public policy that integrates school districts. In both cases, after the change in public policy, the location of housing no longer determines the quality of schooling. Opposition to educational vouchers can be expected from administrators of government schools who oppose the competition introduced by school vouchers. At the same time, people (not just parents) who own houses that are valuable because of capitalized values of good schools have reason to oppose the introduction of school vouchers.

10.2.6 Private managers for government schools

A government school system can be administered by private managers. Private management of government schools is a means of implementing the bidding solution for natural monopolies that we considered in Chapter 8. Private managers can be asked to bid on costs and indicators of educational achievement, or private management companies can bid for contracts to manage school districts based on reputation in achieving cost reductions and quality improvement.

Private management of government schools facilitates change to vouchers and provides incentives consistent with competition when vouchers finance education. Vouchers expose government schools to competition with private schools in attracting students. In private schools, successful managers and owners of private schools are personally rewarded through the voucher system by additional payments from additional students. When salaries in an administrating bureaucracy are fixed by terms of government employment, the same personal financial rewards from attracting more students are not available in government schools. However, the administrating bureaucracy of government schools faces the risk that the government school system will contract due to competition with private schools, diminishing employment and perhaps incomes in the school bureaucracy as a result.[12] Therefore, the administering bureaucracy has an incentive to preempt the competition that vouchers introduce, in particular by playing on the uncertainties confronting parents when changes to vouchers are proposed. When private managers who can be readily hired and fired administer government schools, the opposition to change by an entrenched bureaucracy is not present.

10.2.7 Initial inequality and equal opportunity

Affirmative action is a public policy intended to compensate for inequalities due to family background. Problems of initial inequality also arise when children have different abilities.

Affirmative action

Affirmative action provides preferential access to limited places in colleges and universities with the intention of compensating for initial inequalities or educational disadvantages. Affirmative action could also be applied under a voucher system. Good schools at all levels could be required to make compensating adjustments for differences in children's initial conditions.

Affirmative action is controversial. The case for affirmative action is that historically disadvantaged peoples should be compensated for past injustices by preferential access to education. The case for affirmative action may also be that admission standards discriminate by being based on the knowledge and understanding that comes from particular types of home environments.

---

[12] The government monopoly of publicly financed schooling can be a source of rents for the administering bureaucracy. The rents are threatened by competition.

Initial conditions can be difficult to apply based on need, if affirmative action is not to be based on detailed evaluations of individuals' family circumstances but rather on broad criteria such as ethnicity and family name.

Students from the preferentially targeted groups who satisfy standard criteria for admission to a college or university on their own merit can feel that affirmative action is disparaging because of the presumption that they have benefited from discriminatory privilege when their successes are the result of their own efforts and achievements.

People from outside the groups targeted for affirmative action can feel that there has been injustice when they discover that they have been denied admission to a college or university while others with inferior academic records have been admitted in their place.

Affirmative action is a complex issue because advocates for and against claim to have justice on their side. Advocates against point out that, inside a college or university, personal evaluations are based on personal achievement and personal merit; therefore, it would seem that admissions should be based on the same criteria. Advocates in favor point out that not making allowance for initial inequality due to family background contradicts the principle of equal opportunity through education.

Differences in childrens' abilities

Children differ in abilities. Faster-learning and slower-learning children both benefit from specialized attention. Should children who have learning disabilities receive special attention, but not children who are fast learners and who become bored with the normal progress of class learning? If children or students are not "equal" in aptitudes and abilities, does equality in educational opportunity imply the same educational means and pace of teaching for everybody? To address individual differences in ability, some school systems screen children at young ages and place higher-ability children in special classes that advance at a faster pace than regular classes. In other school systems, students are kept together independently of abilities, on the grounds that separating better students into special classes disadvantages the students who remain behind in regular classes by lowering classroom standards. Children who are slow learners or have learning disabilities are also sometimes removed from mainstream classes, to allow these children to be taught by special methods that are suitable for their learning problems, and to allow the rest of the class to advance. Policy responses to different abilities therefore differ.

10.2.8 Financing higher education

Public policy toward education also confronts the question: if the intention of policy is to provide educational opportunity, where does the responsibility of government end? Should education be free and compulsory to the end of high school, or should free education extend to college and university? Should anyone who wishes to keep studying after high school be permitted to do so at public expense? Or should only good students be permitted to attend college or university at public expense? What of graduate school, or professional education in law, business administration and finance, and medicine? That is, does the principle of publicly financed equal opportunity in education continue to higher education, or should the market and private payment take over? If children prefer not to finish high school but leave their studies to obtain qualifications as electricians, plumbers, secretaries, or hairdressers, should government also finance these types of studies? These questions are answered through the public policy chosen toward higher education.

Student loans as means of providing equal opportunities

The alternative to free access to publicly financed education is private payment. Students may, however, lack the means to pay for their education and may wish to borrow to finance their education costs. Private lenders may be unwilling to lend. The impediment to lending is asymmetric information that results in moral hazard. The asymmetric information is that students know their own effort input and motivation, but lenders can observe neither effort put into studying nor the motivation to study. Repayment of loans is based on the expectation of future earnings, and the risk of default facing the lender depends on the unobserved effort of the student in studying and preparing for exams. A moral-hazard problem arises because the nonobservable behavior of the student determines whether education will provide an income that will allow the loan to be repaid.[13]

Moral hazard introduces government involvement into student loans. Government can provide loans directly through a government agency or security to the private lender by guaranteeing repayment of loans. As noted in Chapter 5, government does not, however, have an advantage over private markets in solving problems of moral hazard.

There are other types of problems. If a person withdraws from the labor force after completing studies, should the loan be forgiven? Or should the loan become an obligation of family members? If a woman withdraws from the labor force to raise a family, should the husband be responsible for repaying his wife's student loans? What happens to the responsibility to repay the loan if the couple subsequently separates? Should students who repay their own loans also be held responsible for repaying loans of others who have defaulted? If the interest rate on student loans includes the risk of default, students who repay their loans are subsidizing those who do not.

Free or subsidized higher education

When education is free or sufficiently subsidized, student loans are not required. Free and subsidized higher education benefits people who can afford to take

---

[13] In a slave state, the lender could stake claim to the person of the borrower in default.

advantage of the "free" opportunities.[14] Some poorer people may be unable to take advantage of free educational opportunities because they are obliged to work full-time. Income differences are reinforced when students from middle (and upper) class households systematically receive the benefits of free education.

Scholarships

Public policies of guaranteeing student loans and providing free or subsidized education apply to all students. Scholarships target good students and are a reward for superior scholastic achievement. However, judgments often must be made with respect to a balance between academic performance and lower family income and other adverse initial personal circumstances in determining criteria for scholarships.[15]

10.2.9 Summary

As with health care, which we considered in Section 10.1, public goods, externalities, paternalism, issues of social justice and entitlements, choice between user pricing and public finance, and natural monopoly are present when we consider education. Education can be privately provided through payment of user prices and began that way. The public-good aspects enter through collective benefit in classrooms (although this cannot be any more of a reason for government schools than it could be a reason for government movie theaters). Externalities are present through social benefits from a more-educated population.[16] Paternalism is present through the legal requirement that schooling is compulsory. Attributes of social justice or social insurance are present through the entitlement to educational opportunity independent of parents' income or inclination to educate their children. Natural monopoly is present if children are obliged to attend the closest neighborhood school. The choice between tax-financing and user prices is present, through alternatives offered by government and private schools. The principal-agent problem between taxpayers and government can be present to affect choice of public policy: educational vouchers allow a market for publicly financed education, but administrators of government schools lose from market competition. Homeowners gain or lose because of changes in housing prices when school assignment is no longer determined by location. Because of the redistribution of wealth, changes in

---

[14] Recall from Chapter 6 that publicly financed public-good spending tends to benefit middle-income people (or the median voter).

[15] Often scholarships are not financed by government, but by the college or university. The criteria for scholarships can then involve nonscholastic aptitudes including athletic ability. Good sports teams can be a major part of the prestige of a college or university. University and college administrators may feel that success in sports enhances student pride and also increases demand for admissions. Successful sports teams are also sources of profit through payments for attendance at games and through fees from television and radio coverage.

[16] If education provides no lasting benefits and does no more than signal achievement, private benefits exceed social benefits, and externalities are negative. We have noted that education is then a form of rent seeking.

public policies can be resisted when housing prices change because the locational eligibility to attend government schools has been redefined.

We have noted that increased spending does not necessarily increase the quality of education. Social norms, parents' attitudes, teacher motivation, and personal objectives within the administrative bureaucracy of the school district also affect the quality of education.

We have also noted that adverse-selection problems arise when superior private and inferior government schools coexist. The adverse-selection problem becomes more severe when, with more voters' children in private schools, less public finance is provided for government schools.

Vouchers eliminate adverse selection based on parents' willingness or ability to pay, allowing sorting of children to take place according to aptitude and scholastic merit, and also the educational preferences of parents. Vouchers sustain segmentation between children from lower- and higher-income families, if school admission is based on academic merit, and if children's educational achievements are influenced by incomes or backgrounds of their parents.

We have also noted the benefits of private management of government schools, and in particular that private management is consistent with the incentives of a voucher system.

With or without educational vouchers, differing initial conditions complicate a definition of equal opportunity through education. A case can be made for and against affirmative action intended to compensate for differing initial conditions. Problems of defining equal educational opportunity also arise because of differences in abilities and scholastic aptitudes.

We have also considered financing of higher education. Students may be admitted to schools on academic merit, but they may not have the means to pay school fees. Moral-hazard problems limit the willingness of private lenders to lend for costs of education. While government can assist in providing guarantees for student loans, moral-hazard problems remain, to confront governments as guarantors of the loans.

In the end, if entitlements to education are to be the basis for social mobility, the responsibility of government is to find a way to avoid the adverse-selection problems that leave children and students segmented into groups with different educational benefits and opportunities. A public policy of educational vouchers for compulsory schooling avoids the adverse-selection problem by eliminating locational and financial impediments and opening opportunities for everybody in educational choice.

A solution to the adverse-selection problem is also to have good government schools. Good government schools may be inconsistent with enforced monopoly of government schools for publicly financed education. Also, because government policies are determined by voting and political processes, there may be insufficient political will to improve the quality of government schools after sufficient numbers of children and students leave government schools for private schools.

References and related literature

On determinants of the quality of education, see Card and Krueger (1992), Peltzman (1993, 1996), Borjas (1995), Toma (1996), Cutler and Glaeser (1997), and Angrist and Lavi (1999). For evidence on the effects of locational competition on government schools, see Hoxby (2000). On government schools as a source of uniformity, see Lott (1990). On vouchers and public and private education, see Epple and Romano (1998). On adverse selection through voting, see Glomm and Ravikumar (1998). On child labor, see Horrell and Humphries (1995). On financing of education, see Nerlove (1975), Inman (1978), and Fernández and Rogerson (1998). On the effectiveness and consequences of affirmative action, see Coate and Loury (1993). On incentives facing colleges and universities in admission policies, see Danziger (1990).

Angrist, J. and V. Lavi, 1999. Using Maimonides rule to estimate the effect of class size on scholastic achievement. *Quarterly Journal of Economics* 114, 533–75.

Borjas, G., 1995. Ethnicity, neighborhoods, and human capital externalities. *American Economic Review* 85, 365–90.

Card, D. M. and A. B. Krueger, 1992. Does school quality matter? Returns to education and the characteristics of public schools in the United States. *Journal of Political Economy* 100, 1–40.

Coate, S. and G. L. Loury, 1993. Will affirmative action policies eliminate negative stereotypes. *American Economic Review* 83, 1220–40.

Cutler, D. M. and E. L. Glaeser, 1997. Are ghettos good or bad? *Quarterly Journal of Economics* 112, 827–72.

Danziger, L., 1990. A model of university admission and tuition policy. *Scandinavian Journal of Economics* 92, 415–36.

Epple, D. and R. E. Romano, 1998. Competition between private and public schools, vouchers, and peer group pressures. *American Economic Review* 88, 33–63.

Fernández, R. and R. Rogerson, 1998. Public education and income distribution: A dynamic quantitative evaluation of education-finance reform. *American Economic Review* 88, 813–33.

Glomm, G. and B. Ravikumar, 1998. Opting out of publicly provided services: A majority voting result. *Social Choice and Welfare* 15, 187–99.

Horrell, S. and J. Humphries, 1995. The exploitation of little children: Child labor and the family economy in the industrial revolution. *Explorations in Economic History* 32, 485–516.

Hoxby, C. M., 2000. Does competition among public schools benefit students and taxpayers? *American Economic Review* 90, 1209–38.

Inman, R. P., 1978. Optimal fiscal reform of metropolitan schools. *American Economic Review* 68, 107–22.

Lott, J., 1990. An explanation for public provision of schooling: The importance of indoctrination. *Journal of Law and Economics* 33, 199–231.

Nerlove, M., 1975. Some problems in the use of income-contingent loans for the finance of higher education. *Journal of Political Economy* 83, 157–83.

Peltzman, S., 1993. The political economy of the decline of American public education. *Journal of Law and Economics* 36, 331–70.

Peltzman, S., 1996. Political economy of public education: Non-college bound students. *Journal of Law and Economics* 39, 73–120.

Schansberg, D. E., 1996. *Poor Policy: How Government Harms the Poor*. Westview Press, Boulder, Colorado.

Toma, E. F., 1996. Public funding and private schooling across countries. *Journal of Law and Economics* 39, 121–48.

Questions for discussion

1. In the place where you live or study, when was schooling made compulsory for children? Was education made compulsory at the same time for both boys and girls? Until what age was it at first compulsory for children to attend school? When education of children was made compulsory, was it already the accepted custom to send children to school?

2. Education is, up to certain limits of class size, a public good. However, education historically began as a privately supplied private good. Why did education become a publicly supplied public good? That is, why do you believe that compulsory education was introduced through government schools, rather than making education compulsory through private schools?

3. If free-access education is a basic entitlement through a social insurance contract that makes access to education independent of parental wishes and independent of parental income, up to which age or level of studies, and for what types of studies, do you believe that the entitlement should apply? Explain.

4. When education is provided through locational choice, what are the effects on the distribution of wealth and income of a public policy that changes the locational criteria for determining the government schools that children can attend? Do you believe that anyone should be compensated for changes in property values that result from the change in public policy? Explain.

5. When government and private schools coexist, how can problems of adverse selection arise?

6. Does more spending on schools necessarily result in better-quality schools? Explain. What do you believe are the main differences between "good" and "bad" elementary schools? What do you believe are the main differences between "good" and "bad" high schools? How can public policy close the gap between good and bad schools?

7. Compare user prices and Lindahl prices as means for financing a private school.

8. If there are no educational vouchers, should parents who pay taxes and also pay private-school fees obtain a tax credit for fees paid to the private schools? Do you believe that it is "fair" that parents who send their children to private schools pay twice? Explain.

9. If vouchers allow public finance to be used to provide a wider range of choice, why should anyone object to using vouchers to finance compulsory education? Where does the opposition to vouchers come from?

10. When a government school is a monopoly for publicly financed education (there are no vouchers), what effects would you expect private management of government goods to have? Why is private management of government schools beneficial when vouchers are proposed and introduced?

11. How do school vouchers affect "sorting" of children among schools, compared to locational sorting of children into schools based on school districts and associated sorting through some children attending private schools?

12. Do you believe that access to education should be based on personal academic merit alone? Or should affirmative action programs allow students from groups in the population defined as disadvantaged to be admitted to college or university in place of

students with higher grades who are from other groups in the population? Explain. Do you believe that all children from immigrant families should benefit from preferential admissions, on the grounds that they may speak a foreign language at home, which limits their skills of expression?

13. Should public policy provide additional resources for scholastically superior children? Should public policy make additional resources available to children with learning problems? Explain.

14. Why do private markets not provide loans for education without government guarantees of repayment? Do government guarantees solve moral hazard problems? Explain.

15. Should government guarantee student loans for everybody, or provide scholarships for needy deserving students, or both? Explain.

16. "Government schools are justified because government has an important responsibility in controlling the content of education." Explain why you agree or disagree.

10.3
Providing for Retirement

In the usual course of events, people reach a stage of their lives where they retire and cease the activities that earned them their incomes over the course of their lives. Sometimes retirement is compulsory, and sometimes it is a matter of personal choice. When people do eventually retire, they require a source of income to finance consumption during their nonworking lives. Governments are usually involved in providing this post-retirement consumption. We shall now consider reasons for the government's involvement in providing for consumption during retirement. We shall also ask why the involvement of the government is necessary, since people can predict that they will eventually reach a stage in their lives when they will no longer be earning incomes, and they can privately save in anticipation of these circumstances. We shall see also that the problems that arise in financing retirement consumption affect not only retired people but also young people.

10.3.1 An intergenerational social contract

We begin with circumstances where private saving and investment are not available as a means of personally providing for old-age consumption. This occurs in a society where food cannot be stored, and where there are no financial or real assets that can be owned and sold in the future to finance consumption during years of retirement. These are the conditions of a primitive hunter-gatherer society, where food is obtained by hunting animals and by gathering fruit and vegetables that grow in the wild. In these circumstances, the old can survive only if the young give them food.[1]

---

[1] There is no money in this primitive society. If there were money, people could store money and use the money to finance consumption during old age.

The young might be willing to provide the old with food only if the old provide something in return. The old have, however, nothing with which they can pay the young because the old no longer work and have been unable to store food or assets during their productive years.

Now let us introduce money, or certificates of entitlement to consumption, which the old can trade for food with the young. The young generation will be happy to accept the certificates of entitlement in exchange for food, if the certificates can later be exchanged for food when the young have themselves become old and have themselves retired from productive activity.

The transferable certificates of entitlement to old-age consumption allow a social contract whereby the productive generation always provides food for the retired generation. Under the social contract, no two generations engage in bilateral exchange with one another. The transfers of consumption are always unilateral, between productive young persons at any point in time to the retired generation.

The social contract involves generations as yet born unborn, who, in the future, accept certificates of entitlement from old people, provide the old people with food, and receive food when they themselves are old. The unborn generations are, of course, not present when the conditions of the social contract are set out.

The social contract may specify the amount of food that is to be provided to the old. Generations as yet unborn would be obliged under the contract to make the designated future transfers of food, even though they did not participate in the decision to establish the social contract.

Everyone in each generation gains from the social contract. Because of the social contract, all people are cared for in their old age.

If a generation of productive people were to renege on the social contract by refusing to provide food for the old, the reneging generation would have more to consume during its productive years. In a hunter-gatherer society, the reneging generation cannot, however, keep food for its retirement years because food cannot be stored. The reneging generation, when old, would have to rely on the next generation of young to feed them. They would have to hope that the next generation of young workers did not copy their own behavior in refusing to feed the old. If the social contract whereby the young provide for the old cannot be reestablished, the society is in an unfortunate situation. The old starve, and, because everybody eventually becomes old, everyone's life span is shortened.

It is clearly not in the self-interest of any productive generation to break the chain of intergenerational transfers because the continuation of the precedent of intergenerational transfers is the source of the working generation's own future survival. Abrogating the contract would make each and every generation worse off. That is, annulling the social contract of intergenerational transfers violates Pareto efficiency.

There have been societies without a social contract of intergenerational transfers. In these societies, by not providing for the old, the younger productive generations set the precedent for their own early demise.

Demonstration effects

The intergenerational contract is based on a continued precedent of caring for and feeding the old. Can the precedent be based on a demonstration effect? Under a demonstration effect, a productive generation provides for the old with the intention of setting an example to be followed that will be the basis for their own survival in old age. That is, a generation provides for the old, as an example to be copied by the younger generation in future years when the present generation providing for the old is itself old.

If a demonstration effect were the reason for the transfers, the intergenerational transfers would break down. Members of a young productive generation would reason: "We do not need to provide for the old in order that our children will provide for us when we are old. Our children will provide for us in any event. Our children will want to provide for us because, by providing for us, they demonstrate the act of making the transfers to their young, so that their young will provide for them in the future."

If each productive generation thinks this way, no intergenerational transfers take place. Therefore, a demonstration effect does not provide a rational basis for intergenerational transfers from young to the old.

Intergenerational transmission of ethical norms

An alternative to a demonstration effect as the basis for ongoing transfers from the young to the old is the intergenerational transmission of ethical norms to support the old.[2] The ethical norm ensures continuation of the efficient contract that ensures the young will be cared for when they are themselves old. That is, ethical behavior of providing for the old is efficient.

The social contract and pay-as-you-go transfers

Honoring one's parents places the ethical norm of support for the old within the family. A government can collectivize the intergenerational transfers by levying taxes on young people and transferring the tax revenue to retired people. Such publicly financed intergenerational transfers are known as pay-as-you-go schemes for providing for old-age consumption. Under a pay-as-you-go scheme, taxes paid by working generations are not used to accumulate assets to provide for that generation's future consumption. That is, there is no accumulated fund that finances old-age consumption. Rather, the tax payments of the working generation are directly transferred to the retired generation to finance the retired generation's consumption.

Taxation as the solution to a free-riding problem

Pay-as-you-go intergenerational transfers from working to retired persons are a case of collective supply of private goods. The collective supply is the income

---

[2] Such an ethical norm is expressed in the injunction: "Honor your father and mother so that your days on earth may be long."

provided to the old through the taxes paid by the young working generation. The income is shared among the old retired generation.

The collective nature of the transfer from the productive population to retired persons introduces free-riding incentives whereby a young person may want to leave the financing of transfers to the old to other young people. Without taxation, some members of the young working population might choose to consume all their output rather than make transfers to the old, while relying on a "social safety net" of tax-financed consumption to provide for them when they are old and have retired. Compulsory taxes paid during productive years preempt such free-rider behavior.

10.3.2 Demographics of intergenerational transfers

Pay-as-you-go schemes of intergenerational transfers are sensitive to demographic changes. The schemes can become unsustainable if the number of people working declines compared to the number of people receiving income transfers.

The number of people working can decline and the number of retired people receiving income transfers can increase because pension and social security payments encourage people to take earlier retirement. The payment obligations on the young are also increased when improvements in health standards result in people living longer after retirement. Imbalance between the number of people working and retired people is also created by declines in birth rates.

We shall now look more closely at demographic problems of pay-as-you-go intergenerational transfer schemes. In considering demographic problems, we stay in the framework of a hunter-gatherer society where old people can only survive if the young provide them with food.

Pay-as-you-go schemes can specify the contributions that people make when working, or the benefits that people receive when retired, or both contributions and benefits. We begin with demographic effects where the contributions of the working population are specified but the benefit received when retired is not.

Designated contributions

For simplicity we shall consider a situation where all members of the same generation earn the same income. Suppose that a rate of tax t is levied on the lifetime income y of each member of a productive generation. The purpose of this tax is exclusively to finance transfers to retired persons. Therefore, each working person has an income during his or her working life of $y(1 - t)$ after paying the tax.

Consider a young working generation B with n_b people. The total value of the taxes collected from generation B is $n_b t y$. This sum is transferred to a retired generation C. The value of the post-retirement transfer received by an individual in retired generation C is

$$\tau_{bc} = \frac{n_b t y}{n_c}, \tag{10.1}$$

where n_c is the number of people in the retired generation C.

In expression (10.1), the value of the transfer received by a retired person depends on the size of the working population relative to the size of the retired population, that is, on the ratio n_b/n_c. The retired population is better off, the fewer people in its generation and the greater the number of people in the generation that is working.

Let us now denote the rate of population increase between generations by g. That is,

$$n_b = n_c(1 + g). \tag{10.2}$$

By substituting the expression (10.2) into (10.1), we obtain the transfer received by an individual in retired generation C in the alternative form

$$\tau_{bc} = (1 + g)ty. \tag{10.3}$$

An individual in generation C will have paid $t \cdot y$ in taxes when working and receives, when retired, the amount given by expression (10.3).

The rate of population growth of g is the rate of return from the intergenerational pay-as-you-go transfer scheme. If population size does not change between generations, so that $g = 0$, the rate of return from the intergenerational transfer scheme is zero. Or, if g is negative, the return from the pay-as-you-go scheme is negative.

Even with g zero or negative, the intergenerational transfer scheme is beneficial. The transfers allow consumption to be transferred from the productive period of a person's life to the period when the person is not working. Without the scheme of intergenerational transfers, retired people would starve.

If population is growing, so that $g > 0$, the pay-as-you-go scheme of intergenerational transfers yields a positive rate of return. Each retired generation then receives a bonus. Retired persons not only are provided with old-age consumption but also receive back more than they originally contributed.

We have been looking at pay-as-you-go schemes of intergenerational transfers with designated payments by the young working population. The designated payment has been set by the rate of income taxation t. In practice, the taxes are given other names, such as social security taxes.

Designated benefits for retired persons

Rather than designated payments by the young working population, pay-as-you-go intergenerational transfers can be based on designated benefits to retired people. For example, suppose that all retired people are entitled to a specified post-retirement income or pension P. The total pension payments to a retired population of size n_c are $P \cdot n_c$.

The total tax payment per member of the working population (with n_b people working) required to finance the designated benefit P for retired persons is

$$T = \frac{Pn_c}{n_b}. \tag{10.4}$$

The value of the tax payment T depends on the relative size of the two generations, or on demographics.

For example, suppose $n_c = 100$ and $n_b = 800$. For each retired person, there are then eight people working who share and finance the cost of one retired person's pension or social security payment P.

The tax burden of the pension scheme on the working population remains unchanged if the population remains constant over time (so that there remain, for example, eight people working and financing the pension scheme for each retired person).

If the population is increasing, more people are working per retired person in successive generations, and the effect of demographic change is to decrease the tax burden on the working population over time. However, the burden on each consecutive working generation increases overtime, if population declines from one generation to the next.

High designated benefits for retired persons benefit initial participants in a pay-as-you-go intergenerational transfer scheme. The first beneficiaries will have paid nothing (the scheme did not exist when they were working) and benefited from the contributions made by the working generation.

Pay-as-you-go social security and pension schemes that provide high designated benefits to retired persons can be like a Ponzi scheme.[3] Initial participants gain, while later participants lose. There is a fundamental difference between a Ponzi scheme and pay-as-you-go intergenerational transfers. Participation in a Ponzi scheme is voluntary. Participation in tax-financed intergenerational transfer scheme of social security is compulsory.

When earlier retirement, increased longevity of retired people, and low birth rates increase the tax burden of financing benefits for retired people, the tax-paying working population might propose a downward revision of retirement benefits. The retired population, and persons close to retirement, might be expected to object to a proposal to reduce retirement benefits. Such a proposal might be viewed as an unfair violation of the intergenerational social contract. The retired population financed retirement benefits at a specified level of benefits at the time when it was working and paying taxes. When retired and no longer working, the older population expects to receive the same benefits that it provided when financing retirement benefits for others.

---

[3] In a Ponzi scheme (named for Charles Ponzi, the first well-known perpetrator of chain letters), high returns to initial investors are financed by borrowing at high interest rates from other investors. The scheme breaks down when no more investors can be found to finance the high interest rates for previous investors. In the chain letter version, people receive a letter or e-mail with a list of people to whom they are asked to send money. The new participants in the scheme are invited to add their names to the list of future recipients of money and to forward the letter to other people who are invited to join by sending money to the new participant in the scheme and to the others on the original list. No investment takes place by the initial investors in a Ponzi scheme. Unidirectional transfers take place as in pay-as-you-go intergenerational transfer schemes. Initial investors receive high returns, while later investors lose their money when the Ponzi scheme ultimately breaks down (as it must because the population of participants is finite).

To decrease their tax burden, members of the young working population might propose an increase in the age at which retirement benefits become available. People nearing retirement might object to this proposal.

Another approach to reducing the tax burden for financing pay-as-you-go retirement benefits is to attempt to increase the productivity (or productiveness) of the working population. Productivity growth increases the pre-tax per capita income y of the working population. Even if population is declining, sufficient growth in productivity can provide a positive return from an intergenerational transfer scheme. Therefore, fewer young people may be providing for more old people, but, if the young are more productive than the working persons in the generation before them, the increased productivity of the young can more than compensate for decline in the number of taxpayers whose tax payments finance the benefits of retired people.[4] Demographic problems can therefore be solved or moderated by increased investment in education that increases a working generation's productivity. A working generation that will benefit in the future when retired has an incentive to increase spending on education of the young.

Another solution to the problem of an increasing tax burden on the young working population is to expand the tax base for intergenerational transfers through immigration of a working aged population.[5] Large numbers of immigrants may be required to sustain the defined benefits of an intergenerational transfer scheme. In that case, immigration as a solution to the problem of intergenerational demographic imbalance requires willingness of the local population to be receptive to the large numbers of immigrants.

Eventually the immigrants themselves will retire and become eligible for intergenerational transfers. Increasing immigration may be required over time to sustain the benefits to which the old have become accustomed.

While immigration can be part of the solution, emigration can be part of the problem. Faced with high taxes because of demographic imbalance, young productive people can choose to emigrate to tax jurisdictions where taxes to finance intergenerational transfers are lower. Such emigration deteriorates the demographic imbalance further.

There is a problem of adverse selection for the society from which the productive young are emigrating. As more young productive people leave, the tax burden on those productive people remaining behind increases, and they too might be inclined to emigrate – and their emigration further increases the tax burden on those who have so far remained. The opportunities offered by location in different government tax jurisdictions can unravel the population of young productive people who support the old.

---

[4] For example, if people are twice as productive, in expression (10.4) the tax burden per taxpayer is halved because it is as if twice as many taxpayers were financing the designated benefits to the retired population.

[5] Immigration is possible as a solution when incomes in a country are higher than in foreign locations so that immigrants can be attracted to leave their homes.

The demographic prisoners' dilemma

Suppose, only hypothetically, that children provide no intrinsic personal benefit to parents and that the cost of having and raising children falls exclusively on parents. However, children, when grown, pay taxes that finance income transfers to all members of the older population. The conditions of a prisoners' dilemma are then present. Each person will wish personally to have no children and will wish to impose the burden of having children on others. The dominant strategy is to attempt to free ride for support in old age on the children of others, and there will be no children in the Nash equilibrium of the prisoners' dilemma.[6] This society will eventually die out because of absence of reproduction, and in particular the old will starve.

An escape from the demographic prisoners' dilemma can take place if the pay-as-you-go scheme under which all people's children are collective resources for financing intergenerational transfers is cancelled. Children then become a personal, and not a collective, means of providing intergenerational transfers. Each family internalizes the intergenerational transfer, and grown working children take care only of their own aged parents. People who do not have children then condemn themselves to an early death because they do not have children who will provide them with food in their old age.

In the less-developed regions of the world, social security has been based on the extended family. Governments have not provided social security, and children have been a form of personal insurance within the extended family. The output of the extended family is shared among all family members.[7]

When the extended family is the means of providing social security, some children might not provide for their parents and so leave their parents destitute in old age. Some people may simply not have children.[8] Because some people may have uncaring children or may not have children for no fault of their own, strict reliance on one's own children for survival during advanced years can be, of course, capricious and unjust. A government can provide insurance against not having had children through a collective scheme of intergenerational transfers that pools all children's contributions to provide old-age consumption. That is, the government provides social insurance against the risk that people find themselves without children. Then, however, the society can confront the demographic prisoners' dilemma because of the collectivization of benefits from having had children. A government providing old-age social insurance cannot precisely identify reasons why people have not had children. Therefore, the free riding of people who have chosen not to have children is part of a government-sponsored pay-as-go scheme of intergenerational transfers.

---

[6] Each person makes the calculation: if others have children, my best response is not to have children, and if others do not have children, again my best response is not to have children.

[7] The older retired generation often contributes by caring for the young children when the parents who are the productive generation are at work.

[8] They may not have been able, or the opportunities for having children may not have presented themselves.

Privatized social security through the family is a response to the demographic prisoners' dilemma, but, as we see, is not a satisfactory response because of people who cannot rely on a family for old-age support. People who do not have children could, however, compensate those who do. We observe tax deductions and direct transfer payments based on the number of children. Transfers also take place in the form of subsidized schooling and child health services. Childless people contribute to the cost of other people's children through taxes that finance education and health care for children.

Through pay-as-you-go social security, the benefits of having children are shared with other people. If people without children locate in areas where they are not required to finance schools, but they receive retirement benefits through a national or federal level of government, childless people are free riding for old-age provision on people who have children.

When locational sorting between people with children and childless people does not take place, so that both people with children and childless people are in the same tax jurisdiction, free riding is nonetheless present if many of the costs of having and rearing children are private and fall upon the parents.[9]

Generational accounting

Changes in the attractiveness of having children and the free-riding problem of the prisoners' dilemma, as well as increased longevity and early retirement, can cause intergenerational accounting imbalances. The imbalances reflect intergenerational income redistribution. In particular, the first generation of beneficiaries of a pay-as-you-go scheme necessarily gains from the scheme because this generation made no payments and only receives benefits, whereas the last working generation before a scheme becomes bankrupt necessarily loses since this generation pays into the scheme but receives no payout.

Table 10.1 shows gains and losses from the U.S. social security system for different generations or age groups, for males and females. The numbers indicate the present value in the year 1998 of investments made through U.S. social security payments, computed for tax payments and retirement benefits. The investment is that individuals lend the government money when they work through payment of social security taxes, and the government repays the money when people retire according to the rate of return from the system.

Positive values in Table 10.1 indicate losses through net tax payments. Negative values indicate gains from the excess of social security payments over taxes. We see the following.

(1) Women aged 60 and over in the year 1998 gain, as do men aged 70 and over. Everybody else loses.

---

[9] Personal costs arise when people feel that children limit entertainment and life-style opportunities. People may feel that changing diapers is unpleasant, as is waking in the night to feed babies. A child increases the cost of switching partners and can interfere with personal career advancement. People who enjoy having children willingly or happily bear these costs.

TABLE 10.1. INTERGENERATIONAL GAINS
AND LOSSES FROM U.S. SOCIAL SECURITY
(PRESENT VALUE IN THOUSANDS OF 1998
U.S. DOLLARS)

Age in 1998	Net tax payment	
	Males	Females
0	122.1	61.1
10	169.4	82.0
20	238.2	109.4
30	268.1	111.4
40	236.9	77.8
50	152.8	10.5
60	10.8	−95.6
70	−92.4	−135.9
80	−83.6	−112.3
90	−61.5	−74.3
Born after 1999	142.5	71.3

Note: Discount rate 6%, growth of labor productivity 2.2%.
Source: Gokhale et al. (2000).

(2) For men aged 60 and under, compulsory participation in social security
    is a net tax. The tax is substantial for men aged 50 and below.
(3) Participation for women aged 50 and under was also not worthwhile.
    Women however lost less because they contributed less on average.
(4) The clear beneficiaries were people in the older generations, or earlier
    entrants into the system of pay-as-you-go intergenerational transfers.

The viability of a pay-as-you-go intergenerational transfer scheme can be examined as an exercise in generational accounting. Viability requires that the present
value of the government's tax receipts be greater than or equal to the present
value of the government's payment obligations in the future. If the present value
of a government's future commitments to pay exceeds the present value of tax
receipts, the pay-as-you-go scheme of intergenerational transfers is technically
bankrupt. Restoring viability requires increased tax payments, reduced benefits,
or a combination of both.

In Table 10.1, the returns to tax-paying generations are already negative. Increasing taxes further increases losses for working generations. Reducing benefits
meets with resistance from retired generations. Yet balance inevitably must be
achieved between money paid in and money paid out.

Table 10.2 shows generational accounts for a number of countries. Column (1)
shows the difference between the present value of contributions and expenditures

TABLE 10.2. INTERNATIONAL COMPARISON OF PENSION SCHEMES

Country	Imbalance as percentage of GDP (1)	Public pension payments as percentage of GDP		Increase in tax/GDP ratio required to keep net debt constant	
		1995 (2)	2030 (3)	2005 (4)	2030 (5)
Denmark	−234.5	6.8	10.9	−1.9	3.8
New Zealand	−212.8	5.9	8.3	–	–
Belgium	−152.6	10.4	13.9	−2.0	5.9
Sweden	−132.3	11.8	15.0	−0.6	4.0
Norway	−124.1	5.2	10.9	−2.7	3.8
Portugal	−109.2	7.1	13.0	0.5	8.2
Spain	−108.6	10.0	14.1	0.9	7.4
France	−102.1	10.6	13.5	0.8	7.1
Canada	−100.7	5.2	9.0	−3.2	3.6
Australia	−96.7	2.6	3.8	−1.3	2.4
Austria	−92.5	8.8	14.4	3.8	15.4
Japan	−70.0	6.6	13.4	3.5	9.6
Germany	−61.6	11.1	16.5	2.8	9.7
Italy	−59.7	13.3	20.3	1.8	11.4
United Kingdom	−23.8	4.5	5.5	1.7	3.5
United States	−23.0	4.1	6.6	−0.3	5.3
Ireland	−17.8	3.6	2.8	−0.3	1.8

Source: Kotlikoff and Ferguson (2000).

for retirement consumption as a percentage of a country's gross domestic product.[10] All the numbers are negative. Therefore, retirement schemes of all countries in Table 10.2 are actuarially bankrupt.

Higher productivity growth and a lower discount rate reduce the imbalances between the present value of payment obligations and receipts. The age of mandatory retirement and the level of benefits that were set when the retirement schemes were initiated also affect the degree of imbalance. We see from column (1) in Table 10.2 that the imbalances of the United States, the United Kingdom, and Ireland are relatively favorable when compared with other countries.

Column (2) shows public pension payments as a percentage of GDP in the year 1995. Column (3) shows the projected share of public pension payments in GDP in the year 2030. In all countries with the exception of Ireland, the share of public pensions in GDP increases.

Columns (4) and (5) show the tax adjustments required to balance the generational accounts and to finance the pay-as-you-go intergenerational transfers

[10] The values are computed up to the year 2070, using 1994 as the base year for the value of gross domestic product, with productivity in each country set as growing by 1.5 percent per year. The discount rate used in computing present value is 5 percent.

without increasing government debt. If taxes are not increased, governments must borrow to finance their social-security or public-pension obligations. If neither taxes nor borrowing increase, balance of revenues against payment obligations as a last resort can be achieved by inflationary financing, or simply printing money (which we saw in Chapter 7 is also a tax).

Column (4) shows the increase in taxes relative to GDP required in the year 2005, and sustained thereafter, to keep the debt/GDP ratio constant as of the year 1995. Column (5) shows the same number if the tax increase is deferred until the year 2030. We see substantial differences in the required magnitudes of tax increases between confronting the problem of imbalance in 2005 and deferring the problem until the year 2030.

The adjustment in 2005 places the burden of tax increases on a different generation than if adjustment is deferred until 2030. Tax increases are politically unpopular. Politicians who seek political support in 2005 are in general not the same politicians who will confront the problem of imbalance in the year 2030.

10.3.3 Personal voluntary provision for retirement

The intergenerational pay-as-you-go transfers that we have been considering are the only means of providing for the old in a hunter-gather society where there are no financial or real assets that can be personally accumulated for old-age consumption. Where financial and real assets exist, there is an alternative to pay-as-you-go intergenerational transfers for providing for old-age consumption. People can make their own personal voluntary provision for retirement through financial markets.

Let us first take one step beyond a hunter-gatherer society, to consider a society where money or gold or silver provides a store of value over time. There is also a market in food and shelter. During their working years, people can voluntarily save for their old age; when they are old, they can use their savings to buy food and shelter. Markets thereby allow intertemporal transfer of consumption from working to retired years.

In a further step, we can introduce financial assets, such as government bonds.[11] People can buy the bonds during the working period of their lives and sell the bonds during their retirement years to finance their old-age consumption. The bonds might be sold back to the government; that is, the government might redeem the bonds. The bonds can also be sold to people who are working and who wish to provide for their own old age. Therefore, transactions in the bond market allow deferral of consumption from working to retired years.[12]

Bonds perform the same function as a pay-as-you-go intergenerational transfer scheme. Intertemporal transfers from young to old are, however, now voluntary through markets. The old sell their bonds for money in the bond market and use

[11] In Chapter 2, we described the use of bond financing by government for public projects.
[12] Supplement 10E shows that intertemporal competitive markets are efficient. Intertemporal markets are no different in principle from markets in which there are buyers and sellers at a point in time. The price in an intertemporal market is the interest rate.

the money to buy food. Later the bonds will be sold again to finance old-age consumption by the working generation that bought the bonds.

Intertemporal transfers through the voluntary transactions of a bond market are subject to the demographic problems that we have noted affect a pay-as-you-go intergenerational transfer scheme. The young still produce for both themselves and the old. If there are fewer young people relative to old people at any point in time, less is available for consumption per person in the society.

Negative interest rates

In a society where population is declining, consider people who are 50 years old and who wish to finance consumption in 20 years time at age 70. If they buy a bond for $100 that can be redeemed for $100 in 20 years time, the interest rate on the bond is zero. The purpose of the bond is to enable consumption to be transferred over time, and the persons wishing to defer consumption to the future accept the zero interest rate on the bond.

Suppose that bread costs $1 a loaf when the bond is purchased, but costs $2 per loaf in 20 years time when the bond is sold to finance consumption. The increase in price has not occurred because of inflation but because of demographic changes. Because population is declining, there will be fewer young productive people in the future whose output feeds the entire population of working and retired people.

The real rate of interest over the period of the bond is therefore minus 50 percent. Suppose that the negative real rate of interest is known in advance. Nonetheless, people will still wish to buy the bond when 50 years old and sell the bond when 70 years old because the only way that they can assure their survival at age 70 (when they will not be working and earning income) is to use the bond market to transfer consumption over time.

We saw that, with declining population, pay-as-you-go tax-financed intergenerational transfer schemes yield negative rates of return. Demographic problems are not exclusive to compulsory pay-as-you-go intergenerational transfer schemes. The returns to voluntary intertemporal transfers through bond markets can also be negative for the same demographic reasons that compulsory pay-as-you-go schemes can yield negative returns. In both cases, people are provided with future consumption, and how much will be available for consumption in both cases, depends on how many people are working relative to how many people are consuming, when only the young work and both the young and the old consume.

Durable productive assets

Let us now introduce private ownership of durable productive assets. Remember that until now we have been looking at a hunter-gatherer society. Although we introduced financial assets, our picture of the society has not included privately owned durable productive assets. Privately owned durable productive assets allow the old to release themselves from dependence for old-age consumption on the young because the old can receive income from ownership of the productive assets.

The first change from a hunter-gatherer society is in general to an agrarian society. With private ownership of agricultural land, the old can pay the young to work the land and can live from the surplus returns from the land. In modern society, housing and stock markets similarly permit old-age consumption through asset ownership.

When durable productive assets exist, the rate of interest is in general positive. The rate of interest is equal to the marginal benefit provided by capital over time (or the value of the marginal product of capital), which is positive.

Still, suppose that population is in decline, so that there are fewer and fewer people of working age over time. The decrease in available labor relative to capital or productive land increases the real income of labor and reduces the real incomes of people (the elderly and retired) who live from interest income. The demographic problems are still present. Fewer people are working to sustain the total population of young and old, and market returns to durable productive assets change to redistribute income from the old to the young.

Compulsory or voluntary savings?

Financial markets and private asset ownership allow private voluntary savings for old age but do not ensure that everyone will have adequate means of support during retirement years. Some people may have been unable to save in the course of their working lives because they did not earn enough income.

Also, some people may have made a decision not to save for retirement. The reason for not saving may be failure to recognize the need to provide for post-retirement consumption. People at age 20 may fail to envisage their needs at age 30 or 40, let alone at age 60 or 65. People do not like to think of themselves as being old one day. The future may seem so far off, and the enjoyment of present life may be so compelling, that all income is used for present consumption. People may, therefore, live their lives according to the principle, "I want it all, and I want it now." Even as time passes, old age and retirement may remain too far off to provide a motive for saving for old age. By the time the recognition of the need to provide for old-age consumption takes hold, it may be too late to accumulate adequate savings to allow a reasonable living standard during retirement years.

Moral hazard can also be present. People may decide not to save, but rather to rely on the conscience of society to save them from destitution when old.

People who fail voluntarily to provide for old age will have to be provided with food and shelter when they are old, either through private charity or through the public finance of government. Public finance will require taxation. The taxpayers will be the working generation and other retired persons who were prudent and saved for their old age.

To preempt the need for such tax-financed payments to people who did not make provision for their old age, a society can decide that personal saving for old age should be compulsory. That is, people can be legally required to invest in pension funds that will provide them with income after retirement.

Compulsory saving and investment in pension funds do not solve the problem of people who lack the means to save for their old age. Such people will in all likelihood have received income transfers from government during their younger years and will continue to receive tax-financed income transfers in their later years.

Pooled or personal savings

When saving to provide for old age is compulsory, we confront the further question whether the compulsory savings should be pooled or personal. Pooled and personal retirement funds provide insurance against different types of risks.

A personal payment scheme protects against *biometric risk*. Biometric risk is the risk that an individual, or dependent family members, will live long enough to reach an age where income is no longer earned. This is a personal risk.

A pooled system protects against an unstable family life, against lack of investment in education, and against unemployment or illness during working years. Therefore, the pooled or collective scheme provides social insurance.

With a pooled scheme, we return to the moral-hazard and adverse-selection problems of social insurance. In pooled scheme, income redistribution takes place through insurance and through moral hazard. Income redistribution also takes place when people die and leave a dependent spouse and children who are cared for through social security. People who die after marrying a number of times can have multiple past spouses with dependent children to be cared for.

All people pay into the pooled fund when they earn income, but all people do not survive to reach the age when payouts begin. Therefore, income redistribution takes place from people who have shorter lives to people who live longer. If richer people tend to live longer than poorer people, the income redistribution is from poor to rich because the poor are less likely to reach retirement age to obtain the benefits.

A means test

Under a pooled scheme, benefits to retired people can be subject to a means test, which determines payments for retired persons according to "need." The need is defined by other income that retired people have available to them and by their wealth. There is an incentive to avoid a means test by relinquishing ownership of property and other assets, which can be passed to children and other beneficiaries while alive. When assets are not relinquished, a means test in combination of progressive taxation has the consequence that, the more money people pay in taxes during their life times, the less they receive back in return. Individuals or families that have been financially successful may have paid considerable parts of income as taxation and, because of a means test, may receive little or no benefit when reaching the age of retirement. An individual or family that has not been financially successful will have paid in little, and, not having much, when retired can receive a considerable return from the pension or social-security scheme.

Effects on savings and growth

When intergenerational transfers take place through a pay-as-you-go scheme, people may think that their taxes have been "invested" to create a fund that will be the source of the payouts when they retire. Their future retirement payments are, however, based on an "unfunded" scheme of transfers because their taxes have directly financed income transfers to the old. Because of the future intergenerational transfers that will provide for them in their old age, people may quite rationally feel that they do not need to save and accumulate personal assets to finance old-age consumption. That is, under a pay-as-you-go scheme, people may perceive themselves as saving for old age through their social-security or tax contributions. Their savings are, however, transformed into consumption for the old and are not true investment. On the other hand, when assets are accumulated to finance old-age consumption, savings are invested to create productive assets that provide for future consumption. Growth is therefore higher when personal savings are transformed to productive assets than when pay-as-you-go intergenerational transfers are used to provide for old-age consumption.

Risk spreading

There is a risk that personal savings may be lost in unwise investment decisions or because of bad fortune. Such risk can generally be avoided by spreading private risk through diversified personal investments. Mutual funds and private pension schemes allow people to diversify as well as delegate investment decisions to professionals. Or people can buy assets linked to broad stock indexes. In the long run, a diversified portfolio of stocks tends to provide a return that reflects the fundamentals of the growth of the economy.

Political decisions

Personal savings for old age or payments into a social security fund are personal property accumulated through personal contributions. Political decisions cannot be readily made to appropriate or redistribute this private property. Public pensions payments funded through taxation are not based on personal contributions. A government-funded collective pension scheme is more susceptible to change through political decisions than a scheme that identifies and records personal contributions.

10.3.4 Transition from intergenerational dependence

A pay-as-you-go intergenerational transfer scheme is an investment. An individual will prefer to "invest" in a pay-as-you-go intergenerational transfer scheme rather than in financial or productive assets if the rate of population growth, which we have denoted g, exceeds the market rate of return on investments in assets. We can denote the return from investment in assets by r. The intergenerational scheme is therefore a preferred investment if

$$g > r. \tag{10.5}$$

When people are having children and the rate of growth of population g is high, the intergenerational transfer scheme is attractive. When the demographic problems that we considered are present and r comes to exceed g, the preferred investment for a young person is in financial or asset markets. In particular, the market rate of return r can be positive when the return g from intergenerational transfers can be negative. In these circumstances, younger people have an incentive to switch from the social contract of intergenerational transfers to funded investments based on personal asset accumulation that yield market rates of return.

To invest in assets that yield a market rate of return, the young might attempt to reduce pay-as-you-go transfers to the old. The young and the retired generation are then in distributional conflict.

Both the young working generation and the retired generation can appeal to social justice. The case for social justice made by the people in the retired generation is that they honored the intergenerational contract when they were working and earning income. The social justice of the case of the young generation is that they too want a reasonable standard of living in the future when they retire, and that continuation of the pay-as-you-go system will not provide such reasonable living standards. The young generation can also claim that they did not participate in the decisions about benefits to the retired generation and may feel no obligation to honor an arrangement to which they did not agree, especially if defined benefits for retired people seem inordinately high.

The young can also claim that the retired generation deserved its predicament because, when young, the retired generation failed to have enough children to provide a future working-age generation that could adequately support them through intergenerational transfers. Moreover, knowing that their generation did not have enough children, the retired persons should have supplemented their social-security taxes with private savings. The means of private savings should have been available because members of the retired generation did not have the high personal expenses required to rear children.

Terminating the pay-as-you-go intergenerational contract would violate Pareto efficiency. The young generation would be made better off and the retired generation would be made worse off. The working generation could not (and would not) compensate the retired generation for its losses.

With a low or negative rate of population growth g, the change from intergenerational transfers to a funded scheme with accumulated assets would benefit all future generations who would receive the rate of return r from their personal investments rather than the low or negative return g that is determined by the rate of population growth.

The excess burden of taxation

There are efficiency losses due to the excess burden of taxation when taxes redistribute income between different generations.[13] The efficiency losses can be

---

[13] Recall from Chapter 5, that efficiency losses are incurred when taxes finance income redistribution. In Chapter 5, we looked at redistribution of income among members of one generation.

eliminated by changing from pay-as-you-go transfers that require payment of social security taxes to voluntary saving for old age, which does not require taxation.

The beneficiaries of the efficiency gains from elimination of the excess burden of taxation are the young, who are the taxpayers. The young not only benefit from replacing the intergenerational transfers by voluntary savings and so not having to pay taxes but also benefit by avoiding the excess burden of the taxes. The old lose in the change from a pay-as-you-go to a funded scheme because they no longer receive the pay-as-you-go transfers.

The young gain more than the old lose, but the young cannot compensate the old.[14] For example, suppose that under a pay-as-you-go scheme, the young are paying taxes of 1,000, which is transferred to the old, and that the excess burden of the taxation on the young is 300. Ending the pay-as-you-go intergenerational transfers provides the young with a benefit of 1,300, and the old lose their previous transfers of 1,000. Compensating the old requires giving them 1,000, which requires taxes on the young of 1,000 and which again incurs the 300 excess burden.

That is, compensating the old would require a return to the status quo of intergenerational transfers, and therefore a return to the previous inefficiency of the excess burden of taxation. We are back with the excess burden that we set out to eliminate.

Although the young cannot compensate the old for ending the pay-as-you-go transfers, the change from tax-financed intergenerational transfers to a voluntary saving scheme is efficient for society in aggregate because of the elimination of the excess burden of taxation. The young, however, obtain the entire benefits from the change, and all losses fall on the old.[15]

Bond financing to spread the cost of the change

The cost of ending pay-as-you-go intergenerational transfers can be spread more evenly if bond financing is used to maintain the consumption of the old. Future taxpayers then share the costs of change, in the same way as bond financing spreads the cost of a durable public good over future generations. A government can issue bonds and use the revenue from the sale of the bonds to finance consumption of the retired generation. The bonds are bought by the working generation, which will redeem the bonds when it retires, at which time a new working generation can be taxed to provide the revenue for the bond redemption.

Voting for change

The decision whether to end pay-as-you-go transfers could be put to a vote. Retired persons would vote to retain the pay-as-you-go scheme. People beginning their

---

[14] In Chapter 1, we considered compensation as an accompaniment of the criterion of Pareto efficiency. We noted that a change was Pareto efficient, if the gainers could compensate the losers and still be better off.

[15] In our example, the young gain 1,300 and the old lose 1,000. The total benefits from the change exceed the total costs, but the old cannot be compensated for their loss.

working careers would vote to end the pay-as-you-go transfers. What of people in between?

Because past personal contributions to the pay-as-you-go transfer system have been consumed by the retired generation and cannot be restored, a middle-aged person has nothing to show for past personal social-security taxes that have been paid (other than an obligation to be repaid in the future through the pay-as-you-go scheme).

For example, with the market rate of return for investment exceeding the rate of population growth, let us consider a person who begins to work at the age of 24. This person would vote to end the pay-as-you-go scheme because of the higher market rate of return from investment in assets.

A person aged 44 is some time from retirement but might vote to continue the pay-as-you-go intergenerational transfers. At age 44, the present value of future retirement payments through future pay-as-you-go transfer entitlements might exceed the benefits from switching to private asset accumulation to obtain the market return because only the future matters. All past "investments" through payment of pay-as-you-go social security taxes have been lost.

Therefore, among the working population, there can be majority support to retain the pay-as-you-go transfer scheme, even though the return from asset market investments exceeds the return from the pay-as-you-go transfers.

Outcomes of voting decisions are also affected by demographic trends that determine the number of voters in different age groups. With population declining and older people living longer, the older population has a political advantage in determining outcomes by majority voting.[16]

Pay-as-you-go transfer schemes can therefore continue to have majority support, even though the schemes provide returns that are inferior to the returns from investments in real and financial assets.

10.3.5 Intergenerational risk sharing

An entire generation can suffer from an adverse shock to its income. Such an adverse shock occurred, for example, during the Great Depression of the 1930s, when a large part of the population reached old age without means of support. The U.S. pay-as-you-go social security scheme was introduced during this time, and retired persons received free retirement benefits financed by the pay-as-you-go taxes of people earning income.

A society can also confront an adverse shock from a natural disaster such as an earthquake that wipes out the value of the population's accumulated assets. Pay-as-you-go transfers allow for intergenerational risk sharing in face of the possibility of such disasters. The living standards (or lives) of the population whose assets were wiped out are sustained when these people reach retirement age.

---

[16] The retired and near-retired population can also have an advantage in acting as an interest group to influence public-policy decisions because of the focus on one policy issue. See Chapter 6.

Suppose that generation A has been subject to the adverse shock that has wiped out its assets. When generation A retires, a younger generation B that is working would, through a pay-as-you-go scheme, transfer goods for consumption to the retired generation A. There is however no gain through risk-sharing to members of generation B from transferring consumption to the retired generation A. The younger working generation has already witnessed the adverse outcome for the older retired generation and loses from being in an insurance pool with a generation that is already known to need the insurance with certainty (which is then not insurance).

There is a problem of adverse selection. Members of generation B would maximize their personal lifetime incomes by not making the consumption transfers to generation A. Without government to enforce compulsory income transfers through taxation, social insurance, as insurance against idiosyncratic intergenerational shock, break downs – unless the younger generation acts as if it adheres to an intergenerational social contract.

10.3.6 Conclusions

Insurance protects against risk. In this section, we have noted the presence of a number of different types of risks that are related to provision for old age. There is risk associated with how long a person will live, or biometric risk. This form of risk differs from other risks because the uncertain event against which people seek insurance is beneficial rather than disadvantageous. More usually, insurance is sought in the face of adverse outcomes, such as bad health or loss due to theft or damage. Biometric risk involves the risk that an individual achieves the outcome of living a long life.

Another form of risk is associated with personal lifetime circumstances. A nonsupportive family background or a life history of bad health and unemployment can leave a person with inadequate personal means of support in old age. Social security covers people against the risk of reaching old age with such inadequate means of personal support.

There is also capital-market risk. People may save and make investments that are intended to provide for post-retirement consumption, but the investments may turn out to be unsuccessful.

We have seen that pay-as-you-go intergenerational transfers are subject to demographic risk. The demographic risk gives rise to a political risk: people who contributed to a pay-as-you-go intergenerational transfer scheme during their working lives confront the risk that the pay-as-you-go transfers will be discontinued because better returns are available from investments in asset markets.

In societies with pay-as-you-go intergenerational transfers, viability of the intergenerational social contract can be compromised not only by demographic change but also by early retirement and high benefits offered on retirement. Problems due to demographic change can be alleviated by changing to an asset-backed system for financing post-retirement consumption. The accumulated assets provide a means of financing consumption during retirement, so ending reliance on transfers from the younger working generation for old-age survival. We have seen that issues arise regarding whether the asset-backed scheme should be compulsory or voluntary, and whether the scheme should be personal or pooled.

A change from a pay-as-you-go transfer system to an asset-backed system has distributional affects. With the asset-backed or funded system having a greater rate of return, a majority of voters may nonetheless favor retaining the pay-as-you-go system, including older voters in the working population. Nonetheless the pay-as-you-go scheme may not be viable in the long term.

Whether pay-as-you-go transfer schemes are viable is revealed through generational accounting. When generational accounting reveals pay-as-you-go intergenerational transfer schemes to be technically bankrupt in having a present value of payout obligations that exceed the present value of tax revenues, political decision makers might prefer to leave changes for the next generation of politicians.

We can conclude with a parable that reflects the political incentives. A king once offered to pay a large reward to anybody who would teach his dog to talk within ten years. The penalty for failure after accepting the obligation and the reward was, however, severe (death). For a long time, no one dared to accept the challenge of teaching the king's dog to talk. Then, finally, one person (a politician) came forward and declared to the king that he would teach the dog to talk. The king gave the politician his reward for accepting the challenge, and the politician took the dog and left the palace. Outside the palace, a crowd of people that had gathered asked the politician: how could you agree to such an impossible assignment? The politician replied: be patient. In the course of ten years, the dog might die, the king could die, or I might die. Or the dog might learn to talk. Teaching the dog to talk is the challenge of sustaining the social contract of pay-as-you-go intergenerational transfers in the face of imbalance in generational accounts. The death of the dog, or of the king, is spontaneous resolution of the problem from a source not explained (or is wishful thinking). The immediate reward for the politician is in the next election, by declaring the feasibility of the prospect that the dog can be taught to talk. If the king lives, and if the dog lives and does not learn to talk, there will be a problem. The obligation to teach the dog to talk will, however, have been passed on to future politicians or a future government.

References and related literature

On the history of social security, see Verbon (1988). On approaches to providing for old age in different societies, see Gruber and Wise (1999). On the theory of intergenerational transfers, see Samuelson (1958), Aaron (1966), Diamond (1977), Kotlikoff and Spivak (1981), Veall (1986), Hubbard and Judd (1987), Hansson and Stuart (1989), and Cigno (1993). On demographics, see Bental (1989), Disney (1996), Kolmar (1997), and de Nardi, İmroharoğlu, and Sargent (1999); for an optimistic view of U.S. social security, see Bohn (1999). On education and growth as a solution to demographic problems, see Zhang (1995),

Marchand, Michel, and Pestieau (1996), and Kaganovich and Zilcha (1999). On migration as a solution, see Hillman (2000) and Storesletten (2000). On the problem of emigration to a response to demographic problems, see von Hagen and Waltz (1995). On generational accounting, see Kotlikoff (1992), Auerbach, Kotlikoff, and Liebfritz (1999), and Kotlikoff and Rafelhuschen (1999). On political decisions and social security, see Browning (1975), Boadway and Wildasin (1989), Breyer (1994), Cooley and Soares (1999), and Casamatta, Cremer, and Pestieau (2000); for a survey of political economy models of social security, see Galasso and Profeta (2002). On change from pay-as-you-go transfers, see Brunner (1996), Feldstein (1998), Diamond (1999), Disney (2000), and Sinn (2000). On intergenerational risk sharing, see Gordon and Varian (1988). On intertemporal markets and intertemporal transfers, see Eckstein, Eichenbaum, and Peled (1985).

Aaron, H. J., 1966. The social insurance paradox. *Canadian Journal of Economics* 32, 371–4.

Auerbach, A., L. J. Kotlikoff and W. Liebfritz, 1999. *Generational Accounting around the World*. University of Chicago Press, Chicago.

Bental, B., 1989. The old age security hypothesis and optimal population growth. *Journal of Population Economics* 1, 285–301.

Boadway, R. and D. Wildasin, 1989. A median voter model of social security. *International Economic Review* 30, 307–28.

Bohn, H., 1999. Will social security and Medicare remain viable as the U.S. population is aging? *Carnegie Rochester Series on Public Policy* 50, 1–53.

Breyer, F., 1994. The political economy of intergenerational redistribution. *European Journal of Political Economy* 10, 61–84.

Browning, E. K., 1975. Why the social insurance budget is too large in a democracy. *Economic Inquiry* 13, 373–88.

Brunner, J. K., 1996. Transition from a pay-as-you-go to a fully funded pension system: The case of differing individuals and intergenerational fairness. *Journal of Public Economics* 60, 131–46.

Casamatta, G., H. Cremer and P. Pestieau, 2000. Political sustainability and the design of social insurance. *Journal of Public Economics* 75, 341–64.

Cigno, A., 1993. Intergenerational transfers without altruism. *European Journal of Political Economy* 9, 505–18.

Cooley, T. and J. Soares, 1999. A positive theory of social security based on reputation. *Journal of Political Economy* 107, 135–65.

de Nardi, M., S. İmroharoĝlu, and T. Sargent, 1999. Projected U.S. demographics and social security. *Review of Economic Dynamics* 2, 575–615.

Diamond, P. A., 1977. A framework for social security analysis. *Journal of Public Economics* 8, 275–98.

Diamond. P. (ed.), 1999. *Issues in Privatizing Social Security: Report of an Expert Panel of the National Academy of Social Insurance*. MIT Press, Cambridge, Massachusetts.

Disney, R., 1996. *Can We Afford to Grow Older: A Perspective on Aging*. MIT Press, Cambridge, Massachusetts.

Disney, R., 2000. Crises in public pension programmes in OECD: What are the reform options? *Economic Journal* 110, F1–23.

Eckstein, Z., M. Eichenbaum and D. Peled, 1985. Uncertain lifetimes and the welfare-enhancing properties of annuity markets and social security. *Journal of Public Economics* 26, 303–26.

Feldstein, M. (ed.), 1998. *Privatizing Social Security*. Chicago University Press, Chicago.

Galasso, V. and P. Profeta, 2002. Political economy models of social security: A survey. *European Journal of Political Economy* 18, 1–29.

Gokhale, J., B. Page, J. Potter and J. Sturrock, 2000. Generational accounts for the United States: An update. *American Economic Review Papers and Proceedings* 90, 293–6.

Gordon, R. and H. R., Varian 1988. Intergenerational risk sharing. *Journal of Public Economics* 37, 185–202.

Gruber, J. and D. Wise (eds.), 1999. *Social Security and Retirement around the World*. University of Chicago Press, Chicago.

Hansson, I. and C. Stuart,1989. Social security as trade among living generations. *American Economic Review* 79, 1182–95.

Hillman, A. L., 2002. Immigration and intergenerational transfers. In *Economic Policy for Aging Societies*, H. Siebert (ed.). Springer, Berlin, 213–26.

Hubbard, R. G. and K. Judd, 1987. Social security and individual welfare. *American Economic Review* 77, 630–46.

Kaganovich, M. and I. Zilcha, 1999. Education, social security, and growth. *Journal of Public Economics* 40, 37–56.

Kolmar, M., 1997. Intergenerational redistribution in a small open economy with endogenous fertility. *Journal of Population Economics* 10, 335–56.

Kotlikoff, L. J., 1992. *Generational Accounting*. Free Press, New York.

Kotlikoff, L. J. and N. Ferguson, 2000. The degeneration of EMU. *Foreign Affairs* 79, 110–21.

Kotlikoff, L. J. and B. Rafelhuschen, 1999. Generational accounting around the globe. *American Economic Review* 90, 161–6.

Kotlikoff, L. J. and A. Spivak, 1981. The family as an incomplete annuities market. *Journal of Political Economy* 89, 320–91.

Marchand, M., P. Michel and P. Pestieau, 1996. Optimal intergenerational transfers in an endogenous growth model with fertility changes. *European Journal of Political Economy* 12, 33–48.

Samuelson, P. A., 1958. An exact consumption-loan model of interest with and without the social contrivance of money. *Journal of Political Economy* 66, 467–82.

Sinn, H-W., 2000. Why a funded pension system is useful and why it is not. *International Tax and Finance Journal* 7, 389–410.

Storesletten, K., 2000. Sustaining fiscal policy through immigration. *Journal of Political Economy* 108, 300–23.

Veall, M. R., 1986. Public pensions as socially optimal contracts. *Journal of Public Economics* 31, 237–51.

Verbon, H. A. A., 1988. *The Evolution of Public Pension Systems*. Springer-Verlag, Berlin.

von Hagen, J. and U. Waltz, 1995. Social security and migration in an aging Europe. In *Politics and Institutions in an Integrated Europe*, B. Eichengreen, J. Frieden, and J. von Hagen (eds.). Springer, Heidelberg, 177–92.

Zhang, J., 1995. Social security and endogenous growth. *Journal of Public Economics* 58, 185–213.

Questions for discussion

1. In a hunter-gatherer society, the old who can no longer fend for themselves can only stay alive through food and shelter provided by the young who gather food and hunt. A social contract allows intergenerational transfers so that the old in every generation can continue living. Why is a demonstration effect not a rational basis for the intergenerational transfers from the young to the old? What is a basis for behavior that sustains the intergenerational transfers? Why are the intergenerational transfers in this society precisely like a pay-as-you-go (unfunded) social security or pension scheme?

2. Why would you expect the social contract of intergenerational transfers to be successfully sustained in the family without enforcement, whereas the enforcement by government is required when the contract covers a large number of anonymous people?

3. How does demographic change affect the returns from pay-as-you-go intergenerational transfers when the transfers are based on (i) designated contributions or (ii) designated benefits for retired persons?

4. How do externalities affect pay-as-you-go intergenerational transfers through decisions regarding the number of children a person has? How do externalities arise through decisions to educate children?

5. What is a Ponzi scheme? Why have intergenerational transfers where initial generations define high retirement entitlements for themselves been likened to a Ponzi scheme?

6. When demographic trends threaten the viability of a pay-as-you-go intergenerational transfer scheme, what are the public-policy responses that a government can adopt? What are the political impediments to the public policies? What do you expect to happen eventually if there is no public-policy response when intergenerational transfer schemes are not viable?

7. What is generational accounting? How does generational accounting reveal whether a pay-as-you-go intergenerational transfer scheme is viable in the long run? How does generational accounting reveal the costs of deferring solutions to balance generational accounts? Why is there an incentive for political decision makers to shift a solution to the future?

8. Does the government oversee a pay-as-you-go intergenerational transfer scheme in the place where you live or study? What are the characteristics of the scheme (is the scheme based on defined contributions, defined benefits, or a combination of both)? How does the pay-as-you-go scheme fare in terms of generational accounting (have doubts been voiced about the future viability of the scheme)?

9. How do pay-as-you-go schemes redistribute income between high- and low-income people, or between married and unmarried people? Are the redistributions consistent with social justice?

10. Suppose that we leave a hunter-gatherer society and allow for personal savings, which allows individuals to prepare themselves personally for a time when they will no longer be earning income. How would you expect the presence of a pay-as-you-go transfer scheme to affect personal savings decisions? Is a government pay-as-you-go scheme a form of "saving for old age"?

11. Rather than receive transfers through a pay-as-you-go intergenerational scheme, people could save for their old age by buying government bonds. How does a bond market differ from a pay-as-you-go intergenerational transfer scheme? Does a bond market solve demographic problems?

12. How could the interest rate on bonds be negative?

13. When a retirement scheme is funded (the money people save is used to invest in financial or real assets that provide interest payments or can be sold in the future), people can make their own personal voluntary decisions about investments to provide for their old age. The government can also make the investments compulsory and compel people to pool their savings through mandatory mutual funds. Should government make savings for old age compulsory? Should the government insist on pooling? Explain.

14. When taxes are used to finance intergenerational income transfers, there is an excess burden of taxation, just as when taxes finance income redistribution within a generation. Elimination of the excess burden of taxation is the source of an efficiency gain when a change is made from a pay-as-you-go scheme to an asset-backed scheme. Does this efficiency gain allow compensation that makes both the working and

retired generations better off from the change in the means of financing retirement consumption? Explain.

15. How can bond financing alleviate problems when a decision is made to change from an unfunded (not-asset-backed) pay-as-you-go scheme to a funded (asset-backed) scheme?

16. What should be the response of government when young generations complain that continued compulsory participation in compulsory pay-as-you-go social security yields inferior returns to investment in bonds or the stock market? Suppose that the question whether to change from a pay-as-you-go scheme to a funded scheme is put before voters and that the decision is made by majority voting. What do you expect the decision of the median voter to be? Explain. How is the position of the median voter influenced by demographic trends?

17. What are the different types of risks involved when people wish to provide for their old age? How can pay-as-you-go intergenerational transfer schemes be interpreted as intergenerational risk sharing?

18. Before pay-as-you-go intergenerational schemes based on taxation were first introduced, how did people survive during their old age?

19. It is sometimes proposed that social security or pension schemes should consist of both unfunded and funded components (see, for example, Hans-Werner Sinn, 2000). The argument is that if people did not have enough children to allow the viability of an unfunded pay-as-you-go scheme, they should realize that they need to accumulate assets to make up the shortfall resulting from the smaller number of people in the younger generation contributing to the pay-as-you-go transfers to the old generations. These people should have the means of personally saving for their old age through a funded scheme because they did not spend their money on children. What implications follow from the fact that some people have more children than others, or that some people have children when others have none? Do you believe that the existence of a government-implemented pay-as-you-go scheme of intergenerational transfers is itself a reason why people have chosen to have fewer children, so making the scheme nonviable because of demographic problems? Explain.

20. In summary, what do you believe should be the responsibility of government regarding providing for old age?

POSTSCRIPT: WHY VIEWS CAN DIFFER

Economists sometimes find themselves disagreeing with one another. Lack of consensus can be found in other fields of research and enquiry. For example, professors of physics might disagree about the existence of dark matter to account for the distribution of observable matter in the universe. Medical researchers might disagree about the underlying reasons for the malfunctioning of cells. Historians can disagree about what happened and why. Psychologists can disagree about the reasons for pathological human behavior. Disagreement is common, and the task of ongoing research is to reduce disagreement.

Disagreement among economists can be normative or positive. When disagreement is normative, the disagreement is about what is desirable. Disagreement can also be positive, about facts, explanations, and predictions. These disagreements can in principle be resolved by empirical economic research. For example, the size of the excess burden of an income tax, which affects efficient public spending on public goods and socially desirable income redistribution, is determined by empirical measurement of how increased taxation affects hours worked or effort. Measurement can, however, give different results. A position regarding the excess burden of taxation can also be normative. The normative position is that incentives and efficiency should not stand in the way of decisions about taxation to redistribute income.

One economist may be expressing a normative preference when another is making a positive statement. The economist making the normative statement is describing behavior or outcomes that he or she *would like* to see. The economist making the positive statement is offering an explanation or a prediction. For example, one person may declare that there *ought to be* no political principal-agent problem, while another (who agrees) is declaring that there is *in fact* a political principal-agent problem. An informed economic evaluation requires identifying the questions under discussion as normative or as positive. After that step has been taken, attempts to resolve disagreements can begin.

The disagreements that can arise among economists can be expressed in terminology that distinguishes left and right.[1] Economists on the left may regard the principal-agent problem between citizens and government as minimal, and take the position that government can be broadly trusted to choose and bureaucracies trusted to implement public policies in the public interest. A view from the left might also regard information limitations as not serious impediments to assigning responsibilities to government. The judgment might be made that personal incentives are not important in influencing personal economic decisions. That is,

---

[1] The terminology "conservative" and "liberal" could also be used, although, as we have noted, the term liberal is used in precisely contrary ways by different people. In the United States, liberal identifies a position favoring high taxation to finance high public spending and a general predisposition to support assigning responsibilities to government. In Europe and elsewhere, the term "liberal" refers to the opposite predisposition of wishing as far as possible to see people free to make their own decisions in markets and to be free of constraints imposed through public finance and public policy. In this respect, Adam Smith was a liberal. To avoid the confusion of using the term "liberal" with its different meanings, we use the terms "left" and "right" to distinguish predispositions of economists.

excess burdens of taxation are small, and governments can therefore set high taxes to redistribute income without significant efficiency losses. A view from the left may also be that, when all is said and done, people have more or less the same preferences about public spending because people are more or less alike. Because inefficient or unjust outcomes of majority voting require diversity of preferences, a belief that preferences should be uniform (which is normative) or the claim that preferences are in fact uniform (which is positive) is beneficial for collective decision making through government.

A view from the left may tend to favor centralized over multiple government. Centralized government allows income to be redistributed through centralized taxation. Centralized government also moderates the impediment to taxing income from capital and other mobile factors by preempting tax competition, and provides more limited opportunities for individuals to escape high taxes. A view from the left emphasizes the need for social justice and sees tax competition among governments as restricting the scope of social insurance programs because of the locational adverse selection problem. Tax competition may thus be viewed as causing social harm rather than providing a basis for competitive choice among governments.

A belief that people do not differ much in personal preferences for public spending diminishes the scope for benefit from locational choice as a means of matching public spending with personal preferences. A view from the left might also see little scope for benefit to voters from observations on comparative political performance, again because of the belief that the political principal-agent problem is not significant. Competitive discipline on governments is, of course, not required if there is no political principal-agent problem so that government acts in the interest of taxpayers and citizens.

Most basically, the view from the left gives priority to social justice and equality over efficiency. Income redistribution is regarded as the primary justification for public finance and public policy.

Because of the greater perceived benefits from government, the view from the left may de-emphasize the limitations on assigning responsibilities to government. A view from the right stresses these limitations. Therefore, a view from the right stresses the problems of asymmetric information, in particular the moral-hazard problem when government provides social insurance. A view from the right also stresses the inefficiencies, as well as the social injustices, that can accompany majority voting because of diversities in voters' preferences. A view from right stresses the information problems that governments face in making efficient public-spending decisions and in designing efficient corrections for externality problems.

A view from the right points out that government is made up of *people* who, like people everywhere, have self-interests and personal objectives and can be expected to wish to increase their incomes and status. There may be reluctance in the view from the right to believe in the effectiveness of the Thomas-à-Beckett effect. Greater emphasis is placed on the consequences for public policies of the need by

politicians for special-interest money and the personal benefits to government bureaucracy from public spending. With government having a legal monopoly to tax
and to choose and administer public policies, a view from the right expresses concern about whether the political and bureaucratic principal-agent problems are
impediments to voters and taxpayers being able to achieve normatively desirable
objectives through public finance and public policy. The excess burden of taxation and rent-seeking behavior also suggest caution about proposals to increase
taxation and public spending.

Because of the priority given to personal freedom and incentives expressed
through markets, a view from the right stresses the importance of the rule of law
to protect private property. A classic view from the left, on the other hand, sees private property as reflecting and preserving past inequalities. A more contemporary
view from the left may regard private property and rights of personal possession
as subordinate to extensive redistribution justified by social insurance and social
justice.

A view from the right sees multiple government as beneficial. The personal
ability to choose among governments and tax competition among governments
are restraints on the legal monopoly of governments to tax and to decide who
benefits from public spending. The presence of multiple government is also seen
as advantageous because of the information on comparative political performance
that allows voters to judge the competence and honesty of their political representatives. Because of the limitations of government, there is greater receptiveness to
the idea of constitutional restraint that specifies how the authority of government
can be exercised over citizens. A view from the right also places more emphasis
on possible private resolution of problems of efficiency and social justice without
government. There may be greater patience for exploring possibilities of private
voluntary finance for public goods through user prices, private resolution of externality problems by specifying legal rights, and private voluntary giving to help
people in need.

The role of ethics or trust might be emphasized in a view from the right. Ethical
or caring behavior and reciprocated trust diminish the need for the authority
of government. There would be competitive market prices if no one ever took
advantage of monopoly power (in natural as well as ordinary monopoly). If all
people were to respect the natural property rights and freedom of others, the rule
of law through government would not be required. If all people were to reveal
their true benefits from public goods and were voluntarily to pay efficient Lindahl
prices, taxation would not be required to pay for public goods. Public policy and
public finance would not be required to resolve externality problems, if people
were considerate in taking into account how their decisions affect others. The
responsibility of government to provide social insurance would be unnecessary, if
private charity were adequately to provide for the poor and disadvantaged; there
would no accompanying moral-hazard problem, if people did not change their
behavior to take advantage of the presence of social insurance. There would be no
political principal-agent problem and no ambivalence about relying on politicians

and government bureaucracies, if people in government never made personally self-interested decisions that compromise the public interest.

However, the behavior that is here being sought contradicts the principle of personal decisions made for self-benefit that led Adam Smith to find virtue in the market. Hoping for personal behavior not based on personal self-interest returns us to the observations made by Friedrich von Hayek about the unlikely prospects for success of attempts to re-engineer human beings to contribute according to ability rather than personal reward. Yet if we view people as only acting in their self-interest, we make the error of dismissing the possibility of altruistic motives and of ignoring the genuine desire of people to help others in adverse circumstances. Personal self-interest is nonetheless the underlying behavioral principle of economic analysis. We have seen in this book that efficiency and social justice in general require more than voluntary decisions based on personal self-interest. The responsibilities that are consequently required to be assigned to government through public finance and public policy lead us to encounter the different views from the left and the right on the limitations of government and on the priority that should be given to efficiency or to social justice when one objective is only attainable at the expense of the other.

Somewhere between left and right, we must as citizens and voters make our own choices. This book has been about making the choices.

SUPPLEMENTS

Supplements to Chapter 1

1A The efficiency of a competitive market
This supplement looks more closely at the efficiency of a competitive market.

Maximal benefit from consumption
When the market price is P, a buyer or consumer (whom we denote by i) maximizes utility by choosing to purchase a quantity q_{bi} such that marginal benefit from consumption equals the market price:

$$P = MB_i(q_{bi}). \tag{S1.1}$$

Figure S1.1 shows two buyers who choose the consumption quantities q_{b1} and q_{b2} when the market price is P. Because the two buyers confront the same market price, their marginal benefits from consumption are equal. In Figure S1.1, we see that

$$P = MB_1(q_{b1}) = MB_2(q_{b2}). \tag{S1.2}$$

If there are n buyers, the MBs of all n buyers are equal to the market price,

$$P = MB_1(q_{b1}) = MB_2(q_{b2}) = MB_3(q_{b3}) = \cdots = MB_n(q_{bn}). \tag{S1.3}$$

Total market demand is the sum of the n individual demands,

$$Q_b = \sum_{j=1}^{n} q_{bj}. \tag{S1.4}$$

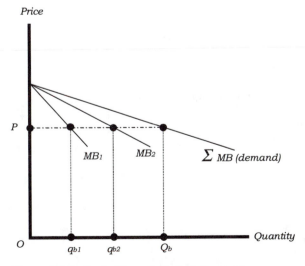

Figure S1.1. Derivation of market demand.

The total benefit $B(Q_b)$ from consumption depends on how the output Q_b is distributed among the population of n consumers:

$$B(Q_b) = B(q_{b1} + q_{b2} + q_{b3} + q_{b4} + \cdots + q_{bn}). \tag{S1.5}$$

An allocation of goods among the population of buyers maximizes total benefit given by (S1.5) when

$$MB_1(q_{b1}) = MB_2(q_{b2}) = MB_3(q_{b3}) = \cdots = MB_n(q_{bn}). \tag{S1.6}$$

We see that condition (S1.6) is the same as condition (S1.3), which describes the market outcome when individual buyers make independent purchase decisions. Therefore, we conclude that total benefit from consumption is maximized when individual buyers make self-interested market decisions.

Minimum cost of supply
In a competitive market, an individual supplier j pursues self-interest by maximizing profit. Profit is maximized by choosing supply of output so that market price equals marginal cost of production:

$$P = MC_j(q_{sj}). \tag{S1.7}$$

Figure S1.2 shows two suppliers' output decisions, for which

$$P = MC_1(q_{s1}) = MC_2(q_{s2}). \tag{S1.8}$$

The sum of the two suppliers' MC functions in Figure S1.2 is market supply.
  With m individual sellers, all sellers' marginal costs are equal,

$$P = MC_1(q_{s1}) = MC_2(q_{s2}) = MC_3(q_{s3}) = \cdots = MC_n(q_{sm}), \tag{S1.9}$$

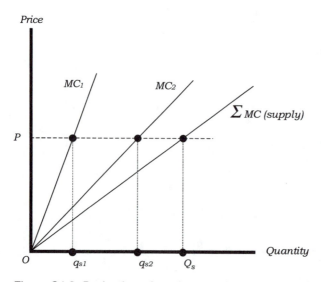

Figure S1.2. Derivation of market supply.

and total output supplied is

$$Q_s = \sum_{j=1}^{m} q_{sj}. \tag{S1.10}$$

For efficiency, we require outputs supplied by different suppliers to minimize total cost $C(Q_s)$. The total cost of supply depends on the quantities provided by each supplier:

$$C(Q_s) = C(q_{s1} + q_{s2} + q_{s3} + q_{s4} + \cdots + q_{sm}). \tag{S1.11}$$

To minimize total cost given by (S1.11), we require marginal cost of production MC to be equal for all m suppliers:

$$MC_1(q_{s1}) = MC_2(q_{s2}) = MC_3(q_{s3}) = \cdots = MC_n(q_{sm}). \tag{S1.12}$$

When individual suppliers make the independent market decisions described in (S1.9), the condition (S1.12) is satisfied. Therefore, the independent supply decisions of competitive suppliers minimize the total cost of market supply.

Efficiency
We define efficiency as maximization of $W = B - C$, where B is total benefit to buyers and C is total cost of sellers. Hence, efficiency requires that

$$MB(Q) = MC(Q). \tag{S1.13}$$

Additionally, a maximum for W requires

$$\frac{\partial MB}{\partial Q} < \frac{\partial MC}{\partial Q}. \tag{S1.14}$$

This condition is satisfied in the usual market equilibrium where demand has a negative slope and supply has a positive or constant slope.

Unstable market equilibria
Figure S1.3 shows a market where the market supply function is negatively sloped. Such a negative slope for market supply, for example, arises if expanding total market supply reduces costs for the different competitive suppliers through the availability of a pool of skilled employees and supportive service industries. Knowledge-based firms tend to concentrate in the same location to take advantage of such cost-reducing benefits. In Figure S1.3, there are market equilibria at points 1 and 2. Both points satisfy the condition that $MB = MC$, but only point 2 satisfies condition (S1.14). At point 1, $W = (B - C)$ is therefore (locally) minimized. The total social loss when the market provides the quantity Q_1 is the shaded area. Society is better off with zero supply than with the quantity Q_1 supplied to buyers at point 1. In the market equilibrium at the point 2 where Q_2 is supplied, condition (S1.14) for maximization of W is satisfied, and W attains a maximum.

Under the competitive adjustment mechanism, the undesirable market equilibrium at the point 1 in Figure S1.3 is unstable. Beginning from any output below

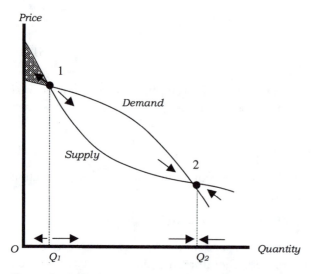

Figure S1.3. Stable and unstable market equilibria.

Q_1, supply will decline to zero. From an output above Q_1, supply will increase to Q_2. The market is thus attracted away from the inefficient equilibrium at the point 1. The desirable equilibrium at point 2 is, on the other hand, stable. The market moves toward efficient supply Q_2 when supply is either above or below Q_2. The competitive output adjustment mechanism ensures that the market will either be at the efficient equilibrium, or that there will be no production (in principle, it is possible for a market to find itself at an inefficient equilibrium, but any small change in supply or demand would displace the equilibrium).

1B The efficiency of a competitive economy

Supplement 1A demonstrated that a competitive market is efficient by looking at a single market in isolation from the rest of the economy. The picture in supplement 1A was partial-equilibrium – partial because of the focus on one market among the many in an economy. We shall now demonstrate the efficiency of an economy with competitive markets through a *general-equilibrium* picture that portrays the many interrelated markets of an entire economy. We shall simplify our picture. We shall look at an economy populated by two people, where two factors of production are used to produce two final consumption goods. We are interested in questions of allocation. We shall show that, in an economy with competitive markets, (1) factors of production (or resources) are efficiently allocated to production of different goods, (2) the combination of goods produced in the economy maximizes the value of output, and (3) the goods produced are allocated efficiently for consumption among the population.

Efficient allocation of resources

Figure S1.4 shows an economy with two factors of production, which we identify as labor and capital. In general, quantities of factors supplied depend on factor

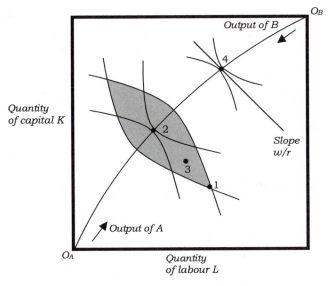

Figure S1.4. Allocation of factors of production.

payments or incentives. Figure S1.4 adopts the simplification that the supply of factors of production is fixed without regard for factor payments.

A point in Figure S1.4 defines an allocation of factors of production between production of goods A and B. Pareto-efficient allocations in Figure S1.4 lie along the *contract curve* $O_A O_B$, which is defined by points where isoquants of the two goods are tangential. Point 2 on the contract curve is a Pareto-efficient allocation, because no move is possible from point 2 to obtain more of one good without giving up a quantity of the other.[1] Point 1 is an inefficient allocation because all points inside the shaded area between the two isoquants that intersect at point 1 provide greater supply of both goods. Moving along any one of the isoquants through point 1 provides more of one good without a decrease in the supply of the other good. From any Pareto-inefficient point such as 1, the allocation can be changed to a point such as 3, which is Pareto-superior in providing more of both goods. From any point such as 3, the allocation can be changed to a point such as 2, which is Pareto-efficient (and Pareto-superior to point 3).

When individuals make decisions about the use of factors of production in competitive factor markets, an economy is on the contract curve, and resource allocation is Pareto-efficient. In a competitive economy, all firms, no matter which goods they produce, obtain factors of production in the same competitive factor markets; therefore, they pay the same price for the services of factors of production that they employ. Let w be the market-determined wage paid by all firms for labor

---

[1] Moving away from point 2 up the contract curve increases the quantity of good A but decreases the quantity of good B. Moving down the contract curve from point 2 increases the quantity of good B at the expense of good A. Moving off the contract curve from point 2 decreases the supply of both goods, or increases the supply of one good while decreasing the supply of the other.

and let r be the cost of capital that confronts each firm (we view r as the return that firms are obliged to pay to the people who provide investment funds). The production technologies for the two goods shown as the isoquants in Figure S1.4 are

$$q_i = F^i(K_i, L_i) \qquad i = A, B. \tag{S1.15}$$

Profits of a firm j producing good A are

$$\pi_A^j = P_A F^A(K_A, L_A) - w L_A^j - r K_A^j. \tag{S1.16}$$

A firm producing good A chooses profit-maximizing employment of labor and use of capital to satisfy

$$\frac{\partial \pi_A^j}{\partial L_A^j} = P_A \frac{\partial F^A}{\partial L_A^j} - w = 0, \qquad \frac{\partial \pi_A^j}{\partial K_A^j} = P_A \frac{F^B}{\partial K_B^j} - r = 0. \tag{S1.17}$$

Therefore,

$$w = P_A \frac{\partial F^A}{\partial L_A^j} \equiv P_A MP_L^A, \qquad r = P_A \frac{\partial F^A}{\partial K_A^j} \equiv P_A MP_K^A. \tag{S1.18a}$$

The same relationships apply for firms producing good B, for which we have

$$w = P_B \frac{\partial F^B}{\partial L_B^j} \equiv P_B MP_L^B, \qquad r = P_B \frac{\partial F^B}{\partial K_B^j} \equiv P_B MP_K^B. \tag{S1.18b}$$

The slope of an isoquant is defined as

$$\frac{MP_L^i}{MP_K^i} \qquad i = A, B. \tag{S1.19}$$

On the Pareto-efficient contract curve, since slopes of isoquants are equal,

$$\frac{MP_L^A}{MP_K^A} = \frac{MP_L^B}{MP_K^B}. \tag{S1.20}$$

Competitive factor markets ensure that the condition (S1.20) is satisfied. Combining expressions (S1.18a) and (S1.18b), we see that, when firms make factor employment decisions in competitive markets,

$$\frac{MP_L^A}{MP_K^A} = \frac{w}{r} = \frac{MP_L^B}{MP_K^B}, \tag{S1.21}$$

where w/r is the relative factor price of labor and capital. Looking at point 4 in Figure S1.4, we see that this price ratio is equal to the slope of the straight line tangential to the A and B isoquants on the contract curve. Firms guided by the competitively determined relative price of labor and capital thus choose combinations

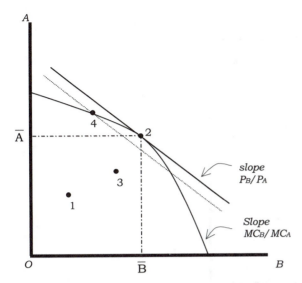

Figure S1.5. Competitive product markets.

of factors of production on the contract curve. In so doing, competitive firms
ensure that an economy's resources are efficiently allocated.

Choice of the combination of goods to produce
By using the information on outputs from the isoquants, we can derive the economy's production possibility frontier as in Figure S1.5. Points 1 and 3 in Figure S1.5
are inside the production possibility frontier because these factor allocations are
not Pareto-efficient. The Pareto-efficient allocations 2 and 4 are on the production
possibility frontier.

At point 2, where the quantities $\bar{A}$ and $\bar{B}$ are produced and P_A and P_B are the
prices of the two goods, the value of the economy's national output (or national
income)

$$Y = P_A\bar{A} + P_B\bar{B}. \tag{S1.22}$$

is maximized. We want the economy to produce at point 2 when the relative price
is P_B/P_A and not for example at point 4 where the value of national output is lower.
At point 2, the relative price line is tangential to the slope of the production possibility frontier. The slope of the frontier is the ratio of marginal costs of production
MC_B/MC_A. In competitive output markets, firms choose the quantity of output
to supply by setting

$$P_A = MC_A, \qquad P_B = MC_B. \tag{S1.23}$$

Therefore, when markets are competitive, it follows that

$$\frac{P_B}{P_A} = \frac{MC_B}{MC_A}. \tag{S1.24}$$

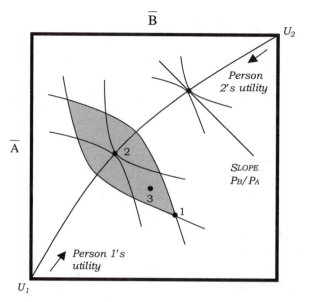

Figure S1.6. Pareto-efficient allocations of goods for consumption.

Competition in product markets accordingly ensures that the economy produces the value-maximizing combination of national output at point 2 in Figure S1.5. If the relative price P_B/P_A were to change, the value-maximizing production point would change from point 2 to another tangency point, as firms adjust to equalize marginal costs of production to the changed prices.

Efficient consumption
The goods produced at point 2 in Figure S1.5 are distributed among the population. Figure S1.6 shows the indifference curves of two consumers, 1 and 2. The dimensions of the box in Figure S1.6 indicate the quantities of two goods available for distribution to the population.[2] The allocation of goods at point 1 in Figure S1.6 is Pareto-inefficient. Point 3 is Pareto-superior to point 1. Point 2 is Pareto-superior to point 3 and is Pareto-efficient. The Pareto-efficient point 2 is on the contract curve.

The contract curve is defined by tangency of consumers' indifference curves. The slope of an indifference curve is defined by

$$MRS^i_{AB} \equiv \frac{MB^i_B}{MB^i_A}, \qquad i = 1, 2 \text{ consumers.} \tag{S1.25}$$

Along the contract curve, since indifference curves are tangent,

$$MRS^1_{AB} = MRS^2_{AB}. \tag{S1.26}$$

---

[2] Figure S1.6 differs from Figure S1.4 only in that outputs, rather than inputs, are being allocated.

An allocation of goods for consumption is Pareto-efficient when (S1.26) is satisfied. In competitive markets, individuals choose quantities of goods to buy by setting the market price equal to the marginal benefit from consumption,

$$P_A = MB^i_A, \qquad P_B = MB^i_B \qquad i = 1, 2 \text{ consumers.} \qquad \text{(S1.27)}$$

Because consumers in competitive markets confront the same market prices when making their consumption decisions, as we see in Figure S1.6,

$$MRS^1_{AB} = \frac{P_B}{P_A} = MRS^2_{AB}. \qquad \text{(S1.28)}$$

The expression (S1.28) is equivalent to (S1.26). In a competitive economy, market-determined allocations determined by individual purchase decisions are therefore on the contract curve, and so are Pareto-efficient. From (S1.28), we see that allocation of goods among buyers through market decisions is efficient if there is no discrimination in prices that different people pay. Price discrimination can be unjust when some people benefit from favors that others do not. We observe that price discrimination is also inefficient.

Simultaneity

We have now looked sequentially at three decisions: (1) how to allocate inputs in production, (2) how to choose the combination of goods to produce, and (3) how to allocate goods for consumption. These decisions require simultaneously available information. In Figure S1.5, the value of the relative price of output is, for example, based on information in Figure S1.6 that is provided by individuals' preferences in consumption.

Efficiency and the initial income distribution

Figure S1.7 shows two individuals with different incomes and different preferences in consumption. As long as the two individuals confront the same market prices when making consumption decisions, consumption determined through competitive markets is on the contract curve in Figure S1.6, and so is Pareto-efficient. The effect of income distribution is to determine where on the contract curve the efficient allocation will be.

International trade

Figure S1.8 shows opportunities for international trade along the line joining points 2 and 5. Through international trade, the value of national output is maximized at tangency point 2, and total consumption is at the point 5, which is outside the domestic production possibilities frontier. To consume at 5, the economy trades $(\tilde{A} - \overline{A})$ of good A for $(\overline{B} - \tilde{B})$ of good B. We see that an economy where the population confronts opportunities for international trade has consumption possibilities that are Pareto-superior to those offered when the economy is closed to international trade.

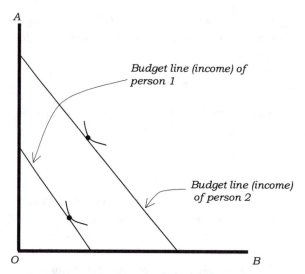

Figure S1.7. Income distribution and efficiency.

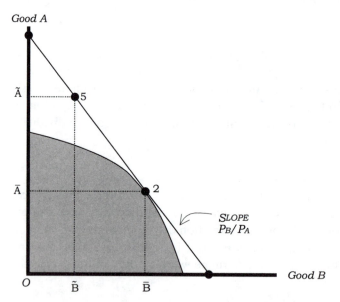

Figure S1.8. The efficiency of free international trade.

Conclusions

We have shown how a competitive economy accomplishes three efficiency objectives: (1) efficient allocation of resources among production alternatives, (2) production of combinations of goods that maximize the value of national output (or national income), and (3) efficient assignment of goods for consumption. The efficiency is achieved by individuals making personal market decisions with no more information than is necessary for their own personal decisions. Efficiency is consistent with different income distributions, and efficiency is enhanced by opportunities for international trade.

1C Why choose collective property?

Section 1.3 describes an economy with collective property that is the basis for maximal government. The rule of law with private property provides efficiency and personal freedom through minimal government. A case was nonetheless made that a society is better off with maximal government. Collective property was proposed as desirable because social inequality and differences in personal wealth are eliminated. The case was also made that markets "exploit." The idea that markets "exploit" contradicts the mutual benefit to buyers and sellers from voluntary market transactions. For how can people be exploited when they voluntarily choose to buy or sell? The answer was that employers in a market economy collude to set exploitative low wages at which people have no choice but to work to survive. Collusion among employers was also the explanation given for the existence of unemployment in a market economy with private property. Unemployed workers wait as a "reserve army" at the gates of the factory. Employed workers see the unemployed waiting at the factory gates and are reminded each day not to complain about their wages or working conditions. With centralized control over economic decisions and collective property, labor markets can be abolished (along with other markets), and people can be assigned jobs. Full employment is ensured, and the business cycles of the market economy do not exist. Workers' job security and incomes are thus not subject to the expansions and contractions of the private-property market economy.

Collective property owned by all workers was also justified by the argument that everything that had ever been produced was the result of past efforts of labor, and thus legitimately belonged only to labor. That is, capital or property existing today was the creation of yesterday's labor, and, because yesterday's workers created the wealth that exists today, all wealth or capital rightfully belongs to the workers.[3] Therefore, if today's capital was not entirely owned by today's workers, there has been theft or exploitative appropriation of workers' property. That is, property not belonging to the workers had been stolen.

Reference

Marx, K., 1994. Ideology and method on political economy. In *The Philosophy of Economics*, 2nd edition, D. M. Hausman (ed.). Cambridge University Press, New York, 119–42.

---

[3] In the words of Karl Marx, (1994, original 1857–58, p. 121): "No production (is) possible without an instrument of production, even if this instrument is only the hand. No production (can take place) without stored-up past labor. Capital is objectified past labor."

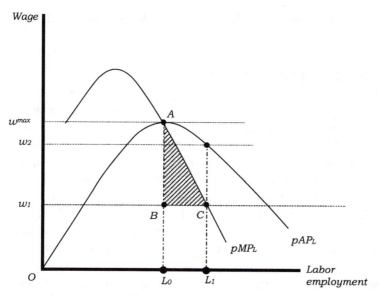

Figure S1.9. Employment decisions in a labor-managed firm.

1D A labor-managed firm

Under collective property, there are no private owners of capital to make labor employment decisions. With a system known as labor management, workers
themselves then make labor employment decisions. A labor-managed firm has
"members" who have an objective of maximizing profits per worker and not total
profit. A firm under private ownership views wage payments as a cost. Members
of a labor cooperative view wage payments not as a cost but as a benefit. Because they pay themselves, workers wish the wage that they receive to be as high
as possible. In Figure S1.9, the highest wage that workers can pay themselves is
w^{max}, which is the maximized value of the average product of labor pAP_L. This
maximum wage is achieved by choosing a number of members of the cooperative
equal to L_0.

A competitive firm chooses labor employment to maximize profits given by
$pY - wL$, where Y is output and w is the market wage. Therefore, profits are
maximized by choosing a number of employees such that $pMP_L = w$, that is, the
value of marginal product equals the wage. This is efficient because pMP_L is the
marginal benefit of hiring an additional worker, and w is the marginal cost of
an additional worker. Figure S1.9 shows a market wage w_1, for which the profit-
maximizing (and efficient) number of employees is L_1, which exceeds the number
of workers L_0 who are members of the labor-managed cooperative.

The inefficiency of having L_0 workers rather than L_1 is revealed by the value
of output lost from the smaller labor employment. Adding $(L_1 - L_0)$ workers
increases the total value of output by the area under the pMP_L function between L_0 and L_1, while the cost of employing the additional workers is the area
$w_1(L_1 - L_0)$. The difference is the shaded area ABC, which is the loss in efficiency,

and in profits, from the labor cooperative's decision to maximize the wage of its members.

The members of the labor cooperative face a dilemma. If they hire the additional $(L_1 - L_0)$ workers at the market wage, they gain profits of ABC; however, they would be acting contrary to the egalitarian principles of their cooperative by paying the hired workers a lower wage than they receive. If egalitarian principles are to be maintained, additional workers must be allowed to become members of the cooperative. By admitting the additional $(L_1 - L_0)$ workers as members, the cooperative reduces the average wage in the cooperative to w_2. This is inconsistent with maximizing the incomes of the cooperative's members.

Supplements to Chapter 2

2A Efficiency with public and private goods

In Section 2.1, we established the condition $\sum MB = MC$ for efficient supply of a public good without referring to the rest of the economy. Figure S2.1 shows an economy's production possibilities frontier for a private good X and public good G. Competitive supply of factors of production ensures that production in the economy is efficient and so on the production possibility frontier (see Supplement 1B). Private goods are distributed through markets to individuals for consumption. The public good is simultaneously available to the entire population. The question is where to produce along the production possibility frontier. Suppose that the

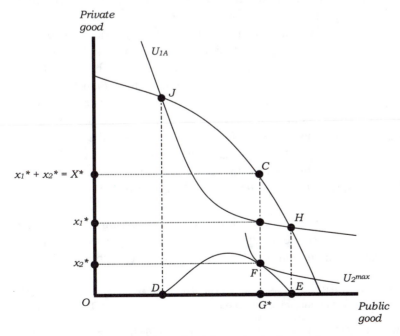

Figure S2.1. Efficient choice of public and private goods.

economy has two inhabitants. To establish Pareto-efficient outcomes for the two inhabitants, we hold the utility of one person constant and maximize the utility of the second person. This ensures that no person can be made better off without making someone worse off. In Figure S2.1, we hold person 1's utility constant at U_{1A}. The curve DE shows the consumption possibilities available to person 2 when person 1 is ensured the level of utility U_{1A}.

If the economy were producing at point J on the production possibility frontier, no quantity of private good would be available for person 2. Person 2's consumption would consist exclusively of the public good, which is available simultaneously to both persons. Person 2 similarly has no private-good consumption if the economy produces at point H on the production possibility frontier. Between points J and H on the production possibility frontier, maintaining person 1's utility at U_{1A} provides the positive quantities of private goods for consumption by person 2 given by the height of DE.[1] We can now maximize the utility of person 2 from among the possible outcomes available along the frontier DE. Highest utility U_2^{max} for person 2 is at point F. Pareto-efficient production for the economy is then established at point C on the production possibility frontier. At C, total production of the private good in the economy is $X^* = (x_1^* + x_2^*)$. Person 1 receives x_1^*, and person 2 receives x_2^* of the private good. At C, the economy produces a quantity G^* of the public good, which is available to both persons (or to the entire population).

The slope of U_{1A} is MRS_1, and the slope of the production possibility frontier is MRT (see Supplement 1B). Therefore, the slope of person 2's consumption possibility frontier DE is $MRT - MRS_1$. At the efficient point F, $MRS_2 = MRT - MRS_1$, which implies the efficiency condition $\sum MRS = MRT$. By the definitions of MRS and MRT, this is equivalent to $\sum MB_G = MC_G$.[2]

Instead of choosing U_{1A} as utility for individual 1, we can choose some other level of utility to hold constant. We then find another Pareto-efficient allocation between private- and public-good production. Figure S2.2 shows how an alternative efficient outcome is obtained. When utility promised to person 1 decreases from U_{1A} to U_{1B}, the frontier DE moves down to $D'E'$ because less of the private good is now available for person 2 for any quantity of the public good supplied. At the new location of the tangency point F', person 2 has less of the private good and less of the public good (we treat the public good as a normal good, that is, as a good for which demand increases with income). Because the quantity of the public good is common to both individuals, a smaller quantity of the public good is now supplied, at C'.

C' is efficient, as is C. For different utility levels held constant for person 1, we obtain different Pareto-efficient outcomes. In an economy with only private goods, there are likewise many Pareto-efficient outcomes (see Supplement 1B).

---

[1] To obtain DE, we vertically subtract the private-good consumption that is required for the level of utility U_{1A} from private-good production on the production possibility frontier. This leaves, along DE, the quantity of private-good consumption available to person 2.

[2] MRS is MB_G/MB_X, and MRT is MB_G/MB_X. Substituting the relation from competitive markets, $MB_X = P_X = MC_X$, into $\sum MRS = MRT$ gives $\sum MB_G = MC_G$.

*Private
good*

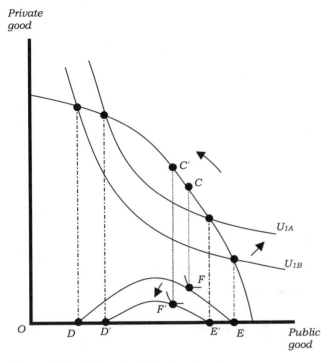

Figure S2.2. Different efficient outcomes.

2B Group size and voluntary collective action

This supplement considers the relation between group size and the effectiveness of voluntary collective action. We shall want to be able to compare sizes of different groups. Therefore, we shall treat individuals as identical. We begin with an individual i who has income y_i to allocate between personal private-good consumption x_i and a contribution g_i to a public good from which n other people benefit. With P_G the relative price of the public good, the individual's budget constraint is

$$y_i = x_i + P_G g_i. \tag{S2.1}$$

The total supply of public good available is

$$Q = g_i + G_i, \tag{S2.2}$$

where G_i is the amount provided by the others. The individual's utility function is

$$U^i = U^i(x_i, Q). \tag{S2.3}$$

In Figure S2.3, we see the individual's income y_i (expressed in terms of the quantity of private consumption that can be purchased with the given income) and the quantity of the public good G_i provided to individual i by the voluntary contributions of others. The contribution G_i by others moves the origin for the individual's choice of allocation of expenditure between public- and private-good

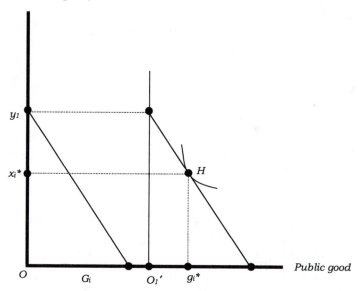

Figure S2.3. Individual choice of Nash contribution.

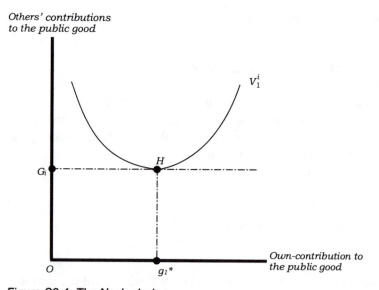

Figure S2.4. The Nash choice.

consumption from O to O'. The utility-maximizing choice is at point H, where x_i^* of the private good is purchased and the individual makes the Nash contribution to the public good g_i^*.

The choice at H in Figure S2.3 is also shown in Figure S2.4. To arrive at Figure S2.4 from Figure S2.3, we use the individual's budget constraint to express utility as

$$U^i = U^i[y_i - P_G g_i, G + g_i] = V^i[g_i, G_i, P_G, y_i], \tag{S2.3a}$$

which shows that utility depends on the choice of the own-contribution g_i to the public good, *given* others' contributions G_i to individual i, the relative price P_G of the public good, and the individual's income y_i. The only decision that a person makes here is the own-contribution g_{i*}.

Just as utility is constant along the indifference curve U_1^i in Figure S2.3, so utility is constant along V_1^i in Figure S2.4. Along V_1^i,

$$dV^i = 0 = \frac{dV^i}{dg_i} \cdot dg_i + \frac{dV^i}{dG_i} \cdot dG_i, \tag{S2.4}$$

and so the slope of an indifference curve in Figure S2.4 is

$$\frac{dG_i}{dg_i} = -\left(\frac{dV^i}{dg_i}\right) \bigg/ \left(\frac{dV^i}{dG_i}\right). \tag{S2.5}$$

Thus, the slope of the indifference curve is the ratio of two marginal benefits (or utilities) of the *same* public good. The difference is in *who* pays for the public good. The own-contribution g_i is personally financed at a marginal cost MC and so

$$\frac{\partial V^i}{\partial g_i} = MB_i - MC. \tag{S2.6}$$

Other people's contributions G_i, however, provide marginal benefit MB_i at no personal cost, and

$$\frac{\partial V^i}{\partial G_i} = MB_i. \tag{S2.7}$$

Substituting equations (S2.6) and (S2.7) into equation (S2.5), we obtain the expression for the slope of the indifference curve in Figure S2.4 as

$$\frac{dG_i}{dg_i} = \frac{MB_i - MC}{MB_i}. \tag{S2.8}$$

At the point H in Figure S2.4, the individual chooses a personally best or utility-maximizing own-contribution g_i^*, when others are providing G_i. At H,

$$\frac{dV^i}{dg_i} = 0 = MB_i - MC. \tag{S2.9}$$

The choice at H is a Nash response. Given contributions of others G_i, the individual has chosen a personal utility-maximizing own-contribution to the public good that satisfies $MB_i = MC$.

The individual response to changes to contributions by others

How does the individual respond when others provide a larger quantity of the public good? In Figure S2.5, the quantity of the public good provided by others

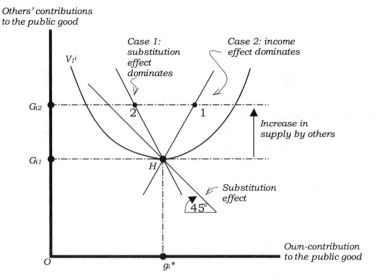

Figure S2.5. The change in the contribution by others.

increases from G_{i1} to G_{i2}. The individual's response is given by

$$\frac{dg_i}{dG_i} = -1 + P_G \cdot \frac{dg_i}{dI_i}.$$
(S2.10)

The value -1 is a one-for-one negative substitution effect. The substitution effect is one-for-one because of the perfect substitutability in consumption between the public good provided by own spending and the public good provided by the spending of others. The second term in (S2.10) is an income effect. The income effect occurs because the increase in the public good provided by others is like receiving a gift of money. The income effect is positive if the public good is a normal good, which we take to be the case.

Figure S2.5 shows two alternatives. In case 1, the substitution effect dominates the income effect, and the own-contribution declines as the contribution of others increases. In case 2, the income effect dominates, and the own-contribution increases. If there were *only* a substitution effect (if the income effect were precisely zero), the slope of the reaction function would be precisely -1, or $45°$.

The Nash equilibrium for individual voluntary contributions

We now consider two people whom we denote A and B. Figure S2.6 shows the derivation of the reaction function $R_B R_B$ of individual B, who chooses personal utility-maximizing public-good contributions in reaction to changes in the contributions of individual A. $R_B R_B$ shows a dominant substitution effect (the slope of the reaction function is negative).

Figure S2.7 shows the Nash equilibrium at point N where the reaction functions of the two persons intersect. At point N, the choices of own-contributions are mutually consistent given the contributions each is making to the public good.

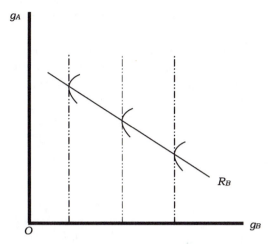

Figure S2.6. The reaction function of person B.

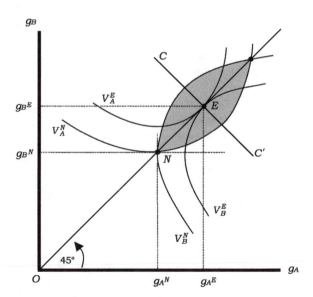

Figure S2.7. The Nash equilibrium for individual contributions.

The total quantity of the public good that is voluntarily supplied at N is

$$Q^N = g_A^N + g_B^N. \tag{S2.11}$$

If the individuals are identical, then their contributions to the public good are also identical.

Point N in figure S2.7 is the inefficient outcome obtained in the prisoners' dilemma. This outcome can be improved upon for both persons. The potential for mutual improvement is clear in Figure S2.7. The indifference curves V_A^N and V_B^N show utility at point N (the indifference curves pass through point N). The shaded area depicts possibilities for Pareto-improvement for a move away from the Nash equilibrium.

Pareto-efficient combinations of private contributions to the public good lie along the contract curve CC′ in Figure S2.7. Since indifference curves are tangential along the contract curve, we can equate the slopes of the two individuals' indifference curves, to obtain

$$\frac{MB_A - MC}{MB_A} = \frac{MB_A}{MB_B - MC}. \tag{S2.12}$$

We can rearrange (S2.12) to establish

$$\sum MB_i = MC, \tag{S2.12a}$$

which is the efficiency condition for public good supply.

In Figure S2.7, E is an efficient point on the contract curve, with utilities V_A^E and V_B^E on a ray from the origin through N. Let us denote the total amount provided at E by Q^E. We can then use Q^N/Q^E to measure the relative inefficiency of Nash provision of the public good.

We can now see how the Nash outcome changes when group size increases. With n identical individuals, each person contributes

$$g_i = g = \frac{\dot{Q}}{n}. \tag{S2.13}$$

We can transform this expression to

$$g = \frac{G + g}{n} \tag{S2.13a}$$

and therefore

$$g = \frac{G}{(n-1)}. \tag{S2.13b}$$

For example, in Figure S2.7, since $n = 2$, we have $g = G$, and the Nash outcome is on the 45° line from the origin. As the size of the group increases beyond 2, the ray from the origin along which the Nash equilibrium is located moves to the left, as in Figure S2.8.

We see in Figure S2.8 that

$$\frac{dg_i}{dn} < 0 \quad \text{and} \quad \frac{d(ng_i)}{dn} = \frac{dQ^N}{dn} > 0. \tag{S2.14}$$

Therefore, (1) as group size increases, individuals increasingly free ride by reducing individual contributions (i.e., the average personal contribution falls); (2) at the same time, the total value of the contributions made by the population (including a newly added member) increases.

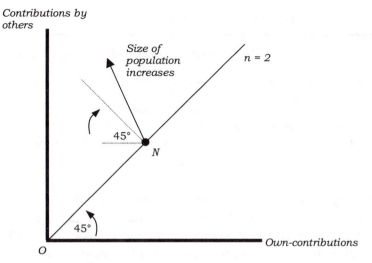

Contributions by others

Size of population increases

n = 2

45°

N

45°

O

Own-contributions

Figure S2.8. Changes in Nash equilibria when group size increases.

The measure of relative efficiency of voluntary private contributions is Q^N/Q^E. Total voluntary contribution Q^N and the efficient contribution Q^E both increase with group size n. For a wide class of utility functions,

$$\frac{\partial(Q^N/Q^E)}{\partial n} < 0, \tag{S2.15}$$

and so the group becomes relatively less efficient as a voluntary provider of public goods as group size increases.

In the additively separable case with $U(x, Q) = x + B(Q)$, there is no income effect on choice of own-contribution to the public good when the contribution of others increases. Because of the one-to-one substitution effect, individuals reduce their own supply commensurately with increases in anyone else's supply. Therefore, total Nash contributions are independent of group size. Because the efficient quantity Q^E increases with group size, larger groups are relatively less efficient voluntary providers of public goods than smaller groups.

Deviations from cooperation

Nash behavior supposes that people act independently of one another. We could begin with the alternative hypothesis that members of a group cooperate but nonetheless free ride according to the ability of the other members of the group to identify free-riding behavior. As group size increases, there is more anonymity in the group and less enforcement, and the effectiveness of the group in obtaining contributions from its members for collective action declines. This view of voluntary collective action begins with cooperation and looks at reasons for deviations from cooperation. Nash behavior begins from individually rational behavior and look for ways to achieve Pareto-improving cooperation.

References and related literature

Chamberlin, J., 1976. A diagrammatic exposition of the logic of collective action. *Public Choice* 26, 59–74.

Cornes, R. and T. Sandler, 1996. *The Theory of Externalities, Public Goods, and Club Goods.* Cambridge University Press, New York.

McGuire, M., 1974. Group size, group homogeneity, and aggregate provision of a pure public good under Cournot behavior. *Public Choice* 18, 107–26.

Olson, M., 1965. *The Logic of Collective Action: Public Goods and the Theory of Groups.* Harvard University Press, Cambridge, Mass.

2C Income distribution and voluntary collective action

With independent noncooperative Nash behavior as underlies the prisoners' dilemma, the total voluntary contributions for paying for a public good made by members of a group depend on the total combined income of members of the group and not on the distribution of income within the group – provided the individuals in a group have more or less equal incomes. This result arises because a person benefiting from a public good is indifferent between being given a gift of money and being given a gift of more of a public good through someone else's increased spending on the public good. When person 2 increases personal spending on a public good by $100, person 1 can decrease spending on the same public good by $100, can spend the $100 on private goods, and be just as well off as if person 2 had given him or her $100 directly. If $100 is taken from person 1 and given to person 2, person 1 reduces spending on the public good, but person 2 who received the $100 increases spending. In the Nash equilibrium, the decrease and increase in personal public-good expenditure precisely match, provided both persons contribute to the public good before and after the income redistribution.

To demonstrate, we return to the budget constraint for person i. The total quantity of the public good available is again own-provision g_i by person i plus the amount provided by others. Own-provision is $g_i = Q - G_i$, so we can express the budget constraint as

$$y_i = x_i + P_G(Q - G_i). \tag{S2.16}$$

Therefore, from the budget constraint,

$$Q = \frac{(Y_i - x_i)}{P_G} + G_i. \tag{S2.17}$$

The utility function can accordingly be expressed as

$$U^i(x_i, Q) = U^i\left(x_i, \frac{y_i - x_i}{P_G} + G_i\right) \tag{S2.18}$$

or

$$U^i(x_i, Q) = U^i\left(x_i, \left(\frac{y_i}{P_G} + G_i\right) - \frac{x_i}{P_G}\right). \tag{S2.19}$$

We see that utility depends on the sum,

$$\left[\left(\frac{y_i}{P_G}\right) + G_i\right],$$

and not on the composition of own-income and others' public-good provision. We can now consider an initial Nash equilibrium for public-good contributions by two individuals where an income transfer made from individual 1 to individual 2 leads to a new Nash equilibrium, and where in both Nash equilibria both individuals are contributing to the public good. Individual 1 (who has lost income) decreases personal spending on the public good by the amount of income lost, and individual 2 increases personal spending on the public good by the amount of the income transfer. Therefore, total spending on the public good in the initial Nash equilibrium is equal to total spending in a Nash equilibrium after the income redistribution, reflecting the indifference between losing income and having others finance public-good consumption. We have used an example of a group consisting of two people, but the same conclusion applies for any number of people who voluntarily contribute to a public good. Provided all members of the group make positive contributions before and after income redistribution, total voluntary contributions by a group of people to a public good do not depend on the distribution of income among members of the group.

Income distribution when incomes differ

Let us now consider a group of diverse individuals. The diversity can be in income or in personal benefit from a public good. Figure S2.9 shows who in a group of people with diverse incomes contributes to providing a public good (see Andreoni and McGuire, 1993). With income y_1 and relative price as shown, the individual chooses consumption at N_1 if (in the Nash equilibrium) no one else has provided a quantity of the public good. At N_1, the individual contributes g_1 to the public good. When others provide a positive quantity G_1, the individual's budget constraint moves out reflecting the equivalence between own-income and others' public-good contributions. The new consumption point is at N_2 where the own-contribution to the public good is g_2. At N_2, total availability of the public good is $(g_2 + G_1)$. The own-contribution reaches zero at point N_3 when the contribution by others reaches G_m. A sequence of substitution effects has taken place in response to the increase in contributions by others. The negative substitution effects have reduced the own-contribution to zero.

It follows from Figure S2.9 that it requires only one other person in the population whose income is sufficiently high, or whose preference for consumption of the public good is sufficiently great, for a person's own-provision (in a Nash equilibrium) to be zero.

Figure S2.10 shows marginal benefits from a public good for three people. In a Nash equilibrium where the group is composed of only persons 1 and 2, person 2 contributes g_2 and person 1 contributes nothing. High-benefit (or high-income) person 3 then joins the group. In the new Nash equilibrium, person 3 supplies g_3

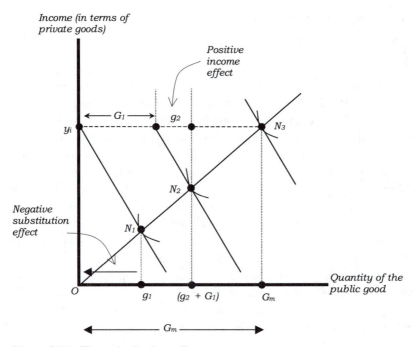

Figure S2.9. The substitution effect.

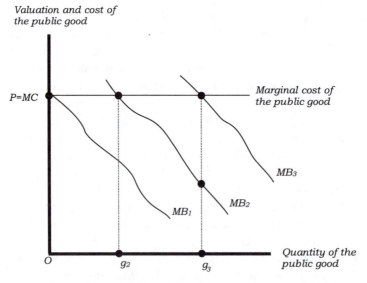

Figure S2.10. Diverse individuals and voluntary contributions.

and person 2 joins person 1 in not contributing because, when g_3 is supplied by person 3, the marginal benefit to person 2 from the public good is less than the MC of supply (the price P that has to be personally paid to increase supply). The larger group after person 3 has joined provides more of the public good, but only

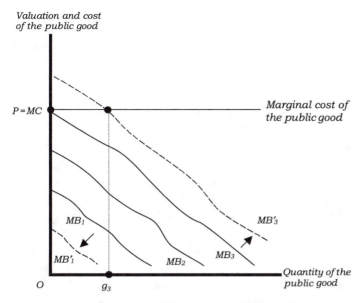

Figure S2.11. Increased diversity in the population results in positive supply.

because the increase in group size has taken place by adding a high-income (or high-benefit) person.

We are not here describing charitable giving. The high-benefit person has a *personal demand* for the public good. Because of nonexcludable benefit, all members of the group benefit.

Figure S2.11 shows a three-person group whose members make no voluntary private contributions in a Nash equilibrium. Efficient supply for the group determined by $\sum MB = MC$ is, however, positive. This is a limiting example of underprovision of public goods through voluntary independent Nash decisions.

Now, in Figure S2.11, income distribution or preferences change so that MB_1 declines to MB'_1 and MB_3 increases to MB'_3. The increased diversity in the population results in positive supply because person 3 supplies g_3. Increased diversity in the population has increased the effectiveness of the group in voluntary collection action by creating a sufficiently high-income or high-benefit member of the group.

References and related literature

Andreoni, J. and M. McGuire, 1993. Identifying the free riders: A simple algorithm for determining who will contribute to a public good. *Journal of Public Economics* 51, 447–54.

Bergstrom, T., L. Blume and H. Varian, 1986. On the private provision of public goods. *Journal of Public Economics* 29, 25–49.

Konrad, K. A., 1994. The strategic advantage of being poor: Public and private provision of public goods. *Economica* 61, 79–92.

Warr, P., 1983. The private provision of a public good is independent of the distribution of income. *Economics Letters* 13, 207–11.

2D Sequential voluntary financing of public goods

When voluntary contributions to financing a public good are made sequentially over time, there is an incentive for high-valuation persons to wait for low-valuation persons to contribute first. A high-valuation person wants a large quantity of a public good, whereas a low-valuation person wants a small quantity. By contributing first, a high-valuation person may spend enough on the public good to satisfy the demand of the low-valuation person, and the low-valuation person would then contribute nothing. For example, suppose that a high-valuation person is prepared to contribute $5,000 for a neighborhood park if no one else contributes, and that a low valuation person is satisfied with spending $1,000 if no one else contributes. The higher-valuation person knows that if he or she contributes more than $1,000 today, the low-valuation person will contribute nothing tomorrow, and so waits for the low-valuation person to contribute first. The low-valuation person knows that the high-valuation person values having a park very highly and waits for the high-valuation person to pay for the public good. If the period of time over which contributions are made is long enough, total contributions could approach efficient spending on the public good.

A public good might require a minimal contribution before any benefit is provided. In that case, people may make pledges, which become contributions only if total pledges by everyone reach the threshold required for minimal supply of the public good. When nearly enough money is available to finance the minimal quantity of the public good, individuals have an incentive to add pledges because additional contributions become critical to reaching the threshold required for providing the public good. The free-riding problem diminishes as total pledges approach the minimum required spending. For example, if a million dollars has been pledged for medical equipment for a children's hospital, and only $10 more is required to reach the price of the equipment, obtaining the additional $10 will not be difficult.

Related literature

Fershtman, C. and S. Nitzan, 1991. Dynamic voluntary provision of public goods. *European Economic Review* 35, 1057–67.

Gradstein, M., 1992, Time dynamics and incomplete information in the private provision of public goods. *Journal of Political Economy* 100, 581–97.

Gradstein, M., 1994. Efficient provision of a discrete public good. *International Economic Review* 35, 877–97.

Marx, L. M. and S. A. Matthews, 2000. Dynamic voluntary provision to a public project. *Review of Economic Studies* 67, 327–58.

2E Income effects and the excess burden of taxation

Taxes have both income and substitution effects. The substitution effect is negative; that is, people respond to taxes by substituting free time for income-earning activity or by substituting relatively less expensive for more expensive goods. For normal goods, for which demand increases with income, the income effect of an increase in taxation is also negative: increased taxes reduce real income and reduce demand.

If free time is a normal good, increased taxes reduce demand for free time, and so labor supply increases through the income effect. The substitution response to a tax is to work less, which increases free time. Income and substitution effects thus affect labor-supply decisions in opposing ways. In principle, the net effect could go either way.

When taxes finance a public good, the income paid as taxes is returned to taxpayers through public spending on public goods, leaving only the substitution effect. The excess burden of taxation is measured only by the substitution effect. Without a substitution effect, there is no excess burden of taxation.

We observed in Section 2.3 that two questions can be asked to identify the excess burden of taxation. We can ask how much compensation a person requires for a tax that has been levied, or how much the same person is prepared to pay to avoid the tax. When asking these questions, we defined an individual's labor-supply function as showing only the substitution effect. In that case, both questions have the same answer. The answers to the questions, and therefore the measures of the excess burden of taxation, differ when income effects of taxes are taken into account.

To see how income effects affect the excess burden of taxation, we look at Figure S2.12. Figure S2.12 shows the effect of a tax on a good X. Rather than on a good X, the tax could also be on labor supplied.

The horizontal axis measures the quantity of X, and the quantity of all other goods is measured on the vertical axis. OY is income earned before tax. The budget constraint at the pre-tax relative price is YA, and the individual chooses to consume at point 1. Point 1 is on an income-consumption curve ICC_1 for the pre-tax relative price of good X. An income-consumption curve shows how demand changes when income changes and relative price remains constant: the income effect is a move along the income-consumption curve. The substitution effect is a movement along an indifference curve.

When the government imposes a tax on good X, the budget constraint becomes YB instead of YA, and the individual chooses post-tax consumption at point 2. Point 2 is on a different income-consumption curve ICC_2 because of the new post-tax relative price. The individual pays the government the amount (2–3) in taxes.

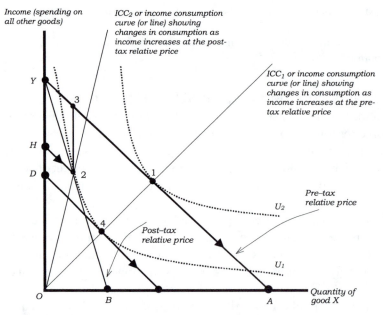

Figure S2.12. The excess burden of a tax as the amount of income the taxpayer is prepared to pay to avoid the tax.

By consuming at point 2 and paying (2–3) in taxes, the taxpayer returns to the original pre-tax budget constraint YA.

Now let us ask the taxpayer how much he or she is prepared to pay to avoid the tax. If payment of the tax can be avoided, the taxpayer can stay on ICC_1, which shows consumption at the pre-tax relative price. If the tax is not levied, the taxpayer has utility U_2. The most the taxpayer is prepared to pay to avoid the tax is the amount of income that gives this utility while being on ICC_1. Therefore, to avoid the tax, the individual is prepared to pay the amount of income that would give the utility U_1 at point 4. The individual is therefore prepared to pay income YD to avoid the tax.

The tax revenue that the government collects if the tax is levied is YH, which is equal to (2–3). The difference HD is the additional personal loss due to the excess burden of the tax.

We can also ask the taxpayer the question how much he or she needs to be compensated if the tax is levied. In Figure S2.13, after the tax has been levied, the taxpayer faces the new post-tax relative price. Having paid the tax, the taxpayer is at the point 2 on ICC_2.

How much income does the taxpayer now have to be given to allow a return to the original level of utility U_2? To find this compensating level of income, we look for the point where ICC_2 meets U_2. This is at point 5. If the taxpayer were to have additional income FY, he or she would be as well off after the tax at point 5 as before the tax at point 1. The income required as compensation for the tax is equal to the distance (2–6), which exceeds the tax revenue (2–3) by the

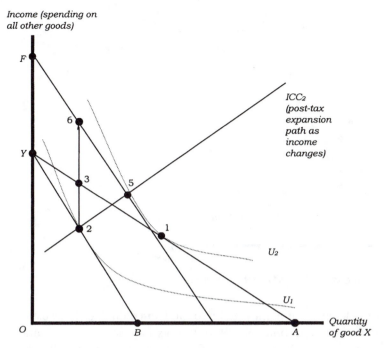

Income (spending on all other goods)

Figure S2.13. The excess burden as compensation for imposition of a tax.

distance (3–6). The distance (3–6) is the personal loss due to the excess burden of taxation.

2F Empirical measurement of the excess burden of taxation

Figure S2.14 shows a labor market with a tax of t percent. The shaded area is the revenue from the tax and the striped area is the excess burden of the tax. The excess burden of the tax is measured by

$$\text{excess burden} = \frac{1}{2} \frac{w L t^2}{\left(\frac{1}{\varepsilon_D} + \frac{1}{\varepsilon_S} \right)}$$

where w is the market wage, L is total hours of labor supplied, ε_D is the labor-market demand elasticity, and ε_S is the labor-market supply elasticity.

The excess burden is measured by computing the striped area BDE. What information do we require to compute the area BDE?

If we were observing the market depicted in Figure S2.14, we would observe points B and D. We would know the tax rate t, and we would observe the tax revenue given by the gray area. We would know pre- and post-tax wages w and $w(1 - t)$.

To measure the area of the triangle BDE, we need to know the location of point E. We would not observe point E because point E is the market equilibrium without the tax, and we are observing the market with the tax imposed. Econometric

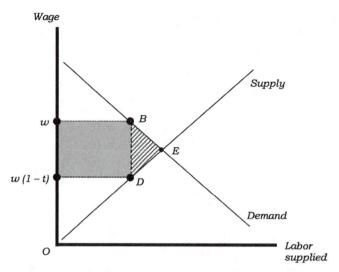

Figure S2.14. The excess burden of taxation in a market.

techniques allow the location of point E to be found from data that allow estimation of the supply and demand functions. With the tax imposed, we seek data to estimate the tax-inclusive supply or demand function (it does not matter where the tax is included in the supply function or the demand function). When we know the tax-inclusive supply or demand function, and given that we know the level of the tax, we can locate point E. We would also establish whether BDE is indeed a triangle, that is, whether the segments BE and DE are straight lines. Whether there is a triangle or the lines are curved of course affects the size of BDE.

After we have located point E in Figure S2.14, we need to separate income and substitution effects, so as to isolate the substitution effect that underlies the excess burden of taxation. Market data do not reveal the separation between income and substitution responses. The data show the two effects together. A decomposition of income and substitution effects follows from the utility function from which supply of labor is established.

Supplement to Chapter 3

3A Political competition with many candidates

Although there is no stable equilibrium with political competition with three candidates, stability is restored when a fourth candidate enters the political contest (see Selten, 1971).

Figure S3.1 shows the Nash equilibrium for four candidates. G^{max} is the maximal quantity af a public good sought in the population and G^m is the amount sought by the median voter in the uniform distribution over (O, G^{max}). Candidates 1 and 2 locate themselves at point A at 25 percent of the maximal quantity and

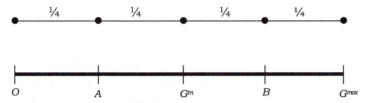

Figure S3.1. *Political competition with four candidates.*

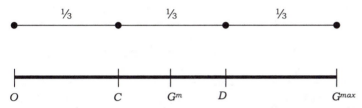

Figure S3.2. *Political competition with five candidates.*

candidates 3 and 4 locate themselves at the point B at 75 percent of the maximal quantity. Neither policy A nor B is the policy sought by the median voter.

Figure S3.2 shows the outcome when a fifth candidate enters the political contest. In the Nash equilibrium two candidates locate themselves at point C at one-third of the maximal quantity and two candidates locate themselves at the point D at two-thirds of the maximal quantity. The fifth candidate chooses the position of the median voter.

With a sixth candidate, the Nash equilibrium is that three sets of candidates share one-third of the vote. However, other Nash equilibria are possible. We shall stop with six candidates. For more detail, see Selten (1971).

Reference

Selten, R., 1971. Anwendungen der Spieltheorie auf die Politische Wissenschaft. In *Politik und Wissenschaft*, H. Maier (ed.). Beck, München, 287–320.

Supplements to Chapter 4

4A The tragedy of the commons

The grazing of animals demonstrates the common-access externality, or the tragedy of the commons. Let the total number of goats grazing in a field be A. There are n different owners. Each owner i has a_i animals, and the sum of everybody's animals is the total, so

$$A = \sum_{i=1}^{n} a_i. \tag{S4.1}$$

The goats produce cheese, and the field yields a quantity of cheese $F(A)$ that depends on the number of goats. The price of cheese is one. Output of cheese is subject to diminishing marginal product because of the fixed size of the field so that

$$\frac{\partial F}{\partial A} \equiv MP_A, \quad \frac{\partial MP_A}{\partial A} < 0. \tag{S4.2}$$

The average product of an animal placed in the field is declining, since

$$\frac{F(A)}{A} \equiv AP_A > 0, \quad \frac{\partial AP_A}{\partial A} = \frac{1}{A}[MP_A - AP_A] < 0. \tag{S4.3}$$

That is, because marginal product is declining, marginal product lies below average product (where the product is the cheese of the goats). Efficient use of the field is established by allowing the number of goats to graze that maximizes the value of the cheese output of the animals. Let P_A denote the fixed market price of a goat. A single owner of the field would choose a number of goats to maximize profits,

$$\pi(A) = F(A) - P_A A. \tag{S4.4}$$

The efficient choice of the number of goats to graze is determined by

$$\frac{\partial \pi}{\partial A} = MP_A - P_A = 0. \tag{S4.5}$$

The efficient solution is shown as A_e in Figure S4.1, where the price of a goat is equal to the marginal product of adding a goat to the grazing field, that is, where

$$MP_A = P_A. \tag{S4.6}$$

The declining MP_A function for goats is depicted in Figure S4.1.

When the field has no recognized owner and there is free access to the field, each of many owners of goats uses the common field to maximize personal profits. We denote the share of the goats of person 1 by s_1 where

$$s_1 \equiv \frac{a_1}{A}. \tag{S4.7}$$

Owner 1 chooses a number of goats a_1 to maximize his or her share s_1 of total profits from use of the field,

$$s_1 \pi \equiv \pi(a_1) = s_1 \left[F\left(\sum_{k=1}^{n} a_k \right) \right] - P_A a_1. \tag{S4.8}$$

The negative externalities that are present here are expressed in the reduced profits of one goat herder when another goat herder adds an additional goat to the flock grazing the common.

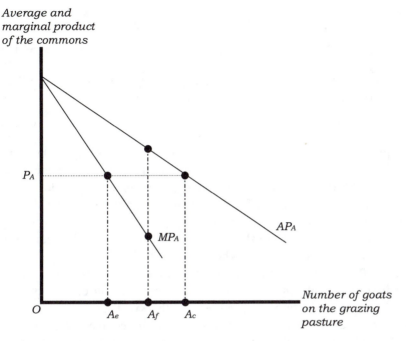

Figure S4.1. The commons.

When goat herder 1 increases the number of his goats on the field, the profits of any other goat owner j decline by

$$\frac{\partial \pi_j}{\partial a_1} = s_j[MP_A - AP_A] < 0. \tag{S4.9}$$

The decline in the profits of goat herder j when goat herder 1 increases the number of his or her goats on the common field is thus the difference between the marginal and average products of goats, weighted by the share of goat herder j in the total flock. The total negative externalities imposed by goat herder 1 when he or she adds a goat to the common is the sum of externalities over all other goat herders,

$$\sum_{k=2}^{n} \frac{\partial \pi_k}{\partial a_1} = \sum_{k=2}^{n} s_k[MP_A - AP_A] < 0. \tag{S4.10}$$

In a noncooperative Nash equilibrium, each one of many owners of goats chooses a number of goats to graze on the common, taking the sizes of the herds of all other goat-owners as constant. The outcome is inefficient choice of the total number of animals on the common. Too many goats graze the common. With private ownership of the field, the private owner internalizes the interaction among goats by valuing the marginal contribution of a goat to total profit taking into account the "congestion" on the field. The individually privately profitable number of goats is determined by the solution to

$$\frac{\partial \pi_1}{\partial a_1} = \frac{\partial s_1}{\partial a_1}[F(A) - P_A A] + s_1[MP_A - P_A] = 0, \tag{S4.11}$$

which implies

$$\frac{\partial s_1}{\partial a_1}[F(A) - P_A A] = s_1[P_A - MP_A] > 0. \tag{S4.12}$$

From (S4.12), we see that $P_A > MP_A$. Also, $P_A < F(A)/A = AP_A$. Figure S4.1 shows the outcome of free access to the common at A_f, where

$$MP_A < P_A < AP_A. \tag{S4.13}$$

Efficiency requires $P_A = MP_A$. The source of the inefficient crowding on the common is that, by adding a goat, an individual goat herder increases his or her share of the total profit $[F(A) - P_A A]$ available from the common pasture field. A private owner is not subject to this inefficiency because for him or her the share s is fixed and equal to one. In the competitive limiting case where a large number of people use the common and the share of any one user approaches zero, the outcome approaches A_c in Figure S4.1, where $P_A = AP_A$.

The tragedy of the commons thus occurs because people who seek a larger individual share of the total benefit (access to the common resource) do not take into account the output reductions they impose on others on the common. Private ownership internalizes the externality. The goat herders confront a prisoners' dilemma. All goat herders would be better off if they all simultaneously reduced the size of their goat herds because they would thereby mutually benefit each other by increasing the productivity of the use of the field. Although collectively rational, such behavior is not individually rational, hence the prisoners' dilemma.

4B An impediment to replicating missing markets

This supplementary note describes a technical impediment to using public policy to correct externality problems. Figure S4.2 shows a discontinuous supply function consisting of the segment OA, and then BC, with a discontinuous jump between the points A and B. Because of the discontinuous supply function, demand and supply functions do not intersect, and an equilibrium price does not exist. If Figure S4.2 shows the missing market that is the source of an externality, then, even with full information about market supply and demand, a government cannot set a corrective tax or subsidy because the price that the government is seeking to duplicate does not exist.

What reason is there to believe that the circumstances of Figure S4.2 might arise? Let us consider again a factory that disrupts Robinson Crusoe's fishing by polluting a stream. In Figure S4.3, the vertical axis indicates the number of fish Crusoe catches, and the horizontal axis indicates the output of the factory, which directly translates into the extent of environmental damage of the stream. The maximum number of fish that Crusoe can catch is Y_1, when the factory does not produce and so does not pollute.

As the factory begins to produce, Crusoe's catch of fish declines along the production possibility frontier, and falls to zero when the output (and environmental damage) of the factory is X_1. After Crusoe's fishing has been reduced to

Price

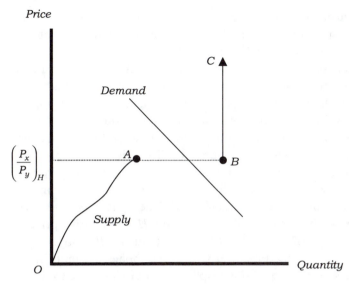

Figure S4.2. A discontinuous supply function and no equilibrium price.

Quantity of fish

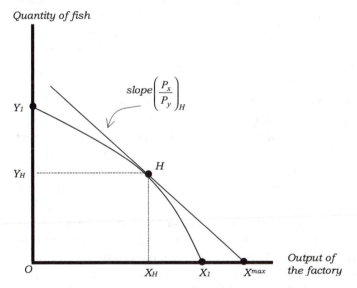

Figure S4.3. The source of the discontinuous supply function in the missing market.

zero, the factory can however continue producing (and polluting). The maximum production and pollution of the factory is X^{max}.

Therefore, the production possibility frontier between fishing and output by the factory begins at Y_1 and ends at X^{max}. The production possibility frontier follows the path $Y_1 X_1 X^{max}$ and is nonconvex.

Now let us introduce a "missing market" for the right to pollute. We give legal rights in this market to Crusoe. Crusoe can therefore sell units of the right to pollute to the factory.

When he sells a unit of the right to pollute, Crusoe incurs a loss due to the adverse effect on his fishing. The opportunity cost of environmental damage, in terms of fish foregone, is measured by the slope of $Y_1 X_1$.

Crusoe can, however, sell the right to pollute beyond X_1. He can continue selling the right to pollute after environmental damage has destroyed all his fishing prospects, by selling a further $(X^{max} - X_1)$ units of the right to pollute; without the right to pollute supplied by Crusoe, the factory cannot produce.

When we look at Crusoe's supply function for the right to pollute, we see that the supply function is discontinuous as in Figure S4.2. To derive the supply function, we look at the tangency point H in Figure S4.3. The slope of the frontier $Y_1 X_1$ is the relative supply price of the right to pollute, and between points Y_1 and H Crusoe supplies profit-maximizing quantities of the right to pollute in response to a relative price given by this slope. At point H, the relative price of the right to pollute (in terms of fish lost) is $(P_X/P_Y)_H$ (which is the slope of the frontier at H). Once he has reached point H where he supplies X_H units of the right to pollute, Crusoe's profit-maximizing response is not to continue to supply the right to pollute along the frontier beyond H, but to jump to the endpoint X^{max}. That is, Crusoe's profit-maximizing response beyond the quantity of fish caught Y_H at H is to cease fishing altogether and to supply to the factory all the rights to pollute for which the factory is prepared to pay. Therefore, Crusoe's supply response is discontinuous between H and X^{max}. We see this discontinuous jump in supply between X_H and X^{max} in Figure S4.2 at the relative price $(P_X/P_Y)_H$.

The profit motive underlying the discontinuous jump in supply between H and X^{max} is expressed in Figure S4.3, where we see that all points on the segment of the frontier HX_1, which Crusoe ignores in making the jump, are Pareto-inferior to points along the price line HX^{max}. Because fish and the factory's right to produce are valuable, profit maximization in trading off fish for the right to pollute (or equivalently for the factory's right to produce) entails being as far out as possible from the origin. All points along HX^{max} offer more fish and more rights to pollute (which translates into increased factory output) than the continuation of the frontier HX_1; therefore, Crusoe ignores HX_1 in making his profit-maximizing supply decisions regarding the right to pollute (and fish not caught).

Points along HX^{max} are not feasible. Such points are not attainable because they lie outside of the feasible frontier $Y_1 X_1 X^{max}$ – with the exception of the endpoints H and X^{max}. Hence the jump takes place from H to X^{max}, and there is a discontinuity in supply of the right to pollute.

Crusoe has lost nothing in being obliged to jump between H and X^{max}. All points along the line HX^{max} are of equal value in terms of fish and the right to pollute; hence, they are also equal in profitability in trading off fish caught for supplying the right to pollute.

What are we to conclude from such "fundamental nonconvexities" in the theory of externalities? The nonconvexities impose a conceptual limitation on the idea that governments can use taxes or subsidies to replicate the missing efficient prices of missing markets. Replicating missing markets can, in principle, be more complex than we might have at first thought.

Related literature

Baumol, W. J. and D. F. Bradford, 1972. Detrimental externalities and non-convexity of the production set. *Economica* 39, 160–76.

Starrett, D. A., 1972. Fundamental non-convexities in the theory of externalities. *Journal of Economic Theory* 4, 180–99.

4C Protection of dolphins

In tropical areas of the Pacific Ocean, dolphins swim over the top of schools of tuna. The dolphins become entangled in nets that are used to catch the tuna. In the 1980s, public awareness of the plight of dolphins caught in tuna nets led U.S. consumers to boycott tuna. In 1988, the U.S. Congress amended the Marine Mammal Protection Act of 1972 to apply U.S. pro-dolphin standards to imports. Imports of dolphin-unfriendly tuna were banned in 1990 (after the pro-environment Earth Island Institute took court action against the U.S. Department of Commerce for failure to enforce the pro-dolphin policy for imports). In 1990, the U.S. Congress also passed the dolphin-protection consumer information bill that prohibited canned tuna caught in the eastern tropical Pacific (principally by Mexican fishermen) from being labeled dolphin-friendly.

Protection of dolphins became a subject of international dispute when European governments rejected the right of the U.S. government to ban imports of Mexican-caught tuna that had been canned in Europe. Despite the European protests, the U.S. government maintained its pro-dolphin policy.

Domestic consumer sentiment had changed government policy in the United States to protect dolphins. At the same time, the U.S. pro-dolphin policy also appeared to benefit the dominant suppliers of tuna to the U.S. market.

In the late 1980s, the suppliers, who had previously opposed a ban on dolphin-unfriendly tuna, shifted their position to support a ban on imports of the tuna. In the face of competition from low-cost foreign canned tuna, the U.S. canners moved their canneries from the continental United States to off-shore U.S. territories, where they could benefit from lower labor costs and tax concessions. In the new locations, the U.S. suppliers did not themselves use tuna from dolphin-unfriendly waters.

The U.S. pro-dolphin policy resulted in closure of competing smaller U.S. processing plants that relied on dolphin-unfriendly tuna while also eliminating competition from imports of dolphin-unfriendly tuna. Environmentally concerned consumers found an ally in the tuna-processing producers that supplied the U.S. market. There was a domestic consensus to protect the dolphins; as observed by

Achim Körber (1998), everyone – consumers, producers, and government – had come to love Flipper.

Reference

Körber, A., 1998. Why everybody loves Flipper: The political economy of the U.S. dolphin-safe laws. *European Journal of Political Economy* 14, 475–509.

Supplements to Chapter 5

5A *An impossibility theorem for social aggregation*

The social welfare function that we considered in Chapter 5 is a measure of the total welfare of the members of a society. Principles of democracy suggest that we would want the social welfare function to consistently include all individuals' preferences. The members of a society have preferences over their own consumption, the consumption of others, and the different public goods in society. Social welfare should somehow ideally acknowledge these different individual preferences. Kenneth Arrow of Stanford University (1950, Nobel Prize in economics 1972) concluded from an investigation of attempts at aggregation of individual preferences into social preferences that:

> *If we exclude the possibility of interpersonal comparisons of utility, then the only methods of passing from individual tastes to social preferences which will be satisfactory and which will be defined for a wide range of individual orderings are either imposed or dictatorial.* (p. 164 in Arrow and Scitovsky, 1969).

Arrow required that the social preferences expressed in the social welfare function satisfy a number of reasonable conditions. The conditions include that a social choice can always be made between alternatives. If social state A is preferred to B and B is preferred to C, then A is preferred to C, that is, preference relations are transitive. Another condition is "independence of irrelevant alternatives" (a person who has decided to vote for a political candidate in preference to rival candidates does not change his or her vote when one of the rival candidates drops out of the political contest). Arrow also required "the condition of citizens' sovereignty," which is that individuals in a society "be free to choose, by varying their values, among the alternatives available. That is, alternatives are not externally excluded from the possibilities of citizens' choices by some outside rule." The social welfare function should also not be dictatorial, that is, there should be no person in society whose personal preferences dictate the outcome for the rest of the society. Arrow concluded that the only social welfare functions that can be assured to exist are imposed (exclude some choices) or are dictatorial (one person decides for society).

Arrow's "impossibility theorem" rules out interpersonally comparable utility functions. We have adopted interpersonal comparisons of utility in viewing all people in society as identical when choosing the social welfare function behind a veil of ignorance. We treated people as identical or equal because we acknowledged that we had no way of making interpersonal comparisons between the utilities of people. If the social welfare is chosen before people know who they are, we can only presume that people are identical when choosing the social welfare function. The social welfare function is chosen before people know whether they will be rich or poor, or in good or bad health, and so on. If we want to construct a social welfare function by aggregating over preferences of individuals whom we acknowledge are different and have different visions of how society ought to distribute income and provide public goods, Arrow's impossibility theorem tells us that we must set aside democracy and allow a dictator to choose on behalf of society, or that we must limit the range of outcomes over which social choices are made.

Reference

Arrow, K. J., 1950. A difficulty in the concept of social welfare. *Journal of Political Economy*, 58, 328–46. Reprinted 1969 in *Readings in Welfare Economics*, K. J. Arrow and T. Scitovsky (eds.), Richard D. Irwin, Homewood, Illinois, 147–68.

5B Measurement of income inequality

If social justice is related to income inequality, we require means of measuring the extent of inequality. An often-used measure of inequality is known as the Gini coefficient. Figure S5.1 shows how the Gini coefficient is computed. With a given population and a given distribution of income among the members of the population, the vertical axis of Figure S5.1 measures the proportion of income, and the horizontal axis measures the proportion of the population. Along the 45° line, there is complete equality of incomes: 25 percent of the population has 25 percent of the income, 50 percent of the population has 50 percent of the income, and so on. The curved line, which is known as a Lorenz curve, shows the actual income distribution. At point 1, 50 percent of the population has 50 percent of the income, but point 2 on the Lorenz curve indicates that 50 percent of the population has more than 50 percent of the income.

The Gini coefficient is the shaded area divided by the area on one side of the diagonal (half the box). The smaller the shaded area is, the more equal the income

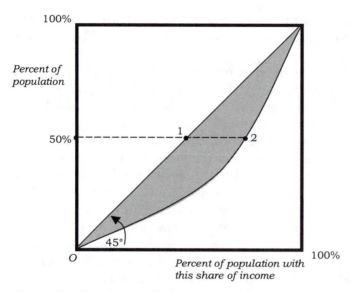

Figure S5.1. The Gini coefficient as a measure of economic inequality.

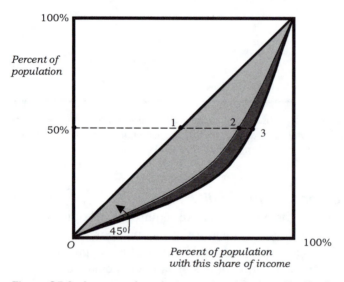

Figure S5.2. A comparison between two income distributions.

distribution is. When the Lorenz curve and the 45° line coincide, the shaded area disappears and the Gini coefficient reaches its minimum value of zero, at which there is complete income equality.

Figure S5.2 shows a comparison between income distributions in two societies. We see that one society has a more unequal distribution of income than the other. At point 1, 50 percent of the population would have 50 percent of the income. Comparing points 2 and 3, we see that, at point 2, 50 percent of the population has a smaller share of income than at point 3. For any percentage of the population, the society with the larger Gini coefficient (whose Lorenz curve is further to the right) has a more unequal income distribution.

Suppose that two people together earn $100 of income. The value of the Gini coefficient is then defined by the percentage of income above 50 percent earned by the higher-income person. For example, if one person earns $70 and the other earns $30, the Gini coefficient is 0.2. If one person earns $90 and the other earns $10, the Gini coefficient is 0.4. When each person earns $50, the Gino coefficient is zero, indicating complete equality.

Suppose that there are N people in the population with incomes

$$y_1, y_2, y_3, \ldots, y_N \tag{S5.1}$$

and that the average income for the population is y_a. The Gini coefficient is then computed as

$$\text{Gini} = \frac{1}{N^2 y_a} \sum_{i=1}^{N} \sum_{j=1}^{N} \frac{|y_i - y_j|}{2}. \tag{S5.2}$$

For example, for a population of four people with incomes of $2,000, $3,000, $4,000, and $7,000 per month, the Gini coefficient is 0.22.

If the highest-income person becomes more productive and earns $15,000 instead of $7,000, the new value of the Gini coefficient is 0.46. By Rawls's definition of social welfare, such an increase in income of the highest-income person is irrelevant. By Bentham's social welfare criterion, society is better off. We see that, by the Pareto criterion (which Bentham satisfies), there has been an improvement because one person is better off due to the higher income, and no one is worse off. The total income of the population has also increased. At the same time, the Gini coefficient tells us that inequality has increased.

Another measure of income inequality is based on Bentham's social welfare criterion. Recall that, without the leaky bucket of income distribution, the Bentham measure of social welfare is maximized when post-tax incomes are equal. Therefore, income inequality reduces social welfare. Anthony Atkinson (1970) of Oxford University proposed a measure of inequality based on the welfare loss from deviation from the full-equality Bentham maximum social welfare. Let y_a again be the average income in the population, and let everybody have the same utility function. Social welfare is maximized by giving everyone this average income (there is no leaky bucket; that is, there are no adverse incentive effects of redistribution involved here). Maximal social welfare is greater than (or not less than) the social welfare attained with the actual distribution of income, that is,

$$\max W = \sum_{i=1}^{N} u(y_a) \geq \sum_{i=1}^{N} u(y_i). \tag{S5.3}$$

Let the certainty-equivalent income that provides the same utility as the mean income y_a of the population be y_c. That is, the risk premium is $(y_a - y_c)$. Atkinson's proposed measure of inequality is

$$A \equiv \frac{\text{Risk premium}}{\text{Mean income}} = \frac{y_a - y_c}{y_a}. \tag{S5.4}$$

This measure is invariant to the scale on which income is measured if relative risk aversion r is constant, that is if

$$u(y) = \frac{y^{1-r}}{1-r} \qquad \text{for } r > 0, r \neq 1,$$

or

$$u(y) = \ln y \qquad \text{for } r = 1.$$

With constant relative risk aversion, the measure of inequality is

$$A \equiv 1 - \frac{1}{y_a} \left[\frac{1}{N} \sum_{i=1}^{N} y_i^{1-r} \right]^{1/(1-r)} \qquad r > 0, r \neq 1,$$

or

$$A \equiv 1 - \frac{1}{y_a} (y_1 \, y_2 \, y_3 \cdots y_N)^{1/N} \qquad \text{for } r = 1.$$

If the population is risk neutral so that utility is linear in income, then inequality would not matter. Because the population is risk-averse, inequality reduces expected utility and social welfare. In particular, progressive transfers increase social welfare by making incomes more equal. Progressivity in taxation is therefore beneficial in reducing inequality.

Suppose now that social welfare is measured by the Bentham sum of utilities for identical people with the same concave utility function. Take two distributions of income

$$\begin{aligned} y_1, \, y_2, \, y_3, \ldots, y_N \\ y_1^*, \, y_2^*, \, y_3^*, \ldots, y_N^* \end{aligned} \tag{S5.7}$$

with the same mean. When we evaluate social welfare for these income distributions, we find that

$$\sum_{i=1}^{N} u(y_i) \geq \sum_{i=1}^{N} u(y_i^*). \tag{S5.8}$$

if and only if, when we compare the Lorenz curves for the two income distributions, the Lorenz curve for the y distribution dominates the Lorenz curve for the y^* distribution.

It is possible to have income distributions where the Lorenz curves cross. In that case, we need another way of comparing inequality. Whether two Lorenz curves cross is a property of the income distributions on which the Lorenz curves are based. Measures of inequality that allow for such crossing have been devised (see for example Anthony Shorrocks, 1983).

References and related literature

Atkinson, A. B., 1970. On the measurement of economic inequality. *Journal of Economic Theory* 2, 244–63.

Silver, J. (ed.), 1999. *Handbook on Income Inequality*. Kluwer Academic Publishers, Dordrecht.

Shorrocks, A. F., 1983. Ranking income distributions. *Economica* 50, 1–17.

5C Social status and private charity

Charitable donations are sometimes part of the quest for social status that attracts people to charity balls and dinners. Charitable causes then gain through self-interest of the donors. Amihai Glazer and Kai Konrad (1996) suggested that conspicuous publicized charitable donations serve the purpose of displaying wealth to others. Thorstein Veblen (1857–1929), in his book *The Theory of the Leisure Class* (1899/1934), proposed that people display their wealth through conspicuous consumption. Conspicuous giving to charity is a more socially worthy means of displaying wealth.

Is social status, however, also an impediment to voluntary charitable transfers? Giacomo Corneo and Hans-Peter Grüner (2000) suggested that wealth and high income can be a source of a person's social status. Voluntary charitable redistribution of wealth or income then reduces the social status that people value. Desire to preserve social status thus counters personal charitable inclinations, because of the personal benefit when people who perceive themselves as having high social status (through education or pedigree) are able to identify one another and interact socially. The social interaction is made possible through the consumption activities associated with wealth and high incomes. That is, Corneo and Grüner propose that people view wealth and high income as an exclusion device that allows enjoyment of the company of other people with high social status, who might, for example, appreciate good cigars, malt whiskey, and the best vintages of wine. This argument is a variation on the theme of conspicuous consumption proposed by Thorstein Veblen. The consumption activities that reveal social status need to be conspicuous in order to allow people of social status to identify one other and to keep each other's company. Without wealth and high income, people would not be able to meet and identify each other at exclusive schools, hotels, and country clubs, and in the first class compartments of travel.

Wealth and high income are not necessary when there are other visible indicators of social status. For example, in many societies, incomes of university professors have been low, reflecting the view that high incomes are unnecessary because of the social status of being a professor. For example, in the prestigious English universities in Oxford and Cambridge, the presumption was, following on from monastic traditions of learning, that scholars do not marry but dedicate themselves to learning with no family obligations, and high incomes are unnecessary for the consequent modest means of living. Perhaps also the monastic tradition of social status reflected the perceived threat to the hereditary nobility from reproduction by people who were thought to be too clever. The clever were encouraged to choose confinement to monastic learning. The hereditary nobility married, and often intermarried. Excessive intermarriage of the hereditary mobility was perhaps a reason for the encouragement of monastic traditions for the clever.

References and related literature

Corneo, G, and H-P. Grüner, 2000. Social limits to redistribution. *American Economic Review* 90, 1491–1507.

Glazer, A. and K. A. Konrad, 1996. A signaling explanation for charity. *American Economic Review* 86, 1019–28.

Veblen, T., 1934 (1899). *The Theory of the Leisure Class*. Modern Library, New York.

Supplements to Chapter 6

6A *Probabilistic voting*

The theory of probabilistic voting proposes (see Section 6.2) that the probability that a voter will vote for a candidate C rather than for a candidate D depends on the difference in personal benefit to a voter from the two candidates' policy proposals. The probability that voter 1 will vote for candidate C is therefore

$$P_1^C = f\left(B_1^C - B_1^D\right) \tag{S6.1}$$

where the Bs are the benefits to voter 1 from the policies of candidates C and D. Voter 1 votes for either candidate C or candidate D so

$$P_1^C + P_2^D = 1. \tag{S6.2}$$

We define

$$\Delta B_i \equiv B_i^C - B_i^D, \quad i = 1, 2. \tag{S6.3}$$

so that

$$P_i^C = f(\Delta B_i), \quad i = 1, 2. \tag{S6.4}$$

Candidate C chooses a policy that maximizes

$$P_1^C + P_2^C. \tag{S6.5}$$

The policy decision is how to allocate public expenditure E between public spending on x and y. The policy chosen is determined by forming a Lagrangean function:

$$\sum_{i=1}^{2} p_i^C(\Delta B_i) - \lambda(x + y - E). \tag{S6.6}$$

This yields the condition for choice of policy by candidate C

$$\frac{\partial P_1^C}{\partial \Delta B_1} ML_1^C = \frac{\partial P_2^C}{\partial \Delta B_2} ML_2^C, \tag{S6.7}$$

where

$$\left(\frac{\partial \Delta B_1}{\partial x} - \frac{\partial \Delta B_1}{\partial y}\right) \equiv ML_1^C < 0$$

is voter 1's loss from the deviation of candidate C's policy from voter 1's preferred policy and

$$\left(\frac{\partial \Delta B_2}{\partial y} - \frac{\partial \Delta B_2}{\partial x}\right) \equiv ML_2^C < 0$$

is the similar loss for voter 2. In Section 6.2, we expressed (S6.6) as

$$a_{C1} ML_1^C = a_{C2} ML_2^C,$$

where

$$a_{C1} \equiv \frac{\partial P_1^C}{\partial \Delta B_1}, \qquad a_{C2} \equiv \frac{\partial P_2^C}{\partial \Delta B_2}.$$

Therefore, the candidate chooses a policy where marginal losses of the two voters from departures from the voters' preferred policies are weighted by the sensitivity of voting decisions to the difference in benefits offered by the candidates' policies.

6B A case of extreme corruption

From time to time, evidence of political corruption emerges. Extreme cases are interesting in showing the scope of what is possible where there are no bounds. To find extreme cases, we generally need to leave democratic societies. However, as a case study, we can consider the activities of Mr. Asif Ali Zardari during a period in the mid 1990s when his wife was prime minister of Pakistan. Mr. Zardari's activities were far reaching. *The International Herald Tribune*, January 10–11, 1998, reported that Mr. Zardari benefited from bribes involving "defense contracts, power plant projects, the privatization of state-owned industries, the awarding of broadcast licenses, the granting of an export monopoly for the country's huge rice harvest, the purchase of planes for Pakistan International Airways, the assignment of textile export quotas, the granting of oil and gas permits, authorization to build sugar mills, and the sale of government lands, and rake-offs from government welfare schemes." With the norms of behavior that prevailed, Mr. Zardari could use his wife's position as prime minister to enrich himself. He benefited personally when the government was buying (for defense or for the state-owned airline) and when government was selling (or privatizing) state property. He also benefited personally by selling rights to be monopolists to private interest groups and also by selling permission to receive government welfare payments.

If Mr. Zardari's wife were to lose political office, the benefits would cease for Mr. Zardari. Mr. Zardari's wife lost her position as prime minister in 1995. In 1997 Mr. Zardari was in a Pakistani jail. He was in jail because he was charged with complicity in organizing a *police* ambush that resulted in the death of his wife's brother – in an internecine dispute over the division of wealth – not because of corruption.

The value of Mr. Zardari's personal wealth at the time was estimated to be $1.5 billion U.S. in a country where most ordinary people were very poor.

Mr. Zardari used a small part of his wealth ($4.5 million U.S.) to purchase an English country estate. When questioned about the source of finance for his English country estate, Mr. Zardari pointed out that the person who had followed his wife as prime minister had already purchased two properties in England that were considerably more valuable than his property: "Those Park Lane flats (belonging to the new prime minister who had replaced his wife in 1995) are worth more than (my English property) twice over," Mr. Zardari declared.

We might have expected corruption on the scale that Mr. Zardari could achieve to be stopped short by information provided by the press, and by impeachment or resignation. Mr. Zardari was himself not a corrupt politician. His wife was the politician.

6C *Theoretical models of rent seeking*

A theoretical literature on rent seeking infers losses from rent seeking by modeling rational behavior by rent seekers and political decision makers who dispense rents. Rent-seeking behavior is in general not observable but is conducted behind closed doors. Often however the gain obtained by rent seekers (known in the rent-seeking literature as the rent-seeking prize) can be observed. Theoretical models of rent seeking attempt to link the value of resources used in seeking the rent-seeking prize to the value of the prize (or the value of the rent that was obtained). There are many different models of rent seeking, with different descriptions of how rent seeking takes place. The value of the resources used in seeking a rent depends on how a rent-seeking contest is described. The rule determining the identity of the successful rent seeker (known as the contest-success function) affects the resources used in rent seeking. Other influences include risk aversion, valuations of a rent-seeking prize, abilities of rent seekers, and information available to rent seekers. The number of people eligible or able to take part in a contest and the responsiveness of government to rent seeking (i.e., whether political decision makers are willing or reluctant participants) also influences the use of resources in rent seeking. The characteristics of the rent-seeking prize affect rent-seeking incentives, that is, it matters whether the prize provides private benefit, is shared among a number of winners, or is a public good. Rent seeking can also be delegated rather than undertaken personally and directly. A rent-seeking contest can have different stages. The rent may preexist and have a predetermined value, or the objective of rent seeking may be to seek public policies that create or increase the value of rents. The political decision makers whose policy decisions provide rents might also consider how they can most benefit from rent seekers who seek to influence public-policy decisions and may design rent-seeking contests accordingly. People who are attempting to prevent the policies that would provide rent seekers with rents can also use resources to affect outcomes. Such resources are used with good intentions but are also used in a socially wasteful way because the resources could have been used productively. We shall not review the entire literature on the formal modeling of rent-seeking contests here. We shall consider some basic elements of rent seeking that affect whether we can reliably approximate social loss from rent seeking from the observed the value of a rent-seeking prize.

The participation condition

We can consider a rent of value V. The rent yields an equally valued known private benefit to any one of n individuals who are active contenders in a contest to obtain the rent and who also have the same initial wealth A and the same utility from wealth U. One of the active contenders might be the incumbent claimant to the rent, but he or she has no advantage over the other contenders in contesting the claim. Each individual confronts a decision regarding how much of initial wealth A to allocate to contesting the claim to the rent. If active in the contest, an individual allocates resources of value x to the contest. The utility achieved with certainty by not participating in rent seeking is $U(A)$. The expected utility from participating is

$$EU = \left(\frac{n-1}{n}\right) U(A-x) + \left(\frac{1}{n}\right) U[A-x+V].   \tag{S6.8}$$

Expected utility EU here reflects the two possible outcomes of winning or not winning the contest. Only one person wins the contest. A person who is not successful is left with $(A-x)$, which gives utility $U(A-x)$. If everybody is identical and behaves identically in choosing the allocation x to contesting the rent, the probability of not being successful is $(n-1)/n$. The probability of being successful is $1/n$, and the winner has $(A-x+V)$. An individual will not participate in rent seeking if $EU < U(A)$. If $EU > U(A)$, an individual has an incentive to contest the prize V. The identical active contenders use resources of value nx in rent seeking. Rent dissipation is given by the ratio nx/V. If nx is equal to V, there is complete rent dissipation. In that case, the observed value of the prize V indicates the unobserved value of resources used in contesting the prize.

Competitive rent seeking

Suppose that rent-seeking contests are open to all, with no entry barriers to participation – and suppose no one has moral qualms about being a rent seeker. As the number of active contenders n becomes larger, the probability of any one person winning the contest decreases. The change in nx determines the effect on the dissipation rate nx/V, since V is given. With risk-neutral rent seekers, rent dissipation is complete in the limit as the number of contenders expands without bound, that is, competitive rent seeking results in complete rent dissipation (for a proof, see Hillman and Katz, 1982).

Small numbers and strategic behavior

Rather than a large number of contenders and competitive rent seeking, we can consider contests where the number of contenders is sufficiently small that contenders behave strategically. A contest-success function is then required indicating how strategic behavior affects the determination of the winner of a contest. General forms of contest-success functions have been considered by Hirshleifer (1989) and Skaperdas (1996). Two popularly applied contest-success functions are (1) a probabilistic rule that "the more you spend in a contest, the greater your chance of winning" (Tullock, 1980) and (2) an all-pay auction where "the highest outlay made in a contest wins" (Hillman and Samet, 1987). In either case, we seek a Nash equilibrium in outlays $\{x_1, \ldots, x_n\}$ when a person i chooses a rent-seeking outlay x_i to maximize expected utility

$$EU_i = \rho_i(x_1, \ldots, x_i, \ldots, x_n)V - x_i, \tag{S6.9}$$

where ρ_i is the probability of person i being the successful rent seeker who wins V, and $\Sigma\rho_i = 1$.

Contests where the highest outlay wins

When the rule is that the highest outlay wins, in (S6.9)

$$\rho_i = 1 \quad if \quad x_i > x_k \quad k \neq i,$$
$$\rho_i = 0 \quad if \quad x_i < x_k \quad k \neq i.$$

The outcome with identical risk-neutral contenders is, under this rule, complete rent dissipation on average. Complete dissipation on average is moreover the outcome for any number of active contenders in a contest, that is, even the minimum number of two contenders (see Hillman and Samet, 1987).

In these contests, contenders choose their rent-seeking outlays x as a mixed strategy; that is, the Nash equilibrium is a probability distribution from which contenders draw their outlays at random. We can readily see that there is no pure-strategy equilibrium. If all contenders were to make the same outlay, this could not be an equilibrium because the contenders would wish to revise their strategy to outlay a little more than everybody else and thereby win the contest. All contenders choosing the same x therefore cannot be an equilibrium. Choice of different xs can also not be an equilibrium because the persons whose xs are lower than the highest x would be better off choosing $x = 0$. If they choose $x = 0$, then the person who chose the highest x has an incentive to revise his or her outlay to ε (a very small positive number). However, then contenders who chose to outlay zero have an incentive to revise their behavior and outbid ε. Therefore, there is also no pure-strategy equilibrium when active contenders make different bids. Because there are no pure-strategy equilibria where contenders choose the same outlay and where contenders choose different outlays, there is no pure-strategy equilibrium.

There is however a mixed-strategy equilibrium (see Hillman and Samet, 1987, for the formal derivation). When $n = 2$, the mixed-strategy equilibrium is to choose x from the uniform distribution ranging over $\{0, V\}$. When $n = 3$, the equilibrium distribution changes to place more weight on lower bids over the range $\{0, V\}$, because of the increased competition. The change in the equilibrium distribution, whereby greater weight is placed on lower outlays, continues as n increases. The expected value of a person's outlay Ex is determined by the probability distribution describing the Nash equilibrium, which depends upon the number of active contenders n. It is always the case that rent dissipation is complete in an expected sense, that is,

$$\frac{nEx}{V} = 1 \qquad \text{for all values of } n \geq 2. \tag{S6.10}$$

As n increases, the mean outlay Ex of the distribution defining the equilibrium mixed strategy falls, but the increase in the number of persons outlaying (on average) Ex precisely balances the reduced average outlay.

Different valuations of rents

Valuations of the prize could differ among contenders (Hillman and Riley, 1989). Where the prize is to be a successful political candidate, different candidates can, for example, have different personal benefits from winning. Contenders may also have different costs of contesting a prize, resulting in different net values for the prize. We can rank valuation for n contenders:

$$V_1 > V_2 > V_3 > \cdots > V_n. \tag{S6.11}$$

When the highest bid wins the prize, only the two highest-valuation contenders take an active role in a contest. Neither active participant spends more than the valuation V_2 of the lower-valuation contender. A high-valuation contender who spends a little more than the valuation V_1 of the low-value opponent would win with probability one because the low-valuation contender will never outlay more than the personal valuation V_2. A pure strategy of $x_1 > V_2$ and $x_2 = 0$ is not, however, a Nash equilibrium because if $x_2 = 0$, then the high-valuation contender will wish to choose $x_1 = \varepsilon$, in which case the second contender would not choose $x_2 = 0$ but would outbid the ε outlay of the first contender. Again, there is no pure-strategy equilibrium.

The low-valuation contender is inhibited from actively participating in the contest (i.e., from choosing x_2 strictly positive) because of the known greater valuation of the opponent. Still, the low-valuation contender does not choose $x_2 = 0$ with certainty. An outlay of zero would guarantee the prize to the high-valuation rival. Both contenders choose their outlays from a distribution over the range of $\{0, V_2\}$. The low-valuation contender makes a strictly positive outlay with probability V_2/V_1. That is, in the distribution defining the low-valuation contender's equilibrium mixed strategy, the likelihood of a positive bid by the low-valuation contender increases with his or her valuation of the prize relative to the high-valuation opponent. However, the high-valuation contender always makes a positive bid. The expected value of total rent-seeking expenditures is then (for the detailed derivation, see Hillman and Riley, 1989)

$$Ex_1 + Ex_2 = \left(\frac{V_2}{V_1}\right)\left(\frac{V_2 + V_1}{2}\right). \tag{S6.12}$$

Rent dissipation is always incomplete because

$$Ex_1 + Ex_2 = V_2\left(\frac{V_2 + V_1}{2V_1}\right) \qquad \text{where} \left(\frac{V_2 + V_1}{2V_1}\right) < 1; \tag{S6.13}$$

hence,

$$Ex_1 + Ex_2 < V_2 < V_1. \tag{S6.14}$$

Complete rent dissipation is approached as V_2 approaches V_1 in value.

   This outcome is consistent with the many cases where contests have small numbers of contenders or in particular there are two rivals. Other potential contenders whose net valuations of the prize are lower stay out of the contest. This is understandable because outlays are lost independently of the result of the contest. Low-valuation contenders confronting known high-valuation contenders are consequently disinclined to allocate their time and money to a contest. The contender with the second-highest valuation is the sole active challenger but also chooses a zero outlay with a positive probability depending on by how much the low valuation differs from the high valuation.

Uncertain valuations of rents

Contenders may not know each other's valuations of the prize with certainty. Suppose contenders are uncertain about each other's valuations, but that valuations are known to be independently drawn from the uniform distribution where $V \in (0, V^*)$. Let us consider equilibria where each contender's spending level is increasing in his or her valuation of the prize. Then (see Hillman and Riley, 1989) the value of total expected outlays is obtained as

$$E\left(\sum_{j=1}^{n} x_j\right) = \left(\frac{(n-1)}{(n+1)}\right) V^*. \tag{S6.15}$$

Thus, if $n = 2$, rent dissipation is one-half of the maximal valuation. As n increases, rent dissipation becomes larger. When $n = 10$, rent dissipation is around 82 percent; when $n = 20$, rent dissipation is around 90 percent. As the number of contenders increases, each participant judges that even if he or she has a high valuation, there will now be increasing numbers of others who also have high valuations, and hence that more has to be spent to win; consequently, rent dissipation increases.

Probabilistic contests

In probabilistic contests, the contest-success function has the interpretation of a probability of winning. For example, a person i spending x_i has a probability of winning given by (see Tullock, 1980)

$$\rho_i(x_1, \ldots, x_i, \ldots, x_n) = \frac{x_i^r}{\sum\limits_{j=1}^{n} x_j^r} \tag{S6.16}$$

where r is a scale parameter. In the preceding case where the highest bid wins, $r = \infty$. The expected utility of individual i is now

$$EU_i = \frac{x_i^r}{\sum\limits_{j=1}^{n} x_j^r} V - x_i. \tag{S6.17}$$

In a symmetric Nash equilibrium, with $n = 2$, and for $r \leq 2$, there is a unique pure-strategy equilibrium where the contenders choose

$$x = \frac{rV}{2}.$$

Therefore, rent dissipation is

$$\frac{2x}{V} = \frac{r}{2}.$$

Thus, where $r = 1$, rent dissipation is 50 percent.

When $n > 2$, there are multiple Nash equilibria (see Baye, Kovenock, and de Vries, 1996), which complicates the computation of rent dissipation (rent dissipation depends on the equilibria that emerge). Where $\infty > r > 2$, the solution is a mixed-strategy equilibrium (Baye, Kovenock, and de Vries, 1994).

When valuations differ, we can evaluate the harmonic mean of the valuations. For two contenders,

$$\tilde{V} \equiv \frac{n}{v_1 + v_2}.$$

Denoting the sum of rent-seeking outlays of n contenders by S_n, we have

$$S_n = \frac{1}{2}\tilde{V}.$$

Risk aversion

Risk aversion can either decrease or increase individuals' rent-seeking spending (see Konrad and Schlesinger, 1997). This is so for any general contest-success function with the property that own-expenditures on rent seeking increase the probability of success and expenditure by any other contender reduces the probability of success. The ambiguity is the consequence of two effects when a rent seeker increases rent-seeking outlays. An increase in spending on rent seeking reduces wealth in all states of the world (whether individual i wins or loses in the contest) and at the same time increases the likelihood of the favorable outcome of winning the rent-seeking prize. That is, in increasing the likelihood of winning, increases in rent-seeking outlays provide a form of self-insurance. More risk-averse persons will seek more insurance by spending more on rent seeking to increase the likelihood of success, but they will also be inclined to spend less on rent seeking because of the risky nature of spending on rent seeking.

Design of rent-seeking contests

Political decision makers who benefit from part of the effort and resources used by rent seekers have an interest in designing contests that provide maximal political benefit.[1] One question of design concerns the number of prizes.[2] The design of a rent-seeking contest can also involve delegation to others.[3] Limits can also be placed on the resources that can be used in rent-seeking activity. Che and Gale (1998) use the rule that the highest bid wins to investigate the effects of placing maximum limits on spending in political contests: total resources used in a contest increase because of the increased contestability of the prize.

Countervailing opposition

We can distinguish contests where a rent is a predetermined available prize from contests where the rent is to taken from or financed by another group (Hillman and Riley, 1989). In the latter case, we expect countervailing opposition, for example, from consumers resisting quests for monopoly power or protectionist international trade policies. The opposition makes the task of rent seekers more difficult and affects decisions to use resources in rent seeking. At the same time, resources are used in resistance.[4]

Attempts to change behavior of rent seekers

Guttman, Nitzan, and Spiegel (1992) have considered the role of education as a means of attempting to change personal behavior so that people refrain from rent seeking. Hardened rent seekers have reason to support investment in education that convinces people that rent seeking is socially undesirable. Education that leads some people to refrain from rent seeking is to the advantage of the people who remain unconvinced about the impropriety of rent seeking, by reducing competition for rents.

Rent seeking by groups

Rent seeking is often a group activity. We can consider a population of n rent seekers divided into m competing groups. Each individual makes a Nash decision

---

[1] On the design of rent-seeking contests, see Applebaum and Katz (1987), Michaels (1988), Glazer (1993), and Gradstein and Konrad (1999).
[2] See Moldovanu and Sela (2001). On rent seeking with multiple prizes, see also Clark and Riis (1998).
[3] See Congleton (1984) and Baik and Kim (1997).
[4] On rent seeking with countervailing opposition, see for example Ellingsen (1991), Paul and Wilhite (1991), Fabella (1995), Keem (2001), and Epstein and Nitzan (2003).

about a personal contribution to the group effort. The individual contributions to a group's effort depend on incentives that reflect how the rent is shared among group members (if the group is successful in its rent-seeking contest).[5]

Suppose that the rent is an income transfer (a sum of money) and that, if a group is successful, a share of the money a is divided equally among the group and the remaining share $(1 - a)$ is divided among group members according to observed individual contributions. With the probabilistic rule for winning the contest and $r = 1$, the proportion of a rent dissipated in individual rent seeking efforts is (see Nitzan, 1991)

$$\frac{(1 - a)n + ma - 1}{n}. \tag{S6.18}$$

As a special case, if $a = 1$, the entire rent is equally shared without regard for individual contributions, and the proportion of the rent dissipated is $(m - 1)/n$. The greater the number of groups for a given population is, the greater rent dissipation is because of the greater between-group competition. For any given number of groups, rent dissipation declines with the total number of rent seekers because the equal-sharing rule within a group diminishes the personal incentive to contribute to the group objective. When $a = 0$, the rent is shared within the group solely on the basis of personal contributions. In that case, the share of the rent dissipated is $(n - 1)/n$, which is the same as when each of the n persons competes individually for the rent. We see in expression (S6.18) that rent dissipation declines as the share a of the rent distributed within the group without regard for individual contributions increases.

Rather than being shared, the rent might be a public good for the members of the rent-seeking group (see Ursprung, 1990). For example, the group might be seeking a (noncongested) road that would principally serve them, government support for the local opera company or symphony orchestra, more funds for the local school, or increased attention to the quality of the environment. When the prize is a public good, all persons in the group benefit without regard for their personal contributions, and there is a personal incentive to free ride. On the other hand, the rent does not need to be shared; everyone in the group benefits from the entire rent. When the prize is a public good, individual rent seekers are making private contributions to a public good that the group wins with some probability. The public good has an expected value, and the results described in Supplement 2B apply for individual Nash contributions to providing the public good. If there is no income effect, in a Nash equilibrium, the amount spent in rent seeking is independent of the number of rent seekers in a group. With m groups competing, rent dissipation is $(m - 1)/m$. Rent dissipation then depends on the number of groups and not on the size of the population that has been divided among the groups.

---

[5] Shared rents with risk aversion were studied by Ngo Van Long and Neil Vousden (1987).

Experimental evidence

Experiments have been conducted with rent seeking. Potters, de Vries, and van Winden (1998) conducted experimental contests with probabilistic contest success functions (with $r = 1$) and contest success functions where the highest bid wins. Participants (who were students) competed in pairwise rent-seeking contests, one against another. The results of the experiments revealed irrational bids in both types of contests. In some cases, the bids exceeded the value of the prize. The behavior of the participants differed in the two types of contests. The mean of bids was significantly different from the Nash equilibrium for the probabilistic contests, and the hypothesis of bids drawn from a uniform distribution was rejected for contests with the rule that the highest bid wins. In the probabilistic contests, rent dissipation was persistently higher than the prediction of 50 percent, but as rent-seeking games continued to be played, rent dissipation showed a tendency to move toward the predicted level. In the contests where the highest bid wins, the level of dissipation fluctuated around the predicted complete dissipation. Rent dissipation was smaller in the probabilistic contents. The study revealed three types of behavior. Some participants thought strategically and understood quickly what to do. Some learned from experience and adapted their behavior. Some remained confused throughout.

References and related literature

Applebaum E. and E. Katz, 1987. Seeking rents by setting rents: The political economy of rent seeking. *Economic Journal* 97, 685–99.

Baik, K. H. and I-G. Kim, 1997. Delegation in contests. *European Journal of Political Economy* 13, 281–98.

Baye, M. D., D. Kovenock and C. de Vries, 1994. The solution to the Tullock rent-seeking game when $R > 2$: Mixed strategy equilibria and mean dissipation rates. *Public Choice* 81, 363–80.

Baye, M. D., D. Kovenock and C. de Vries, 1996. The all-pay auction with complete information. *Economic Theory* 8, 291–305.

Che, Y-K. and I. L. Gale, 1998. Caps on political lobbying. *American Economic Review* 88, 643–51.

Clark, D. J. and C. Riis, 1998. Influence and the discretionary allocation of several prizes. *European Journal of Political Economy* 14, 605–25.

Congleton, R. D., 1984. Committees and rent seeking effort. *Journal of Public Economics* 25, 197–209.

Ellingsen, T., 1991. Strategic buyers and the social cost of monopoly. *American Economic Review* 81, 648–57.

Epstein, G. S. and S. Nitzan, 2003. The social cost of rent seeking when consumer opposition influences monopoly behavior. *European Journal of Political Economy* 18, 61–9.

Fabella, R. V., 1995. The social cost of rent seeking under countervailing opposition to distortionary transfers. *Journal of Public Economics* 57, 235–47.

Glazer, A., 1993. On incentives to establish and play rent-seeking games. *Public Choice* 75, 139–48.

Gradstein, M. and K. A. Konrad, 1999. Orchestrating rent seeking contests. *Economic Journal* 109, 536–45.

Guttman, J., S. Nitzan and U. Spiegel, 1992. Rent seeking and social investment in taste change. *Economics and Politics* 4, 31–42.

Hillman, A. L. and E. Katz, 1982. Risk-averse rent seekers and the social cost of monopoly power. *Economic Journal* 94, 104–10.

Hillman, A. L. and J. Riley, 1989. Politically contestable rents and transfers. *Economics and Politics* 1, 17–39.

Hillman, A. L. and D. Samet, 1987. Dissipation of rents and revenues in small-numbers contests. *Public Choice* 54, 63–82.

Hirshleifer, J., 1989. Conflict and rent-seeking success functions: Different models of relative success. *Public Choice*, 63, 101–12.

Keem, J. H., 2001. The social cost of monopoly when consumers resist. *European Journal of Political Economy* 17, 633–9.

Konrad, K. and H. Schlesinger, 1997. Risk aversion in rent-seeking and rent-augmenting games. *Economic Journal* 107, 1671–83.

Long, N. V. and N. Vousden, 1987. Risk-averse rent seeking with shared rents. *Economic Journal* 97, 971–85.

Michaels, R., 1988. The design of rent seeking competition. *Public Choice* 56, 17–29.

Moldovanu, B. and A. Sela, 2001. The optimal allocation of prizes in contests. *American Economic Review* 91, 542–58.

Nitzan, S., 1991. Collective rent dissipation. *Economic Journal* 101, 1522–34.

Paul, C. W., II and A. W. Wilhite, 1991. Rent seeking, rent defending, and rent dissipation. *Public Choice* 71, 61–70.

Potters, J., C. de Vries and F. van Winden, 1998. An experimental examination of rational rent seeking. *European Journal of Political Economy* 14, 783–800.

Skaperdas, S., 1996. Contest success functions. *Economic Theory* 7, 283–90.

Tullock, G. 1980. Efficient rent seeking. In *Toward a Theory of the Rent Seeking Society*, J. M. Buchanan, R. D. Tollison and G. Tullock (eds.). Texas A & M Press, College Station, 97–112.

Ursprung, H. W., 1990. Public goods, rent dissipation, and candidate competition. *Economics and Politics* 2, 115–32.

6D Rents and protectionist international trade policies

Protectionist policies provide rents for import-competing domestic producers. At the same time, when protection is provided through a quota, the persons with the right to import are also provided with rents. Figure S6.1 shows domestic demand and supply, and a world price P^{world} at which a good can be bought or sold in a competitive world market. When there are no restrictions on the quantity of goods that can be imported, a quantity of output Q_1 is produced domestically, domestic consumption is Q_4, and the quantity imported is $(Q_4 - Q_1)$. A government might decide to set a limit on imports and allow no more than the quantity $(Q_3 - Q_2)$ to be bought from foreign suppliers. The market equilibrium with the quota in Figure S6.1 is point E where imports are the quantity $(Q_3 - Q_2)$ allowed under the quota. Because of the restriction on purchases from foreign suppliers, the domestic price has increased from the world price P^{world} (when the domestic market was part of an integrated world market) to $P^{domestic}$. A government could equivalently limit imports to the quantity $(Q_3 - Q_2)$ by imposing a tariff on imports equal to

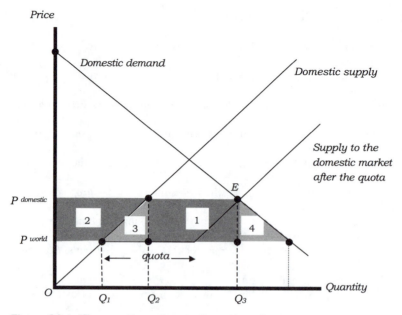

Figure S6.1. The creation of rents through an import quota.

the difference between $P^{domestic}$ and P^{world}. Whether imports are taxed or a quota limits allowable imports, the excess burden (or efficiency loss) of the protectionist policy is the sum of the areas 3 and 4. The area 3 is the excess cost of producing goods that were previously imported, and the area 4 is the loss in consumer benefit from the reduction in domestic consumption. The area 2 is the gain or rent provided through the protectionist policy to the domestic industry.

The only difference in Figure S6.1 between an import duty and an import quota is in the interpretation of the area 1. With a tariff (or import duty), the area 1 is the revenue received by the government. With the quota, the area 1 is a rent to persons who have received the right to import the restricted quantity of imports. The quota provides a rent by allowing these persons to buy at the price P^{world} and sell at the price $P^{domestic}$. This right is a privilege that is the equivalent of a gift of money equal to the area 1. If the quota rent is entirely dissipated in contests to secure the rights to the quota, the total loss to society from the restriction of imports through the quota is the sum of the areas $(1 + 3 + 4)$. The area 1, which under an import duty was not a social loss but instead a transfer of revenue to the government, becomes a social loss under the quota, measured as the value of resources attracted to rent seeking (see Anne Krueger, 1975).

Free trade would eliminate the rent for domestic producers given by area 2, which exists only because of the public policy that restricts imports. Free trade would convert this rent to benefit for consumers. Rent seeking may take place to persuade political decision makers to maintain the rent for domestic producers. In that case, the value of the resources and time used in rent seeking by domestic producers to sustain the protectionist policy is an additional loss to society. With rent seeking for the quota rights taking place, and with complete dissipation of rents, areas 1, 2, 3, and 4 all indicate values of social losses. Free trade, and a commitment to free trade that credibly ensures that rent seeking has no purpose, transforms these social losses to consumer benefit.

Reference

Krueger, A. O., 1975. The political economy of the rent seeking society. *American Economic Review* 64, 291–303.

Supplements to Chapter 7

7A *Measuring the size of the shadow economy*

The estimates of the shadow economy in Table 7.1 in Section 7.3 are based on the demand for cash for shadow economy transactions. Alternative methods of estimating the size of the shadow economy have been used. For example, a sample of people can be asked to indicate their true incomes and the incomes that they report to the tax authorities. The problem then is that tax evasion is illegal and people are being asked to admit to illegal activities, which they may be reluctant to do for fear that the information may not remain confidential, or that the survey is a device for detection organized by the tax authorities.

Studies of the size of the shadow sector also use electricity consumption as an indirect measure of true economic activity. Electricity consumption is compared with reported income, and the difference is attributed to the informal economy. Of course, not all activities in the informal economy require electricity, and not all activities require equal use of electricity. Changes also take place over time in the amount of electricity required for different economic activities.

Another method uses official statistics of national income and national expenditures. If income is underreported or not reported to evade taxes but national expenditures can be measured, the difference can be used as a measure of the size of the shadow economy. A problem with this approach is that expenditures of non-reported incomes are also hidden. People transact with one another in cash, and one person's nonreported expenditure is another person's nonreported income. A further problem with this approach is that aggregate economy-wide statistical measures of income and expenditure are imperfect and include an errors-and-omissions term to balance the national accounts. It is difficult or impossible to distinguish true errors and omissions from the evidence on the size of the shadow economy. The government statistical offices that provide the data for the national accounts perceive their competence as reflected in the size of the errors and omissions term. A perfect reporting of the national accounts from the perspective of the government statistical offices would have zero errors and omissions. The national statistical offices therefore have incentives to bias their reporting toward minimal error and omissions by finding ways to reduce the value of the error and omissions term. To the extent that the error and omissions term reflects the size of the shadow economy, the quest to balance the national accounts leads to underestimation of the size of the shadow economy. The same applies to the errors and omissions term in the balance of payments, which can reflect capital flight or transfer abroad of income earned in the shadow economy.

Employment statistics have been used to measure the size of the shadow economy. If official statistics indicate a decrease in employment, but unemployment has not increased, then people may have moved to the shadow economy where their economic activities (as well as their incomes) are not reported. People may, however, work in the shadow economy and also receive unemployment or welfare benefits, and people may work in the shadow economy in addition to their regular jobs.

7B Tax evasion and the value-added tax

A value-added tax (see Section 7.2) has an advantage over a sales tax for monitoring taxpayer compliance for the value-added tax, and also for income taxes. With a value-added tax, intermediate buyers report their expenditures to the tax administration to claim the deduction against their own value-added tax liabilities. Sellers who do not report the income from a sale must therefore, for consistency, also ensure that the buyer does not report the purchase for the purpose of obtaining the credit from value-added tax. Buyers have, however, an incentive to report purchases from sellers to receive the tax credit for their purchase of inputs. This self-policing aspect of the value-added tax makes tax evasion difficult. The weak link in the chain of self-policing of a value-added tax is when the good reaches the final purchaser. The final purchaser sells to no one else, and so receives no tax credit for the purchase. The final purchaser accordingly has no personal incentive to report the purchase to the tax authorities, nor usually is the final purchaser obliged to do so.

One solution to the problem that information is not reported by final purchasers is to make purchase without an official receipt illegal and to offer prizes in a government lottery where the lottery tickets are the receipts of the final purchasers. For example, the final consumer pays a tradesman, obtains a receipt, and sends the receipt to an advertised address. The receipt is like a lottery ticket; tickets are drawn, and prize winners are publicly announced. The government uses the receipts that have been sent in as lottery tickets to check against reported sales. For each receipt that a purchaser has sent in as a lottery ticket, there should be an exact copy in the receipt book of the seller. The disciplining effect on sellers does not require all final purchasers to send in their receipts to participate in the lottery. The likelihood that a purchaser will send in a receipt acts as an incentive for sellers to include the revenue from their sales in their statements of taxable income.

7C Tax evasion through expense accounts

Expense accounts are a means of evading payment of taxes. The expenses are a deduction from the taxes payable by the employer, and so cost the employer less than the amount spent on the expense account. However, expense accounts can provide payments for personal use of cars (including insurance and gasoline), superior hotel accommodations, gourmet meals, and other entertainment expenses. The beneficiary of an expense account can be asked how much he or she is prepared to accept in money in place of the expense account. This is similar to the question that was asked in Chapter 2 to determine the excess burden of a tax. The answer will reveal the excess burden or efficiency loss from the expense account. For example, an employee may receive $10,000 of expense-account expenses that he or she values at only $6,000.

An expense account is a subsidy. The personal price of a gourmet meal, for example, falls to zero. We have seen there are efficiency losses (like excess burdens of taxes) associated with subsidies. The efficiency loss due to the subsidy is the reason why $10,000 of expense account spending might be valued at $6,000.

The inefficiency would not exist, if true business-related expenses could be separated from personal benefits financed through expense accounts. Taxation authorities attempt to monitor for the separation and attempt to tax income received in kind through expense accounts in the same way as income received in money. Nonetheless, ambiguities of business expenses allow tax-deductible payments to be paid through expense accounts. It can be difficult for the tax authorities to distinguish between a business conference and a good time at a hotel resort, or between travel for business purposes and travel for personal enjoyment, or between accompaniment on a trip by a companion and accompaniment by a business associate.

In Section 7.2, we investigated justifications for a corporate income or profits tax and found no particular justification. If the rate of corporate taxation is low relative to personal income tax rates, individuals have incentives to incorporate and to take personal benefits through corporate expense accounts that allow tax deductions for vehicles, entertainment, and other expenses.

Supplements to Chapter 8

8A Public finance and private supply

The relation between public finance and government supply of education and health care in the United States in the late 1990s is shown in Table S8.1. Education at the elementary and secondary school level was 92 percent publicly financed with 89 percent direct government supply. Hospitals were 62 percent publicly financed, with 17 percent of beds in state-owned hospitals. Public finance accounted for

TABLE S8.1. PUBLIC SUPPLY AND PUBLIC FINANCE

Type of entitlement	Share of state supply	Share of public finance
Hospitals	17	62
Nursing homes	9	53
Elementary and secondary education	89	92
Post-secondary education	78	38
Childcare	7	30

Source: Blank (2000).

39 percent of child care, with 7 percent of children in state facilities. Only in post-secondary education did the proportion of direct state supply exceed the proportion of public finance.

Reference

Blank, R. M., 2000. When can public policy makers rely on private markets? *Economic Journal* 110, 34–49.

8B User pricing and prisons

Prisons provide a public-good benefit as part of the credible deterrence that maintains the rule of law. Potential victims are also separated from criminals, although the criminals may themselves be victims of underprivilege, lack of opportunity, and lack of appropriate role models. Prisons have traditionally been owned and administered by governments, yet prisons can be privately owned with different private suppliers competing on a price and quality basis – just as, for example, there is competition among privately owned homes for the elderly. In the case of both prisons and sheltered care for the aged, government regulation may be required to ensure that the private-profit motive does not result in adverse conditions.

Rather than financing through taxes, could the user-pays principle be applied to financing of prisons? The elderly are in general voluntarily in homes for the aged and are willing to pay, whereas prisoners are involuntarily incarcerated. Nonetheless, prisoners have personal assets and also are in most cases able to work. Should not prison inmates pay for their food and accommodation and for the costs of prison personnel from accumulated private wealth or savings or from the value of output they produce when in prison? The question is whether society should pay through the crime and through public finance for the police and justice system, and pay again for the upkeep of the prisoners? The case against prisoners' paying on a user-pays basis for their stay in prison is possible adverse incentives. Just as care for the aged is in general profitable, privately owned user-pays prisons can be profitable, in which case there are private incentives to lock people up and have the prisoners pay for their imprisonment.

8C Supplemental user pricing

Where governments finance and supply public goods by taxation, possibilities may also be present for taxpayers to supplement public services provided by the government through user prices in private markets. For example, there is a supplementary market in private security services. People who seek more protection than is offered by publicly financed security can choose to pay for additional security. Supplemental user pricing also takes place through private lessons after school hours.

8D Privatization

Consumers can gain from privatization through lower prices and better-quality service. After privatization, shareholders and management of the private firm can also gain. In the case of electricity supply in the United Kingdom, after privatization there were claims of "unfair" gains to private shareholders and management at the expense of consumers. Electricity supply, as a natural monopoly, remains subject to price regulation after privatization. Estimates had been made of the cost reductions that were expected to be achieved under private ownership, and regulated prices were set according to anticipated costs. However, cost reductions achieved through private ownership exceeded expectations. Profits increased, and stock prices rose. In recognition of the cost savings and profits, management was also paid more.

The government regulator of electricity prices now faced a problem. The high profits under private ownership from sales of electricity at the regulated electricity prices were interpreted as unfair to consumers and overly advantageous to shareholders and management. However, a reduction in the regulated price of electricity would be unfair to shareholders because the stock price would fall and shareholders would suffer a capital loss, in particular those who bought stock when the true low cost of supply under private ownership was already known and was capitalized into the share price. Management whose efforts had yielded the efficiency gains would also lose because their remuneration was linked to profits. Higher user prices than warranted by costs are, however, inefficient. Also, more users of electricity vote than shareholders or management. The press gave the issue wide coverage. The regulator decided to decrease the regulated price of electricity.

Supplements to Chapter 10

10A Employer-provided health insurance

Health care is subsidized if private health-care expenses are a personal tax deduction. The tax-deductible health-care expenses might be paid directly by taxpayers, or employers may provide health insurance as a payment-in-kind benefit to employees. A substantial part of the cost of health insurance may well be paid by employees, even if employers make the payments to health-insurance companies. We saw in Chapter 2 that the true burden of payment is determined by supply and demand elasticities in a market and not by who transfers the money. However, independently of on whom the true burden of payment falls, if the cost of providing health insurance is a tax-deductible expense for the employer, then by subsidizing health insurance government is participating in the cost.

10B Markets and publicly financed health care for the elderly

Elderly people tend to have high health costs. In the United States, health care for elderly people is covered by the federal government's Medicare program. If elderly people were to receive health care through health management organizations, competition among HMOs might be expected to contain costs. In the 1990s, this line of thought led to a government policy that encouraged participation by the elderly in HMOs. The HMOs offered "medicare plus choice" programs that were attractive to the elderly, and many elderly people joined the private health-insurance programs. The HMOs sought to counter adverse selection by basing the personal insurance premium on the participant's age, on whether the participant received government income assistance (whether the person was on welfare), on where the participant lives, and whether the health insurance was being provided to a man or woman. The policy of using HMOs to provide health care for the elderly soon encountered difficulties. The HMOs were happy to take the senior citizens when they were relatively younger and relatively healthy. As age advanced, however, so did costs of providing health care, and the HMOs were victims of their own success. Good health care kept people alive into more advanced years, where their health costs increased even more. HMOs responded to the increasing costs by refusing to renew participation of elderly people in their programs. Costs could have been contained by reducing health-care standards. The elderly patients' complaints about changes in health care were taken up by the press, and HMOs therefore faced adverse publicity when they attempted to contain costs. HMOs had originally competed for participants by offering generous benefits. When the time came to pay the benefits, profitability declined, and the elderly were denied further health insurance.

The selection response of the HMOs reflects a general problem that arises in private health-insurance markets. The insurer is happy to receive the premium payment and to stand ready to finance medical care when health is good. When health deteriorates and costs of care increase, the health insurer has an incentive to end the insurance contract.

10C Costs of medical education and training

Market-based systems of health care are in general accompanied by private financing of medical education and training. The high private cost of medical school
is a personal investment that will yield future returns in the private market for
health care. In societies that choose socialized health care provided through government, medical education and training are subsidized. Incomes of doctors and
medical staff are determined by government and are systematically lower than
market-determined incomes in societies that rely on market provision of health
care. When emigration and immigration can freely take place, the medical practitioner who has received free training in the country with socialized medicine has
an incentive to move to a country where medical services are provided through
a private market and to practice medicine there, to take advantage of the high
income that is available in the private market. The doctors who emigrate from
countries with socialized medicine to countries with market-provided medicine
could be viewed as breaking an implicit social contract. The contract is that they
will receive an education for free and in return will accept the low income that
comes with the free medical education. Society has financed the investment in
medical training in order to allow lost-cost provision of medical services to the
population. By emigrating, the doctor takes away the investment of society and
uses that investment for personal gain.

To deal with this problem, some societies impose bonds on medical students.
The bonds require repayment of the educational investments of society if the
newly graduated doctor does not remain within the country's socialized system of
medicine for a sufficient number of years.

In a free society, a person has the right to leave when he or she wishes. The
problem is the embodiment in people of investments paid for by society with the
anticipation of social benefit. This problem is absent when medicine is provided
through the market. People make their private decisions about education and
medical training and after graduation receive their private returns. They are free
morally to go and come as they please because, when they move around, they take
with them their own personally financed human investment, and not a personal
investment in their education that has been publicly financed with the anticipation
of future social benefit through a universal coverage socialized health-care scheme.

10D Administrative expenses of providing for old age

Costs of administration are a consideration in the choice of how to provide for
post-retirement consumption. Such costs can take around 40 percent of annual
contributions for government administered pay-as-you-go schemes. The costs are
incurred in the bureaucracy required to monitor designated contributions and/or
to oversee the payouts to beneficiaries. For private asset accumulation, there are
corresponding portfolio management costs and custodian fees that could, for example, amount to between 1 and 3 percent annually of the value of the assets under
management. These fees, which are compounded over a typical person's working
life, also take significant proportions of the lifetime value of private savings. There

are further costs incurred in advertising when asset management companies compete for people's retirement savings.

10E Intertemporal markets

Intertemporal markets allow people to make private provision for retirement. Figure S10.1 shows an individual who is aware that life is divided into working and retirement periods. In period 1 the person works and consumes. In period 2 the person is retired, earns no income, and only consumes. Income Y is earned during the working period and no income is earned during the retirement period. In period 1, the income Y can be used for present consumption or can be saved and invested at a risk-free rate of return of r_1 percent. If all period 1 income were invested, the individual would have the income $Y(1 + r_1)$ available for consumption in retirement period 2. The line joining Y (on the present consumption axis) and $Y(1 + r_1)$ (on the future consumption axis) is therefore the individual's intertemporal budget constraint. All feasible choices of present and future consumption when the interest rate is r_1 are on this line.

   If interest rate were zero, the intertemporal budget constraint would be the dashed 45° line. When the interest rate is r_1, the individual in Figure S10.1 chooses the intertemporal consumption combination (C_1, F_1) at point 1 to maximize utility subject to available intertemporal income. The individual saves and invests $(Y - C_1)$ in period 1. The savings provide future income of $(Y - C_1)(1 + r)$ in

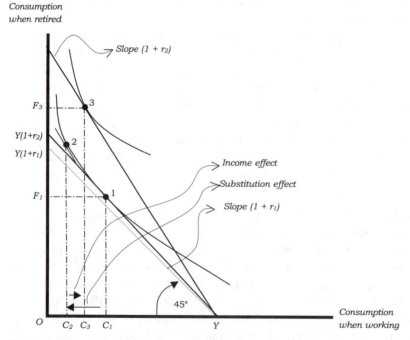

Figure S10.1. An intertemporal market allows people to make private provision for retirement.

period 2, which is spent to finance retirement consumption F_1. Asset (or capital) markets therefore resolve the personal problem of providing post-retirement income.

Present consumption and future consumption are different goods distinguished by time of consumption. The slope of the intertemporal budget constraint gives the relative price of the two goods. The equation of the intertemporal budget constraint is

$$C(1+r) + F = Y(1+r). \qquad (S10.1)$$

In expression (S10.1), all values are expressed in terms of future (period 2) values. In period 2, income of Y becomes $Y(1+r)$ because of the interest received. Similarly, consumption C deferred to period 2 becomes $C(1+r)$. F in the expression (S10.1) is already in terms of a period 2 value.

When we divide equation (S10.1) by $(1+r)$, we convert from future value terms to present value terms:

$$C + \frac{F}{1+r} = Y. \qquad (S10.2)$$

In this form, the intertemporal budget constraint tells us that the value of present consumption plus the present value of future consumption are equal to the present value of income. The present value of future consumption is discounted by the interest rate. We obtain the slope of the intertemporal budget constraint from either equation (S10.1) or (S10.2) as

$$\frac{dF}{dC} = -(1+r). \qquad (S10.3)$$

The slope of the individual's indifference curves in Figure S10.1 expresses the individual's subjective rate of time preference, which indicates the compensation the individual requires for deferring present consumption to the future. At the utility-maximizing intertemporal consumption choice at point 1, this subjective rate of time preference is equal to $(1+r_1)$, which reflects through r_1 the return offered by the market for deferring a dollar of consumption to the future. Therefore, we have a usual market equilibrium, in which a market price is equal to a subjective valuation (in relative terms).

When the interest rate increases from r_1 to r_2, present income Y can be converted to higher future income $Y(1+r_2)$. Utility is then maximized at point 3 where consumption when working is C_3 and consumption when retired is F_3.

We cannot predict how an increase in the interest rate will affect savings and the choice of present consumption. The substitution effect on present consumption is negative (the opposite of the substitution effect for future consumption). The income effect is positive because present consumption (like future consumption) is a normal good. Savings can increase or decline because either the substitution effect or the income effect could be greater. In the case shown in Figure S10.1, the negative substitution effect on present consumption ($C_1 - C_2$) is greater than the positive income effect $(C_3 - C_2)$, and savings increase from $(Y - C_1)$ to $(Y - C_3)$ in response to the higher interest rate.

The increase in the market rate interest results in higher consumption during the second retirement period. Future consumption increases because of a substitution effect (the move from point 1 to point 2) and further increases because of an income effect (the move from point 2 to point 3). The substitution effect increases future consumption because at the higher interest rate it is more worthwhile to invest and defer consumption to the future. The income effect increases future consumption because future consumption is a normal good, and total available income for present and future consumption has increased because of the higher interest rate. Therefore, a higher interest rate encourages people to increase provision for old age. An increase in the interest rate makes people saving for retirement unequivocally better off whether they save more or save less. The losers from an increase in the interest rate are borrowers.

Subject Index

Author Index